T0328387

Equilibrium, Trade, and Growth

Lionel W. McKenzie, circa 1960. Photo by Duncan Studio, Pittsford, NY.

Equilibrium, Trade, and Growth

Selected papers of Lionel W. McKenzie

edited by Tapan Mitra and Kazuo Nishimura

The MIT Press
Cambridge, Massachusetts
London, England

This book was set in Palatino on 3B2 by Asco Typesetters, Hong Kong.

Library of Congress Cataloging-in-Publication Data

McKenzie, Lionel W.
Equilibrium, trade, and growth : selected papers by Lionel W. McKenzie / edited by Tapan Mitra and Kazuo Nishimura.
    p. cm.
Includes bibliographical references and index.
ISBN 978-0-262-13501-6 (hardcover : alk. paper)—978-0-262-52638-8 (pb.)
1. Economics, Mathematical. 2. Equilibrium (Economics). 3. Economic development.
I. Mitra, Tapan, 1948–. II. Nishimura, Kazuo, 1946–. III. Title.
HB135.M413   2009
330—dc22   2008029323

Contents

Introduction

1 Lionel W. McKenzie

Tapan Mitra and Kazuo Nishimura

1.1 Preamble

Lionel McKenzie is one of the giants of twentieth-century neoclassical economics. The most productive period of his research coincided with the twenty-five years of the postwar period, which saw the major themes of neoclassical economics crystallized, and which also saw the development and use of more fundamental mathematical methods toward this end. He contributed greatly to both facets of this research program and, indeed, helped to shape the direction in which it developed.

To us, his students at the University of Rochester in the seventies, there is another dimension to Lionel McKenzie. We had the privilege of learning from him firsthand much of what we know about how to approach economic theory. The learning experience from his classroom lectures was supplemented by the handwritten lecture notes he would circulate and followed by presentations by students on a set of papers (typically unpublished current work by researchers from all over the world) selected by him. For us, that entire experience was to have permanent effects. The definitive books by Debreu (1959), Nikaido (1968), and Arrow and Hahn (1971), dealing with roughly the same subject matter, were illuminating on a variety of issues, but were *different* in their approaches from McKenzie's. The way we understand the subject matter even today was decided years back by the way we first understood some of the central concepts, the way McKenzie introduced them to us.

We wished for the lecture notes to be published in book form someday, so our experience could be at least partially shared by others in the profession. We felt encouraged when, upon his retirement, Lionel McKenzie began organizing his lecture notes for publication. And, our hope was realized when *Classical General Equilibrium Theory* was published by the MIT Press in 2002.

When the book was in preparation, we had the benefit of looking at early drafts of the manuscript. It occurred to us at that point that it would be ideal to publish a companion volume, consisting of a selection of Lionel McKenzie's papers. The idea, met with immediate approval from Lionel McKenzie himself, comes to fruition with this book.

It is often desirable in such collections to provide the reader with an overview of the selected papers, a guide which could be used to explore some papers in greater depth than others, depending on one's tastes. But this task has already been accomplished by our teacher. In a paper which he contributed to a special issue of the *Nagasaki Prefectural University Review* in memory of Professor Yasuo Uekawa, McKenzie reviewed his own contributions to equilibrium, trade, and capital accumulation. A slightly revised version of the paper was published in the *Japanese Economic Review*, and it provides the perfect lead article of the present collection.

The purpose of this chapter is therefore somewhat different. We provide here a sketch of McKenzie's academic career with the hope that it will help illuminate his contributions to the areas of equilibrium, trade, and growth, by providing us with the relevant backdrop as well as hints about possible influences. The chapter relies on McKenzie's own recent retrospective, "A Scholar's Progress," his reminiscenses in "The First Conferences on the Theory of Economic Growth," as well as on Roy Weintraub's account of the development of the theory of competitive equilibrium in his *Journal of Economic Literature* article (1983) and book (1985). However, it also relies on our own reading of McKenzie's papers.

1.2   A Life in Academia

1.2.1   In Search of a Specialization

Lionel McKenzie was born in 1919 in Montezuma, Georgia. His mother, in her youth a teacher, encouraged him to read the Harvard Classics. He attributes his introduction to economics to a reading of Adam Smith's *Wealth of Nations* one summer, while he attended Middle Georgia College in Cochran.

After graduating from junior college, he transferred to Duke University to enter an honors course in philosophy, politics, and economics.

The Great Depression of the 1930s was probably responsible for his choosing to concentrate in economics. In his final year at Duke, he won a Rhodes scholarship to pursue the same course at Oxford, but his plan was postponed indefinitely by the Second World War.

In 1939, he entered the Princeton Graduate College to work toward a Ph.D. in economics. There, he was greatly influenced by Frank Graham, who introduced him to multisector, many-country models of international trade, and by Oskar Morgenstern, whose course on economic theory included a critical study of *Value and Capital* by John Hicks. In 1941, with the United States at war, McKenzie left Princeton and spent a year with the Office of Civilian Supply in the War Production Board, and then in the Navy up to 1945.

In 1946, he obtained an appointment as an instructor at MIT. It appears that, even though he was familiar with Samuelson's work, his stay at MIT had no lasting influence on his academic interests, and after a couple of semesters there he resigned to take up his deferred scholarship at Oxford.

At Oxford, he was entered in the D.Phil. program, where his supervisor was John Hicks. While at Oxford, he spent a significant amount of his time studying philosophy and did not pursue the mathematical approach to economics. He embarked on a research project on modern welfare economics and wrote a draft of a thesis on the subject. His examiners (Roy Harrod and Hibert Henderson) ruled that it was not a finished product and would need to be revised. When he did not agree to do this, McKenzie had to settle for a B.Litt. degree.

Upon returning to the United States in 1948, he joined Duke University as an assistant professor. There, he wrote his paper "Ideal Output and the Interdependence of Firms," published in the *Economic Journal* in 1951. McKenzie refers to this work as an indirect outcome of his research project at Oxford, although it was not included in his thesis. At Duke, he became acquainted with Tjalling Koopmans's work on activity analysis. The theory of activity analysis immediately appealed to McKenzie as providing the sort of method that he could have used in his paper on ideal output. But, it also must have had a more profound influence, for in 1950, after teaching at Duke for two years, he applied to Jacob Marschak to visit the Cowles Commission in Chicago and became a University of Chicago graduate student in economics, a decisive turn in his academic career.

1.2.2 The Year at the Cowles Commission

At the Cowles Commission, McKenzie devoted considerable time to learning mathematics, taking courses from Paul Halmos, Irving Kaplansky, Saunders MacLane, and Jimmy Savage. He attended the classes of Tjalling Koopmans on activity analysis and econometrics and of Jacob Marschak on decision making under uncertainty. His colleagues in these courses included Martin Beckmann, John Chipman, and Edmond Malinvaud. Karl Brunner, Gerard Debreu, Leonid Hurwicz, and Harry Markowitz were also in the Cowles Commission group at that time.

In Koopmans's class, McKenzie wrote a term paper entitled "Specialization in Graham's Model of World Trade," a revised version of which appeared in 1954 in the *Review of Economic Studies* under the title "Specialization and Efficiency in World Production." Koopmans was pleased with the term paper and suggested that McKenzie work on the factor price equalization theorem of Samuelson in an activity analysis model. But McKenzie did not follow up on this suggestion until several years later.

On the walk back from a class by Koopmans on the relation between activity analysis and competitive equilibrium, McKenzie asked Koopmans about the issue of existence of a competitive equilibrium. Koopmans indicated that the existence question had not yet been answered. While at the Cowles Commission, McKenzie began thinking seriously about the question, especially in the context of Graham's models of international trade. It is perhaps significant (in view of developments that followed over the next year) that during his year in Chicago, McKenzie acquired a set of notes from a seminar on convex sets given by Marston Morse at Princeton, as well as a Cowles Commission paper by Morton Slater on Kakutani's fixed point theorem.

1.2.3 On the Existence of Competitive Equilibrium

Upon returning to Duke, McKenzie studied the papers by Abraham Wald (1951) and John von Neumann (1945) on the existence of equilibrium, and proceeded to write his own paper "On Equilibrium in Graham's Model of World Trade and Other Competitive Systems," which he presented at the Chicago meeting of the Econometric Society in December 1952. The Arrow-Debreu paper on the existence of a competitive equilibrium was presented at the same meeting, and both were later published in *Econometrica* in 1954. The approaches taken in the two papers on this central problem of general equilibrium theory were quite different. The Arrow-Debreu paper, which viewed competitive equilibrium as the outcome of a game, was directly influenced by the paper of Nash (1950) on non-cooperative games, and by the generalization of a Nash equilibrium to a social equilibrium by Debreu (1952). McKenzie's paper was inspired by the papers of Wald (1951) and the theory of activity analysis developed by Koopmans (1951).

According to McKenzie, while writing his term paper on specialization at the Cowles Commission, the idea came to him of mapping the social demand from the origin on the world production possibility frontier as a possible device for proving the existence of competitive equilibrium. As his 1954 paper showed, this device, when combined with the price support property of efficient points, makes it possible to view a competitive equilibrium as a fixed point of an upper semicontinuous correspondence from the price simplex to subsets of that simplex. The map itself suggests use of the Kakutani fixed point theorem (1941) as a natural method of establishing the existence of a competitive equilibrium.[1]

The map constructed by McKenzie is a composition of three maps, and it is possible to explain in geometric terms what each component map does. In fact, McKenzie has indicated that the notes on convex sets by Marston Morse allowed him to understand the existence problem geometrically. Moving somewhat ahead of the story, it is interesting to note that when Dorfman, Samuelson, and Solow published their classic *Linear Programming and Economic Analysis* in 1958, they chose to present the proof of existence of competitive equilibrium very much along the lines of McKenzie's 1954 paper.

1.2.4 Research at Duke

As already noted, Koopmans had suggested McKenzie work on the factor price equalization theorem, which is where McKenzie turned his attention next; he showed that if there is a choice of factor prices that put each country's factor supply in the interior of the diversification cone, then those factor prices would have to prevail in all countries in a world equilibrium under free trade. This result was published in *Econometrica* in 1955 and still remains the state-of-the-art result on the subject.

McKenzie then continued his research on the existence of competitive equilibrium; while his earlier contribution had started with demand functions, his new approach focused on consumer preferences as the primitive objects of study. This led him to give a simple approach to demand theory starting from assumptions on consumer preferences, in the paper "Demand Theory without a Utility Index," published in the *Review of Economic Studies* in 1957. This elegant paper forms the basis of demand theory, and a version of it is now covered in every standard graduate text on microeconomic theory.

His research on preference orderings led him to introduce preferences of consumers that depend on what other consumers buy. His paper on the existence of equilibrium with such *dependent* consumer preferences was presented at a Symposium on Linear Programming and published in its proceedings in 1956. At this symposium, Oskar Morgenstern indicated that he would make a proposal to the Princeton economics department to grant McKenzie a Ph.D. So, McKenzie obtained his degree by putting together the papers he had written and submitting them to Princeton.

It was around this time that McKenzie completed his definitive work on existence of competitive equilibrium, weakening the assumptions made by Arrow-Debreu (1954) and by himself in his earlier papers on the subject in 1954 and 1956. This was accomplished by introducing the notion of an irreducible economy, following a suggestion from David Gale. This paper was later published in *Econometrica* in 1959.

In the spring semester of 1956, while still at Duke, McKenzie visited the Cowles Foundation at Yale University. There he worked on the Ramsey theory of optimal taxation, and on a study of matrices with dominant diagonals, with applications to economics. The research on the Ramsey theory of optimal taxation was reported at the summer meeting of the Econometric Society in Ann Arbor, Michigan, but never submitted for publication. The study on dominant diagonal matrices later became McKenzie's contribution to the conference on Mathematical Methods in the Social Sciences held at Stanford in 1959. It showed the wide range of economic problems to which the concept of a dominant diagonal matrix could be applied fruitfully.

1.2.5 Move to Rochester

During his visit to the Cowles Foundation in 1956, McKenzie was approached by the University of Rochester to head an economics department there, with the aim of developing a Ph.D. program. He accepted the offer and moved from Duke to Rochester in the fall of 1957. During his first academic year, McKenzie recruited Ronald Jones, and the program's first Ph.D. student in economics, Akira Takayama, was admitted in that year. Richard Rosett and Edward Zabel joined the faculty the following year, and a full-fledged doctoral program was put into place. Some of the first students to join that program were Akihiro Amano, Hiroshi Atsumi, and Yasuo Uekawa. The graduate program grew in strength and reputation over the years, and the faculty expanded rapidly under McKenzie's chairmanship from 1957 to 1966. In 1995, when the National Research Council published its definitive study ranking departments of universities in the United States in the various disciplines, the economics department of the University of Rochester ranked among the top ten, as judged by the quality of its graduate program.

1.2.6 Final State Turnpike Theory

In 1958 Dorfman, Samuelson, and Solow (DOSSO) had published *Linear Programming and Economic Analysis*. The book analyzed a planning problem in which the objective was to maximize terminal stocks of capital goods (in certain prespecified proportions) over a long but finite horizon. It was indicated in DOSSO that plans that were optimal with respect to such an objective should stay, for most of the planning horizon, near the von Neumann equilibrium,[2] representing a balanced growth path with the maximum rate of growth. Drawing its analogy from the effectiveness of using the turnpike while driving over long distances, it came to be known as the *turnpike conjecture*.[3] McKenzie read the book very soon after moving from Duke to Rochester and spent the next twenty-five years exploring various aspects of the turnpike conjecture and establishing turnpike theorems that have greatly enriched the literature on economic dynamics.

In 1960 McKenzie, Morishima, and Radner independently provided the first formal proofs of the (final-state) turnpike theorem. It appears that all of them were influenced to some extent by John Hicks, who gave seminars at various universities around this time, reporting on the difficulty of formally establishing a turnpike theorem (see also, in this connection, the paper by Hicks (1961)). McKenzie (1963) and Morishima (1961) used Leontief models of production in their papers, but their approaches were very different from each other. Radner (1961) modeled the production set as a convex cone, which had become the standard generalization of the von Neumann model, but his assumption that the input-output combinations on the von Neumann ray were the only profit-maximixing combinations at the von Neumann prices made the technology quite restrictive. Radner's method of proof was elegant and it conveyed the sense of the original turnpike conjecture; it was to influence almost all of McKenzie's future writings on turnpike theory.

McKenzie quickly recognized that Radner's technique of proof was ideally suited for proving turnpike theorems for more general models of capital accumulation. He applied it to the dynamic Leontief model[4] and to the von Neumann model,[5] both of which are examples of well-known models in which Radner's "unique profitability condition" fails to hold. McKenzie showed that Radner's method can be used to establish the very general theorem that paths optimal with respect to the final state would have to lie close to a facet of the technology set (containing the von Neumann ray) consisting of all those activities that maximize profits at the von Neumann equilibrium prices.

These results might suggest that proximity of optimal paths to the von Neumann ray itself was not to be obtained in general. However, further investigations by McKenzie[6] indicated that paths on the facet have an additional stability property. This ensured the proximity of optimal paths to a subset of the facet activities, a subset that degenerated to the von Neumann ray in many important cases. The definitive account of this theory was presented by McKenzie in 1968, using the theory of matrix pencils developed by Gantmacher.[7]

1.2.7   The Uniqueness Debate

As an interlude to these exciting developments of turnpike theory, McKenzie wrote two pieces on the inversion of cost functions. To place them in the proper context requires going back more than a decade to a paper by Samuelson in 1953 in which, generalizing his own two-by-two-by-two factor price equalization result, a condition on the Jacobian matrix of the cost functions was conjectured by him to be sufficient for inversion of cost functions and therefore for factor price equalization (in the case of non-joint production) under "incomplete specialization." As we have already indicated, the most general result on factor price equalization (in a model that included cases of joint production and nonsmooth production relations, and allowed for specialization) was established by McKenzie in 1955. However, Samuelson's conjecture remained an issue of interest for the inversion of cost functions and for the uniqueness of competitive equilibria arising in contexts other than in international trade. Nikaido[8] gave a counterexample to Samuelson's conjecture in the context of global univalence of solutions to a system of nonlinear equations in general, and subsequently Gale and Nikaido

(1965) established that a stronger condition than Samuelson's was sufficient.[9] But, Nikaido's counterexample itself lacked the restrictions that cost functions would impose on the relevant equation system.

Pearce and James (1952) had rightly observed that if the Jacobian of the cost function were nonsingular, it would allow a local inversion of the cost function, but this condition was not guaranteed to ensure global inversion. However, Pearce (1959) had made the conjecture that the nonvanishing Jacobian condition might be sufficient after all for global invertibility of cost functions.

McKenzie set the matter to rest in 1967 by providing a definitive counterexample to the global invertibility of cost functions under the nonvanishing Jacobian condition.[10] This counterexample established the important result that determinateness of equilibrium was not to be expected as a generic outcome. It is an important instance of the sheer power of mathematical reasoning. Under the nonvanishing Jacobian condition, what one can see from the inverse function theorem is that the cost function must be locally invertible. But, the condition is clearly weaker than the Gale-Nikaido conditions, so whether global inversion holds or not is not easy to guess. The matter must be settled with a theorem or a counterexample, where the mathematics plays the important role, and economic intuition can provide only limited assistance.

In 1970 Debreu showed, using Sard's theorem, that the generic outcome of equilibrium systems was a *finite number* of equilibria, thereby providing a formal justification for *local* comparative static exercises. Following his influential paper, mathematical economists conducted a considerable amount of research on uniqueness of solutions to systems of nonlinear equations, defined by *smooth functions*, with the hope of producing stronger results on uniqueness of equilibria arising in economics by exploiting the methods of differential topology. However, McKenzie's counterexample clearly defined the limits to which this research program could be pushed.[11]

1.2.8   On the Ramsey Turnpike

Apart from this detour, McKenzie's research remained firmly focused on turnpike theory. While growth of capital stocks might be a reasonable objective in the initial stages of modernization for planned economies, researchers recognized that the motivation for studying such an objective was somewhat forced. Consumer preferences were ignored in planning exercises over such horizons, but the more basic objection was that if growth of capital stocks were indeed a reasonable goal for planned economies in the initial phases of their development, that should be the *consequence* of attaining a more fundamental objective rather than being imposed as an *objective* itself.

Such a fundamental objective should reflect consumer preferences and ideally should extend over an indefinite future, since specifying some fixed terminal date would itself be an ad hoc imposition on the problem.[12] This brought the profession's interest to focus precisely on Ramsey's classic 1928 paper on optimal savings.[13]

McKenzie was a leading contributor in establishing this shift of focus, which principally was accomplished in two conferences on optimal economic growth. The first was at the University of Rochester, led by McKenzie; the second was at Stanford University, led by Kenneth Arrow. Several papers initially presented at these conferences later were published in a *Review of Economic Studies* symposium in 1967.

The reformulation of the objective function along the lines of Ramsey meant that utility at each point in time would be derived from consumption and leisure choices, and future utilities would be treated as current ones in the planner's objective function, since Ramsey considered discounting of the future utilities to be "ethically indefensible." This brought to the forefront the question of existence of optimal paths over an infinite horizon, which had not been a major issue in the final-state turnpike literature. On the other hand, the similarity of the two theories derived from the similarity of the methods used to establish asymptotic properties of optimal paths. While the papers of Gale and McFadden,[14] and later Brock,[15] primarily were concerned with the first topic, Atsumi[16] and McKenzie recognized that Radner's "value-loss lemma" could be adapted to the new setting to obtain turnpike theorems for both finite- and infinite-horizon optimal paths when future utilities were undiscounted, with the golden-rule equilibrium (associated with a program yielding maximum sustainable utility) replacing the notion of the von Neumann equilibrium. McKenzie's comprehensive treatment of this topic was his contribution to the Hicks *festschrift* in 1968.

In light of later developments in this area of research, it is worth mentioning at this point that in the first conference on optimal growth (mentioned above), McKenzie introduced the formulation of utility derived at each point in time, which has come to be known as the "reduced form" version of the optimal growth model. In this formulation, utility is derived from beginning- and end-of-period stocks of goods.[17] Consumption, leisure, and stock effects on returns all can be captured in this formulation, but these "primitive" variables determining utility do not appear explicitly in the reduced form version. The formulation has the advantage over other formulations in providing the essential mathematical form of the *intertemporal* problem, where the *atemporal* problem already has been "solved" in arriving at the reduced form utility function. This has become the standard formulation of the utility function used in optimal growth theory.

1.2.9 Discounting and Long-Run Behavior

Along with a shift in emphasis of many economies away from planning at the national level was a corresponding change in interpretation of dynamic optimization problems of the Ramsey type. The problem being solved was previously viewed as a normative problem that the "social planner" ought to solve but came to be viewed as a descriptive problem a typical representative agent (more precisely, an infinitely lived dynasty of the typical agent) solves. The Ramsey objection to discounting future utilities as "ethically indefensible" on the part of the social planner was no longer relevant. If the representative agent did discount the future, the optimization problem would have to reflect this. Thus, the central problem to be solved in describing the agent's behavior would be a discounted dynamic optimization problem of the Ramsey type.

This reformulation of the focus of the subject had two significant consequences. The issue of the existence of an optimal program, which had occupied center stage for undiscounted dynamic optimization models, became a relatively unimportant aspect of the theory for discounted models because it was a relatively straightforward exercise, under discounting, to establish the existence of an optimal program. In contrast, description of dynamic behavior of optimal programs became considerably more difficult.

Examples due to Kurz (1968) for continuous-time models and Sutherland (1970) for discrete-time models indicated that multiple stationary optimal states could exist. Further, even if the stationary optimal state were unique, optimal programs starting from other initial states need not converge to it over time. Then, Samuelson (1973) presented an example due to Weitzman, which showed that optimal programs could cycle around a unique stationary state independent of the magnitude of the discount factor, and these cycles were not "boundary phenomena." While this destroyed any hope of a general turnpike theorem for discounted models, Samuelson conjectured that with (differential) strict concavity of the utility function, a turnpike property for optimal programs would continue to hold for high discount factors. This led to a considerable literature on the discounted turnpike problem. In alternative frameworks, Samuelson's conjecture was shown to be valid by Brock and Scheinkman (1976), Cass and Shell (1976), Rockafellar (1976), and Scheinkman (1976).

McKenzie was very much part of these developments. The Mathematical Social Sciences Board Conference in Squam Lake, where these papers (among others) were presented, received his encouragement as well as close scrutiny, as was quite common with McKenzie's oral presentations. A more concrete evidence of his contribution can be found in the proof of the turnpike theorem presented by Brock and Scheinkman (1978) in a discrete-time setting.

McKenzie also remained somewhat distant from this line of research, though. He was on a quest for the general result of the subject, and the theory of global asymptotic stability of optimal paths when the discount factor is sufficiently close to 1 had not come to terms with the Weitzman-Samuelson example. In 1980–1981, McKenzie spent a year away from Rochester as Taussig Research Professor at Harvard University. There, he wrote his paper on the "neighborhood turnpike theorem" when future utilities are discounted. This paper was published in the *Journal of Economic Theory* in 1982, and its generalization (to the case where no strictness in concavity of the utility function is assumed) was published in the same journal the following year. They represent a full account of what rightly can be regarded as the general result of the subject.

When the discount factor is close to 1, a stationary optimal stock is close to the golden-rule stock (of maximum sustainable utility). McKenzie had always regarded Jose Scheinkman's (1976) "visit lemma" as a basic result in the discounted case. This said that an optimal path must visit any preassigned small neighborhood of the golden-rule stock at least once, when the discount factor is sufficiently close to 1. This is, of course, different from the typical global asymptotic stability result. The latter result (when the discount factor is close to 1) can be obtained by ensuring that the "basin of attraction" of the stationary optimal stock (which clearly exists when the discount factor equals 1) does not vanish for discount factors close to 1.

The last requirement is fairly strong; it is a kind of uniform local asymptotic stability condition with respect to the discount factor. In particular, it rules out cyclical paths, and therefore it does not accommodate examples (of the Weitzman-Samuelson type) where cycles persist for all discount factors, no matter how close to 1. Now, if the only cycles that persist are cycles of small amplitude around the turnpike, the turnpike still would be a good approximation to long-run optimal behavior. So, McKenzie's idea was to use the "visit lemma" to make optimal paths visit a neighborhood of the golden-rule stock and then trap them in a (possibly somewhat larger) neighborhood of the stationary optimal stock by showing that the stationary optimal stock was stable in the sense of Lyapounov. This allows optimal paths to cycle or even exhibit more complicated behavior while being confined to this neighborhood.

1.2.10   A Presidential Lecture
In 1977, Lionel McKenzie was elected President of the Econometric Society. For his presidential lecture, he chose the topic of existence of competitive equilibrium, addressing one of the most severe shortcomings of general equilibrium theory up to that time. This was the issue of ensuring survival of agents in equilibrium, without assuming that agents can survive on their own.

In their proofs of existence of a competitive equilibrium, Arrow and Debreu (1954) and McKenzie (1956) had maintained the assumption that agents can survive on their own. Koopmans (1957), evaluating the contributions made to general equilibrium, had regarded this area as one needing additional research, remarking, "In modern society few of us can indeed survive without engaging in exchange." McKenzie (1959) had maintained this assumption in slightly modified form and had changed it to the more direct version used in Arrow-Debreu when in 1961 he published his corrections to the 1959 contribution. Arrow and Hahn (1971) had introduced the alternative notion of resource relatedness, but this implied in a very strong sense that agents could survive without trading.

The assumption that individuals can survive without trading was needed to ensure continuity of demand functions, as McKenzie had recognized even in his 1954 paper, where demand functions were primitives, and not derived from assumptions of consumer preferences on their consumption sets. Jim Moore (1975) was able to overcome this problem by using the method of Negishi instead of dealing with properties of demand functions. He showed that the assumption that individuals can survive can be dropped if the economy were assumed to be irreducible in the sense of McKenzie (1959, 1961).

McKenzie (1981) drew attention to this issue as one of considerable importance for general equilibrium theory by providing an alternative approach to the same result. Other assumptions also were relaxed, but the lecture primarily was a major contribution to the survival issue. Of course, as in the 1959 contribution, the economy as a whole must be assumed to be able to survive.

This contribution makes McKenzie's concept of irreducibility of primary importance in the study of famines. As Sen (1981) has noted, "Starvation is a matter of some people not having enough food to eat, and not a matter of there being not enough food to eat." That is, the typical situation in a famine is that the economy as a whole can survive (by, for example, a "command system"), and it is a failure of the market mechanism that not all agents can survive. This market failure can then be attributed to a failure of irreducibility.

1.3   Summary

As students of McKenzie, we have shared a common experience. When we teach *our* students aspects of equilibrium, trade, or growth and encounter difficult terrain, we are led to look at original papers by McKenzie to see how he dealt with it. Invariably, we find the issue has been addressed by him, and more often than not a general way of overcoming the difficulty has been suggested. It is clear to us that in developing a theory, McKenzie aimed at a complete understanding of what makes such a theory work. With that aim, over roughly a forty year period, he made contributions of extraordinary depth on a wide range of important questions in economic theory.

In putting together this selection of his papers, we were principally guided by two objectives. First, we firmly believe that there is no better way to perceive the development of McKenzie's ideas than to look at the original papers in which they appeared together, not in isolation. Second, in contrast to the simplified versions of his contributions that have been readily available for years, the many state-of the-art results achieved by McKenzie in the original papers present a much more sophisticated theory, which will continue to be important in future developments of the discipline.

Notes

1. Our exposition of McKenzie's 1954 paper, and indeed of his subsequent papers on the existence of competitive equilibrium, is deliberately brief. In a book of this size and scope, we would not be able to do justice to the technical aspects, which are an integral part of the subject matter. A comprehensive discussion of McKenzie's four papers on the subject (published in 1954, 1956, 1959, and 1981) can be found in the paper by Ali Khan (1993).

2. This is the notion of equilibrium examined by von Neumann in the paper, previously mentioned in our discussion of McKenzie's contributions to the theory of existence of a competitive equilibrium. In that context it was primarily of interest for the novelty of the methods introduced, since it provided a result, which was effectively a generalization of Brouwer's fixed point theorem before Kakutani's well-known contribution on the same topic. In the turnpike theory context, von Neumann's concept of equilibrium itself was shown to be of interest by the conjecture of DOSSO, a point made most clearly in the expository piece by Koopmans (1964).

3. The demonstration of this result was sketched in DOSSO, but it was incomplete and restricted to two goods. Further, in its demonstration, although clearly not in its formulation, it was a "local result"; this local result was formally demonstrated in its full generality later by McKenzie in a paper published in the *International Economic Review* in 1963.

4. This was published later in a paper in *Econometrica* in 1963.

5. This was later published in a conference volume of the International Economic Association, titled "Activity Analysis in the Theory of Growth and Planning" in 1967.

6. This was first undertaken in the paper published in *Econometrica* in 1963, already mentioned.

7. This was published in a special issue in 1971 of the *Journal of Economics*, devoted to "Contributions to the von Neumann Growth Model."

8. His counterexample is contained in a manuscript written in 1962 but never published. It was reproduced in the paper by Gale and Nikaido in their 1965 paper in *Mathematische Annalen*.

9. Their famous global univalence result imposed the condition that the relevant Jacobian matrix have all its principal minors positive in a domain, which was taken to be rectangular, and has come to be known as the "P-matrix" condition.

10. This was published in the *International Economic Review* in 1967.

11. See, in particular, Mas-Collel's (1979) contribution to the first McKenzie *festschrift* for an account of the developments for the issue of global inversion of cost functions.

12. A systematic study of the nature of such preferences over an infinite horizon was initiated by Koopmans in 1960. Becker and Boyd (1998) provide a comprehensive account of the literature that since has developed on this theme.

13. Interest in studying the themes of Ramsey's paper had surfaced before, most notably in the research of Tinbergen (1956) and Chakravarty (1962), but it was not shared more broadly by the profession at that time.

14. See the *Review of Economic Studies* symposium of 1967, mentioned earlier.

15. See his beautiful and definitive contribution on the existence problem in the *Review of Economic Studies* (1970).

16. Atsumi's contributions were part of his doctoral thesis at the University of Rochester, under McKenzie's supervision, and were published in the *Review of Economic Studies* in 1965 and 1969.

17. Equivalently, one writes the transition possibility set as transforming a vector of beginning-of-period stocks of goods to a vector consisting of end-of-period stocks of goods and a "utility good." It is this formulation that appears in McKenzie's contribution to the Hicks *festschrift*. The "reduced form utility function" would then be obtained by fixing a pair of (feasible) beginning-of-period and end-of-period stocks of goods, and maximizing the component of the "utility good."

References

Arrow, K. J., and G. Debreu. (1954). Existence of an Equilibrium for a Competitive Economy. *Econometrica* 22, 265–290.

Arrow, K. J., and F. H. Hahn. (1971). *General Competitive Analysis*. Holden-Day: San Francisco.

Atsumi, H. (1965). Neoclassical Growth and the Efficient Program of Capital Accumulation. *Rev. Econ. Studies* 32, 127–136.

Atsumi, H. (1969). The Efficient Capital Program for a Maintainable Utility Level, *Rev. Econ. Studies* 36, 263–288.

Becker, R., and J. Boyd. (1997). *Capital Theory, Equilibrium Analysis, and Recursive Utility*. Basil Blackwell: Oxford.

Brock, W. A. (1970). On Existence of Weakly Maximal Programmes in a Multi-sector Economy, *Review of Economic Studies* 37, 275–280.

Brock, W. A., and J. Scheinkman. (1976). Global Asymptotic Stability of Optimal Control Systems with Applications to the Theory of Economic Growth. *J. Econ. Theory* 12, 164–190.

Brock, W. A., and J. Scheinkman. (1978). On the Long-Run Behavior of a Competitive Firm, in G. Schwodiauer (ed.), *Equilibrium and Disequilibrium in Economic Theory*. Dodrecht: D. Reidel.

Cass, D., and K. Shell. (1976). The Structure and Stability of Competitive Dynamical Systems. *J. Econ. Theory* 12, 31–70.

Chakravarty, S. (1962). The Existence of an Optimum Savings Programme, *Econometrica* 30, 178–187.

Debreu, G. (1952). A Social Equilibrium Existence Theorem, *Proc. Nat. Acad. Sci., USA* 38, 886–893.

Debreu, G. (1959). *Theory of Value*. Wiley: New York.

Debreu, G. (1970). Economies with a Finite Set of Equilibria, *Econometrica* 38, 387–392.

Dorfman, R., P. Samuelson, and R. Solow. (1958). *Linear Programming and Economic Analysis*. McGraw-Hill: New York.

Gale, D. (1955). The Law of Supply and Demand. *Math. Scand.* 30, 155–169.

Gale, D. (1967). On Optimal Development in a Multi-Sector Economy. *Rev. Econ. Stud.* 34, 1–18.

Gale, D., and H. Nikaido. (1965). The Jacobian Matrix and the Global Univalence of Mappings, *Math. Ann.* 159, 81–93.

Hicks, J. R. (1939). *Value and Capital.* Oxford: Oxford University Press.

Hicks, J. R. (1961). The Story of a Mare's Nest, *Rev. Econ. Stud.* 76, 77–88.

Kakutani, S. (1941). A Generalization of Brouwer's Fixed Point Theorem, *Duke Math J.* 8, 457–459.

Khan, M. Ali. (1993). Lionel McKenzie on the Existence of Competitive Equilibrium, in R. Becker, M. Boldrin, R. Jones, and W. Thomson (eds.), *General Equilibrium, Growth and Trade II.* Academic Press: New York.

Koopmans, T. C. (1951). Analysis of Production as an Efficient Combination of Activities, in T. C. Koopmans (ed.), Activity Analysis of Production and Distribution. New York: Wiley.

Koopmans, T. C. (1957). *Three Essays on the State of Economic Science.* McGraw-Hill.

Koopmans, T. C. (1960). Stationary Ordinal Utility and Impatience, *Econometrica* 28, 287–309.

Koopmans, T. C. (1964). Economic Growth at a Maximal Rate. *Quart. Journ. Econ.* 78, 355–394.

Kurz, M. (1968). Optimal Economic Growth and Wealth Effects. *Int. Econ. Rev.* 9, 155–174.

Mas-Colell, A. (1979). Two Propositions on the Global Univalence of Syatems of Cost Function, in J. Green and J. A. Scheinkman (eds.), *General Equilibrium, Growth, and Trade.* Academic Press: New York.

McFadden, D. (1967). The Evaluatin of Development Programmes. *Rev. Econ. Studies* 34, 25–50.

McKenzie, L. W. (1951). Ideal Output and the Interdependence of Firms, *Economic Journal*, 785–803.

McKenzie, L. W. (1954). On Equilibrium in Graham's Model of World Trade and Other Competitive Systems, *Econometrica*, 147–161.

McKenzie, L. W. (1954). Specialization and Efficiency of World Production, *Review of Economic Studies*, 165–180.

McKenzie, L. W. (1955). Equality of Factor Prices in World Trade, *Econometrica*, 239–257.

McKenzie, L. W. (1955). Specialization in Production and the Production Possibility Locus, *Review of Economic Studies*, XXIII (1), 56–64.

McKenzie, L. W. (1956). Competitive Equilibrium with Dependent Consumer Preferences, in H. A. Antosiewicz (ed.), *Second Symposium in Linear Programming*, vol. I. National Bureau of Standards, Washington, DC, 277–294.

McKenzie, L. W. (1957). Demand Theory without a Utility Index, *Review of Economic Studies*, XXIV (3), 185–189.

McKenzie, L. W. (1957). An Elementary Analysis of the Leontief System, *Econometrica*, 456–462.

McKenzie, L. W. (1959). On the Existence of General Equilibrium for a Competitive Market, *Econometrica*, 54–71.

McKenzie, L. W. (1959). Matrices with Dominant Diagonals and Economic Theory, in K. J. Arrow, S. Karlin, and P. Suppes (eds.), *Mathematical Methods in the Social Sciences*. Stanford University Press, 47–62.

McKenzie, L. W. (1960). Stability of Equilibrium and the Value of Excess Demand, *Econometrica*, 606–617.

McKenzie, L. W. (1961). On the Existence of General Equilibrium: Some Corrections, *Econometrica*, 247–248.

McKenzie, L. W. (1963). The Dorfman-Samuelson-Solow Turnpike Theorem, *International Economic Review*, 29–43.

McKenzie, L. W. (1963). Turnpike Theorems for a Generalized Leontief Model, *Econometrica*, 165–180.

McKenzie, L. W. (1963). Turnpike Theorem of Morishima, *Review of Economic Studies*, 169–176.

McKenzie, L. W. (1967). Maximal Paths in the Von Neumann Model, in E. Malinvaud and M. O. L. Bacharach (eds.), *Activity Analysis in the Theory of Growth and Planning*. Macmillan: London, 43–63.

McKenzie, L. W. (1967). The Inversion of Cost Functions: A Counter-Example, *International Economic Review*, 271–278.

McKenzie, L. W. (1967). Theorem and Counter Example, *International Economic Review*, 279–285.

McKenzie, L. W. (1968). Accumulation Programs of Maximum Utility and the Von Neumann Facet, in J. N. Wolfe (ed.), *Value, Capital, and Growth*. Edinburgh University Press, 353–383.

McKenzie, L. W. (1971). Capital Accumulation Optimal in the Final State, in G. Bruckmann and W. Weber (eds.), *Contributions to the Von Neumann Growth Model*. Springer-Verlag: New York, 107–120.

McKenzie, L. W. (1974). Turnpike Theorems with Technology and Welfare Function Variable, in J. Los and M. Los (eds.), *Mathematical Models in Economics*. North Holland: Amsterdam, 271–288.

McKenzie, L. W. (1976). Why Compute Competitive Equilibria? in J. Los and M. Los (eds.), *Computing Equilibria: How and Why*. North Holland: Amsterdam, 3–19.

McKenzie, L. W. (1977). Turnpike Theory, *Econometrica*, 841–865.

McKenzie, L. W. (1977). A New Route to the Turnpike, in R. Henn and O. Moeschlin (eds.), *Mathematical Economics and Game Theory*. Springer-Verlag: New York, 683–694.

McKenzie, L. W. (1981). The Classical Theorem on Existence of Competitive Equilibrium, presidential address to the Econometric Society, *Econometrica*, 819–841.

McKenzie, L. W. (1982). A Primal Route to the Turnpike and Liapounov Stability, *Journal of Economic Theory* 27, 194–209.

McKenzie, L. W. (1983). Turnpike Theory, Discounted Utility, and the Von Neumann Facet, *Journal of Economic Theory* 30, 330–352.

McKenzie, L. W. (1986). Optimal Economic Growth, Turnpike Theorems and Comparative Dynamics, in K. J. Arrow and M. D. Intriligator (eds.), *Handbook of Mathematical Economics*, vol. III, North Holland: Amsterdam, 1281–1355.

McKenzie, L. W. and J. H. Boyd III. (1993). The Existence of Competitive Equilibrium over an Infinite Horizon with Production and General Consumption Sets, *International Economic Review* 34, 1–20.

McKenzie, L. W. (1999). A Scholar's Progress, *Keio Economic Studies* 36, 1–12.

McKenzie, L. W. (1999). Equilibrium, Trade, and Capital Accumulation, *The Japanese Economic Review* 50, 371–397.

McKenzie, L. W. (2002). Some Early Conferences on Growth Theory, in G. Bitros and Y. Katsoulacos (eds.), *Essays in Economic Theory, Growth, and Labor Markets*. Edward Elgar: Cheltenham, UK.

Moore, J. (1975). The Existence of Compensated Equilibrium and the Structure of the Pareto Efficiency Frontier, *Int. Econ. Rev.* 16, 267–300.

Morishima, M. (1961). Proof of a Turnpike Theorem: The No Joint Production Case, *Rev. Econ. Studies* 28, 89–97.

Nash, J. F. (1950). Equilibrium Points in N-Person Games, *Proc. Nat. Acad. Sci., USA* 36, 48–59.

Negishi, T. (1960). Welfare Economics and Existence of Equilibrium for a Competitive Economy, *Metroeconomica* 12, 92–97.

Nikaido, H. (1956). On the Classical Multilateral Exchange Problem. *Metroeconomica* 8, 135–145.

Nikaido, H. (1968). *Convex Structures and Economic Theory*. Acadmic Press: New York.

Pearce, I. (1959). A Further Note on Factor Commodity Price Relationships, *Econ. J.* 69, 725–732.

Pearce, I. F., and S. F. James. (1952). The Factor Price Equalization Myth, *Rev. Econ. Stud.* 19, 111–120.

Radner, R. (1961). Paths of Economic Growth That Are Optimal with Regard Only to Final States. *Rev. Econ. Stud.* 28, 98–104.

Ramsey, F. P. (1928). A Mathematical Theory of Saving. *Econ. J.* 38, 543–559.

Rockafellar, R. T. (1976). Saddle Points of Hamiltonian Systems in Convex Lagrange Problems Having a Non-Zero Discount Rate. *J. Econ. Theory* 12, 71–113.

Samuelson, P. A. (1953). Prices of Factors and Goods in General Equilibrium, *Rev. Econ. Stud.* 21, 1–20.

Samuelson, P. A. (1973). Optimality of Profit-Including Prices under Ideal Planning, *Proc. Nat. Acad. Sci., USA* 70, 2109–2111.

Scheinkman, J. (1976). On Optimal Steady State of N-Sector Growth Models When Utility Is Discounted, *J. Econ. Theory* 12, 11–30.

Sen, A. (1981). Ingredients of Famine Analysis: Availability and Entitlements, *Quarterly Journal of Economics* 96, 433–464.

Sutherland, W. (1970). On Optimal Development in a Multi-sectoral Economy: The Discounted Case, *Rev. Econ. Studies* 37, 585–589.

Tinbergen, J. (1956). The Optimum Rate of Saving, *Econ. J.* 66, 603–609.

von Neumann, J. (1945). A Model of General Economic Equilibrium, *Rev. Econ. Stud.* 13, 1–9 (translated from the original German paper of 1935–1936 by G. Morton).

Wald, A. (1951). On Some Systems of Equations of Mathematical Economics, *Econometrica* 19, 368–403 (translated from the original German paper of 1936 by O. Eckstein).

Weintraub, E. R. (1983). The Existence of a Competitive Equilibrium: 1930–1954, *Journal of Economic Literature*, 1–39.

Weintraub, E. R. (1985). *General Equilibrium Analysis*. Cambridge University Press.

2 Equilibrium, Trade, and Capital Accumulation

Lionel W. McKenzie

2.1 Introduction

My work in economic theory is usually referred back to Walras, and it might be said that I have devoted myself to the task of finishing the analysis of the competitive economy along the lines that he first laid out. Along with many other authors of the 1950s, when modern theory that uses mathematics freely was being developed, I proved theorems on the existence and uniqueness of competitive equilibrium, the stability of the *tâtonnement* and the efficiency of competitive equilibrium. However, there were some particular characteristics of my work. It usually departed from well-known models of the competitive economy that had been put to use in policy contexts or empirical contexts. For example, my first existence theorem was concerned with Frank Graham's model of international trade (McKenzie, 1954a), which he had used to criticize the classical trade theory and its policy implications. His model had been criticized because no proof of existence or of uniqueness was supplied. On the other hand, when I proved turnpike theorems for optimal paths of capital accumulation, I dealt first with the simple open Leontief model (McKenzie, 1963a) with variable coefficients; later, in developing a theorem that would apply to the neoclassical model with independent industries and constant returns at the industry level, I used a Leontief model (1963b) with durable capital goods present. In both cases, of course, I went on to models that were more general, but the initial steps were taken in simple models which had been given rather concrete applications.

A second aspect of my work has been to preserve the vision of the competitive economy which I found in Walras (1874–7). In this vision the basic facts about the economy are the tastes of consumers, the supplies of factors and the productive processes that are available. The processes are treated as independent and linear, at least on the industry scale. This is in contrast with the Hicksian model (Hicks, 1939) of a set of firms that own idiosyncratic production sets where no provision is made for the entry of new firms. This agrees with my use of Graham's model and the Leontief model, which have linear production processes in each industry. Arrow and Debreu (1954) took the other route. Mathematically the models can be shown to be equivalent, but economically I think they are not. The linear model can represent the dissolution and formation of firms in terms of the flow of entrepreneurial factors between activities that may use them in different proportions. This is not a natural development of the Arrow–Debreu model.

I believe my inspiration actually goes back to a hundred years before Walras, to Adam Smith. I first read Adam Smith's *Wealth of Nations* (1776) one summer when I was attending a small junior college in Cochran, Georgia, a town no larger than my home town of Montezuma and close by it. I was struck by Smith's description of the competitive economy, which is indeed the Walrasian description in embryo. The price of a commodity is equated to the cost of the factors that enter into its production, and the factors migrate to the activities where they can earn the largest returns. Moreover, production can be extended by the duplication of activities, so from the economy-wide standpoint activities can be treated as linear.

I found Smith in the Harvard Classics, so it is possible that my entry into economics depended on a travelling salesman persuading my mother, who had been a schoolteacher in her youth, to buy the Harvard Classics. In another summer I read Darwin's *Origin of Species* from the same set of classics, and the professor who recommended me to Duke University for scholarship support was a biologist. Perhaps my preference for economics arose from the pressing economic problems of the time. However, the most serious competitor as my main subject of study was physics, and my decision in favour of economics may have arisen from a tension between doing a scientific subject or a literary one: economics seemed in prospect to be a fair compromise between them. But in retrospect, the scientific side (or at least the mathematical side) seems to have won out!

My plan for this chapter is to discuss some of the ideas for which I can claim a degree of originality—the activities model of competitive equilibrium, irreducible economies, minimum income functions, quasi-dominant diagonals and positive excess demand for *tâtonnement* stability, non-neutral cycles and comparative advantage, maximal balanced growth and von Neumann equilibria, von Neumann facets, and neighbourhood turnpike theorems. These ideas are applied to general equilibrium theory for the competitive economy, international trade theory and the theory of capital accumulation.

2.2   Existence and the Economy of Activities

A characteristic feature of my treatment of general equilibrium for the competitive economy is the use of a social production set which is a convex cone with vertex at the origin. This means, in more familiar terms, that production functions show constant returns to scale. In the light of other assumptions, made by Arrow and Debreu as well, of divisibility of goods and convexity of the production sets, one might think that constant returns is only to be expected. Indeed, one may reason that any tendency towards diminishing returns to scale must result from some indivisibility of a productive factor. In that case, assuming constant returns is the same type of approximation to reality that is involved in assuming divisibility of goods in the first place. However, I believe my motivation comes largely from the vision of Walras as I interpret it, where the basic fact about production is the existence of potential productive activities that may be undertaken by any people possessing the requisite knowledge and able to obtain the additional factors, not the existence of a set of firms, given *a priori*, that own convex production sets. This leads to the zero profit condition of competitive equilibrium assumed by Walras, and indeed by Marshall as well.

If we assume that demand functions are single-valued (that is, are functions rather than correspondences), a simple proof of existence is available which can be displayed geometrically. The proof passes from a normalized price vector to the market demand that it implies, then back to the possible production set by projection, and then to the set of normalized prices at which this production is profit-maximizing. An initial price may be found which is contained in the set of prices into which it maps. This is a competitive equilibrium price. Figure 2.1 illustrates the proof.

If one wishes to introduce firms into production, perhaps it should be done by treating firms as coalitions of entrepreneurs which may dissolve and reform and whose stable configurations lie in the core of a profit game where the profits arise from prices that are competitive equilibria, given the set of coalitions. That is, the competitive equilibria would be the strong Nash equilibria where no group of entrepreneurs

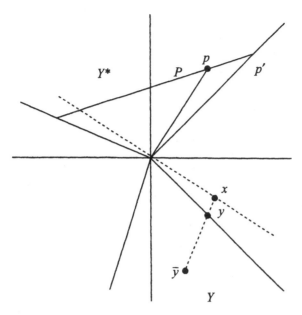

Figure 2.1
Y is the set of outputs. Y^* is the set of prices that meet the zero profit condition. P is the set of normalized prices. p is a normalized price vector from P. $x = \sum_1^H x^h = \sum_1^H f^h(p) = f(p)$ is the market demand at prices p. $\bar{y}$ lies in the interior of Y and y is the projection of x on the boundary of Y from $\bar{y}$. Let $F(p) = g(h(f(p)))$. By Kakutani's fixed point theorem, there is $p^* \in F(p^*)$. Then $(p^*, y^*, x^{1*}, \ldots, x^{H*})$ is a competitive equilibrium.

sees an opportunity to earn larger incomes from forming new firms and trading at the existing prices.

An alternative way to interpret the assumption of constant returns is to use a correspondence between convex cones and convex sets. The Arrow–Debreu model can be mapped into the constant returns model by introducing a specific factor for each firm whose ownership is shared among the stockholders in proportion to their ownership of stock in the firm, as assumed in that model. This ploy also has the advantage that the profits are realized as prices of the specific factors in the same way as other prices of goods in the equilibrium. Of course this does not alter the Arrow–Debreu model, but it has proved to have some mathematical advantages in exploring the properties of the model.

I believe that irreducibility and constant returns are the principal characteristics that have attracted attention in my general equilibrium theory. However, I also (1956) showed how the existence theory could be extended to models where consumer tastes were allowed to depend on quantities bought by other consumers and on levels of production of the different goods. I did not see how to include external effects on production sets or on possible consumption sets for the general case of both economies and diseconomies in an economically acceptable manner. And in my opinion this has not been done to this day. The difficulty is that the feasible set then need not be simply connected except by an *ad hoc* assumption.

2.3   Existence of Equilibrium and Irreducibility

One of my chief contributions to general equilibrium, following a suggestion from David Gale, is the concept of irreducibility for a competitive economy. This replaces the assumption used by Arrow and Debreu that everyone owns a factor that is always able to increase the output of a good which is always desired in larger quantities by everyone. This assumption implies irreducibility, but it is rather implausible. Loosely speaking, irreducibility means that the economy cannot be divided into two groups where one group has nothing to offer the other group which has value for it. This idea was first defined and used in my paper on the existence of equilibrium published in 1959, where various generalizations were made of the theory announced by Arrow and Debreu and myself in 1954 and by me in 1956.

In addition to replacing the assumption just described, negative prices were allowed, free disposal and irreversibility of production were dispensed with, and a model was developed which allowed for the entry of new firms and the dissolution of old firms, but which could accommodate the Arrow–Debreu model as well. The assumption that the production set has an interior was also dropped. However, it was still assumed that each consumer could survive without trading with other consumers. This assumption may be implausible even for the primates who were ancestors of *Homo sapiens*, but it seems in any case undesirable to make for modern man. It was first seen from the work of John Moore (1975) that irreducibility made this assumption unnecessary, although he did not call attention to the generalization. He applied a fixed-point theorem to a mapping of a set of normalized utility possibility vectors into itself in the manner of Negishi (1960) and Arrow and Hahn (1971). This suggested that the survival assumption for isolated consumers had been needed only because the mappings were defined by demand functions in the commodity and price spaces. I was able to confirm this in my presidential address to the Econometric Society (1981) by showing that demand functions based on the pseudo-utility functions of Shafer with some rather difficult indirect arguments allowed a commodity space approach to the existence proof where survival for isolated individuals is not assumed. The new approach was essential in order to achieve the further generalization of the existence theorem without individual survival to the case of intransitive preferences, since in the absence of transitivity the utility functions do not exist. Thus, a mapping in the space of utility vectors is not available.

Since my 1959 paper there has been some discussion about the meaning of the irreducibility assumption. I made a small amendment in 1961 to take account of an objection raised by Gerard Debreu in private correspondence. When Arrow and Hahn wrote their book (1971), which expounds the basic general equilibrium theory for competitive economies, they chose not to use irreducibility but to introduce a notion of resource relatedness, which implies individual survival. Thus, resource relatedness does not permit a generalization which only assumes survival by the whole body of consumers. Also in Debreu's paper of 1962, "New Concepts and Techniques for Equilibrium Analysis," individual survival still appears. In that paper the basic theorem establishes the existence of a quasi-equilibrium and an implication of irreducibility is introduced at the end to convert the quasi-equilibrium into a full equilibrium. In a quasi-equilibrium consumers minimize the cost of reaching the equilibrium level of preference, but they do not necessarily maximize preference over the budget set. More recently, Hammond (1993) and Ali Khan (1993) analysed and extended the concept of irreducibility in papers delivered to a Rochester conference.

I think the best formulation of the irreducibility assumption for present purposes may be derived from the statement of strong irreducibility in the paper of Boyd and McKenzie (1993) on existence over an infinite horizon. Index the set of consumers by $\{1, \ldots, H\}$. Let C^h be the set of possible trades for the hth consumer and P^h denote his preference relation over trades. Then C^h is the set of possible consumption bundles less the initial stocks held by the hth consumer. Let x_I denote $\sum_{h \in I} x_h$. Y is the production set for the economy, which is assumed to be a convex cone with vertex at the origin. I showed (McKenzie, 1959) that this is not inconsistent with diminishing returns to scale for each firm in an Arrow–Debreu model once entrepreneurial factors are introduced. The definition is as follows.

Definition An economy is irreducible if, whenever I_1, I_2 is a nontrivial partition of $\{1, \ldots, H\}$ and $x_{I_1} + x_{I_2} \in Y$ with $x^h \in C^h$, there are $z_{I_1} + z_{I_2} \in Y$ and $\alpha > 0$, with $z^h \in C^h$ and $z^h P^h x^h$, for $h \in I_2$, and $z_{I_1} \in \alpha C_{I_1}$.

It is easily seen how this assumption implies that a quasi-equilibrium must be a competitive equilibrium. In a quasi-equilibrium each consumer minimizes the cost of reaching the preference level he is in. This will imply that he maximizes his preference level under his budget constraint provided there is a point in his budget set that costs less than his income. If this condition holds, the quasi-equilibrium is a competitive equilibrium. Since the income of consumers arises from the sale of productive services or initial stocks, the value of the consumer's actual trade cannot exceed 0. Thus, in a quasi-equilibrium a better trade must cost more than 0. Irreducibility implies that, should a feasible allocation place some consumers, those in I_1, in the position that their trading sets lie above their budget planes, the consumers whose consumption sets contain points that lie below their budget planes, those in I_2, are not satiated in all the commodity bundles that can be obtained from positive multiples of trades that are possible for the consumers in I_1 (disregarding the equilibrium trade) together with adjustments in production. However, in the quasi-equilibrium the balance condition requires

$$z_{I_1} + z_{I_2} = y.$$

Let the prices of the quasi-equilibrium be represented by the vector p. Because of the zero profit condition for the quasi-equilibrium, we have $py = 0$. But $pz_{I_2} > 0$ must hold by the demand condition of equilibrium. However, by assumption $pz_{I_1} \geqslant 0$, so we arrive at a contradiction. This implies that the set I_1 is empty. Therefore if any consumer has points in his consumption set, then all do. But someone must be in this position because of the survival assumption made for the set of consumers as a whole. In the simplest statement of this assumption, there is a point z interior to the production set such that $z = \sum w^h$ where $w^h \in C^h$ and the sum is over all consumers. Such a point z will satisfy $pz < 0$ by the profit condition. Thus, all consumers will maximize their preferences under their budget constraints and the quasi-equilibrium is in fact a competitive equilibrium. This is how the assumption of irreducibility was used in my 1959 article.

Notice that irreducibility does not require that any subset of consumers smaller than the whole body of consumers can survive alone.

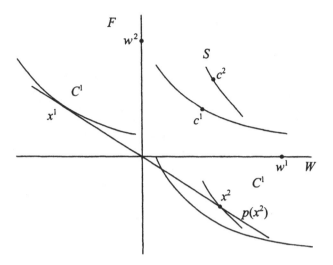

Figure 2.2
S is the possible consumption set for both traders. C^h is a possible trading set. w^h is an endowment. c^h is a consumption for consumer h. x^h is a trade for consumer h. x^1 lies on the boundary of C^1. $P(x^2)$ is the preferred set of x^2. The economy is irreducible.

The very simple example illustrated in Figure 2.2 shows this. There are two goods, called "food" and "water." The first consumer has more water than he needs to survive but not enough food; the second consumer has more food than he needs to survive but not enough water. Clearly, they either trade or die. The possible consumption sets are translated into possible trading sets by the subtraction of initial stocks. In the trading sets, negative quantities represent amounts of goods given up and positive quantities, amounts of goods received. However, when the first consumer is on the boundary of his trading set and is providing all the water possible, retaining just enough to survive, given the quantity of food he is receiving, the second consumer is not satiated in the trade implied by this allocation but would like to receive more water from the first consumer on the same terms. Since the analogous condition prevails when the second consumer is on the boundary of his trading set, the economy is irreducible. Of course, an equilibrium exists at an intermediate price ratio despite the absence of individual survival. In trading models of this type without production Hammond (1993) has given conditions that are necessary and sufficient for turning a quasi-equilibrium into a competitive equilibrium. These conditions do not imply a cheaper point. Irreducibility is designed to provide cheaper points, but it is important that it also allows us to dispense with the condition that consumers must be able to survive without trading.

The condition of resource relatedness will always provide a cheaper point at a compensated equilibrium if each consumer's trading set contains a point in the negative orthant with negative components for the initial resources, and zeros otherwise. This is precisely what is assumed by Arrow and Hahn (1971, p. 77) in their Assumption 2. It is a strong survival assumption for individual consumers without trade. In this sense, irreducibility represents a much weaker assumption for the proof of existence than resource relatedness.

The example we have used did not include production possibilities. However, to include them one may replace the trading sets C^h with $C^h - Y$, when there is, for example, a technology for turning water into food. It still may not be possible for consumers to survive alone. The use of irreducibility to turn a quasi-equilibrium into a competitive equilibrium is quite straightforward and easily seen. However, its use to dispense with the survival of individual consumers without trade in establishing that an equilibrium exists is quite subtle and cannot be presented in such an intuitive way. There is good discussion of this proof in Khan (1993).

At the time of my retirement conference in Rochester (in 1989), Ali Khan correctly pointed out that I had not contributed to existence theory for competitive equilibria when there is an infinite number of commodities. However, I had made a practice of introducing the paper of Peleg and Yaari (1970) into my classes. When I came to write up my notes on their paper, I thought it would be nice to make use of a consumption set that was not assumed to have the shape of the positive orthant, which I felt to be highly inappropriate for economic reasons. This assumption implies that the lower bound of the possible consumption set lies in this set; for example, the lowest consumption possible for me in this period is independent of my consumption in earlier periods. Also, there is no substitution on the subsistence boundary of the consumption set in a given period. However, I found that this assumption was virtually universal. Kerry Back (1988) was apparently a major exception, but his argument was very laconic and his assumptions were not entirely satisfactory in some respects. In a collaboration with my colleague John H. Boyd III (Boyd and McKenzie, 1993) we were able to prove a satisfactory theorem using a line of argument suggested by Peleg and Yaari.

It did not turn out to be possible to prove existence in the case of an infinite number of goods without introducing the assumption that isolated consumers can survive, as well as a stronger irreducibility assumption than the finite case requires. The irreducibility assumption may be taken in the following form, which is somewhat stronger than in the Boyd–McKenzie paper.

Assumption   An economy is strongly irreducible if it is irreducible; and, in the definition of irreducibility, whenever x_{I_2} does not lie on the relative boundary of C_{I_2}, the corresponding value of α may be taken to be 1.

The relative boundary of C_{I_2} is the boundary in the smallest affine subspace or flat containing C_{I_2}. This means that the improvement for consumers in I_2 may be obtained by increasing the allocation to I_2 by some quantity that is large enough to sustain the consumers in I_1. Thus, it is not enough that members of I_2 may reach a preferred position by adding to their current trade (the negative of) some fraction of a trade that I_1 could accept initially: they must reach a preferred position when receiving that trade itself. If there is only one other consumer in the economy, the condition is rather severe. However, if there are many other consumers, it would appear not to make a very significant difference. The reason this strengthening is needed for the proof in the infinite case is that the method of proof uses a generalization of the Debreu–Scarf (1963) theorem. This theorem says that, when an economy is replicated indefinitely often, an allocation that remains in the core is a competitive equilibrium. The core consists of allocations that no subset of consumers can improve upon using only their own resources. We need strong irreducibility to prove that replicates of a given consumer receive allocations in the core that are indifferent. Another method of proof might eliminate this embarrassment.

The need for the survival of consumers without trade may also arise from the line of proof. We combine the theorem of Debreu and Scarf with that of Scarf (1967), that the core is not empty for a balanced game. The Scarf argument assumes the ability of every coalition to survive in isolation. In the finite case, the stronger assumption is known not to be needed (Border, 1985), so some suspicions must be aroused that the stronger assumption is not needed for the infinite case, either.

2.4   Demand Theory and Minimum Income Functions

I may be forgiven for intruding here a contribution to demand theory which was not itself a major advance but which led to some develop-

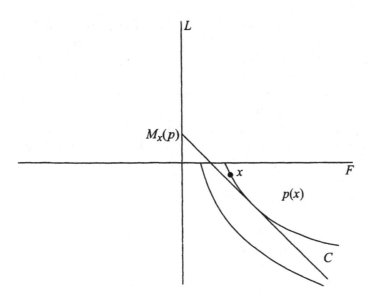

Figure 2.3
The goods are labour (L) and food (F). Labour is the numeraire. $M_x(p)$ is the minimum income needed at price p to reach the preference level given by the consumption vector x.

ments in the hands of Leo Hurwicz and his collaborators. I showed (McKenzie, 1957) how the Slutsky equation for the separation of the effect of price change on demand between a pure substitution effect and an income effect and other results in the theory of demand could be derived by the use of properties of the minimum income function. The minimum income is the smallest income, given prices, that allows the consumer to reach a given level of preference, determined by a reference consumption bundle.

I wrote this function as $M_x(p)$. It is illustrated in Figure 2.3. The matrix of second partial derivatives of $M_x(p)$ (the Hessian matrix) is equal to the substitution matrix (or to the matrix of first derivatives of the compensated demand functions (the Jacobian of those functions)). Since $M_x(p)$ is a concave function, this matrix is negative semidefinite, from which the results of pure demand theory follow. Unlike the classical approach, this derivation of demand theory avoids the use of the mathematics of determinants and Jacobi's theorem. Also, the results do not depend on goods being divisible or utility being a quasi-concave function. Since $M_x(p)$ is concave, it has a well defined Hessian at almost every point in the price space.

Hurwicz was in the audience when my paper was presented to the Econometric Society. Later Hurwicz (1971) and Hurwicz and Uzawa (1971) used this approach to demand theory to do some definitive work on the old problem of integrability, the problem that asks when a field of indifference directions can be integrated into a set of indifference curves. Today the minimum income function is often referred to as the minimum cost function or the minimum expenditure function, sometimes with the qualifier "minimum" omitted. I do not regard this change of terminology as an improvement.

2.5 *Tâtonnement* Stability and Positive Excess Demand

In addition to my work on the existence problem, I also looked into the question of stability of the Walrasian *tâtonnement*. Interest in this question had been revived by papers of Arrow and Hurwicz (1958), in which for the first time a dynamic stability was proved using meaningful economic assumptions. Although interest has lapsed in recent years, I do not regard the subject as completely obsolete. If equilibrium prices are defined by equality of supply and demand, it would seem to be implied that a dynamic system is present where inequality of supply and demand has consequences for the evolution of prices. Then it is natural to associate an excess of demand over supply with a price rise and an excess of supply over demand with a price fall, as Walras did. If there are unsatisfied traders, as there might be for perishable goods, the excess demand is easy to define and the dynamics are appealing. However, there may also be unsatisfied traders in markets for durable goods if they are not literally auctions. Then for the very short run the evolution of prices may display the dynamics of the *tâtonnement*, for example on Marshall's market day (Marshall, 1890). So when expectations are not treated as necessarily correct and the longer-term development of prices is analysed in a sequence of temporary equilibria, there is still a place for *tâtonnement* stability in the Walrasian sense for the attainment of temporary equilibrium. My work on stability made use of the notions of a quasi-dominant diagonal and of positive excess demand.

A square matrix has a dominant diagonal by columns if there are positive numbers by which the rows may be multiplied, so that the diagonal element in any column is larger in absolute value than the sum of the absolute values of the off-diagonal elements. *Mutatis mutandis* for a dominant diagonal by rows. A square matrix has a quasi-dominant diagonal by columns if we replace "larger than" by "at least as large as" and require "larger than" for at least one column in each submatrix that is symmetric around the diagonal. It may be proved that a quasi-dominant diagonal implies a dominant diagonal. Nevertheless, we introduce the notion of a quasi-dominant diagonal since this condition is naturally implied in some economic situations with the prices as multipliers. This is true at equilibrium for columns in Leontief models because of the profit condition. When the gross substitute condition holds, it is true for columns in the Jacobian of market demand functions, omitting the numeraire row and column, by Walras's Law, and for rows in this reduced Jacobian by homogeneity of zero degree.

Let $e_i(p)$ be the excess demand for the ith good when the price vector is p. Most of the theory developed for global *tâtonnement* stability used the assumption of gross substitutes $(\partial e_i(p)/\partial p_j > 0$ for $i \neq j)$ or weak gross substitutes $(\partial e_i(p)/\partial p_j \geq 0$ for $i \neq j)$. "Gross substitutes" means that an increase in the price of one good with the prices of other goods constant increases the demand for all other goods. "Weak gross substitutes" means that the demand for other goods does not fall under these conditions. In a paper delivered at the 1959 Stanford conference on mathematical methods in the social sciences (McKenzie, 1960a), I used the properties of the gross substitute matrix, whose elements are the rates of change of demand as prices rise, to prove global stability for the simplest *tâtonnement* dynamics, under the assumption of weak gross substitutes.

Consider the reduced gross substitute matrix where the numeraire is omitted. The assumption of weak gross substitutes implies that the gross substitute submatrix containing only the rates of change of the goods with positive excess demand, with respect to their prices, has a negative dominant diagonal in its columns, and nearly so in its rows. To see the meaning of this condition, we may choose units of measurement so that all prices equal 1. The dominant diagonal in columns means that the marginal effect on the demand for a given good that is in excess demand of an increase in its price is larger in absolute value than the sum of the effects on all other goods that are in excess demand. In rows, a slightly modified condition requires that the sum of marginal effects of raising the price of one good that is in positive excess demand on the demand for this good *at least equals* in absolute value the sum of the marginal effects of own price increases on the demands for all other goods that are in positive excess demand.

Table 2.1

$$\begin{bmatrix} -0.6 & 0.6 & 0 \\ 0.2 & -0.7 & 0.5 \\ 0.2 & 0.0 & -0.2 \\ -0.2 & -0.1 & 0.3 \end{bmatrix} \begin{matrix} 0 \\ 0 \\ 0 \end{matrix}$$

A possible gross substitute matrix is given in Table 2.1. The column sums equal minus the excess demands, which may be seen by differentiating Walras's Law, and the row sums equal zero by homogeneity. Each column corresponds to a good and each row to the price of a good (arranged in the same order). Any good may be chosen as numeraire, but to have a non-trivial submatrix for the goods in excess demand, excluding the numeraire, choose the third good. In the *tâtonnement* where the rate of price change is proportional to the excess demand, the dominant diagonal implies that the length of the excess demand vector for the goods in excess demand, exclusive of the numeraire, is always falling away from equilibrium. As a consequence, the market prices converge to the set of equilibrium prices when they start from any positive initial prices. (I first proposed a false conjecture along these lines when discussing the first Arrow–Hurwicz paper on stability at a meeting of the Econometric Society. I did not immediately recognize the special role of the goods in excess demand. Fortunately, I was able to pass a note containing the correct proof to Ken Arrow before the meeting ended.)

Formally, the simple adjustment model for the *tâtonnement* is

$$dp_i/dt = k_i e_i(p),$$

where p is the price vector and k_i is some positive constant. Thus, the rate of price change is the same for a given level of excess demand, however high or low the price of the good may be. (Recall that excess demand will also depend on other prices.) I do not think this is a reasonable assumption. The weakest assumption for the Walrasian *tâtonnement* is that excess demand causes a price to increase and excess supply causes a price to fall where the rate of change is not specified.

I defined (McKenzie, 1960b) a Liapounov function $V(p)$ equal to the value of positive excess demand and used it to prove the global stability of this general model of the *tâtonnement* under the assumption of weak gross substitutes. Formally, let P be the set of goods with non-negative excess demand. Then

$$V(p) = \sum_{i \in P} p_i e_i(p).$$

The function $V(p)$ is positive away from equilibrium and zero at equilibrium. Its derivative with respect to time is non-negative everywhere and it converges to zero over time. This implies that the prices approach the set of equilibria, which I showed to be a convex set under the assumption of weak gross substitutes. I learned later (from Negishi, 1962) that Allais had conjectured in the 1940s that an argument of this type could prove the stability of the *tâtonnement*.

If our attention is turned to local stability, which I now regard as the central problem, it may be shown that the local stability of any well behaved nonlinear price adjustment mechanism for the Walrasian *tâtonnement* is locally equivalent to the simple model where the rate of price change for any good is proportional to the level of excess demand for that good. In this setting, I believe that the most meaningful assumption for stability is that the weak axiom of revealed preference holds in a neighbourhood of equilibrium. Other conditions for stability that are recommended by economic theory imply the weak axiom, for example small net income effects or weak gross substitutes. It has been shown by Anjan Mukherji (1989) that local stability is actually equivalent to the weak axiom or its analog after a transformation of coordinates.

On the other hand, there is the evolution of prices along an equilibrium path over time, of the kind studied in the theory of capital accumulation or in the theory of the equilibrium business cycle, where it is assumed that the future prices are foreseen, at least in a probabilistic sense. If the movement is towards a path that remains constant thereafter, or is represented by a constant probability distribution thereafter, it is natural to speak of stability in this context too.

2.6   The Graham Model: Existence and Comparative Advantage

The other major areas in which I have worked are the theory of international trade and the theory of optimal growth. My initial excursion into existence theory was to prove the existence of equilibrium in F. D. Graham's model of international trade (McKenzie, 1954a) which I had studied with Graham at Princeton. Graham had us solve, purely by hand, using trial and error, small general equilibrium models of trade with a few countries and a few goods, assuming the simplest production and demand functions in each country. While we always found solutions, and never more than one for a given model, no one had found a proof that this must be the case, and von Neumann had informed Graham that no analytical solution was to be expected. Actually, the problem can be reduced to a nonlinear programming problem under the particular demand functions used by Graham, which are derivable from Cobb–Douglas utility functions and are assumed to be the same for all countries. That is, Graham assumed that the same proportion of income is spent on all goods in all countries. Under these conditions, the world demand maximizes a utility function over the production possibility set, so fixed-point methods are not needed. However, even a small generalization of these assumptions, say that the proportions in which income is spent in different countries differ, will invalidate this approach.

My theorem was proved under much more general demand conditions and extended to more general production models as well, so that the application of a fixed-point theorem was essential. My initial proof was to smooth the production set and apply Brouwer's fixed-point theorem followed by an approximation argument; but, having in my hands a discussion paper from the Cowles Commission by the mathematician Morton Slater suggesting that the Kakutani theorem might be useful in economics, I saw that this was the perfect theorem for the problem. This paper (McKenzie, 1954a) and that by Arrow and Debreu (1954) were first presented to the meeting of the Econometric Society in Chicago in December 1952. They were written independently.

However, my principal papers in trade theory proper were concerned with comparative advantage (1954b) and factor price equalization (1955). The comparative advantage paper was written in its first version for Tialling Koopmans in his class on activity analysis at Chicago in 1950. He then urged me to tackle the factor price equalization problem and seemed to be somewhat disappointed when I first proved a theorem on the existence of equilibrium. The major point of the comparative advantage paper was to show by elementary arguments that efficient specialization in production in Graham's model is equivalent to the existence of prices at which the profit conditions of competitive equilibrium are satisfied. The sufficiency of the profit conditions for efficiency is rather obvious and very quickly proved; but the proof that efficient production implies the existence of prices at which the profit conditions are satisfied requires the use of a theorem on the separation of convex sets by hyperplanes.

Table 2.2

	A	B	C	D
Cloth	10	10	10	10
Linen	19	20	15	28
Corn	42	24	30	40

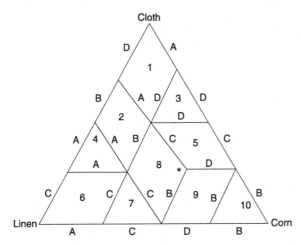

Figure 2.4
At the vertex marked "Cloth" only cloth is produced. Similarly, only linen is produced at "Linen" and only corn at "Corn." In the sector labelled 1, country A is changing from cloth to corn on the right boundary from the vertex and country D is changing from cloth to linen along the left boundary from the vertex. Similarly for other boundaries. In the interior of any sector, all countries produce all the goods they produce at any vertex of that sector. The diagram is qualitative, since the metric changes from one sector to another.

I also argued that bilateral comparisons of comparative advantage in the classical manner were not adequate to determine whether a specialization in production is efficient. To illustrate this point, I used a Graham model which is summarized in Table 2.2, where each number represents the quantity of the good in the row produced by one unit of labour in the country in that column.

The efficient specializations in production are presented schematically in Figure 2.4, where all countries are specialized to one good at the vertices and all are moving from one specialization to another along the lines of the diagram. At the points where lines meet, each country is producing one good. Within the lines, some countries are producing two goods and substitutions are possible at constant rates

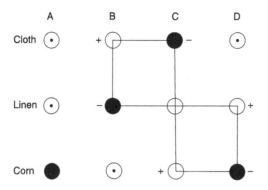

Figure 2.5
The location Linen, B represents production of linen in country B and similarly for other locations. Solid dots represent activities mistakenly used in an inefficient specialization at vertex * of figure 2.4. The lines describe a non-neutral circuit. When the circuit is traversed, output increases at locations labelled +, decreases at locations labelled −. When the changes are complete, the specialization is that of vertex * as it appears in figure 2.4. This specialization is efficient. There are no non-neutral circuits when it is used.

between these goods. In the interior of the spaces outlined by the lines, substitutions are possible at constant rates between all three goods and countries are producing all the goods they produce at some vertex of the enclosed space. The metric changes from one enclosed space to another. The lines lie between points of complete specialization which are efficient and where the change of specialization involves only one country. As Richard Rosett pointed out to me when he was still a student of Koopmans at Yale, my original diagram is incorrect and the error illustrates very nicely the dangers of bilateral comparison. I had the specialization that is indicated by an asterisk to be A and D in corn, C in cloth and B in linen. It is now shown correctly to be A and C in corn, B in cloth and D in linen. It is ironic that this specialization is one vertex of the facet labelled 5 in the diagram which was used correctly in the paper to illustrate the assignment of prices to support an efficient specialization. One of the results proved in the paper is that a specialization is efficient if and only if there is no non-neutral circuit of substitution, that is, no series of substitutions leading to a net increase in world output. The non-neutral circuit in this case is outlined in Figure 2.5, where solid dots indicate active production processes and circles indicate inactive processes in the inefficient specialization. The vertical lines indicate substitutions in production between processes. A + sign represents an increase in output and a − sign, a reduction in output. If linen is reduced in output by 1 unit and the circuit is followed, the result is

$$1 \times (10/20)(30/10)(28/40) - 1 = 21/20 - 1 = 1/20.$$

Thus, the output of linen has risen by $1/20$ and all other goods are produced in the same amounts. So the specialization is not efficient. This possibility is not seen from bilateral comparisons, since every country has a comparative advantage in the good it is producing compared with any other country.

The product of ratios used in identifying the non-neutral circuit is in general the product of the terms a_{sj}/a_{rj}, where a_{sj} is the amount of the sth good produced by a unit of labour in the jth country and a_{rj} is the amount of the rth good produced by a unit of labour in the jth country. Suppose we consider all such products where the denominator of one ratio and the numerator of the next always have the same first subscript and a_{rj} appears in a denominator only if the jth country is producing the rth good in a positive amount. Then for efficiency it must not be possible to form such a product which is greater than 1. Ronald Jones (1961) showed that this condition is equivalent to requiring that an efficient specialization minimize the product of the labour requirements $1/a_{rj}$ over all patterns of specialization that have a given number of countries in each good. Using the direct labour requirements, this criterion can be extended to the case where intermediate goods are traded. However, the world production frontier must be intersected with the positive orthant to prevent the inputs of intermediate goods from exceeding their outputs. Then some "efficient" specializations are seen to be infeasible.

2.7 Factor Price Equalization and the Cone of Diversification

The analysis of specialization was conducted in the Graham model, where each country was treated as though it held only one factor of production, called labour, which differs in relative productivity between different lines of production in different countries. At least, the analysis depends on the possibility of making substitutions in the production of traded goods without encountering seriously diminishing returns, a possibility that Harry Johnson (1966, p. 697) argued is realistic. On the other hand, the theory of factor price equalization involves the exact opposite viewpoint, in which there are multiple factors of production and these are uniform in quality between countries but are

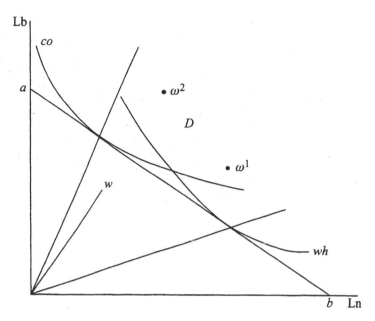

Figure 2.6
Ln labels the land axis and Lb the labour axis; w is the vector of factor prices; co is a set of minimal factor combinations able to produce \$1 worth of corn; wh is a similar set for wheat; ω^1 and ω^2 are the vectors of factor endowments for countries 1 and 2, respectively; D is the cone of diversification. Since the factor endowments lie in the interior of D, the factor price vector w, converted to their respective currencies, must prevail in both countries. That is, at the price for goods implied by the \$1 isoquants, there must be factor price equalization.

differing in quantity. My main contribution to the theory of factor price equalization was the introduction of the cone of diversification (so labelled by John Chipman in his survey article: Chipman, 1965–6). Given a set of production processes, also assumed to be the same between countries, and a set of goods prices, for any given factor prices there will be one or more least-cost combinations of factors for operating a process at unit level, defined as the level where the process produces a unit value of output, which may include several goods. The cone of diversification lies in the factor space. It is the convex cone with its vertex at the origin spanned by the least-cost combinations for the processes present which meet the zero profit conditions. In equilibrium, all other factor combinations on the unit value isoquants must have more than a unit cost. The cone of diversification is illustrated in Figure 2.6.

My central result is that, given the goods prices, factor price equalization can occur only if the factor supplies of the countries involved lie within the cone of specialization for some choice of factor prices. Moreover, if the factor supplies for some countries lie in the interior of the cone of specialization for some choice of factor prices, factor price equalization for these countries must occur in competitive equilibrium, and these factor prices must prevail in all countries. This result does not depend on smooth production functions or on an assumption of nonjoint production. However, as is usual in this subject, costs of transport are being neglected. Allowance may be made for goods that cannot enter into international trade because transport costs are prohibitive. Then the resource vector should include the resources that remain after the domestic goods have been produced. Of course this is a considerable complication, since the resources absorbed by domestic goods will depend both on the prices for traded goods and on the factor prices.

2.8   The von Neumann Model and Turnpike Theory

My contributions to the existence and stability of competitive equilibrium and the theory of international trade were made in the 1950s, when economic theory using mathematics was burgeoning. My only contribution to optimality theory in this period was my first substantial article, which was published in the *Economic Journal* in 1951. This was concerned not with the perfectly competitive economy, but with monopolistic competition. It argued that an efficient distribution of resources among firms could not be achieved in a competitive market unless price and marginal cost were equated everywhere. No system of proportionality would suffice.

In the 1960s I moved to Rochester and shifted my attention to the theory of optimal capital accumulation, where the models do not necessarily refer to competitive markets. The analysis of optimal capital accumulation attracted many economists in this period. The subject was started by Dorfman, Samuelson and Solow (1958), following a conjecture by Samuelson. I read their book around 1959. (Indeed, I can recall deciding to pursue this topic upon reading their chapter on the turnpike theorem while waiting for a flight south in Newark airport.) There was also a paper of Samuelson and Solow (1958) which the literature has neglected, although it dealt with a generalized Ramsey model with a proper economic objective in the form of a social utility function.

The modern period began with three papers in the early 1960s by Radner (1961), Morishima (1961) and myself (McKenzie, 1963). The papers of Radner and Morishima were inspired by a lecture given by Hicks as he travelled from Rochester to Berkeley to Tokyo in 1958. My work was inspired by the theorem in the book of Dorfman *et al.* (1958), where the model was a Leontief model with variable coefficients and two goods. However, their proof was somewhat incomplete. I related my model to Morishima's since his paper became available to me before mine was published, although my work was independent of his. These papers were all concerned with a von Neumann model with the objective of reaching the largest possible stock of capital goods in pre-assigned ratios after a given time. Radner's model assumed a convex social production cone with vertex at the origin and strictly convex cross sections, at least in the neighbourhood of the ray along which maximal balanced expansion occurs. This means that expansion at the maximal rate requires that all goods be jointly produced. Thus, Radner's model is not consistent with the neoclassical production model. The neoclassical model has independent industries which operate together. In the neoclassical model with more than one industry, the production possibility set always has flats on the efficient part of its boundary. Morishima dealt with a Leontief-type model without fixed capital, assuming one nonproduced factor of production, a finite number of alternative processes for each industry and no joint production. I also used a type of Leontief model (1941) where inputs are initial capital stocks and outputs are terminal capital stocks and the input coefficients in each industry are assumed to be continuously variable. My paper (McKenzie, 1963a) was delivered to the Econometric Society meeting in St Louis in December 1960. Radner's paper was scheduled for the same meeting in the preliminary programme, but I believe he did not take part in the final programme.

My method of proof was to appeal to an old theorem of Samuelson and Solow (1953) on the convergence of optimal growth paths to a balanced path. Their theorem was not really appropriate for optimal growth paths, since it assumed that higher levels of capital stocks this period imply higher levels of capital stocks next period. However, this condition is an implication for levels of prices in the Leontief model when the technology matrix is assumed to be indecomposable. As a consequence, prices do converge over time. Once convergence has occurred, the Samuelson–Solow theorem may be applied to the transformation of capital stocks, now with coefficients that are approximately fixed because of the nearly constant prices, to obtain a convergence of capital stocks to a balanced path except for a limited number of initial and terminal periods. The path is traced back from the terminal stocks, so the transitions are from capital stocks in one period to capital stocks in the previous period. The Samuelson–Solow assumption is implied for capital stocks on this path since the inverse of the Leontief input–output matrix is a positive matrix. This proof has the feature that one argument (on prices forwards) is used to obtain convergence to a face of the production cone which I later called the "von Neumann facet." The facet is generated by the activities meeting the profit conditions at the prices that support growth at the maximal rate. Another argument, on stocks backwards, is used to obtain convergence in the neighbourhood of the facet to the maximal balanced growth path lying on it. This method is the characteristic feature of my work on optimal growth problems. In the general model I use the value loss argument due to Radner for the first stage to obtain convergence to a face of the production cone, which I named the von Neumann facet. The argument of the second stage is analogous to the argument for the simple Leontief case.

The paper in which the von Neumann facet was explicitly recognized (McKenzie, 1963b) uses a generalized Leontief (1953) model with variable coefficients and durable capital goods. This paper was given at the Econometrics Society summer meeting at Stillwater, Oklahoma, in 1961. The von Neumann facet in this model is characterized as the smallest face of the production cone that contains a von Neumann ray. A von Neumann ray, which need not be unique, is the locus of paths that achieve the maximal rate of balanced growth of the capital stocks possible in the technology. The analogy of the role of this path to the role of an express highway led Samuelson to call it a "turnpike." Ever since, the theorems proving asymptotic convergence for optimal paths of capital accumulation have been termed "turnpike theorems." Like the previous papers, with the notable exception of that by Samuelson and Solow (1958), the objective is pure capital accumulation over a given time interval. Radner's idea of value loss for paths off the von Neumann ray is used. However, the loss is no longer associated with the von Neumann ray in the production cone, but rather with the flat in the efficiency boundary of the production cone which properly contains the von Neumann ray. The dimension of the flat is equal to the number of industries, that is, the number of goods that are produced. It is shown that the rate of increase in the value of the input–output vector on an optimal path, valued at the prices supporting the von Neumann facet, cannot fall short of the rate of increase for paths on the facet by an $\varepsilon > 0$ for more than a fixed number of periods. This forces convergence of the optimal path to the facet, in angular distance.

Indeed, the optimal path cannot stay out of a given angular neighbourhood of the von Neumann facet for more than a finite number of periods, however long the path might be.

The continuation of the argument is to show that a path converging to the von Neumann facet must converge to a path that is permanently on the facet. Then the turnpike result will follow if the technology spanning the facet requires that any path remaining on the facet permanently must converge to a unique von Neumann equilibrium. A von Neumann equilibrium is a balanced path of expansion that is supported by prices in the sense that each process in use earns zero profits and all other processes earn zero or negative profits. This is analogous to the argument of the second stage of the St Louis paper. The convergence to a von Neumann facet can also be proved for the general von Neumann model described by Kemeny, Morgenstern and Thompson (1956), in which several von Neumann equilibria with different rates of balanced growth are possible. Kemeny *et al.* considered only those equilibria whose outputs have positive value at the supporting prices. In a paper of mine (McKenzie, 1967) given to a conference in Cambridge, UK, in 1963 of the International Economic Association, I proved that the growth rate of such an equilibrium is the supremum of the rates of balanced growth in which some particular set of goods can participate. The associated von Neumann facets are the only faces of the production cone that have the turnpike property, i.e. the property that optimal paths which are long enough can be made to spend an arbitrarily large fraction of the accumulation time arbitrarily near a von Neumann facet. This property gives the economic significance of the requirement introduced by Kemeny *et al.* that the output should have positive value in the von Neumann equilibrium.

2.9 The Ramsey Model and Turnpike Theory

Of course, the objective of maximal accumulation of capital goods in preassigned ratios has limited interest to economists. The von Neumann model with its maximal balanced growth equilibria is important chiefly because it led to models with alternative processes and joint production where the objective is defined in terms of utility for consumers. A model of capital accumulation whose objective is based on consumer utility was introduced by Ramsey (1928) in a one-sector economy a few years before von Neumann presented his multi-sectoral model. The fusion of the von Neumann and Ramsey models was done by McFadden (1967), Gale (1967) and myself (McKenzie, 1968). The papers by Gale and myself were presented to a summer workshop at Stanford in 1965 which was sponsored by the Mathematical Social Science Board. In the previous summer, in a workshop at Rochester, I had introduced the idea of a reduced model in which an initial stock of capital and a final stock in each period are associated with the maximal consumer utility per capita achievable over the period.

For finite paths, define an optimal path as one that achieves the largest sum of per capita utility over the entire programme. Consider the one-period utility function $u(k_{t-1}, k_t)$ defined on the initial and terminal stocks of the tth period. If this function is assumed to be concave, the set of input–output vectors that lie below its graph, called its subgraph, will be convex. For any point on the upper boundary of the subgraph, there is a hyperplane which contains the point and has the subgraph lying below it. A vector is perpendicular to this hyperplane and may be treated as a price vector. The length of the price vector may be chosen so that utility has the price 1.

A facet here is the set of points in the subgraph that are contained in a flat part of its boundary. They lie in a supporting hyperplane of the subgraph. The von Neumann facet is the smallest flat in the boundary that contains all the points of maximal sustainable utility per capita. At a point of maximal sustainable utility, the terminal capital stocks must be at least as large as the initial stocks, and the utility must be as large as possible given this condition. A von Neumann facet is represented in Figure 2.7. In this case, the graph of the utility function is a lined surface, so the von Neumann facet is a line segment. The figure represents a projection of the facet on the input–output space for capital stocks. My theorem says that an optimal path from any initial stocks that are large enough to allow a path starting there to reach a point of maximal sustainable utility will converge to the von Neumann facet, in the sense that, given any neighbourhood of the facet, an optimal path cannot remain outside this neighbourhood more than a certain fixed number of periods, however long the path may be. Again, if the facet is stable in the sense that any path that remains on the facet indefinitely must converge to a point of maximal sustainable utility, called by me a von Neumann point, an optimal path also converges to a von Neumann point for all but a finite number of periods.

Von Weizäcker (1965) and Atsumi (1965), in the same issue of the *Review of Economic Studies*, introduced a criterion for optimality over an infinite horizon which made it unnecessary to select a terminal stock in considering optimal paths. Atsumi used this criterion to prove a turnpike theorem for infinite optimal paths in a two-sector model.

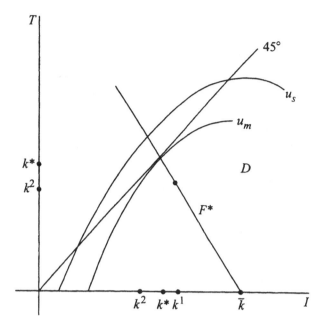

Figure 2.7
I is the axis of initial capital stocks and T the axis of terminal capital stocks. The input–output combinations on u_s can only provide subsistence levels of utility for consumers. Those on u_m provide the maximum sustainable level of utility. k^* is the capital stock of the path of maximal sustainable utility; $\bar{k}$ is the maximal sustainable stock; k^1 to k^2 is a path that cannot be continued on F^*, which is the von Neumann facet. Since there are no paths on F^* which can be continued indefinitely except the balanced path at k^*, the facet F^* is said to be stable. If F^* made an angle of less than $45°$ with the horizontal axis to the left, all paths would converge to k^* and F^* would again be stable. Only facets with non-trivial cyclic paths fail to be stable.

Gale extended the turnpike result to a multi-sector model using the assumption that utility defined on capital stocks is strictly concave near the point of maximum sustainable utility. In loose terms, the criterion is that a path from given initial stocks is optimal if the utility sum for finite initial segments of the path permanently overtakes the utility sum from an alternative path from the same initial stocks, after a time T which depends on the alternative path. More exactly, if $\{k_t\}$ is the optimal path and $\{k'_t\}$ is the alternative, for an arbitrary $\varepsilon > 0$ there is a time T such that

$$\sum_{t=1}^{r} u_t(k'_{t-1}, k'_t) - \sum_{t=1}^{r} u_t(k_{t-1}, k_t) < \varepsilon,$$

for all τ greater than T. The utility sum for all later times along the alternative path does not exceed the utility sum along the optimal path by as much as ε. The turnpike result is convergence to the balanced path along which maximum sustainable utility is achieved, using strict concavity of the utility function so that the path is unique and the von Neumann facet is trivial.

In subsequent years, the turnpike theorems for infinite paths in the multi-sector Ramsey model were generalized in various ways. I showed, in my Fisher–Schultz lecture to the Econometric Society (McKenzie, 1976; see McKenzie and Yano, 1980, for some corrections) that the proper setting for the turnpike theorems in general models, where it is not assumed that the reduced utility function is constant over time, is convergence of optimal paths to each other, provided one path is reachable from the other and utility is strictly concave. This removes the special position of balanced paths, none of which may be optimal when utility and production functions vary over time.

I gave a simple proof for this result (McKenzie, 1982), adapting an argument given by Jeanjean (1974) for the stationary stochastic model. It uses the fact that the chord of a concave function lies beneath the graph of the function. Put utility along the first optimal path equal to 0 in every period. (We are free to do this, since adding an arbitrary constant to utility in each period makes no difference to the relative sizes of utility sums along different paths.) Let K be the set of stocks from which this path can be reached in finite time. Then the optimal paths from any initial stock in K will have a utility sum greater than $-\infty$. Also assume that the initial stock of the first path is relative interior to K. The fact that the first path can be reached from the starting point of the second implies that the finite utility sums along the second path are uniformly bounded below. But strict concavity implies that a path halfway between the two does better than the average of the two. Suppose the paths do not converge and the concavity of the utilities is uniformly bounded from zero. Then the gain of the midpath is bounded above 0. Thus, the finite utility sums along the midpath are unbounded above. Since the initial stock of the first path is relative interior to K, it may be expressed as a convex combination of the midpath and some third path with its initial stock in K, both of which have their utility sums bounded below. By concavity of u, this implies that the first path also has utility sums unbounded above over finite periods. However, these sums are identically 0 by the normalization. This contradiction implies that the paths must converge. Note that the argument does not

require either path to be stationary and the utility function may depend
on t. However, discounting is excluded, since then uniform strict concavity is lost. It is astonishing that we took so long to find this simple
argument although we were quite conscious of the fact that we had no
direct proof of convergence. We used a dual argument which is a
roundabout way through support prices. I recall William Brock early
predicting to me in conversation that some day a primal proof would
be found because the convergence properties really had nothing to do
with duality.

2.10   The Neighbourhood Turnpike Theorem

The von Neumann facet plays a crucial role in the multi-sector Ramsey
model once the assumption of strict concavity of the reduced utility
function is dropped. This is true for the model in which future utility
is discounted as well as for the model in which it is not. Indeed, strict
concavity is inconsistent with the neoclassical model. It is not the lack
of strict concavity for consumer's utility that causes the problem, but
the lack of strictly convex cross sections in the production cone.

   The dimensionality of the von Neumann facet may be seen intuitively in the case of a Leontief model with capital coefficients, where
there may be alternative activities in each industry and each industry
produces a single net output. (Gross outputs include the capital stocks
that are not completely consumed in the period.) In a Leontief model
labour is the only unproduced factor. Integrated activities may be
defined whose inputs are labour and initial stocks and whose net outputs are consumption goods and additions to the initial stocks entering
the activity. If the total labour input to the set of such integrated activities producing capital goods is held constant, while activity levels are
changed by shifting labour between the integrated activities, there is
no effect on the output of consumption goods and services. The utility
level is constant while the inputs of initial stocks and the outputs of
terminal stocks are changing. Suppose the stocks from which these
changes are made are the stocks of an optimal stationary path and the
changes are confined to integrated activities which operate at positive
levels. Then, by the argument of the last paragraph, all the resulting
points on the graph of the utility function are in the von Neumann
facet. This follows from the fact that the same prices are supporting,
together with the definition of the von Neumann facet as the smallest
facet of the subgraph containing the points of maximum sustainable
utility.

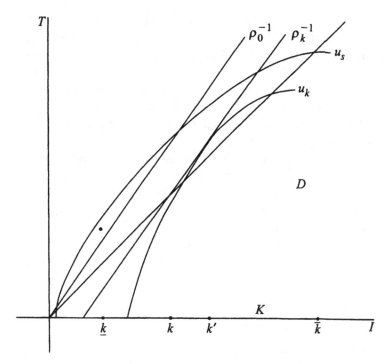

Figure 2.8
The line labelled ρ_0^{-1} has slope ρ^{-1} and passes through the origin. $\underline{k}$ is a capital stock that can be expanded in a ratio larger than ρ^{-1}. ρ_k^{-1} is a line with slope ρ^{-1} that passes through the point (k, k). u_k is the highest level of utility for any point in the feasible set D that lies above the line ρ_k^{-1}. This utility is achieved at a point with initial stock k'. This procedure defines a mapping of the set K of capital stocks less than or equal to $\bar{k}$ into convex subsets of K. There is a fixed point by Kakutani's theorem which is an optimal stationary path for the discount factor ρ.

The generalized Leontief case is discussed at length in Takahashi (1985). If there are n capital goods, the dimension of the von Neumann facet associated with any optimal stationary path will be $n - 1$. Thus, if we are considering a model with a single good in addition to labour, the facet is trivial unless the utility function for consumption is linear in some direction around the consumption bundle on the optimal stationary path. In other words, the example in Figure 2.8 requires linearities other than those arising from variations of activity levels.

The first turnpike theorems with discounting were proved independently by Cass and Shell (1976) and by José Scheinkman (1976). These assumed strict concavity and differentiability of the utility functions so that the von Neumann facets are single points on the graph of the utility function which correspond to optimal stationary paths. When the discount factor is near enough to 1, an optimal stationary path lies in a small neighbourhood of the path of maximal sustainable utility. The optimal stationary path is also unique (see Brock, 1973) and globally stable. Scheinkman's method of proof is to show that an optimal path must approach close to the path of maximal sustainable utility at least once, which brings it within the basin of stability of the optimal stationary path for p near 1.

Turnpike theory has been extended to quasi-stationary models where differentiability is not assumed (McKenzie, 1982, 1983). However, the basic theorem with discounting proves convergence of the optimal path to a neighbourhood of the von Neumann facet rather than to the facet itself. The neighbourhood depends on the discount factor and converges to the facet as the discount factor approaches 1. The utility function in the tth period is $p^t u(x, y)$ with $0 < p < 1$. The proof uses support prices for optimal paths. If k_t, $t = 1, 2, \ldots$, is an optimal path, support prices p_t satisfy the relation

$$u_t(k_t, k_{t+1}) + p_{t+1}k_{t+1} - p_t k_t \geq u_t(x, y) + p_{t+1}y - p_t x,$$

for all input–output vectors (x, y) of initial and terminal stocks which are consistent with the technology. Weitzman (1973) found these prices for any model where the utility sum $\sum_{r=1}^{r=\infty} u_r(k_{r-1}, k_r)$ is finite, whether or not the model is quasi-stationary. His results were extended by me (McKenzie, 1974) to paths for which this utility sum is finite only after utility is normalized relative to an optimal path. It is important that these prices support the value function as well as the period-wise utility function. The value function $V_t(x)$ has capital stocks at the start of the tth period as its argument. Utility in each period along an optimal path is set equal to 0. In the quasi-stationary model, a stationary optimal path may be chosen for the normalization. Suppose that any infinite path from x is valued at the largest number that its finite utility sums do not fall below permanently. Then the value $V_t(x)$ is the smallest number that is not exceeded by the value of any path from x. Support of the value function means that the following relation is satisfied:

$$V_t(k_t) - p_t k_t \geq V_t(y) - p_t y,$$

for all y from which there are infinite paths of accumulation. Of course, $V_t(k_t) = 0$ for all t along the optimal path. This allows the definition of a Liapounov function $L_t(y)$. The Liapounov function L_t is non-negative everywhere, positive, decreasing at a point that is not on the von Neumann facet, and zero on the von Neumann facet. In the quasi-stationary case of discounted utility, it may be shown under rather general assumptions that a stationary optimal path $\{\bar{k}_t\}$ exists where $\bar{k}_t = k^\rho$ for all t.

This proof is illustrated in Figure 2.8. The proof uses an assumption that a capital stock exists which can be expanded in one period by a factor at least as great as ρ^{-1}. A stationary optimal path is supported by prices $\bar{p}_t = \rho^t p^\rho$. Let $\{k_t\}$ be an optimal path of accumulation and let $\{p_t\}$ be prices that support $\{k_t\}$ in the sense that both the period-wise utility and the value functions are supported.

Put $q_t = \rho^{-t} p_t$. Then it is possible to use the Liapounov function,

$$L_t(y) = (q_t - q^\rho)(k_t - k^\rho),$$

to prove a convergence property for k_t. The result was proved assuming that the reduced utility function is strictly concave in the neighbourhood of a von Neumann facet $F(k^\rho)$ which contains the optimal stationary path with capital stock k^ρ. This will be true in the neoclassical model if each capital good appears in some activity in use which comes from a process whose production cone has a strictly convex and smooth cross section at the activity used for generating $F(k^\rho)$. However, if the correspondence from stationary capital stocks to facets is lower semi-continuous, the strict concavity can be weakened to concavity. The convergence is not asymptotic, as it is in the case of a discount factor equal to 1. Also, the neighbourhood of convergence depends on ρ. Define a neighbourhood $N(\varepsilon)$ of $F(k^\rho)$ as all k such that the distance of (k_t, k_{t-1}) from $F(k^\rho)$ is less than $\varepsilon > 0$. It may be shown that for any $\varepsilon > 0$ there is a discount factor $\bar{\rho}$, less than one, and a time T such that k_t lies in $N(\varepsilon)$ for all $t > T$ for any ρ greater than $\bar{\rho}$ and less than 1. I call this a neighbourhood turnpike theorem (McKenzie, 1983).

It is worth remarking that the neighbourhood turnpike theorem is consistent with optimal paths that are cyclic or even chaotic. Thus, the many recent results that find optimal paths of this type, for example Benhabib and Nishimura (1985), Boldrin and Montruchio (1986), Majumder and Mitra (1994) and Nishimura et al. (1994), do not conflict with the neighbourhood turnpike theorem. Indeed, Nishimura et al. point out that in their model, as $\rho \to 1$, the chaotic attractor converges to an optimal stationary path. The cyclic or chaotic paths will eventually be confined to a neighbourhood of a von Neumann facet and the extent of the neighbourhood will depend on ρ. There is a turnpike or asymptotic result no matter how far $\rho(> \bar{\rho})$ is from 1, although if it is too far away the neighbourhood may be too large to be of interest.

By introducing differentiability near $k(1)$ and assuming certain regularity properties there, asymptotic convergence to the optimal balanced paths $k(\rho)$ call be proved for ρ sufficiently near to 1. In particular, there should be no cyclic paths on the von Neumann facet for $\rho = 1$, and the Hessian at $k(1)$ should be negative definite on the complement of the von Neumann facet for $k(1)$, in a small neighbourhood of $k(1)$.

A further step in this line of research was the demonstration by Bewley (1982) and, following him, Yano (1984) that turnpike theory can be extended to competitive equilibria with consumers who have diverse tastes so long as their utilities are separable over time and they have the same discount factors. This theory uses the approach that Negishi (1960) used to prove the existence of competitive equilibrium. Negishi shows that at a competitive equilibrium an appropriately weighted sum of the utility functions of the consumers is maximized. Bewley and Yano apply this theorem to intertemporal utilities. Coles (1985) introduces the von Neumann facet into the equilibrium theory. Marimon (1989) generalized the results of Bewley and Yano in the equilibrium theory to allow for uncertainty. Others have carried the programme to certain cases where utility can be recursive (Lucas and Stokey, 1984), so discount rates are endogenous and may differ for different consumers. Since the weighted sum of utilities may be regarded as belonging to a representative consumer, this line of argument supports the use of a representative consumer in dynamic models like those of Kydland and Prescott (1982) and the other real business cycle theorists.

Thus, one application of the analysis of optimal growth paths is the theory of the equilibrium business cycle, the cycle that can appear in an economy where markets are complete and Pareto optimality is attained. In such a theory the asymptotic properties of optimal growth paths would be realized if the reduced utility function of the representative consumer satisfies the conditions of a turnpike theorem. Although it is extremely unlikely that the required conditions would be satisfied exactly, this does not exclude the possibility that a significant approximation to actual dynamics will be observed in some realistic conditions. On the other hand, David Cass (1991) has shown persuasively that incomplete financial markets will lead to indeterminacy of the intertemporal equilibrium, even under conditions where traders are agreed on future prices, so the extent to which the equilibrium approach to business cycles is applicable is an empirical question.

Note

An earlier version of this chapter was published in the special issue of the *Nagasaki Prefectural University Review* (Vol. 28, No. 1) in memory of Professor Yasuo Uekawa.

References

Arrow, K. J. and G. Debreu (1954) "Existence of an Equilibrium for a Competitive Economy," *Econometrica*, Vol. 22, pp. 265–290.

—— and F. H. Hahn (1971) *General Competitive Analysis*, San Francisco: Holden-Day.

—— and L. Hurwicz (1958) "On the Stability of the Competitive Equilibrium, I," *Econometrica*, Vol. 26, pp. 522–552.

Atsumi, H. (1965) "Neoclassical Growth and the Efficient Program of Capital Accumulation," *Review of Economic Studies*, Vol. 32, pp. 127–136.

Back, K. (1988) "Structure of Consumption Sets and Existence of Equilibria in Infinite Dimensional Commodity Spaces," *Journal of Mathematical Economics*, Vol. 17, pp. 88–99.

Benhabib, J. and K. Nishimura (1985) "Competitive Equilibrium Cycles," *Journal of Economic Theory*, Vol. 35, pp. 284–306.

Bewley, T. F. (1982) "An Integration of Equilibrium Theory and Turnpike Theory," *Journal of Mathematical Economics*, Vol. 10, pp. 233–268.

Boldrin, M. and L. Montrucchio (1986) "On the Indeterminacy of Capital Accumulation Paths," *Journal of Economic Theory*, Vol. 40, pp. 26–39.

Border, K. C. (1985) *Fixed Point Theorems with Applications to Economics and Game Theory*, Cambridge: Cambridge University Press.

Boyd, J. H. III and L. W. McKenzie (1993) "The Existence of Competitive Equilibrium over an Infinite Horizon with Production and General Consumption Sets," *International Economic Review*, Vol. 34, pp. 1–20.

Brock, W. A. (1973) "Some Results on the Uniqueness of Steady States in Multisector Models of Optimum Growth when Future Utilities Are Discounted," *International Economic Review*, Vol. 14, pp. 535–559.

Cass, D. (1991) "Perfect Equilibrium with Incomplete Financial Markets: An Elementary Exposition," in L. W. McKenzie and S. Zamagni (eds.), *Value and Capital: Fifty Years Later*, London: Macmillan, pp. 121–144.

—— and K. Shell (1976) "The Structure and Stability of Competitive Dynamical Systems," *Journal of Economic Theory*, Vol. 12, pp. 31–70.

Chipman, J. S. (1965–6) "A Survey of the Theory of International Trade," *Econometrica*, Vol. 33, pp. 477–519, 685–760; Vol. 34, pp. 18–76.

Coles, J. L. (1985) "Equilibrium Turnpike Theory with Constant Returns to Scale and Possibly Heterogeneous Discount Factors," *International Economic Review*, Vol. 26, pp. 671–680.

Debreu, G. (1962) "New Concepts and Techniques for Equilibrium Analysis," *International Economic Review*, Vol. 3, pp. 257–273.

——— and H. Scarf (1963) "A Limit Theorem on the Core of an Economy," *International Economic Review*, Vol. 4, pp. 235–246.

Dorfman, R., P. A. Samuelson and R. Solow (1958) *Linear Programming and Economic Analysis*, New York: McGraw-Hill.

Epstein, L. G. (1987) "The Global Stability of Efficient Intertemporal Allocations," *Econometrica*, Vol. 55, pp. 329–355.

Gale, D. (1967) "On Optimal Development in a Multi-Sector Economy," *Review of Economic Studies*, Vol. 34, pp. 1–18.

Graham, F. D. (1948) *The Theory of International Values*, Princeton, NJ: Princeton University Press.

Hammond, P. J. (1993) "Irreducibility, Resource Relatedness, and Survival in Equilibrium with Individual Nonconvexities," in R. Becker, M. Boldrin, R. Jones and W. Thomson (eds.), *General Equilibrium, Growth, and Trade*, Vol. II, New York: Academic Press.

Hicks, J. R. (1939) *Value and Capital*, Oxford: Oxford University Press.

Hurwicz, L. (1971) "On the Problem of Integrability of Demand Functions," in J. S. Chipman, L. Hurwicz, M. K. Richter and H. F. Sonnenschein (eds.), *Preferences, Utility, and Demand*, New York: Harcourt, Brace, Jovanovich.

——— and H. Uzawa (1971) "On the Integrability of Demand Functions," in J. S. Chipman, L. Hurwicz, M. K. Richter and H. F. Sonnenschein (eds.), *Preferences, Utility, and Demand*, New York: Harcourt, Brace, Jovanovich.

Jeanjean, P. (1974) "Optimal Development Programs under Uncertainty: The Undiscounted Case," *Journal of Economic Theory*, Vol. 7, pp. 66–92.

Johnson, H. (1966) "Factor Market Distortions and the Shape of the Transformation Curve," *Econometrica*, Vol. 34, pp. 686–698.

Jones, R. (1961) "Comparative Advantage and the Theory of Tariffs: A Multi-Country, Multi-Commodity Model," *Review of Economic Studies*, Vol. 28, pp. 161–175.

Khan, M. A. (1993) "Lionel McKenzie on the Existence of Competitive Equilibrium," in R. Becker, M. Boldrin, R. Jones and W. Thomson (eds.), *General Equilibrium, Growth, and Trade*, Vol. II, New York: Academic Press.

Kemeny, J. G., O. Morgenstern and G. L. Thompson (1956) "A Generalization of the von Neumann Model of an Expanding Economy," *Econometrica*, Vol. 24, pp. 115–135.

Kydland, F. and E. C. Prescott (1982) "Time to Build and Aggregate Fluctuations," *Econometrica*, Vol. 50, pp. 1345–1370.

Leontief, W. (1941) *The Structure of the American Economy, 1919–1929*, Cambridge, MA: Harvard University Press.

—— (1953) *Studies in the Structure of the American Economy*, New York: Oxford University Press.

Lucas, R. E. Jr (1980) "Methods and Problems in Business Cycle Theory," *Journal of Money, Credit, and Banking*, Vol. 2, pp. 696–715.

—— and N. Stokey (1984) "Optimal Growth with Many Consumers," *Journal of Economic Theory*, Vol. 32, pp. 139–171.

Majumdar, M. and T. Mitra (1994) "Periodic and Chaotic Programs of Optimal Intertemporal Allocation in an Aggregative Model with Wealth Effects," *Economic Theory*, Vol. 4, pp. 677–688.

Marimon, R. (1989) "Stochastic Turnpike Property and Stationary Equilibrium," *Journal of Economic Theory*, Vol. 47, pp. 282–306.

Marshall, A. (1890) *Principles of Economics*, Vol. I, London: Macmillan.

McFadden, D. (1967) "The Evaluation of Development Programmes," *Review of Economic Studies*, Vol. 34, pp. 25–31.

McKenzie, L. W. (1951) "Ideal Output and the Interdependence of Firms," *Economic Journal*, Vol. 61, pp. 785–803.

—— (1954a) "On Equilibrium in Graham's Model of World Trade and Other Competitive Systems," *Econometrica*, Vol. 21, pp. 147–161.

—— (1954b) "Specialization and Efficiency in World Production," *Review of Economic Studies*, Vol. 23, pp. 165–180.

—— (1955) "Equality of Factor Prices in World Trade," *Econometrica*, Vol. 22, pp. 239–257.

—— (1956) "Competitive Equilibrium with Dependent Consumer Preferences," in H. A. Antosiewicz (ed.), *Second Symposium in Linear Programming*, Vol. I, Washington: National Bureau of Standards, pp. 277–294.

—— (1957) "Demand Theory without a Utility Index," *Review of Economic Studies*, Vol. 24, pp. 185–189.

—— (1959) "On the Existence of General Equilibrium for a Competitive Market," *Econometrica*, Vol. 27, pp. 54–71.

—— (1960a) "Matrices with Dominant Diagonals and Economic Theory," in K. J. Arrow, S. Karlin and P. Suppes (eds.), *Mathematical Methods in the Social Sciences*, Stanford, CA.: Stanford University Press, pp. 47–62.

—— (1960b) "Stability of Equilibrium and the Value of Excess Demand," *Econometrica*, Vol. 28, pp. 606–617.

—— (1961) "On the Existence of General Equilibrium: Some Corrections," *Econometrica*, Vol. 29, pp. 247–248.

—— (1963a) "Turnpike Theorem of Morishima," *Review of Economic Studies*, Vol. 30, pp. 169–176.

—— (1963b) "Turnpike Theorems for a Generalized Leontief Model," *Econometrica*, Vol. 31, pp. 165–180.

——— (1967) "Maximal Paths in the von Neumann Model," in E. Malinvaud and M. O. L. Bacharach (eds.), *Activity Analysis in the Theory of Growth and Planning*, London: Macmillan.

——— (1968) "Accumulation Programs of Maximum Utility and the von Neumann Facet," in J. N. Wolfe (ed.), *Value, Capital, and Growth*, Edinburgh: Edinburgh University Press, pp. 353–383.

——— (1976) "Turnpike Theory," the Fisher–Schultz Lecture for 1974, *Econometrica*, Vol. 43, pp. 841–865.

——— (1981) "The Classical Theorem on Existence of Competitive Equilibrium," Presidential Address to the Econometric Society, *Econometrica*, Vol. 49, pp. 819–841.

——— (1982) "A Primal Route to the Turnpike and Liapounov Stability," *Journal of Economic Theory*, Vol. 27, pp. 194–209.

——— (1983) "Turnpike Theory, Discounted Utility and the von Neumann Facet," *Journal of Economic Theory*, Vol. 30, pp. 330–352.

——— (1986) "Optimal Economic Growth, Turnpike Theorems, and Comparative Dynamics," in K. J. Arrow and M. Intriligator (eds.), *Handbook of Mathematical Economics*, Vol. III, Amsterdam: North-Holland, pp. 1281–1355.

——— and M. Yano (1980) "Turnpike Theory: Some Corrections," *Econometrica*, Vol. 48, pp. 1839–1840.

Moore, J. (1975) "The Existence of 'Compensated Equilibrium' and the Structure of the Pareto Efficiency Frontier," *International Economic Review*, Vol. 16, pp. 267–300.

Morishima, M. (1961) "Proof of a Turnpike Theorem: The No Joint Production Case," *Review of Economic Studies*, Vol. 28, pp. 89–97.

Mukherji, A. (1989) "On *Tâtonnement* Process," Working Paper, Jawaharlal Nehru University, New Delhi.

Negishi, T. (1960) "Welfare Economics and Existence of an Equilibrium for a Competitive Economy," *Metroeconomica*, Vol. 5, pp. 22–30.

——— (1962) "Stability of a Competitive Economy," *Econometrica*, Vol. 30, pp. 635–669.

Nishimura, K., G. Sorger and M. Yano (1994) "Ergodic Chaos in Optimal Growth Models with Low Discount Rates," *Economic Theory*, Vol. 4, pp. 705–717.

Peleg, B. and M. E. Yaari (1970) "Markets with Countably Many Commodities," *International Economic Review*, Vol. 11, pp. 369–377.

Radner, R. (1961) "Paths of Economic Growth that are Optimal with Regard Only to Final States," *Review of Economic Studies*, Vol. 28, pp. 98–104.

Ramsey, F. (1928) "A Mathematical Theory of Savings," *Economic Journal*, Vol. 38, pp. 543–559.

Samuelson, P. A. and R. W. Solow (1953) "Balanced Growth under Constant Returns to Scale," *Econometrica*, Vol. 21, pp. 412–424.

——— and ——— (1958) "A Complete Capital Model involving Heterogeneous Capital Goods," *Quarterly Journal of Economics*, Vol. 70, pp. 537–562.

Scarf, H. (1967) "The Core of an N-Person Game," *Econometrica*, Vol. 35, pp. 50–49.

Scheinkman, J. (1976) "On Optimal Steady States of n-Sector Growth Models when Utility is Discounted," *Journal of Economic Theory*, Vol. 12, pp. 11–70.

Smith, A. (1776) *An Inquiry into the Nature and Causes of the Wealth of Nations*, 5th edn, ed. E. Cannan, London: Methuen, 1906.

Takahashi, H. (1985) "Characterizations of Optimal Programs in Infinite Horizon Economies," PhD thesis, University of Rochester.

von Weizsäcker, C. C. (1965) "Existence of Optimal Programs of Accumulation for an Infinite Time Horizon," *Review of Economic Studies*, Vol. 32, pp. 85–104.

Walras, L. (1874–7) *Elements d'économie politique pure*, Lausanne: Corbaz; trans. by W. Jaffé from the 1926 definitive edn as *Elements of Pure Economics*, London: George Allen & Unwin, 1954.

Weitzman, W. L. (1973) "Duality Theory for Infinite Horizon Convex Models," *Management Science*, Vol. 19, pp. 783–789.

Yano, M. (1984) "The Turnpike of Dynamic General Equilibrium Paths and its Insensitivity to Initial Conditions," *Journal of Mathematical Economics*, Vol. 13, pp. 235–254.

Equilibrium

3 On Equilibrium in Graham's Model of World Trade and Other Competitive Systems

Lionel W. McKenzie

3.1 Introduction

I shall prove the existence and uniqueness of equilibrium in a particular economic model, that of Frank D. Graham for world trade ([4], ch. 5, 6).[1,2] It will be apparent from the proof, however, that the results apply to quite general economic systems, in which perfect competition is assumed and problems of uncertainty are suppressed. The directions of generalization will be indicated more exactly in the conclusion. It is especially appropriate to investigate these questions for Graham's model, since Graham conjectured on them himself[3] and evidently was not provided a solution. However, the power of the proof which is used in dealing with Graham's model will permit a considerable extension of the results.

The first general and rigorous theorems on the existence and uniqueness of equilibrium in economic systems were developed by John von Neumann in 1932 [9] and Abraham Wald in 1934 [12, 13]. Wald confined his attention to an extension of Cassel's system of general equilibrium in which only one process of production is present for each output. However, in the extended system factors of production can be in surplus supply and become free goods. For this system he showed that an equilibrium exists if the demand functions satisfy certain conditions. In particular, his existence proof imposes a severe restriction on the demand functions which we use only in the proof of uniqueness, namely that $p \cdot \Delta y \leq 0$ implies $(p + \Delta p) \cdot \Delta y < 0$, for $\Delta y \neq 0$.[4] This restriction cannot be allowed in general because of the redistribution of income accompanying price changes. Graham's demand functions do satisfy the restriction (although his production system does not meet Wald's conditions). It is my purpose, however, to develop a more general existence proof where the demand functions are not confined so narrowly.

Von Neumann's discussion[5] allows alternative processes of production and joint products, and introduces capital accumulation. He formulates, however, a rather different problem from ours. In particular, all income except workers' subsistence is saved, and the labor supply expands exactly in proportion to the supply of subsistence goods. In the solution the economy, including the labor supply, expands at a maximal rate, while individual consumption levels are constant.

The essential idea of the present proof is the conjunction of a fixed point theorem and the notion, familiar in activity analysis, of an efficiency frontier to the convex set of attainable outputs. In our initial proofs generality will be sacrificed wherever there is a gain in simplicity.

3.2   Graham's Model

In its production aspect the model of world production and trade used by Frank D. Graham is a linear activities model in which the primary goods are the labor supplies of the several countries. The intermediate goods do not appear explicitly, but each productive process converts the labor of a certain country into a single final good. Each country's labor is confined to its boundaries, and, therefore, the labor supplies are distinct resources. The technology of the jth country may then be represented by the matrix[6]

$$A^j = \begin{bmatrix} a_1^j & & & \\ & \cdot & & 0 \\ & & \cdot & \\ 0 & & & \cdot \\ & & & a_k^j \\ -1 & \cdots & & -1 \end{bmatrix} = \begin{bmatrix} A_{\text{fin}}^j \\ A_{\text{pri}}^j \end{bmatrix}, \tag{2.1}$$

where there are k final goods. a_i^j is the quantity of the ith good produced by a unit of labor of the jth country. A_{fin}^j is the diagonal matrix formed of the first k rows of A^j. A_{pri}^j is the $(k+1)$st row of A^j, and its elements are all -1.

The world technology may now be represented by the matrix[7]

$$A = \begin{bmatrix} A_{\text{fin}}^1 & \cdots & A_{\text{fin}}^n \\ A_{\text{pri}}^1 & & 0 \\ & \cdot & \\ & \cdot & \\ 0 & & A_{\text{pri}}^n \end{bmatrix} = \begin{bmatrix} A_{\text{fin}} \\ A_{\text{pri}} \end{bmatrix}, \tag{2.2}$$

assuming that n countries are present.

Let x^j be a column vector whose typical component x_i^j is the level in the jth country of the activity that produces the ith good. Then the vector

$$x = \begin{bmatrix} x^1 \\ \cdot \\ \cdot \\ \cdot \\ x^n \end{bmatrix} \tag{2.3}$$

is the vector of activity levels for the world economy. x is not allowed to have negative components.

Finally, let η be a vector whose typical component η_j is the labor supply available to the jth country. Then the Graham model may be summarized in the following way:[8]

Production system:

$$\begin{bmatrix} A_{\text{fin}} \\ A_{\text{pri}} \end{bmatrix} x = \begin{bmatrix} y_{\text{fin}} \\ y_{\text{pri}} \end{bmatrix}, \tag{2.4}$$

$$x \geq 0, \tag{2.5}$$

$$y_{\text{pri}} \geq -\eta < 0. \tag{2.6}$$

Demand functions:

$$w_{j\,\text{pri}} = -\eta_j, \quad p_{j\,\text{pri}} > 0, \quad (j = 1, \ldots, n). \tag{2.7}$$

$$w_{i\,\text{fin}} = b_i \frac{r}{p_{i\,\text{fin}}}, \quad \left(b_i > 0, \sum b_i = 1, i = 1, \ldots, k \right). \tag{2.8}$$

$$r = p_{\text{fin}} \cdot y_{\text{fin}}, \quad p_{i\,\text{fin}} > 0. \tag{2.9}$$

It is assumed that each country is able to produce each good, that is, in (2.1)

$$a_i^j > 0 \text{ for all } j \text{ and all } i. \tag{2.10}$$

y_{fin} is the vector of final output, y_{pri} the vector of labor input, for the world economy. $w_{j\,\text{pri}}$ is the quantity of the jth country's labor supplied by consumers at positive prices. $w_{i\,\text{fin}}$ is the quantity of the ith final good demanded by consumers. p_{fin} is the vector of prices for final goods. p_{pri} is the vector of labor prices. r is the level of world income. The demand functions (2.8) imply that the same proportion, b_i, of total world income is devoted to the ith final good regardless of its price. In other words, the price and income elasticities of world demand are unity. The supply of labor is constant at positive prices.

3.2.1

The linearity of the model involves the assumption that multiplying the input to an activity by a number $\alpha \geq 0$ will multiply the output of the activity by the same number α, independently of the levels of other activities.[9] Thus there are no indivisibilities and no external economies in production. Also, joint production is absent and every process is completely integrated, so that intermediate products do not appear explicitly. As Samuelson and Arrow have shown [11, 1], it is legitimate[10] to assume a single integrated activity for each output in linear production models provided there is only one primary resource and no joint production.[11] But this is the case in each country considered separately. Therefore, Graham's simplification only involves as an additional assumption that intermediate products do not enter international trade. This assumption seems to be implicit in most of the classical trade theory.

3.3 Implications of the Model

3.3.1

Let X denote the set of vectors x of activity levels which satisfy the restrictions of the production system (2.4), (2.5), and (2.6). X is bounded, closed, and convex.[12] X is bounded, since each activity uses a finite quantity of labor at the unit level and the labor supplies are finite. X is closed, since the restrictions (2.5) and (2.6) on x and y_{pri} are closed, and y_{pri} is by (2.4) a continuous[13] function of x. To prove X convex, assume x' and x'' are two vectors of X, then if $x = \alpha x' + (1 - \alpha)x''$, with $0 \leq \alpha \leq 1$, x is also a permissible vector of activity levels. Clearly $x \geq 0$, and $y_{\text{pri}} = A_{\text{pri}}x = A_{\text{pri}}(\alpha x' + (1 - \alpha)x'') \geq -\alpha\eta - (1 - \alpha)\eta = -\eta$.

In the remainder of section 3.3 all vectors are vectors of final outputs. Therefore, the subscript "fin" will be omitted. Let Y be the set of all vectors y of final output which can be attained within the restrictions of the model.[14] Then by (2.4) $y = A_{\text{fin}}x$ for $x \in X$. Therefore, Y is the linear transform of X by A_{fin}. Thus Y is also closed, bounded, and convex.

3.3.2
Next we note that if z is any vector of final output, there is a number $\alpha > 0$ such that $\alpha z \in Y$. In other words, it is possible to produce output in any proportions. This is easily seen within the technology (2.1) of a single country. Choose any $y \geq 0$. Then put $\alpha x_i^j = \alpha y_i / a_i^j$. For $\alpha > 0$ and sufficiently small, $\alpha x_i^j \geq -\eta_j$. Thus $\alpha y \in Y$.

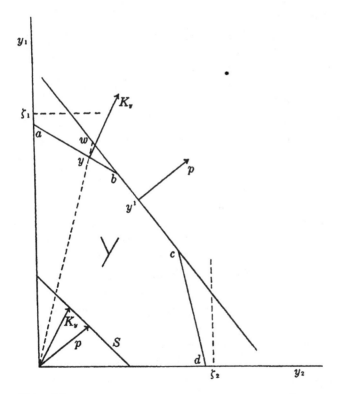

Figure 3.1

Let us refer to a vector z of final output as efficient if

$$z \in Y \text{ and } z + w \notin Y \text{ for } w \geqslant 0. \quad [15] \tag{3.1}$$

Thus z is efficient if no component output can be increased without some other output being reduced.[16] However, in the present model we can show that "z is efficient" is implied by

$$z \in Y \text{ and } \alpha z \notin Y \text{ for } \alpha > 1. \tag{3.2}$$

For suppose $z + w \in Y$, $w \geqslant 0$. Reduce w to 0. Then, since each country can produce every good, the labor supplies released may be used to produce final goods in the same proportions as they appear in z. The resulting output vector y will equal αz for some $\alpha > 1$, and, therefore, inefficiency implies $\alpha z \in Y$ for some $\alpha > 1$. Since final goods can be produced in any proportions, this means that for any $z \neq 0$, $y = \alpha_0 z$ where α_0 is the largest positive number such that $y \in Y$, will be efficient. Since Y is closed, there is an efficient output vector with final goods in any desired proportions.

Outputs satisfying (3.2) will be called "extreme outputs." The extreme points of a set of attainable outputs will be in the boundary and, in general, will include the efficient points.

3.4 Competitive Equilibrium

We shall interpret Graham's model according to the usual static assumptions. Price anticipations have no explicit role. The presence of competition means that everyone accepts prices as given and beyond the scope of his influence. If the input-output vector of a process is z (where input components are negative numbers) and the corresponding vector of prices is p, define profits earned from the process as $p \cdot z$. Then managers of productive processes (firms) do not initiate changes in output unless their profits will be increased. Consumers may derive income from profits or from the sale of primary goods (productive services) to the firms. Thus income for the economy is equal to $p \cdot y + p_{pri} \cdot y_{pri}$ or $p_{fin} \cdot y_{fin}$, where y is the vector of net inputs and outputs for all productive processes together. It is assumed that consumers wish to spend all their income on output and that the pattern of demand (including the offer of primary goods) is a function of the price vector p. We shall then regard an equilibrium position as a price vector p and an attainable input-output vector y, which (1) satisfy the demand functions and (2) leave producers with no opportunity for increasing profits.[17] Condition (1) may be termed the demand condition and condition (2) the profit condition of competitive equilibrium.

Let us apply these principles to Graham's model. The profit from an activity A_i^j operated at a level x_i^j is $p \cdot x_i^j A_i^j = p \cdot z$ where z is the input-output vector of this activity. Since x_i^j may assume any nonnegative value, aside from resource limitations which are not apparent to the individual manager, it is clear that any profit $p \cdot z$ from A_i^j which is nonnegative can always be expanded by increasing x_i^j unless $p \cdot A_i^j = 0$, and thus $p \cdot z = 0$. On the other hand, if an activity is used, $p \cdot A_i^j$ must not be negative. For then profits could be increased to 0 by putting $x_i^j = 0$. Thus in Graham's model the profit condition of competitive equilibrium takes the form:[18]

$$p \cdot A_i^j \leqq 0 \text{ and } p \cdot A_i^j = 0 \text{ if } x_i^j > 0. \tag{4.1}$$

Since in an equilibrium every activity in use earns zero profits, no profits are disbursed, and all income is derived from the sale of primary goods. Furthermore, the condition $p \cdot A_i^j = 0$ where $x_i^j > 0$ determines the wage rate in the jth country once the price of the ith good is known. For, by (2.1), $p \cdot A_i^j = p_{i\,\text{fin}} a_i^j - p_{j\,\text{pri}} = 0$. Therefore, consumers' demand in this model can be represented as a function of output prices alone. The demand functions for final output then depend, implicitly, both on the ownership of the primary goods and on the technology.[19] Of course, Graham's own demand functions were recommended by their simplicity. It should be noted that the demand functions (2.7), (2.8), with (2.9) allow only for positive prices. Indeed, as we shall see later, the demand for a final good grows without limit as its relative price approaches zero.

We may now state that (p, y) is a competitive equilibrium in the Graham model if and only if

(a) y_{fin} is attainable according to (2.4), (2.5), and (2.6).
(b) The profit condition (4.1) is met.
(c) p and y satisfy the demand functions (2.7), (2.8), with (2.9) and $w = y$.

$$\tag{4.2}$$

On the other hand, Koopmans has shown[20] that, in a model of production with a finite number of activities and given supplies of primary goods, a vector of final output z_{fin} is efficient[21] if and only if (a) and (b) of (4.2) can be satisfied with p and y, where $y_{\text{fin}} = z_{\text{fin}}$, and where $p_{\text{fin}} > 0$, $p_{\text{pri}} \geqq 0$, and $p_{j\,\text{pri}} = 0$ if $y_{j\,\text{pri}} > -\eta_j$. Let us call such a p a vector of efficiency prices associated with z_{fin}. However, in Graham's model $p_{fin} > 0$ together with the profit condition implies $p_{pri} > 0$. Therefore, efficiency requires $y_{j\,pri} = -\eta_j$. On the other hand, in a competitive equilibrium (c) of (4.2) requires that $y_{j\,pri} = -\eta_j$. Otherwise, labor would be in surplus supply (2.7). And the demand functions for final goods (2.8) require $p_{fin} > 0$.

A comparison of the conditions for competitive equilibrium and for efficiency in this model shows that if (p, y) is a competitive equilibrium, then y_{fin} is efficient and p is a vector of efficiency prices associated with y_{fin}. Furthermore, if y_{fin} is efficient and p is an associated vector of efficiency prices, then (p, y) is a competitive equilibrium if the demand functions for final goods are satisfied by p_{fin} and y_{fin}. For then all the conditions (4.2) are met.

However, it is not necessary to introduce the primary goods and their prices explicitly in order to identify efficient outputs when the primary goods are in fixed supply. For y_{fin} is efficient if and only if y_{fin} is attainable and there exists a price vector $p_{fin} > 0$ such that $p_{fin} \cdot y_{fin} = $ max $p_{fin} \cdot z_{fin}$ for $z_{fin} \in Y$ where Y is the set of attainable outputs. This means, by the definition of normal, that p_{fin} is normal to Y at y_{fin}.[22] Furthermore, any such p_{fin} can be extended to a price vector p for all goods which satisfies the profit condition (4.1). [7], pp. 85–91.

We may conclude, then, that (p_{fin}, y_{fin}) can be extended to a competitive equilibrium in the Graham model if and only if

(a) y_{fin} is attainable.
(b) p_{fin} is normal to Y at y_{fin}, with $p_{fin} > 0$.
(c) p_{fin} and y_{fin} satisfy the demand functions (2.8) and (2.9) with $w_{fin} = y_{fin}$. (4.3)

(In the following two sections (3.5 and 3.6), since the discussion will concern final output vectors only, the subscript "fin" will be dropped, and (p, y) will denote (p_{fin}, y_{fin}).)

3.5 Uniqueness

I shall first prove that if an equilibrium output exists in the Graham model it is unique. In the proof only these properties of the model are actually used:

(a) The set Y of attainable outputs is closed and convex (section 3.3.1).

(b) Any equilibrium output lies on the boundary of Y and the corresponding equilibrium price vector is normal to Y at y (4.3).

(c) The demand functions satisfy the condition $p \cdot \Delta y \leqq 0$ implies $(p + \Delta p) \cdot \Delta y < 0$, for $y \neq 0$.[23]

It is clear that these properties far transcend the Graham model.

Suppose that y and $y + \Delta y$ are distinct boundary points of Y and p and $p + \Delta p$ are corresponding normals. Then by the definition of a normal $p \cdot y \geqq p \cdot (y + \Delta y)$, or $p \cdot \Delta y \leqq 0$. However, by the same token $(p + \Delta p) \cdot (y + \Delta y) \geqq (p + \Delta p) \cdot y$, or $(p + \Delta p) \cdot \Delta y \geqq 0$. This is in conflict with property (c), so the proof is finished if we show that Graham's model has property (c).

In order to prove property (c), I shall first prove that when income is constant $p \cdot \Delta y \leqq 0$ and $\Delta y \neq 0$ implies $\Delta p \cdot \Delta y < 0$ for the Graham demand functions. Let $p \cdot y = (p + \Delta p) \cdot (y + \Delta y) = r_0$. Then from (2.8) we obtain for each i, $\Delta y_i = b_i r_0 [1/(p_i + \Delta p_i) - 1/p_i] = b_i r_0 [-\Delta p_i / p_i (p_i + \Delta p_i)]$. Then $\Delta p_i \Delta y_i = b_i r_0 [-(\Delta p_i)^2 / p_i (p_i + \Delta p_i)]$, which is negative. Therefore, for this special case $\Delta p \cdot \Delta y < 0$.

Now let Δp be any shift in prices for which prices remain positive. Define a new shift in prices $\Delta' p = \Delta p - (\Delta r / r) p = \Delta p - kp$. Thus $\Delta p = \Delta' p + kp$. Since income will remain positive, $\Delta r > -r$, and $k = \Delta r / r > -1$. For $\Delta' p$, income is constant, and $\Delta' p \cdot \Delta' y < 0$. But the shift in prices from p to $p + kp$ or $(1 + k)p$ has no effect on y, since p is only multiplied by a positive constant and the demand functions are homogeneous (of zero degree). Therefore, $\Delta' y = \Delta y$, and $(p + \Delta p) \cdot \Delta y = (1 + k) p \cdot \Delta y + \Delta' p \cdot \Delta y$. Since $\Delta' p \cdot \Delta y < 0$, $p \cdot \Delta y \leqq 0$ implies $(p + \Delta p) \cdot \Delta y < 0$. Thus any equilibrium output of the Graham model is unique.

Suppose $\Delta y = 0$ but $\Delta p \neq 0$. Then by the demand functions (2.8), for every i, $r/p_i = (r + \Delta r)/(p_i + \Delta p_i)$ or $(p_i + \Delta p_i)/p_i = (r + \Delta r)/r$. Thus $p_i + \Delta p_i = p_i (r + \Delta r)/r = (1 + k) p_i$, for each i. In other words, $p + \Delta p = kp$. Thus any equilibrium price vector in the Graham model is unique up to multiplication by a positive constant. Therefore, we may state:

Theorem 1 Any competitive equilibrium in the Graham model is unique, except for multiplication of the price vector by a positive constant.

3.6   Existence

The existence of an equilibrium point is more difficult to show and involves a deep theorem from topology. However, the meaning of the theorem is easy to grasp, and its importance is great enough that economists may well benefit from acquaintance with it.

3.6.1

The properties[24] of Graham's model which will actually be used in the existence proof are:

(a) The set Y of attainable outputs of final goods is closed, bounded, and convex (section 3.3.1).

(b) For final goods in any proportions there is an extreme output[25] with a nonnegative normal (section 3.3.2).

(c) Any extreme output and a positive normal to it[26] define a competitive equilibrium if the demand conditions are met (4.3).

(d) The demand functions for final goods are homogeneous, nonnegative, and continuous for positive prices of final goods (section 3.6.5).

(e) All income is spent (2.8).

(f) If income remains finite and the price of a final good approaches zero, demand for this good eventually exceeds the maximum production attainable (section 3.6.5).

In the ordinary language of economics we shall consider all social budget planes which touch the production transformation surface. Then we assume that total purchases, when the goods are available, will always lie on the budget plane (ignoring an extension of the demand functions, which is a technical point of the proof). Finally, we will prove that there is a budget plane for which the chosen point lies in the section of the plane which touches the production transformation surface, assuming the demand functions to be continuous functions of the prices of final goods. I should conjecture that elementary proofs do not exist of this theorem unless the demand functions are drastically restricted.

3.6.2

It will not be necessary to consider all possible price vectors. Indeed, we will confine attention to the price vectors which lie in the closed simplex S, defined as all p such that $\sum p_i = 1$, $p_i \geq 0$, where the p_i are components of p. Every vector of S is normal to some point y of Y, since the continuous function $p \cdot z$ must attain a maximum on the closed and bounded set Y. Moreover, y must be an extreme output. For if y were not extreme, then, by definition, there is an α with $\alpha y \in Y$ for $\alpha > 1$. But this would imply $p \cdot \alpha y > p \cdot y$, so that p could not be a normal at y. Furthermore, by section 3.3.2, y is also efficient.

3.6.3
In order to prove the existence theorem it will be necessary to use two results from the theory of convex sets. These results can be proved without great difficulty, and I do so in an appendix. Here I merely state them. First, the function $r(p) = \max p \cdot z$ for $z \in Y$ is continuous. Second, if w is an arbitrary vector, not in the interior of Y, $w \geqslant 0$, and $h(w)$ is the intersection of the ray from the origin containing w with the set of extreme outputs of Y, then $h(w)$ is continuous. We know the ray contains an extreme output by property (b). The definition may also be stated as

$$h(w) = \alpha w, \; \alpha \leq 1, \; \alpha w \in Y, \; kw \notin Y \text{ for } k > \alpha. \tag{6.1}$$

In both cases continuity is intuitively appealing, if not "obvious."

3.6.4
Next, we note that the set of normals to Y at a point y is convex and closed. To show convexity, let p^1 and p^2 be normal at y. Then $p^1 \cdot y = \max p^1 \cdot z$ for $z \in Y$, and $p^2 \cdot y = \max p^2 \cdot z$ for $z \in Y$. Let $p = ap^1 + (1 - a)p^2$ with $0 \leq a \leq 1$. Then clearly $p \cdot y = \max p \cdot z$ for $z \in Y$, and p is a normal at y. The set of normals is closed by the continuity of the function $r(p)$ and of the inner product as a function of both vectors. Thus $p_i \to p$ implies $r(p) = p \cdot y$, so that p is normal at y.[27]

3.6.5
The demand w_i for the ith good is given by (2.8) and (2.9) as a function of both p and y. However, we may ignore values of y which are not contained in the set of extreme outputs since they either are not contained in Y or they do not have nonnegative normals. Therefore, they can never appear in a competitive equilibrium (4.3). These restricted demand functions may be written

$$f_i(p) = b_i r(p)/p_i, \quad (p_i > 0),$$

$$r(p) = \max p \cdot z \text{ for } z \in Y, \quad \left(\sum b_i = 1, b_i > 0 \right). \tag{6.2}$$

Since the demand functions are not defined for zero prices, it is necessary either to bound the price vectors which are considered in the proof away from zero or to modify the demand functions so that they are continuous at zero. The latter method is both simpler and more general. First, we note that no competitive equilibrium is possible when $f_i(p)$ exceeds ζ_i where ζ_i is larger than the maximum attainable production of the ith good. Therefore, we are free to modify the demand functions in any manner that excludes an equilibrium for values of p where an $f_i(p) > \zeta_i$. Define

$f_i^*(p) = f_i(p)$ if $f_i(p) \leq \zeta_i$, and

$f_i^*(p) = \zeta_i$ if $f_i(p) > \zeta_i$ or $p_i = 0$,   for $p \in S$.   (6.3)

The function $f_i^*(p)$, defined on S, must be shown to be continuous.

For $p_i > 0$ and $f_i(p) \leq \zeta_i$, $f_i^*(p)$ is continuous by (6.2) and the continuity of $r(p)$. Therefore, it is only necessary to prove that $f_i^*(p)$ is continuous when $f_i(p) > \zeta_i$ or $p_i = 0$. Suppose $p^j \to p'$, where $f_i(p') > \zeta_i$ and $p_i \neq 0$. Since $f_i(p)$ is continuous, for j large enough $f_i(p^j)$ will remain greater than ζ_i and $f_i^*(p^j)$ will be equal to ζ_i. Since $f_i^*(p') = \zeta_i$, continuity exists for this alternative. Suppose now $p^j \to p''$ where $p_i'' = 0$. Assume $r(p)$ is always larger than a positive number δ. Then we see from (6.2) that $f_i(p^j) \to \infty$, and for j_0 large enough, $f_i(p^j)$ remains greater than ζ_i for $j > j_0$. Therefore, $f_i^*(p^j) = \zeta_i$ for $j > j_0$. But $f_i^*(p'') = \zeta_i$, so $f_i^*(p)$ is continuous for the second alternative as well. Hence $f_i^*(p)$ is continuous if $r(p)$ can be bounded away from zero.

Suppose $r(p)$ cannot be bounded away from zero on S. Then there is a sequence p^j such that $r(p^j)$ converges to zero. Since S is closed and bounded,[28] there is a subsequence p^{j_i} converging to a vector $p' \in S$. By the continuity of $r(p)$, $r(p^{j_i})$ converges to $r(p')$. Therefore $r(p') = 0$. But $p' \geqslant 0$ and thus some $p_i' > 0$. Moreover, there is a $y \in Y$ with $y_i > 0$. For this y, $p' \cdot y > 0$, and thus $r(p') = \max p' \cdot z$ for $z \in Y$ cannot be equal to zero. Therefore, there must be a δ such that $r(p) > \delta$ for all $p \in S$, where $\delta > 0$.

3.6.6
In order to proceed to the proof of the theorem, we define mappings f^*, h, and g. To gain an intuitive notion of the mappings, the reader may refer to the figure. For $p \in S$ let $f^*(p) = w$, where $w_i = f_i^*(p)$, as already defined (6.3). The mapping f^* is continuous since f_i^* is continuous. $h(w)$ is defined by (6.1).[29] It is proved to be continuous in the appendix. If y is in the set of extreme outputs, let $g(y) = K_y$, where K_y is the intersection of the set of normals to y with S. This intersection is not empty, since every extreme point has, by property (b), a normal $p \geqslant 0$ and $p / \sum p_i$ is an element of S. K_y is convex as it is the intersection of convex sets.

Lemma The mapping g is upper semi-continuous.

To prove the lemma, we must show that if $y^i \to y'$ and $p^i \to p'$ where p^i is normal at y^i, then p' is normal at y'. Since $r(p)$ is a continuous function, $r(p^i) \to r(p') = \max p' \cdot z$ for $z \in Y$. Also $p^i \cdot y^i \to p' \cdot y'$. But $r(p^i) = p^i \cdot y^i$, so $r(p') = p' \cdot y'$. Then p' is indeed normal at y'.

We must now cite the fixed point theorem of Kakutani:[30]

If F maps a closed simplex S into the set $\{K_d\}$ of convex subsets of S, and F is upper semi-continuous, then there is an $x \in S$ such that $x \in F(x)$.

Let $F = g \circ h \circ f^*$, the composition of the mappings f^*, h, and g. Since f^* and h are continuous and g is upper semi-continuous, F is also upper semi-continuous (the proof is immediate from the definition of upper semi-continuity). But F is a mapping of S into a set $\{K_y\}$ of convex subsets of S. Therefore, the fixed point theorem applies, and there is a p which is contained in the set K_y into which it maps.

Let us consider the possibility that a fixed point p of F and $y = h(f(p))$ define a competitive equilibrium according to (4.3). y is attainable by the definition of h. p is normal to Y at y by the definition of g. Thus $p \cdot y = \max p \cdot z$ for $z \in Y$, and $p \cdot y = r(p)$ by (6.2). On the other hand, $p \cdot w = \sum p_i f_i^*(p)$, and $f_i^*(p) \leq f_i(p)$ by (6.3), except when $p_i = 0$. Therefore, $p \cdot w \leq \sum p_i f_i(p) = \sum b_i r(p) = r(p)$ by (6.2).[31] But by definition (6.1) of h, $y = h(w) = \alpha w$, $\alpha \leq 1$. Thus we have $p \cdot y = p \cdot \alpha w \geq p \cdot w$, where $\alpha \leq 1$. The inequalities are impossible unless $\alpha = 1$. This implies, by h, that $y = w$. Now $y \in Y$, so $w \in Y$. But $f_i^*(p) = \zeta_i$ unless $p_i > 0$, and any vector z with $z_i = \zeta_i$ lies outside Y by the definition of ζ_i. Thus p is greater than zero and $f^*(p) = f(p)$ by (6.3). This means that the original demand functions (2.8) with (2.9) are satisfied with $w = y$. Since all the conditions of (4.3) are met, (p, y) can be extended to a competitive equilibrium. Therefore, we have proved:

Theorem 2 Any Graham model has a competitive equilibrium.

3.7 Generalization of the Results

It is already apparent from the fact that each proof was based on a very general statement of properties for the Graham model that the validity of the theorems extends much beyond this model.[32] However, the necessary assumptions can be relaxed further without departing from the design of our proofs. Let us consider first the properties used in the existence proof as announced in section 3.6.1.

Property (b) (an extreme output for final goods in any proportions) is really not needed so long as the demand for each final good is insatiable as prescribed by property (f). For because of (f) the demand functions can be extended to allow some zero prices as in section 3.6.5, without introducing any equilibria where a price is zero. This permits us to assume that final goods can be disposed of without cost when they are not wanted. In the extended set of attainable outputs final goods are producible in any proportions if only there is some $y_{\text{fin}} \in Y$ with $y_{\text{fin}} > 0$. Disposal will never actually occur in an equilibrium position, because demand for a final good exceeds the maximum quantity producible when its price is zero, while its disposal activity will be unprofitable if the price is not zero. The mapping F is still well defined. One only needs to show that the extended Y has a normal $p_{\text{fin}} \geqslant 0$ at every extreme point when free disposal activities are present. As a result of giving up (b), we no longer have to require that every country be able to produce each good. Also joint production may be allowed.

If joint production is not present, or if there are, in fact, free disposal activities for jointly produced goods, (f) (the insatiability of demand) can be given up so long as demand is, in fact, continuous even when some prices are equal to zero, that is, if (d) (section 3.6.1) holds for $p_{\text{fin}} \geqslant 0$. This depends, however, on proving that (c) can be extended so that any point $y_{\text{fin}} \in Y$ such that $\alpha y_{\text{fin}} \notin Y$ for $\alpha > 1$ is a competitive equilibrium if the (new) demand conditions are met by y_{fin} and a normal $p_{\text{fin}} \geqslant 0$ to Y at y.[33]

Next the labor supplies may be variable if the demand for labor (that is, supply by consumers) also satisfies (d) (except for assuming only nonpositive values), where demand now depends on the prices of labor as well as on those of final goods. We must, however, replace Y with the set Y^* of net input-output vectors which are compatible with the technology, in the space of all primary goods and final goods.[34] Then S is replaced with S^* defined as all vectors $p \geqslant 0$, $\sum p_i = 1$, which are normal to Y^*. S^* is then the intersection of a simplex and the convex cone of normals to Y^*. A mapping F^* can be defined just as before except that the projection will now be from the point $(0, -\eta)$, which corresponds, of course, to the point 0 of Y. The argument is entirely analogous to that of section 6. A fixed point of F^* will be a pair (p, y) where y is extreme[35] and p is normal at y with $p \geqslant 0$. Since p is normal at y, the profit condition is satisfied. (p, y) also satisfies the demand conditions. Therefore, it is a competitive equilibrium by (4.2).

Finally, we may admit many ultimate resources (primary goods) in each country. The method remains essentially the same. It becomes rather acute, however, to discuss the conditions in which it is possible to suppose the demand functions to be continuous over a sufficiently wide domain. For example, it is impossible that the demand functions should be continuous at a price vector p which has a zero price for some final outputs and a zero price for a primary good, if some consumers depend entirely on this primary good for income, while they do consume some of the free goods. Since these consumers have no income at p, their demand for a free good will be entirely cut off at any positive price, however small. But this discussion is too extended to justify its inclusion in the present paper.[36]

The uniqueness of the net input-output vector in the competitive equilibrium of the model with many variable primary goods can be proved by replacing Y with Y^* and by using the same conditions as those of section 3.5 when extended to cover the consumer demand functions for primary goods. Uniqueness of p, save for positive multiplication by a scalar, will follow if $\Delta p \neq 0$ and $\Delta y = 0$ implies $\Delta p = kp$ for $k > 0$.

Appendix

First, I prove that any function $H(z)$ on a finite dimensional vector space is continuous if it satisfies the two conditions, (a) $H(z + z') \geq H(z) + H(z')$, (b) $H(\mu z) = \mu H(z)$ for $\mu \geq 0$.[37] By (a), $H(z) \geq \Sigma|z_i|H(\pm\pi^i)$, where the π^i are the coordinate unit vectors and the sign is taken to agree with that of z_i. But $\Sigma|z_i|H(\pm\pi^i) = m\Sigma|z_i|$, where $m \geq \max H(\pm\pi^i)$ for all π^i and both signs. Moreover, $m\Sigma|z_i| \geq m(n\Sigma(z_i^2))^{1/2} = mn^{1/2}|z|$. Therefore, $H(z) \geq k|z|$, with $k = mn^{1/2}$. From this it may be seen that $-k|\varepsilon| \geq -H(-\varepsilon) \geq H(z + \varepsilon) - H(z) \geq H(\varepsilon) \geq k|\varepsilon|$, which proves the continuity of $H(z)$.

Now, the continuity of $r(p)$ follows directly from the obvious relations, (a) $\max(p' + p'') \cdot z \geq \max p' \cdot z + \max p'' \cdot z$, each maximum being over Y, and (b) $\max \mu p \cdot z = \mu \max p \cdot z$, for $z \in Y$ and $\mu \geq 0$.

In the case of $h(w)$, assume that 0 is an interior point of Y and w is not an interior point of Y. Let $h(w) = w/p(w)$ with $p(w) = $ g.l.b. $\lambda > 0$ such that $w/\lambda \in Y$. We shall prove $h(w)$ continuous for w not an interior point of Y. Relation (b), $p(\mu w) = \mu p(w)$ for $\mu \geq 0$, may be seen to hold directly, but (a) requires proof. Clearly $p(w) \neq 0$ if w is not in the interior of Y. Also $w \in Y$ implies $p(w) \geq 1$. Let w, w' be points which are not in the interior of Y. Then

$$p\left(\frac{p(w)}{p(w) + p(w')} \frac{w}{p(w)} + \frac{p(w')}{p(w) + p(w')} \frac{w'}{p(w')}\right) \geqq 1.$$

This implies

$$\frac{1}{p(w) + p(w')} p(w + w') \geqq 1,$$

or $p(w + w') \geqq p(w') + p(w)$. Therefore, (a) also holds and $p(w)$ is continuous over the prescribed domain. But then so is $h(w) = w/p(w)$, since $p(w) \neq 0$. To apply this result to Graham's model, note that Y can be extended to include 0 as an interior point without altering $h(w)$ for $w \geqq 0$. For example, take the convex hull of Y and $z = (-1, \ldots, -1)$.

Notes

1. I wish to dedicate this article to the memory of my friend and teacher, Frank D. Graham. An earlier version was presented to the Econometric Society in December, 1952.

2. Gerard Debreu and Kenneth Arrow have been working, independently, along similar lines. Their method seems closely related to the theory of competitive games developed by John Nash [8], while my motivation comes directly from the work of Abraham Wald and Tjalling Koopmans.

3. Graham felt confident a solution always existed. He was less sure of uniqueness. See [4], p. 95.

4. p is a vector of prices. Δy is a vector of increments in quantities demanded. The dot symbol is used to indicate the inner product of two vectors. $\Delta y \neq 0$ means that not all components of Δy can be zero at the same time. p and y are connected by the demand functions.

5. This paper was first presented to a seminar in Princeton in 1932, although it was published later than Wald's paper.

6. The ith column of this matrix represents an activity which converts 1 unit of labor into a_i^j units of the ith final good.

7. Denote the $(j - 1)k + i$th column of the matrix A by A_i^j. This column represents in the world technology the activity described in the last footnote, located in the jth country and producing the ith final good.

8. This model is an analytical statement of the arithmetic models which Graham constructs. The fin and pri subscripts are used to distinguish submatrices or subvectors containing final output or primary good components respectively. Taking account of the zero elements of A (2.4) can be written more explicitly as

$$x_i^1 a_i^1 + \cdots + x_i^n a_i^n = y_{i\,\text{fin}} \qquad (i = 1, \ldots, k)$$

$$-x_1^j - \cdots - x_k^j = y_{j\,\text{pri}} \qquad (j = 1, \ldots, n).$$

9. Consequently the set of input-output vectors which are consistent with the technology is a cone in the space of all primary goods and final goods [7].

10. In the sense that the attainable combinations of primary goods used up and final goods produced remain the same.

11. In other words, by the elimination of intermediate goods we arrive at a constant cost production possibility locus for each country of the form $\Sigma_i y_i^j / a_i^j = \eta_i$, where y_i^j is the quantity of the ith final good produced in the jth country.

12. X is closed means the following. If $x^1, x^2, \ldots$ is a sequence of vectors contained in X which converges to a vector x, then x is also contained in X.

13. A function, say $r(p)$, is continuous if for every sequence of vectors $p^1, p^2, \ldots$ in the domain of definition which approaches a limit p also in the domain of definition, the sequence $r(p^1), r(p^2), \ldots$ approaches the limit $r(p)$.

14. The figure represents a model with two final goods and three countries. Y is enclosed by the positive axes and the line $\overline{abcd}$. On each segment of this line, moving in the counter-clockwise direction, one country is changing from y_2 to y_1.

15. $w \geqslant 0$ means that some but not all components of w may be zero, and the nonzero components are positive. $w \geqq 0$ allows all components to be zero together.

16. In the figure this is obviously true for points on the line $\overline{abcd}$ and for no others in Y.

17. Through trading at the prices p and using the available technology.

18. It should be obvious that these conditions are independent of the number of processes and apply to any competitive economy with homogeneous production functions. Our analysis treats the integration of production as though it were actually achieved in centrally managed processes. However, it should be said that (4.1) is equivalent to the same conditions for the processes using intermediate products.

19. Indeed, strictly speaking, they should not be regarded as defined except when the profit condition is satisfied.

20. See [7], pp. 93–95 and the earlier theorems cited there.

21. In the sense of (3.1).

22. In the figure the vector p is normal to Y at y^1, and, indeed, at all points of the segment of the set of efficient outputs containing y^1. For the theory of the function max $p \cdot z$ for $z \in Y$ (the tac-function of Y), see [2], pp. 19–24. The profit condition is equivalent to the condition that the price vector be normal to the cone of input-output vectors which are consistent with the technology [7].

23. This is Samuelson's fundamental postulate for the theory of demand for the single consumer. See [10], p. 111. Wald believed that the condition probably held also for the body of consumers [15]. However, the results obtained by Hotelling [5], on which Wald's argument depends cannot be deduced from the requirement that consumers choose consistently.

24. Not necessarily independent.

25. In fact, an efficient output with a positive normal.

26. So the output is also efficient.

27. The arrow symbol is used in an expression $p^i \to p$ to mean that the sequence $p^1, p^2, \ldots$ approaches p as a limit.

28. The essential theorems on continuity for the arguments of this paper can be found in calculus texts (for example, Courant, R., *Differential and Integral Calculus*, Vol. I, pp. 58–68) for the case of one real variable. The extension to Euclidean vector spaces is quite straightforward.

29. Note that w is never in the interior of Y, either because $p \cdot w = r(p)$, or because $w_i = \zeta_i$ for some i.

30. See [6]. By a corollary S is allowed to be any closed and bounded convex subset of a Euclidean space. Further generalizations of the theorem exist. For example, [3].

31. Note that property (e) is used at this point.

32. For example, these properties do not require the prohibition of trade in intermediate products, or the presence of only a finite number of activities.

33. This is one of the two or three proofs we avoided by using the more limited results achieved by Koopmans for his somewhat different problem.

34. The role of boundedness in our proof is replaced by the continuity of the demand for labor by consumers.

35. In the sense that $y \in Y^*$ and $-\eta + \alpha(y - \eta) \notin Y^*$ for $\alpha > 1$.

36. A fuller treatment was given by the author in a paper read to the Econometric Society at Kingston, Ontario, in September, 1953.

37. These proofs are simplifications for present uses of theorems in [2].

References

[1] Arrow, Kenneth J., "Alternative Proof of the Substitution Theorem for Leontief Models in the General Case," *Activity Analysis of Production and Allocation*, ed. by Tjalling C. Koopmans, New York, 1951.

[2] Bateman, P. T., "Introductory Material on Convex Sets in Euclidean Space," Ch. 1 of *Seminar on Convex Sets* (mimeographed), Princeton, 1951.

[3] Eilenberg, S. and D. Montgomery, "Fixed Point Theorems for Multi-valued Transformations," *American Journal of Mathematics*, 1946, pp. 214–222.

[4] Graham, Frank D. *The Theory of International Values*, Princeton, 1948.

[5] Hotelling, Harold, "Demand Functions with Limited Budgets," *Econometrica*, January 1935, Vol. 3, pp. 66–78.

[6] Kakutani, Shizuo, "A Generalization of Brouwer's Fixed Point Theorem," *Duke Mathematical Journal*, 1941, pp. 457–459.

[7] Koopmans, Tjalling C., "Analysis of Production as an Efficient Combination of Activities," *Activity Analysis of Production and Allocation*, see [1].

[8] Nash, J. F., "Non-Cooperative Games," *Annals of Mathematics*, 1951, pp. 286–295.

[9] von Neumann, John, "Über ein ökonomisches Gleichungssystem und eine Verallgemeinerung des Brouwerschen Fixpunktsatzes," *Ergebnisse eines Mathematischen Kolloquiums*, No. 8, Vienna, 1937. Translated in *Review of Economic Studies*, 1945–6.

[10] Samuelson, Paul A., *Foundations of Economic Analysis*, Cambridge, 1947.

[11] ———, "Abstract of a Theorem Concerning Substitutability in Open Leontief Models," *Activity Analysis of Production and Allocation*, see [1].

[12] Wald, Abraham, "Über die eindeutige positve Lösbarkeit der neuen Produktionsgleichungen," *Ergebnisse Mathematischen Kolloquiums*, No. 6, Vienna, 1935.

[13] ———, "Über die Produktionsgleichungen der ökonomischen Wertlehre," *Ergebnisse Mathematischen Kolloquiums*, No. 7, Vienna, 1936.

[14] ———, "Über einige Gleichungssysteme der mathematischen Ökonomie." *Zeitschrift für Nationalökonomie*, 1936. Translated in *Econometrica*, October, 1951, Vol. 19, pp. 368–403.

[15] ———, "On a Relation between Changes in Demand and Price Changes," *Econometrica*, April, 1952, Vol. 20: pp. 304–305.

4 Competitive Equilibrium with Dependent Consumer Preferences

Lionel W. McKenzie

In this chapter I shall try to do three things. First, show that the dependence of consumer preferences on various economic factors need not prevent a proof of competitive equilibrium under general conditions. Second, give a proof of the existence of an equilibrium in terms familiar to economists. Third, employ methods of proof simpler than have been used heretofore for this problem.[1]

4.1 The Model of Production

The model of production is essentially that of Walras [8]. Although his model may appear rather special, it can be shown to include the system of [1] where there are a finite set of firms each owning an initial endowment of unmarketable resources.[2] The use of Walras' model will simplify the proof and bring it into touch with methods of activity analysis.

The productive activities are assumed to be linear, that is, if y is a vector of inputs (negative numbers) and outputs (positive numbers) representing a possible combination of inputs and outputs for a productive activity, then αy, $\alpha \geq 0$, also represents a possible combination of inputs and outputs for this activity. Moreover, the input-output vectors which belong to an activity do not depend on the levels at which other activities are operated. Then the productive system is a linear activities model in the sense of activity analysis [4]. The number of available activities is assumed finite. This is not, however, an essential restriction.

Since the activities are linear, each may be represented by a normalized vector. Let a^j be the vector of unit length belonging to the j-th activity. a^j is a column vector and A is the matrix whose j-th column is a^j. A is $n \times m$ where there are n commodities and m activities in the model. Let x be the column vector with m components such that the input-output vector of the j-th activity equals $x_j a^j$. Then the vector of inputs and outputs for the economy is $y = Ax$. The set of input-output vectors compatible with the productive system is the set Y of all y such that $y = Ax$ with $x \geq 0$.

It is not necessary to regard the inputs and outputs as contemporaneous or located in the same place. Of course, commodities at different places or times must be treated as different commodities, and the number of places and times must be finite. However, the finiteness restrictions are not essential. Thus capital investment and the location of industry are not excluded from the model.

Y is a convex, closed polyhedral cone in the n dimensional (Euclidean) commodity space. The following assumptions are made with respect to Y.

(1.1) Y has an interior point $\bar{y}$.

(1.2) Y is pointed.

(1.3) $Y \cap I = 0$, where I is the positive orthant.

The first assumption involves a certain richness of the technology. The second assumption is usually justified by the fact that every activity has labor as an input and none has labor as an output. Thus $y \in Y$ implies $-y \notin Y$. The third assumption excludes the production of something from nothing.

4.2   The Demand Functions

Let W^i be the set of combinations of commodities demanded and supplied which the i-th consumer can support. W^i lies in the n dimensional commodity space. We assume, for every i,

(2.1) W^i is convex, closed, and bounded from below.

"Bounded from below" means that the consumer can only supply limit quantities of any commodity. The set W is defined as $\sum W^i$, that is, $y \in W$ if and only if $y = \sum w^i$ and $w^i \in W^i$. The set $\mathcal{W}$ is defined as πW^i, that is, $w \in \mathcal{W}$ where $w = (w^1, \ldots, w^s)$. W lies in the n dimensional commodity space. $\mathcal{W}$ lies in a Euclidean space of dimension ns.

Define P as all p such that $p \cdot y \leq 0$ for $y \in Y$ and $p \cdot \bar{y} = -1$.[3] P lies in the n dimensional commodity space and $p \in P$ represents a normalized vector of commodity prices. Let X be the set of $x \geq 0$. Let Z be the Cartesian product $P \cdot \mathscr{W} \cdot X$. An element z of Z has the form (p, w, x). Z lies in a Euclidean space of dimension $(n + 1)s + m$.

Now consider the subset S of Z defined by $z \in S$ if and only if $z \in Z$ and $\sum w^i = Ax$. Then $z = (p, w, x)$ is an element of S means that p is a price vector normal to Y at the origin, w^i is a possible consumption vector for the i-th consumer, and $y = \sum w^i$ is a possible input-output vector for the productive system. S is closed, convex, and bounded. Closure is immediate. Suppose $z \in S$ and $\tilde{z} \in S$. Let $\tilde{\tilde{z}} = \alpha z + (1 - \alpha)\tilde{z}$, $0 \leq \alpha \leq 1$. $\tilde{\tilde{z}} \in Z$ by the convexity of P, $\mathscr{W}$, and X. Also $\alpha \sum w^i + (1 - \alpha) \sum \tilde{w}^i = A(\alpha x + (1 - \alpha)\tilde{x})$. Therefore, $z \in S$ and S is convex. If S is unbounded, there is a sequence $\{z^t\}$ where z^t_h is unbounded for some h. Suppose p^t is unbounded. Consider $\{p^t / |p^t|\}$. Since this sequence lies in a bounded region, there is a convergent subsequence. Let $\tilde{p}$ be the limit of the subsequence. Then $\tilde{p} \cdot y = 0$ for $y \in Y$, in contradiction to (1.1). On the other hand, w^{it} unbounded implies y^t unbounded where $y^t = \sum w^{it} = Ax^t$, that is where $y^t \in W \cap Y$. However, w^{it} is bounded from below by (2.1). Therefore, y^t is also bounded from below. Consider $\{y^t / |y^t|\}$. Again there is a convergent subsequence. Let y be the limit of this subsequence. Since the vectors y^t are bounded from below $y \geq 0$. But by convexity and closure of Y, $y \in Y$, which contradicts (1.3). Therefore, S must be bounded.[4]

The individual demand function $f^i(z)$ is defined over S[5] and takes values in W^i. Let $f = \pi f^i$ be the collective demand function, which takes values in $\mathscr{W}$. Let $\zeta_k > y_k$ for y in $W \cap Y$. Two assumptions are made with regard to f.

(2.2) f is single-valued and continuous.

(2.3) $p \cdot f(z) \leq 0$, and, if $f_k(z) \leq \zeta_k$ for all k, equality holds in this relation.

The first assumption requires a special discussion which will be given later. The implication (from continuity) that f is bounded on S is harmless, since any bounds greater than ζ_k may be imposed on f without affecting the proof. The second assumption means that all income is spent when demand lies within the bounds ζ_k, and more than all income cannot be spent. Income is defined as receipts from the sale of commodities by consumers. This assumption may be justified by the fact that no consumer can attain complete satiation within these bounds (although the assumption is much weaker than the justification).

4.3 Competitive Equilibrium

The characteristic of a competitive equilibrium is that everyone behaves as though he were unable to influence the levels of market prices or the actions of other producers and consumers. The individual demand functions give the amounts which individual consumers will wish to buy or sell given the prices, the activity levels, and the consumption patterns of other consumers. The classical procedure is to derive the individual demand function from a consistent preference ordering of the set W^i. This will be done later.

The managers of activities are regarded as maximizing profit where profit per unit level of the j-th activity is given by $p \cdot a^j$. However, in this model, a maximum is only possible if $p \cdot a^j \leq 0$, since a positive profit could always be increased by increasing the activity level. Moreover, if $p \cdot a^j < 0$, the maximum is attained at a zero level of activity. Thus, we have as the profit conditions of competitive equilibrium,

(3.1) $p \cdot a^j \leq 0$, $j = 1, \ldots, m$, $p \cdot a^j = 0$, if $x_j > 0$.

A competitive equilibrium requires that the profit conditions (3.1) be met and that demand equal supply for all commodities. The demand conditions may be written formally,

(3.2) $\sum f^i(z) = Ax$.

The competitive equilibrium may be represented by a vector $z = (p, m, r)$ whose components satisfy (3.1) and (3.2) when $w = f(z)$.

4.4 Existence of an Equilibrium

The proof that an equilibrium vector z exists under the assumptions made depends on an upper semi-continuous mapping of the set S into the set of convex subsets of S. A fixed point exists by Kakutani's theorem.[6] It will be shown to be a competitive equilibrium. The upper semi-continuity of the mapping results from the continuity of the demand functions and the upper semi-continuity of the inverse supply function. The upper semi-continuity of the inverse supply function is provided by the fact that Y has an interior point $\bar{y}$.[7] The scheme of the mapping is

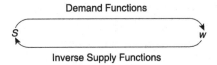

A two dimensional illustration is provided in Figure 4.1.
   The definition of the mapping uses an assumption

(4.1) $W \cap \text{int } Y \neq \emptyset$.

We may suppose that $\bar{y} \in W \cap \text{int } Y$. Let $\bar{y} = \sum \bar{w}^i$ where $\bar{w}^i \in W^i$.
$w' = f(z)$ defines a continuous single valued mapping of S into $\mathcal{W}$ by
(2.2). Let $y'' = \sum w^{i''}$. Define $w'' = \bar{w} + \gamma_{w'}(w' - \bar{w})$ where $\gamma_{w'}$ is a

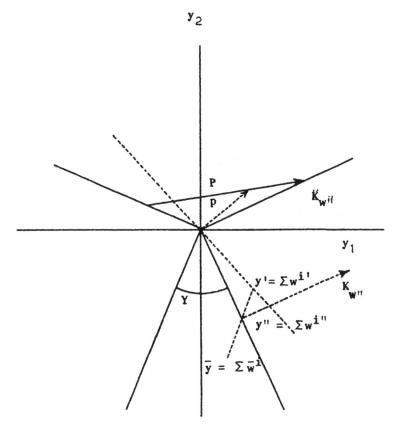

Figure 4.1
The mapping F is represented here without the explicit mention of the set X.

maximum for $y'' \in Y$. Then w'' is a continuous function [2] of w'. Write $w'' = h(w')$. Finally, define $g(w'') = K_{w''}$ where $K_{w''}$ is the set of $z = (p, w, x)$ such that $p \cdot y'' = 0$, $w = w''$, and $z \in S$. $K_{w''}$ is not empty, since every boundary point of Y has a normal $p \in P$ and may be expressed as Ax for some x. $K_{w''}$ is convex, since the set of normals to Y at y'' is convex and S is convex.

Let $F = g \circ h \circ f$. Then $F(z) = K_{w''}$ is a mapping of S into the set of convex subsets. Moreover, F is upper semi-continuous. Since f and h are continuous, we need only show that g is upper semi-continuous. Suppose $\{w^t\}$ is a sequence converging to w such that y^t is a boundary point of Y, where $y^t = \sum w^{it}$. Let $z^t \in g(w^t)$ and suppose $\{z^t\}$ converges to $\tilde{z} = (\tilde{p}, \tilde{w}, \tilde{x})$. Then $p^t \cdot y^t = 0$, implies $\tilde{p} \cdot \tilde{y} = 0$. Also $\tilde{y} = \sum \tilde{w}^i$ and $\tilde{z} \in S$ by the closure of $\mathcal{W}$ and S. Hence $\tilde{z} \in g(\tilde{y}) = K_{\tilde{w}}$ and g is upper semi-continuous.

A fixed point z^* exists by Kakutani's theorem. z^* is also a competitive equilibrium. Let $y^* = \sum w^{i*}$. The profit condition (3.1) follows immediately from the definition of g, since $p^* \cdot y^* = 0$ implies $p^* \cdot a^j = 0$ for $x_j > 0$ and $p^* \cdot y \leq 0$ for $y \in Y$ implies $p^* \cdot a^j \leq 0$, $j = 1, \ldots, m$. It remains to show that $\gamma_{w'} = 1$, where $w' = f(z^*)$. Then $w' = w^*$ where $y^* = Ax^*$ and (3.2) is met. By (2.3) $p^* \cdot y' \leq 0$ for $y' = \sum w^{i'}$. Also $p^* \cdot \bar{y} < 0$. But $p^* \cdot y^* = p^* \cdot (\bar{y} + \gamma_{w'}(y' - \bar{y})) = 0$ by definition of h. Moreover, $0 < \gamma_{w'} \leq 1$, since (2.3) implies that $y' \notin \text{int } Y$. Therefore, $\gamma_{w'} = 1$, and $w' = w^*$. Since both the profit condition and the demand condition are met, z^* is a competitive equilibrium.

4.5 Continuity of the Demand Functions

The validity of the foregoing proof depends on the demand assumptions (2.2) and (2.3). However, (2.2) is unlikely to hold unless each f^i is single-valued and continuous over S. This, in turn, is unlikely unless the i-th consumer is always able to subsist for $z \in S$ and, indeed, always earns a positive income in excess of subsistence requirements.[8] For subsistence, it is necessary that there should be some w^i such that $p \cdot w^i \leq 0$ for any $p \in P$. Thus subsistence is provided for if we assume

(5.1) $W^i \cap Y \neq \emptyset$,

since if $w^i \in W^i \cap Y$, $p \cdot w^i \leq 0$ for all $p \in P$. To provide a positive income above subsistence requirements for all p, it is necessary that $p \cdot w^i < 0$ be satisfied for some w^i at any given p. It is sufficient, of course, to have

(5.1') $W^i \cap \text{int } Y \neq \emptyset$.

Then, for $w^i \in W^i \cap \text{int } Y$, $p \cdot w^i < 0$ for $p \in P$ by the definition of P. However, (5.1') requires that the i-th consumer have a positive supply of every unproduced commodity, so that it is very restrictive.

Fortunately, assumption (2.2) is not needed in the final proof. Assume that (5.1) holds. Then define Y^t as the cone spanned by the activity vectors $a^j + \delta/2^t(a^j - \bar{y})$ where $\delta > 0$ is small enough so that Y^0 is pointed and $Y^0 \cap I = 0$. $Y \subset \text{int } Y^t$. Therefore, $w^i \in W^i \cap Y$ implies $w^i \in \text{int } Y^t$. Then (5.1') holds and the demand functions f^i are continuous over $S^t = P^t \cdot \mathscr{W} \cdot X$, where $p \in P^t$ if and only if $p \cdot y \leq 0$ for $y \in Y^t$ and $p \cdot \bar{y} = -1$.

Let t increase without limit. For each t there is an equilibrium vector z^t by the argument of section 4. Since $z^t \in S^t \subset S^0$, the sequence lies in a closed and bounded set. Then there is a convergent subsequence $\{z^{t_s}\}$ approaching $z^* \in S$. z^* is an equilibrium for the original problem if p^* is normal to Y at y^* and $y^* = f(z^*)$. However, $p^{t_s} \cdot y^{t_s} = 0$ for all s implies $p^* \cdot y^* = 0$. Also $p^{t_s} \cdot y \leq 0$ for $y \in Y^{t_s}$ implies $p^{t_s} \cdot y \leq 0$ for $y \in Y$, since $Y \subset Y^{t_s}$. Thus $p^* \cdot y \leq 0$ for $y \in Y$ since $p^{t_s} \to p^*$. This shows that the profit condition (3.1) is satisfied.

The demand condition (3.2) is more difficult. In the limit W^i does not have a point interior to Y. Therefore, it is necessary to introduce assumptions[9] sufficient to give $p^* \cdot w^i < 0$ for some $w^i \in W^i$.

Let D be the set of commodity indices such that every consumer's demand for the k-th commodity exceeds ζ_k when $p_k \leq 0$ for $k \in D$. Let G be the set of indices such that $k' \in G$, $y \in Y$ implies there is $y' \in Y$ and $k \in D$ with $y'_h = y_h$ for $h \neq k$, $h \notin D$, and $y'_k > y_k$, $y'_{k'} < y_{k'}$. Then $p^*_h > 0$ for $h \in D$ and (3.1) implies $p^*_{k'} > 0$. G contains the indices of commodities which can always be used to increase the output of some commodity with index in D. Let $\delta^k_k = \delta > 0$ and $\delta^k_h = 0$ for $h \neq k$. We make the assumption

(5.2)   For every i, there is a $w^i \in W^i \cap Y$ such that $w^i - \delta^k \in W^i \cap Y$ and $k \in G \cup D$.

From the assumption (4.1) it must hold for some consumer, say the i-th, that $p^* \cdot \bar{w}^i < 0$. Otherwise, $p^* \cdot \bar{y} \geq 0$ in contradiction to $\bar{y} \in \text{int } Y$. Thus $f^i(z)$ is continuous at z^*. Then $f^i_k(z^*) > \zeta_k$ would imply $f^i_k(z^{t_s}) > \zeta_k$ for s large enough. But for large enough s, $\zeta_k > y_k$ for $y \in Y^{t_s}$. This contradicts the fact that z^{t_s} is an equilibrium of Y^{t_s}. Therefore, $f^i_k(z^*) \leq \zeta_k$ and $p^*_k > 0$ for $k \in G \cup D$. By (5.2) it then holds for every i that

$p \cdot \tilde{w}^i < 0$ where $\tilde{w}^i \in W^i$ and $\tilde{w}^i = w^i - \delta^k$, with $w^i \in W^i$. This assures a positive income above subsistence requirements for every consumer at z^*, so that it is not unreasonable to suppose the individual demand functions continuous at z^*. Consequently, $y^{t_s} = f(z^{t_s})$ implies $y^* = f(z^*)$ and the demand condition (3.2) is met. Thus z^* is an equilibrium vector.

4.6   Demand as Consistent Preference

The argument of section 4.5 depends on the supposition that the individual demand functions are continuous at $z \in S$ if $p \cdot w^i < 0$ for some $w^i \in W^i$ for every i, where $z = (p, w, x)$. If the consumers choose consistently, we may place conditions on their preference ordering which will ensure this result. We must also define the conditions more carefully that allow us to take the demand functions to be single valued.[10]

The only case in which the single valued demand function seems unrealistic is that of commodity stocks which the consumer may possess and to which, as such, he is indifferent. However, the prices of these commodities clearly cannot fall below zero. Therefore, it is possible to regard them as always supplied to the economy and include among the a^j a free disposal activity for each. Let the indices of such goods lie in sets R^i. Then we assume

(6.1)   For $k \in R^i$ for some i there is a^j with $a^j_h = 0$ for $h \neq k$ and $a^j_k = -1$.

Let the stock of the k-th commodity held by the i-th consumer for $k \in R^i$ be r^i_k.

Define V^i as the set of $w^i \in W^i$ such that $w^i_k = r^i_k$ for $k \in R^i$. V^i is convex, closed, and bounded from below. In the following argument the i superscript will be suppressed. A preference ordering[11] on V will be said to be closed if $z^t \to z$, $z^t \in S$, and $v^t \gtrsim v''$, for $v^t \to v$ and $v'' \to v'$, implies $v \gtrsim v'$. v^t, v'', v, v' all lie in V. For a given z, closure implies that every closed and bounded subset of V has at least one maximal element.[12]

Let C^s be the set of v such that $v \in V$ and $p^s \cdot v \leq 0$. Suppose $p^s \to p$ where there is v^0 such that $p \cdot v^0 < 0$. Then for every $v \in C$, there is a sequence $v^s \to v$, where $v^s \in C^s$, $s = 1, 2, \ldots$ We may assume without loss of generality that $p^s \cdot v^0 < 0$. Let $v^s = \alpha^s v + (1 - \alpha^s) v^0$ where α^s is a maximum for $0 \leq \alpha^s \leq 1$ and $v^s \in C^s$. $v^s \to v$ is equivalent to $\alpha^s \to 1$.

$\alpha^s < 1$ implies $p^s \cdot v^s = 0$. If α^s does not converge to 1, a subsequence α^{s_t} converges to $\alpha < 1$. Then $p^{s_t} \cdot v^{s_t} = 0$ and $p^{s_t} \to p$ implies $p \cdot (\alpha v + (1 - \alpha)v^0) = 0$. Thus $p \cdot v > 0$ in contradiction to the assumption $v \in C$. Therefore, v^s does converge to v.

A preference ordering will be called strictly convex if $v \gtrsim v'$ implies $v'' \succ v'$ where $v'' = \alpha v + (1 - \alpha)v'$ for $0 < \alpha < 1$. If a simple ordering is strictly convex, there can be but one maximal element in each closed and bounded subset. In order to insure the boundedness of C we may impose on W^i the bounds $\zeta_k + \delta$, for $\delta > 0$. This restriction has no effect on the proof, as the reader may easily discover.[13]

Let us assume

(6.2)   The preference ordering on V is simple, closed, and strictly convex.

Let v^* be the maximal element in C defined by z and v^{s^*} the maximal element in C^s defined by z^s. Let $z^s \to z$, where there is $v^0 \in C$ and $p \cdot v^0 < 0$, then $v^{s^*} \to v^*$. Otherwise, a subsequence $v^{s_t^*} \to v \neq v^*$. But there is a sequence $v^{s_t} \to v^*$ and $v^{s_t^*} \succ v^{s_t}$. This implies by closure and strict convexity that $v \succ v^*$, which is a contradiction.

It is now possible to define the demand function $f^i(z)$. Let $f^i(z) = v^{i^*}$. f^i is continuous at z if $p \cdot \tilde{v}^i < 0$ for some $v^i \in V^i$. But this is equivalent to the existence of $w^i \in W^i$ with $p \cdot w^i < 0$, since $p_k \tilde{w}_k \leqq 0$ for $k \in R^i$. Therefore, (5.2) implies (2.2) over the domain needed in the proof of section 5. (2.3) is assured by the fact that D is not empty, together with the strict convexity of the preference ordering.

Notes

1. Abraham Wald first solved a problem of the existence of a competitive equilibrium rigorously in [6] and [7]. However, his model did not admit joint production or the variability of productive coefficients, and subjected the demand functions to severe conditions. A more general production model with relaxed demand conditions was introduced by the author in [5]. Kenneth Arrow and Gerard Debreu treated a general production model with further relaxation of the demand conditions in [1]. However, they did not allow negative prices (free disposal activities for jointly produced goods and productive services are implicitly assumed), and preferences are required to be independent. Nonetheless, their treatment of demand has been fundamental to this chapter.

2. Arrow and Debreu assume each firm to have available a convex set of possible input-output vectors, including the origin. The entrepreneurial resources can be treated as always sold by their owners to the firms where each firm can dispose of them without cost if necessary. The convex set of possible input–output vectors then becomes a cone in a space which includes a dimension for each firm's entrepreneurial resources. The fact that

the firm has to use its entire batch of entrepreneurial resources, no more and no less, and the batch may, indeed, be indivisible, does not interfere with the proof. Of course, if the batches of entrepreneurial resources could be broken up and reorganized, the problem might be greatly complicated.

3. $p \cdot y \leq 0$ for $y \in Y$ implies $p \cdot \bar{y} < 0$ for $y \in$ int Y.

4. y^t bounded implies x^t bounded by (1.2).

5. f^i does not, in fact, depend on w^i, but it simplifies the notation to admit w^i as a dummy variable.

6. Kakutani's theorem is "If F maps a closed and bounded convex set S in a finite dimensional Euclidean space into the set $\{K_\alpha\}$ of its convex subsets and F is upper semi-continuous, there is $z \in S$ with $z \in F(z)$." See [3].

7. The presence of such a point in [1] is guaranteed by the disposal activities which must be assumed to be present.

8. To convince oneself of the need for some such assumption, consider a price vector which leaves the i-th consumer with no commodities having a positive price, which he can supply, but enough free goods to allow him to subsist. Neighboring price vectors may exist in P with some of these commodities having positive prices. The i-th consumer will have to cease consuming such commodities abruptly, if his resources continue to be free. But this is quite possible.

9. These assumptions were discovered by Arrow and Debreu. See [1], p. 280.

10. It is possible to allow set valued demand functions which are upper semi-continuous, but the proof is somewhat complicated thereby, and a more powerful fixed point theorem has to be used.

11. The ordering will be denoted by the usual symbols placed inside circles. V is presumed to be simply ordered.

12. The set of rational points in V is denumerable. Select a strictly monotonic subsequence (in the preference ordering) from any arbitrary sequential arrangement of this set, by omitting from the sequence any element which is not superior to all elements preceding it. If the subsequence is finite, the last number z^n is maximal in the set of rational points. If it is infinite, there is point of accumulation z, which is superior to any rational point. But any point in V is a limit of a sequence of rational points. Thus z^n or z is maximal in the subset of V.

13. If set valued demand functions were allowed, it would be appropriate to require only convexity for the preference ordering.

Bibliography

[1] Arrow, Kenneth J., and Gerard Debreu, "Existence of an Equilibrium for a Competitive Economy," *Econometrica*, July, 1954.

[2] Bateman, P. T., "Introductory Material on Convex Sets in Euclidean Space," Ch. 1 of *Seminar on Convex Sets* (mimeographed), Princeton, 1951.

[3] Kakutani, Shizuo, "A Generalization of Brouwer's Fixed Point Theorem," Duke Mathematical Journal, 1941, pp. 457–459.

[4] Koopmans, Tjalling C., "Analysis of Production as an Efficient Combination of Activities," *Activity Analysis of Production and Allocation*, edited by Koopmans, New York, 1951.

[5] McKenzie, Lionel W., "On Equilibrium in Graham's Model of World Trade and Other Competitive Systems," *Econometrica*, April, 1954.

[6] Wald, Abraham, "Über die eindeutige positive Lösbarkeit der neuen Produktionsgleichungen," *Ergebnisse Mathematischen Kolloquiums*, No. 6, Vienna, 1935.

[7] ———, "Über die Produktionsgleichungen der ökonomischen Wertlehre," *op. cit.*, No. 7, Vienna, 1936.

[8] Walras, Leon, *Éléments d'Économie Politique Pure*, Paris, 1926.

5   Demand Theory without a Utility Index

Lionel W. McKenzie

The modern revolution in the theory of demand has been to replace utility as a measurable quantity with a utility index which is arbitrary up to a strictly monotonic transformation. It is my purpose here to describe an approach to the theory of demand which dispenses with the utility index entirely. This use of Occam's razor does not, however, complicate the derivation of the major propositions of demand theory, but rather, in at least the case of the Slutsky equation, leads to an important simplification. My approach can be related to three developments by other authors, the revealed preference analysis of Samuelson [7], the use of the indirect utility function[1] by Houthakker [5], and the use of convex set methods by Arrow and Debreu [1].

The Slutsky equation asserts that, for compensated price changes, the rate at which the consumer varies the consumption of the i-th good per unit change of the j-th price equals the rate at which the consumer varies the consumption of the j-th good per unit change of the i-th price. By compensated price changes is meant that income changes are made at the same time of the proper magnitude to keep the consumer on the same indifference locus [7, pp. 103–104]. In other words, if $f_i(p, M)$ is the demand function for the i-th good, where p is the vector of prices and M is money income,

$$\frac{\partial f_i}{\partial p_j} + k_j \frac{\partial f_i}{\partial M} = \frac{\partial f_j}{\partial p_i} + k_i \frac{\partial f_j}{\partial M}, \tag{1}$$

where k_i is the appropriate compensation per unit change of p_i.

Let $\frac{\delta f_i}{\delta p_j} = \frac{\partial f_i}{\partial p_j} + k_j \frac{\partial f_i}{\partial M}$. Then $\frac{\delta f_i}{\delta p_j}$ is the effect of a compensated price change. It is written by Hicks x_{ji} [4, p. 309] and by Samuelson $k_{ij} = \left(\frac{\partial x_j}{\partial p_i}\right) U = \text{constant}$ [7, p. 103]. Hicks calls x_{ji} the substitution term.

Define $M_x(p)$ as the minimum income[2] which allows the consumer to attain a commodity combination at least as good as x when the price vector is p. If C_x is the set of commodity combinations at least as good as x, then:

$$M_x(p) = \min \ p \cdot x' \text{ for } x' \text{ in } C_x.\text{[3]} \tag{2}$$

I shall show that $\frac{\delta x_i}{\delta p_j}$ and $\frac{\delta x_j}{\delta p_i}$ are cross partial derivatives of the function $M_x(p)$, differing only in the order of derivation, and therefore equal whenever the second differential exists.[4]

Let S be the set of combinations x of goods which the consumer is capable of consuming. S is often taken to be all x such that $x_i \geqq 0$ for each i and, if the i-th good is indivisible, x_i is an integer. I assume that the set S is completely ordered by a preference ordering, which I will write with inequality signs in parentheses. The preference ordering of S is assumed to be closed. By closure, I mean:

If $\bar{x}^1, \ldots, \bar{x}^i, \ldots \to \bar{x}$ and $x^1, \ldots, x^i, \ldots \to x$, and
$\bar{x}^i \ (\geqq) \ x^i, \text{ then } \bar{x} \ (\geqq) \ x. \tag{3}$

The arrow symbol should be read "converges to."

As a consequence of (3), the set C_x of combinations of goods indifferent with or preferred to x will be closed if S is closed. This means that the minimum in (2) may be expected to exist for any non-negative p. The consumer is presumed to choose a combination of goods which is at least as good as any combination available to him when he is restrained by the budget condition:

$$p \ x \leqq M. \tag{4}$$

In order to carry through our demonstrations we must provide for two things. First, we must ensure that the consumer has to spend all his income to achieve a best combination of goods subject to the budget restraint. Then the chosen combination x will be a least cost combination in C_x. Second, we must require that the nearby combination to which the consumer is led to move when a compensated price change is made is actually indifferent to the initial combination. In other words, compensation in the Slutsky sense must be possible for the price change in question. Notice, however, that neither of these requirements represents a limitation on the analysis, for they are needed to make the Slutsky equation meaningful in any case.

The first requirement is met if the consumer is not satiated in some good which is divisible, at points of S which lie within the budget limitation. That is to say, for a combination x in S and within the budget limitation, there is a j-th good and a quantity x_j^* of it, with $x_j^* - x_j$, such that any combination x^1 lies in S and is preferred to x if $x_i^1 = x_i$ for $i \neq j$ and $x_j^* > x_j^1 > x_j$. Indeed, it is enough for this condition to hold at the chosen point.[5]

This assumption implies that any chosen point x involves the expenditure of all income, that is, $p \cdot x = M$. For if $p \cdot x < M$, there would be, by the assumption, an x^1 $(>)$ x and $p \cdot x^1 < M$, where $x_i^1 = x_i$ for $i \neq j$ and $x_j^1 > x_j$. Thus x could not be a chosen point. Moreover, we must have $p \cdot x = M_x(p)$. Necessarily, $p \cdot x \geq M_x(p)$, since x does lie in C_x. But if $p \cdot x > M_x(p)$, by the definition of $M_x(p)$ it would not be necessary to spend as much as $M = p \cdot x$ to reach a point in C_x, in contradiction to the proposition just proved.

The second requirement can be met if we assume the existence of a point $\tilde{x}$ in S cheaper than the chosen point x and such that the points also lie in S, which are intermediate between $\tilde{x}$ and any point x^1 of S in a small neighbourhood of x. Let x^1 lie in the small neighbourhood of x, and suppose x^1 is chosen at p' and $M_x(p')$. Then x^1 $(\geq)$ x. Now consider a sequence of points x_i which lie on the line segment from $\tilde{x}$ to x_i and which converge to x^1 in the limit as $i \to \infty$. Since x_i is in S but does not lie in C_x, x $(>)$ x_i. Therefore, by the closure of the preference relation, x $(\geq)$ x^1. Thus x $(=)$ x^1. A basis for the proof has now been prepared (Figure 5.1).

Let $f_x(p) = f(p, M_x(p))$, that is, $f_x(p)$ is the combination chosen at p and a value of M equal to $M_x(p)$. Consider $\frac{\partial M_x(p)}{\partial p_i}$, or equivalently $\frac{\partial p \cdot f_x(p)}{\partial p_i}$. Assume that the requirements of non-satiation in a divisible good and of the existence of the cheaper combination in S are met at x. Write $f(p)$ for $f_x(p)$. Then, by the argument just made, points $x^1 = f(p^1)$ are indifferent with x if they lie close enough to x. If the minimum cost combination in C_x is unique in the neighbourhood of p, then $f(p)$ is well defined and continuous. It is also differentiable. Performing the derivation:

$$\frac{\partial p \cdot f(p)}{\partial p_i} = f_i + \sum_k p_k \frac{\partial f_k(p)}{\partial p_i}.$$

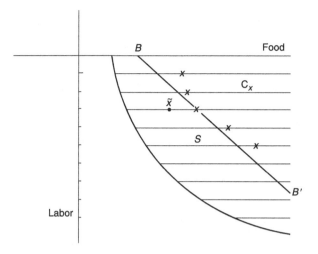

Figure 5.1
If food is divisible and labor performances are not, the set S is composed of the parallel lines and C_x is composed of the portion of these lines to the right of the crosses. If both goods are divisible, the set S is bounded by the arc on the left. BB' establishes the budget restriction.

But the derivatives $\frac{\partial f_k(p)}{\partial p_i}$ are defined by values of $x^1 = f(p')$ which lie arbitrarily near $x = f(p)$, and which are consequently indifferent with x. Thus:

$$\frac{\partial p \cdot f(p)}{\partial p_i} = x_i + p \cdot \frac{\delta x}{\delta p_i},$$

where the symbol δ has its earlier meaning.

We may now show that $p \cdot \frac{\delta x}{\delta p_i} = 0$. Choose Δp_i small enough so that $p \cdot \Delta x$ has the sign of the first differential $p \cdot \frac{\delta x}{\delta p_i} \Delta p_i$. Choose the sign of Δp_i so that the first differential is negative. Then $p \cdot (x + \Delta x) < p \cdot x$ in contradiction to the requirement that $p \cdot x = \min p \cdot x^1$ for $x^1 \in C_x$. Therefore, $p \cdot \frac{\delta x}{\delta p_i} = 0$ and $\frac{\partial p \cdot f(p)}{\partial p_i} = x_i$.

Write $M(p)$ for $M_x(p)$. If $\frac{\partial M(p)}{\partial p_i}$ exists, it is equal to f_i or x_i. Therefore, if $\frac{\partial M(p)}{\partial p_i \partial p_j}$ exists, it must be $\frac{\partial f_i}{\partial p_j} = \frac{\delta x_i}{\delta p_j}$. Similarly, $\frac{\delta x_j}{\delta p_i} = \frac{\partial M(p)}{\partial p_j \partial p_i}$. Therefore, wherever the second differential exists, $\frac{\partial M(p)}{\partial p_i \partial p_j} = \frac{\partial M(p)}{\partial p_j \partial p_i}$ and $\frac{\delta x_i}{\delta p_j} = \frac{\delta x_j}{\delta p_i}$, but since

$M(p)$ is a concave function, this differential exists for "almost every" value of p.

As we have seen, $M = M_x(p)$ for movements along the indifference locus of x. But $\frac{\partial M_x(p)}{\partial p_i} = x^i$. This shows that k_i in (1) is equal to x_i, or the compensation needed per unit change of p_i is x_i. Then the Slutsky equation appears in its traditional form:

$$\frac{\partial f_i}{\partial p} + x_j \frac{\partial f_i}{\partial M} = \frac{\partial f_j}{\partial p_i} + x_i \frac{\partial f_j}{\partial M}, \tag{5}$$

where f_i is now written for $f_i(p, M)$.

The other relations satisfied by the substitution terms $\frac{\delta x_i}{\delta p_i}$ can be proved through the manipulation of the inequality $p \cdot x \leqq p \cdot x^1$ for x^1 in C_x. This proof corresponds so closely to that used by Samuelson in his revealed preference approach that it does not require repeating. Therefore, I will merely indicate the implication from properties of $M_x(p)$.

As we have noted, $M_x(p)$ is a concave function. It is a fundamental property of concave functions that the second differential is non-positive [2, p. 88] where it exists. Thus, $\sum_i \sum_j \frac{\partial^2 M_x(p)}{\partial p_i \partial p_j} dp_i \, dp_j \leqq 0$. Therefore, by our results:

$$\sum_i \sum_j \frac{\delta x_i}{\delta p_j} dp_i \, dp_j \leqq 0. \tag{6}$$

In other words, (6) is a negative semi-definite quadratic form. In particular, we may set $dp_k < 0$ and $dp_i = 0$ for $i \neq k$. This shows that $\frac{\delta x_k}{\delta p_k} \leqq 0$.

The strict inequality cannot hold in (6), for, as appeared earlier, $p \cdot \frac{\delta x}{\delta p_i} = 0$ for every i. However, it may happen that the strict inequality holds whenever dp is not proportionate to p. This means that the indifference surface does not have a corner at x in any direction. Then $\frac{\delta x_k}{\delta p_k} < 0$ for each k.

Notes

This paper was first written independently, but it has since benefited from the very similar approach in Professor Hicks' new book [3]. The chief virtues of the presentation here are perhaps the mathematical form, and brevity. This is a technical report of research undertaken by the Cowles Commission for Research in Economics under contract with the Office of Naval Research. Reproduction in whole or in part is permitted for any purpose of the United States Government.

The argument was also partly anticipated by R. G. D. Allen in his Article "The Substitution Effect in Value Theory," *Economic Journal*, 1950.

1. The indirect utility function represents the level of utility as a function of prices and income, rather than as a function of quantities of goods consumed.

2. $M_x(p)$ is called a concave function of p. A function $g(p)$ is said to be concave if $g(tp + (1 - t)p') \geqq tg(p) + (1 - t)g(p')$ when $0 \leqq t \leqq 1$. That is, every chord of the surface defined by the function lies on or below the surface. Write $M_x(p) = M(p)$. That $M(p)$ is concave is clear, for suppose $p'' = tp + (1 - t)p'$ and $p'' \cdot x = \min p'' \cdot x'$ for x' in C_x. Then $tp \cdot x + (1 - t)p' \cdot x = p'' \cdot x = M(p'')$. But $p \cdot x \geqq M(p)$ and $p' \cdot x \geqq M(p')$. Thus $tM(p) + (1 - t)M(p') \leqq M(p'')$. The second differential exists for a concave function (technically speaking) "almost everywhere" [2, pp. 87, 102, 142].

3. $p \cdot x$ equals $\sum p_i x_i$, the inner product of p and x, which are vectors in an n-dimensional vector space, n being the number of goods.

4. By Young's theorem: see La Vallée Poussin, *Cours d'analyse infinitessimale*, Vol. I, pp. 122–3.

5. The strategic role of a divisible good was made clear by Professor Hicks [3, p. 38]. He suggested that savings might play this role.

References

[1] Arrow, Kenneth, and Gerard Debreu, "Existence of an Equilibrium for a Competitive Economy," *Econometrica*, July, 1954.

[2] Fenchel, W., *Convex Cones, Sets, and Functions*, Department of Mathematics, Princeton University, September, 1953.

[3] Hicks, J. R., *A Revision of Demand Theory*, Oxford, 1956.

[4] Hicks, J. R., *Value and Capital*, Oxford, 1939.

[5] Houthakker, H. S., "Compensated Changes in Quantities and Qualities Consumer," *Review of Economic Studies*, October, 1951.

[6] McKenzie, Lionel, "Competitive Equilibrium with Dependent Consumer Preferences," *Second Symposium in Linear Programming*, Vol. I, Bureau of Standards, Washington, 1955.

[7] Samuelson, Paul A., *Foundations of Economic Analysis*, Cambridge, 1947.

6   On the Existence of General Equilibrium for a Competitive Market

Lionel W. McKenzie

In the past few years several writers have presented sets of postulates for an abstract market and then proved that the market has a position which satisfies conditions of competitive equilibrium [for example, 1, 6, 10, 12, 13, 14].[1] In this chapter I shall start from a significantly weaker set of postulates. Also, I shall use a more direct, and mathematically simpler, proof that the equilibrium position exists.

The postulates are weaker in three ways. First, there are no restrictions on the dimensionality of the production and consumer sets. In earlier papers such restrictions were used to safeguard the income of consumers so that the demand functions would be continuous in the neighborhood of equilibrium.[2] Either the production set was directly assumed to have an interior point, or else free disposal of unwanted supplies of goods was assumed, which implies the interior point. The new postulates may also be interpreted as involving some vestiges of disposal, but the role of disposal is reduced to what is needed to insure the participation of consumers, and the disposal processes need not be free. This is analogous to the assumption in activity analysis that production is possible. Some such minimal provision for economic activity can hardly be avoided.

Second, the assumption that there are always desired goods and always productive goods is replaced by the assumption that the economy is irreducible. In loose terms, an economy is irreducible if it cannot be divided into two groups of consumers where one group is unable to supply any goods which the other group wants.[3] A restriction of this type is also needed to protect consumer income.

A third relaxation is that production processes may be reversible. The negative of an input-output combination which is technically possible may also be possible.

The argument uses the most elementary of the fixed point theorems, that of Brouwer, without introducing additional complications. The Brouwer theorem is applied to a point-to-point mapping of a normalized price set. Earlier writers have used the more powerful fixed point theorems [1, 3, 10, 12, 13, 14] or have been involved in substantial extensions of a similar nature [6].

Two further features of the argument may be worth mention. As in my earlier paper [12] I first prove the existence theorem for a model with constant returns to scale of production and then show that the general case can be handled through an appropriate introduction of entrepreneurial factors. Actually, it is not unreasonable to consider the constant returns model as the truly general competitive model, approximating to the situation with freedom of entry and firms which are small compared to their industries. In any case, this approach facilitates the handling of returns to the owners of firms, and simplifies the initial proofs. The second feature is that I do not define a utility function, again as in [12], but proceed directly from the preference ordering. This is not a weakening of the assumptions of Arrow and Debreu, but an exercise of Occam's Razor.

The idea of the new proof can be described in a few words. Let Y be the set of possible net output combinations, and, given a set of prices p, let $C(p)$ be the set of combinations of goods that can be distributed so that no one is worse off than when he trades freely at these prices. Consider a competitive equilibrium which is also a Pareto optimum.[4] The value of net output in this equilibrium is maximized, at the equilibrium prices, over the production set Y and minimized over the preferred set $C(p)$. But the shortest vector reaching from Y to $C(p)$ has a similar property. It has a maximum inner product over Y at the point where it starts, and a minimum inner product over $C(p)$ at the point where it ends. This suggests a mapping of prices by shifting them towards the shortest vector joining the production set and the preferred set (which depends on the prices). A fixed point of this mapping implies that the shortest distance is zero, and there is a competitive equilibrium associated with it.

In Sections 6.1–6.3 definitions and assumptions will be introduced to characterize the abstract market. In Section 6.4 the competitive equilibrium for this market is defined. Then in Sections 6.5 and 6.6, existence theorems are proved using the constant returns model. However, in Section 6.7 the model with constant returns is shown to include the apparently more general case of a convex production set generated by a finite number of firms who experience decreasing returns in the classical sense. Section 6.8 presents several lemmas on the set $C(p)$ which were assumed in the earlier proofs. The last two sections are brief comments on Wald's counter-example and on our Assumption 6.

6.1   The Consumer Sets

There are n goods whose combinations are represented as vectors in n-dimensional Euclidean space. There are m consumers. Let X_i be the *i-th consumer set*. Then X_i is the set of vectors x_i corresponding to the feasible trades of the ith consumer. Quantities of goods taken are represented by positive numbers and quantities of goods supplied by negative numbers. Two assumptions are made about the X_i.

Assumption 1 X_i is convex, closed, and bounded from below.

Assumption 2 X_i is completely ordered by a convex and closed preference relation.

Assumption 1 is the same as II in Arrow and Debreu [1, p. 268]. Assumption 2 is equivalent to their III.a and III.c, which are stated in terms of the utility function [1, p. 269].

That X_i is *bounded from below* means that, for x_i in X_i, $x_i > \xi_i$ for some vector ξ_i.[5]

The preference relation will be written $(\geqq)$, which may be read "preferred to or indifferent with." Then "preferred to" $(>)$ and "indifferent with" $(=)$ may be defined as usual in terms of $(\geqq)$.[6]

Convexity of $(\geqq)$ means that $x_i (>) x_i'$ implies $x_i'' (>) x_i'$ where $x_i'' = tx_i + (1-t)x_i'$ for $0 < t < 1$.

Closure of $(\geqq)$ means that $x_i^s \to x_i$ and $x_i^{s'} \to x_i'$ and $x_i^s (\geqq) x_i^s$, implies $x_i (\geqq) x_i'$.

Sets of prices for the n goods are represented as vectors p in the same n-dimensional Euclidean space. For any price vector p, define the *i-th available set* $H_i(p)$ as all combinations of goods in X_i which lie within a zero budget restriction. Thus, $H_i(p) = \{x_i \mid p \cdot x_i \leqq 0 \text{ and } x_i \in X_i\}$. Then we define the *i-th preferred set* $C_i(p)$ as all combinations of goods in X_i to which the consumer prefers no available trade. Thus, $C_i(p) = \{x_i' \mid x_i' (\geqq) x_i \text{ for all } x_i \in H_i(p)\}$. Let $C(p) = \sum_{i=1}^{m} C_i(p) \cdot C(p)$ is a generalized preferred set in the sense of Pareto. We will say that the ith consumer is *satiated at* x_i if $x_i (\geqq) x_i'$ for all $x_i' \in X_i$. The ith consumer is *satiated at* p if $x_i (\geqq) x_i'$ for all $x_i, x_i' \in C_i(p)$. It is not difficult to prove as a consequence of Assumptions 1 and 2 that

Lemma 1 Suppose X_i is bounded, and $H_i(p) \neq \varphi$. Then $H_i(p) \cap C_i(p) \neq \varphi$.

Lemma 2 If the i-th consumer is not satiated at p, $p \cdot x_i \geq 0$ for $x_i \in C_i(p)$.

Lemma 3 $C_i(p)$ is convex and closed and $C(p)$ is convex.

Lemma 4 Suppose X_i is bounded. $C_i(p)$ is a continuous set-valued function at p when $\min x_i \in X_i$ $p \cdot x_i < 0$. Also $C(p)$ is continuous over a neighborhood where each $C_i(p)$ is continuous.

We shall find in the sequel that the X_i may be regarded as bounded for the purpose of establishing an equilibrium. Lemmas 1, 2, 3 and 4 will be proved in section 6.8. Lemma 1 says, in effect, that $H_i(p)$ has a maximal point in the preference ordering. Lemma 2 will imply that consumers who are not satiated spend all their incomes.

6.2 The Production Set

There is a set Y of possible input-output combinations of the productive sector. Outputs are represented by positive numbers, inputs by negative numbers. Two assumptions are made with respect to Y.

Assumption 3 Y is a closed convex cone.

Assumption 4 $Y \cap \Omega = \{0\}$.

Ω is the positive orthant, so Assumption 4 says that it is not possible to produce something from nothing. These assumptions correspond to I.a and b in Arrow and Debreu [1, p. 267] except that they do not assume Y to be a cone. We omit assumption I.c of Arrow and Debreu which requires that $Y \cap -Y = \{0\}$. In other words, production may be reversible. The assumption that Y is a cone means that $y \in Y$ implies $ty \in Y$ for $t \geq 0$. This assumption is usually accepted in orthodox competitive theory on the basis of an adjustment in the number of firms, which are supposed to be small in size compared to the industry. The actual production set then approximates a cone if external economies, in the real technological sense, are absent. The apparently weaker assumption of convexity must rely on much the same defenses. In any case, the formal advantage of the weaker assumption is removed if the entrepreneurial factor is introduced properly. See Section 6.7.

The pattern of decentralized control in production can be recognized in the model by distinguishing the basic input-output combinations as those combinations which can be realized under a single direction. Then the whole set Y will be the convex cone which is spanned by the vectors corresponding to the basic input-output combinations.

6.3   Relations between Consumer and Production Sets

In addition to the assumptions made for the X_i and Y separately two further relations are postulated between them. Let $X = \sum_{i=1}^{m} X_i$ be the *aggregate consumer set*, i.e., $x \in X$ means $x = \sum_{i=1}^{m} x_i$ and $x_i \in X_i$ for each i.

Assumption 5 $X_i \cap Y \neq \varphi$. Moreover, there is a common point $\bar{x}$ in the relative interiors[7] of Y and X.

Assumption 5 will guarantee that *all* consumers can participate, and that *some* consumer *always* has income, in the sense that he can trade with a budget whose value is below zero. The assumption in Arrow and Debreu corresponding to the first part of 5 is included in IV'.a, and that corresponding to the second part is V [1, p. 280], including, in both cases, the implicit assumption of free disposal present in Condition 4 of the definition of competitive equilibrium [1, p. 271]. Note that Assumption 5 lays no restrictions on the dimensions of Y and X.

In the proof of existence, however, we require that *every* consumer should have positive income in the neighborhood of the equilibrium prices. Thus some means must be provided to guarantee that the income protected by Assumption 5 is spread through the entire market. We will be able to dispense with the categories of always desired goods and always productive goods used by Arrow and Debreu. An always desired good appears particularly implausible. It requires that every consumer be insatiable in this good within the supplies attainable by the whole market.

Let I_1 and I_2 be non-empty sets of indices for consumers such that $I_1 \cap I_2 = \varphi$ and $I_1 \cup I_2 = \{1, \ldots, m\}$. Let $x_{I_k} = \sum_{i \in I_k} x_i$ and $X_{I_k} = \sum_{i \in I_k} X_i$, for $k = 1, 2$. We make as our final assumption:

Assumption 6   However I_1 and I_2 may be selected, if x_{I_1} lies in $Y - X_{I_2}$, then there is also $w \in Y - X_{I_2}$ such that $w = x'_{I_1} - x_{I_1}$ and $x'_i \, (\geqq) \, x_i$ for all $i \in I_1$, and $x'_i \, (>) \, x_i$ for some $i \in I_1$.

This assumption says that however we may partition the consumers into two groups if the first group receives an aggregate trade which is an attainable output for the rest of the market, the second group has within its feasible aggregate trades one which, if *added* to the goods already obtained by the first group, can be used to improve the position of someone in that group, while damaging the position of none there. Of course, this implies immediately that some member of the first group is not satiated. Since I_1 may consist of one arbitrarily chosen index, no consumer can be satiated with an $x \in X \cap Y$. We may say that a market which satisfies Assumption 6 is *irreducible*.

The effect of Assumption 6 for equilibrium positions is that all consumers must have income if even one does.[8] Together with Assumption 5 this means that every consumer can participate with a budget of negative value in the neighborhood of equilibrium.

The assumptions in Arrow and Debreu corresponding to irreducibility are IV'.a, VI, and VII [2, p. 280], and III.b [2, p. 269]. III.b is an assumption of insatiability. It is immediately implied by Assumption 6, within the limits of attainable outputs. VI and VII provide that an always desired and an always productive good exist. IV'.a provides that each consumer can always supply an always productive good.

6.4 Competitive Equilibrium

The competitive equilibrium of the abstract market is given by a price vector p, an output vector y, and vectors $x_1, \ldots, x_m$ of consumer trades, which satisfy certain conditions.

(I) $y \in Y$ and $p \cdot y = 0$, and for any $y' \in Y$, $p \cdot y' \leq 0$.

(II) $x_i \in C_i(p) \cap H_i(p), i = 1, \ldots, m$.

(III) $\sum_{i-1}^{m} x_i = y$.

Prices p may be interpreted as defining opportunities for exchange present somewhere in the market. Then (I) is the familiar zero profit condition of competitive theory[9]. It is explained by the efforts of consumers to maximize their satisfactions. If there were a basic input-output combination y' for which $p \cdot y' > 0$, it would be possible for consumers as owners of resources to form new productive combinations proportional to y'. Some of them could then receive higher returns for their resources. This would permit them to make preferred trades which were formerly excluded. Thus the situation would not be stable. On the other hand, some returns would be reduced if combinations were formed for which $p \cdot y' < 0$. Since every combination in Y is a sum of positive multiples of basic combinations, (I) follows.

(II) implies the optimization of choice in the set of available trades for each consumer. In traditional terminology the budget restraint is $p \cdot x_i \leq 0$ for the ith consumer since in this model all income is derived from the sale of goods (productive services and resources). Then if x_i lies in $C_i(p)$, it is, by definition of $C_i(p)$, as well as the ith consumer can do. (III) is the familiar requirement that demand equal supply.

Definition   A *competitive equilibrium* is a set $(p, y, x_1, \ldots, x_m)$ which satisfies conditions (I), (II), and (III).

The conditions of competitive equilibrium given by Arrow and Debreu [1, pp. 268, 271] are similar except that they restrict prices to be nonnegative (their Condition 3) and allow goods whose prices are zero to be in excess supply (their Condition 4). Thus their Conditions 3 and 4 imply free disposal. Their Conditions 1 and 2 correspond to (I) and (II) here. The differences are due to the explicit recognition of profit in their system. Condition (III) is a stronger version of their 4, since it does not allow excess supply in equilibrium.

6.5   The Special Existence Theorem

In proving the existence of an equilibrium for the abstract market it is sufficient to confine attention to price vectors p which satisfy condition (I), the profit condition of competitive equilibrium, for an appropriate choice of y. Let $Y^* = \{p \mid p \cdot y \leq 0 \text{ for } y \in Y\}$. The homogeneity of the conditions of equilibrium suggests that the non-zero vectors in Y^* may be normalized. Let $P = \{p \mid p \in Y^* \text{ and } |p| = 1\}$.

The special existence theorem is concerned with the case where $C(p)$ is continuous over the whole set of non-zero price vectors in Y^*. To this end we replace Assumptions 5 and 6 with

Assumption 5′ $X_i \cap Y$ has an interior point $\bar{x}_i$ for $i = 1, \ldots, m$.

Assumption 6′   Either $C(p) \cap Y = \varphi$, or no consumer is satiated at p.

Assumption 5′ corresponds to IV.a of Arrow and Debreu [2, p. 270], where it is assumed that each consumer can supply a positive amount of every good. Assumption 6′ replaces their III.b, an assumption of insatiability throughout X_i. Assumption 6′, on the other hand, says that if a consumer is satiated while *trading* at prices p, then *total* demand at p will exceed the possibilities of production. Assumption 6′ is, of course, a good deal weaker than 6. The reader will recognize that the major generalization which our discussion contributes appears in

Assumptions 5 and 6 underlying the general theorem. However, the new method of proof is used in establishing the special theorem.

It is useful to introduce a second normalization for Y^* in proving the special theorem. Define $S = \{p \mid p \in Y^* \text{ and } p \cdot \bar{x} = -1\}$, where $\bar{x} = \sum_{i=1}^{m} \bar{x}_i$. By Assumption 5', $\bar{x}_i$ is an interior point of Y. Thus $p \cdot \bar{x}_i < 0$ for $p \in S$, and Lemma 4 will be applied to show that $C(p)$ is continuous over S.

Lemma 5 S is convex and compact.

Proof Convexity and closure are obvious. To show that S is bounded, suppose on the contrary there is an unbounded sequence p^s contained in S. Consider $p^s/|p^s|$. This normalized sequence lies in a compact set and, therefore, has a subsequence converging to a vector p' which also lies in S. Consider $p^s \cdot \bar{x}/|p^s|$. Since $|p^s|$ is unbounded and $p^s \cdot \bar{x} = -1$, in the limit $p' \cdot \bar{x} = 0$, which contradicts Assumption 5' that $\bar{x}_i$ is interior to Y. Thus there can be no such unbounded sequence p^s.

For any $p \in S$, we wish to consider the set of vectors joining the production set Y and the preferred set $C(p)$. Let $Z = \{z \mid z = x - y\}$, for some $x \in C(p)$, $y \in Y$. Z is convex by Lemma 3 and Assumption 3. Now define $h(p)$ as the shortest such link. That is $h(p) = z$ where $|z| \leq |z'|$ for $z' \in Z$.

Lemma 6 $h(p)$ is single valued.

Proof Suppose $h(p) = z$ and $|z| = |z'|$. Consider the element z'' of Z where $z'' = (z + z')/2$. $4(|z|^2 - |z''|^2) = 2|z|^2 + 2|z'|^2 - 4|z''|^2 = |z|^2 + |z'|^2 - 2z \cdot z' = |z - z'|^2 > 0$. Thus, $|z''| < |z|$, contradicting $h(p) = z$.

Lemma 7 If $h(p) = x - y$, then

(1) $h(p) \cdot x \leq h(p) \cdot x'$ for $x' \in C(p)$;

(2) $h(p) \cdot y = 0$;

(3) $h(p) \in Y^*$.

Proof (1) Suppose $h(p) = z$ and $z \cdot x' < z \cdot x$. Let $z' = x' - y$ and $z^t = x^t - y$, where $x^t = tx' + (1 - t)x$. Since, by Lemma 3, $C(p)$ is convex, for $0 \leq t \leq 1$, x^t also lies in $C(p)$. However, at $t = 0$, $\partial |z^t|^2/\partial t = 2z \cdot x' - 2z \cdot x < 0$. Thus, $|z^t| < |z|$ for t sufficiently small in contradiction to $h(p) = z$.

(2) Similarly, if $h(p) = z$, $z \cdot y \geq z \cdot y'$ for $y' \in Y$. This implies $z \cdot y \geq 0$, since $0 \in Y$. But $z \cdot y > 0$ would give $z \cdot ty > z \cdot y$ for $t > 1$, which contradicts $z \cdot y$ maximal over Y.

(3) It follows immediately from the foregoing that $h(p) \cdot y' \leq 0$ for $y' \in Y$. Thus $h(p) \in Y^*$.

In order to prove the continuity of $h(p)$ over S, we need two further lemmas (similar results are in Arrow and Debreu [1, pp. 276–7]).

Lemma 8 $X \cap Y$ is compact.

Proof   Suppose $X \cap Y$ is not bounded. Then there is an unbounded sequence y^s lying in $X \cap Y$. Consider $y^{s'} = y^s/|y^s|$. Since $y^{s'}$ is bounded, there is a subsequence converging to a point y'. Since X is bounded from below by Assumption 1, $y' \geq 0$. But y' is also in Y, since Y is closed, and this contradicts Assumption 4 that $Y \cap \Omega = \{0\}$.

To see that $X \cap Y$ is closed consider a convergent sequence $x^s \to x$. By closure of Y, Assumption 3, $x \in Y$. However, x_i^s is bounded for each i, where $\sum_{i=1}^m x_i^s = x^s$. Otherwise, since X_i is bounded below for each i, some positive component of x_i^s would be unbounded, and, therefore, the corresponding component of x^s would be unbounded. This contradicts the convergence of x^s to x. Then each x_i^s has a subsequence converging to x_i, where $\sum_{i=1}^m x_i = x$.

Lemma 9   All equilibrium consumer trades x_i lie in a bounded region.

Proof   By Lemma 8 all $x = \sum_{i=1}^m x_i$, $x_i \in X_i$, such that $x = y$ for $y \in Y$, lie in a bounded region. Thus by condition III of equilibrium all equilibrium aggregate trades x have $x_h < \xi$ for some ξ. However, by Assumption 1, $x_{hi} > \xi'$ for all i for some ξ'. Then $x_{hi} < \xi - (m-1)\xi'$ for any i and any h.

Since the only x_i which can appear in an equilibrium lie within sufficiently large bounds, no artificial equilibria are introduced by imposing these bounds. Therefore, we will introduce as a formal restriction the

Auxiliary Assumption 1   The X_i are bounded.

Lemma 10 $h(p)$ is continuous over S.

Proof   Let $p^s \to p$. Suppose $|z^s|$ is minimal for $z = x - y$, where $x \in C(p^s)$ and $y \in Y$, and $|z^0|$ is similarly minimal for $C(p)$. We must show that $z^s \to z^0$. But by Auxiliary Assumption 1 the X_i and thus X are bounded. Then z^s lies in a bounded region, and a subsequence z^r converges to a limit z', where $z' = x' - y'$, and $y^r \to y'$, $x^r \to x'$. $y' \in Y$, since Y is closed, and $x' \in C(p)$, since $C(p)$ is continuous. The continuity of $C(p)$ follows from Lemma 4, for consumer trades are

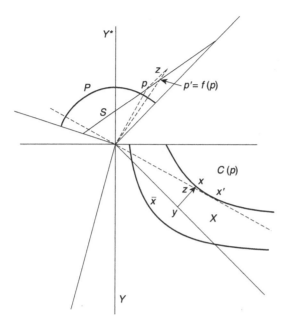

Figure 6.1
$z = h(p)$. x' is chosen at p.

bounded by Auxiliary Assumption 1 and each consumer has income by Assumption 5′. On the other hand, $|z^r| < |z^{r''}|$ for any $z^{r''}$ with $y^{r''} + z^{r''} = x^{r''}$, $y^{r''} \in Y$, $x^{r''} \in C(p^r)$. Since $C(p)$ is continuous and Y is fixed, any y and x, with $y \in Y$, $x \in C(p)$, are limits of properly chosen sequences $y^{r''}$ and $x^{r''}$. Then, continuity of the norm implies $|z'| \leq |z|$ for any z with $y + z = x$. Therefore, $z' = h(p) = z^o$, so that $h(p^s)$, or z^s, converges to $h(p)$, and $h(p)$ is continuous.

The ground has now been prepared for the Special Existence Theorem.

Theorem 1   Under Assumptions 1, 2, 3, 4, 5′, and 6′, the abstract market has a competitive equilibrium position.

Proof   Define a mapping of S into itself by

$$f(p) = -\frac{p + h(p)}{(p + h(p)) \cdot \bar{x}} = -\frac{p + h(p)}{-1 + h(p) \cdot \bar{x}}. \tag{1}$$

This mapping is illustrated in Figure 6.1. Since $h(p) \in Y^*$, and $\bar{x}$ is interior to Y, $h(p) \cdot \bar{x} < 0$, and the denominator does not vanish. $h(p)$ is also continuous by Lemma 10. Therefore, $f(p)$ is a continuous (vector valued) function of p. Moreover, $f(p) \in S$, since $p + h(p) \in Y^*$ and $f(p) \cdot \bar{x} = -1$.

By Lemma 5 and the Brouwer fixed point theorem[10] [11, p. 117] there is p such that $p = f(p)$. For this p we have by substituting in the definition (1) of $f(p)$, that $(-1 + h(p) \cdot \bar{x})p = -p - h(p)$ or

$$h(p) = -(h(p) \cdot \bar{x})p = tp, \ t \geq 0 \ \text{(since } h(p) \in Y^*\text{)}. \tag{2}$$

Consider $x = y + h(p)$ for $x \in C(p)$ and $y \in Y$. Assume $h(p) \neq 0$. By Lemma 7, $h(p) \cdot y = 0$, so $h(p) \cdot x = |h(p)| > 0$. Also by Lemma 7, $h(p) \cdot x' \geq h(p) \cdot x$ for any $x' \in C(p)$. Therefore $h(p) \cdot x' > 0$ for $x' \in C(p)$. Then by (2) $p \cdot x' > 0$. On the other hand, by Lemma 1 $C_i(p) \cap H_i(p) \neq \varphi$ for any i. Thus $p \cdot x' \leq 0$ must hold for some $x' \in C(p)$. This is a contradiction. Therefore, the assumption $h(p) \neq 0$ is untenable, and $x = y$. We have proved condition (III) of competitive equilibrium.

The first part of condition (II), $x_i \in C_i(p)$, $i = 1, \ldots, m$, is immediate from the definition of $C(p)$. It remains to satisfy the second part of condition (II), $p \cdot x_i \leq 0$, and condition (I), $p \cdot y = 0$. Since $p \in Y^*$ and $y \in Y$, $p \cdot y \leq 0$. Consider $y = x = \sum_{i=1}^{m} x_i$. By Assumption 6' no one is satiated at p. By Lemma 2, it then holds that $p \cdot x_i \geq 0$ for $x_i \in C_i(p)$. Thus $p \cdot y = p \cdot x \geq 0$, or, in other words $p \cdot y = p \cdot x = 0$. Then $p \cdot x_i = 0$, for all i.

Since all the conditions of competitive equilibrium have been established, $(p, y, x_1, \ldots, x_m)$ is an equilibrium for the special case.

6.6 The General Existence Theorem

The general theorem is proved by an approximation process in which Assumptions 5 and 6 play the key roles.

Theorem 2   Under Assumptions 1, 2, 3, 4, 5, and 6, the abstract market has a competitive equilibrium position.

Proof   The discussion may be confined to the smallest linear subspace which contains Y and all the X_i. Indeed, the essential part of Y^*, the other set we use, also lies here, since adding an arbitrary vector from the orthogonal subspace has no effect on the budget restrictions over the X_i nor on profit maximization over Y. Consider the smallest linear subspace L containing the convex hull of X and Y. L does contain all the X_i. Indeed, they lie in $X - Y$.[11] Since $X_i \cap Y \neq \varphi$ by Assumption 5, y may be selected from Y so that $y = \sum_{i \neq i_0} x_i$. Then $x - y = x_{i_0}$, where

x_{i_0} may be any element of X_{i_0}. Now any convex set has an interior in the smallest flat[12] (affine subspace) which contains it. But a flat which contains Y contains 0, and, therefore, it is a linear subspace. Hence, the convex hull of X and Y has an interior in L, and it is innocuous to introduce

Auxiliary Assumption 2   The convex hull of X and Y has an interior.

It is then implied by Assumption 5, on the presence of a common point relative interior to X and Y, that X and Y cannot be separated by a hyperplane. That is, there is no vector p such that $p \cdot x \geq 0$ for $x \in X$ and $p \cdot y \leq 0$ for $y \in Y$. For at least one of the sets does not lie in the separating hyperplane. Else the convex hull would lie there and have no interior. Then the relative interior points of this set lie on one side of the hyperplane, and none of them can be common to both sets, contradicting Assumption 5. Therefore, for any $p \in Y^*$, $p \cdot x < 0$ for some $x \in X$.

In order to apply the special existence theorem, we must provide the production set with an interior.[13] If Y has no interior, expand Y to $\tilde{Y}$ by adding to the generators of Y the vectors lying in a small n-sphere about the point $\bar{x}$ mentioned in Assumption 5. That is, if int $Y = \varphi$, $\tilde{Y} = \{\tilde{y} \mid \tilde{y} = t_1 y + t_2 y', \text{ for } y \in Y \text{ and } |y' - \bar{x}| \leq \delta_1, t_1 \text{ and } t_2 \geq 0\}$. δ_1 is chosen >0 and small enough so that $\tilde{Y} \cap \Omega$ is still $\{0\}$. On the other hand, if Y has an interior, let $\tilde{Y} = Y$.

If we are to meet Assumption 5', each consumer set must contain an interior point of $\tilde{Y}$. To this end, each consumer set will be displaced toward $\bar{x}$. Let $\tilde{X}_i$ be the set $\{\tilde{x}_i \mid \tilde{x}_i = \delta_2 \bar{x} + (1 - \delta_2)x_i \text{ for } x_i \in X_i\}$,[14] where $0 < \delta_2 < 1$. Take the ordering of $\tilde{X}_i$ to correspond to that of X_i. That is $\tilde{x}_i (\geq) \tilde{x}_i'$ if and only if $x_i (\geq) x_i'$. Assumptions 1 and 2 are then satisfied by $\tilde{X}_i$. Since $\bar{x}$ lies in the interior of $\tilde{Y}$, any point of $X_i \cap Y$ will be interior to $\tilde{Y}$. Such a point exists for each i by Assumption 5. $\tilde{P}$ and $\tilde{C}(p)$ are defined for $\tilde{Y}$ as P and $C(p)$ were for Y.

Assumption 6' is implied by Assumption 6 for δ_1, δ_2 small, since X contains $C(p)$ and $\tilde{X} \cap \tilde{Y}$ lies in an arbitrarily small neighborhood of $X \cap Y$ as $\delta_1, \delta_2 \to 0$. If there were an x leading to satiation in every neighborhood of $X \cap Y$, there would be a limit point of such x's, which would lie in $X \cap Y$, by Lemma 8. It would lead to satiation for some i by closure according to Assumptions 1 and 2. Therefore the assumptions of the special theorem are satisfied, with the new production and consumer sets, and there is an equilibrium. If we let δ_1 and $\delta_2 \to 0$ together, a sequence of equilibria $(\tilde{p}^s, \tilde{y}^s, \tilde{x}_1^s, \dots, \tilde{x}_m^s)$ is generated. Consider the sequences $\tilde{p}^{s'} = \tilde{p}^s / |\tilde{p}^s|$, $\tilde{y}^s$, and $\tilde{x}_i^s \cdot \tilde{p}^{s'}$ lies in the compact set $P \cdot \tilde{y}^s = \sum_{i=1}^{m} \tilde{x}_i^s$ where $\tilde{x}_i^s$ lies in the convex hull of X_i and $\bar{x}$, which is bounded, and thus compact, by Auxiliary Assumption 1. Then there are subsequences $\tilde{p}^r$, $\tilde{y}^r$, $\tilde{x}_i^r$ converging to limits p^*, y^*, x_i^*. Since $p \cdot \tilde{y}^r = p \cdot \tilde{x}_i^r = 0$ and $\tilde{y}^r = \tilde{x}^r$, it follows from continuity of sum and inner product that $p^* \cdot x_i^* = p^* \cdot y^* = 0$, $y^* \in Y$, $p^* \in P$ and $y^* = x^*$, or the second part of condition (II) and conditions (I) and (III) of competitive equilibrium are met in the limit for the original production and consumer sets. Therefore, if the first part of condition (II) can be shown to hold for them, the general existence theorem will be proved.

We must show that $x^* \in C(p^*)$. This will be true if $C(p)$ is continuous at p^*. For sequences $\tilde{x}^r \in \tilde{C}^r(\tilde{p}^r)$ and $x^r \in C(\tilde{p}^r)$ have the same limits as $\delta^r \to 0$, and, at $\delta = 0$, $\tilde{C}(p^*) = C(p^*)$. Now, we have seen that for $p \in P$ there is an x such that $p \cdot x < 0$, $x \in X$. Therefore, for some i_0 there is $x_{i_0} \in X_{i_0}$ and $p^* \cdot x_{i_0} < 0$. By Lemma 4, using Auxiliary Assumption 1, $C_{i_0}(p)$ is continuous at p^*. Let I_1 be the set of indices i for consumers such that there is $x_i \in X_i$ and $p^* \cdot x_i < 0$. Let I_2 be the set of indices for consumers which do not lie in I_1. We shall show that I_2 is empty. $C_{I_1}(p) = \sum_{i \in I_1} C_i(p)$ is continuous at p^*. On the other hand, for the equilibrium values $\tilde{x}_{I_1}^r \in \tilde{C}_{I_1}^r(\tilde{p}^r) \cap (\tilde{Y}^r - \tilde{X}_{I_2})$ and $p^r \cdot \tilde{x}_{I_1}^r \leq 0$. Thus we can conclude from continuity that $x_{I_1}^* \in C_{I_1}(p^*) \cap (Y - X_{I_2})$ and $p^* \cdot x_{I_1}^* \leq 0$. Assume that I_2 is not empty. Then by Assumption 6 there is an $\omega \in (Y - X_{I_2})$, such that $\omega = x_{I_1} - x_{I_1}^*$, where $x_i (\geq) x_i^*$ for all $i \in I_1$, and $x_{i_1} (>) x_{i_1}^*$ for some $i_1 \in I_1$. Since x_{i_1} is in the preferred set, x_{i_1} cannot be available, or $p^* \cdot x_{i_1} > 0$. On the other hand, by Assumption 6 the ith consumer is not satiated at $x^* \in X \cap Y$, nor, therefore, at p^*, for any $i \in I_1$. Then Lemma 2 implies $p^* \cdot x_i \geq 0$ for any $x_i \in C_i(p^*)$ for $i \in I_1$. Since $p^* \cdot x_{I_1}^* \leq 0$, this gives $p \cdot \omega > 0$. However, $\omega = y - x_{I_2}$ where $y \in Y$ and $x_{I_2} \in X_{I_2}$. Also $p^* \cdot y \leq 0$, because $p^* \in P$. Consequently $p^* \cdot x_{I_2} < 0$ must hold. Then $p^* \cdot x_i < 0$ must hold for some $i \in I_2$, where $x_i \in X_i$. This contradicts the definition of I_2, so I_2 is empty.

Since $C(p^*) = C_{I_1}(p^*)$, and $C_{I_1}(p)$ is continuous at p^*, we have proved $C(p)$ to be continuous at p^*. This establishes the first part of condition (II) of competitive equilibrium. Therefore, the equilibrium exists for the original production and consumption sets.

6.7 Concordance with Hicksian Model

The model of production described here includes the model which uses a finite number l of firms each of which owns a production set Y_j. Let $Y = \sum_{i=1}^{l} Y_j$.[15] The new assumptions are

Assumption 3′ Y_j is closed and convex. $0 \in Y_j$.

Assumption 4′ $Y \cap \Omega = \{0\}$. Y is closed.

This is the model used by Arrow and Debreu [1, p. 267] except that they also require $Y \cap -Y = \{0\}$. However, we allow the possibility that some production processes may be reversed. To bring this model within the linear model we have described, we must introduce the entrepreneurial factor which is private to the firm and not marketed [1, p. 267n.] The ownership of this factor is divided among the owners of the firm according to their rights to participate in profits. Then all the receipts of the firm, above its payments to hired factors, can be imputed to the entrepreneurial factor.

Lemmas 8 and 9 apply equally well to the new model where 1, 2, 3′, and 4′ are assumed. Then, as we saw in Section 5, the X_i may be taken to be compact. Formally, we introduce a new dimension for each entrepreneurial factor. Then $\hat{y}_j \in \hat{Y}_j$ in the enlarged space, if $y_j \in Y_j$, and $\hat{y}_{hj} = y_{hj}$ for $h = 1, \ldots, n$, $\hat{y}_{n+j,j} = -1$, and $\hat{y}_{hj} = 0$ for all $h \neq 1, \ldots, n$, $n + j$. $\hat{Y}$ is the convex cone spanned by the elements of the $\hat{Y}_j$. That is, $\hat{Y} = \{\hat{y} \mid \hat{y} = \sum_{j=1}^{l} t_j \hat{y}_j$ for $t_j \geq 0$ and $\hat{y}_j \in \hat{Y}_j\}$.

The owners of entrepreneurial factors are assumed always to supply them, and the total supply of each type is one unit. Of course, the price of the entrepreneurial factor will be nonnegative in the set $\hat{P}$, corresponding to $\hat{Y}$, since there is $\hat{y}_j$ in $\hat{Y}$, where $\hat{y}_{n+j,j} = -1$, and $\hat{y}_{hj} = 0$ for $h \neq n + j$. Then the projection of an equilibrium $\hat{y}$ into the original space will be in $Y = \sum_{j=1}^{l} Y_j$, and an equilibrium $\hat{x}$ goes into $x \in X$.

The set $\hat{Y}$ satisfies Assumptions 3 and 4, except that it may not be closed. However, it is obviously closed as a result of Assumption 4′ in the flat defined by $\hat{y}_{hj} = -1$ for $h = n + 1, \ldots, n + l$. But $\hat{X}$ lies in this flat by the assumption that entrepreneurial factors are always supplied, and, therefore, so do all possible equilibrium points. Thus no equilibria are introduced by taking the closure of $\hat{Y}$ and using this in the proof of Section 6. Arrow and Debreu do not directly assume that Y is closed, which is the basis for this argument. However, their assumptions of irreversibility and closure for the Y_j are easily shown to imply that Y is closed. They also use irreversibility to place bounds on the Y_j, but these bounds are not needed in our proofs.

Let us define a competitive equilibrium in the model where 1, 2, 3′, 4′, 5, and 6 are assumed by (II), (III), and [see 1, p. 268]

(I′) $p \cdot y_j \geq p \cdot y_j'$ for $y_j' \in Y_j$, for each j.

Except for the condition that $p \geq 0$, and $y \geq x$, which we omit, this is the definition of Arrow and Debreu. We may now state

Theorem 3 There is a competitive equilibrium in the sense of (I′), (II), and (III) on Assumptions 1, 2, 3′, 4′, 5 and 6.

Proof The foregoing discussion showed that there was an equilibrium in the sense of (I), (II), and (III) for the analogue model in the extended space. This immediately implies conditions (II) and (III) for the reduced space. If (I′) does not hold, $p \cdot y_j < p \cdot y_j'$ for some j. Then $\hat{p} \cdot \hat{y}_j' > \hat{p} \cdot \hat{y}_j = 0$, which directly violates (I). Thus (I′) also holds and the conclusion follows.

We may note that in view of the entrepreneurial factor it is not unreasonable to bound Y_j from the beginning. In this case Assumption 4′ can be eliminated, since it is no longer needed for the proof of Lemma 8.

6.8 Properties of $C_i(p)$

Several lemmas stating important properties of $C_i(p)$ and $C(p)$ have been used in the preceeding arguments and remain to be proved.

Lemma 1 Suppose X_i is bounded, and $H_i(p) \neq \varphi$. Then $H_i(p) \cap C_i(p) \neq \varphi$.

Proof The available set $H_i(p)$ is non-empty and compact, by hypothesis. Let N_δ be a finite set of points such that for any $x_i \in H_i(p)$ the distance of x_i from some point $x_i' \in N_\delta$ is less than δ. Let x_i^δ be a point of N_δ such that $x_i^\delta \, (\geq) \, x_i$ for $x_i \in N_\delta$. Consider a sequence $x_i^{\delta s}$ as $\delta_s \to 0$. A subsequence $x_i^{\delta r} \to x_i''$ for some $x_i'' \in H_i(p)$. I assert $x_i'' \, (\geq) \, x_i$ for $x_i \in H_i(p)$. Take a sequence $x_i^r \to x_i$. Then $x_i^{\delta r} \, (\geq) \, x_i^r$ and the conclusion follows by Assumption 2.

Lemma 2 If the i-th consumer is not satiated at p, $p \cdot x_i \geq 0$ for $x_i \in C_i(p)$.

Proof Suppose $p \cdot x_i^1 < 0$ and $x_i^1 \in C_i(p)$. By hypothesis, there is also $x_i^2 \, (>) \, x_i^1$. By the definition of $C_i(p)$, it must be that $p \cdot x_i^2 > 0$. Consider $x_i^3 = tx_i^1 + (1-t)x_i^2$. For an appropriate t with $0 \leq t < 1$, $p \cdot x_i^3 = 0$. But by convexity of the preference ordering, Assumption 2, $x_i^3 \, (>) \, x_i^1$. Since x_i^3 is available, $x_i^1 \notin C_i(p)$, which contradicts the hypothesis. Therefore, $p \cdot x_i^1 \geq 0$.

Lemma 3 $C_i(p)$ is convex and closed, and $C(p)$ is convex.

Proof   The closure of $C_i(p)$ is immediate from Assumptions 1 and 2. Moreover, the convexity of $C(p)$ is easily derived from the convexity of $C_i(p)$. Thus we only need to show convexity for $C_i(p)$. For points which are not equivalent, convexity follows from Assumption 2. The cases where $C_i(p)$ is empty or where all points of X_i are saturation points are trivial. However, if x_i^1 is not a saturation point, every neighborhood of x_i^1 has a point x_i^3 (proof of Lemma 2) such that $x_i^3 \, (>) \, x_i^1$. Simply take t small enough. Now suppose $x_i' \, (=) \, x_i''$ where $x_i' x_i'' \in C_i(p)$, and x_i'' is not a saturation point. Let $x_i = tx_i' + (1-t)x_i''$, $0 < t < 1$. Then there is a sequence $x_i^{s''} \to x_i''$ and $x_i^{s''} \, (>) \, x_i''$. Consider $x_i^s = tx_i' + (1-t)x_i^{s''}$. By convexity, Assumption 2, $x_i^s \, (>) \, x_i'$. Therefore, $x_i \, (\geqq) \, x_i'$ by closure, Assumption 2, and $x_i \in C_i(p)$. If x_i'' is a saturation point, there is a sequence $x_i^{s''} \, (<) \, x_i''$. Then, by a similar argument, $x_i \, (\geqq) \, x_i''$, so again $x_i \in C_i(p)$. There is a different proof of the analogous result in [1, p. 269].

Lemma 4   Suppose X_i is bounded. Then $C_i(p)$ is a continuous set valued function at p when $\min_{x_i \in X_i} p \cdot x_i < 0$. Also $C(p)$ is continuous over a neighborhood where each $C_i(p)$ is continuous.

Proof   The proof of continuity for $C_i(p)$ falls into two parts. First, we show that every convergent sequence of vectors $x_i^s \in C_i(p^s)$, where $p^s \to p$, converges to a vector $x_i \in C_i(p)$. This is upper semi-continuity and uses the conditions of the lemma. Second, we show that every $x_i \in C_i(p)$ is, in fact, the limit of a sequence x_i^s with $x_i^s \in C_i(p^s)$. This is lower semi-continuity, and the two types of continuity together are what is meant by continuity for $C_i(p)$.

We will see that lower semi-continuity for the available set $H_i(p)$ implies upper semi-continuity for $C_i(p)$. Suppose $H_i(p)$ is lower semi-continuous. Then for $p \cdot x_i \leqq 0$ there is $x_i^s \to x_i$ and $p^s \cdot x_i^s \leqq 0$. Now $x_i^{s'} \in C_i(p^s)$ means that $x_i^{s'} \, (\geqq) \, x_i^s$ for $x_i^s \in H_i(p^s)$. Suppose $x_i^{s'} \to x_i'$. Then, by Assumption 2, $x_i' \, (\geqq) \, x_i$. Since x_i is an arbitrary element of $H_i(p)$, $x_i' \in C_i(p)$ and $C_i(p)$ is upper semi-continuous. Thus it suffices for the first part of the proof to show that $H_i(p)$ is lower semi-continuous.

By hypothesis there is $\bar{x}_i \in X_i$ and $p \cdot \bar{x}_i < 0$. Therefore, if $p^s \to p$, $p^s \cdot \bar{x}_i < 0$, for s sufficiently large. Take an arbitrary point x_i of $H_i(p)$. Let $x_i^s = t^s x_i + (1-t^s)\bar{x}_i$, where t^s is a maximum, for $0 \leqq t^s \leqq 1$ and $x_i^s \in H_i(p^s)$. $x_i^s \to x_i$ is equivalent to $t^s \to 1$. $t^s < 1$ implies $p^s \cdot x_i^s = 0$.

Otherwise, t^s could be larger without making x_i^s unavailable. If t^s does not converge to 1, a subsequence t^r converges to $t < 1$. Then, for large r, $p^r \cdot x_i^r = 0$, and since $p^r \to p$, we have $p \cdot (tx_i + (1 - t)\bar{x}_i) = 0$. Since $p \cdot \bar{x}_i < 0$, this implies $p \cdot x_i > 0$, which contradicts the assumption that $x_i \in H_i(p)$. Therefore, t must converge to 1, and x_i^s converges to x_i. Thus $H_i(p)$ is lower semi-continuous. This completes the first part of the proof of continuity for $C_i(p)$.

For the proof of lower semi-continuity suppose $x_i \in C_i(p)$ and $p^s \to p$. Let x_i^s be the closest point of $C_i(p^s)$ to $x_i \cdot C_i(p^s)$ is not empty by Lemma 1, and since it is closed and convex by Lemma 3, a closest point exists and is unique as we saw in the proof of Lemma 6. We will show that $x_i^s \to x_i$. If x_i is a saturation point, $x_i \in C_i(p^s)$ for all s, and the x_i^s may be selected equal to x_i. If x_i is not a saturation point, there is a sequence of preferred points converging to x_i, as we saw in the proof of Lemma 3. Then if it should be true that for every x_i' $(>)$ x_i, $x_i' \in C(p^s)$ for all s large enough, the distance from $C_i(p^s)$ to x_i must go to zero. But if for some x_i' $(>)$ x_i it is not the case that $x_i' \in C_i(p^s)$ for large s, there must be a subsequence p^r of p^s for which there exists x_i'' with x_i' $(<)$ x_i'' and $x_i'' \in H_i(p^r)$. By the compactness of X_i there is a further subsequence of x_i'' converging to $x_i'' \in H_i(p)$ and, by Assumption 2, x_i' $(\leqq)$ x_i''. Since x_i $(<)$ x_i', x_i $(<)$ x_i'' and x_i cannot be in $C_i(p)$. This contradicts the hypothesis, so $x_i' \in C_i(p^s)$ must hold for large s. Then, the distance from $C_i(p^s)$ to x_i does go to zero, x_i^s converges to x_i, and $C_i(p)$ is lower semi-continuous.

That $C(p)$ is lower semi-continuous follows directly from the lower semi-continuity of the $C_i(p)$. That is, a sequence converging to $x \in C(p)$ may be found as the sum of sequences converging to any x_i for which $\sum_{i=1}^m x_i = x$. For upper semi-continuity, the case is a little less simple. We must show, when $x^s \to x$, $x^s \in C(p^s)$ and $p^s \to p$, that $x \in C(p)$. This requires $x = \sum_{i=1}^m x_i$ where $x_i \in C_i(p)$. Take $x^s = \sum x_i^s$ where $x_i^s \in C_i(p^s)$. By the compactness of X_i, a subsequence x_i^r converges to a limit x_i' for each i. Then $\sum_{i=1}^m x_i' = x$ by continuity of the sum, and $x_i' \in C_i(p)$ by the upper semi-continuity of $C_i(p)$.

6.9 Wald's Counter-Example

The famous counter-example to the existence of equilibrium proposed by Abraham Wald [15, p. 389] fails to upset our theorem, although it is, of course, subject to it. The production cone in Wald's case is simply the negative orthant. The only processes are disposal processes.

Each of the three consumers holds the entire supply of one good. The marginal utility of each good increases without limit as the quantity taken falls. Each consumer is insatiable in the first good, held by the first consumer. Thus no consumer can be satiated. However, if the first consumer is awarded the whole supply of the goods held by the second consumer and the third consumer, he is satiated in those goods. Thus the rest of the market then has no attainable combination of goods which can improve the position of the first consumer. (We do *not* mean the obvious fact that they cannot give more than their whole supply of goods, but that even the addition of their *original* supplies to the amounts now taken by the first consumer would have no value for him.) This violates Assumption 6.

As it happens, in Wald's example, the violation of Assumption 6 by itself would not eliminate the equilibrium. The fatal blow is that the preference order is not closed on the boundary of X_i. For the second consumer, for example, the indifference curves for quantities retained approach the boundary of the first quadrant in the limit. But this boundary, which is the boundary of X_i (after a translation of the origin to the point representing the initial stock), is not an indifference curve, or rather is not *treated* as one. It would not be unreasonable to treat this boundary as an indifference curve. In that case, there *would* be an equilibrium with prices 1, 0, and 0, for the goods held by consumers 1, 2, and 3 respectively, and the first consumer receiving all supplies of the three goods. With equal logic, this boundary would be excluded from X_i. Since at the boundary one good has infinite marginal utility, each is presumably a necessity. Then it is Assumption 1 that is violated, for X_i is not closed. I think it must be concluded that Wald did not present a plausible example from the viewpoint of economics. Unless the goods were absolute necessities, marginal utilities should not have been allowed to become indefinitely large. But if they are, some minimum requirement, greater than zero, should be stated for each person and each good.

6.10 Weakening of Assumption 6

Assumption 6 as it has been given is somewhat stronger than the argument of Section 6.6 requires. This version has been used because it is straightforward and easily understood. It is not entirely clear what the weaker assumption implies for the basic consumer and production sets. Nonetheless, the weaker assumption has a strong intuitive appeal.

Let I_1 be the set of indices for consumers with income at p, and I_2 the set of indices for other consumers. We can replace Assumption 6 with

Assumption 6*   (a) If a consumer is satiated at p' for $\{\tilde{X}_i, \tilde{Y}\}$ in a sufficiently small neighborhood of $\{X_i, Y\}$, then $\tilde{C}(p') \cap \tilde{Y} = \varphi$.

(b) If no consumer is satiated at p' for $\{\tilde{X}_i, \tilde{Y}\}$ in arbitrarily small neighborhoods of p, $\{X_i, Y\}$ and $\tilde{C}(p') \cap \tilde{Y} \neq \varphi$, then no consumer is satiated at p for $\{X_i, Y\}$.

(c) If neither I_1 nor I_2 is empty, either $C_{I_1}(p) \cap (Y - X_{I_2}) = \varphi$, or there is an $\omega \in (Y - X_{I_2})$ such that $\omega = \sum_{i \in I_1}(x_i - x_i')$ for $x_i' \in H_i(p)$, $x_i \in C_i(p)$, and for some $i_0 \in I_1$, $x_{i_0} \; (>) \; x_{i_0}''$ for all $x_{i_0}'' \in H_{i_0}(p)$.

Part (a) of 6* provides the needed non-satiation required for the use of Theorem 1, since it implies Assumption 6' for the modified sets. Part (b) implies nonsatiation at p^* for $\{X_i, Y\}$, a fact which is appealed to in the last stage of the proof of Theorem 2. Part (c) provides for irreducibility. Since the main body of the proof proceeds within a bounded region, there is no difficulty in giving appropriate definitions of the neighborhoods employed. Of course, more general variations of the basic sets can be allowed than those defined in proving Theorem 2. However, the displacement of X_i should preserve the preference order, as well as being continuous in the metric sense. The appeal of 6* is that we no longer say that no one can possibly be satiated, but that if some one is, demand will be excessive in the way described.

Notes

1. I should like to acknowledge the value to me of the many conversations on this subject which I have had with Gerard Debreu. I am also grateful to the Cowles Foundation for numerous courtesies. David Gale proved very helpful at strategic moments in the revision of the chapter, as did Debreu.

2. Arrow and Debreu [1] give as their condition 3 in the definition of equilibrium that prices are nonnegative and, as condition 4, that excess demand is nonpositive and the price of a good is zero if its excess demand is negative. This is equivalent to assuming free disposal for all goods, so that the negative orthant lies in the production set. "V asserts that it is possible to arrange the economic system by choice of production and consumption vectors so that an excess supply of all commodities can be achieved" (p. 280). This assumption is used p. 287, line 9, to ensure that productive labor has a positive price in the neighborhood of equilibrium, or, in other words, that demand is continuous there.

McKenzie [12] assumes the production set to have an interior point (assumption (1.1), p. 279), and assumes the aggregate consumer set to have a point lying in the interior of the production set (assumption (4.1), p. 284). Gale [6] allows excess demand to be negative if price is zero in the manner of Arrow and Debreu. However, he does not discuss the general problem but assumes each consumer to hold initial supplies of every good. Thus the individual consumption sets have points in the interior of the production set (p. 167).

3. I was led to this assumption through the insistence of David Gale.

4. That is, no one can be made better off within the limitations of production unless someone is made worse off.

5. $x \geqq x'$ means $x_h \geqq x'_h$. $x > x'$ means $x_h > x'_h$. $x > x'$ means $x \geqq x'$ and $x \neq x'$. x_h is the hth component of x.

6. $x \ (>) \ x'$ means $x \ (\geqq) \ x'$ and not $x' \ (\geqq) \ x$. $x \ (=) \ x'$ means $x \ (\geqq) \ x'$ and $x' \ (\geqq) \ x$.

7. A point x is relative interior to a set X if x is interior to X in the smallest flat containing X. See footnote 12 below.

8. This revision in the assumptions which protect consumer income follows a method used by Gale [6] in building a model with linear utility functions. In a later section we will see how Assumption 6 may be relaxed further.

9. See Tjalling Koopmans [9] for a discussion of the significance of this condition. Our description of competitive equilibrium closely parallels Walras [16].

10. If $g(z)$ maps continuously into itself a compact convex subset V of a Euclidean space, there is $z^* \in V$ such that $g(z^*) = z^*$.

11. I am indebted to Gerard Debreu for correcting an error in the initial statement of this point.

12. A flat is a set of vectors F such that x and x' in F implies $tx + (1 - t)x'$ in F for any real number t. If $0 \in F$, then F is a linear subspace. For this and related questions see [4, pp. 29–41].

13. This method was used in Debreu [2]. We suppose, for simplicity, Y is not a linear subspace.

14. A similar move was made in [12].

15. A model of this type may have been first stated in full blown mathematical form by J. R. Hicks [8]. Of course, the elements are much older.

References

[1] Arrow, Kenneth J., and Gerard Debreu: "Existence of an Equilibrium for a Competitive Economy," *Econometrica*, July 1954.

[2] Debreu, Gerard: "Market Equilibrium," *Proceedings of the National Academy of Sciences*, 1956.

[3] ———, "A Social Equilibrium Existence Theorem," *Proceedings of the National Academy of Sciences*, 1952.

[4] Fenchel, W.: *Convex Cones, Sets, and Functions*, offset, Princeton, 1953.

[5] Gale, David: *General Equilibrium for Linear Models*, Rand p-1156, 1957.

[6] ———, "The Law of Supply and Demand," *Mathematica Scandinavia*, 1955.

[7] Hicks, J. R.: *Value and Capital*, Oxford, 1939.

[8] Kakutani, Shizuo: "A Generalization of Brouwer's Fixed Point Theorem," *Duke Mathematical Journal*, 1941.

[9] Koopmans, Tjalling: "Analysis of Production as an Efficient Combination of Activities," *Activity Analysis of Production and Allocation*, edited by Koopmans, New York, 1951.

[10] Kuhn, Harold W.: "A Note on 'The Law of Supply and Demand'," *Mathematica Scandinavia*, 1956.

[11] Lefshetz, S.: *Introduction to Topology*, Princeton, 1949.

[12] McKenzie, Lionel W.: "Competitive Equilibrium with Dependent Consumer Preferences," *Second Symposiom on Linear Programming*, Washington, 1955.

[13] Nikaido, H.: "On the Classical Multilateral Exchange Problem," *Metroeconomica*, 1956.

[14] Uzawa, Hirofumi: "Note on the Existence of an Equilibrium for a Competitive Economy," *Technical Report No. 40*, Department of Economics, Stanford University, Stanford, California.

[15] Wald, Abraham: "On Some Systems of Equations of Mathematical Economics," translation, *Econometrica*, 1951.

[16] Walras, Leon: *Elements of Pure Economics*, translated by Jaffé, London, 1954.

7 Stability of Equilibrium and the Value of Positive Excess Demand

Lionel W. McKenzie

7.1 Weak Gross Substitutes

I shall prove two theorems using a new method in the problem of stability of equilibrium based upon the second method of Liapounov [4, p. 256ff.].[1] The novelty of method lies in the selection of the function $V(p)$ whose decrease with time leads to the equilibrium position.[2] This is the price weighted sum of the positive excess demands. I shall first prove the existence and stability[3] in the large of the set of equilibrium points in the case of cross-elasticities which are nonnegative. The set of equilibrium points is compact and convex, and if the gross substitution matrix is indecomposable at equilibrium, the equilibrium is unique. When a numéraire is not present, it is possible to proceed beyond the limitation of nonnegative cross-elasticities to consider cases where certain weighted sums of the partial derivatives of excess demands with respect to prices are positive. This appears to be a natural generalization. Although the second theorem is primarily of local interest, one hardly need apologize for that. Global stability is not to be expected in general.

This type of study was initiated by Walras [8, p. 170] and given its present formulation by Samuelson [5, p. 269]. I shall not elaborate on its limitations. Suffice it to say that, strictly interpreted, the groping for equilibrium which occurs here is prior to the conclusion of any trades. Of course, the analysis may be relevant to the more realistic market processes nonetheless. The subject derives interest from the significance of the underlying Walrasian model. It is a part of the large problem of exploring the properties of this model as amended and developed by Pareto, Hicks, and Samuelson.

I shall proceed formally in the interest of expedition and clarity. There are n goods indexed by the integers 1 to n. p denotes a price vector. $f_i(p)$ is the excess demand for the ith good. p is an equilibrium means $f_i(p) = 0$, $i = 1, \ldots, n$. $h_i(p)$ is the rate of change of the ith price. S is the gross substitution matrix. Formally, we make the following

Definitions

(1) $I = \{1, \ldots, n\}$. $P = \{i \mid f_i \geqslant 0, i \in I\}$. $N = \{i \mid f_i < 0, i \in I\}$. $P' = \{i \mid h_i \geqslant 0, i \in I\}$. $N' = \{i \mid h_i < 0, i \in I\}$.

(2) $p, f, h \in E_n$, the n dimensional Euclidean space.

(3) $z > w$ means $z_i > w_i$, $i \in I$, and similarly for $\geqslant$ and $=$.

(4)   The norm of $z \in E_n$ is $|z| = \sum_{i \in I} |z_i|$. The length of $z \in E_n$ is $\|z\| = (\sum_{i \in I} z_i^2)^{1/2}$. The inner product $w'z = \sum_{i \in I} w_i z_i$, for $w, z \in E_n$.

(5) $f_{ij}(p) = \partial f_i(p)/\partial p_j$.

(6) $S = [f_{ij}]$, an $n \times n$ matrix.

(7) $S^* = [p_i f_{ij}/p_j] = [s_{ij}]$.

(8) $V(p) = \sum_{i \in P} p_i f_i(p)$. $V'(p) = \sum_{i \in P'} p_i f_i(p)$.

(9) $dV/dt = dV(p(t))/dt$, and similarly for V'.

The set P is the set of indices of goods whose excess demand is non-negative, and N is the set of indices of goods whose excess demand is negative. $P \cup N = I$, of course. It is also useful to consider P' as the set of indices of goods whose prices are constant or rising, and N' as the set of indices of goods whose prices are falling. P' and N' differ from P and N, under the assumptions we shall use, only when there is a numéraire, whose price is constant regardless of the excess demand for it. Then the index of the numéraire is always in P' but it may not be in P. P, N, P', and N' are functions of the price vector p, since $f_i(p)$, the excess demand for the ith good, and $h_i(p)$, the rate of change of the ith price, are functions of p and their signs determine which indices are in these sets.

$V(p)$ is the Liapounov function which we shall use. $V'(p)$, however, plays a similar auxiliary role. A Liapounov function is used to prove that equilibrium is stable for a differential equation system. To serve in this role a function of the dependent variables, in this case, the p_i, $i \in I$, must be monotone decreasing. $V(p)$, however, and $V'(p)$ do not have derivatives everywhere, and, if there is a numéraire, $V(p)$ is not strictly decreasing. These facts cause some complications in our proofs.

There will be a set of assumptions for each theorem.

Assumptions I

(1) $f_i(p)$ is defined for $p > 0$. It is continuous with continuous first partial derivatives.

(2) $p'f(p) = 0$, for $p > 0$.

(3) $f_i(kp) = f_i(p)$ for $k > 0$, $p > 0$.

(4) (a) There is $\varrho > 0$ such that $p > 0$, $p_n = 1$, $|p| \geqslant \varrho$ implies $f_n(p) \geqslant \varepsilon$, for some $\varepsilon > 0$.
   (b) There is $\delta > 0$ such that $p > 0$, $p_n = 1$, and $p_i \leq \delta$, for any $i \neq n$, implies $f_i(p) \geqslant \varepsilon$, for some $\varepsilon > 0$.

(5) $f_{ij} \geq 0, i \neq j$.

(6) $dp_i/dt = h_i(p)$, $i \in I$. $h_i(p)$ is defined for $p > 0$. It is continuous with continuous first partial derivatives.

(7) Sign $h_i(p) \equiv$ sign $f_i(p)$, $i \neq n$. $h_n(p) \equiv 0$.

Assumption (2) is the famous Walras's Law which is also fundamental for the existence of equilibrium in more general models. It is a consequence of the budget restraints on traders. (3) is homogeneity of zero degree for the excess demand functions, which are assumed here to be single valued. Homogeneity may be derived from the maximization of preference by traders subject to their budget restraints. (4) is important in the proof of existence. It is fairly weak because of Assumption (5), which is an assumption of gross substitutability or independence. (5) is the key substantive assumption for Theorem 1. It means that, if any price falls, while other prices are constant, no other good experiences an increase of demand. The term "gross" is used because income effects are not removed. (6) is the system of differential equations whose equilibrium is to be studied. (7) is intended to represent the action of a (recontracting) competitive market, where prices in terms of the numéraire rise if excess demand is positive, fall if excess demand is negative, and otherwise remain constant. Note that (7) is a qualitative assumption, and the rate of price change is not required to be proportional to excess demand.

Theorem 1 The differential equation system of Assumptions I has a unique solution $p(t; p^\circ)$ for any initial prices $p^\circ > 0$. $p(t; p^\circ)$ approaches the set M of equilibria as t increases without limit. M is compact and convex. For $p^* \in M$, $M = \{p^*\}$, if S is indecomposable at p^*.

In preparation for the proof of Theorem 1, a number of lemmas will be established. The first and fourth will be useful for the proof of Theorem 2. The first lemma establishes the positivity of the Liapounov function.

Lemma 1 $V(p) > 0$, unless $f(p) = 0$, for $f > 0$. $V'(p) \geqslant 0$.

Proof By Walras's Law, Assumption (2), $p'f(p) = 0$. Since $p > 0$ by hypothesis, $f(p) \neq 0$ implies $f_i(p) > 0$ for some $i \in P$. Thus $V(p) = \sum_{i \in P} p_i f_i(p) > 0$. If $V'(p)$ were negative, $V'(p) + \sum_{i \in N'} p_i f_i < 0$, or $p'f(p) < 0$, contradicting Walras's Law.

Lemma 2 helps in proving that dV'/dt is negative if $V' > 0$. Let E and F be disjoint sets with $E \cup F = I$.

Lemma 2 Suppose $\sum_{i \in E} p_i f_i \geqslant \varepsilon > 0$ and $p \geqslant 0$. Then $f_{ij} > 0$ for some $i \in E$, $j \in F$, if f_{ij} exists for all $i, j \in I$.

Proof Differentiating Walras's Law with respect to p_j,

$$\sum_{i \in I} p_i f_{ij} = -f_j. \tag{1}$$

Thus, $\sum_{i \in I} \sum_{j \in E} p_i f_{ij} p_j = -\sum_{j \in E} p_j f_j \leqslant -\varepsilon$. But $f_{ij} \geqslant 0$ for $i \in F$, $j \in E$. Therefore,

$$\sum_{i \in E} \sum_{j \in E} p_i f_{ij} p_j \leqslant \varepsilon. \tag{2}$$

By homogeneity $\sum_{j \in I} f_{ij} p_j = 0$ so

$$\sum_{i \in E} \sum_{j \in I} p_i f_{ij} p_j = 0. \tag{3}$$

Then (2) and (3) imply

$$\sum_{i \in E} \sum_{j \in F} p_i f_{ij} p_j \geqslant \varepsilon. \tag{4}$$

Since $p_i \geqslant 0$, there must be an $f_{ij} > 0$ with $i \in E$, $j \in F$.

We now show that the derivatives of V and V' are not positive.

Lemma 3 $dV'/dt \leq 0$, if the derivative exists, and, if $V'(p) > 0$, the strict inequality holds. $dV/dt \leq 0$, where it exists.

Proof   At a point where the derivative exists,

$$\frac{dV'}{dt} = \frac{d}{dt}\sum_{i \in P'} p_i f_i = \sum_{i \in P'} h_i f_i + \sum_{i \in P'} p_i \frac{df_i}{dt} = \sum_{i \in P'} h_i f_i + \sum_{i \in P'} p_i \sum_{j \in I} f_{ij} h_j. \qquad (5)$$

Substituting for f_i in (5), by use of (1),

$$\frac{dV'}{dt} = -\sum_{j \in P'} h_j \sum_{i \in I} p_i f_{ij} + \sum_{i \in P'} p_i \sum_{j \in I} f_{ij} h_j.$$

By cancellation of terms,

$$\frac{dV'}{dt} = -\sum_{i \in N'} \sum_{j \in P'} p_i f_{ij} h_j + \sum_{i \in P'} \sum_{j \in N'} p_i f_{ij} h_j. \qquad (6)$$

Since $f_{ij} \geq 0$, $i \neq j$, $p_i > 0$, $h_j < 0$ for $j \in N'$, and $h_j \geq 0$ for $j \in P'$, $dV'/dt \leq 0$. But, $V'(p) > 0$ and Lemma 2 (with $E = P'$) imply $f_{ij} > 0$ for some $i \in P'$, $f \in N'$. Thus the second term in (6) is negative and $dV'/dt < 0$.

The second part of the lemma follows from formula (6) when N and P are substituted for N' and P'. Then $h_j \leq 0$ for $j \in N$, $h_j \geq 0$ for $j \in P$, and $f_{ij} \geq 0$, so $dV/dt \leq 0$.

V and V' do not always have derivatives. Therefore, to prove the monotone properties of V and V', we also require.

Lemma 4[4]   Let $V'(t) = V'(p(t))$, where $p(t) > 0$ is a solution of the differential equations of Assumptions I. dV'/dt is Lebesgue integrable and $\int_{t_0}^{t} dV'/dt = V'(t) - V'(t_0)$. The analogous proposition is true for $V(t) = V(p(t))$.

Proof   Consider the functions $p_i(t) f_i(p(t))$, $i \in I$. These are continuous, and their derivatives $h_i f_i + \sum_{j \in I} p_i f_{ij} h_j$ are continuous, and thus bounded over a finite interval. Hence the $p_i f_i$ satisfy a Lipshitz condition and are absolutely continuous [3, p. 203]. It follows that the functions $V_n(t) = p_n(t) f_n(t)$, $V_i(t) = \{\max p_i(t) f_i(p(t)), 0\}$, $i \neq n$, and, therefore, $V'(t) = \sum_{i \in P'} V_i(t)$, are absolutely continuous. Then the Lemma is implied by the fundamental theorem of the integral calculus

[3, p. 207]. A similar proof applies to $V(t)$. With the help of Lemma 4, the properties of the derivatives derived in Lemma 3 can be effectively used.

Finally, the path $p(t)$ must be bounded so that limit points will exist. These will be the equilibria. With this end in view we state

Lemma 5 $|p| \to \infty$, where $p_n \equiv 1$ and $p > 0$, implies that $f_n(p)$ increases without limit.

Proof We may represent any such p in the form $u + tq$, where $u_n = 1$, $u_i = 0$, $i \neq n$, and $q_n = 0$, $|q| = 1$. t is a positive number. Rewrite formula (6) as

$$\frac{dV^*}{dt} = -\sum_{i \in F} \sum_{j \in E} p_i f_{ij} h_j + \sum_{i \in E} \sum_{j \in F} p_i f_{ij} h_j. \tag{6'}$$

(6') is valid for any fixed partition of I into disjoint sets E and F if $V^*(p)$ is defined as $\sum_{i \in E} p_i f_i(p)$ and p is a differentiable function of a parameter t. Let $E = \{n\}$ and F be the set of all other indices in I. Let $p(t) = u + tq$ and $t \to \infty$. Then $V^*(p) = f_n$, and $h_i = dp_i/dt = q_i$. Suppose $f_n \geq \varepsilon > 0$. Then, by (4) in the proof of Lemma 2, $\sum_{i \in E} \sum_{j \in F} p_i f_{ij} h_j = \sum_{j \in F} f_{nj} q_j \geq \varepsilon$, since n is the only index in E. But the first term in (6') is zero since $h_n = q_n = 0$, and $dV^*/dt = \sum_{j \in F} f_{nj} q_j \geq \varepsilon$. Thus $df_n/dt = dV^*/dt \geq \varepsilon$. By Assumption (4), however, there is a ϱ such that $|p| > \varrho$ implies $f_n \geq \varepsilon$. Therefore, $t > \varrho$ implies $df_n/dt \geq \varepsilon$ and $f_n \geq (t - \varrho)\varepsilon$. This shows that f_n is unbounded as $t \to \infty$. Since ϱ is independent of q, this condition holds uniformly over $p > 0$ with $p_n \equiv 1$.

Let $H = \{p \mid p \in E_n, p_n = 1, p_i \geq \delta, i \neq n\}$, where δ satisfies Assumption (4). The bounding of $p(t)$ is accomplished in

Lemma 6 If $p(t; p^\circ)$ is a solution of the differential equation system of assumptions I for $t \geq 0$, where $p(0, p^\circ) = p^\circ \in H$, there is a compact set B, depending on p°, such that $p(t; p^\circ) \in B$ for all $t \geq 0$, and $B \subset H$.

Proof $p_i(t; p^\circ) < \delta$, $i \neq n$, cannot occur, since assumptions (4), (6), and (7) imply that $p_i(t)$, $i \neq n$, is increasing in the neighborhood of $p_i = \delta$, if $p > 0$. Let $V^\circ = V(p^\circ)$. By Lemmas 3 and 4, V is nonincreasing, thus $V(p(t; p^\circ)) \leq V^\circ$. But by Lemma 5, there is $\omega > 0$ such that $|p| \geq \omega$ implies $f_n(p) > V^\circ$. By Lemma 1, $V^\circ \geq 0$. This shows that $n \in P$, so that $V(p) > V^\circ$ for $|p| > \omega$. This is a contradiction, and $|p(t; p^\circ)| \leq \omega$ must hold for $t \geq 0$. We define $B = \{p \mid p \in H, |p| \leq \omega\}$.

We are now prepared for

Proof of Theorem 1   The existence of a solution $p(t; p^\circ)$ for $p^\circ > 0$ is provided by the Cauchy–Lipshitz theorem in view of assumption (6) [2, p. 20]. By Lemma 6 this solution exists for $p^\circ \in H$ for all $t \geqslant 0$. Let B be the compact set of Lemma 6. B is contained in H. By consulting definitions, we see that $V = V'$, if $f_n \geqslant 0$, and $V = V' - f_n$, if $f_n < 0$. Thus $V = V' - \min(0, f_n)$. Since $dV'/dt < 0$, where the derivative exists, and the derivative is integrable, it is not difficult to show that V' becomes small. Then the proof will be completed if we can prove that V cannot remain large if V' is small.

To prove that V' becomes small, assume

$$V'(p(t; p^\circ)) \geqslant \varepsilon' > 0 \tag{7}$$

for all $t \geqslant 0$. Since $p(t; p^\circ)$ remains in B by Lemma 6, and B is compact, there is a sequence t_s, $s = 1, 2, \ldots$, with $t_s \to \infty$ and $p(t_s; p^\circ) \to \bar{p}$. But $p(t; p^\circ)$ is a continuous function of the initial position. Also $p(t; p(t_s; p^\circ)) = p(t + t_s; p^\circ)$, and $V'(t) = V'(p(t; p^\circ))$ is a continuous function of t. Then $\bar{V}' = V'(\bar{p}) = \lim_{s \to \infty} V'(p(t + t_s; p^\circ)) = \lim_{s \to \infty} V'(p(t; p(t_s; p^\circ))) = V'(p(t; \bar{p})).^5$ Because $t_s \to \infty$, these equalities are independent of t. Thus $\int_0^t dV'(p(t; \bar{p}))/dt = 0$ for $t \geqslant 0$, where the integral exists by Lemma 4. But, by Lemma 3 and (7) above, $dV'/dt < 0$. This is a contradiction, and (7) cannot continue to hold indefinitely. For some t', $V'(p(t'; p^\circ)) < \varepsilon'$. Since $dV'/dt \leq 0$ by Lemma 3, $V'(p(t; p^\circ)) < \varepsilon'$ for all $t \geqslant t'$. If $\bar{p}$ is a limit point of $p(t)$ in B, (7) cannot hold for any ε'. Then by Lemma 1, $V'(\bar{p}) = 0$.

We must now explore the consequences of V large relative to V'. Assume

$$V(p(t; p^\circ)) \geqslant \varepsilon > 0, \text{ for } t \geqslant 0. \tag{8}$$

By Walras's Law, $V'(p) = -\sum_{i \in N'} p_i f_i(p)$. Moreover, since $p \in B$, $-\sum_{i \in N'} p_i f_i \geqslant -\delta \sum_{i \in N'} f_i$. Thus, $-\sum_{i \in N'} f_i(p) \leq V'(p)/\delta$. However, $V'(p(t)) \to 0$ as $t \to \infty$. Therefore, $-\sum_{i \in N'} f_i(p(t)) \to 0$ as $t \to \infty$. By Assumption 7, f_i and h_i have the same signs. Also they are continuous as functions of p. Suppose $-\sum_{i \in N'} h_i(p(t))$ does not converge to 0. Then there is a sequence t_s, $s = 1, 2, \ldots$, $t_s \to \infty$, and $-\sum_{i \in N'} h_i(p(t_s)) \geqslant \varepsilon'' > 0$ holds for all s. Since $p(t)$ is contained in the compact set B, there is a subsequence $t_{s'}$ for which $p(t_{s'}) \to \bar{p}$ and $-\sum_{i \in N'} f_i(\bar{p}) = 0$. But $-\sum_{i \in N'} h_i(\bar{p}) \geqslant \varepsilon''$, which contradicts Assumption 7. Therefore, $-\sum_{i \in N'} h_i(p(t)) \to 0$ as $t \to \infty$.

On the other hand, $V(p(t)) = \sum_{i \in P} f_i(p(t)) \geq \varepsilon$ by (8). Then by a repetition of the foregoing argument, $\sum_{i \in P} h_i(p) \geq 2\varepsilon''$ for $t \geq 0$, for some $\varepsilon'' > 0$. Consider

$$\frac{d|p(t)|}{dt} = \sum_{i \in P} h_i(p(t)) + \sum_{i \in N'} h_i(p(t)).$$

Take t' so large that $-\sum_{i \in N'} h_i(p(t')) < \varepsilon''$. Then $d|p(t)|/dt \geq \varepsilon''$, for $t \geq t'$. In other words, $|p(t)| \geq |p(t')| + \varepsilon''(t - t')$, for $t \geq t'$. This implies that $|p(t)|$ is unbounded as $t \to \infty$ in contradiction to Lemma 6. Therefore, (8) cannot continue to hold indefinitely. There is t'' such that $V(p(t''; p°)) < \varepsilon$. Since $dV/dt \leq 0$, and $V(p(t)) - V(p(t'')) = \int_{t''}^{t} dV/dt\, dt$ by Lemma 4, $V(p(t; p°)) < \varepsilon$ for all $t \geq t''$.

Let $U = \{p \mid p \in B$ and $V(p) \leq \varepsilon > 0\}$. U is closed. By the foregoing argument, U is not empty for any ε. Let $\varepsilon^s \to 0$ in the definition of U^s. Then $M = \bigcap_{s=1}^{\infty} U^s \neq \varphi$. $p \in M$ implies $V(p) < \varepsilon^s$ for all s or $V(p) = 0$. Thus, $f(p) = 0$, by Lemma 1, and p is an equilibrium. Since the U^s are nested sets and $p(t)$ remains in U^s once it has entered, $p(t) \to M$ as $t \to \infty$.

Suppose p^1 and p^2 are both elements of M and $p^1 \neq p^2$. By homogeneity $f(kp^2) = 0$ for $k > 0$. Let $p(t) = tkp^2 + (1 - t)p^1$, and $h_i = dp_i/dt = kp_i^2 - p_i^1$. Let E, F be a partition of I where $i \in E$ implies $h_i \geq 0$, $i \in F$ implies $h_i < 0$. If k is chosen very large, $kp_i^2 - p_i^1 > 0$ for all $i \in I$, and all prices will be rising as t goes from 0 to 1. If k is chosen very small, all prices will be falling. As k is increased, the goods pass from the falling to the rising class in the order of the fractions p_i^2/p_i^1, that is, in the order of the relative price increases from p^1 to p^2. With a proper choice of k, E will include any subset of goods each of whose prices is rising or constant relative to each good in the complementary subset. Let $i_1, \ldots, i_n$ be an indexing of I such that $p_{i_k}^2/p_{i_k}^1 \geq p_{i_{k+1}}^2/p_{i_{k+1}}^1$. Let $V_k(p(t)) = \sum_{i=i_1}^{i_k} p_i f_i(p(t))$, where $k = 1, \ldots, n - 1$. Letting $V_k = V^*$ in (6') and using the argument of Lemma 3, we see that $dV_k/dt \leq 0$. If $V_k = 0$ for all k, clearly $f_i = 0$, $i = 1, \ldots, n$. Therefore, unless every p for $0 < t < 1$ is an equilibrium, at some t' in this range and for some choice of k, $V_k(p(t')) < 0$ must hold. Then $V_k(p(1)) = V_k(kp^2) = V_k(p^2) < 0$ must also hold. Since this is a contradiction, all $p = tp^2 + (1 - t)p^1$ for $0 \leq t \leq 1$ must be equilibria. Thus M is convex.

Suppose S is indecomposable at p^1 where p^1 and p^2 are elements of M. We may choose E, F, k so that F is not empty and $j \in F$ implies $h_j < 0$. Since S is indecomposable at p^1, there is $f_{ij} > 0$, $i \in E$, $j \in F$, in a neighborhood of p^1. Then $dV^*/dt < 0$ for t near 0. Then $V^*(p^1) = 0$ implies $V^*(p^2) < 0$, which contradicts $p^2 \in M$. Thus $M = \{p^1\}$.

This completes the proof of Theorem 1. If there is no numéraire, the stability proof is simpler, since then V and V' are the same. Existence of equilibrium, however, may need to be proved, or assumed, in order to bound $p(t; p^\circ)$.

7.2   A Limiting Case for This Method

The second theorem does not require $f_{ij} \geq 0$. Although it can be stated as a theorem on global stability, it uses the assumption that $h_i(p) \equiv f_i(p)$. This is only reasonable for a small neighborhood of equilibrium, provided $h_{ij} = 0$ is equivalent to $f_{ij} = 0$ at equilibrium. Then, if assumption (7) holds, $h_i(p)$ and $k_i f_i(p)$ will have the same first order approximations, for some $k_i > 0$, near equilibrium. When the rank of S is $n - 1$, the local behavior of the system defined for $dp_i/dt = k_i f_i(p)$ will not differ significantly from that with $dp_i/dt = h_i(p)$. With proper choice of units $k_i = 1$, $i \in I$. Finally, the theorem is for the case where a numéraire commodity is absent. The problem of bounding $p(t)$ is not serious in the neighborhood of equilibrium for our assumptions.

For the sake of the second theorem we list new assumptions.

Assumptions II

(1), (2), (3), (6) as before.

(4′)   There is p^*, $f(p^*) = 0$, $p^* > 0$.

(5′)   At p^*, for any partition of I into proper subsets I_1, I_2, $\sum_{i \in I_1} s_{ij_2} + \sum_{i \in I_2} s_{ij_1} > 0$ for any $j_1 \in I_1$, $j_2 \in I_2$.

(7′) $h_i(p) \equiv f_i(p)$, $i \in I$.

The Assumption (4′) that $p^* > 0$ is not stronger than assuming $p_i^* > 0$ or $f_i^* < 0$ for $i \in I$. What we avoid is $p_i^* = 0$ and $f_i^* = 0$, which would be a complication. (5′) is the weakest assumption that will give $dV/dt < 0$ everywhere in a neighborhood of p^* when S is indecomposable, that is, has rank $n - 1$. As we will find in Lemma 5′, Assumption (7′) suffices to bound $p(t)$, for all t. This suggests that a global theorem could be proved in which (4′) would be omitted. We shall not pursue this question here, however. We shall prove

Theorem 2 The differential equation system of Assumptions II has a unique solution $p(t; p^\circ)$ for any initial prices p° in a small enough neighborhood of $p^* \cdot p(t; p^\circ)$ approaches αp^* as t increases without limit, where $\|\alpha p^*\| = \|p^\circ\|$.

Lemma 1 and Lemma 4 are not affected by the change of assumptions, and will be useful again. In addition we shall need.

Lemma 3′ Under Assumptions II, $dV/dt < 0$, or $f(p) = 0$, in a small enough neighborhood of p^*.

Proof By Walras's Law, $\sum_{i \in I} p_i f_i = 0$. Assume $f(p) \neq 0$. Choose $j_0 \in N$ so that $\sum_{i \in P} p_i f_{ij_0}/p_{j_0} \leq \sum_{i \in P} p_i f_{ij}/p_j$, $j \in N$.

$$p_{j_0} f_{j_0} = -\sum_{j \neq j_0} p_j f_j, \quad \text{or} \quad f_{j_0} = -\sum_{j \neq j_0} \frac{p_j f_j}{p_{j_0}}. \tag{9}$$

We shall now once more use the equation (6), with P and N rather than P' and N' as the sets over which the summations occur. By Assumption (7′), h_j in (6) may be replaced by f_j. Then f_{j_0} may be eliminated from the second summation of (6) by use of (9). This will introduce the elements of the j_0th column of S, which lie in the rows with indices in P, as coefficients of each f_j, $j \neq j_0$. The result is

$$\frac{dV}{dt} = -\sum_{j \in P} \left(\sum_{i \in N} p_i f_{ij} + \sum_{i \in P} p_i p_j \frac{f_{ij_0}}{p_{j_0}} \right) f_j + \sum_{i \in P} \sum_{j \in N} p_i \left(f_{ij} - \frac{p_j f_{ij_0}}{p_{j_0}} \right) f_j. \tag{10}$$

Thus if $f(p) \neq 0$, $dV/dt < 0$, if

$$\sum_{i \in N} p_i f_{ij} + \sum_{i \in P} \frac{p_i p_j f_{ij_0}}{p_{j_0}} > 0, \quad j \in P,$$

$$\sum_{i \in P} p_i \left(f_{ij} - \frac{p_j f_{ij_0}}{p_{j_0}} \right) \geq 0, \quad j \in N.$$

or,

$$\sum_{i \in N} \frac{p_i f_{ij}}{p_j} + \sum_{i \in P} \frac{p_i f_{ij_0}}{p_{j_0}} > 0, \quad j \in p, \tag{11}$$

$$\sum_{i \in P} \frac{p_i f_{ij}}{p_j} - \sum_{i \in P} \frac{p_i f_{ij_0}}{p_{j_0}} \geq 0, \quad j \in N. \tag{12}$$

However, (12) is implied by the choice of j_0. Thus (11) is sufficient for $dV/dt < 0$. But (11) may be written $\sum_{i \in N} s_{ij} + \sum_{i \in P} s_{ij_0} > 0$, for $j \in P$, $j_0 \in N$. This is precisely Assumption (5') applied to the sets P and N and a particular choice of j_0 in N. Thus (11) will hold for all choices of P, N, and j_0. Since the f_{ij} are continuous, (11) will also hold in a small neighborhood of p^*. Then the conclusion follows.

Finally, we may prove

Lemma 5' $\frac{d\|p\|}{dt} = 0$, under Assumptions II.

Proof $\frac{d\|p\|^2}{dt} = 2 \sum_{i \in I} p_i f_i = 0$ by Assumptions 7' and 2.

We may now proceed to the

Proof of Theorem 2 Let $D = \{p \mid \|p - p^*\| \leq \varepsilon\}$, and ε is small enough so that (11) holds throughout D. The existence of a unique solution in D is provided by the theorem of Cauchy-Lipshitz and Assumptions (1), (6) and (7'). Suppose $p^\circ \in D$.

Let $D_1 = \{p \mid p \in D \text{ and } \|p\| = \|p^\circ\|\}$. Let $\|\alpha p^*\| = \|p^\circ\|$. Then $\alpha p^* \in D_1$. By homogeneity $f(\alpha p^*) = 0$. We will first show that αp^* is an isolated equilibrium point in D_1. Let U be a small neighborhood of αp^* relative to D_1. Let $\overline{V} = \min V(p)$ on the boundary of U. Suppose $\overline{V} = 0$, and this value is assumed at $\bar{p}$. Consider the path $p(t) = t\alpha p^* + (1 - t)\bar{p}$, which passes through $\bar{p}$ and αp^* where t is a real number. Consider the value of $V'(p)$ along this path. If $\bar{p} \neq \alpha p^*$, $dp_i/dt = h_i = \alpha p_i^* - \bar{p}_i \neq 0$ for some $i \in I$. Also, since the norms of $\bar{p}$ and αp^* are equal, $p'h = 0$ except for terms of order higher than the first. As a consequence, dV'/dt may replace dV/dt in Lemma 3', and h_i may replace f_i in the definition (9) of the substitution. Then $dV'/dt < 0$. But this implies $V'(\alpha p^*) < 0$, which is a contradiction, so $\overline{V} > 0$ for U small enough and αp^* is isolated in D_1.

Choose a neighborhood W of αp^* relative to D_1 contained in U and so small $p \in W$ implies $V(p) < \overline{V}$. Let $p(0; p^\circ) = p^\circ \in W$. By Lemma 5', $d\|p\|/dt = 0$, $t \geq 0$, and by Lemma 3', $dV/dt < 0$. Therefore, $p(t; p^\circ)$ remains in D_1 and cannot approach the boundary of U. Thus $p(t; p^\circ) \in \overline{U}$ for $t \geq 0$, where $\overline{U} = \{p \mid V(p) \leq \overline{V} \text{ and } p \in U\}$. $\overline{U}$ is closed and contained in U. Let p^1 be a limit point of $p(t; p^\circ)$. Such a point obviously exists. Using Lemma 4 once more, we may repeat the argument which in the proof of Theorem 1 was used to show that $V'(\bar{p}) = 0$ at any limit point $\bar{p} \in B$. Then $V(p^1) = 0$, and by Lemma 1, p^1 is an equilibrium.

Therefore, $p^1 = \alpha p^*$, since αp^* is the only equilibrium point in $\overline{U}$, and $p(t; p^\circ) \to \alpha p^*$ as $t \to \infty$.

The strategic Assumption (5′) uses the matrix S^*. In S^* the jth column of S has been divided by p_j and the ith row has been multiplied by p_i. If the sum of all the elements in any single column of S^* is taken, this will be zero by Walras's Law, since $f(p^*) = 0$, and $\sum_{i \in I} p_i f_{ij}(p) = -f_j(p)$. Now the Assumption (5′) says that for any two columns the sum of n off-diagonal elements from different rows is positive. Since the diagonal elements are most likely to be negative, there is this much presumption in favor of (5′). However, it is possible to provide a more explicit rationale than this. The commodity units have been chosen so that the rate of change of price with excess demand equals unity at p^* for each good. If the prices are not normalized in this way, the columns must also be multiplied by the speeds of adjustment k_j. Then the elements of S^* will appear as $\frac{k_j p_i}{p_j} f_{ij}$. However, $\frac{dp_j}{dt} = k_j x_j$, or $k_j = \frac{1}{x_j} \frac{dp_j}{dt}$, that is, the rate of increase of the jth price per unit of the jth excess demand, and $f_{ij} = \partial x_i / \partial p_j$. Thus in more explicit form the typical element of S^* is

$$s_{ij} = \frac{p_i (\partial x_i / \partial p_j)(dp_j / dt)}{x_j p_j}. \tag{13}$$

This represents the time rate of change in the value of excess demand for the ith good (at the initial price) in so far as this change is due to a change in the jth price, all per unit value of excess demand for the jth good. In other words, it is the effect of a dollar's worth of the jth excess demand (at initial prices) on the value of the ith excess demand (at initial prices). s_{ij} is, of course, independent of the choice of units, since the numerator and denominator of (13) are each invariant for changes of units of measurement.

The formula (13) shows that the s_{ij} are commensurable and the summations in Assumption (5′) are meaningful. This assumption may be interpreted as follows. Whatever goods may be in excess demand the effect of any dollar's worth of excess demand on the (negative) value of the excess supply plus the effect of any dollar's worth of excess supply (which is negative) on the value of the excess demand is positive. This is a natural generalization of the Assumption (5) that $f_{ij} \geqslant 0$. Since the value of excess demand equals the negative of the value of excess supply, the assumption implies that the effect of a dollar's worth of excess demand is to reduce the value of excess demand.

If a numéraire is introduced, the arguments would no longer be effective. Let the nth good be the numéraire. The fact that $h_n \equiv 0$ removes the first of the summations from the member of (11) or (12) where $j = n$. Then Assumption (5′) no longer suffices to guarantee the inequalities.

It is possible for the condition $f_{ij} \geqslant 0$ to hold for $p > 0$, if the net substitution terms off the diagonal are large and positive. However, the question whether this condition holds does not seem to be independent of the original distribution of commodities. It may also be shown that $f_{ij} \geqslant 0$ for $p > 0$ implies the following proposition: If a good is ever in excess demand for $p > 0$, then should its price approach zero while other prices are positive, its demand is unbounded.

Notes

1. I received much valuable advice from Gerard Debreu, who discussed this chapter at the meetings of the Econometric Society in December, 1958. My initial stimulus was an elegant lecture by Kenneth Arrow at Stanford before the Summer Institute in Social Science for College Teachers of Mathematics, held in 1957. The work on this problem has been supported by research funds granted to the Department of Economics of the University of Rochester by the Ford Foundation.

2. Several applications of Liapounov's approach have been made in recent years. The original discoveries are due to Arrow and Leonid Hurwicz. My knowledge of their approach was derived from Arrow's lecture, but an article [1] has now appeared in *Econometrica* for January, 1959. There have also been some closely related papers by Hirofumi Uzawa [6, 7]. These did not treat the case of a numéraire, while Arrow and Hurwicz assumed cross-elasticities to be strictly positive. A result of Uzawa's has enabled me to strengthen my argument at one point. See footnote 5 below.

3. It is a stronger stability than the "quasi-stability" of Uzawa [7]. There are no unstable equilibria or saddle points. However, we have replaced the unique equilibrium with a compact convex set of equilibria.

4. The need for a rigorous argument on integrability was rightly urged by Debreu.

5. This argument is due to Uzawa [6]. It is used by him to discuss a weaker type of stability, which he calls "quasi-stability," and which does not exclude equilibrium points with features of instability. However, it is also a useful method in our problem.

References

[1] Arrow, Kenneth, H. D. Block, and Leonid Hurwicz: "On the Stability of the Competitive Equilibrium, II," *Econometrica*, January, 1959.

[2] Coddington, Earl A., and Norman Levinson: *Theory of Differential Equations*, New York, 1955.

[3] Graves, Lawrence M.: *The Theory of Functions of Real Variables*, New York, 1946.

[4] Liapounov, M. A.: *Problème Général de la Stabilité du Mouvement*, Princeton, 1947.

[5] Samuelson, Paul A.: *Foundations of Economic Analysis*, Cambridge, 1947.

[6] Uzawa, Hirofumi: "An Alternative Proof of the Stability in the Gross Substitute Case," *Technical Report No. 60*, Department of Economics, Stanford University, Stanford, California, 1958.

[7] ———: "On the Stability of Dynamic Processes," *Technical Report No. 61*, Ibid., 1958.

[8] Walras, Léon: *Elements of Pure Economics*, translated by Jaffé, London, 1954.

8 On the Existence of General Equilibrium: Some Corrections

Lionel W. McKenzie

A careful audit of the argument of my chapter "On the Existence of General Equilibrium for a Competitive Market" [2] by Gerard Debreu has exposed a weakness in the definition of irreducible markets which should be corrected. As the definition now stands, the extension of the results to nonlinear models in Theorem 3 cannot be made. The necessary amendment, however, is not difficult. Also, for the purpose of this Theorem, Assumption 5 needs a small revision.

The definition of irreducible markets as it now stands is contained in Assumption 6, [2, p. 58]:

However I_1 and I_2 may be selected, if x_{I_1} lies in $Y - X_{I_2}$, then there is also $w \in Y - X_{I_2}$ such that $w = x'_{I_1} - x_{I_1}$ and $x'_i \ (\geqq) \ x_i$ for all $i \in I_1$ and $x'_i \ (>) \ x_i$ for some $i \in I_1$.

The difficulty with this definition is that the I_1 consumers will be unable to take w if it contains a resource whose supply they cannot increase above what is offered in x_{I_1}. On the convention which is used in Section 6.7, in approaching Theorem 3, this difficulty always arises with respect to the I_1 entrepreneurial resources. Thus these resources must not appear in w, and Y is effectively reduced to production which employs only I_2 entrepreneurial resources.[1] The restriction could be recognized by applying Assumption 6 to the extended model directly, replacing the variables with their capped analogues. Such a restriction is, however, unnecessary. Indeed, a difficulty can easily arise when no entrepreneurial resources are present, with land, for example, when none of it is withheld for direct use by the consumers.

The preferable solution is to revise Assumption 6. It may be rephrased as follows:

However I_1 and I_2 may be selected, if $x_{I_1} = y - x_{I_2}$ with $y \in Y$ and $x_{I_2} \in X_{I_2}$, then there is also $y' \in Y$ and $w \in X_{I_2}$, such that $x'_{I_1} = y' - x_{I_2} - w$ and $x'_i \ (\geqq) \ x_i$ for all $i \in I_2$, and $x'_i \ (>) \ x_i$ for some $i \in I_1$.

This revision actually corresponds better with the verbal discussion of the Assumption on p. 59 [2] than the present version. Now the Assumption implies its capped analogue and the extension of Section 6.7 to the model with firms can go forward. It should be noted, however, that w and x_{I_2} may swell the quantity of I_2 resources beyond what is useful for I_1 consumers. Then the surplus must be disposed of in some way. This is no bother with the entrepreneurial resources, since they are freely disposed of in the extended model.

Neither the old nor the new version of Assumption 6 implies the other. Thus an even weaker assumption would present the two versions as alternatives. The gain from preserving the old version in the new, however, seems too slight to justify the complication.

The change in the statement of Assumption 6 requires a corresponding modification of the proof of Theorem 2. The new argument is simpler. From the middle of line 6, it should now read:

"Then by Assumption 6 there is $y \in Y$ and $w \in X_{I_2}$ such that $w = y - x^*_{I_2} - x_{I_1}$, where $x_i \ (\geqq) \ x^*_i$ for all $i \in I_1$, and $x_{i_1} \ (>) \ x^*_{i_1}$ for some $i_1 \in I_1$. Since x_{i_1} is preferred, it cannot be available, or $p^* \cdot x_{i_1} > 0$. On the other hand, by Assumption 6 the ith consumer is not satiated at $x^* \in X \cap Y$, nor, therefore, at p^*, for any $i \in I_1$. Then Lemma 2 implies $p^* \cdot x_i \geqq 0$ for any $x_i \in C_i(p^*)$ for $i \in I_1$. Thus $p^* \cdot x_{I_1} > 0$. But $p^* \cdot y \leqq 0$, because $p^* \in P$, and $p^* \cdot x^*_{I_2} = 0$ by continuity. Therefore, $p^* \cdot w_i < 0$ for some $i \in I_2$, which contradicts the definition of I_2. So I_2 is empty."

The other revision which Section 6.7 demands is also a consequence of the presence of entrepreneurial resources in the extended model. Either we must apply Assumption 5 directly to the extended model, or we must revise the first part of the assumption. The first part now reads:

"$X_i \cap Y \neq \phi$."

The analogue version of this is not implied, however, since the ith consumer lacks some of the entrepreneurial resources.[2] We must either apply the assumption to the analogue model directly, or change the assumption. The former is more general, but the gain is slight over assuming

"$0 \in X_i$."

This says that each consumer can survive without trade. It is one of the assumptions of Arrow-Debreu [1].[3]

With these corrections Theorem 3 may be established. Theorem 2 of Arrow-Debreu is a special case of Theorem 3. Finally, part (c) of Assumption 6* [2, p. 71] needs a revision parallel to the revision I have described for Assumption 6.

Notes

1. This was observed by Debreu. I am very grateful to him for the care he has taken to examine my arguments.

2. This was also noticed by Debreu.

3. Their explicit assumption, in my terminology, is $X_i \cap -\Omega \neq \phi$. Since, however, there is free disposal, by implicit assumption, if $x \in X_i$, then $x + \Omega \in X_i$. Thus $0 \in X_i$ is implied, on the interpretation of X_i which I envisage.

References

[1] Arrow, Kenneth J., and Gerard Debreu: "Existence of an Equilibrium for a Competitive Economy," *Econometrica*, July, 1954.

[2] McKenzie, Lionel W.: "On the Existence of General Equilibrium for a Competitive Market," *Econometrica*, January, 1959.

9 Why Compute Economic Equilibria?

Lionel W. McKenzie

When I was a student of Frank Graham in the academic year 1939–40, he gave us a simple general equilibrium model of world trade as an exercise for his course. This model involved several countries and several commodities, and we knew no algorithm for solving it. We used trial and error. Presenting these general equilibrium exercises to his class was a regular practice of Graham, and he used such models in his writing to establish presumptions of the effects of changes in circumstances on the course of trade, or to refute the conclusions of earlier trade theorists by counter-example. The exploration of these models was the principal method of his book, *The Theory of International Values*, published in 1948.

The technology is given by a table which records for each country the output that is obtained from one unit of its "productive power", or "labor."

	A	B	C	D
Cloth	10	10	10	10
Linen	19	20	15	28
Corn	42	24	30	40

Also total quantities of labor are specified for each country, 1,000 units in A, 2,000 in B, 3,000 in C, and 4,000 in D. Demand is determined by the rule that one-third of expenditure in each country is devoted to each good. The world production possibility set for this model may be represented in schematic form in Figure 9.1,[1] where the country named beside a one dimensional facet is changing over from the output of one vertex to that of another. Inside any facet a country produces every good that it produces at some vertex of that facet. As Graham shows,

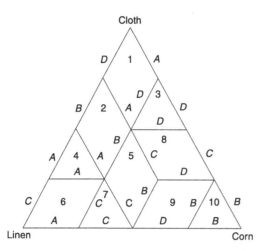

Figure 9.1

the equilibrium falls in the interior of facet 8, where A and B are specialized respectively to corn and cloth, while C produces cloth and corn and D produces linen and corn. Graham shows that this equilibrium refutes the claim made by Mill that under the conditions of constant cost and zero transport costs, no country would make anything for itself that it did not make for other countries. Graham goes on in the following chapters to use the equilibria of more complex models (10 countries, 10 goods) to modify other conclusions of the classical trade theorists.

Graham and his students knew no algorithm for finding the equilibria of these models, even in the case where all countries had the same demand functions derived from a Cobb–Douglas utility function. In this special case the problem can be set as a problem in concave programming. He has a footnote [Graham, 1948, p. 95], which deserves to be quoted in full,

The ratio that will solve the problem can ordinarily be ascertained only through a tedious process of trial and error in which the whole course of trade must be worked out before one can know whether the exchange ratio with which he is experimenting will, in fact, provide a solution. It has been suggested that a mathematical formula should be developed which would provide the solution instanter. This would, surely, be desirable, but mathematicians of great repute, to whom I have submitted the problem, have been unable to furnish any such formula (perhaps because they were not sufficiently interested to devote to it the necessary time). The difficulty is that any shift in the ratio will set in motion kaleidoscopic changes not only in consumption but in produc-

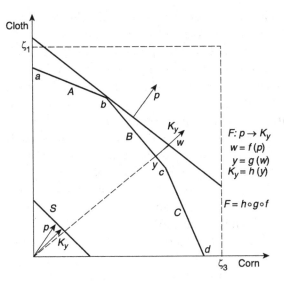

Figure 9.2

tion, will immediately take countries completely out of the production of at least one commodity and, perhaps, put them into others, and will change their consumption in varying proportions according to the varying net changes in the total income of each country and the opportunity cost, in trade, of each of the commodities. The data change, unevenly, with every change in the (tentative) solution. If therefore, anyone thinks that there is more than one solution to any set of data, or that a formula is readily at hand, I can only invite him to try to find them. On the other hand, *some* solution is, of course, always possible.

The verbal tradition at Princeton was that the mathematician of the footnote was John von Neumann, who was in Princeton at the time in the Institute of Advanced Study. We are not surprised today that no mathematical formula was produced. It is also part of graduate student lore that a famous colleague chided Graham for having no existence proof and no proof of uniqueness of equilibrium. Since Graham drew comparative static conclusions from his examples a proof of uniqueness was certainly desirable. Later I was able to provide proofs of existence, for general demand functions, and of uniqueness, for Graham's demand functions [McKenzie 1954b].

The proof of existence, which may be extended to much more general situations, may be illustrated by Figure 9.2, where the number of commodities is reduced to two and the number of countries to three. Also the implied technology table and the demand functions are omitted. The world production possibility set is *abcd*. The mapping *F* sends price vectors in the unit simplex into convex subsets. *F* is the composition of three functions, *f* that takes *p* into the world demand point *w* lying on a social budget plane[2] supporting the production possibility set, *g* that projects *w* from the origin on the production possibility set at *y*, and *h* associating *y* with the convex set of normals in *S* to the production set at *y*. *F* is upper semi-continuous so that it has a fixed point, by Kakutani's theorem, and it is easily seen that any fixed point is an equilibrium. Uniqueness of equilibrium follows for any world demand function that satisfies the weak axiom of revealed preference, as Graham's do. Of course, these demand functions are very special but they serve to provide counterexamples.

The solution of a general equilibrium model is an essential step of most of Graham's arguments in *The Theory of International Values*. Of course, earlier trade theorists also dealt with general equilibrium situations, either numerically as Ricardo and Mill did, or with geometry as Marshall did. However, their models usually involved two countries and two goods and could be solved without difficulty in the case of constant costs, or where countries were permanently specialized to one good each. However, Graham showed the simpler models could be misleading.

Another possibility is to complicate the model to the point that geometry and arithmetic do not provide easy solutions but to explore the variation of the solution with a variation of parameters, only in a small neighborhood of an initial equilibrium. This method was developed by Hicks [1939] and applied to international trade by Mosak [1944] in the *n* good *m* country case. Indeed, the method of elasticities, that is, local variations, has been the most extensive way of drawing conclusions from small models of trade as well, since they quickly become too complex for geometry. The difficulty with this approach is that it cannot deal with large changes, or with critical values of the parameters where even small changes have large effects.

I will look at some places in the literature where efficient algorithms for finding equilibrium points of large scale economic models might be useful. By necessity the survey will be rather cursory, but perhaps it will at least turn up some typical cases of possible application. First, I will note that the Graham tradition of solving numerical models in order to explore the implications of changes in circumstances for the course of international trade is being continued at Harvard by Hendrik Houthakker and his students. They have complicated the Graham model by introducing intermediate goods and transport costs. In the paper delivered to the European meeting of the Econometric Society in Grenoble in September, 1974, Houthakker [1974] assumed there were two countries which actually reduces the number of prices to one, the exchange rate between the labor services of these countries. This simplification allows a special algorithm to be used. When even two independent prices are allowed, because of a third country or a second factor, a more sophisticated algorithm of the Scarf type[3] will surely be needed. One possibility is that the conditions are met for factor price equalization, so that the two prices might be the common prices of the two factors in several countries. In the absence of joint production it may in any case be expedient to reduce the system to a mapping of factor prices since all other prices would be implied by them.

A second example to consider is a long term forecasting model based on a Leontief system with capital coefficients. This model was used by Clopper Almon [1966] to make a projection of the American economy for 1975. The coefficients of the model are fixed except for technological trends. Although the technological trends must be expected to alter relative prices of the outputs of different industries, the price changes are not allowed to influence the input structure. The dynamic Leontief model that Almon fits may be summarized by

$$x(t) = A(t)x(t) + DB(t)x(t) + f(t). \tag{1}$$

Final demand except for investment in the expansion of capacity is $f(t)$, which is estimated by projecting disposable income and applying income elasticities. D is the differential operator, so expansion investment is explained by the acceleration principle. Thus the model corresponds closely to what Kornai and Martos [1973] term a system with autonomous control. Gross outputs of the sectors are the components of $x(t)$, and $A(t)$ is the input-output matrix in the tth period. $B(t)$ is the matrix of capital coefficients. In application (1) is replaced by a system of equations that is linear in $x(t)$ and applies to the whole forecast period simultaneously. This system is written by Almon, not too accurately, I think, as

$$X = \hat{A}X + \hat{C}\hat{B}X + F, \tag{2}$$

where X, $\hat{A}$, $\hat{B}$ are T-fold expansions of the elements of the one period model and $\hat{C}$ is a matrix that translates the differential operator into a discrete form.

Almon obtains an approximate solution of (2), or something like (2), by iteration. This provides a set of x's that are consistent with the input-output and capital coefficients, and with the projected final demands. However, the sequence of x's may not be consistent with projected employment. In that case, the final demands $f(t)$ are changed by changing projected disposable income, until x's are found that fit the projected employment figures as well. The important point is that the variables being determined by the general equilibrium system are the sector outputs, the x's, which must be mutually consistent and consistent with labor supplies and final demands. I doubt that Almon has a complete proof that the iteration converges. He just finds that it does, well enough anyway.

It should also be mentioned that prices are not really absent from consideration. In projecting final demands, and input-output and capital coefficients, prices are taken into account. However, they are independently forecast. They are not derived from the general equilibrium model, so they are not subjected to consistency requirements, as the outputs are. In the terminology of socialist planning, Almon's model is concerned with material balances. I should add that a new model has now been developed by Almon [1974] making projections to 1985.

In runing through the literature, I found one paper in which prices were fully integrated into a general equilibrium model. In this paper, Mitsuo Saito [1971] uses a Leontief format, but interprets the input-output table, according to a suggestion of Klein, as a distribution of expenditure given Cobb–Douglas production functions embracing all inputs including intermediate products. Whereas Almon makes independent estimates of final demand, other than investment for capacity expansion. Saito independently estimates final demand, except for consumer demand, which is explained by income and prices. Thus prices, outputs, and consumer demand are determined consistently in a general equilibrium system. A second feature of the Saito paper is that he forecasts one year ahead, and uses the differentiated system for this purpose, in the manner of the comparative statics of Hicks' appendix [1939].

Saito obtains an excess demand function for each sector's output that depends on relative prices and predetermined final demand,

$$E_i = f_i(\pi, G), \quad i = 1, 2, \ldots, 26.$$

Differentiating he obtains

$$\left[\frac{\partial f_i}{\partial \pi_j}\right]\left[\frac{d\pi_j}{dG_k}\right] + \left[\frac{\partial f}{\partial G}\right] = 0.$$

Thus the solution for the price change resulting from a change of final demand only requires a matrix inversion. In the case he deals with, he finds the condition of gross substitutability approximately satisfied by the Jacobian of excess demand, and the inverse is mostly negative off the diagonal. Of course, this is classical procedure for general equilibrium theory. However, it requires that the changes be small enough to justify using a local approximation by derivatives. Also the Cobb–Douglas assumption for intermediate product inputs is a bit strained.

The most widely used general econometric model is the short term forecasting model, pioneered by Tinbergen, but usually associated nowadays with the name of Lawrence Klein. An example of this type of model is the Brookings quarterly model of the United States economy [Duesenberry *et al.*, 1965]. The industry structure of the model is much more highly aggregated than for Almon's model. Indeed, while Almon assumes an employment level and seeks the changing structure of the economy over a long period of technical change, capital accumulation, and population growth, Klein and his associates aim at the level of general activity in the next quarter, or at most the next year. As a consequence the presence of lags leads to a highly regressive structure. What is found is not an equilibrium of the system, but the next step of a disequilibrium process. On the other hand, the set of variables is comprehensive since there is a full-fledged price and financial subsystem. Also there are consistency conditions to be met, not only by prices among themselves but between prices and outputs. An equilibrium solution, in the sense of full employment over time, need not, I suppose, even exist within the model as set. An extended solution by iteration would reduce the role of initial conditions although the resulting path might not be very relevant. Almon avoids the possibility of a wild path by smoothing the investment series and fitting the whole forecast period at once.

The Brookings model is solvable by linear methods despite its non-linear terms because of a block recursive structure. The system may be decomposed into four blocks, each of which is linear in its own variables. The first block is composed of equations that link a single dependent variable to predetermined (exogenous and lagged) variables. This block, $B^{(1)}$, explains investment in durable capital. Next is a "real" block $B^{(2)}$ composed of equations linear in output, employment, and income, when fixed investment and prices have been specified. Then comes a "price" block $B^{(3)}$ composed of equations linear in prices and wages, when fixed investment, and output, employment, and income, are given. Finally, a block $B^{(4)}$ determines profits by sector recursively from the predetermined variables and the solutions of the first three blocks. The solution is straightforward except for the interdependence of $B^{(2)}$ and $B^{(3)}$. A simple method of solution is to take an initial approximation of prices and wages $Y^{(3)}$, which allows the solution for $Y^{(2)}$ by inversion of $B^{(2)}$. Then using this $Y^{(2)}$, a new approximation of $Y^{(3)}$ may be derived by inverting $B^{(3)}$. If this iteration converges, an approximate solution of the whole system may be reached. Gary Fromm and Klein report that convergence occurs in less than 10 iterations in the cases they have tried. However, the iteration is not guaranteed to converge. One would think given the bilinearity of the block structure, conditions for convergence would be fairly simple.

The basic non-linearities of the Brookings model are products of price and quantity variables to give components of GNP and quotients of price variables to give relative prices. However, if the system were treated as a set of difference equations to be solved completely, the nonlinearities would be much more complex, since ratios often appear in the lagged terms. The solution procedures used for carrying the system forward from predetermined variables would not work. Of course, to achieve any solution in this sense, one would need to specify the exogenous variables as functions of time.

The system is linear in essence and subject to the disability of a linear system that it is likely to be inapplicable outside a small neighborhood of the initial position. It must be recognized that even if we had ways of solving large non-linear systems, we might not have the data to estimate them. All Klein models have been highly aggregated and their use has been for macroeconomic forecasts of GNP, employment, and price levels. It is still a matter of dispute whether they have an advantage over "naïve" extrapolation schemes that ignore economic analysis. It seems doubtful that more efficient solution procedures for nonlinear systems would do much to improve the situation. However, W. E. Diewiert of the University of British Columbia has undertaken a project of designing a Klein model that makes better use of economic theory and allows more complex functions to appear. It is expected that dependence on lagged relations will be less and the role of interdependence in the current period greater. It is likely that better solution procedures for non-linear systems will help in this effort.

It is clear from the example of the Graham model that solving a model of an economy for an equilibrium may be represented as finding a fixed point of an appropriate mapping. The new methods for finding such points, due in the first instance to Herbert Scarf [1973], have now been applied to several problems. These include models where real data is introduced to estimate the effects of a specific policy change in existing economies, and purely theoretical models used to explore theoretical possibilities in the manner of Graham and Houthakker. I will briefly examine an example of each type.

John Shoven and John Whalley [1972] have used the Scarf algorithm to estimate the effects of taxation of income from capital at higher rates than other income. The estimate is made for a highly aggregated model of the American economy averaged over the period 1953–59. This is compared with a similar estimate of Harberger [1966] which is facilitated by linearization and the assumption that all consumers are alike. The Shoven and Whalley model has two sectors,[4] the corporate where capital is taxed heavily, and the noncorporate. Each has a production function with constant elasticity of substitution between two factors labor and capital. These are written

$$Q_i = \gamma_i [a_i L_i^{-\rho_i} + (1 - \alpha_i) K_i^{-\rho_i}]^{-1/\rho_i}. \tag{3}$$

L_i and K_i are the quantities of factors in the ith industry, $\frac{1}{1+\varrho_i}$ is the elasticity of substitution and α_i is proportional to the share of wages in output. There are two kinds of consumers that represent the top 10% of income receivers and the remainder. Each has the type of demand function assumed by Graham, that is, a constant proportion of expenditure is devoted to each product, sometimes including leisure. This system is solved with differential taxation of income from capital removed, and the solution is compared with the actual situation (loosely speaking). The Shoven–Whalley results differ substantially from Harberger's especially when a choice is allowed between work and leisure. However, both differ dramatically from estimates of other investigators who did not determine a new full general equilibrium.

Harberger's method is comparative statics in the manner of Hicks. A three equation system in the excess demand for one good and the two factors is differentiated to provide a linear system that may be solved for the price and quantity derivatives with respect to the tax bias. This is surely superior to a partial equilibrium estimate but one may question the adequacy of a linear approximation for such a large parameter shift. On the other hand, the propriety of the particular functions used by Shoven and Whalley and the relevance of such highly aggregated models may be questioned as well.

The theoretical model was developed by James MacKinnon [1974] for the problem of urban location. He uses an improved version of the Scarf simplicial search algorithm, called "the sandwich method". This method makes it practicable to find approximate fixed points for larger models and with greater accuracy. The MacKinnon model includes a utility function in which the consumption of housing services, consumption of goods, and travel time appear as arguments, a production function for housing services with goods and land as inputs, a cost function for transportation depending on distance from the city center, and a budget constraint in which an initial endowment of goods less transportation costs is spent on goods and land. The land is located in a discrete number of rings around the city center. Within each ring land is treated as homogeneous. The prices are prices of land in each ring and the price of goods. Once again the utility function is Cobb–Douglas, as is the production function, so the demand functions are of the Graham type. Given the prices, a consumer chooses to live in a ring where his utility is maximized. In some cases, two classes of consumers are introduced and a cost is allowed for congestion of the roads. The simplest model is given by

$$U = H^{\alpha}(X - X')^{\beta}(a - T)^{\gamma}, \tag{4}$$

$$H = X'^{\delta}L^{1-\delta}, \tag{5}$$

$$E_i = \overline{X} - 2w(i - \tfrac{1}{2})c, \tag{6}$$

$$P_i L_i + P_x X = P_X E_i, \tag{7}$$

$$\sum_j L_i^j \leq \overline{L}_i, \quad \text{all } i. \tag{8}$$

The utility function is (4) with housing services H, goods consumption X, and travel time T. Housing services are produced according to (5), where X is goods input and L is land input. In (6) $\overline{X}$ is the initial endowment of a consumer in goods, $w(i - \tfrac{1}{2})$ is distance to the city center form ring i, and c is cost of transportation. (7) is the budget equation, where the P's are prices, and (8) is the constraint on land use. Consumers are indexed by i, and a, w, and c are constants.

By solving this model for various values of the parameters, Mac-Kinnon is able to estimate the effects of various changes in conditions on prices of land and on the area of the city when land is given an alternative use. For example, introduce the equation

$$L_i^j = 0 \quad \text{if} \quad P_i < P_x r, \quad \text{all } i, j,$$

where r is agricultural rent in terms of goods. Then an increase of $\overline{X}$, i.e. income, leads to an expansion of the area but little change in the rate of price rise as the city center is approached.

There are continuous models in the urban field that can be solved analytically, but the fixed point algorithms are more flexible and powerful. In any case, beyond quite simple models, qualitative features cannot be derived analytically and even the continuous models must be solved by numerical methods.[5] The introduction of more than one type of consumer seems to be a critical step. I have been told by trade theorists that the two country, two factor, two good trade model, which is perhaps the *locus classicus* of global comparative statics,[6] can be solved by geometry without much bother until this point is reached. It must be admitted, however, that the examples we have before us can only be regarded as timid first steps in the use of the fixed point methods.

Let us look briefly at one more field where a beginning has been made in computing equilibria, at least for theoretical models. This is optimal growth theory. Jinkichi Tsukui [1968] has fitted an input-output model with durable capital and fixed coefficients to Japanese data. The model describes marginal changes in output and consumption from a base year. Marginal consumption is absorbed into the input matrix as a linear function of marginal value added in each sector. Activity levels $\bar{x}$ are calculated for a stationary state, and marginal activity levels are expressed by $z(t) = x(t) - \bar{x}$. Also an activities vector z^* that gives the direction of maximal balanced growth is calculated and the following problem is solved. Maximize u subject to

$$(I - \overline{A} + B)z(t) - Bz(t+1) \geqq 0,$$

$$(I - \overline{A} + B)z(\tau - 1) - uBz^* \geqq 0, \tag{9}$$

$$z(t) \geqq 0.$$

Here $\overline{A}$ is the augmented matrix of current inputs. B is the matrix of capital stock inputs. The relevance of this problem comes from turnpike theorems that guarantee that any efficient path tends to the proportions of z^*. The coefficients were estimated from 1955 data and the maximum problem was solved for 1956–60. The actual course of output was found to correspond reasonably well to the maximum solution, that is, to the path that maximizes the size of increments to capital stocks in the proportions given by z^*. Although it is an optimality problem that is set, an equilibrium solution is also approximated if foresight is not too bad. The model has since been generalized to allow the consumption coefficients to be piecewise linear functions of value added [Tsukui, 1972]. However, the changing shadow prices of the maximum problem have no effect on either consumption or production coefficients. Also the level of aggregation is very high, twelve sectors.

Tsukui's model is patterned on the von Neumann model of the expanding economy. On the other hand, the Ramsey model of optimal savings is the source of the problem attacked by Hansen and Koopmans [1972] using the fixed point methods of Scarf. They compute an optimal stationary state in a multisector growth model of the type due to Gale in which a von Neumann technology is combined with a utility function defined on activity levels. Given a reproducible stock z, the one period optimality problem for a stationary stock is to maximize utility $v(x)$ subject to

$$-Ax \geqq -z,$$

$$Bx \geqq z,$$

$$-Cx \geqq -w, \tag{10}$$

$$x \geqq 0,$$

where A is the input matrix for intermediate goods, B is the output matrix for intermediate goods, C is the input matrix for primary goods, and w is the vector of primary good supplies. Since $v(x)$ is concave, $\hat{x}$ solves this problem if and only if there are vectors q_1, q_2, and r satisfying

$$(q_1, q_2, r) \geqq 0,$$

$$v'(\hat{x}) - q_1 A + q_2 B - rc \leqq 0, \tag{11}$$

$$v'(\hat{x}) - q_1 z + q_2 z - rw = 0.$$

The Ramsey problem is to choose a path of activity levels and capital stocks (x_t, z_t) which is feasible, given an initial stock z, and which maximizes $\sum_{t=1}^{\infty} \alpha^{t-1} v(x_t)$, for $0 < \alpha < 1$. Suppose, however, that z is chosen so that the solution of the infinite horizon problem is $x_t = x$, $z_t = z$, for all t. Then it is equivalent to solve the one period problem with $q_2 = \alpha q_1$. After this constraint is placed on the dual variables of the optimum problem, it is natural to seek a solution by way of a fixed point theorem. Hansen and Koopmans use the Scarf method, applied to a simplex of activity vectors rather than price vectors. Their approach is dual to the approach to the general equilibrium of a Walras economy described by Scarf. As in the case of Tsukui's model, explicitly it is an optimum rather than an equilibrium that is sought, although the optimum problem is an equilibrium problem for an economy with a single consumer and thus a first step toward a more general problem of equilibrium over time where there are many consumers. Hansen and Koopmans solve a numerical example and call attention to a comparative static result in one place. However, they have not undertaken a general comparative study of examples in the style of Graham or MacKinnon, though such an analysis might be useful. Also they do not introduce economic data in the manner of Shoven and Whalley or Tsukui, and empirical application may be even more difficult for their model. Presumably such applications would be possible for programs of capital accumulation, or natural resource decumulation, with an appropriate adjustment of the model.

We have now surveyed a reasonable sample of attempts to use estimates of general equilibria either in testing theoretical possibilities or in explaining or projecting the performance of actual economies. This should provide some basis for judging whether such efforts are worth pursuing and also whether the new fixed point methods are likely to help. First, in theoretical studies such as those of Graham or MacKinnon the solution of numerical examples is surely useful. If systems are at all complex, qualitative analysis with geometry or calculus does not lead very far. General theorems are few and abstract. If concrete possibilities are to be explored, numerical analysis seems needed. If one has a dynamic system in reduced form, the path of the system may be simulated. If, however, a reduced form is not available, this procedure may not be possible. Moreover, the equilibria of the system may have primary interest, for a comparative static analysis, and a solution for these equilibria would be required.

On the other hand, the studies where quantitative prediction from current data is sought seem to be further from their objectives. Of course, they depend on adequate data as well as appropriate models. The models described by Almon, and Klein et al., do claim to be helpful for making better forecasts. They are linear, or bilinear, and seem not to need fixed point methods. However, this may be due to the primitive role prices play in them. Almon's model, in particular, is essentially a method of material balancing with fixed coefficients of production, except for time trends. For this reason, the linear methods used in dealing with other Leontief systems suffice. I am not qualified to judge to what degree the Leontief and Klein models of long run and short run forecasting have been useful, but certainly their use is growing and vast resources are devoted to them. It is at least possible that numerical methods permitting the solution of large systems, with as many prices as there are sectors, could bring this activity nearer to the break even point. I think we must regard the empirical essays of Saito and Tsukui as suggestive rather than operative at this time. However, the simple character of their models may once again be the consequence, at least in part, of the need to stick to linear solution techniques, that is, matrix inversion and linear programming. Shoven and Whalley have shown that even in a two sector model, the availability of fixed point algorithms can significantly modify the results of a computation done after linearization of a model. Additional examples of promising applications to theory and prediction of general equilibrium methods have been presented to this conference, but it would not be appropriate for me to discuss them.

In the course of surveying the literature for this paper, I came upon an interesting essay by James Mirrlees [1969] on the Price Mechanism in a Planned Economy. I will conclude with some of his observations. Although the explicit reference is to a planned economy, the proposals are also relevant to free enterprise. His central message is that efficient performance by an economy depends on reasonably good prediction by the decision makers of future prices. But for the prediction of prices large scale computations and data collections are important and they are expensive. Thus it is appropriate that central authorities engage in these activities. Decentralization as such offers limited advantages except as a trial of different methods. To quote him at some length [Mirrlees, 1969, p. 189],

In "normal" times, when no hostile external forces threaten the economy, it does seem that both the demand pattern and the production potential of actual economies progress evenly and undramatically. Under these circumstances, I cannot see that *very* much in terms of human welfare is likely to be gained by an improved balance between supply and demand once the long-term investment decisions are rightly made; and I suspect too that in a smoothly developing economy, the prediction and allocation of prospective demands between enterprises would not greatly improve the scale decisions. Granted large-scale production units, for the reasons discussed above, it may be that good price predictions are the most important contribution that central computations can make to the workings of a free-market price system. Without them, I doubt whether, however smoothly the economy adjusts actual supplies to actual demands, we should have much reason to approve of the result.

The Mirrlees view appears to favor an attempt to use long range forecasting à la Almon to provide price predictions as well as the quantity predictions which the Almon model now concentrates on. The prices would be sector-wide indices just as the quantities are. Special studies would be needed to derive the implications of these figures for a single enterprise. One would need, as Almon already has done for quantity indices, to attach a supplement to the input-output tables specializing to the small sector in question [Almon et al., 1974].

To romanticize a bit, one could imagine a very long run projection on growth theoretic grounds as in Tsukui's model, integrated with a medium range forecast of the type of Almon's model, and with a short term forecast in a Klein model, all aimed to guide enterprises in their investment planning. I am told that fixed point methods are near to handling as many as 80 prices simultaneously. Perhaps this brings such possibilities closer. Note that the whole program could be undertaken with equal justification in a planned or a free enterprise economy. The general equilibrium of an economic system has claim to support only to the degree that the expected prices which are implicit in it are correct, as compared with the foresight of an alternative scheme, of course.

Notes

1. This analysis was presented in my paper [1954a]. The diagram here is a correction of the one appearing in the original paper, provided by Richard Rosett, then (1955) a Yale graduate student.

2. The budget plane is intersected with a cube large enough to contain the world production set in its interior. Thus no equilibria are introduced.

3. Scarf [1973] developed an algorithm for locating an approximate equilibrium for a Walrasian economic model. There have been several subsequent alternative algorithms for approximating fixed points of correspondences, for example, Kuhn [1968], Merrill [1971], and Eaves [1971].

4. An early example of the formal two sector model is Meade [1955]. It has since become a favorite model for trade theory, for example, Jones [1965], and for growth theory, for example, Uzawa [1961]. Its applications today are legion.

5. For example, the model described by Solow [1972].

6. Perhaps the earliest full fledged application of the method of comparative statics in a formal model is Marshall [1879].

References

C. Almon, 1966, The American economy to 1975—an interindustry forecast, Harper and Row, New York).

C. Almon *et al.*, 1974, 1985, Interindustry forecasts of the American economy (D. C. Heath, Lexington, Mass.)

S. Duesenberry, G. Fromm, L. R. Klein and E. Kuh, eds., 1965, The Brookings Quarterly Econometric Model of the United States (Rand Mc Nally and Co., Chicago).

B. C. Eaves, 1971, Computing Kakutani fixed points, SIAM Journal of Applied Math. **21**, 236–244.

F. D. Graham, 1948, The theory of international values (Princeton University Press, Princeton).

T. Hansen and T. C. Koopmans, 1972, On the definition and computation of a capital stock invariant under optimization, Journal of Economic Theory **5**, 487–523.

A. C. Harberger, 1966, Efficiency effects of taxes on income from capital, in: Effects of the corporation income tax, ed. M. Kryzaniak, Detroit.

J. R. Hicks, 1939, Value and capital (Clarendon Press, Oxford).

H. S. Houthakker, 1974, The calculation of bilateral trade patterns in a general equilibrium model, mimeo, European Meeting of the Econometric Society, Grenoble, 1974.

R. W. Jones, 1965, The structure of simple general equilibrium models, Journal of Political Economy, **73**, 557–572.

J. Kornai and B. Martos, 1973, Autonomous control of the economic system, Econometrica **41**, 509–528.

H. Kuhn, 1968, Simplicial approximation of fixed points, Proc. Nat. Acad. Sci. **65**, 1238–1242.

J. MacKinnon, 1974, Urban general equilibrium models and simplicial search algorithms, Journal of Urban Economics **1**, 161–183.

A. Marshall, 1879, The pure theory of foreign trade, The pure theory of domestic values, privately printed; reprinted by The London School of Economics, 1930.

L. W. McKenzie, 1954a, Specialization and efficiency in world production, Review of Economic Studies **21**, 56–64.

L. W. McKenzie, 1954b, On equilibrium in Graham's model of world trade and other competitive systems, Econometrica **22**, 147–161.

J. E. Meade, 1955, Trade and welfare, Mathematical Supplement (Oxford University Press, Oxford).

O. H. Merrill, 1971, Applications and extensions of an algorithm that computes fixed points of certain non-empty convex upper semi-continuous point to set mappings, Technical Report No. 71–7, Dept. of Industrial Engineering, University of of Michigan.

J. Mirrlees, 1969, The price mechanism in a planned economy, in: Planning and Markets: Modern trends in various economic systems, eds. J. T. Dunlop and N. P. Fedorenko (McGraw–Hill, New York), pp. 177–189.

J. L. Mosak, 1944, General equilibrium theory in international trade (Principia Press, Bloomington, Indiana).

M. Saito, 1971, An interindustry model of price formation, Review of Economics and Statistics 53, 11–24.

H. Scarf (with the collaboration of T. Hansen), 1973, The computation of economic equilibria (Yale University Press, New Haven).

J. B. Shoven and J. Whalley, 1972, A general equilibrium calculation of the effects of differential taxation of income from capital in the U.S., Journal of Public Economics 1, 281–321.

R. M. Solow, 1972, Congestion, density and the use of land in transportation, Swedish Journal of Economics, 74, 161–173.

J. Tsukui, 1968, Application of a turnpike theorem to planning for efficient accumulation: An example of Japan, Econometrica 36, 172–186.

J. Tsukui, 1972, Optimal path in a non-linear dynamic input-output system—A generalization of the turnpike model, in: Input-output techniques, eds. A. Brody and A. P. Carter (North-Holland, Amsterdam), pp. 551–561.

H. Uzawa, 1961, On a two sector model of economic growth, Review of Economic Studies 29, 40–47.

10 The Classical Theorem on Existence of Competitive Equilibrium

Lionel W. McKenzie

My purpose is to discuss the present status of the classical theorem on existence of competitive equilibrium that was proved in various guises in the 1950's by Arrow and Debreu [1], Debreu [5, 6], Gale [8], Kuhn [14], McKenzie [17, 18, 19], and Nikaido [22].[1] The earliest papers were those of Arrow and Debreu, and McKenzie, both of which were presented to the Econometric Society at its Chicago meeting in December, 1952. They were written independently. The paper of Nikaido was also written independently of the other papers but delayed in publication.

The major predecessors of the papers of the fifties were the papers of Abraham Wald [31, 32] and John von Neumann [30], all of which were delivered to Karl Menger's Colloquium in Vienna during the 1930s. The paper of von Neumann was not concerned with competitive equilibrium in the classical sense but with a program of maximal balanced growth in a closed production model. However, he first used a fixed point theorem for an existence argument in economics and provided the generalization of the Brouwer theorem that was the major mathematical tool in the classical proofs. Wald achieved the first success with the general problem of the existence of a meaningful solution to the Walrasian system of equations. The proofs which were published used an assumption that later became known as the Weak Axiom of Revealed Preference. This axiom virtually reduces the set of consumers to one person, since it is equivalent to consistent choices under budget constraints. In a one consumer economy the existence of the equilibrium becomes a simple maximum problem and advanced methods are not needed. When many consumers with independent preference orders are present, it has been shown (Uzawa [29]) that fixed point methods are necessary. Wald also wrote a third paper whose main theorem was announced in a summary article [33], but which never reached publication in the disturbed conditions of Vienna of the period. This theorem does not make the Weak Axiom assumption and presumably fixed point methods were used in the proof. However, the paper apparently has not survived and did not directly influence the writers of the fifties.

The classical theorem is characterized above all by its use of assumptions of finiteness and convexity. That is, the economy comprises a finite number of economic agents or consumers who trade in a single market under conditions of certainty. The goods are finite in number and, as a consequence, the horizon is finite. Goods are divisible, and production is modeled either as a set of linear activities in the space of goods or as convex input-output sets belonging to a finite list of firms. Consumption sets and preference relations are also convex in an appropriate sense. Consumption and production activities are mutually independent.

In subsequent years the abstract model of an economy has been complicated for the existence theorems in many directions, principally weakening the crucial finiteness and convexity assumptions. However, somewhat surprisingly, in recent years the classical theorem itself has been improved in basic ways by Andreu Mas-Colell and James Moore. Mas-Colell [16] and Gale and Mas-Colell [9] showed that preferences need not be assumed transitive or complete. On the other hand, Moore [21] showed that the assumption that agents may survive without trade is superfluous for an irreducible economy.

In this paper I will introduce these innovations into an exposition based on the use of demand functions and production sets. I believe this order of proof is best for economic understanding and also for achieving the weakest assumptions. In particular, the Mas-Colell-Gale assumptions are weakened and a way is found to incorporate a version of the Moore result without returning to classical preferences. I shall also discuss three other themes that have been pursued in recent papers, the inclusion of external economies affecting production and consumption sets, the representation of firms as coalitions of economic agents, and the elimination of the free disposal assumption by new means.

10.1 The Classical Theorem

I will use the theorem of my paper of 1959 to represent the classical theorem on existence in fully developed form. The assumptions of this theorem fall naturally into three groups, assumptions on the consumption sets X_i, on the total production set Y, and on the relations between these sets. First, for the consumption sets, which lie in R^n, the Cartesian product of n real lines, we assume

(1) X_i is convex, closed, and bounded from below.

(2) X_i is completely ordered by a convex and closed preference relation.

X_i is interpreted as the set of feasible trades of the ith consumer. There are m consumers. That X_i is *bounded from below* means that there is ξ_i such that $x > \xi_i$ holds for all $x \in X_i$. *Convexity* of the preference relation $\succsim_i$ means that $x \succ_i x'$ implies $x'' \succ_i x'$ where $x'' = tx + (1 - t)x'$, for $0 < t < 1$. *Closure* of $\succsim_i$ means that $x^s \to x$ and $x^{s'} \to x'$, where $x^s \succsim_i x^{s'}$, implies $x \succsim_i x'$.

For the total production set Y, which also lies in R^n, we assume

(3) Y is a closed convex cone.

(4) $Y \cap R_+^n = \{0\}$.

R_+^n is the nonnegative cone of R^n.

The assumption that Y is a cone recognizes the role of constant returns to scale as a basis for perfect competition. It may be defended as an approximation when efficient firm sizes are small, and in this sense was accepted by both Marshall and Walras. It may be argued that the error of this approximation is of the same order as the error introduced by the assumption of convexity in the presence of indivisible goods. In any case the assumption of convex production sets for firms may be shown to be mathematically equivalent to Assumption (3) (McKenzie [19, pp. 66–67]; also see McKenzie [20]). Assumption (4) is not a real restriction. It amounts to ignoring goods that are available in any desired quantities without cost. In this model the consumption sets X_i are net of initial stocks, that is, the elements of X_i are possible trades.

Finally, there are two assumptions on the relations between the X_i and Y. Let $X = \sum_1^m X_i$, where m is the number of consumers. Then the first assumption is:

(5) $X_i \cap Y \neq \emptyset$. Moreover, there is a common point $\bar{x}$ in the relative interiors of Y and X.

The first part of this assumption states that any consumer can survive without trade. The second part implies that we may choose the price space so that any price p that supports Y will have $p \cdot x < 0$ for some $x \in X$. In other words, if p is compatible with equilibrium in the production sector, there is a feasible trade for the group of all consumers with negative value. This may be interpreted as saying that some consumer has income, in the sense that he is not on the boundary of his consumption set.

Suppose there are m consumers. Let I_1 and I_2 be nonempty sets of indices for consumers such that $I_1 \cap I_2 = \varnothing$ and $I_1 \cup I_2 = \{1, \ldots, m\}$. Let $x_{I_k} = \sum_{i \in I_k} x_i$ and $X_{I_k} = \sum_{i \in I_k} X_i$, for $k = 1, 2$. The second relation between the X_i and Y is:

(6)   However I_1 and I_2 may be selected, if $x_{I_1} = y - x_{I_2}$ with $x_{I_1} \in X_{I_1}$ $y \in Y$, and $x_{I_2} \in X_{I_2}$, then there is also $y' \in Y$, and $w \in X_{I_2}$, such that $x'_{I_1} = y' - x_{I_2} - w$ and $x'_i \gtrsim_i x_i$ for all $i \in I_1$, and $x'_i \succ_i x_i$ for some $i \in I_1$.

An alternative way of expressing the condition of (6), by substituting for x_{I_2}, is $x'_{I_1} - x_{I_1} = y' - y - w$. That is, I_1 may be moved to a preferred position by the addition of a vector $y' - y$ from the local cone of Y at y (see Koopmans [13, p. 83]) plus a feasible trade from I_2. The resource relatedness assumption of Arrow and Hahn [2, p. 117], implies Assumption (6), but the converse is not true. Since they assume that a household can survive with less of all the resources it holds (p. 77), they are able to take w equal to a small fraction of the resources held by I_2 consumers. Then it is supposed that I_1 consumers can be benefited with this w.

The purpose of Assumption (6) is to insure that everyone has income, if someone has income, at any price vector that supports the production set Y at y as well as the sets of consumption vectors at least as good as x_i, at the points x_i. Then if we choose I_1 to contain just the indices of the consumers with income, nonempty by Assumption (5), $p \cdot x'_{I_1} > 0$ must hold. Also Assumption (6) with Assumption (2) implies local nonsatiation within the feasible set $X \cap Y$ so that $p \cdot x_{I_1} = 0$. Since $p \cdot y = 0$ and $p \cdot y' \leqslant 0$, it follows that $p \cdot w < 0$. But $w \in X_{I_2}$ so some consumer in I_2 has income in contradiction to the choice of I_1. Thus I_2 must be empty, and the result follows.

Competitive equilibrium is defined by a price vector $p \in R^n$, an output vector y, and vectors $x_1, \ldots, x_m$ of consumer trades that satisfy

(I) $y \in Y$ and $p \cdot y = 0$, and for any $y' \in Y$, $p \cdot y' \leqslant 0$.

(II) $x_i \in X_i$ and $p \cdot x_i \leqslant 0$, and $x_i \gtrsim_i x'$ for any $x' \in X_i$ such that $p \cdot x' \leqslant 0$, $i = 1, \ldots, m$.

(III) $\sum_{i=1}^{m} x_i = y$.

The first condition corresponds to Walras' requirement that in equilibrium there should be "ni bénéfice, ni perte" [34, p. 225]. It is not possible for a combination of resources to be formed that allows larger payments to some resource than those implied by p. Resources belonging to "entrepreneurs" are priced along with hired factors, and the entire income of a productive activity is imputed to the cooperating factors. This is the traditional picture of perfect competition in Marshall [15], as well as in Walras.

The second condition implies that consumers maximize preference over their budget sets. Debts and taxes are ignored in the classical theorems, though many writers have introduced them subsequently. The third condition says that consumer trades sum to the total production. Given $p \cdot y = 0$ and $p \cdot x_i \leqslant 0$ it follows from condition (III) that $p \cdot x_i = 0$.

We make the following definition.

Definition   A *competitive equilibrium* is a set of vectors $(p, y, x_1, \ldots, x_m)$ that satisfy conditions (I), (II), and (III).

An *economy* E may be defined by $E = (Y, X_i, \gtrsim_i, i = 1, \ldots, m)$. One form of the classical theorem on the existence of a competitive equilibrium is:

Theorem 1   If an economy E satisfies the Assumptions (1), (2), (3), (4), (5), and (6), there is a competitive equilibrium for E.

Debreu [7] has defined a weaker notion of equilibrium which he calls "quasi-equilibrium." A quasi-equilibrium in our setting satisfies (I) and (III), but in place of (II) there is:

(IIq) $x_i \in X_i$ and $p \cdot x_i \leqslant 0$, and $x_i \gtrsim_i x'$ for any $x' \in X_i$ such that $p \cdot x' \leqslant 0$, or $p \cdot x_i \leqslant p \cdot x'$ for all $x' \in X_i$, $i = 1, \ldots, m$.

Debreu's strategy for proving existence of equilibrium in this paper is to prove that a quasi-equilibrium exists and then introduce a further assumption which implies that a quasi-equilibrium is a competitive equilibrium. Arrow and Hahn [2], and James Moore [21], follow the same strategy using the closely related notion of a "compensated equilibrium." A compensated equilibrium replaces (II) by:

(IIc) $x_i \in X_i$ and $p \cdot x_i \leqslant 0$, and $p \cdot x_i \leqslant p \cdot x'$ for any $x' \in X_i$ such that $x' \gtrsim_i x_i$.

If indifference sets may be thick, (IIq) is a weaker condition than (IIc). In particular, when all consumers have income (IIc) implies Pareto optimality, while (IIq) does not. However, under our assumptions, these concepts are equivalent. The assumption that converts a proof that a quasi-equilibrium exists, given Assumption (2), into a proof of existence for competitive equilibrium is essentially irreducibility, our Assumption (6). These assumptions insure that all consumers have income at a quasi-equilibrium, so the second alternative of (IIq) does not occur and the condition of (IIq) implies (II). Since we are primarily interested in competitive equilibrium, we will not use this order of proof.

10.2   The Survival Assumption

Perhaps the most dramatic innovation since 1959 is the discovery that the survival assumption, that is, the first part of Assumption (5), $X_i \cap Y \neq \varnothing$, can be dispensed with in the presence of the other assumptions, in particular in the presence of Assumption (6) that the economy is irreducible. In retrospect this seems a plausible result. However, it was hidden by the character of the mappings used in the early proofs. These mappings involve demand functions defined on price vectors that are normal to the production set. Then $p \cdot y \leqslant 0$ for all $y \in Y$, and in particular for $y \in X_i \cap Y$. This means that the budget set is never empty and the demand function is always well defined. The demand function may not be upper semi-continuous when the budget plane supports X_i, but the modified function defined by Debreu [7] even has this property. The modified function defines the demand set, when the budget plane supports X_i, as the intersection of X_i and the budget set. Then condition (IIq) of the quasi-equilibrium will be satisfied.

On the other hand, the mapping used by Arrow and Hahn to prove that a compensated equilibrium exists avoids mapping by means of a demand function by giving the Pareto frontier in the space of consumers' utilities a central role. Then the mapping can go forward even if prices are used for which the budget set, defined relative to X_i, is empty. Arrow and Hahn map a Cartesian product of a normalized price set, a set of normalized utility vectors from the Pareto efficient frontier, and a set of feasible allocations of goods into convex subsets. The Pareto efficient frontier is the set of feasible utility allocations $\{u_i\}$,

$i = 1, \ldots, m$, such that there exists no feasible allocation $\{u_i'\}$ with $u_i' > u_i$ for all i. If indifference sets may be thick, this mapping need not be upper semi-continuous, so it cannot be used with Debreu's assumptions. Moreover, a compensated equilibrium is Pareto efficient if someone has income, though not necessarily Pareto optimal, while a quasi-equilibrium may not be even Pareto efficient. The key to this distinction is that at a quasi-equilibrium spending is maximized for the utility levels achieved. Therefore, it may be possible to increase everyone's utility without increasing total spending. But when spending is minimized for the utility levels achieved, and there is someone with income, this is no longer possible since to increase this consumer's utility his spending must go up, and no one can reduce spending without losing utility.

Arrow and Hahn still made the survival assumption, but James Moore [21] who uses the Arrow-Hahn mapping with small modifications dispenses with this assumption and replaces it for the purpose of compensated equilibrium by a weakened version of irreducibility. Moore also uses a slightly different Pareto frontier defined as the set of utility allocations $\{u_i\}$ such that $u_i \leq u_i'$ for all i, for some feasible $\{u_i'\}$, but there is no feasible $\{u_i''\}$ such that $u_i'' > u_i$ for all i. This allows him to drop the free disposal assumption implicitly made by Arrow and Hahn when they define equilibrium [2, p. 108].

I think there are advantages to the use of the demand function, or correspondence, in proofs of existence, both for mathematical power and for understanding the proof. I will show how the demand correspondence may be used in a mapping of the Cartesian product of the price simplex and the social consumption set into itself whose fixed points are competitive equilibria even in the absence of the survival assumption. At the equilibrium the budget sets will not be empty, the demand correspondences will be well defined and upper semi-continuous, but these conditions need not be satisfied for non-equilibrium prices. We will avoid the difficulties posed by this possibility by using an extension of the demand correspondence which reduces to the original correspondence whenever the original correspondence is well defined and nonempty. The extended demand correspondence will be well defined and nonempty for all price vectors.

We will first prove the special existence theorem in which an interiority assumption is made. Then the general theorem is proved by a limiting argument in which the interior is removed. This argument will be sketched later. Therefore, we make the six assumptions listed in Section 10.1 except that Assumption (6) is slightly weakened, and Assumption (5) is replaced by

(5′) $X \cap \text{interior } Y \neq \varnothing$.

Assumption (5′) is used as we explained earlier to insure that someone has income at any price vector that supports Y. Then Assumption (6) will provide income to everyone in equilibrium. The interior point of (5′) is a temporary expedient for proving the special theorem. It is needed for the order of proof that we use since we project points of the social consumption set on the boundary of Y from an interior point of Y. The projection is then continuous.

I will sometimes appeal to the results of my *Econometrica* paper of 1959 [19] and Debreu's paper of 1962 [7] in the subsequent argument. Let $\overline{X}_i$ be the convex hull of X_i and $\{0\}$. Since $0 \in Y$, the survival assumption is met in its original form of Assumption (5) in the economy with $\overline{X}_i$. We also introduce:

Auxiliary Assumption   The X_i are bounded.

This assumption is innocuous since $X \cap Y$ is bounded as a consequence of Assumption (1), X_i bounded below, and Assumption (4), $Y \cap R_+^n = \{0\}$. See Lemmas 8 and 9 of McKenzie [19].

Assumption (6) is weakened by choosing w from $\overline{X}_{I_2}$ rather than X_{I_2}.

(6′)   However I_1 and I_2 may be selected, if $x_{I_1} = y - x_{I_2}$ with $x_{I_1} \in X_{I_1}$, $y \in Y$, and $x_{I_2} \in X_{I_2}$, then there is also $y' \in Y$, and $w \in \overline{X}_{I_2}$, such that $x'_{I_1} = y' - x_{I_2} - w$ and $x'_i \succsim_i x_i$ for all $i \in I_1$, and $x'_i \succ_i x_i$ for some $i \in I_1$.

This revision of (6) is a significant weakening unless $0 \in X_i$. If $0 \in X_i$ is assumed as in McKenzie [20], X_{I_2} and $\overline{X}_{I_2}$ are the same. The revision is in accord with Assumption (e.4′) used by Moore [21].

We will define an extension of the demand correspondence to the set $\overline{X}_i$. We first define a correspondence

$$\xi_i(p) = \{x \mid p \cdot x \leqslant 0 \text{ and } x \succsim_i z \text{ for all } z \in X_i \text{ such that } p \cdot z \leqslant 0\}.$$

This is the usual demand correspondence adapted to our case where income is zero, since entrepreneurial resources absorb profits and all resources are included as components of the vectors in X_i. The correspondence ξ_i will be upper semi-continuous when there is a cheaper point in X_i, that is, a point x such that $p \cdot x < 0$. However, this property fails on the boundary of X_i. Therefore, we define a modification of the demand correspondence in the manner of Debreu by

$\psi_i(p) = \xi_i(p)$ if there is $x \in X_i$ and $p \cdot x < 0$,

$\psi_i(p) = \{x \in \overline{X}_i \mid p \cdot x = 0\}$,   otherwise.

Then $\psi_i(p)$ is well defined for all p, since $0 \in \overline{X}_i$ by the definition of $\overline{X}_i$. It is easily seen that $\psi_i(p)$ is upper semi-continuous (see Debreu [7, Lemmas 1 and 2]).

We will use a mapping of the Cartesian product of a normalized price set S with the extended consumption set $\overline{X}$, which can be interpreted as taking prices into demand sets, by means of the demand correspondences, and possible consumptions into the normalized price set by an inverse supply correspondence. The mapping is so defined that a fixed point will be an equilibrium. The mapping of prices into a social demand set is given by $f(p) = \sum_{i=1}^{m} \psi_i(p)$. Let $\bar{y}$ lie in the interior of Y. The normalized price set S is defined as $S = \{p \mid p \cdot y \leqslant 0$, for all $y \in Y$, and $p \cdot \bar{y} = -1\}$. The set S is convex and compact since Y has an interior and $Y \neq R^n$ (see McKenzie [19, Lemma 5]).

In order to map possible consumptions into the price set S, we define a projection on the boundary of Y from $\bar{y}$. Let $\pi(x)$ be the maximum number π such that $\bar{y} + \pi \cdot (x - \bar{y}) \in Y$. It is possible to choose $|\bar{y}|$ large enough so that the function $\pi(x)$ is well defined for $x \in \overline{X}$. See Appendix I for a proof. Then let $h(x) = \bar{y} + \pi(x)(x - \bar{y})$. Then define, for any $y \in$ boundary Y, $g(y) = \{p \in S \mid p \cdot y = 0\}$. It may be shown that h is continuous, and also that $g(y)$ is upper semi-continuous. We may think of $g \circ h$ as an inverse supply correspondence.

Now define the correspondence $F(p, x) = ((g \circ h)(x), f(p))$. F maps $S \times \overline{X}$ into the collection of subsets of $S \times \overline{X}$. The subsets $(g \circ h)(x)$ and $f(p)$ are convex and not empty. Also f is upper semi-continuous, since ψ_i is for each i, h is continuous, and g is upper semi-continuous. Since g and h are correspondences whose values lie in compact sets, their composition $g \circ h$ is upper semi-continuous, in the sense that $p^s \to p$, $p^{s'} \to p'$, and $p^{s'} \in (g \circ h)(p^s)$ for $s = 1, 2, \ldots$, implies $p' \in (g \circ h)(p)$. Thus F is upper semi-continuous and convex valued. Since $S \times \overline{X}$ is convex, and compact by the Auxiliary Assumption, there is (p^*, x^*) such that $(p^*, x^*) \in F(p^*, x^*)$ by the fixed point theorem of Kakutani [12]. The mapping is illustrated in Figure 10.1.

To show that a fixed point of F leads to a competitive equilibrium for the economy $E = (Y, X_i, \succsim_i, i = 1, \ldots, m)$, we must show that

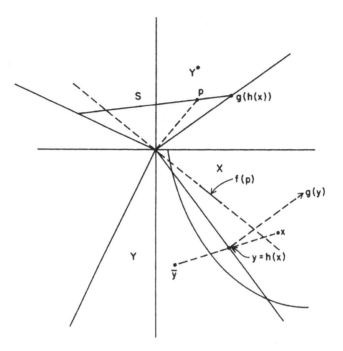

Figure 10.1
For $(p, x) \in S \times \overline{X}$, $F(p, x) = (g(h(x)), f(p)) \subset S \times \overline{X}$, where $\overline{X}$ is the convex hull of X and 0.

Conditions (I), (II), and (III) are met by $x_i^* \in \psi_i(p^*)$, $y^* = h(x^*)$, and $p^* \in g(h(x^*))$. Consider $p^* \in g(h(x^*))$. From the definition of g it follows that $p^* \cdot y^* = 0$, where $y^* = h(x^*)$, and $p^* \cdot y \leqslant 0$ for all $y \in Y$. Thus Condition (I) is met for p^* and y^*. Now suppose that all consumers have income, that is, for all i there is $x_i \in X_i$ such that $p^* \cdot x_i < 0$. Then $\psi_i(p^*) = \xi_i(p^*)$ and $x_i^* \in X_i$. Then insatiability within $X \cap Y$ implies that $p^* \cdot x_i^* = 0$ if $x^* \in Y$. In any case $p^* \cdot x_i^* \leqslant 0$ must hold, and $x_i^* \gtrsim_i x_i$ for x_i such that $p \cdot x_i \leqslant 0$ by definition of ξ_i. Thus Condition (II) holds for p^* and x^*. To prove Condition (III), consider $y^* = h(x^*) = \alpha x^* + (1 - \alpha)\overline{y}$ where α is maximal for $y^* \in Y$. Then $p^* \cdot y^* = 0 = \alpha p^* \cdot x^* + (1 - \alpha)p^* \cdot \overline{y}$. Since $\overline{y} \in$ interior Y, $p^* \cdot \overline{y} < 0$, and by definition of f, $p^* \cdot x^* \leqslant 0$. If $\alpha > 1$ it follows that $x^* \in Y$. Then non-satiation in $X \cap Y$ implies $p^* \cdot x^* = 0$. This is incompatible with $p^* \cdot y^* = 0$. However, if $0 < \alpha \leqslant 1$, $p^* \cdot y^* = 0$ requires $\alpha = 1$ and $p^* \cdot x^* = 0$. Thus $x^* = y^*$ and Condition (III) of competitive equilibrium also holds.

This proves that a fixed point of F is a competitive equilibrium if all consumers have income at p^*. Some consumers must have income since $z \in$ interior Y implies $p^* \cdot z < 0$, and by Assumption (5') there is $\bar{x} \in X \cap$ interior Y. Therefore, $p^* \cdot \bar{x}_i < 0$ holds for some i where $\bar{x}_i \in X_i$. Let $I_1 = \{i \mid p^* \cdot x_i < 0 \text{ for some } x_i \in X_i\}$. Let $I_2 = \{1, \ldots, m\} - I_1$ and suppose I_2 is not empty. Suppose there is $x \in f(p^*)$ and $x \in X \cap Y$. By Assumption (6'), there is $y' \in Y$ and $w \in \overline{X}_{I_2}$ such that $x'_{I_1} = y' - x_{I_2} - w$ and $x'_i \gtrsim_i x_i$ for all $i \in I_1$, and $x'_i \succ_i x_i$ for some $i \in I_1$. These relations are well defined since $x_i \in X_i$ for $i \in I_1$ from the definition of ξ_i. Also non-satiation in $X \cap Y$ and the definition of ξ_i imply that $p^* \cdot x'_{I_1} > 0$ must hold. On the other hand, $p^* \cdot y' \leqslant 0$, and $p^* \cdot x_{I_2} = 0$ by definition of ψ_i. This implies $p^* \cdot w < 0$ contradicting $w \in \overline{X}_{I_2}$, since $p^* \cdot x \geqslant 0$ for all $x \in \overline{X}_{I_2}$, that is, no one in I_2 has income. Then it must be that $I_2 = \varnothing$ and all consumers have income. In other words, $(p^*, y^*, x_i^*, i = 1, \ldots, m)$ is an equilibrium of E.

On the other hand, if $f(p^*) \cap (X \cap Y) = \varnothing$, that is, $\xi_{I_1}(p^*) \subset Y - \overline{X}_{I_2}$, but $\xi_{I_1}(p^*) \cap (Y - X_{I_2}) = \varnothing$, the transitivity of preference for the members of I_1 will be violated on the boundary of $Y - X_{I_2}$ in the relative topology of $Y - \overline{X}_{I_2}$. That is:

Lemma 1 If (p^*, x^*) is a fixed point of F, $f(p^*)$ and $X \cap Y$ have a nonempty intersection.

Define the feasible set F_1 for consumers in I_1 as $F_1 = Y - X_{I_2}$. The extended feasible set for I_1 is $\overline{F}_1 = Y - \overline{X}_{I_2}$. F_1 is properly contained in $\overline{F}_1$, and F_1 and $\overline{F}_1$ are convex and closed with nonempty interiors. Let B be the boundary of F_1 in the relative topology of $\overline{F}_1$, and let $B' = B \cap X_{I_1}$. Assume $f(p^*) \cap (X \cap Y) = \varnothing$. Then there is $x_{I_1}^* \in \psi_{I_1}(p^*)$ where $x_{I_1}^* \in \overline{F}_1 - F_1$. By Assumption (5') there is a point $\bar{x}_{I_1} \in F_1$. Since $X_{I_1}, \overline{F}_1$, and F_1 are all convex, the line segment from $\bar{x}_{I_1}$ to $x_{I_1}^*$ must lie in $X_{I_1} \cap \overline{F}_1$ and intersect B'. Thus B' is not empty.

If no members of I_1 are satiated at p^*, Assumption (2) implies that $\{x_i^*\}_{I_1}$ is a Pareto optimal allocation for I_1 over all allocations feasible in $\overline{F}_1$. Assumptions (1) and (2) imply that the preference relation $\gtrsim_i$ may be represented on X_i by a real valued utility function that is continuous and positive valued. See Debreu [6, pp. 56–59]. We may take 0 to be the greatest lower bound of u_i on X_i for all i and 1 to be the least upper bound. Let $\overline{U}_1$ be the utility possibility set for I_1 consumers over $\overline{F}_1$, and let U_1 be the utility possibility set for I_1 consumers over F_1. Let $u_i^* = u_i(x_i^*)$. Since $u^* = \{u_i^*\}_{I_1}$ is undominated in $\overline{F}_1$, it is undominated in F_1. If there were a point $x = \{x_i\}_{I_1} \in F_1$ with $u_i(x_i) = u_i(x_i^*)$ for $i \in I_1$, $x = \sum_{i=1}^m x_i$ would lie in $f(p^*)$ with $x \in X \cap Y$. This contradicts the assumption that $f(p^*) \cap (X \cap Y) = \varnothing$. Therefore u^* is not an element of U_1.

Define the social utility function for I_1, $v(x) = \max \alpha$ such that $u_i(x_i) \geq \alpha u_i^*$, $i \in I_1$, where the maximum is taken over allocations $\{x_i\}_{I_1}$ such that $\sum_{i \in I} x_i = x$, $x_i \in X_i$. To see that v is continuous, consider $x_i^s \to x_i$, $\alpha^s \to \alpha$ where α^s is maximal for $x^s = \sum_{i \in I_1} x_i^s$. It is clear from the continuity of u_i that $u_i(x_i) \geq \alpha u_i^*$ must hold in the limit. But if there were $\epsilon > 0$ such that $u_i(x_i) \geq (\alpha + \epsilon)u_i^*$ held for $i \in I_1$, $u_i(x_i^s) \geq (\alpha^s + (\epsilon/2))u_i^*$ would hold, for large s, contradicting the maximality of α^s. Also v inherits the quasi-concavity properties of u_i, derived from Assumption (2).

I claim v has no maximum on the set B'. Suppose b provided a maximum for v over B'. It must be that $v(b) < 1$, that is, $u_i(b_i) < u_i^*$ holds for some i, where $\{b_i\}_{I_1}$ is a maximizing allocation of b. Otherwise $u_i(b_i) \geq u_i(x_i^*)$, $i \in I_1$, and $u^* \in U_1$, which we have seen to be impossible. Since $b \in F_1$, it is feasible and by Assumption (2) and (6′) there is a point $w \in \bar{F}_1$ such that $c = b + w$ and $v(c) \geq v(b)$. Since c lies in the cone from the origin spanned by F_1 and $x_{I_1}^* \in \bar{F}_1 - F_1$, the line segment from c to $x_{I_1}^*$ cuts B in a point z. Indeed, c and $x_{I_1}^*$ both in X_{I_1} implies that $z \in B'$. It is shown in Appendix II that z may be chosen distinct from c. Therefore, Assumption (2) and the definition of v imply that $v(z) > v(b)$, so b does not provide a maximum for v over B'. This is a contradiction of the fact that B' is compact and v is continuous. Thus the assumption that $f(p^*) \cap (X \cap Y) = \emptyset$ must be rejected.

If some members of I_1 are satiated, it follows from the impossibility of satiation in the feasible set according to Assumption (6′) that u^* does not lie in U_1. Then the proof proceeds as before and Pareto optimality of $\{x_i^*\}_{I_1}$ in $\bar{F}_1$ is not needed. This completes the proof of Lemma 1. The argument is illustrated for the case where $Y = R^n$ in Figure 10.2.

Lemma 1 together with the previous argument implies that the case where all consumers have income at p^* is the only possible case. Therefore, the equilibrium proved to exist for this case must exist in general.

We have proved the following theorem.

Theorem 2   If an economy $E = (Y, X_i, \succsim_i, i = 1, \dots, m)$ satisfies the Assumptions (1), (2), (3), (4), (5′), and (6′), there is a competitive equilibrium for E.

The interiority assumption of (5′) is easily removed. We will say more about this when recent remarks on free disposal are discussed later. However, two assumptions are weakened following Moore. The survival assumption is removed and the assumption of irreducibility is weakened.

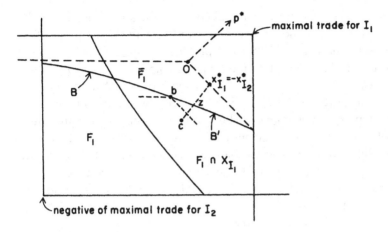

Figure 10.2

$v(x_{I_1}^*) > v(b)$.
$v(c) \geqslant v(b)$.
$\therefore v(z) > v(b)$.
$\therefore b$ does not max v on B'.

I_2 cannot survive without trade.
$Y = R_-^n, F_1 = R_-^n - X_{I_2}$.
No equilibrium exists in F_1, but $(p^*, x_i^*, i = 1, \ldots, m)$ is an equilibrium with $\sum_1^m x_i^* = x_{I_1}^* \in \bar{F}_1 - F_1$.
v has no maximum on $B' = B \cap X_{I_1}$.
This may be viewed as an Edgeworth box with the initial allocation at 0.

The proof of Lemma 1 allows us to see with clarity why a weaker irreducibility assumption used by James Moore [21, p. 272–273], suffices to establish the existence of a compensated equilibrium. His result requires that all the fixed points of F should have $x^* \in X \cap Y$. This is true if Lemma 1 holds. However, in the proof of Lemma 1 only the weak inequality $v(b + w) \geqslant v(b)$ was used, where $w \neq 0$ and $w \in Y - \bar{X}_{I_2}$.

10.3   A Weaker Preference Relation

The other direction in which the classical theorem has been substantially strengthened is to remove the requirement that the preference relation be transitive and complete. This process was begun by Sonnenschein [28] and brought to fruition by Mas-Colell [16] and Gale and Mas-Colell [9]. Later a more general theorem was proved in a very efficient way by Shafer and Sonnenschein [26] and applied to competitive equilibrium by Shafer [25]. Sonnenschein showed that the existence of a well defined demand function does not depend on the transitivity of preference. He also showed that the demand function would be upper semi-continuous if preferences are continuous. However, this still does not allow the demand correspondence to be used in the customary ways in proofs of existence of equilibrium since the value of the correspondence need not be a convex set, even though the preferred point set is convex. The proof of existence of equilibrium without transitivity was given first by Mas-Colell, and then in a slightly different form by Mas-Colell and Gale. Whether the preference relation $\gtrsim_i$ is complete seems to be a matter of definition, since x incomparable with y can be replaced harmlessly by x indifferent to y in the absence of transitivity.

Let $P_i(x)$ be the set of commodity bundles y such that $y \succ_i x$. Assumption (2) may be weakened to:

(2′)   A preference correspondence P_i is defined on X_i into the collection of subsets of X_i, $i = 1, \ldots, m$. The correspondence P_i is open valued relative to X_i and lower semi-continuous. Also $x_i \notin$ convex hull $P_i(x_i)$.

Assumption (2′) is a major weakening of (2) since it does not require $\succ_i$ to be transitive, or even asymmetric, and no convexity assumption is made on the relation $\gtrsim_i$ (defined by $x \gtrsim_i y$ if and only if $\sim y \succ_i x$). As mentioned above, even though transitivity and asymmetry of $\succ_i$ were introduced and $P_i(x)$ were assumed convex, the non-convexity of $\gtrsim_i$ would still require a new proof of existence since the value of the demand correspondence need not be convex or even connected. On this point, see Mas-Colell [16].

Because Assumption (2′) does not include convexity and transitivity of preference in the sense of Assumption (2), the argument that excluded fixed points of F involving $x_i^* \in \overline{X}_i - X_i$ in the proof of Theorem 2 can no longer be made. Therefore, to prove existence with the preference correspondences P_i we introduce a stronger assumption of irreducibility. We assume:

(6″)   However I_1 and I_2 may be selected, if $x_{I_1} = y - x_{I_2}$ with $x_{I_1} \in X_{I_1}$, $y \in Y$, and $x_{I_2} \in \overline{X}_{I_2}$, then there is also $y' \in Y$ and $w \in \overline{X}_{I_2}$, such that $x'_{I_1} = y' - x_{I_2} - w$ and $x'_i \in P(x_i)$ for all $i \in I_1$.

Assumption (6″) is stronger than (6′) in two respects. The point x_{I_2} may be in the enlarged possible consumption set $\overline{X}_{I_2}$, and it must be possible for an additional trade from $\overline{X}_{I_2}$ to improve the position of all consumers belonging to I_1. Then Lemma 1 is no longer needed.

A device introduced by Shafer [24] and exploited by Shafer and Sonnenschein [26] will allow us to use a mapping of the social consumption set on the boundary of the production possibility set, as before. Then the proof of existence for a production economy under quite weak conditions may be derived. The trick is to define a new preference relation that is transitive, by means of a preference correspondence R_i conditioned on $x \in \overline{X}_i$. First, define P'_i by $P'_i(x) = $ convex hull $P_i(x)$ for $x \in X_i$. It is easily seen that P'_i satisfies Assumption $(2')$ and, in addition, it is convex valued. Let G_i denote the graph of P'_i, and denote by $d((x,z), G_i)$ the Euclidean distance from $(x,z) \in \overline{X}_i \times X_i$ to G_i. Define $R_i(x, y)$ for $x \in \overline{X}_i$ and $y \in X_i$ by

$$R_i(x, y) = \{z \mid d((x,z), G_i) \leqslant d((x, y), G_i)\}, \quad \text{if } y \notin P'_i(x), \quad \text{and}$$

$$R_i(x, y) = \{z \mid d((x,z), G^c_i) \geqslant d((x, y), G^c_i)\}, \quad \text{if } y \in P'_i(x).$$

G^c_i is the complement of G_i in $X_i \times X_i$. For any given $x \in \overline{X}_i$, $R_i(x, y)$ defines a transitive and symmetric preference relation on X_i. Because $d((x,z), G_i)$ is a continuous function of (x,z), $R_i(x, y)$ is a continuous correspondence. This justifies the following lemma.

Lemma 2 R_i is a continuous correspondence mapping $\overline{X}_i \times X_i$ into the collection of subsets of X_i, $i = 1, \ldots, m$.

Now we use R_i to define a pseudo-demand correspondence $\xi'_i(p, x)$, where p is a price vector and $x \in \overline{X}_i$. Let $\xi_i(p, x) = \{y \in X_i \mid p \cdot y \leqslant 0$ and $p \cdot z \leqslant 0$ implies $y \in R_i(x, z)\}$. That is, $\xi_i(p, x)$ is the set of commodity bundles y such that (x, y) is as close to G_i (or as far from G^c_i) as (x, z) for any commodity bundle z in the budget set defined by p. Let ξ'_i be the convex hull of this set. It is clear that $\xi'_i(p, x)$ is contained in the budget set.

I claim that $\xi'_i(p, x)$ is upper semi-continuous at (p, x) if there is $z \in X_i$ such that $p \cdot z < 0$, that is, if the ith consumer has income. Suppose $p^s \to p$, $x^s \to x$, $y^s \to y$, $s = 1, 2, \ldots$, where $y^s \in \xi'_i(p^s, x^s)$ and $(x^s) \in \overline{X}_i$. Consider $w \in X_i$ where $p \cdot w \leqslant 0$. The existence of z implies that the budget set $B(p') = \{z \in X_i \mid p' \cdot z \leqslant 0\}$ is a continuous correspondence at $p' = p$. Then, for s large, there is $w^s \in X_i$ such that $p^s \cdot w^s \leqslant 0$ and $w^s \to w$. By definition of $\xi'_i(p^s, x^s)$, $y^s = \sum_1^{n+1} \alpha^s_j z^s_j$

where $z_j^s \in B(p^s) \cap R_i(x^s, w^s)$ and $\sum_1^{n+1} \alpha_j^s = 1$, $\alpha_j^s \geqslant 0$, all j. Since the X_i are bounded by the Auxiliary Assumption, z_j^s is bounded for each j, and a subsequence may be chosen which converges for z_j^s and α_j^s. Retaining notation, let $z_j^s \to z_j$, $\alpha_j^s \to \alpha_j$, all j. Then $y = \sum_1^{n+1} \alpha_j z_j$. But, by Lemma 2, R_i is continuous, so $z_j \in R_i(x, w)$. Since w is an arbitrary element of $B(p)$, this implies $z_j \in \xi_i(p, x)$ and, therefore, $y \in \xi_i'(p, x)$. Thus ξ_i' is upper semi-continuous. It is convex valued by definition. We have shown the following lemma to be true.

Lemma 3 The correspondence ξ_i' is upper semi-continuous and convex valued at (p, x) if there is $w \in X_i$ such that $p \cdot w < 0$.

We define $f_i'(p, x)$ in a manner similar to the definition of $\psi_i(p)$, that is,

$$f_i'(p, x) = \xi_i'(p, x) \quad \text{if there is } w \in X_i \text{ and } p \cdot w < 0,$$

$$f_i'(p, x) = \{y \in \overline{X}_i \mid p \cdot y = 0\}, \quad \text{otherwise.}$$

We may prove the following lemma.

Lemma 4 The correspondence f_i' is upper semi-continuous and convex valued for any (p, x) with $p \in S$, $x \in \overline{X}_i$.

The result follows from Lemma 3 if there is w such that $p \cdot w < 0$. If $p \cdot w \geqslant 0$ for all $w \in X_i$, $f_i'(p, x)$ is the intersection of the budget set with $\overline{X}_i$ and thus convex valued. Upper semi-continuity follows from the arguments of Debreu appealed to earlier in the case of $\psi_i(p)$.

We may now define a mapping F' whose fixed points will be competitive equilibria for an economy $E = (Y, X_i, P_i, i = 1, \ldots, m)$ that satisfies (1), (2'), (3), (4), (5'), and (6''). First, define f' on $S \times \prod_1^m \overline{X}_i$ by $f'(p, \prod_1^m x_i) = \prod_1^m f_i'(p, x_i)$. Thus $f'(p, \prod_1^m x_i) \subset R^{mn}$. Correspondences h and g may be defined as before in the definition of the mapping F. Let $F'(p, \prod_1^m x_i) = ((g \circ h)(\sum_1^m x_i), f'(p, \prod_1^m x_i))$. Then F' maps $S \times \prod_1^m \overline{X}_i$ into the collection of subsets of $S \times \prod_1^m \overline{X}_i$. Since the values of g, h, f', and f_i' lie in compact sets and each is continuous or upper semi-continuous, F is upper semi-continuous. Since $g \circ h$ is convex valued and not empty as before, and $\prod_1^m f_i'$ is also convex valued and not empty, F' has these properties. Then the Kakutani fixed point theorem provides a fixed point for F' on $S \times \prod_1^m \overline{X}_i$.

We must show that the fixed point of F' is a competitive equilibrium. However, first we will slightly modify condition II to read

(II′) $x_i \in X_i$ and $p \cdot x_i \leqslant 0$, and $p \cdot z > 0$ for any $z \in P(x_i)$, $i = 1, \ldots, m$.

This condition implies (II) whenever $\succsim_i$ can be consistently defined as a complete weak ordering over X_i. However, (II′) is not as restrictive as (II) since (II′) allows both $x \in P_i(y)$ and $y \in P_i(x)$.

Lower semi-continuity of P_i, and thus of P_i', plays a role like local non-satiation in the present context to imply the spending of all income for the pseudo-demand functions at a fixed point.

Lemma 5   If $x \in f_i'(p, x)$, then $p \cdot x = 0$.

The definition of $f_i'(p, x)$ implies $p \cdot x \leqslant 0$. Suppose $p \cdot x < 0$. Then $f_i'(p, x) = \xi_i'(p, x)$. Thus we only need consider the case $x \in \xi_i'(p, x)$. Suppose there is $z \in \xi_i(p, x)$ and $(x, z) \in G_i$, that is, $z \in P_i'(x)$. Then $y \in \xi_i(p, x)$ implies $y \in P_i'(x)$, that is, $(x, y) \in G_i$. This implies $x \in P_i'(x)$ by convexity of P_i', contradicting Assumption 2′. Therefore, $\xi_i(p, x) \cap P_i'(x) = \varnothing$. On the other hand, $p \cdot x < 0$ implies there is $y \in \xi_i(p, x)$ and $p \cdot y < 0$. Thus the result follows if $p \cdot y < 0$ implies that (x, y) cannot be a closest point to G_i of the form (x, z) for which $p \cdot z \leqslant 0$.

Suppose otherwise and let $(\bar{x}, \bar{z})$ be a point of G_i closest to (x, y). Let $x^s \to \bar{x}$, $s = 1, 2, \ldots$, where x^s lies on the line segment from x to $\bar{x}$. By lower semi-continuity of P_i' there is a sequence $z^s \to \bar{z}$ where $(x^s, z^s) \in G_i$. Choose a sequence $(x, w^s) \to (x, y)$, where $w^s = \alpha_s y + (1 - \alpha_s) z^s$ and $0 < \alpha_s < 1$. Convexity of X_i implies $w^s \in X_i$. Also $z^s - w^s = \alpha_s(z^s - y)$. We may choose α_s so that $\alpha_s|z^s - y| < |\bar{z} - y|$ for large s. This together with $|x^s - x| < |\bar{x} - x|$ implies for large s, $|(x^s, z^s) - (x, w^s)| < |(\bar{x}, \bar{z}) - (x, y)|$. But for s large $p \cdot w^s < 0$. Since $(x^s, z^s) \in G_i$, $y \notin R_i(x, w^s)$ for large s. This contradicts $y \in \xi_i(p, x)$, and the lemma is proved.

Consider $(p^*, x_1^*, \ldots, x_m^*) \in F'(p^*, x_1^*, \ldots, x_m^*)$. Let $x^* = \sum_1^m x_i^*$, where $x_i^* \in f_i'(p^*, x_i^*)$. Then by Lemma 5, $p^* \cdot x^* = 0$. Also $y^* \in h(x^*)$. Then $p^* \cdot \bar{y} < 0$, together with $y^* = \alpha x^* + (1 - \alpha)\bar{y}$, from the definition of h, and $p^* \cdot y^* = 0$ from the definition of g, gives $\alpha = 1$. Thus $x^* = y^*$. Since $p^* \cdot y \leqslant 0$ for $y \in Y$ follows from the definition of g, and $y^* \in Y$ from the definition of h, Conditions (I) and (III) are satisfied.

The verification of Condition (II′) like that of Condition (II) is less simple than the verification of (I) and (III), in this instance because the maximization of preference in $f_i'(p^*, x_i^*)$ is relative to x_i^* by way of a pseudo-preference ordering. As before, make the provisional assumption that all consumers have income at p^*, that is, for each i there is $w \in X_i$ and $p^* \cdot w < 0$. Then $f_i' = \xi_i'$ and $x_i^* \in \xi_i'(p^*, x_i^*)$. By definition of

ξ_i' it must hold that $x_i^* \in X_i$ and $p^* \cdot x_i^* \leq 0$. Also $x_i^* = \sum_1^{n+1} \alpha_j z_j$, $\alpha_j \geq 0$, $\sum_1^{n+1} \alpha_j = 1$, where $z_j \in \xi_i(p^*, x_i^*)$, that is, $z_j \in R_i(x_i^*, y)$ for all j and for any $y \in X_i$ such that $p^* \cdot y \leq 0$, and $p \cdot z_j \leq 0$. Let F_i be the smallest affine subspace containing X_i. We will need the following lemma:

Lemma 6   If $y \in$ interior $P_i'(x)$ relative to F_i, then $(x, y) \in$ interior G_i relative to $X_i \times X_i$.

The proof follows from the fact that P_i' is lower semi-continuous and convex valued. Suppose $y \in$ interior $P_i'(x)$ relative to F_i. Then there is a neighborhood N of y in F_i such that $N \subset P_i'(x)$. Indeed, we may choose N to be the interior, relative to F_i, of the convex hull of points $w_j \in P_i'(x)$, $j = 1, \ldots, n_i + 1$, where n_i is the dimension of F_i. Let y be an arbitrary element of N. Then $y = \sum_1^{n_i+1} \alpha_j w_j$ for unique α_j with $\sum \alpha_j = 1$, and $\alpha_j > 0$, all j. We must show that any point (x^s, y^s) sufficiently near (x, y) belongs to G_i. Suppoes not. Then there is a sequence $(x^s, y^s) \to (x, y)$ and $y^s \notin P_i'(x^s)$. However, by lower semi-continuity for any sequence $x^s \to x$, there is a sequence $w_j^s \in P_i'(x^s)$ with $w_j^s \to w_j$, for all j. The affine independence of the w_j implies the affine independence of w_j^s for large s. Therefore, $y^s = \sum_j^{n_i+1} \alpha_j^s w_j^s$ for unique α_j^s for large s, where $\sum \alpha_j^s = 1$. Since $y^s \to y$ and $w_j^s \to w_j$, it must be that $\alpha_j^s \to \alpha_j$. Otherwise, a subsequence of α_j^s could be chosen converging to α_j', where $\alpha_j' \neq \alpha_j$ for some j, and $y = \sum_1^{n_i+1} \alpha_j' w_j$, in contradiction to the uniqueness of the α_j. Thus $\alpha_j^s > 0$ for s large, and $y^s \in P_i'(x^s)$ by the convexity of $P_i'(x^s)$. This proves the lemma.

To verify Condition (II'), we must show that $y \in P_i(x_i^*)$ implies $p^* \cdot y > 0$. Assume the contrary, that is, $y \in P_i(x_i^*)$ and $p^* \cdot y \leq 0$. However, $y \in P_i(x_i^*)$ implies $y \in P_i'(x_i^*)$. Since all consumers have income, there is $w \in X_i$ satisfying $p^* \cdot w < 0$. It is clear that w may be chosen interior to X_i relative to F_i. Let $S_\epsilon(w)$ be an ϵ-ball in F_i about w contained in X_i. Consider $N_\alpha = \alpha y + (1 - \alpha) S_\epsilon(w)$. N_α is an open set relative to F_i and contained in X_i for all α with $0 \leq \alpha < 1$. Since $y \in P_i'(x_i^*)$ and $P_i'(x_i^*)$ is open relative to X_i, for α near 1, $N_\alpha \subset P_i'(x_i^*)$. Let $y' \in N_\alpha$, so that $y' \in$ interior $P'(x_i^*)$ relative to F_i. Then $(x_i^*, y') \in$ interior G_i relative to $X_i \times X_i$ by Lemma 6, and $d((x_i^*, y'), G_i^c) > 0$. But x_i^* is a convex combination of $n + 1$ points $z_j \in \xi_i(p^*, x_i^*)$. Thus $p^* \cdot y' < 0$ implies that $z_j \in R_i(x_i^*, y')$. Then, by definition of R_i, $d((x_i^*, z_j), G_i^c) > 0$ must hold for all j. In other words, $(x_i^*, z_j) \in G_i$, or $z_j \in P_i'(x_i^*)$, all j. Since P_i' is convex valued, it follows that $x^* \in P_i'(x_i^*)$. But $P_i'(x_i^*)$ is the convex hull of $P_i(x_i^*)$, which contradicts Assumption (2') and establishes Condition (II') of competitive equilibrium. This argument is analogous to an argument of Shafer and Sonnenschein [26], where G_i was assumed to be an open graph.

An argument parallel to that in the case of Theorem 2 shows that on the basis of (5′) and (6″) every consumer does in fact have income for any fixed point of F'. We have shown for a fixed point (p^*, x^*) of F' that $x^* = y^*$ where $x^* \in f'(p^*, \prod x_i^*)$ and $y^* \in Y$. Thus by the definition of f' we find $x^* \in \overline{X} \cap Y$. As before, Assumption (5′) implies that someone has income at p^*, so the set I_1 of consumers with income is not empty. Suppose the set I_2 of consumers without income is not empty. Then by Assumption (6″), there is $y' \in Y$ and $w \in \overline{X}_{I_2}$ such that $x'_{I_1} = y' - x^*_{I_2} - w$ and $x'_i \in P_i(x_i^*)$ for all $i \in I_1$. Then $x'_i \in P'_i(x_i^*)$ also holds and $(x_i^*, x'_i) \in G_i$. Since $(x_i^*, x_i^*) \notin G_i$ by Assumption (2′), $x'_i \in R_i(x_i^*, x_i^*)$. Therefore, $p^* \cdot x'_i > p^* \cdot x_i^*$ by definition of $\xi'_i(p^*, x^*)$. Then, by Lemma 5, $p^* \cdot x'_i > 0$ must hold for all i. However, $p^* \cdot x_i^* = 0$ for $i \in I_2$ by definition of f'_i. Also $p^* \cdot y' \leqslant 0$ since p^* supports Y, and $p \cdot w \geqslant 0$ since $w \in X_{I_2}$, which is also supported by p^*. Thus $p^* \cdot x'_{I_1} = p^* \cdot y' - p^* \cdot x^*_{I_2} - p^* \cdot w \leqslant 0$ in contradiction to $p^* \cdot x'_i > 0$. Therefore, $I_2 = \varnothing$ and all consumers have income. Thus we have the following theorem:

Theorem 3   If an economy $E = (Y, X_i, P_i, i = 1, \ldots, m)$ satisfies the Assumptions (1), (2′), (3), (4), (5′), and (6″), there is a competitive equilibrium for E.

Except for the interiority assumption of (5′), this is the modern form of the classical theorem on existence of competitive equilibrium that was promised. Its major improvements are the removal of the survival assumption based on the work of Moore and the discard of transitivity of the preference relation based on the work of Sonnenschein, Shafer, Mas-Colell, and Gale. The interiority assumption is made only for simplicity. A method for its removal will be described in the next section.

However, the greatly weakened assumption on preferences for Theorem 3 required that the irreducibility assumption be significantly stronger than Moore's. Irreducibility was assumed for an economy with expanded consumption sets $\overline{X}_i$ and the improvement for I_2 consumers was positive for all $i \in I_2$. This stronger form of irreducibility would actually be needed even for preferences of the type assumed by Debreu [7] where thick indifference sets were allowed and transitivity was retained. Otherwise, the contradiction that establishes $I_2 = \varnothing$ is not available, since $x'_i \succsim_i x_i^*$ does not imply $p \cdot x'_i \geqslant p \cdot x_i^*$ when indifference sets may be thick, that is, when $x \succ_i y$ and $z = \alpha x + (1 - \alpha)y$ for $0 < \alpha < 1$ only implies $z \succsim_i y$.

10.4   Free Disposal

The question of free disposal, or more generally, the question of interiority, for existence of equilibrium was essentially settled in McKenzie [19]. However, the explicit proof offered in the original paper does not cover the case of production sets that are linear subspaces, in particular, the case where $Y = \{0\}$. A hint was given in the *Econometrica* reprint volume [19, p. 350, fn. 13] on how the gap should be repaired, but the original omission may still lead to confusion. There have been recent articles, in particular Hart and Kuhn [10], and Bergstrom [3], providing alternative proofs that "free disposal" is not needed as an assumption. These proofs are, of course, valuable to have, but the original proof can be recommended for simplicity and intuitive appeal. Thus it may be worthwhile to provide the missing steps from the 1959 argument, particularly since the recent proofs have interiority assumptions stronger than the second part of (5). The final form of the interiority assumption is

(5″)   relative interior $X \cap$ relative interior $Y \neq \varnothing$.

This is the second part of (5), from which the survival assumption has been removed. The interior is taken relative to the smallest linear subspace containing X, or Y, respectively.

The technique for reducing (5′) to (5″) is to expand Y so that it acquires an interior in such a way that a relative interior point given by (5″) is interior to Y, thus re-establishing (5′). Then an equilibrium exists for the modified system. The modification is made to depend continuously on a parameter $\epsilon \geq 0$ in such a way that $\epsilon = 0$ corresponds to the original model. The equilibria for E^s as $\epsilon_s \to 0$, $s = 1, 2, \ldots$, lie in a compact set, and the limit of the equilibria $(p^s, y^s, x_i^s, i = 1, \ldots, m)$ for a converging subsequence is an equilibrium for E. Conditions (I) and (III) hold in the limit from the continuity of sum and inner product. Condition (II) of Theorems 1 and 2 follows from the upper semi-continuity of the demand correspondence, once it is shown that all consumers have income at the limit price vector p, as a consequence of Assumption (5″) and (6) or (6′). The argument of McKenzie [19, p. 64] may be used for this purpose. However, for the case of Theorems 2 and 3, X_i should be replaced by $\overline{X}_i$ and X by $\overline{X}$ in the argument. Assumption (5″) implies that relative interior $\overline{X} \cap$ relative interior $Y \neq \varnothing$. To establish (II′) in the case of Theorem 3 note that $p \cdot x_i \leq 0$ holds by continuity when x_i is a limit point of x_i^s and apply the same argument used to establish (II′) for E^s. The proof is simpler than in McKenzie [19] since it is no longer necessary to move the X_i. Formerly, X_i was moved to provide a point interior to $X_i \cap Y$ that would guarantee income for the ith consumer in the modified economy E^s. This role is now played in the same way in E and E^s by Assumption (6') or (6'').

If Y is not a linear subspace, let $\bar{x} \in$ relative interior $X \cap$ relative interior Y. The existence of $\bar{x}$ results from (5''). Let $S_\epsilon(\bar{x}) = \{y \mid |y - \bar{x}| \leqslant \epsilon\}$, where $\epsilon > 0$ is chosen sufficiently small so that Assumptions (3) and (4) are protected. Let $Y(\epsilon) = \{y \mid y = \alpha w + \beta z, \text{ where } \alpha \geqslant 0, \beta \geqslant 0, w \in Y,$ and $z \in S_\epsilon(\bar{x})\}$. $Y(\epsilon)$ is the convex cone spanned from the origin by Y and $S_\epsilon(\bar{x})$. Then $\bar{x} \in$ int $Y(\epsilon)$ and Assumption (5') is satisfied. Thus there is an equilibrium by Theorem 3 for $E(\epsilon) = (Y(\epsilon), X_i, P_i, i = 1, \ldots, m)$, and similarly for Theorem 2. We must show that the equilibria $(p^s, y^s, x_i^s, i = 1, \ldots, m)$ lie in a compact set as $\epsilon^s \to 0$. Eventually $Y(\epsilon^s) \subset Y(\epsilon)$ for an $\epsilon > 0$, and $Y(\epsilon) \cap R_+^n = \{0\}$. Therefore, X_i bounded below implies that y^s and x_i^s are bounded over s by the usual argument (McKenzie [19, p. 62]). To bound p^s, renormalize the prices given by Theorem 3 by setting $|p^s| = 1$. By letting ϵ tend to 0, the existence of an equilibrium for E is established in the way described above. Note that Y may contain a linear subspace, although it is not equal to a linear subspace.

If Y is a linear subspace, the construction is slightly more complicated. An $n+1$st pseudo-good is introduced into the model. Let $Y' = \{y \in R^{n+1} \mid (y_1, \ldots, y_n) \in Y \text{ and } y_{n+1} \leqslant 0\}$. Since $(0, -1) \in Y'$, the pseudo-good is freely disposable. Let $\bar{x} \in$ relative interior $X \cap$ relative interior Y as before. Define $S_\epsilon(\bar{x}, -1) = \{y \in R^{n+1} \mid |y - (\bar{x}, -1)| \leqslant \epsilon,$ where $\epsilon < |\bar{x}, -1|\}$. Define $X_i' = \{x \in R^{n+1} \mid (x_1, \ldots, x_n) \in X_i \text{ and } x_{n+1} = -1/m\}$. Define $Y'(\epsilon)$ as before and (5'') is satisfied. Then by the previous argument an equilibrium exists for $E'(\epsilon) = (Y'(\epsilon), X_i', P_i'', i = 1, \ldots, m)$, where $y \in P_i''(x)$ if and only if $(y_1, \ldots, y_n) \in P_i(x_1, \ldots, x_n)$. As $\epsilon \to 0$, and the productivity of the pseudo-good disappears, any limit of the p^s has $p_{n+1}^s = 0$. Therefore, a limit $(p, y, x_i, i = 1, \ldots, m)$ of the equilibria for $E'(\epsilon)$, as $\epsilon \to 0$, is an equilibrium for E when the coordinate $n+1$ is ignored. Since $Y = \{0\}$ is a possibility, the pure trade economy without disposal is covered by this argument.

10.5   Role of the Firm

It is an unusual characteristic of my contributions to the theory of existence of equilibrium that the social production set has been represented by a convex cone. I would claim that this properly represents the Walrasian system where production processes rather than firms are featured, but also it is a fair representation of a Marshallian economy of competitive industries where firm size is small relative to the market and firms operate in a small neighborhood of the minimum cost points on their U-shaped cost curves. The representation of the competitive economy as a fixed collection of disparate firms maximizing profit over concave production functions probably dates from Hicks' *Value and Capital* [11], but it was taken up by Arrow and Debreu [1]. Wald [31, 32] had used a simplified Walrasian model. My own initial contribution [17] was in the context of Graham's model of world trade which was also linear. However, I have continued to regard the linear process model to be the appropriate ideal type for the competitive economy.

It should be remarked that in a strict mathematical sense the models of Walras and Hicks are equivalent, without resort to approximations. In one direction this is obvious since linear processes may be assigned to Hicksian firms leading to a social production set that is a cone. This is a Hicksian model without scarce unmarketed resources. In the other direction an artificial construction is needed. An entrepreneurial factor is introduced for each firm which is divided among the owners in proportion to their ownership shares. This factor is always supplied and freely disposable. The production set Y_j of the jth firm is displaced by appending minus one unit of the jth entrepreneurial factor to each of its input-output vectors and setting all other entrepreneurial inputs equal to zero. The new production set $\tilde{Y}^j$, for a unit input of entrepreneurship, lies in a space R^{n+l} when there are l firms. Then the social production set $\tilde{Y}$ is taken to be the closure of the set, $\sum_i^m \alpha_j \tilde{Y}_j$, $\alpha_j \geqslant 0$. The only part of the set $\tilde{Y}$ that contributes to an equilibrium is its intersection with the hyperplane defined by setting entrepreneurial components equal to -1. This set is not affected by taking the closure. The pricing of the entrepreneurial factors will provide for the distribution of profits by the firms and the order of proof is the same as before.

On the other hand, my own preference is to regard the entrepreneurial factors as no different from other goods, suffering indeed from some indivisibilities in the real world, but approximated in the competitive model by divisible goods just as in the case of television sets and steel mills. Viewed this way the use of the production cone approximates the basic competitive notion of free entry more closely than Hicks' unmarketed factors. In the firm model of Hicks and Arrow-Debreu a firm becomes active whenever its profit becomes nonnegative. However, the list of firms is given and for Hicks, at least, identified with the list of consumers. Trouble immediately arises if firms are run by coalitions of people, that is, entrepreneurial factors can be supplied to a firm by more than one consumer. Merely earning a positive return does not then activate a firm, as a potential coalition, unless the profit is sufficient to match the earnings that the coalition members already receive elsewhere. Suppose entrepreneurial factors do not affect preferences directly. Then given the prices of traded goods, an equilibrium would be an allocation of profits in the core of a profit game, in which the firms are coalitions of entrepreneurs rather than single entrepreneurs as in the Hicks theory, or unique unreproducible resources as in Arrow-Debreu.

Let e_j be a point in R^m, where $e_{ij} = 1$ if the ith entrepreneur is in the jth coalition and $e_{ij} = 0$ otherwise. Let e_j be the jth column of the matrix $[e_{ij}]$ which has m rows and 2^m columns. Let π be a point in R^m representing a distribution of profits, and let $v(e_j)$ be the maximum profits attainable by the jth coalition at the ruling prices. Let $e \in R^m$ be the vector all of whose components equal 1. Then π is in the core if $\pi \cdot e_j \geqslant v(e_j)$, for all j, and there exists $\delta \in R^{2^m}$ such that $\delta_j = 0$ or 1, all j, $\sum_j \delta_j e_j = e$, and $\pi \cdot e_j = v(e_j)$ if $\delta_j = 1$. Under these conditions there is a collection of coalitions accomodating all entrepreneurs with sufficient profits to pay their members at the rate π and there is no coalition with enough profits to better these rates of pay.

Unfortunately the conditions that will imply a nonempty core are onerous. Scarf [23] has shown that a game has a nonempty core if it is balanced. A game with transferable utility is *balanced* if, for any $\delta \in R_+^{2^m}$ and $\pi \in R^m$, $\sum_j \delta_j e_j = e$, all i, and $\pi \cdot e_j \leqslant v(e_j)$, all j with $\delta_j > 0$, implies that $\pi \cdot e \leqslant v(e)$. There seems no reason why these conditions should be met. In particular, they imply that the problems of coordination within firms are overcome by economies of scale in production, no matter how large the firms grow. There can always be a single firm embracing all entrepreneurs to realize the core allocation. The role of the market is unimportant.

There seems no way out of this difficulty except to allow the distribution of effort implied by δ to be realized in fact, either by a distribution of time over coalitions by individuals or by the presence of many individuals of each of m types who may be spread over coalitions. Then the managerial structure of the firm appears like a linear activity. The whole set of firms generates Y, a convex cone from the origin in R^{m+1}, spanned by $(v(e_j), -e_j)$, $j = 1, \ldots, 2^m$, with $v(0) = -1$, to allow free disposal of profit. A competitive equilibrium will exist for the reduced economy, impied by given prices for goods and marketed factors, where Y is the production set. The ith consumer supplies one unit of his entrepreneurial factor while demanding π_i units of the output (profit) when the price vector is $(1, \pi)$. In equilibrium prices for entrepreneurial factors may be normalized on the price of profit $= 1$, since every vector in the dual cone is nonnegative by virtue of $v(0) = -1$. Let $\delta^i \in R^m$ have $\delta^i_j = 0$ for $j \neq i$ and $\delta^i_i = 1$. Let $\delta \in R^{2^m}$ satisfy $\delta \geqslant 0$. The equilibrium $((1, \pi), \bar{y}, \bar{x}_1, \ldots, \bar{x}_m)$ will satisfy $(1, \pi) \cdot y \leqslant 0$ for $y \in Y$, $(1, \pi) \cdot \bar{y} = 0$, $\quad \bar{y} = \sum_j \delta_j(v(e_j), -e_j)$, $\quad \sum_j \delta_j e_j = e$, $\quad \sum_j \delta_j v_j = \pi \cdot e$, $\quad \bar{x}_i = (\pi_i, -\delta^i)$, $\bar{y} = \sum_i \bar{x}_i$. Thus π is in the core when δ is allowed to vary continuously with no further assumptions.

However, if this way out is chosen there is no advantage over simply treating entrepreneurial resources like other resources, in particular, without the restriction that the amounts of different entrepreneurial resources in a given activity be used in the same amounts, as the coalition model requires, or the restriction that entrepreneurial resources do not affect preferences. I conclude that whatever resources are brought together to comprise the "unmarketed" resource base of the firm are most reasonably treated symmetrically with other resources. Most goods in the real world are indivisible, so the competitive model is an approximation to reality, but the entrepreneurial resources, or firms' special resources, seem to be no more nor less subject to these reservations than other goods or resources.

10.6 External Economies

Some authors, in particular, McKenzie [18], Arrow and Hahn [2], and Shafer and Sonnenschein [26, 27] have relaxed the assumption that producer and consumer actions are independent except for the balance between demand and supply in equilibrium. My early model made consumer preferences depend on the choices of other consumers, the activity levels, and prices. However, feasible sets for consumers or producers were kept independent. On the other hand, Arrow and Hahn, and Shafer and Sonnenschein, as well as others, have allowed feasibility effects as well. The early model for their analyses was a paper of Debreu [4] which preceded the existence theorem of Arrow and Debreu. However, in the use by Arrow and Debreu of Debreu's results no external economies were allowed.

My omission of feasibility effects from external economies was not an oversight. I did not succeed in formulating such effects in a satisfactory way. It is my view that this question remains unresolved. The difficulties can be illustrated by external economies between firms in an Arrow-Debreu model. It is usual to assume that a set Y_j exists for the jth firm that is closed and convex and includes every input-output combination that this firm could achieve under any conditions that can arise. Then there is a continuous correspondence $\mathscr{Y}_j$ for the jth firm that maps $Y = \prod_1^I Y_j$ into the collection of subsets of Y_j. The value of $\mathscr{Y}_j$ on an element y of Y is interpreted as the set of feasible outputs for the jth firm given that the ith firm, $i \neq j$, is producing y_i. Since y_i is chosen from Y_i there is no guarantee that y is feasible. The technologically feasible outputs are among the fixed points of the product correspondence $\mathscr{Y} = \prod_1^I \mathscr{Y}_j$ which maps Y into the collection of subsets of Y. Since $\mathscr{Y}_j$ is assumed to be convex valued, fixed points do exist. Outside the set of fixed points the points of Y cannot be realized as inputs and outputs even when resource supplies are adequate.

The competitive equilibria are a subset of the fixed points of $\mathscr{Y}$, since technological feasibility is a necessary condition for equilibrium. However, which fixed points of $\mathscr{Y}$ are equilibria will depend on, among other things, what alternative outputs are allowed to the firms, that is, on the precise content of $\mathscr{Y}_j$ for the jth firm. Given the price vector and the output vector y, a necessary condition for equilibrium is that $p \cdot y_j$ be a maximum over $\mathscr{Y}_j(y)$. But $\mathscr{Y}_j(y)$ has no empirical correlates except for the constraints imposed by the set of feasible points of $\mathscr{Y}$, that is, $\mathscr{Y}_j(y)$ contains y_j if y is a feasible point. Moreover, the set of fixed points of $\mathscr{Y}$ may not coincide with the set of technically feasible outputs of the economy, unless the $\mathscr{Y}_j$ can be designed so that they have their assumed properties without introducing new fixed points.

In these circumstances the maps $\mathscr{Y}_j(y)$ are artificial constructions except for the feasible set, that is, the set of fixed points of well defined $\mathscr{Y}_j$'s. What kinds of feasible sets would admit an appropriate set of $\mathscr{Y}_j$'s is unknown. Given that otherwise appropriate $\mathscr{Y}_j$'s exist, the equilibria may then depend on the choice of the correspondences. Since the papers in the literature do not address these problems it is not clear to what extent the subject has been advanced since 1955.

Appendix I

Let $\bar{y} = \alpha z$ for $z \in$ interior Y. Suppose $x \in \bar{X}$ and no matter how large α is chosen the number π is unbounded. Then $(\alpha(1 - \pi)/\pi)z + x \in Y$ for all large π. Let $w(\alpha, \pi) = (\alpha(1 - \pi)/\pi)z + x$. As $\pi \to \infty$, $w(\alpha, \pi) \to w(\alpha)$

$= -\alpha z + x$, which lies in Y since Y is closed. Also $w(\alpha)/\alpha = -z + (x/\alpha)$
$\in Y$, and, as $\alpha \to \infty$, $-z + (x/\alpha) \to -z$, which also lies in Y since Y is
closed. Thus z and $-z$ are in Y, and since z is interior to Y, $Y = R^n$ in
contradiction to Assumption (4). This shows that α exists for any particular $x \in \overline{X}$.

Suppose $w(\alpha, \pi) \notin Y$. Then $(\alpha(1 - \pi)/\pi)z + x' \notin Y$ will also hold for x'
near enough to x. In other words, α is effective for a sufficiently small
open neighborhood of x. Let $U(x)$ be such a neighborhood, relative to
$\overline{X}$, for $x \in \overline{X}$. Since $\overline{X}$ is compact, by the Auxiliary Assumption, there is
a finite set $\{x_i\}$, $i = 1, \ldots, N$, such that $\bigcup_{i=1}^{N} U(x_i) = \overline{X}$. Therefore, we
may choose $\alpha = \max \alpha_i$, where α_i is effective for x_i.

Appendix II

We must show that z may be chosen distinct from c. Let $C \subset R^n$ be a
closed convex set that does not contain 0. Define cone$(C) = \{\alpha x \mid x \in C,$
$\alpha \geq 0\}$, the cone spanned by C from the origin. Let $D = \{x \in C \mid \alpha x \notin C,$
for $0 \leq \alpha < 1\}$. D is the set of points of first contact with C of rays from
the origin. $D \subset C$ and D is contained in the boundary of C in cone(C),
perhaps properly. We have the following proposition:

Proposition   Let $x \in D$ and y be any other point of C. Then
$x - y \notin \text{cone}(C)$.

Suppose $x - y \in \text{cone}(C)$. Then there exists $\alpha > 0$ such that $\alpha(x - y) \in$
C. Since y also lies in C and C is convex, any convex combination of y
and $\alpha(x - y)$ must lie in C. In particular,

$$\frac{\alpha}{\alpha + 1} y + \frac{1}{\alpha + 1} [\alpha(x - y)] = \frac{\alpha}{\alpha + 1} x \in C.$$

Since $\alpha/(\alpha + 1) < 1$, this contradicts the assertion that $x \in D$.

The Proposition must be applied to the closed convex set F_1 and
the cone with vertex at $x_{I_1}^*$ spanned by F_1, denoted cone$(x_{I_1}^*, F_1)$.
Cone$(x_{I_1}^*, F_1) = \{y \mid y = \alpha x + (1 - \alpha)x_{I_1}^*\}, x \in F_1, \alpha \geq 0\}$. Assume that c is
a point of first contact of a ray from $x_{I_1}^*$ with F_1, that is, $c \in F_1$ and
$x_{I_1}^* + \alpha(c - x_{I_1}^*) \notin F_1$ for $0 \leq \alpha < 1$. By choosing $x_{I_1}^*$ to be the origin, we
see that the Proposition implies $x_{I_1}^* + c - b = x_{I_1}^* + w \notin \text{cone}(x_{I_1}^*, F_1)$. We
will show that this contradicts the choice of w to lie in cone$(F_1) =$
cone$(0, F_1)$.

Since $x_{I_1}^* + w \notin \text{cone}(x_{I_1}^*, F_1)$, $x_{I_1}^* + w \neq \alpha x + (1 - \alpha)x_{I_1}^*$ for $\alpha \geq 0$,
$x \in F_1$, or $(1/\alpha)w + x_{I_1}^* \notin F_1$ for any $\alpha \geq 0$. If $x_{I_1}^* = 0$ the contradiction fol-

lows from $w \in \bar{F}_1$. In any case, $y = (1/\alpha)w + x_{I_1}^* \in \text{cone}(F_1)$ for all $\alpha \geq 0$ since F_1 and thus $\text{cone}(F_1)$ are convex. However, $x_{I_1}^* \in \bar{F}_1 - F_1$ and $x_{I_1}^* \neq 0$ imply $\beta x_{I_1}^* \in F_1$ for some $\beta > 1$, and $w \in \text{cone}(F_1)$ implies $\gamma w \in F_1$ for some $\gamma > 0$. Thus $\delta \gamma w + (1 - \delta)\beta x_{I_1}^* \in F_1$ for all δ with $0 \leq \delta \leq 1$. Choose δ such that $(1 - \delta)\beta = 1$. Then $x \notin F_1$ is contradicted for the choice of $\alpha = 1/\delta\gamma$, so $x_{I_1}^* + w \in \text{cone}(x_{I_1}^*, F_1)$ must hold. This implies that c is not a point of first contact of the ray from $x_{I_1}^*$ with F_1. Since $c \in F_1$ and $x_{I_1}^* \notin F_1$, there must be α where $0 < \alpha < 1$ and $x_{I_1}^* + \alpha(c - x_{I_1}^*) \in F_1$. Let $\bar{\alpha}$ be the smallest value of α satisfying these conditions. Choose $z = \bar{\alpha}c + (1 - \bar{\alpha})x_{I_1}^*$. Then $z \neq c$, and $z \in$ boundary F_1 in $\bar{F}_1$, as required.

Note

1. This chapter is a revision of my Presidential Address to the Econometric Society delivered in Ottawa and Vienna in 1977. I have benefited on several occasions when this paper was presented. I would especially like to recall the assistance I received from William Vickery in Ottawa, from Birgit Grodal in Vienna, and from Wayne Shafer in Princeton. I am also grateful to Kenneth Arrow, Gerard Debreu, Charles Wilson, and Makoto Yano for useful comments toward a revised draft, and to Martin Feinberg for the proof of the proposition in Appendix II.

References

[1] Arrow, Kenneth J., and Gerard Debreu: "Existence of an Equilibrium for a Competitive Economy," *Econometrica*, 22(1954), 265–290.

[2] Arrow, Kenneth J., and Frank Hahn: *General Competitive Analysis*. San Francisco: Holden-Day, 1971.

[3] Bergstrom, Theodore C.: "How to Discard 'Free Disposability'—at No Cost," *Journal of Mathematical Economics*, 3(1976), 131–134.

[4] Debreu, Gerard: "A Social Equilibrium Existence Theorem," *Proceedings of the National Academy of Sciences*, 38(1952), 886–893.

[5] ———: "Market Equilibrium," *Proceedings of the National Academy of Sciences*, 42(1956), 876–878.

[6] ———: *Theory of Value*. New York: John Wiley & Sons, 1959.

[7] ———: "New Concepts and Techniques for Equilibrium Analysis," *International Economic Review*, 3(1962), 257–273.

[8] Gale, David: "The Law of Supply and Demand," *Mathematica Scandinavica*, 3(1955), 155–169.

[9] Gale, David, and Andreu Mas-Colell: "An Equilibrium Existence Theorem for a General Model without Ordered Preferences," *Journal of Mathematical Economics*, 2(1975), 9–15.

[10] Hart, Oliver D., and Harold W. Kuhn: "A Proof of Existence of Equilibrium without the Free Disposal Assumption," *Journal of Mathematical Economics*, 2(1975), 335–343.

[11] Hicks, John R.: *Value and Capital*. Oxford: Oxford University Press, 1939.

[12] Kakutani, Shizuo: "A Generalization of Brouwer's Fixed Point Theorem," *Duke Mathematical Journal*, 8(1941), 457–459.

[13] Koopmans, Tjalling C.: "Analysis of Production as an Efficient Combination of Activities," *Activity Analysis of Production and Allocation*, edited by T. C. Koopmans. New York: John Wiley & Sons, 1951.

[14] Kuhn, Harold: "On a Theorem of Wald," *Linear Inequalities and Related Systems*, edited by Harold Kuhn and A. W. Tucker. Princeton: Princeton University Press, 1956, pp. 265–273.

[15] Marshall, Alfred: *Principles of Economics*, 8th edition. London: Macmillan, 1920.

[16] Mas-Colell, Andreu: "An Equilibrium Existence Theorem without Complete or Transitive Preferences," *Journal of Mathematical Economics*, 1(1974), 237–246.

[17] McKenzie, Lionel W.: "On Equilibrium in Graham's Model of World Trade and Other Competitive Systems," *Econometrica*, 22(1954), 147–161.

[18] ———: "Competitive Equilibrium with Dependent Consumer Preferences," *Second Symposium on Linear Programming*. Washington: National Bureau of Standards and Department of the Air Force, 1955, pp. 277–294.

[19] ———: "On the Existence of General Equilibrium for a Competitive Market," *Econometrica*, 27(1959), 54–71. Reprinted in *Selected Readings in Economic Theory from Econometrica*, edited by Kenneth Arrow. Cambridge, Massachusetts: MIT Press, 1971, pp. 339–356.

[20] ———: "On the Existence of General Equilibrium: Some Corrections," *Econometrica*, 29(1961), 247–248.

[21] Moore, James: "The Existence of 'Compensated Equilibrium' and the Structure of the Pareto Efficiency Frontier," *International Economic Review*, 16(1975), 267–300.

[22] Nikaido, Hukukane: "On the Classical Multilateral Exchange Problem," *Metroeconomica*, 8(1956), 135–145.

[23] Scarf, Herbert: "The Core of An *N* Person Game," *Econometrica*, 35(1967), 50–69.

[24] Shafer, Wayne J.: "The Nontransitive Consumer," *Econometrica*, 42(1974), 913–919.

[25] ———: "Equilibrium in Economies without Ordered Preferences or Free Disposal," *Journal of Mathematical Economics*, 3(1976), 135–137.

[26] Shafer, Wayne J., and Hugo Sonnenschein: "Equilibrium in Abstract Economies without Ordered Preferences," *Journal of Mathematical Economics*, 2(1975), 345–348.

[27] ———: "Equilibrium with Externalities, Commodity Taxation, and Lump Sum Transfers," *International Economic Review*, 17(1976), 601–611.

[28] Sonnenschein, Hugo: "Demand Theory without Transitive Preferences, with Applications to the Theory of Competitive Equilibrium," in *Preference, Utility, and Demand*, edited by J. S. Chipman, L. Hurwicz, M. K. Richter, and H. F. Sonnenschein. New York: Harcourt Brace Jovanovich, 1971, pp. 215–223.

[29] Uzawa, Hirofumi: "Walras' Existence Theorem and Brouwer's Fixed Point Theorem," *Economic Studies Quarterly*, 13(1962), 59–62.

[30] von Neumann, John: "Über ein ökonomisches Gleichungssystem und eine Verallge-meinerung des Browerschen Fixpunktsatzes," *Ergebnisse eines Mathematischen Kollo-quiums*, 8(1937), 78–83. Translated in *Review of Economic Studies*, 13(1945), 1–9.

[31] Wald, Abraham: "Über die eindeutige positive Lösbarkeit der Neuen Productions-gleichungen," *Ergebnisse eines Mathematischen Kolloquiums*, 6(1935), 12–20.

[32] ———: "Über die Produktionsgleichungen der ökonomischen Wertlehre," *Ergeb-nisse eines Mathematischen Kolloquiums*, 7(1936), 1–6.

[33] ———: "Über einige Gleichungssysteme der Mathematischen Ökonomie," *Zeits-chrift für Nationalökonomie*, 7(1936), 637–670. Translated in *Econometrica*, 19(1951), 368–403.

[34] Walras, Leon: *Eléments d'Economie Politique Pure*. Paris: Pichon and Durand-Auzias, 1926. Translated as *Elements of Pure Economics* by Jaffé. London: Allen and Unwin, 1954.

11 The Existence of Competitive Equilibrium over an Infinite Horizon with Production and General Consumption Sets

John H. Boyd III and Lionel W. McKenzie

11.1 Introduction

Many theorems have been proved on the existence of competitive equilibrium with an infinite set of goods and a finite set of consumers since the path-breaking papers of Peleg and Yaari (1970) and Bewley (1972).[1] Many of these theorems also allow for production. However, nearly all suffer from a major defect. Their consumption possibility sets are required to equal the positive orthant. See Magill (1981), Aliprantis and Brown (1983), Jones (1984), Mas-Colell (1986), Yannelis and Zame (1986), Zame (1987), and many others. Such consumption sets have two major inadequacies. First, they do not allow trade in personal services, even when production is absent, and a fortiori do not allow for the use of labor services in production. Second, they do not allow for substitution between goods on the subsistence boundary of the possible consumption set.

Three major exceptions are Back (1988), Chichilnisky and Heal (forthcoming) and Stigum (1973). Stigum uses some complex implicit restrictions on the location of the trading set, and also requires that the tail of any vector in the trading set be replaceable by the tail of other suitable vectors in the trading set, while remaining in the trading set. Chichilnisky and Heal use preferences defined on the entire space. Their methods may also apply to more general cases when preferences can be extended to a neighborhood of the positive orthant, but this assumption, which is related to properness, is inappropriate in capital accumulation models. Back describes his consumption set as lying in the positive orthant. However, all that he really requires is that the consumption set have a finite lower bound. Then the net trading set will also have a finite lower bound. Following Arrow and Hahn (1971), add the negative components of the lower bound (with signs changed) to the corresponding components of the vectors in the consumption set, and also to the endowment. The net trading set is unchanged, but the consumption set now lies in the positive orthant. What must be avoided is the requirement that a lower bound lie in the consumption set, which is equivalent to assuming the consumption set *is* the positive orthant.

It was shown in McKenzie (1992) that this constraint on the consumption set could be avoided in a growing economy with consumption and production sets which are sums of periodwise consumption and production sets. This restrictive assumption is avoided in our paper by the use of more powerful topological arguments.

The need to consider economies with an infinite set of goods arises in the study of economies which do not have a definite termination date. It may be reasonable to suppose that an infinity of goods for delivery on one date belong to a compact space which can be adequately approximated by a finite subset of goods. However, if we wish to deal with an economy which has an indefinite or infinite horizon, this approximation is not available. Goods for delivery at different dates must be regarded as different goods. It was a major contribution of *Value and Capital* (Hicks 1939) to provide a full-scale analysis of an economy in which this fact is properly recognized. Then, if the horizon is infinite, the number of goods must be infinite, even when deliveries are scheduled at discrete intervals. The infinity of goods must be dealt with simultaneously since the market is analyzed as though all trades occur at the beginning of time. This is a limiting form of the futures economy of Hicks. When uncertainty is introduced in the manner of Debreu (1959) by also distinguishing goods by the states of the world in which they are delivered, the sets of possible future states in each period must be foreseen. It may be possible to do with only a finite number of states of the world in each period, but to give an infinite horizon a finite approximation is difficult unless an arbitrary truncation of time is used with goods in the terminal period valued in an arbitrary way.

Our method of attack is similar to that used by Peleg and Yaari (1970) for an exchange economy. However, unlike the generalizations of Aliprantis, Brown and Burkinshaw (1987), our results apply not only to the case of an economy with production, but also with trade in a variety of labor services. Their method of proof is based on a theorem of Scarf on the nonemptiness of the core. Scarf's theorem can be used to show that the equal treatment core of every replica economy is non-empty. Peleg and Yaari then show that any point in the intersection of these cores is an equilibrium. In contrast to Back (1988), this approach dispenses with an exclusion assumption, and has the advantage of proving a core equivalence property. An allocation is an equilibrium if and only if it is in the equal treatment core of every replica of the economy. Back uses the commodity space l^∞, as does Bewley (1972). This places an artificial restriction on consumer choices which does not follow from the budget constraint. We use the space s^n of sequences of n-vectors following Peleg and Yaari, where consumers choose freely within budget constraints. In this space, the Mackey topology which is imposed by Bewley and Back does not make sense. By modifying Peleg and Yaari's methods, we are able to avoid interiority or properness conditions, which are not appropriate in our infinite horizon setting.[2]

The proof of existence of equilibrium proceeds in several steps. We first show our economy has a core. Moreover, the core is compact. We then consider equal treatment allocations in the core of replica economies. Each of these is also nonempty and compact. These equal treatment cores are nested, so they have an intersection. The final step is to show that all allocations in the intersection are in fact equilibria. The prices are found by weakly separating the set of weakly preferred trades from zero. We first separate with prices in ba, and then modify these to separate with prices in l^1. This is our candidate equilibrium price vector. The last step of the proof is to show that the candidate price vector yields an equilibrium.

In the course of proving the existence of equilibrium we have shown that any allocation in the equal treatment core of every replica economy must be an equilibrium. Standard arguments show that the converse is true, yielding core equivalence.

In Section 11.2, we set up the equilibrium model. Section 11.3 shows that core allocations exist, and in Section 11.4 we show that the intersection of the cores of replica economies is nonempty. Section 11.5 then proves the main results of the paper. Any allocation that is in the equal treatment core of every replica is in fact an equilibrium. The existence of equilibria is an immediate corollary. In fact, an allocation is an equilibrium if and only if it is in the equal treatment core of every replica. Concluding remarks are in Section 11.6. Basic facts about the space ba of bounded finitely additive measures (or charges) are presented in the Appendix.

11.2   The Model

The commodity space s^n is the Cartesian product $\prod_{t=0}^{\infty} \mathbb{R}^n(t)$, endowed with the product topology were $\mathbb{R}^n(t)$ has the l^1 norm topology (Berge 1963, p. 78). If $z \in s^n$ then $z = \prod_{t=0}^{\infty} z_t$, and $z_t \in \mathbb{R}^n(t)$ represents quantities of goods in period t. We will use $z \geq w$ to mean $z_{it} \geq w_{it}$ for all goods i and times t. The notation $z > w$ means $z \geq w$ and there is a t with $z_{it} > w_{it}$ for all i, and $z \gg w$ means $z_{it} > w_{it}$ for all i and t.

There are a finite number of traders, $1, \ldots, H$. The set of net trades for the hth trader over the infinite horizon is given by the trading set $C^h \subset s^n$. We do not place any additional restrictions on the growth of conceivable consumption sequences, even though the production sequences may be bounded. In a decentralized economy the consumer does not take into account aggregate technical possibilities when choosing a consumption sequence, but rather looks at what is affordable. Any bound on growth of the optimal consumption path must come out of the budget constraint.

In our model any endowments of goods are included in the specification of the trading set. For $w^h \in C^h$, $w_{it}^h < 0$ means that the quantity—w_{it}^h of the ith good is provided by the hth consumer at time t and $w_{it}^h > 0$ means that the quantity w_{it}^h of the ith good is received by the hth consumer at time t. At time zero, the hth consumer will be able to provide any initial stocks of goods which he may possess, including produced goods. Without loss of generality, the consumer offers only labor services and other unproduced goods during later periods.

A binary relation Q is said to be *irreflexive* if zQz does not hold for any z. A relation is said to be *antisymmetric* if zQy implies not yQz, and it is *transitive* if xQy and yQz implies xQz. Note that a transitive, irreflexive relation is automatically antisymmetric. There is an irreflexive and transitive relation P^h of *strict preference* defined on C^h and a correspondence, also denoted by P^h, defined on C^h by $P^h(z) = \{w : w \in C^h$ and $wP^hz\}$.

The production set is denoted Y. Negative components represent inputs; positive components represent outputs. The inputs and outputs of the production sector include the capital stocks. These stocks do not appear in the consumer net trading sets C^h except at $t = 0$. In an economy with certainty, the ownership of capital stocks is inessential. Only the value of investment is significant for the consumer and the sequence of investment values over time is implicit in the pattern of consumption.

The economy $\mathscr{E}$ is given by the list $\{Y, C^1, \ldots, C^H, P^1, \ldots, P^H\}$. Let $P^h(w)$ denote the strictly preferred set to w. If $z \in P^h(w)$, the trade w is less desirable to the trader than the trade z. A *lower section* of the correspondence $f : X \to \{$subsets of $X\}$, at a point $y \in X$, is the set $\{z : y \in f(z)\}$. We define $C = \sum_{h=1}^H C^h$. Let $l^\infty = \{z \in s^n : z_t$ is bounded over $t\}$ and $l^1 = \{z \in s^n : \sum_{t=0}^\infty |z_t|$ is finite$\}$ where $|z_t|$ denotes the l^1 norm on $\mathbb{R}^n$, $|z_t| = \sum_{i=1}^n |z_{it}|$. Define the *preference relation* R^h on C^h by $x^h R^h y^h$ if and only if not $y^h P^h x^h$. We will say that x^h is *indifferent* with y^h, written $x^h I^h y^h$, if $y^h R^h x^h$ and $x^h R^h y^h$.

Recall that x is an *extreme point* of a convex set C if there do not exist distinct $x', x'' \in C$ and α, $0 < \alpha < 1$ with $x = \alpha x' + (1 - \alpha)x''$. We say x^h is *strongly individually rational* if $x^h P^h y^h$ for all $y^h \in C^h \cap Y$. If I is a subset of $\{1, \ldots, H\}$ define $x_I = \sum_{h \in I} x^h$. The economy is *strongly irreducible* if whenever I_1, I_2 is a nontrivial partition of $\{1, \ldots, H\}$, and $x_{I_1} + x_{I_2} \in Y$ with $x^h \in C^h$, there are $z_{I_1} + z_{I_2} \in Y$ with $z^h P^h x^h$ for $h \in I_1$ and for $h \in I_2$, $z^h \in C^h$ when x^h is strongly individually rational and not an extreme point of C^h, and $z^h \in \alpha C^h$ for some $\alpha > 0$ otherwise.

This differs from the standard definition of irreducibility, although it is in the same spirit. Unlike the standard definition, this definition requires in some cases that the I_2 consumers be able to improve the trades of the I_1 consumers by actual moves to other trades in the I_2 possible trading sets. This stronger form of irreducibility is needed to establish that allocations to replicas of a consumer in the core of a replicated economy are indifferent. When endowments are nonnegative and the trading sets are translates of the positive orthant, both irreducibility and strong irreducibility are implied by strict monotonicity.

For any $p \in ba_+$, let $p = p_c + p_f$ be the Yosida-Hewitt decomposition of p (see the Appendix). Define $y(\tau) = (y_1, \ldots, y_\tau, 0, \ldots)$. We can now state the assumptions.

Assumptions

1. Y is a closed convex cone with vertex at the origin that contains no straight lines.

2. For each $\bar{y} \in s^n$ the set $\{y \in Y : y \geq \bar{y}\}$ is bounded.

3. C^h is convex, closed, and bounded below by $\bar{z} \in l^\infty$.

4. For all h the correspondence P^h is convex valued and, relative to C^h, is open valued and has open lower sections. The preference relation P^h is irreflexive and transitive. The weakly preferred set $R^h(x)$ is the closure of $P^h(x)$ for all $x \in C^h$, unless $P^h(x) = \varnothing$.

5. Let $x \in C^h$. If $z > x$ then $z \in P^h(x)$.

6. The economy $\mathscr{E}$ is strongly irreducible.

7. For all h, there is $\bar{x}^h \in C^h - Y$ with $\bar{x}^h \leq 0$. Moreover, $\bar{x} = \sum_{h=1}^H \bar{x}^h$ $\ll 0$ and $\bar{x}_t = \bar{x}_s$ for all s and t. For any x^h, let $z^h \in R^h(x^h) - Y$ and $\delta > 0$. Then there is a τ_0 such that for each $\tau > \tau_0$, there is an $\alpha > 0$ with $(z_0^h + \delta e_0, z_1^h, \ldots, z_\tau^h, \alpha \bar{x}_{\tau+1}^h, \ldots) \in R^h(x^h) - Y$.

The technology exhibits constant returns to scale by Assumption 1. Of course, diminishing returns can be accommodated by introducing artificial entrepreneurial factors (McKenzie 1959). Assumption 2 is needed to establish compactness of the feasible set since s^n is not a Banach space and the usual argument using $Y \cap s_+^n = \{0\}$ does not work. However, the assumption "Given any t and $\delta > 0$ there is $\varepsilon > 0$ such that $|y_t^+| > \delta$ implies $|y_\tau^-| > \varepsilon$ for some $\tau < t$" is equivalent to Assumption 2. Here $y_{it}^+ = \max(y_{it}, 0)$, $y_{it}^- = \min(y_{it}, 0)$. Since closed and bounded subsets of s^n are compact, $\{y \in Y : y \geq \bar{y}\}$ is compact. This then implies that $Y \cap s_+^n = \{0\}$ since $Y \cap s_+^n$ is a compact cone. In Section 2.1 we show that Assumption 2 is satisfied in standard capital accumulation models, where the production set is the sum of periodwise production sets $\bar{Y}_t$. Assumption 2 also holds in "neo-Austrian" capital accumulation models (e.g., Hicks 1973 and Atsumi 1991) even when production cannot be truncated.

In an exchange economy, a lower bound b^h for the net trading set C^h has often been taken to be the negative of a vector of endowments held by the hth trader which lies in the consumption set. In a production economy where productive services are traded, the requirement that b^h lie in C^h would be very restrictive. Even in a trading economy it is not satisfactory since it implies that the subsistence level for consumers allows no substitution between goods. Also, if personal services are traded, and $b^h \in C^h$ (so $C^h = b^h + s_+^n$), labor services provided by the consumer must be measured in units of his labor time without distinguishing the type of labor performed. In our model the last part of Assumption 3 makes $b^h \in C^h$ unnecessary.

Our model allows for differentiated labor services. Consider a consumer who supplies two different types of labor, and consumes an all-purpose consumption good. This consumer has T units of potential labor time. The trading set at time t is $C_t = \{(c_t, l_{1t}, l_{2t}) : c_t \geq 0, T + l_{1t} + l_{2t} \geq 0, T + l_{1t} \geq 0, T + l_{2t} \geq 0\}$. Then $C = \prod_{t=0}^\infty C_t$ satisfies Assumption 3 with $\bar{z}_t = (0, -T, -T)$. Note that the consumer may become satiated in each type of labor when none is being supplied without violating

Assumption 5, provided that the all-purpose consumption good is always valuable. This also permits the use of entrepreneurial factors that do not affect the consumer's utility. This example is a prototype of the kind of trading set we are concerned with. Note that different marginal disutilities for the different types of labor would preclude using aggregate labor time (or leisure) as a good here. From an intertemporal viewpoint $b^h \in C^h$ implies that survival in period t is independent of consumption levels in earlier periods. This is also unsatisfactory.[3]

Assumption 4 will guarantee that preferences can be represented by a continuous utility function. Note that R^h inherits transitivity from P^h. Assumption 5 (periodwise monotonicity) is fairly straightforward. We have already discussed Assumption 6 (strong irreducibility).

The first part of Assumption 7 provides for a path of production and consumption for the economy as a whole in which all goods are in excess supply in every period. This may be thought of as a kind of Slater condition (see Uzawa 1958, p. 34). It is also a weakening of Bewley's (1972) Adequacy Assumption. Requiring $\bar{x}^h < 0$ for all h would be equivalent to the Adequacy Assumption. Also, take $w^h \in C^h$ and $y \in Y$ with $w^h - y = \bar{x}^h \leq 0$. By monotonicity, $w^h - \bar{x}^h \in C^h$. Thus $w^h - \bar{x}^h \in C^h \cap Y \neq \varnothing$, that is, survival is guaranteed for each trader.

The second part of Assumption 7 may seem a bit strange at first glance. It is important to understand Assumption 7 since it plays a key role. Among other things, the second part of Assumption 7 implies that for any consumer, we can replace the tail of his stream of set trades after production with 0 and still remain in $R^h(x^h) - Y$, provided inputs are increased in the first period since $R^h(x^h) + s_+^n \subset R^h(x^h)$ by Assumption 5.

Burke (1988) refers to such conditions as regularity assumptions, and provides examples showing that equilibrium fails to exist without some sort of regularity condition. In particular, his example 1 satisfies all of our assumptions except Assumption 7.

Let's first examine Assumption 7 in the context of an exchange economy $(Y = \{0\})$ where the trading sets are the positive orthant minus the endowment $(C^h = s_+^n - \omega^h$, with $\omega^h \geq 0)$. If $\sum \omega^h$ is bounded below by a constant program, as it would be under Bewley's Adequacy Assumption, we may choose $\bar{x}^h \geq -\omega^h$ to satisfy the first part of Assumption 7. But then the second part of Assumption 7 follows immediately for any $\alpha < 1$ from continuity of preferences in the product topology since the net trading vector with a tail from $\alpha\bar{x}^h$ lies in C^h for any τ.

Now consider models with production. Negative components of vectors in Y represent inputs, as do the positive components of vectors in $-Y$. Thus, Assumption 7 says that if the initial stocks held by a consumer are increased by a positive quantity of all goods, he can supply a uniform amount of all goods in all periods after a time τ, using the production possibilities, and still be as well off. When the trading set is a Cartesian product, $C^h = \prod_{t=0}^{\infty} C_t^h$, it is enough that the production sector be able to supply uniform net outputs of produced goods in late periods while still allowing each consumer to subsist and supply unproduced goods. Capital accumulation models will often obey this stronger condition, which is formalized below.

Assumption For all $y \in Y$ and $\delta > 0$ there is a $b^h \in C^h$ and τ_1 such that for each $\tau > \tau_1$, there is an $\alpha > 0$ with $^\tau y = (-\delta e_0 + y_0, y_1, \ldots, y_\tau, b_{\tau+1}^h - \alpha \bar{x}_{\tau+1}^h, \ldots) \in Y$.

The vector b^h may contain labor services. This assumption can be used to derive the second part of Assumption 7. Suppose $z^h = w^h - y \in R^h(x^h) - Y$ with $w^h \in R^h(x^h)$ and $y \in Y$. Let τ_1, b^h and $^\tau y$ be as in the assumption, and let $^\tau w^h = (\delta e_0 + w_0^h, w_1^h, \ldots, w_\tau^h, b_{\tau+1}^h, \ldots) \in R^h(x^h)$. These vectors are in the trading set and approach $w^h + (\delta e_0, 0, \ldots)$ as $\tau \to \infty$, which is preferred to w^h. The fact that preferred sets are open in C^h implies that there is τ_2 with $^\tau w^h \in R^h(x^h)$ for $\tau > \tau_2$. Now take $\tau \geq \tau_1$, τ_2 and subtract to obtain $^\tau w^h - {}^\tau y = (w_0^h - y_0 + 2\delta e_0, w_1^h - y_1, \ldots, w_\tau^h - y_\tau, \alpha \bar{x}_{\tau+1}^h, \ldots) \in R^h(x^h) - Y$. This implies the second part of Assumption 7.

The set of possible trades with production for the hth consumer is $C^h - Y$. The set of admissible price vectors will be s^n. Unlike the admissible price vectors in most models of the competitive economy, the price vectors in s^n are not all contained in the dual of the commodity space. The elements of the dual space $(s^n)^*$ have only a finite number of non-zero components. This means that the price of all goods must be zero at almost all times, which conflicts with monotonicity. Hence it is totally inappropriate to confine prices to $(s^n)^*$. For $p \in s^n$ the *budget set* of the hth trader is $B^h(p) = \{x : x \in C^h \text{ and } px \leq 0\}$. Bundles with value equal to ∞ are not contained in the budget set. Let $z(\tau) = (z_1, \ldots, z_\tau, 0, \ldots)$.

Competitive Equilibrium A competitive equilibrium for the economy $\mathcal{E} = \{Y, C^1, \ldots, C^H, P^1, \ldots, P^H\}$ is a list $\{p, y, x^1, \ldots, x^H\}$ with $p \in s^n$ which obeys:

1. $px^h \leq 0$ and $z \in P^h(x^h)$ implies $pz > 0$.

2. $y \in Y$, $py = 0$ and $\limsup_{\tau \to \infty} pz(\tau) \leq 0$ for any $z \in Y$.

3. $\sum_{h=1}^{H} x^h = y$.

The first condition is the usual demand condition. The second condition is the profit condition.[4] The lim sup handles cases where the limit may not exist. In these cases, such production paths cannot permanently increase profits over the equilibrium path. It should be recalled that all paths are infinite paths. If a path can be "terminated," this means that it has a zero tail. Then by condition 2, the "terminated" path cannot show a profit. The third condition is the balance condition. Our objective is to prove that an equilibrium exists.

11.2.1 Capital Accumulation Model

The production set is $Y = \sum_{t=1}^{\infty} \bar{Y}_t$ where $\bar{Y}_t \subset \{0\} \times \cdots \times \{0\} \times \mathbb{R}_-^n(t-1) \times \mathbb{R}_+^n(t) \times \{0\} \times \cdots$. The set $\bar{Y}_t$ represents the possibilities of producing goods belonging to the tth period with goods belonging to the $(t-1)^{st}$ period. Let Y_t be the projection of $\bar{Y}_t$ into the coordinate subspace $\mathbb{R}^n(t-1) \times \mathbb{R}^n(t)$. Then $y^t = (u_{t-1}, v_t) \in Y_t$ implies $u_{t-1} \leq 0$ and $v_t \geq 0$. This formulation of production insures that inputs precede outputs, and that production requires inputs. Notice that the firm's profit maximization condition can be written as $p_{t-1}u_{t-1} + p_t v_t = 0$ for $t \geq 1$, and $p_{t-1}u'_{t-1} + p_t v'_t \leq 0$ for all $t \geq 1$ for any $(u'_{t-1}, v'_t) \in Y_t$.

Growth Model The capital accumulation model obeys Assumptions 1 and 2 provided:

1. Y_t is a closed, convex cone with vertex at the origin.

2. $Y_t \subset \mathbb{R}_-^n \times \mathbb{R}_+^n$ with $Y_t \cap (\{0\} \times \mathbb{R}_+^n) = \{(0,0)\}$.

Proof That Y is a convex cone is clear. We next show Y contains no straight lines. If y is in Y, $y_0 = u_0 \leq 0$. Moreover, if $y_0 = 0$, $y = 0$ since outputs require inputs. As a result, $Y - s_+^n$ can contain no straight lines. To see this let $z, -z \in Y - s_+^n$. Then there are y; $y' \in Y$ with $z \leq y$ and $-z \leq y'$. But $0 \leq y + y' \in Y$, so $y + y' = 0$. Finally, $y_0 \leq 0$ and $-y_0 \leq 0$, so $y = 0$ and $y' = 0$. As $z, -z \leq 0$, $z = 0$. That establishes Assumption 1.

Showing that $\{y \in Y : y \geq \bar{y}\}$ is compact for every $\bar{y} \in \mathbb{R}^\infty$ requires several steps. We first show that bounded inputs at time $t - 1$ yield bounded outputs at time t. Suppose not. There is a sequence

$(u_{t-1}^s, v_t^s) \in Y_t$ and constant B with $|u_{t-1}^s| \le B$ and $|v_t^s| \to \infty$. Consider $(u_{t-1}^s, v_t^s)/|v_t^s| \in Y_t$. Since this is bounded, it has a convergent subsequence with limit $(0, v)$ and $|v| = 1$. But Y_t is closed, so $(0, v) \in Y_t$, which contradicts hypothesis (2).

The second step is to show that bounded outputs at time t imply that inputs at t are bounded. Again let $y_t = u_t + v_t$ with $\bar{y} \le y \in Y$. Since $u_t + v_t \ge \bar{y}_t$, so $\bar{y}_t - v_t \le u_t \le 0$. Thus bounded outputs at t imply bounded inputs at t.

Finally, inputs at time zero are bounded since $u_0 \in C$. By induction, both inputs and outputs are bounded at each time t.

Now let $y^s = u^s + v^s$ be a convergent sequence in Y with $y^s \ge \bar{y}$. Both u_t^s and v_t^s are bounded at each time. By passing to a subsequence, we can assume that both u^s and v^s converge to u and v. Since $(u_{t-1}^s, v_t^s) \in Y_t$ and Y_t is closed, $(u_{t-1}, v_t) \in Y_t$ also. Thus $y = u + v \in Y$. This shows $\{y \in Y : y \ge \bar{y}\}$ is closed for each $\bar{y}$. Since it is bounded, it is compact, establishing Assumption 2.[5]   Q.E.D.

Now consider a standard growth model with one produced good, using labor and the produced good as factors of production. Output per unit of labor input is given by a concave function f with $f' > 0$. The set Y is given by the production function F where $F(K, L) = Lf(K/L)$ for $K, L > 0$ and $F(K, L) = 0$ otherwise. Let $Y_t = \{(u_{1t}, u_{2t}, v_{1t}, v_{2t}) : 0 \le v_{1t} \le F(-u_{1t}, -u_{2t}), v_{2t} = 0\}$ where "1" indexes the produced good and "2" indexes labor. There is one consumer with initial endowment $k \ge 0$. The consumer can supply up to one unit of labor in each period. Thus $C_0 = \{(c, l) : c \ge -k, l \ge -1\}$ and $C_t = \{(c, l) : c \ge 0, l \ge -1\}$ for $t = 1, 2, \ldots$. For the sake of simplicity we assume that labor does not affect utility. The utility function is $u(w) = v(c_0 + k) + \sum_{t=1}^{\infty} \delta^t v(c_t)$ where v is a bounded continuous function with $0 < \delta < 1$. Recall that the c_t are quantities traded. The actual consumption is $c_0 + k$ for $t = 0$, due to the initial endowment of k, and c_t for $t = 1, \ldots$. Suppose there is a $0 \le \bar{k} \le k$ and $\beta > 1$ with $f(\bar{k}) \ge \beta \bar{k}$. Set $\bar{x}_t = ((1 - \beta)\bar{k}/\beta, (1 - \beta)/\beta)$ and $b = ((-\bar{k}, -1), (0, -1), \ldots) \in C$. This leaves $(\beta - 1)/\beta$ units of labor for the consumer to devote to leisure or household production. It is easy to see that $\bar{x}$ is in $C - Y$ since $F(\bar{k}/\beta, 1/\beta) = f(\bar{k})/\beta \ge \bar{k}$ allows $v_{1t} = \bar{k}$ and $u_{1t} = -\bar{k}/\beta$ yielding $y_{1t} = (\beta - 1)\bar{k}/\beta$. Let $y \in Y$. Suppose inputs at time zero are increased by δe_0. Maintain consumption levels at each time, while accumulating capital stocks u_{1t}. These will be higher (more negative) at each time period than on the original path. At any time, we may stop following y and devote this capital stock to maintaining steady output. When the capital stock is at least $\bar{k}$, we can follow $y_t' = b_t - \bar{x}_t = ((\beta - 1)\bar{k}/\beta, -1/\beta)$ henceforth. Then Assumption 7 will be satisfied.[6]

This example shows why some sort of joint condition on consumption and production is needed. The production sector alone cannot necessarily produce positive outputs of all goods after the first period. Inputs of labor or other nonproduced goods may be required. A joint condition on consumption and production is then needed to obtain positive output of all goods.

11.3   The Core Is Nonempty

By an *allocation* of net trades we mean a list $\tilde{x} = (x^1, \ldots, x^H)$ such that $x^h \in C^h$ for all h. A *feasible allocation* must also satisfy the condition $\sum_{h=1}^{H} x^h \in Y$. Then the set of feasible allocations for the economy is $F = \{(x^1, \ldots, x^H) : x^h \in C^h \text{ for all } h, \text{ and } \sum_{h=1}^{H} x^h \in Y\}$. Let us say that an allocation $\{z^h\}_{h=1}^{H}$ of net trades admits an *improving coalition* B if there is an allocation $\{w^h\}_{h \in B}$ over the members of B such that $\sum_{h \in B} w^h \in Y$ and $w^h \in P^h(z^h)$ for all $h \in B$. The *core* of the economy $\mathscr{E}$ is the set of feasible allocations which do not admit any improving coalitions.

Lemma 1   The set of feasible allocations is nonempty, compact and convex.

Proof   By Assumption 7, there is $\tilde{x} \in C - Y$ with $\tilde{x} \ll 0$. (Recall $\tilde{x} = \sum_{h=1}^{H} \tilde{x}^h$ and $C = \sum_{h=1}^{H} C^h$.) This implies that $0 \in C - Y$ by Assumption 5. Thus there are $x^h \in C^h$ with $\sum_{h=1}^{H} x^h \in Y$. Then $(x^1, \ldots, x^H) \in F$, so F is nonempty. The set F is convex and closed since Y and all the C^h are both convex and closed. By Tychonoff's Theorem (Berge 1963, p. 79), it is sufficient to prove F is bounded in each factor h.

We first note that $C \cap Y$ is bounded by Assumption 2 and the fact that C is bounded below by $H\bar{z}$. Let $\bar{w}$ be an upper bound for $C \cap Y$ and let $(x^1, \ldots, x^H) \in F$. Then $\bar{z} \le x^h \le \bar{w} - \sum_{j \neq h} x^j \le \bar{w} - (H-1)\bar{z}[l_1 C_1]$.   Q.E.D.

Let F^h be the projection of F into the hth consumer's net trading set C^h. The next proposition uses standard arguments to show that preference order can be represented by a continuous utility function on F^h.

Proposition 1   There exists a continuous function $u^h : F^h \to \mathbb{R}$ such that $x^h P^h z^h$ if and only if $u^h(x^h) > u^h(z^h)$.

Proof Since the preference correspondence is both open-valued and has open lower sections, and F^h is compact, we claim there are best (b) and worst (a) elements of F^h. Suppose there is not a worst element in F^h. For each $y \in F^h$ there is some $x \in F^h$ with $y \in P^h(x)$. It follows that $\{P^h(x) : x \in F^h\}$ is an open cover of F^h. By compactness, it has a finite subcover $\{P^h(x_n)\}_{n=1}^N$. Take a worst element x^* of $\{x_1, \ldots, x_N\}$. By transitivity and irreflexivity, x^* cannot be in any of the $P^h(x_n)$. This contradicts the fact that the $P^h(x_n)$ cover F. It follows that a worst element of F^h exists. A similar argument using open lower sections shows that a best element exists.

Since $R^h(x)$ is the closure of $P^h(x)$ whenever $P^h(x)$ is nonempty, $(1 - \theta)x + \theta b \in P^h(x)$ whenever $b \in P^h(x)$ and $0 < \theta \le 1$. Thus for $0 \le \theta < \theta' \le 1$, either $(1 - \theta')a + \theta'b \in P^h((1 - \theta)a + \theta b)$ or $(1 - \theta)a + \theta b$ is indifferent to b. Moreover, the set of such points indifferent to b is a closed interval $[\theta_0, 1]$. Consider $J = \{(1 - \theta)a + \theta b : 0 \le \theta \le \theta_0\}$ and define $u^h((1 - \theta)a + \theta b) = \theta$ on J. For arbitrary $x \in F^h$, consider $J \cap P^h(x)$ and $J \cap P_-^h(x)$ where $P_-^h(x) = \{y : xP^h y\}$ is the lower section of P^h at x. Both of these sets are open in J. Since J is connected, either one of these sets is empty, or there is a unique θ with x indifferent to $(1 - \theta)a + \theta b$. (There cannot be two values of θ since then, as we have already noted, the corresponding points would not be indifferent.) In the latter case, define $u^h(x) = \theta$. If $J \cap P_-^h(x)$ is empty, x must be indifferent to the worst point of F^h and we set $u^h(x) = 0$. If $J \cap P^h(x)$ is empty, x must be indifferent to the best point of F^h and we set $u^h(x) = \theta_0$.

For any $x \in F^h$, $\{y \in F^h : u^h(y) > u^h(x)\} = P^h(x)$ and $\{y \in F^h : u^h(y) < u^h(x)\} = P_-^h(x)$ by transitivity of P^h and R^h. Since both of these sets are open in F^h, the utility function is continuous.   Q.E.D.

Let u^h be a continuous utility function representing P^h on F^h. Let $U(\tilde{x})$ be the vector of utilities $(u^h(x^h))$ and $\tilde{F} = U(F)$. The set $\tilde{F}$ is the utility possibility set of the economy. Note $\tilde{F}$ is compact as the continuous image of a compact set, hence bounded. For any coalition S define $V(S) = \{\zeta \in \mathbb{R}^H : \zeta_h \le u^h(x^h)$ for all $h \in S$ with $x^h \in C^h$ and $\sum_{h \in S} x^h \in Y\}$. This is the set of utility vectors whose projection on the utility subspace of the coalition S lies in or below the utility possibility set of S. Note that $V(S)$ is closed, nonempty (from Assumption 7), comprehensive ($\zeta \in V(S)$ and $\xi \le \zeta$ implies $\xi \in V(S)$), and bounded above in $\mathbb{R}^S$.

Let $\mathscr{B}$ be a nonempty family of subsets of $\{1, \ldots, H\}$. Define $\mathscr{B}_h = \{S \in \mathscr{B} : h \in S\}$. A family $\mathscr{B}$ is *balanced* if there exist nonnegative weights w_S with $\sum_{S \in \mathcal{B}_h} w_S = 1$ for all h. A *V-allocation* is an element of $V(1, \ldots, H)$. A coalition S can *improve on* a V-allocation ζ if there is a $\xi \in V(S)$ with $\xi_h > \zeta_h$ for all $h \in S$. The *core* of V is the set of V-allocations that cannot be improved upon by any coalition. The following theorem is from Scarf (1967).

Theorem (Scarf) Suppose $\bigcap_{S \in \mathcal{B}} V(S) \subset V(1, \ldots, H)$ whenever $\mathcal{B}$ is a balanced family. Then V has a nonempty core.

Theorem 1 Under Assumptions 1 through 4 and 7 the economy $\mathcal{E}$ has a nonempty core.

Proof Let $\mathcal{B}$ be a balanced family of sets with balancing weights w_S and let $(\zeta_1, \ldots, \zeta_H) \in \bigcap_{S \in \mathcal{B}} V(S)$. For each coalition S there are $x_S^h \in C^h$ for $h \in S$ with $\sum_{h \in S} x_S^h = y^S \in Y$ and $u^h(x_S^h) \geq \zeta_h$ for all $h \in S$. Now consider $x^h = \sum_{S \in \mathcal{B}_h} w_S x_S^h$. Since x^h is a convex combination of the x_S^h, and each x_S^h obeys $u^h(x_S^h) \geq \zeta_h$, $u^h(x^h) \geq \zeta_h$ by quasi-concavity of preferences. Also $\sum_{h=1}^H x^h = \sum_{h=1}^H \sum_{S \in \mathcal{B}_h} w_S x_S^h = \sum_{S \in \mathcal{B}} w_S (\sum_{h \in S} x_S^h) = \sum_{S \in \mathcal{B}} w_S y^S \in Y$. Thus $(\zeta_1, \ldots, \zeta_H)$ is feasible for the entire economy due to the feasibility of $(x^1, \ldots, x^H)$. Therefore $(\zeta_1, \ldots, \zeta_H) \in V(1, \ldots, H)$. Scarf's theorem now shows the core of V is nonempty.

Now let $\tilde{\zeta} = (\zeta^1, \ldots, \zeta^H)$ be in the core of V and take $\tilde{x} \in F$ with $U(\tilde{x}) \geq \tilde{\zeta}$. It is clear that $\tilde{x}$ must be in the core of $\mathcal{E}$. Therefore the core of $\mathcal{E}$ is nonempty.

11.4 Edgeworth Equilibria

We now replicate the economy $\mathcal{E}$. In the rth replica $\mathcal{E}_r$, there are r identical copies of each trader in $\mathcal{E}$. Each copy has the same trading set and preference correspondence as the original trader. We will use the idea of the equal treatment core. The *equal treatment core* K_r is the set of allocations in the core of the replicated economy $\mathcal{E}_r$ such that each trader in $\mathcal{E}_r$ who is a replica of a given trader in $\mathcal{E}$ undertakes the same net trade. Then an allocation in K_r may be represented by $\{x^h\}_r$, where $\{x^h\}$ is the allocation of net trades to the original traders and r is the number of replications. Let K_1 be the core of the economy $\mathcal{E}_1 = \mathcal{E}$. We must first show that the equal treatment core is not empty for any r.

Let $\{x^{hk}\}_r$ represent an arbitrary allocation in the rth replica economy where the kth replica of the hth consumer in $\mathcal{E}$ undertakes the trade x^{hk}.

Lemma 2 If $\{x^{hk}\}_r$, $h = 1, \ldots, H$, and $k = 1, \ldots, r$, is an allocation in the core of $\mathcal{E}_r$, then, for h given, $x^{hj} I^h x^{hk}$ holds for all j and k.

Proof Let the allocation $\{x^{hk}\}$ where $h = 1, \ldots, H$ and $k = 1, \ldots, r$ lie in the core of the economy $\mathscr{E}_r$. Suppose $x^{hj}I^hx^{hk}$ does not hold for some h, j, k. From convexity of $P^h(x)$, it follows that $R^h(x)$ is convex as the closure of $P^h(x)$. Consider a replica of original consumer h with index $hj(h)$ that satisfies $x^{hk}R^hx^{hj(h)}$ for all $k = 1, \ldots, r$. That is, $hj(h)$ has an allocation that is no better, and perhaps poorer, than the allocation of any other replica of h. Consider the coalition $B = \{1j(1), \ldots, Hj(H)\}$ of worst-off replicas, and give $hj(h)$ the net trade $x^h = (1/r)\sum_{k=1}^r x^{hk}$.

For each h it follows that $x^hR^hx^{hj(h)}$ by convexity of $R^h(x)$, and, if $x^{ik}P^hx^{ij(i)}$ for some i, k, then $x^iP^ix^{ij(i)}$. Now $\sum_{h=1}^H x^h = (1/r)\sum_{k=1}^r \sum_{h=1}^H x^{hk} \in Y$ since $\{x^{hk}\}$ is feasible and Y is a cone. Thus $\{x^h\}$ is a feasible allocation. Strong irreducibility and convexity allow us to spread the gain received by $ij(i)$ to all $hj(h)$. Let $I_1 = \{h : h \neq i\}$ and $I_2 = \{i\}$. This yields a feasible allocation $\{z^h\}$ with $z^hP^hx^h$ for $h \in I_1$ since x^i is not an extreme point of C^i, and is clearly strongly individually rational. Take the convex combination $\{\lambda x^h + (1 - \lambda)z^h\}$ for $0 \leq \lambda \leq 1$. This is a feasible allocation, is preferred by all $h \in I_1$ to $\{x^h\}$, and, for λ sufficiently close to 1, is also preferred by i. It follows that $x^hP^hx^{hj(h)}$ for all $hj(h) \in B$. Thus B is an improving coalition, and $\{x^{hk}\}$ cannot be in the core. This contradiction shows $x^{hj}I^hx^{hk}$ for all h, j, k. $\qquad$ Q.E.D.

Lemma 3 The equal treatment core K_r of $\mathscr{E}_r$ is nonempty if the core of $\mathscr{E}_r$ is nonempty.

Proof By Lemma 2, for any core allocation, the allocations received by the replicas of a given h in the original economy are indifferent. Then by the convex valuedness of the relation R^h, the equal treatment allocation in which each replica of h receives $x^h = (1/r)\sum_{k=1}^r x^{hk}$, satisfies $x^hR^hx^{hk}$ for all h, k. Since there is no improving coalition for the allocation $\{x^{hk}\}$, there is certainly not one for $\{x^h\}_r$. Thus $\{x^h\}_r$ is in the core of $\mathscr{E}_r$. $\qquad$ Q.E.D.

Since the core of $\mathscr{E}_r$ is nonempty by Theorem 1, $K_r \neq \varnothing$ is an immediate corollary of Lemma 3.

Corollary $K_r \neq \varnothing$ for any $r \geq 1$.

Our immediate objective is to show there is a common element in all the K_r. Let $K = \bigcap_{r=1}^\infty K_r$. That is, $\{x^h\} \in K$ if $\{x^h\}_r \in K_r$ for all r. Any allocation in K is called an *Edgeworth equilibrium* (Aliprantis, Brown and Burkinshaw 1987).

Theorem 2 K is nonempty.

Proof   Fix r. We first show K_r is closed. Since $K_r \subset F$ and F is compact, this will imply K_r is compact. Let $\{x^{h,s}\}_r \in K_r$, $s = 1, \ldots$, be a sequence of allocations in K_r which converge to a limit $\{x^h\}_r$. Suppose $\{x^h\}_r$ is not in K_r. Let w^{hi} be a net trade for the ith copy of the hth original trader. There is an improving coalition B such that $w^{hi} \in P^h(x^h)$ for $hi \in B$ and $\sum_{hi \in B} w^{hi} \in Y$. By the fact that $P^h(x^h)$ has open lower sections, $w^{hi} \in P^h(x^{h,s})$ will hold when s is large. This implies that B is improving for $\{x^{h,s}\}_r$ for large s, and thus $\{x^{h,s}\}_r$ is not in K_r for large s. Because this contradicts the hypothesis, $\{x^h\}_r$ must be in K_r, which is therefore closed and compact.

It is clear that the K_r form a nested sequence of nonempty compact sets. They have a nonempty intersection K by the finite intersection property.   Q.E.D.

11.5   The Existence of Competitive Equilibrium

To prove the existence of equilibrium we will show that $(x^1, \ldots, x^H) \in K$ implies that there are p and y such that $(p, y, x^1, \ldots, x^H)$ is a competitive equilibrium. Let G be the convex hull of $\bigcup_{h=1}^{H} R^h(x^h)$. The key is to separate $G - Y$ from zero. A vector that performs this separation will be our equilibrium price vector.

The proof proceeds via a series of lemmas. We first show G is closed, hence $G - Y$ is closed. The next step is to show $G - Y$ does not intersect the negative orthant. We then construct a vector $\bar{c}$ which will be used to normalize prices. This allows us to define ε-price sets in ba which approximately separate $(G - Y) \cap l^\infty$ from 0. Lemma 6 shows these sets are nonempty. We use a separation theorem in s^n to find a price vector in $(s^n)^*$ which lies in the ε-price set.

We then show that the ε-price sets form a decreasing sequence of nonempty compact sets, and so have a nonempty intersection. We take an arbitrary vector in that intersection (which does *not* lie in $(s^n)^*$) and use the Yosida-Hewitt theorem to throw away any purely finitely additive part which may be present, leaving us with an l^1 price vector p^*. The normalization by $\bar{c}$ insures that p^* is nonzero.

The last lemma shows that p^* actually separates $G - Y$ from 0, not just $(G - Y) \cap l^\infty$. At this point we have a quasi-equilibrium. Finally, the point $\bar{x}$ together with strong irreducibility guarantees that the cheaper point condition is satisfied, and that the quasi-equilibrium is an equilibrium.

We start by showing G is closed. The lower bound on consumption plays an important role here.

Lemma 4 G is closed in s^n.

Proof   By Assumption 3, each C^h is bounded below by $\bar{z}$, and therefore G is bounded below by $\bar{z}$. Suppose $z^s \in G$ and $z^s \to z$. We must show that $z \in G$. Let $z^s = \sum_{h=1}^{H} w^{hs} = \sum_{h=1}^{H} \alpha_{hs} z^{hs}$ where $\alpha_{hs} \geq 0$, $\sum_{h=1}^{H} \alpha_{hs} = 1$ and $z^{hs} \in C^h$.

The α_{hs} are contained in the unit interval, so we may assume that they converge to α_h, by passing to a subsequence if necessary. If any of the w^{hs} were unbounded, the fact that each w^{hs} is bounded below would imply z^s is also unbounded, contradicting the convergence of z^s. Therefore each of the w^{hs} is bounded. Thus we can choose a further subsequence where each of the w^{hs} converge, $w^{hs} \to w^h$.

Let $I = \{h : \alpha_h > 0\}$. For $h \in I$, $w^{hs}/\alpha_{hs} = z^{hs} \to w^h/\alpha_h \in C^h$. For $h \notin I$, $\alpha_{hs}\bar{z} \leq w^{hs}$ where $\bar{z}$ is the lower bound on C^h from Assumption 3. Taking the limit shows $0 \leq w^h$. Now consider $w^h/\alpha_h + \sum_{i \notin I} w^i$, which is in $R(x^h)$ by periodwise monotonicity. Moreover, $\sum_{h \in I} \alpha_h(w^h/\alpha_h + \sum_{i \notin I} w^i) = \sum_{h=1}^{H} w^h = z$. Therefore $z \in G$.   Q.E.D.

We will need the following theorem adapted from Choquet (1962).

Theorem (Choquet)   If $Z \subset s^n$ is convex, closed in the product topology and contains no straight lines, then for any two closed subsets X, Y of Z, the sum $X + Y$ is closed.

Corollary $G - Y$ is closed in s^n.

Proof   Recall $G - Y \subset \bar{z} + s^n_+ - Y$. Both $G - \bar{z}$ and $-Y$ are closed and contained in $s^n_+ - Y$. Now suppose $z, -z \in s^n_+ - Y$, so there are $y, y' \in Y$ with $z \geq -y$, $-z \geq -y'$. Thus $y + y' \geq 0$. Since Y is a cone, $\lambda(y + y') \in Y$ for every $\lambda \geq 0$. As $\{y \in Y : y \geq 0\}$ is compact, $y + y' = 0$. But then $y = -y'$. Since Y contains no straight lines (Assumption 1), $y = -y' = 0$ and so $z = 0$ too. It follows that $s^n_+ - Y$ contains no straight lines. Thus we need only show $s^n_+ - Y$ is closed and apply Choquet's theorem.

Let $z^n \to z$ with $z^n \in Y - s^n_+$. Then there are $y^n \in Y$ with $z^n \leq y^n$. Since z^n converges, the y^n are bounded below. By Assumption 2, they have a convergent subsequence with limit $y \in Y$. Since $z^n \leq y^n$, $z \leq y$ and $z \in Y - s^n_+$. Thus $Y - s^n_+$ is closed.   Q.E.D.

Lemma 5   If $K \neq \varnothing$ then there is no $z \in G$ and $y \in Y$ such that $z - y < 0$ (i.e., $z - y \leq 0$ and $z_t - y_t < 0$ for some t).

Proof Take $\tilde{x} \in K$. Let $P(\tilde{x})$ be the convex hull of the $P^h(x^h)$. In light of the periodwise monotonicity assumption for preferences, it is sufficient to prove that there is no $z \in P(\tilde{x})$ and $y \in Y$ such that $z - y = 0$. In other words, it is sufficient to show that $Y \cap P(\tilde{x}) = \varnothing$.

Suppose not. There is a set of consumers I and weights α_i such that $\sum_{i \in I} \alpha_i z^i = y \in Y$, $\alpha_i > 0$, $\sum_{i \in I} \alpha_i = 1$, and $z^i \in P^i(x^i)$. An equivalent condition for z^i is that $\sum_{i \in I} \alpha_i(z^i - y) = 0$. For any positive integer k, let a_i^k be the smallest integer greater than or equal to $k\alpha_i$. For each $i \in I$, there is $y^i \in C^i \cap Y$ as a consequence of the first part of Assumption 7. Let $w_k^i = (k\alpha_i/a_i^k)(z^i - y^i) + y^i.$[7] As w_k^i is a convex combination of z^i and y^i, it lies in C^i. Moreover, $w_k^i \to z^i$ as $k \to \infty$. Since the preferred sets are relatively open (Assumption 4), we have $w_k^i \in P^i(x^i)$ for large k, which we now fix.

Also

$$\sum_{i \in I} a_i^k w_k^i = \sum_{i \in I} (k\alpha_i z^i - k\alpha_i y^i + a_i^k y^i) = ky + \sum_{i \in I} (a_i^k - k\alpha_i)y^i.$$

As $0 \leq a_i^k - k\alpha_i \leq 1$, $\sum_{i \in I} a_i^k w_k^i \in Y$. Thus the coalition of a_i^k consumers of type i for $i \in I$ can improve on $\tilde{x}$. The improving coalition can be formed if the original economy has been replicated $\max_i\{a_i^k\}$ times. Therefore $\tilde{x} \notin K$ which contradicts the hypothesis. Hence $Y \cap P(\tilde{x}) = \varnothing$. In other words, $\{x^h\}_r$ in the core for all r implies that the production set Y intersected with the convex hull of the preferred trades of the original consumers, $P^h(x^h)$, is empty.   Q.E.D.

Choose α and τ such that $d^h = (x_0^h + e_0, x_1^h, \ldots, x_\tau^h, \alpha \tilde{x}_{\tau+1}^h, \ldots) \in R^h(x^h) - Y$ for all h by Assumption 7. Let $\bar{d}^h = d^h + (2e_0, 0, \ldots)$. By the definition of d^h and monotonicity, $\bar{d}^h \in l^\infty \cap (G - Y)$, as is $\bar{c}^h = \bar{d}^h - \alpha \tilde{x}^h \geq \bar{d}^h$. Note that $\bar{c}_t^h = 0$ for $t = \tau + 1, \ldots$. Let $\bar{c} = (1/H) \sum_{h=1}^H \bar{c}^h = -\alpha \tilde{x}/H + (1/H) \sum_{h=1}^H \bar{d}^h = -\alpha \tilde{x}/H + \bar{d}$. For $0 < \varepsilon < 1$ we define the price set $S(\varepsilon) = \{p \in ba_+ : p\bar{c} = 1 \text{ and } pw \geq -\varepsilon \text{ for all } w \in (G - Y) \cap l^\infty\}$.

We take an indirect approach, using price vectors in ba. In contrast, Peleg and Yaari use price sets in s_+^n. We could try to define $S(\varepsilon)$ analogously in s_+^n, with $pw \geq -\varepsilon$ for all $w \in G - Y$. However, Peleg and Yaari rely on the fact that a lower bound of the consumption set (or the set of possible net trades) is in the consumption set. This allows them to show their price sets are closed in s_+^n, when boundedness yields compactness. In our case, no lower bound may be in the set of possible net trades. We follow a different route and settle on a price vector first. Our $S(\varepsilon)$ will be compact and have the finite intersection property. We can then take a vector in the intersection of the $S(\varepsilon)$, which may not be admissible. However, this vector can be modified to obtain a price vector in l^1, which will prove to be admissible. The next lemma shows that $S(\varepsilon)$ contains a finitely nonzero vector.

Lemma 6 For any ε, $0 < \varepsilon < 1$, there is $p \in (s^n)^*$ such that $p \in S(\varepsilon)$ with $p \geq 0$ and $|p_0| > 0$. Moreover, whenever $p \in S(\varepsilon)$, $pz \leq 0$ for all $z \in Y \cap l^\infty$.

Proof For $\varepsilon > 0$ let $a(\varepsilon) = (-\varepsilon e_0, 0, 0, \ldots)$ where $e_0 = (1, \ldots, 1)$. By Lemma 5, $a(\varepsilon) \notin G - Y$. By the Corollary to Lemma 4, $G - Y$ is closed in the product topology. Also, $\{a(\varepsilon)\}$ is trivially compact. By a separation theorem (Berge 1963, p. 251) there is a continuous linear functional $f \in (s^n)^*$ with $f \neq 0$ such that $f(z) > f(a(\varepsilon)) + \delta$ for any $z \in G - Y$ and some $\delta > 0$.

Any such f may be represented by a vector $p \in s^n$ with $p \neq 0$ but $p_t = 0$ for all but finitely many t. Thus

$$f(z) = pz = \sum_{t=0}^{\infty} p_t z_t \geq -\varepsilon p_0 \cdot e_0 + \delta,$$

for any $z \in G - Y$ and some $\delta > 0$. Periodwise monotonicity and the separation condition imply that $p \geq 0$, so $p_0 \cdot e_0 = |p_0|$ where $|\cdot|$ is the l^1 norm on $\mathbb{R}^n$. Thus we have for some $p \geq 0$, $p \neq 0$,

$$pz > -\varepsilon |p_0| \text{ for all } z \in G - Y. \tag{1}$$

Now $x^h \in R^h(x^h)$ for all h and $\sum_{h=1}^{H} x^h = y$ for some $y \in Y$ implies that $0 \in G - Y$. Setting $z = 0$ in (1) shows $|p_0| > 0$.

Since $d^h \in G - Y$, we have $pd^h > -\varepsilon|p_0|$ by equation (1). Now $p\bar{c}^h = 2|p_0| + pd^h - \alpha p\bar{x}^h \geq (2 - \varepsilon)|p_0|$ by equation (1). Thus $p\bar{c}^h > |p_0|$ for $0 < \varepsilon < 1$ for all h. This implies $p\bar{c} > |p_0|$ for $0 < \varepsilon < 1$. Define $\hat{p} = p/p\bar{c}$. Consider $z \in G - Y$. If $\hat{p}z \geq 0$, then $\hat{p}z \geq -\varepsilon$. On the other hand, if $\hat{p}z < 0$, $\hat{p}z > pz/|p_0| \geq -\varepsilon$. Thus $\hat{p} \in S(\varepsilon)$ for $0 < \varepsilon < 1$. This is the desired vector in $S(\varepsilon)$.

Now let $p \in S(\varepsilon)$. Since $Y = Y + Y$ and $0 \in G - Y$, it follows that $-Y \cap l^\infty \subset (G - Y) \cap l^\infty$. Therefore $pz < \varepsilon$ for all $z \in Y \cap l^\infty$ by the definition of $S(\varepsilon)$. Since $\alpha z \in Y$ for any $\alpha > 0$, it follows that $pz \leq 0$ for all $z \in Y \cap l^\infty$.   Q.E.D.

Recall that, for two topological vector spaces E and F, $\sigma(E, F)$ denotes the weakest topology on E such that the map $p \mapsto px$ is continuous on

E for each $x \in F$. When E is the dual of a Banach space F, $\sigma(E, F)$ is referred to as the *weak** topology.

Lemma 7 The intersection of the price sets, $S = \bigcap_{0 < \varepsilon < 1} S(\varepsilon)$ is nonempty. Moreover, $\bar{p} \in S$ implies $\bar{p}z \geq 0$ for all $z \in (G - Y) \cap l^\infty$.

Proof Lemma 6 implies $S(\varepsilon)$ is nonempty. Furthermore, $S(\varepsilon)$ is $\sigma(ba, l^\infty)$-closed since the inner product is $\sigma(ba, l^\infty)$-continuous, and the inequalities that define $S(\varepsilon)$ are weak inequalities.

Now let p be an arbitrary element of $S(\varepsilon)$. Consider the point $\bar{d} = \bar{c} + \alpha \bar{x}/H$, which is in $(G - Y) \cap l^\infty$ by construction. Thus $p\bar{c} + \alpha p\bar{x}/H \geq -\varepsilon$, or

$$-p\bar{x} \leq H(1 + \varepsilon)/\alpha. \tag{2}$$

Since $p \geq 0$, and $\bar{x}$ is constant and strictly negative, $S(\varepsilon)$ is bounded by (2). By Alaoglu's theorem (see the Appendix), weak* closed and bounded sets are weak* compact, so $S(\varepsilon)$ is compact.

Finally, the $S(\varepsilon)$ have a nonempty intersection by the finite intersection property. The last statement of the lemma is immediate.   Q.E.D.

Let $\bar{p} \in S$. The Yosida-Hewitt theorem (see the Appendix) allows us to decompose $\bar{p}$ into the sum of an l^1-vector p^* and a pure charge p_f. Since $\bar{c}$ is finitely nonzero, we know $p_f \bar{c} = 0$ and $p^* \bar{c} = \bar{p}\bar{c} = 1$. Thus p^* is nonzero. The next step is to show that p^* separates 0 from $G - Y$, not just from $(G - Y) \cap l^\infty$, in a sense appropriate for our argument.

Lemma 8 The vector p^* satisfies $\lim_{\tau \to \infty} p^* w(\tau) \geq 0$ for all $w \in G$ and $\limsup_{\tau \to \infty} p^* y(\tau) \leq 0$ for all $y \in Y$.

Proof Let $z = w - y$ with $w \in G$ and $y \in Y$. Define $w_{it}^- = 0$ when $w_{it} \geq 0$ and $w_{it}^- = w_{it}$ for $w_{it} < 0$. For $w \in C^h$, $\bar{z}^- \leq w^-$, hence $w^- \in l^\infty$. Now $p^* w = p^* (w - w^-) + p^* w^-$. The first term is either finite or $+\infty$ while the second term is finite. Thus $p^* w$ is either finite or $+\infty$.

Take $z \in G - Y$. Let $\varepsilon > 0$. Write $z = \sum_{h=1}^H \alpha_h z^h$ with $z^h \in R^h(x^h) - Y$. For τ large, $\hat{z}^h(\tau) = (\varepsilon e_0 + z_0^h, z_1^h, \ldots, z_\tau^h, 0, \ldots) \in R^h(x^h) - Y$ by Assumption 7 and monotonicity. Thus $\hat{z}(\tau) = \sum_{h=1}^H \alpha_h \hat{z}^h(\tau) \in (G - Y) \cap l^\infty$. Apply $\bar{p} \in S$ to see $\varepsilon |p_0^*| + \sum_{h=1}^H \alpha_h p^* z^h(\tau) = \bar{p}\hat{z}(\tau) \geq 0$ for τ large. Letting $\tau \to \infty$ we find $\varepsilon |p_0^*| + \liminf_{\tau \to \infty} p^* z(\tau) \geq 0$. Since ε was arbitrary, $\liminf_{\tau \to \infty} p^* z(\tau) \geq 0$. Finally, since $-Y \subset G - Y$, this implies $\liminf_{\tau \to \infty} p^* (-y(\tau)) \geq 0$, or equivalently $\limsup_{\tau \to \infty} p^* y(\tau) \leq 0$ for any $y \in Y$.   Q.E.D.

We claim that $(p^*, y, x^1, \ldots, x^H)$, where $y = \sum_{h=1}^{H} x^h$, is a competitive equilibrium for $\mathscr{E}$. Since C^h is bounded below by $\bar{z}$, $p^* x^h$ either converges or is $+\infty$. Either way, $p^* x^h \geq 0$ for all h since $x^h \in G \subset G - Y$. But then $0 \leq \sum_{h=1}^{H} p^* x^h = p^* y \leq 0$ by Lemma 8. Thus $p^* x^h = 0$ for all h and $p^* y = 0$.

To complete the proof that Condition 1 holds we must show that $w^h \in P^h(x^h)$ implies $w^h \notin B^h(p^*) = \{z^h \in C^h : p^* z^h \leq 0\}$. Any point that is preferred by h to x^h must lie outside the budget set. A final result is the following.

Proposition 2 If there is a $w^h \in C^h$ such that $pw^h < 0$ and $pz^h \geq 0$ for all $z^h \in P^h(x^h)$, then $pz^h > 0$ for all $z^h \in P^h(x^h)$.

Proof Suppose $z^h \in P^h(x^h)$ and $pz^h = 0$. Since $P^h(x^h)$ is open in C^h by Assumption 4, there is a point $y^h = \alpha w^h + (1 - \alpha) z^h$ such that $y^h \in P^h(x^h)$ and $py^h < 0$. This contradicts the hypothesis. Therefore, such a z^h cannot exist.   Q.E.D.

Theorem 3 Under Assumptions 1 through 7 the economy $\mathscr{E}$ has a competitive equilibrium with prices in l^1.

Proof From Proposition 2 we see that Condition 1 will be completed if it can be proved that every consumer has a point w^h in the trading set such that $p^* w^h < 0$. Consider $\bar{x}^h \in C^h - Y$. Then $\bar{x}^h = w^h - y$ for some $w^h \in C^h$ and $y \in Y$. Then $p^* w^h = p^* \bar{x}^h + p^* y \leq p^* \bar{x}^h$. Note that $p^* w^h$ is well defined since $w^h \in C^h$, and $p^* \bar{x}^h$ is well defined since $\bar{x}_t^h$ is constant over t. Thus $p^* y$ is also well defined as $\lim_{\tau \to \infty} p^* y(\tau)$. Since $\bar{x} = \sum_{h=1}^{H} \bar{x}^h < 0$, at least one consumer has $p^* \bar{x}^h < 0$ and hence $p^* w^h < 0$.

Let I_1 be the set of indices h such that there is a $z^h \in C^h$ with $p^* z^h < 0$. Let I_2 be the complementary set of indices. We have just shown that I_1 is nonempty. Suppose that I_2 is nonempty. Use strong irreducibility to obtain $\alpha^h > 0$ and z^h with $z^h \in \alpha^h C^h$ for $h \in I_2$ and $z^h \in P^h(x^h)$ for $h \in I_1$ such that $y' = z_{I_1} + z_{I_2} \in Y$. Taking the inner product of both sides with p^* gives

$$p^* y' = p^* z_{I_1} + p^* z_{I_2}. \tag{3}$$

Also $p^* z_{I_1} > 0$ by Proposition 2 since $z^h \in P^h(x^h)$ for all $h \in I_1$. Now consider the $h \in I_2$. The fact that $z^h \in \alpha^h C^h$ for some $\alpha^h > 0$ yields $p^* z^h \geq 0$ by the definition of I_2. This means the right-hand side of (3) is strictly positive. But $p^* y' \leq 0$ by Lemma 6. This contradiction implies that I_2 is empty. In other words, strong irreducibility of the economy implies that each trading set has points with negative value if any trading set has a point with negative value. Then by Proposition 2, $z^h \in P^h(x^h)$ implies $p^* z^h > 0$ for all h. This establishes the second part of Condition 1 for competitive equilibrium.

Condition 2 is implied by $p^* y = 0$ and Lemma 8, and condition 3 follows from the definition of a feasible trade. Therefore $(p^*, y, x^1, \ldots, x^H)$, where $y = \sum_{h=1}^{H} x^h$, is a competitive equilibrium of $\mathscr{E}$.   Q.E.D.

In fact, we have shown that any Edgeworth equilibrium is a competitive equilibrium. It follows from standard arguments that any competitive equilibrium is an Edgeworth equilibrium.

Corollary   Under Assumptions 1 through 7 an allocation is an Edgeworth equilibrium of the economy $\mathscr{E}$ if and only if there is a price vector $p^* \in l^1$ for which it is a competitive equilibrium.

11.6   Conclusion

Our results have been presented in a general model of intertemporal equilibrium. The advantage of this is that we can make assumptions that are economically natural. The intertemporal structure is more specific than we actually require, and similar results obtain in spaces other than s^n.

If you are willing to start from a utility function, somewhat less continuity of preferences is required. Preferences must still be upper semicontinuous, so that Scarf's theorem applies. However, although lower semicontinuity is used in Lemmas 2 and 5, and Proposition 2, all only require the mapping $t \mapsto u(tx + (1 - t)y)$ be lower semicontinuous on $[0, 1]$ for arbitrary x and y. This is weaker than full lower semicontinuity in the product topology.

These facts suggest that the same proof could be applied to continuous time capital accumulation models, using the compact-open topology.[8] Becker, Boyd and Sung (1989) contains the relevant details on continuity and compactness in this topology.

Another possible application of our results is to a model with uncertainty, such as the model of Debreu and Hildenbrand presented in Bewley (1972). As long as there are countably many states of the world, our techniques could be used in such a setting. By weakening the continuity requirements, our methods may also apply when there are uncountably many states of the world.

Appendix: The Space ba

The dual of l^∞ (under the norm topology) is the space ba of finitely additive measures. A *finitely additive measure* (or *charge*) is a mapping μ from a σ-field $\mathscr{F}$ to the real numbers such that $\|\mu\| = \sup_A |\mu(A)| < \infty$ and $\mu(A \cup B) = \mu(A) + \mu(B)$ whenever $A \cap B = \varnothing$. We can define an integral in the usual way.

In our case, $\mathscr{F}$ is the collection of all subsets of the positive integers. The measure corresponding to $p \in (l^\infty)'$ is defined by $\mu(A) = p \cdot I_A$ where I_A is the indicator function of A. Note that $\|\mu\| = \|p\|$. When A_n are disjoint, $\sum_{n=1}^{N} I_{A_n}$ does not converge in l^∞, since $\|\sum_{n=1}^{N} I_{A_n} - \sum_{n=1}^{N+1} I_{A_n}\| = \|I_{A_{N+1}}\| = 1$. It follows that we cannot conclude that the finitely additive measure μ is countably additive.

An example of a charge that is not countably additive is a Banach limit. Let $c = \{x \in l^\infty : \lim x_t \text{ exists}\}$. Let S be the shift operator $(Sx)_t = x_{t+1}$. A *Banach limit* is any linear functional on l^∞ with $\liminf x_t \le p(x) \le \limsup x_t$, and $p(x) = p(Sx)$. (See Rudin 1973, p. 82.) A Banach limit may be obtained by using the Hahn-Banach theorem to extend $p(x) = \lim x_t$ defined on c to all of l^∞. For $x \ge 0$, $px \ge 0$ since $\liminf x_t = 0$, so a Banach limit must be positive. They also have the interesting property that $p(x) = 0$ whenever there is a T with $x_t = 0$ for $t > T$.

A nonnegative finitely additive measure such that no nonzero countably additive measure v obeys $0 \le v \le \mu$ is called *purely finitely additive* (a *pure charge*). A charge is pure if its positive and negative parts are pure charges. The measure generated by a Banach limit is a pure charge since it assigns zero measure to each point in the positive integers. Yosida and Hewitt (1952, p. 52) prove the following theorem.

Yosida-Hewitt Theorem Any nonnegative finitely additive measure μ has the form $\mu = \mu_c + \mu_f$ where μ_c is nonnegative and countably additive and μ_f is nonnegative and purely finitely additive. Moreover, μ_c and μ_f are unique.

Since countably additive measures on the positive integers correspond to summable sequences, the Yosida-Hewitt theorem lets us uniquely decompose any element of $(l^\infty)'$ into a summable part and a purely finitely additive part.

We also require Alaoglu's Theorem, a form of which may be found in Rudin (1973, p. 66).

Alaoglu's Theorem Any weak* closed, bounded set in the dual of a Banach space is weak* compact.

Since ba is the dual of l^∞, this implies that any $\sigma(ba, l^\infty)$-closed and bounded set is $\sigma(ba, l^\infty)$-compact. We should also note that such sets are not necessarily metrizable. As a result, sequences cannot characterize the topology. In particular, we cannot conclude that a bounded sequence in ba has a convergent subsequence, only that it has a convergent *subnet*.

Notes

1. We thank Andreu Mas-Colell for his comments on an earlier version of this chapter.

2. Aliprantis, Brown and Burkinshaw find that our preference assumptions are incompatible with uniform properness (1989, p. 174), while Back (1988) finds that Inada conditions on utility can generate improper preferences on l^∞.

3. We owe this observation to Darrell Duffie.

4. This profit condition was also used by Stigum (1973).

5. Since in the "neo-Austrian" case, any path is a sum of processes starting at successively later dates, whose initial vectors are composed of inputs, we can argue along similar lines to demonstrate Assumption 2.

6. This argument is easily adapted to stationary multi-sector growth models with diminishing returns and an expansible stock.

7. Except for this step, which has been modified to accommodate our trading sets, we use the argument of Debreu and Scarf (1963). In their case $0 \in C^i \cap Y$, so they can take $y^i = 0$.

8. The compact-open topology is a continuous time analog of the product topology. In fact, in discrete time, it is the same as the product topology.

References

Aliprantis, C. D. and D. J. Brown, "Equilibria in Markets with a Riesz Space of Commodities," *Journal of Mathematical Economics* 11 (1983), 189–207.

———, ——— and O. Burkinshaw, "Edgeworth Equilibria in Production Economies," *Journal of Economic Theory* 43 (1987), 252–291.

———, ——— and ———, *Existence and Optimality of Competitive Equilibria* (New York: Springer-Verlag, 1989).

Arrow, K. J. and F. H. Hahn, *General Competitive Analysis* (Amsterdam: North-Holland, 1971).

Atsumi, H., "On the Rate of Interest in a 'Neo-Austrian' Theory of Capital," in L. W. McKenzie and S. Zamagni, eds., *Value and Capital: Fifty Years Later* (London: Macmillan, 1991).

Back, K., "Structure of Consumption Sets and Existence of Equilibria in Infinite Dimensional Commodity Spaces," *Journal of Mathematical Economics* 17 (1988), 88–99.

Becker, R. A., J. H. Boyd, III, and B. Y. Sung, "Recursive Utility and Optimal Capital Accumulation, I: Existence," *Journal of Economic Theory* 47 (1989), 76–100.

Berge, C., *Topological Spaces* (Edinburgh: Oliver and Boyd, 1963).

Bewley, T., "Existence of Equilibria in Economies with Infinitely Many Commodities," *Journal of Economic Theory* 27 (1972), 514–540.

Burke, J., "On the Existence of Price Equilibria in Dynamic Economies," *Journal of Economic Theory* 44 (1988), 281–300.

Chichilnisky, G. and G. M. Heal, "Competitive Equilibrium in Sobolev Spaces with Unbounded Short Sales," *Journal of Economic Theory* (forthcoming).

Choquet, G., "Ensembles et cônes convexes faiblement complets," *Comptes Rendus de l'Academie des sciences, Paris* 254 (1962), 1908–1910.

Debreu, G., *Theory of Value: An Axiomatic Analysis of Economic Equilibrium* (New Haven: Yale University Press, 1959).

———— and H. Scarf, "A Limit Theorem on the Core of an Economy," *International Economic Review* 4 (1963), 235–246.

Hicks, J. R., *Value and Capital* (Oxford: Oxford University Press, 1939).

————, *Capital and Time: A Neo-Austrian Theory* (Oxford: Oxford University Press, 1983).

Magill, M. J. P., "An Equilibrium Existence Theorem," *Journal of Mathematical Analysis and Applications* 84 (1981), 162–169.

Mas-Colell, A., "The Price Equilibrium Existence Problem in Topological Vector Lattices," *Econometrica* 54 (1986), 1039–1053.

McKenzie, L. W., "On the Existence of General Equilibrium for a Competitive Market," *Econometrica* 22 (1959), 147–161.

————, "Existence of Competitive Equilibrium in a Growing Economy," in Wilhelm Neuefeind, ed., *Economic Theory and International Trade* (Heidelberg: Springer-Verlag, 1992).

Peleg, B. and M. E. Yaari, "Markets with Countably Many Commodities," *International Economic Review* 11 (1970), 369–377.

Rudin, W., *Functional Analysis* (New York: McGraw-Hill, 1973).

Scarf, H., "The Core of an *n*-Person Game," *Econometrica* 35 (1967), 50–69.

Stigum, B. P., "Competitive Equilibria with Infinitely Many Commodities (II)," *Journal of Economic Theory* 6 (1973), 415–445.

Uzawa, H., "The Kuhn-Tucker Theorem in Concave Programming," in K. Arrow, L. Hurwicz and H. Uzawa, eds., *Studies in Linear and Non-Linear Programming* (Stanford: Stanford University Press, 1958).

Yannelis, N. C. and W. R. Zame, "Equilibria in Banach Lattices without Ordered Preferences," *Journal of Mathematical Economics* 15 (1986), 85–110.

Yosida, K. and E. Hewitt, "Finitely Additive Measures," *Transactions of the American Mathematical Society* 72 (1952), 46–66.

Zame, W. R., "Competitive Equilibria in Production Economies with an Infinite Dimensional Commodity Space," *Econometrica* 55 (1987), 1075–1108.

Trade

12 Specialisation and Efficiency in World Production

Lionel W. McKenzie

The fundamental problem of activity analysis is the selection of productive processes which can be used to provide a maximum output from given resources.[1,2,3] This emphasis on the selection of a limited number of productive processes and the suppression of others is rather new in the theory of general equilibrium systems. For example, the systems of Walras, Cassel and Leontiev assume a given set of productive processes which are always in use. There is one field of traditional economics, however, where explicit discrimination between processes to be used and processes to be suppressed has always been the fundamental object of analysis. The problem of specialisation in international trade according to comparative advantage is precisely the problem of selecting a group of productive processes to be used in the interest of maximum world output. The classical analysis, it is true, because of its dependence on bilateral comparisons, was inadequate. To overcome this defect, Frank D. Graham constructed general equilibrium models of world production with many countries and many commodities which he solved by trial and error in the sense of finding points of competitive equilibrium. Although the classical economists would no doubt expect these points to be points of maximum world output, they did not fully expose the relation of maximum output to the possibility of competitive equilibrium. In this chapter I shall begin by presenting an elementary proof of the efficiency of competition and free trade in Graham's model.

The traditional theory of international trade is chiefly concerned with trade between competitive economies which have homogeneous production functions. In the long-run equilibrium of this system, prices must be such that no unused process of production is profitable and all the processes used earn zero profits. I shall refer to these conditions as the profit conditions of competitive equilibrium. Ultimate resources,

however, are assumed to be immobile between countries, so that resources in different countries are essentially different goods and the
processes of each country must be defined in terms of its own resources. Let output include ultimate productive services as negative
goods. Then the profit conditions of competitive equilibrium are necessary and sufficient for a maximum value of world output at given
prices,[4] provided that the productive processes are linear and additive,
that is, that the production functions of traditional analysis are homogeneous (of zero degree) and there are no external economies or diseconomies. On the other hand, the existence of a set of prices for which
world output is a maximum value output is necessary and sufficient
for the output to be in the boundary of the set of outputs which it is
possible to produce with the available productive processes.[5] Thus,
equilibrium points of a linear and additive competitive model always
lie in the boundary of the set of possible outputs, and any point in this
boundary is a possible equilibrium of the competitive model if the demand conditions can be satisfied.

However, it will not be necessary to consider the entire boundary of
the set of possible outputs. Indeed, for most purposes it will suffice to
consider *maximum* outputs, since these are the only outputs for which
the profit conditions can be met with positive prices.[6] But this is just
the efficient point set used by Koopmans in his activity analysis.[7]

The strong parallel between competitive theory and activity analysis
suggests to me that the recent results achieved in activity analysis can
contribute to the analysis of competition. I shall first describe the
Graham model and then prove some propositions on patterns of specialisation in that model which achieve efficiency in the sense of Koopmans. Finally, I will discuss the major limitation of the Graham model.

12.1   The Graham Model

There are two extreme models of world production in which free trade
is efficient. In one, the fundamental reason for trade is the presence of
different productive processes in different countries. It is suggestive to
impute these differences to a general factor, "climate," extending the
meaning of climate to include the total environment. In the second
model, the productive processes are identical between countries. There
are no differences of "climate." But trade occurs because there are differences of tastes and factor endowments, so that countries are led to
produce goods in quantities adapted to their factor supplies but not

necessarily to their tastes. In this chapter I shall be concerned with trade depending upon differences of "climate." It will be convenient to neglect the presence of transport costs and assume that no artificial trade barriers exist. However, we shall suppose that ultimate factors are completely immobile between countries. The analysis will be static. Finally, we will assume that production functions (in their implicit form) are homogeneous of zero degree and mutually independent.

The Graham model is a "climatic" model with productive processes differing between countries. He makes the Ricardian assumption that labour is the only ultimate factor and that the labour cost of each product is constant. However, it is not necessary to assume, to obtain Graham's model, that the activities are *actually* integrated, converting labour directly into final output, or that production coefficients are fixed. It is sufficient that intermediate products do not appear in international trade, or, should they be traded, that they do not contribute to outputs which re-enter trade, and that joint production is absent. As Samuelson and others have shown,[8] if labour is the only unproduced factor for an economy in which each production function is homogeneous and has but one product; then, assuming that production is efficient, each good will be produced by a single process and the rate of transformation between labour and any good will be constant. Thus, the economy may be treated as though its processes were completely integrated.

It is not clear that Graham appreciated the necessity for excluding intermediate products from international trade in his model. At least, he introduces both cloth and linen into his arithmetic examples, though linen presumably will be used largely in making cloth.

For the purpose of illustration, I will present one of Graham's simpler models.[9] He summarises the productivity data in the following table:

		A	B	C	D
Cloth	..	10	10	10	10
Linen	..	19	20	15	28
Corn	..	42	24	30	40

A, B, C and D are four countries trading in the three goods—cloth, linen and corn. In each column of the table are recorded the quantities of linen and corn which can be produced in a certain country by the amount of labour which produces ten units of cloth. I shall take this quantity of labour to be the unit of labour in each country. We are free to do this, since labour does not move from one country to another. Graham also assumes that the labour supply is a given quantity which does not vary with the real wage. In our units of labour the labour supplies in the trading countries are given by Graham as follows:

A   ..   1,000
B   ..   2,000
C   ..   3,000
D   ..   4,000

These data can be introduced into the activities model:

$$\begin{bmatrix} A_{fin} \\ A_{pri} \end{bmatrix} x = \begin{bmatrix} y_{fin} \\ y_{pri} \end{bmatrix},$$

$$x \geq 0, \; y_{pri} \geq -\eta. \tag{1}$$

All of Graham's models have this form. Each column of the partitioned matrix represents the unit level of an integrated activity. A_{fin} is the matrix of output coefficients, and A_{pri} the matrix of input coefficients. x is a column vector of activity levels. y_{fin} is a column vector of outputs. y_{pri} is a column vector of inputs (negative outputs). η is the vector of labour supplies. Inserting the data of our illustration gives:

$$\begin{bmatrix} 10 & & & 10 & & & 10 & & & 10 & & \\ & 19 & & & 20 & & & 15 & & & 28 & \\ & & 42 & & & 24 & & & 30 & & & 40 \\ -1 & 1 & -1 & & & & & & & & & \\ & & & -1 & -1 & -1 & & & & & & \\ & & & & & & -1 & -1 & -1 & & & \\ & & & & & & & & & -1 & -1 & -1 \end{bmatrix} x = \begin{bmatrix} y_{fin} \\ y_{pri} \end{bmatrix}$$

$$x \geq 0, \; y_{pri} \geq - \begin{bmatrix} 1,000 \\ 2,000 \\ 3,000 \\ 4,000 \end{bmatrix} \tag{2}$$

where the empty spaces are to be filled with zeroes.

This model can be used to define a problem in activity analysis, namely, to determine the set of vectors x leading to boundary vectors y which may become competitive equilibria and to determine the set of all such boundary vectors.[10] If we assume that the supplies of labour are constant at positive prices and zero at zero or negative prices, the prices of any final outputs which are produced must be positive if the condition of zero profits is to be met for activities in use. Also, the price of a good which is not produced may be put at a low positive level without making its production profitable, since the cost is positive. Thus any equilibrium output must be a maximum value output for some set of positive prices, and we may confine attention to the boundary points for which this is so. As it happens, the set of such points is Koopmans' efficient point set.[11] Thus our problem is the efficient allocation of resources as Koopmans defines it in his activity analysis. We may refer to a pattern of zeroes and non-zeroes appearing in an activity vector x which generates an efficient point as an efficient specialisation. Then the set of efficient specialisations will be the set of all those specialisations which may appear in a competitive equilibrium when demand conditions, within the restrictions named, are appropriate.

12.2   The Theorem on Efficiency in the Graham Model

I shall show that the basic theorem of activity analysis can be proved directly in Graham's model in an elementary way. First, we define an efficient point as a vector y of primary resources consumed and goods produced such that the net output of intermediate products is zero and no final good can be increased in quantity within the resource limitations unless the condition on intermediate products is violated or the amount of some other final good is reduced. The basic theorem states that a necessary and sufficient condition for an output vector y to be efficient is the existence of a price vector p which satisfies the following conditions. The prices of final goods are positive. The prices of intermediate products may be positive, negative or zero. The prices of primary resources are zero if those resources are in surplus supply and are positive or zero otherwise. At the prices p all activities in use yield zero profits, and all activities not in use would yield zero profits or losses were they put in use.[12]

These conditions are much simplified, however, in the Graham model. Since we can use integrated activities in each country, intermediate products drop out. Moreover, we have only one primary resource in each country, which can be converted into any final good through an integrated activity. Therefore, it will never be efficient to have a primary resource in surplus supply, and since the prices of final goods are positive, the labour supplies must also bear positive prices in order to meet the profit condition. Thus all prices must exceed zero, and for this model the basic theorem takes the form:

If $y = Ax$ with $x \geq 0$, "y is efficient" is equivalent to "$y_{pri} = -\eta$ and there is a p such that $p > 0$ with $p'A_j = 0$ if $x_j > 0$, $p'A_j \leq 0$ if $x_j = 0$." (3)

Here p is the vector of prices, A_j is the vector of input-output coefficients for the jth activity (the jth column of the activities matrix A) and x_j is the level of the jth activity (the jth component of the vector x).

In words, the conditions are that prices are positive, labour supplies are fully used, and the profit conditions of competitive equilibrium are met. When an output is produced, it is efficient if, and only if, these conditions can be satisfied for some set of prices.

The proof of (3) is similar to the proof of an analogous result in a model of transportation by Koopmans.[13] The essential fact seems to be, as Professor Koopmans pointed out to me, that each activity connects only two goods, a final good and a primary resource. Thus each primary resource is an independent origin of final goods and determines a possible ratio of substitution between final goods. This circumstance permits price relations and possibilities of substitution to be represented with a linear graph.

To construct the graph we may replace Graham's table with a table of dots and circles, where dots represent activities at a positive level and circles activities which are unused. Then connect the dots along the rows and along the columns with lines which are regarded as joining only when they meet at a dot. We then have connections between the activities which produce the same good and between activities located in the same country.

Each possible pattern of specialisation will have an associated graph. For example, the graph:

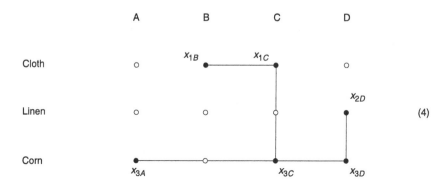

(4)

corresponds to the specialisation that occurs in the solution to the model (2) when Graham's demand conditions are introduced. Note that the x_j's of (3), which represent the activity levels, have now been supplied with two subscripts.

Let us assume first that the conditions of (3) are satisfied. Then if we determine a price for one final good in one country, the condition of zero profits for activities in use will fix a price for labour and therefore for all other goods produced by that country. Also the price of the same good in different countries must be the same. Therefore, setting the price of one good will determine that of all other goods which lie on the same connected subgraph.[14] I shall refer to maximal connected subgraphs as components of the graph.[15] If it should be possible to perform a circuit on a component, that is, to return to the same output from which we departed, without retracing any link, the satisfaction of the conditions of the theorem clearly requires that we should not encounter contradiction by returning to a price different from the one from which we started. I will call these admissible circuits neutral. Thus if the conditions of (3) are met, all circuits, if any, must be neutral and no unused activity can be profitable. The result of selecting prices by this method for the specialisation of (4) is:

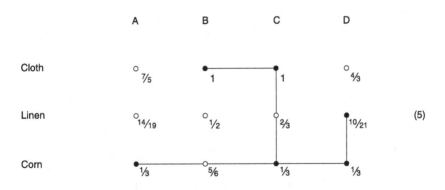

$$(5)$$

Cloth is the *numéraire*. The numbers beside dots represent the resulting prices of final goods. Numbers beside circles represent the costs of production in the unused activities. With a different specialisation, the prices and costs would, of course, be different. It is clear that the profit conditions of (3) are met in this case. Therefore, if the theorem is true, any output of this specialisation which uses the entire labour supply will be contained in the efficient point set, and we may term the specialisation itself efficient.

Let us now consider the graph from the standpoint of substitutions between final goods. We may speak of a move on a vertical branch of the graph when the production of one good is varied at the initial point and the production of a second good is varied at the end point as a result of shifting labour within the country between the two corresponding activities.[16] Then the substitution ratio is, by the profit conditions, the reciprocal of the price ratio. A move on a horizontal branch will be taken to mean that a change in production of the good at the initial point is made up by an opposite change at the end point in another country.[17] If, after a sequence of vertical and horizontal moves, we return to the original good, the initial variation in production may or may not be precisely offset. If it is precisely offset, I shall call the circuit neutral for substitution. This type of neutrality will turn out to be equivalent to the neutrality of price circuits.

In the Graham model every substitution of different final goods is composed of substitutions of final goods within single countries, and if production is not to fall for any good, every decrease in production of a good in one country must be offset by an increase in production of the same good in another. Thus every good must appear in two variations, which creates a horizontal link, and, to keep the use of labour constant, every variation must lie in a country containing another variation, which creates a vertical link. Therefore, if efficiency is preserved, every attempt to increase the production of one or more goods without reducing that of other goods must involve one or more circuits, and if there is no circuit which can cause the production of a final good to increase, the output vector is efficient.

Consider diagram (5) once more. Price and cost in the diagram are proportionate in each country to the quantity of labour required to produce a unit of output, and their reciprocals are proportionate to the quantity of output got from a unit of labour. Thus the reciprocals of prices represent quantities which may be substituted without destroying efficiency when they lie on a vertical segment. It is, on the other hand, equal quantities of a good which are substituted along a horizontal segment, so that total production of the good does not suffer. We may consider circuits which contain activities not in use, but then the variations in output must be such that only positive variations are called for in the levels of heretofore unused activities. In the general case, the result $\triangle y_s$ of traversing a circuit leading from a variation v_{sj} in the production of the sth good in the jth country back to a compensating change in production of the same good in the qth country, when the levels of activities outside the circuit are constant, is given by:

$$\Delta y_s = -v_{sj} \frac{\pi_{sj}}{\pi_{mj}} \cdot \frac{\pi_{mk}}{\pi_{nk}} \cdots \frac{\pi_{pq}}{\pi_{sq}} + v_{sj} \qquad (6)$$

In this formula π_{sj} equals the price p_s of the sth good if the jth country produces it. In any case, π_{sj} equals the cost of producing y_s in the jth country. Each fraction $\frac{\pi_{mk}}{\pi_{nk}}$ is equal to the substitution ratio in the vertical move from a variation of the mth good, which has the sign of the original variation v_{sj}, to a variation of the nth good, of opposite sign, in the output of the kth country. Since the variation of output in an unused activity must be positive, if v_{sj} is positive, π's can differ from price only in the numerators, and if v_{sj} is negative, only in the denominators. But by the profit condition π_{mk} is greater than or equal to p_m. Hence, if any π's exceed price when the circuit introduces unused activities, Δy_s is negative. On the other hand, if no unused activities are included, all the π's cancel and Δy_s is zero.[18] This proves that if the profit conditions can be satisfied in S with positive prices, no circuit can show a gain and hence the specialisation S is efficient.

To prove the converse, note that if y is efficient, then one component of y cannot increase unless another falls. Consequently, every circuit must lead to unchanged production of all goods or must reduce the production of the initial good. Selecting an arbitrary good as *numéraire*, prices may be assigned within a component of the graph by following its subgraph as in (5). Inconsistency can only arise at the completion of a circuit, that is, by (6) if $\pi_{sj} \neq \pi_{sq}$, since the prices associated with goods at intermediate steps in the circuit are carried over from denominator to numerator at each step. But again by (6) in this case the circuit is non-neutral for substitutions and, therefore, by the appropriate choice of v_{sj}, Δy_s can be made positive and y is not efficient.

Suppose, however, that the component is completely traversed without contradiction, but an activity A_{sj} is unused and profitable, where A_{sj} represents that activity of the jth country which can produce the sth good and where the jth country and the sth good are represented, separately, in the component. Then, if we introduce A_{sj} into the component, a circuit is created, and if we give v_{sj} a positive value, Δy_s will be positive according to (6), since $\pi_{sj} < p_s$ by the assumption that A_{sj} is profitable. Therefore, y is not efficient.

If some good is not producible in the specialisation S, it may be assigned any positive price which is less than the lowest cost of production in any country. This is possible, since the lowest cost of production must be positive. Thus we have proved that if y is efficient, the profit condition can be met in the corresponding specialisation S, with prices which are all positive, when S has a single component.

Suppose, then, that more than one component is present. The components are maximal connected subgraphs and, therefore, the set of countries in one component is disjoint[19] from the set in other components and the set of goods produced in one component is disjoint from the set of goods produced in other components. Since efficiency is assumed, it must be possible to set price ratios within each component which are determined by the substitution ratios between the goods produced and which satisfy the profit conditions in this component. However, the relative price levels between components are not thereby determined. Let us select a *numéraire* for each component k_i and assign it a price λ_i. If the conditions of the theorem on efficiency are to be met, it must be possible to choose the λ_i so that all unused activities remain non-profitable.

To simplify the exposition, I shall consider a graph with two components in the pattern:

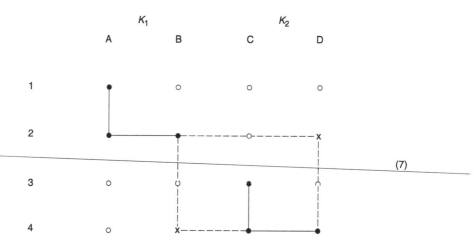

We may fix λ_1 equal to 1. Suppose that it is not possible to find a value of λ_2 greater than zero such that all unused activities remain profitless. Select the maximum value of λ_2 that leaves the unused activities of A and B profitless. There must then be an unused activity in A or B, say the production of 4 in B, which would earn zero profits, if used, and an unused activity in C or D, say the production of 2 in D, which remains profitable, if used. There two activities may be introduced into the graph to create the circuit which is completed in the figure with dashed lines. According to (6), the effect of a positive variation v_{2D} in the circuit is:

$$\Delta y_2 = -v_{2D}\pi_{2D}/p_5 \cdot \pi_{5B}/p_2 + v_{2D} \tag{8}$$

Since $\pi_{5B} = p_5$ and $\pi_{2D} < p_2$, according to the assumptions made, Δy_2 is positive and no output of the specialisation $S = K_1 + K_2$ is efficient.

It should be clear that this argument could be extended to any number of components without difficulty. Therefore, we have proved that if y is an efficient output, the profit conditions can be met in the specialisation which produces y. Thus, "S is efficient" is equivalent to the possibility of satisfying the profit conditions, with positive prices, and if S is efficient, y is an efficient output of S if, and only if, the labour supplies are fully used. This last condition can be slightly relaxed if some countries cannot produce some goods. However, the exception has little interest.

12.3 Efficient Facets

Since every good on a component of the graph is directly or indirectly connected to every other good by vertical links along which substitutions can be made, we see that any good on a given component can be substituted for any other, provided the amount of the substitution is small enough not to require negative production anywhere. Moreover, since the substitutions may be added (that is, may be imposed successively) if r goods are present in the component, the quantities produced of $r - 1$ of the goods may be altered in any proportions so long as the quantity produced of the rth good is properly adjusted, and the variation is sufficiently small. Thus the set of outputs which may be efficiently produced when r goods are present in a connected graph is $r - 1$ dimensional. The theory of activity analysis assures us that when the prices are unique up to a common factor, their ratios are the reciprocals of substitution ratios. In the case of a connected graph, however, this is directly apparent from the profit conditions. Indeed, the prices were assigned by use of the substitution ratios. It is also clear that any efficient output must lie in the boundary of the set of all possible outputs since otherwise all components of the output could be increased simultaneously.

Substitution between goods produced on different components of the graph is not possible, unless the specialisation pattern is changed, since no country has activities in both components. Therefore, the

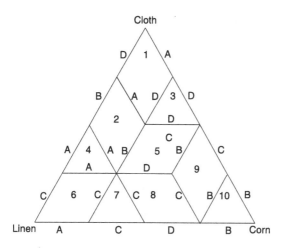

Figure 12.1
The country indicated beside a one-dimensional facet is changing over in that facet from the output of one vertex to that of another. In general, within a facet a country produces every good that it produces at some vertex of that facet. Equal distances do not represent equal quantities in different facets. However, within a facet distances parallel to a side may be interrupted in terms of quantities of the goods being substituted along that side. Then each point of the diagram corresponds to a definite efficient output.

dimension of the set of efficient outputs for a specialisation S is equal to the number r of goods in S diminished by the number t of components. I shall refer to the set of outputs consistent with a specialisation as a facet of the efficient point set. In the extreme case where there is but one good in each component, the dimension $r - t$ of the corresponding set of efficient points is zero, that is, the facet is made up of one efficient point.

It is possible to represent the set of efficient outputs schematically for the model given by (2). This is conveniently done in Figure 12.1 by the subdivision of a triangle whose vertices represent points in which each country is producing the same good. Moving from one vertex to another along a side of the triangle, one country after another is shifting over from the output of the first vertex to that of the second. The other points at which each country is producing only one good may be located symmetrically within the triangle, so that the nearer the point to a vertex the more countries are producing the corresponding good. These points all represent zero-dimensional facets. In our example, there are fifteen such facets. This is the number of ways, consistent with efficiency, in which each of four countries can specialise completely in one of three goods when the rates of substitution differ between countries, so that the order in which countries enter the production of a good is determined. If another good were added, the triangle would have to be replaced by a pyramid, and, in general, the presence of an additional good increases the dimension of the figure by one.

When rates of substitution differ between countries,[20] there is an easy inductive formula for the number of zero-dimensional facets. It is derived from the fact that, when another good is introduced, the number of complete specialisations[21] equals the sum of the number when no country produces the new good, the number when one does, on up to the number with all countries producing the new good. But the number of specialisations in the other goods when an assigned number of countries produce the new good is a problem in specialisation with the smaller number of goods, and by induction is assumed to be known. Thus the formula may be written:

$$C(r, n) = \sum_{i=0}^{n} C(r - 1, i) \tag{9}$$

where $C(r, n)$ is the number of complete specialisations when there are r goods and n countries. The induction begins with $C(2, n) = n + 1$. Then $C(3, n) = \sum_{i=0}^{n} C(2, n) = \sum_{i=0}^{n} (i + 1) = \frac{(n+1)^2 + n + 1}{2}$, which is 15 if $n = 4$.[22]

The one-dimensional facets are represented by line segments drawn between those pairs of zero-dimensional facets for which only one country specialises differently. Each facet of given dimension s is a polygon whose vertices are a maximal set of zero-dimensional facets, between each pair of which s countries or less specialise differently. Moreover, the points of every such maximal set form the vertices of an s-dimensional facet. Within the facet each country produces every good which it produces at some vertex of the facet. In our example, the two-dimensional facets are either quadrangles or triangles, and it is clear that no other possibilities exist for two-dimensional facets. This may also be seen from the graphic representation of the facets. In a two-dimensional facet substitutions may occur between three goods and thus there must be two countries each producing two of the goods, or one producing three. In the former case, the facet is a quadrangle; in the latter case, a triangle. If a neutral circuit exists, however, certain adjacent facets will present the same substitution ratios and will, by the definition usual in activity analysis, form a single facet.[23]

It is also possible to derive a simple relation for the number of activities in a graph and thus in the corresponding facet. Suppose r goods are produced and n countries are present. If there is only one component and no circuits, the number of activities in use must be $r + n - 1$. There must be r activities to ensure that each of the r goods are produced. These activities leave the countries entirely unconnected. Then $n - 1$ additional activities are needed to connect them. If the number of components is larger than one, say equal to k, one activity must drop out to slough off each additional component. Therefore, with no circuits present, the number of activities is $r + n - k$ and the dimension of the facet is $r - k$. If c independent circuits[24] are then introduced, the number of activities must rise by c, since one activity is needed to generate a new circuit in an existing component, and more than one must either alter the number of components or lead to another new circuit.[25] Therefore, the number of activities will be $r + n - k + c$.

In the facet whose linear graph was exhibited in (4), C produces cloth and corn, D produces linen and corn, A produces corn, and B produces cloth. Thus six activities are used. In this example, $r = 3$, $n = 4, k = 1, c = 0$, and $r + n - k + c = 6$, as it should. The facet is number 8 in Fig. 12.1, and since there is only one component, the facet is of maximal dimension and the prices must be in fixed proportions. A reference to the substitutions made on the sides of this facet, which is a quadrangle, show it to be comparatively large. Indeed, within the facet, the change in production in terms of the maximum potential world production of each good is about one-half for corn and linen and one-third for cloth, despite the presence of nine other two-dimensional facets.

12.4   The Equilibrium Position

Graham makes three remarks on the equilibrium position of his model which I will examine briefly. He argues that "limbo" prices corresponding to facets of dimension less than $r - I$ are improbable. He also argues that even large changes in demand are not likely to affect price ratios very much. Finally, he conjectures that with his demand functions the equilibrium of supply and demand is unique.

The demand assumption which Graham uses is that the same proportion of each country's expenditure is devoted to each product regardless of price and that these proportions are equal between countries.[26] Thus redistributions of income between countries will not matter. It is assumed that all income is earned in the production of the goods included in the model. In other words, the proportion of world income devoted to each product is constant.

I have shown elsewhere that Graham's model always has a solution and, indeed, that this solution is unique.[27]

Let us consider the probability that large changes in demand will leave relative prices unaffected. This will depend on the size of the facet within which the original output vector lies. The sizes of the facets with Graham's assumptions of constant costs are determined essentially by the sizes of the countries, and there is little else to be said. If the original point of equilibrium lies in a facet like 8 in Fig. 12.1, large changes may occur in demand without leaving this facet and consequently without changing relative prices in the competitive equilibrium. On the other hand, if the original equilibrium were in facet 4, a much smaller change would suffice to remove the equilibrium to another facet and different relative prices. Graham's own initial solution for the example we have used did lie in facet 8, as we have noted.

Finally, Graham regarded "limbo" prices as very improbable. That is, he thought it quite improbable that an equilibrium point would be found in a facet of dimension less than the maximum, $r - 1$, and in a facet of maximum dimension relative prices are precisely fixed. However, this presumption does not appear to be justified. The dimension of the set of relative prices associated with a facet is $r - f - 1$, where f is the dimension of the facet, for price ratios are fixed just between those outputs which can be substituted in the facet. But then the dimension of the set of outputs, demanded at some set of prices associated with the facet, is also $r - f - 1$. The equilibrium lies in the facet if the facet contains an output with goods in the proportions demanded. There seem no *a priori* grounds for preferring the probability that an $r - 1$ dimensional facet will contain an output with goods in given proportions over the probability that the unique output of a zero-dimensional facet will have goods in the same proportions as some output in the $r - 1$ dimensional set associated with the facet through the demand functions.

12.5 Effect of Trade in Intermediate Products

If intermediate products are traded, the analysis of efficiency in terms of substitution circuits is no longer adequate. The difficulty is that changes in world output can no longer be decomposed into elementary substitutions within single countries, for even substitutions between the products of a single country will typically involve changes in the

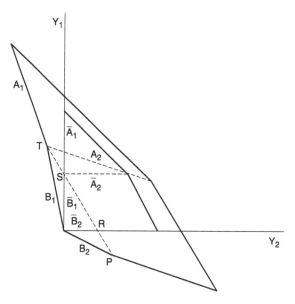

Figure 12.2
B_1 is the input-output vector (exclusive of labour) for the first activity in B when all the labour supply of B is devoted to it, and correspondingly for the other activities. Integrated activities are indicated with a bar. In deriving the set of possible outputs in the free case, draw the vectors representing the activities of A with the point T as origin and slide A_2 along the line $\overline{TP}$. In the integrated case draw the vectors representing the integrated activities of A with S as origin and slide $\overline{A_2}$ along $\overline{SR}$.

supplies of intermediate products from other countries. As a consequence, the effectiveness of one country in the production of a certain good will often depend on the ability of other countries to supply some of the intermediate products needed in its production. The patterns of efficient specialisation may have little relation to those which would appear with integrated activities.

In the competitive model the effect of trade in intermediate products will be reflected in their prices. Clearly, some activities may now be profitable which would have been definitely excluded earlier because of the great cost of producing a necessary intermediate product within the country.

The introduction of trade in intermediate products can be expected, in general, to push the production frontier outwards throughout its entire extent. The effect is most simply illustrated for the case of two countries and two goods where each good enters into the production of the other. In Figure 12.2 the outer frontier combines the activities of the two countries in a completely general way, so that country A produces no y_1 until country B has become entirely committed to y_1. With the inner frontier, however, each country produces its own intermediate products. In other words, it is as though integrated production functions were used.

The appearance of new directions of efficient specialisation may be illustrated in a simple arithmetic model. Suppose the cloth is made of linen, but the linen also has direct uses, and the activities are:

	A			B			C			
	l.	cl.	w.	l.	cl.	w.	l.	cl.	w.	
L_A	−1	−1	−1							
L_B				−1	−1	−1				
L_C							−1	−1	−1	
										(10)
Linen	2	−10		5	−10		10	−10		
Cloth		10			10			10		
Wheat			7			10			10	

Then the table of comparative costs on the basis of integrated activities will be:

				A	B	C	
Cloth	..	..	..	10	10	10	
Linen	..	..	..	12	15	20	(11)
Wheat	..	..	..	42	30	20	

It is clear from (11) that if one country specialised to each product, and intermediate products are not traded, the specialisation will have to be A in wheat, B in cloth, and C in linen.[28] However, it is not difficult to show that this specialisation is never efficient when trade in intermediate products occurs. A cannot profitably produce wheat unless $7p_w \geq 10p_{cl} - 10p_l$ or $10p_{cl} \leq 10p_l + 7p_w$. But B cannot profitably produce cloth unless $10p_{cl} \geq 10p_l + 10p_w > 10p_l + 7p_w$. Thus the profit conditions cannot be satisfied in this specialisation and the specialisation must be inefficient by the general theorem on efficiency in finite linear models.[29]

On the other hand, it *is* efficient to have A produce only cloth, B only wheat, and C only linen. Any price vector for which $10p_l > 10p_w$ and $10p_l + 10p_w > 10p_{cl}$ makes the production of cloth and wheat unprofitable in C. Then if $10p_w > 5p_l$ and $10p_w > 10p_{cl} - 10p_l$, B cannot profitably produce cloth or linen. Finally, if $10p_{cl} > 12p_l$ and $10p_{cl} > 7p_w + 10p_l$, A cannot profitably produce either linen or wheat. These inequalities can be satisfied, for example, by the prices, $p_l = 12$, $p_w = 10$, $p_{cl} = 20$. Consequently, by setting the price of labour in each country just high enough to give zero profits in the one activity which is used, the profit condition is met, and the specialisation is proved to be efficient.

There is nothing shocking to common sense in these results. A moment's consideration will convince one that Lancashire would be unlikely to produce cotton cloth if the cotton had to be grown in England. On the other hand, the production of raw materials, especially the mining of metallic ores, might not be profitable in backward areas without machinery supplied by the industrial countries. The patterns of interdependence are already very complex, but with free trade they would undoubtedly be far more complex than they now are. The low cost of ocean transport would reduce the advantage of internal supply in continental countries.

In discussing the models with trade in intermediate goods, we have implicitly assumed that each country always used the same productive process to produce a given good. However, there is no longer the same justification for this assumption. If the coefficients of production are variable, they will now depend on the prices of intermediate products which will vary with final demand. In other words, what activity it is efficient for a country to use in producing a good will depend on what outputs are being produced in other countries. We have lost the use of Samuelson's theorem, since there are several ultimate factors in the whole interdependent system of world production. Or, looked at differently, imports of intermediate products are like supplies of ultimate factors to a country. Thus, as soon as trade in intermediate products is allowed, the problem loses its special simplicity, and we may as well allow joint production and many factors in each country. The problem of efficient specialisation then assumes the proportions of general activity analysis.

12.6   Efficiency in World Production

It has long been a claim of orthodox economists that, if we assume pure competition and the absence of external economies, free trade will lead to efficiency in world production.[30] The notion of efficiency intended in this claim is no doubt broader than the definition we have used here, but it would surely include efficiency in our sense. Free trade, through promoting proper specialisations in production, would make possible larger outputs of whatever desired composition. However, the methods of the classical economists are entirely appropriate only to the analysis of trade between two countries. Of course, one of these countries may be taken to be "the rest of the world," but this is largely a subterfuge, for we are still left with a problem of specialisation within "the rest of the world."

The deficiency of the classical methods, the method of comparative labour costs in early days, the method of alternative costs as displayed in production possibility curves in later times, is their dependence on bilateral comparison. They are admirably adapted to demonstrating that there are gains to be made from trade when countries begin with different rates of transformation between outputs. But it is not possible through merely bilateral comparison to develop a complete theory of efficient multilateral specialisation.

Graham detected the error of classical ways and introduced a genuinely multilateral method into the study of international trade. We have seen that the efficiency of free trade in his model can be proved through an analysis of the role of substitution circuits. Indeed, the basic theorem on efficiency in linear models can be demonstrated for his model with elementary techniques.

However, we have found that this simplicity is bought at the expense of prohibiting all trade in intermediate products (with a slight exception), which is indeed a heavy price. When the further degree of interdependence which results from trade in intermediate products is recognised, there is no recourse but to use the general methods of activity analysis.

Notes

1. This chapter resulted from research initiated while a guest of the Cowles Commission and will be reprinted in Cowles Commission Papers, New Series, No. 72.

2. I wish to thank Professor Tjalling C. Koopmans for his encouragement and instruction. The debt to my old teacher, Frank D. Graham, will be apparent.

3. Throughout this chapter "an output" means the net quantities of goods produced, by an economy or by an activity, as the case may be. A maximum output is an output in which the quantity of one good cannot be increased unless another is reduced. In activity analysis such an output is called efficient.

4. These being the prices used in the profit conditions. Of course, the maximum value of output must be zero by the profit conditions, since ultimate productive services are included in output.

5. The proof that the profit conditions are sufficient for this result is quite brief. The set of possible outputs is a cone Y and the profit conditions are equivalent to $p'z \leqq 0$ for $z \in Y$ and $p'z = 0$ for $z = y$, where y is the actual output. But these are precisely the conditions for p to be a normal to Y at y. Thus y must lie in the boundary of Y. If, in addition, the demand condition is met and y is the vector of quantities demanded when p is the price vector, y is a competitive equilibrium by definition. (p is a column vector, p' is a row vector, and $p'z$ is the inner product of p and z.) A rather lengthy mathematical argument is needed to prove, in the general case, that the profit conditions are also necessary.

6. That is, the output is maximal for the set of goods which bear non-zero prices. Otherwise, it clearly could not be a maximum value output.

7. Tjalling C. Koopmans, *Activity Analysis of Production and Allocation*, Chapter 3, New York, 1951.

8. Paul A. Samuelson, Chapter VI in *Activity Analysis of Production and Allocation*, ed. by Tjalling C. Koopmans.

9. Frank D. Graham, *The Theory of International Values*, Princeton, 1948, p. 76.

10. It is easily seen that the set of outputs attainable within the model form a closed and bounded convex set. Indeed, a convex cone truncated by hyperplanes expressing the limitations on the supplies of labour. See Koopmans, op. cit., p. 82.

11. Koopmans, op. cit., pp. 60–61.

12. Koopmans, op. cit., p. 82. These results are discussed in non-mathematical terms in Koopmans' "Efficient Allocation of Resources," *Econometrica*, October, 1951, pp. 455–65.

13. Koopmans and Stanley Reiter, "A Model of Transportation," *Activity Analysis*, Chapter XIV, pp. 244–51.

14. A subgraph is a graph formed from some set of activities contained in the original graph. Thus every line segment of the subgraph is contained in the original graph, but not necessarily conversely. A subgraph is connected if there is a line contained in it between any two of its activities.

15. A set defined by stated conditions is maximal if it is not contained in a larger set satisfying those conditions. Thus a connected subgraph regarded as a connected set of activities is maximal if it is not contained in a larger connected subgraph.

16. Consider a change in x_{3C} of the amount $\triangle x_{3C}$. Efficiency demands that the condition $x_{1C} + x_{3C} = \eta_C$ be preserved. Then $\triangle x_{1C}$ must equal $-\triangle x_{3C}$. Thus every variation must lie in a vertical move.

17. Consider again the change $\triangle x_{3C}$. Let a_{3C} be the product per unit level of the activity. Then the change in production of corn is $a_{3C}\triangle x_{3C}$. If total production of corn is to be constant, there must be a change in x_{3D} so that $a_{3C}\triangle x_{3C} + a_{3D}\triangle x_{3D} = 0$.

18. The ratios $\dfrac{\pi_{rj}}{\pi_{sj}}$ are equal to the ratios $\dfrac{a_{sj}}{a_{rj}}$ of elements of A_{fin} when the unit levels of the activities are defined as using a unit of labour. If the determinant of the sub-matrix of (2) which contains the activities appearing in the circuit is expanded, it will be found that only two terms are non-zero. One term is equal to the product of the numerators of the ratios $\dfrac{a_{sj}}{a_{rj}}$. The other is equal to the product of the denominators of these ratios. But they have opposite signs. Thus $\triangle y_r$ is zero if, and only if, this determinant is zero, and, there-

fore, some activity can be expressed as a linear combination of the other activities in the circuit. This is the general form of the problem in activity analysis.

19. Two sets are disjoint if they contain no common elements.

20. Failure of this condition does not vitiate our methods. See the footnote at the end of the next paragraph.

21. That is, specialisations in which each country produces one good.

22. It is easily shown that $C(r,n)$ is the binomial coefficient $\binom{n+r-1}{n} = \frac{(n+r-1)!}{n!(r-1)!}$, which gives the number of distinguishable arrangements of n indistinguishable objects in r cells. Of course, the countries are distinguishable, but when a certain number of countries are assigned to each good, the assignment of individual countries is unique because of comparative advantage. See Wm. Feller, *Probability Theory*, New York, 1950, p. 52.

23. Our definition of facet is easily modified to conform with the standard definition. The facets of activity analysis correspond to maximal efficient specialisations (or maximal efficient graphs). This means that any activity which retains zero profitability for all sets of prices at which the specialisation satisfies (3) must be used. If no circuits ever appear, the definitions are equivalent.

If the substitution ratios between two goods are the same in two countries, the zero-dimensional facets may initially be determined by slightly altering the ratios to make them differ. Then recognising that the ratios are actually the same will eliminate the zero-dimensional facet in which each country produces a different one of the two goods, and some adjacent facets will merge. The final result is independent of the particular perturbation of the ratios in the intermediate step, but it should be small enough to leave other comparative advantages unchanged.

24. That is, no one of the c circuits can be expressed as a sum of the other $c - 1$ circuits. In adding two circuits, give each an orientation. Then branches which appear twice with opposite orientations cancel. Different orientations yield different sums. See D. König, *Theorie der endlichen und unendlichen Graphen*, Leipzig, 1936.

25. It can be shown that the rank of the matrix of input-output coefficients for the activities of a specialisation equals the number of activities reduced by the number of independent circuits, i.e., $r + n - k$.

26. The precise assumption made for the model (2) is that each country spends one-third of its income on each good. Then the solution is in facet 8 and total outputs are approximately 111,302 units of cloth, 239,664 units of linen and 379,714 units of corn. The solution must be found by trial and error.

27. In a paper read before the Econometric Society in December, 1952, and published in *Econometrica*, April, 1954.

28. This may be seen by putting all countries initially in cloth. Then if wheat is to be produced, the largest returns are not only if A switches over, and if linen is desired C provides larger returns for the sacrifice of cloth than does B.

29. If the profit conditions cannot be met, even with negative prices, there is no normal at the output and the output is therefore interior to the cone of possible outputs. Then there is another point interior to the cone using no more resources and providing larger supplies of all outputs.

30. This claim is, at least, implicit in classical discussions of comparative advantage and gains from trade.

13 Equality of Factor Prices in World Trade

Lionel W. McKenzie

The method of the factor price equalization argument has been to assume the same productive processes in each country and then to ask when the profit conditions of competitive equilibrium require that factor prices be the same everywhere.[1,2] In this chapter I shall approach the question of factor price equalization by means of activity analysis.[3] Also I shall not always adhere to the customary assumptions. The usefulness of activity analysis in the equalization problem arises from an assumption which is often made in the field of international trade, that production functions are homogeneous. As a result, the productive system may be represented by a linear activities model. Perhaps we shall find that the activities approach will suggest new theorems and allow general proofs to be reached more expeditiously.

13.1 Description of the Model

Initially I shall use the following assumptions, although later the first two will sometimes be relaxed and the third strengthened.

(1) There is in each trading country, say the kth, a given vector of factor supplies r^k. Thus resources are in completely inelastic supply. Some countries may have no supplies of some resources.

(2) Transport costs for goods are zero and for factors are infinite. No other impediments to trade exist.

(3) The production functions are homogeneous of degree zero (when written in implicit form), and there are no external economies. Joint products are allowed, and intermediate products may appear explicitly. The production functions are not necessarily the same in different countries.

The third assumption is equivalent to requiring that each country have available a basic set of linear activities. An activity may be described by a vector (or list of quantities) of inputs of goods and factors (taken as negative numbers) and outputs of goods (taken as positive numbers) which may be achieved in combination. By linearity, we mean that any positive multiple of this vector also gives a possible set of inputs and outputs of the activity, and that the level at which one activity is operated has no effect on the inputs and outputs which may be achieved in other activities. Linearity of the activities thus has the same force as the absence of external economies in production in classical theory, when the production functions are homogeneous.

A productive process will be defined as the set of all sums of the basic activities in which a given list of inputs and outputs appears. We may regard a sum of activities, each of which uses the same inputs and outputs, as an activity in its own right. Then an activity will be said to be efficient (in its process) if it is not possible to increase an output or reduce an input, by moving to another activity in the process without reducing some other output or increasing some other input. It should not be difficult to see that the classical production function corresponds closely to the set of efficient activities of a productive process, at least, if we suppose that any efficient activity can be the basis of production for a single firm. This must be true, in any case, for the basic activities, which we may take to exclude activities expressible as sums of other activities.

We shall be especially concerned with the combinations of ultimate factor inputs which appear in the activities, as distinguished from the inputs of intermediate products. The inputs of intermediate products are derived from the output of other activities, while inputs of ultimate factor services come from nature, the labor force, or the initial stocks of goods. We may suppose that inputs and outputs are dated, and prices are established for all future dates in an initial Walrasian market.[4] There is no great loss of generality if we assume the dates and the varieties of goods and factors to be finite in number. This model may appear artificial, but there are important reasons for using it. It is awkward to treat capital as homogeneous, since prices and transformation rates will differ in different equilibria. Nor can we suppose that every type of capital is maintained, since sometimes it will not be efficient to replace all the capital goods which wear out. On the other hand, if we confine ourselves to an instantaneous equilibrium in the current flow of goods and services, the current output of intermediate products would play no role in supporting production. Intermediate products flow into stocks as investment, made in anticipation of future production and sales. For the present, they would have to be regarded as final products. However, the notion of a market with determinate prices for all goods and factors, present and future, with an assumption of perfect foresight for wants and production possibilities, provides a model of perfect competition which is free of these difficulties. It will apply to an actual economy in so far as competition exists and anticipations of producers and consumers are, in fact, correct.

13.2   Competitive Equilibrium

Competitive equilibrium is characterized by two conditions:[5] a profit condition and a demand condition. Profits are defined for the sth activity as $\sum_i p_i y_i^s + \sum_j w_j x_j^s$, where the p_i and w_j represent prices of the goods and factors, respectively, and the y_i^s and x_i^s represent the quantities of goods and factors, which appear in the sth activity vector (positive for outputs and negative for inputs). In vector notation we may write for profits $p \cdot y^s + w \cdot x^s$. It is assumed that anyone who governs an activity tries to maximize profits, but since the activities may be operated at any scale, if an activity is used it must realize zero profits. Otherwise there would be no limit to its size. Similarly, an unprofitable activity will not be used at all, so that for unused activities profits will promise to be zero or negative, were they put to use.[6] This is orthodox theory where production functions are homogeneous.

The demand condition is that when income is spent as consumers wish at prevailing prices, the final output will be bought, and, at the factor prices which prevail, the quantities of factor services needed to produce this output will be supplied by the consumers. Income is defined as $-\sum w \cdot x^s$. Profits may be neglected since they are zero in equilibrium. Therefore, in equilibrium the net value of output, $\sum p \cdot y^s$, equals the factor income, $-\sum w \cdot x^s$.

Our approach will be to ignore the consumer demand for final goods, and initially to assume constant factor supplies. Then we are free to consider when the vector p of goods prices implies the vector w of factor prices in a competitive equilibrium. It is clear that if p implies the same w for each country, factor prices must be equalized if p is the vector of world prices for goods.

13.3   The Basic Theorems

In this section I shall first prove that in any country which has given supplies of all factors the prices of goods will uniquely determine the prices of factors in a competitive equilibrium if enough activities may be put to use. The proof depends on the profit condition and does not need advanced mathematics.

Since only relative quantities matter, because of linearity, it is convenient to normalize the activity vectors. We shall select the vector for which $\sum |x_j| = 1$ to represent the unit level of the activity. Then any vector of inputs and outputs belonging to the activity can be obtained by multiplying the normalized vector by the appropriate nonnegative constant.

Suppose the price vector in a competitive equilibrium is $(p\,w)$ and $(y\,x)$ represents an activity which is used in this equilibrium. Then by the profit condition,

$$p \cdot y + w \cdot x = 0. \tag{1}$$

Suppose that $(p\,w')$ is the price vector of another competitive equilibrium which has the same goods prices but different factor prices. Then,

$$p \cdot y + w' \cdot x \leqslant 0. \tag{2}$$

Therefore, subtracting (1) from (2) we obtain

$$\Delta w \cdot x \leqslant 0 \tag{3}$$

where $\Delta w = w' - w$. Suppose now that there are F activities satisfying the profit condition where F is the number of ultimate factors in the country and that the factor input vectors $x^1, \ldots, x^F$ of these activities are linearly independent.[7] Then $|x_j^i|$ is a nonzero determinant. $\Delta w \cdot x^i = 0$ $(i = 1, \ldots, F)$ may be regarded as a system of F linear homogeneous equations in F variables Δw_j. Since, however, the determinant of the system is nonzero, it has no solution other than the trivial one, which is excluded since $\Delta w \neq 0$.[8] Therefore, it must be true for some i that $\Delta w \cdot x^i < 0$. This means that not all of the F linearly independent activities which were available in the first equilibrium remain available in the second equilibrium. At least one must show a loss.

Let $(y'\,x')$ represent an activity (not necessarily from the same productive process) used in the second equilibrium. Again, by the profit condition,

$$p \cdot y' + w' \cdot x' = 0, \tag{4}$$

$$p \cdot y' + w \cdot x' \leqslant 0. \tag{5}$$

Thus, subtracting (5) from (4), we obtain

$$\Delta w \cdot x' \geqslant 0. \tag{6}$$

Let r be the vector of factor supplies. Suppose there is among the available activities a free disposal activity for each ultimate factor. The free disposal activity has a unit input for this factor and no other inputs or outputs. The presence of this activity is equivalent to assuming that the price of the factor will be zero, if it is in surplus supply, and will never become negative (since then the free disposal activity would earn a positive profit).[9] It will always be possible to exhaust the factor supplies with activities which satisfy the profit condition. Thus $r = \sum t_i x^i$, where t_i are the (positive) levels at which the activities in use in the first equilibrium are operated.[10] Suppose the country can use F independent[11] activities at positive levels. Then, there are $t_i > 0$, and Fx^i, such that $\Delta w \cdot r = \Delta w \cdot (\sum t_i x^i) < 0$, from (3) and the fact that $\Delta w \cdot x^i < 0$ for some i, as we have seen. But if t_j are the activity levels in the second equilibrium, then by (6), $\Delta w \cdot r = \Delta w \cdot (\sum t'_j x^{j'}) \geqslant 0$. Thus we have arrived at a contradiction, and the second equilibrium is not possible for $w' \neq w$.[12]

Let us refer to a country as specialized if it uses less than F independent activities.[13] We will say that competitive equilibrium is possible if the factor supplies can be exhausted by activities which meet the profit conditions. Then the foregoing argument allows us to state

Theorem 1   If competitive equilibrium is possible in a country without specialization, when the price vector for goods is p, then the price vector for factors w is uniquely determined by p.

The following corollary is an immediate consequence, although it may seem rather surprising at first sight.

Corollary   At a given price vector p, factor price equalization is necessary, if it is possible without specialization in any country.

Note that we do not require that the countries produce the same goods, nor that any country should *actually* use as many activities as it has factors. Also some of the goods produced may be intermediate products. On the other hand, equalization is *not* a consequence merely

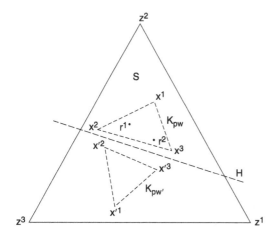

Figure 13.1
The points of S represent factor input vectors whose components sum to -1. At the vertex labelled z^1 the vector is $(-1, 0, 0)$ and correspondingly at other vertices. If we take the altitude of the triangle as equal to 1, the ith component of x is the negative of the perpendicular distance from x to the side opposite the ith vertex.

of the productive systems' being rich in activities. The meaning of the corollary is that if there is a competitive equilibrium, free of specialization, with p and equalized factor prices, there cannot be another equilibrium with p and factor prices not equalized. Since the countries may not have the same factors, we will adopt the convention that equalization of a factor price means equality of price between countries which have supplies of the factor. Otherwise, we should have to assume that each country has positive supplies of each factor.

Theorem 1 shows that the necessity of factor price equality, given its possibility, results from homogeneity of the production functions when factor supplies are constant. It is, however, unlikely that factor price equality *will* be possible, unless the production functions are the same in all countries. For, otherwise, it is conceivable that no $(p\,w)$ which is compatible with the profit conditions (and positive levels of output) in one country will be compatible with the profit conditions (and positive levels of output) in any other country. However, if the activities are the same in all countries, the same $(p\,w)$ will be consistent with the profit conditions everywhere, and the only question will be whether the different r^k can be accommodated. Therefore, let us add assumption.

(3a) The production functions (or activities) are the same in all countries.

Let S be the set of factor input vectors x which satisfy the normalization rule $\sum |x_j| = 1$, where all the factors are included that appear in any country.[14] S is referred to as an $F - 1$ dimensional simplex. In the case of three factors it is a triangle each vertex of which represents an input vector with a unit input of one factor. In the future we will regard r^k as also normalized, so that r^k is the element of S, which represents the factor supply ratios in the kth country. All the factor input vectors lie in S, and for a given $(p\,w)$, which is compatible with the profit conditions, we can consider the set K_{pw} of all elements of S which are expressible as positive linear combinations of x's coming from activities which earn zero profits at $(p\,w)$. In other words, z is in K_{pw} if and only if there are x^i, whose activities earn zero profits at $(p\,w)$, and $z = \sum t_i x^i$ for $t_i > 0$ and $\sum t_i = 1$. K_{pw} is a convex set.[15] Clearly, if it is to be possible to exhaust the given vector of factor supplies for the kth country when the price vector is $(p\,w)$, r^k must lie in K_{pw}. Otherwise, the factors could not be used in the proportions in which they are present.

The points of K_{pw} which can be expressed as positive linear combinations of at least F linearly independent x's lie in the interior of K_{pw}.[16] All other points of K_{pw} lie on the boundary. Suppose $(p\,w')$ is another price vector which is compatible with the profit conditions. Then, as we have seen, $\Delta w \cdot z < 0$ for z in the interior of K_{pw}. Moreover, $\Delta w \cdot z \leqslant 0$ for z in K_{pw} and $\Delta w \cdot z \geqslant 0$ for z in $K_{pw'}$. Thus no z interior to K_{pw} lies in $K_{pw'}$. Indeed, if z lies both in K_{pw} and in $K_{pw'}$, $\Delta w \cdot z = 0$, and z is in the boundaries of both K_{pw} and $K_{pw'}$. The set of all z such that $\Delta w \cdot z = 0$ is called a hyperplane, which we may denote by H. H is said to separate K_{pw} and $K_{pw'}$. Therefore, if r^k is interior to K_{pw}, it cannot lie in any $K_{pw'}$ with $w' \neq w$. But this means that if p is the goods price vector, w must be the factor price vector. We may state

Theorem 2 Given a goods price vector p, if there exists a factor price vector w such that r^k lies in the interior of K_{pw} for all k, factor prices in any competitive equilibrium must be equal to those of w in all countries.

If some country, say the kth, lacks some factors, r^k need only lie in the interior of the K'_{pw} in the simplex S', based on those factors present in the kth country. For the prices of factors which a country does not possess are irrelevant to it. We should note that if r^k lies on the boundary of K'_{pw}, the kth country is forced to specialize to fewer independent activities than it has ultimate factors.

Theorem 2 and the corollary to Theorem 1 show one sense in which specialization may be alternative to factor price equalization. In the set of goods price vectors for which factor price equality is possible, either factor price equalization is necessary or else some country is forced by the goods prices to specialize to less than F independent activities. In the set of goods price vectors which do not permit equalization of factor prices no assured statement about specialization can be made without stronger assumptions.

Thus far we have been concerned with the question when does a price vector p imply equalization of factor prices. It is also possible, however, to ask when does an output vector y imply equalization of factor prices. This will provide another measure of the prevalence of equalization.

Let K_y^k be the region of S spanned by the activities *actually used* in the kth country when the world output is y. We will refer to a pair of countries i and j as connected by a chain if there is a series of countries beginning with the ith and ending with the jth such that the K_y^k of successive countries have interiors which intersect. It is then possible to prove[17]

Theorem 3   With given factor supplies, if a world output y can be produced in competitive equilibrium where every pair of countries is connected by a chain, factor price equalization is necessary for y.

Let $(y^{ki}\, x^{ki})$ be the actual input-output vector of the ith activity in the kth country when y is the world output. Let the price vector for goods be p and for factors w. Factor prices are equalized at p because of the intersections of the K_y^k. Then $p \cdot y^{ki} + w \cdot x^{ki} = 0$, by the profit conditions. Suppose y is also produced when $(p'\, w^k)$ is the price vector in the kth country. Then $p' \cdot y + \sum w^k \cdot r^k = 0$, since the activities used in each country earn zero profits. But $y = \sum_i \sum_k y^{ki}$ and $r^k = \sum_i x^{ki}$. Therefore, $\sum_i \sum_k (p' \cdot y^{ki} + w^k \cdot x^{ki}) = 0$. By the profit conditions, however, $p' \cdot y^{ki} + w^k \cdot x^{ki} \leqslant 0$. This implies that $p' \cdot y^{ki} + w^k \cdot x^{ki} = 0$, and the activities which were used when $(p\, w)$ was the price vector are also available when $(p'\, w^k)$ is the price vector. Thus the sets $K_{p'w^k}$ for successive countries in a chain will contain the sets K_y^k for these countries and, therefore, will have interiors which intersect. Then the w^k of successive countries must be equal. In other words, all the w^k are equal, and factor prices are equalized.

13.4 Variable Factor Supplies

Thus far we have maintained assumption 1 that factor supplies are given in each country. Let us see what can be said if factor supplies are allowed to vary.

Suppose that the factor supplies in each country depend upon $(p\,w)$. If there is no $(p\,w)$ such that all r^k lie in K_{pw}, factor price equality is, in any case, not possible. Suppose, however, that a $(p\,w)$ does exist which leads to r's which even lie in the interior of K_{pw}.[18] Then so long as the r's remain in the interior of this K_{pw}, the goods prices p cannot be associated with a w' with $w' \neq w$. For the r's would then lie in $K_{pw'}$, so that $K_{pw'}$ would intersect the interior of K_{pw}, which is impossible.

Theorem 2′ If the r's remain in the interior of K_{pw} as w varies, factor price equality is necessary for this p.

Recall that for r^k in the interior of K_{pw}, $\Delta w \cdot r^k < 0$, if $\Delta w \neq 0$. Suppose that any change in r^k satisfies the condition $\Delta w \cdot \Delta r^k \leqslant 0$. Then $\Delta w \cdot (r^k + \Delta r^k) = \Delta w \cdot r'^k < 0$. But for z in $K_{pw'}$, $\Delta w \cdot z \geqslant 0$. Thus r'^k cannot lie in $K_{pw'}$, so that $(p\,w')$ cannot provide a competitive equilibrium no matter what the demand for output. We may then state

Theorem 2″ For $\Delta w \cdot \Delta r^k \leqslant 0$, factor price equality is necessary, for given p, if it is possible without specialization.[19]

Loosely speaking, $\Delta w \cdot \Delta r^k \leqslant 0$ means that prices and quantities do not move in opposite directions (quantities, remember, are written with the negative sign). An increase in price for a factor tends to bring out a larger supply. This is what would be expected aside from changes in real income. Changes in real income, however, are likely to have a perverse effect, since any increase of potential earning power is likely to be devoted in part to increased direct use of the factor by its owners, presuming that this use (leisure, for example) is not an inferior good. On the other hand, the income effects will tend to cancel out to the extent that the same people can supply both factors that have risen in price, and factors that have fallen in price. In the labor market, for example, this may, in many cases, overcome the result of a decline in the total quantity of labor offered, should the average wage rate rise. Recall that Δw cannot have components all positive or all negative except in trivial cases.[20] Moreover, substitutions will tend to occur between factors whose relative prices have changed even though their absolute prices change in the same direction.[21]

If the assumption $\Delta w \cdot \Delta r^k \leqslant 0$ is not accepted, however, the case against $r^{\prime k}$ lying in $K_{pw'}$ is still respectable. For not only must r^k pursue $K_{pw'}$, but, if specialization is not present, r^k must move outside the interior of K_{pw} (the absence of specialization insures that K_{pw} does have an interior which contains r^k). Thus an r^k must move perversely in the right direction if some country is to achieve different factor prices. Perhaps we will be allowed to say that this is less "probable" the larger is K_{pw} and the more inelastic are the factor supplies.

13.5 Domestic Goods

In any likely trading situation there will be some goods which, because they are costly or impossible to transport, will not be traded. Many services are of this sort. We can adapt our model to the presence of such goods most easily by combining them with the ultimate factors as commodities whose transport costs are infinite. We will then find that the role they play is very similar to that of factors which are in variable supply.

It is not necessary, however, to include among such goods the intermediate products which are not traded. Such intermediate products have no importance save in facilitating the supply of other goods, and we may suppose the activities to be integrated with respect to them. Then they do not appear explicitly in the activities. We would, of course, fall in error were the intermediate products imported or exported.[22]

The commodities are now divided into two groups, on the one hand, goods, including traded intermediate products, and, on the other hand, factors and untraded final goods. The prices of the first group, the traded commodities, are equalized. Those of the latter group, the untraded commodities, need not be. It is now possible to repeat the foregoing analysis. If the supplies of the factors and the demands for the untraded final goods are fairly inelastic, Theorem 2' is relevant with factor prices augmented by the prices of untraded final goods and with a country able to use F^* independent activities, where F^* is the number of factors and untraded final goods. Activities are considered to be independent when the vectors formed of their factor *and* untraded final goods components are linearly independent. In a similar way, Theorem 2″ may be extended to this case.

Let the set K_{pw}^* be defined by the natural extension of K_{pw}. The larger is K_{pw}^* the more widely diverse are the quantities of untraded commodities which may appear in different countries and yet be accommodated, and, it seems natural to say, the more probable is it that the prices of untraded commodities can be equal without specialization. Similarly, it is less "probable" that the vectors r^{*k} will leave K^*_{pw} when p is constant and w is varied in a fashion consistent with p (including in w the prices of all untraded commodities, in p those of all traded commodities).

13.6 Factor Saturation

Thus far the theorems which we have proved depend not merely on methods of production but also on factor supplies. In this sense it is not really accurate to say that only the profit conditions of equilibrium are involved, since at least part of the demand conditions of equilibrium have been introduced too. In addition to these results, however, our method may be applied to a case where no reference is made to factor supplies.

Suppose there are processes in which the possibilities are limited of substituting factors by moving from one activity efficient in its use of factors to another.[23] If there are F of these, it is possible that any two K's including them will have interiors which intersect. The existence of such processes is not implausible, especially with regard to factors like natural resources and machines. Indeed, I would expect saturation phenomena to be important even though factors are broadly aggregated. But, as we have seen, it is not possible for K_{pw} to intersect the interior of $K_{pw'}$ if $w' \neq w$. Hence as long as F such processes are used in common by two countries, factor prices must be equalized. We may then state

Theorem 4 In a competitive equilibrium, if two countries are able to use a set of independent activities which includes one from each of F processes whose K's always intersect, factor prices must be the same in both countries.

An important application of this theorem arises in the case where each process can be saturated in all factors except perhaps one with which the process may be identified. If we give the same number to the process and its associated factor, it may happen that $|x^i_i| > \sum_{j \neq i} |x^i_j|$ for all activities, efficient in the use of factors, of the ith process for each i.[24] In this case any two K's containing activities from each process will have interiors which intersect.[25] Then if no country is specialized to less than F of *these* processes, factor prices must be equalized. (This is a different sense of specialization from the one we have used earlier.)

The proof of this proposition is not very difficult. If two K's do not have interiors which intersect, they may be separated by a hyperplane H composed of all z such that $q \cdot z = 0$.[26] This is shown for a simple case in Figure 13.1. Let K and K' be two K's which we will suppose to be separated by H, although they contain activities from F processes of the type in question. Then we may suppose[27] $q \cdot x^i \leqslant 0$ for x^i in K and $q \cdot x'^i \geqslant 0$ for x'^i in K'. It is apparent that any component of q of maximum absolute value, say the kth, must be positive. Else $q \cdot x^k \leqslant 0$ would be impossible. Consider then $q \cdot x'^k \geqslant 0$. Since $|q_k| \geqslant |q_j|$ for $j \neq k$, $|q_k x_k'^k| > |\sum_{j \neq k} q_j x_j'^k|$. Therefore, $q_k > 0$ implies $q \cdot x'^k < 0$. Then $q \cdot x'^k \geqslant 0$ is not possible, and K is not separated from K' by H. We may conclude that any two K's containing these F processes must have interiors which intersect.[28] It is apparent that many other cases of saturation can be reduced to this one by redefining the factors so that they become appropriate linear combinations of the natural factors. Note that the only goods prices which need be equalized by trade are the prices of goods appearing in the F processes. Moreover, the processes may be integrated with respect to intermediate products which are not traded between countries.

13.7 The Leontief Model

An interesting special case of the economy with saturation is the Leontief model which has several ultimate factors. The distinctive features of the Leontief model are the absence of joint production and the presence of but one efficient activity for the production of each good. Suppose the number of goods equals the number of factors, and the productive activities are independent. There is a convex set K in S containing all factor ratios which permit the exhaustion of factor supplies without disposal. Indeed, K is a simplex of $F - 1$ dimensions with the input vectors of the *productive* activities as vertices. In addition, there are the free disposal activities represented by the vertices of S.

It is instructive to consider the three dimensional case illustrated in Figure 13.2.[29] A line joins each pair of input vectors. The numbers identify the K_{pw} which use exactly three activities. Apart from singular cases each country will have to use at least one such K_{pw}. We may index the 19 K's which have three vertices by these numbers. S is subdivided by their intersection into 16 elementary divisions. Of course,

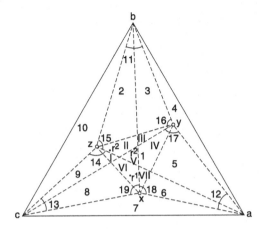

Figure 13.2

x, y, and z are productive activities producing the respective goods. a, b, and c are free disposal activities disposing of the respective factors. Approximately,

$x = (17, 4, 14)/35$,

$y = (15, 16, 4)/35$,

$z = (6, 12, 17)/35$.

The Arabic numbers in the diagram refer to the K's spanned by three activities. The Roman numerals identify the elementary subdivisions of K_1.

for some $(p\,w)$ more or less than three activities will meet the profit conditions. It is apparent that if the r's lie in the interior of the same elementary subdivision of S, the factor prices will always be equal whatever the goods price vector p (or the world output vector y) may be, for then all the K's which contain r's have interiors which intersect. Furthermore, if the r's all lie in the interior of K_1, there can never be more than two sets of factor prices prevailing simultaneously in different countries, since no three K's with disjoint interiors appear in K_1. This is all that can be said, if intermediate products are traded, unless the inputs of intermediate products are specified. If the number of goods is increased, the pattern of subdivision of S and K becomes more complex. Indeed the greater variety of production patterns available may reduce the prevalence of equalization. For example, the divisions of K_1 will be further subdivided. Therefore, even if all the r's formerly lay in the same elementary subdivision, they need not do so when the number of activities is larger.

If intermediate products are not traded, the Leontief model may be completely solved in the three dimensional case by graphical

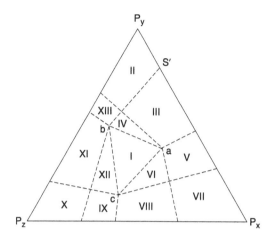

Figure 13.3
S' represents the various possible goods price ratios. The goods price vector at a is the normalization of the goods price vector resulting from the factor price vector $w = (1,0,0)$ and the assumption that all goods are produced, and correspondingly at b and c. Thus

$a = (17,15,6)/38,$

$b = (4,16,12)/32,$

$c = (14,4,17)/35.$

The K_i which is used by a country in the interior of a division of S' is determined by the location of its factor supply vector. For example, the K_i available in the interior of

I are $1,4,7,10,11,12,13$

VI are $2,3,4,7,10,12,13$

VII are $7,18,19.$

For other K_i there is no w consistent with p in the division and the use or disposal of all factor supplies.

techniques.[30] We now suppose there are three final goods and the activities are integrated. The triangle S' in Figure 13.3 represents all possible relative goods prices. It is divided into 13 areas within each of which the K's available to any country are given, depending on its resource vector. On the boundaries of the divisions all the K's are available at a point p which are available in the divisions meeting at this point. The K's available in the interior of a division of S' always exactly exhaust S. Thus, in the interior of a division of S' the K which can be used by a country is uniquely determined by the goods prices provided that the country's resource vector lies in the interior of an elementary subdivision of S.

Suppose, for example, that r^1 lies in VI of K_1, r^2 in II, r^3 in V, factor prices will then be equalized when p lies in I, V, VI, VII, or VIII of S', including the boundaries of these divisions. However, all output ratios which involve a positive output of each good will correspond to I, with its boundaries, and factor prices must be equalized. Note that to the interior of I there corresponds only a single output combination when the r's lie in the interiors of divisions of S, while nearly all output combinations correspond to a vertex of I.[31]

13.8 Substitution and Intermediate Products

In the Leontief model, since the productive processes have but one efficient activity, countries with given factor supplies can specialize to fewer than F productive processes only by having certain particular factor proportions, or by disposing of surplus factor supplies, that is, through the presence of free factors. Moreover, changes in the productive processes used, which might be necessary to reach certain ranges of output, would ordinarily require changes in the list of free factors. These properties will also appear in less extreme form in any economy where saturation is a frequent phenomenon.

In the opposite case, where no process becomes saturated in the region which contains the factor supply vectors, the list of scarce factors will not change and any country will be able to specialize to even a single productive process. Of course, it may not be possible for a country to specialize to some particular processes, even when they do not become saturated, because the corresponding activities may not be efficient from the standpoint of the productive system.[32] This difficulty does not arise if there is but one process for producing each good, or if each process produces at least one good which is produced by no other process.

The extreme cases are quite unrealistic, but it will remain true in other cases that the smaller the incidence of saturation the more often the proximate reason for the failure of factor price equality will be that some country's resource vector strikes the boundary of K_{pw} as prices vary and, therefore, specialization to fewer than F processes becomes necessary for that country.[33]

In order to consider the prevalence of equalization, where saturation is absent we may use Theorem 3 to identify certain world outputs y which imply equalization of factor prices regardless of p. For the sake of concreteness consider Figure 13.4. There are four activities

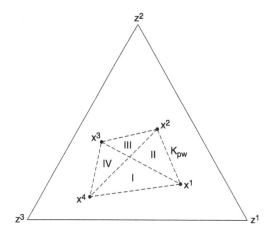

Figure 13.4
With factor supplies given, any output y produced, when all factor supply vectors lie in the interior of the same subdivision of K_{pw}, must always be accompanied by factor price equalization in a competitive equilibrium.

represented by points of S. The lines drawn between these points divide the polygon K_{pw} spanned by the activities into four regions. Suppose all the r's fall into the interior of one of these regions. Then, regardless of what output combination is produced in a competitive equilibrium which uses these four activities (or perhaps only three of them), the K_y of each country intersects that of every other. Therefore, the output cannot be produced except with factor price equality, no matter what activities may be used or what prices prevail.[34] If the activities allow continuous substitution, the polygon K_{pw} may assume various positions, as prices vary, relative to the r's. It would appear then that if the r's are clustered fairly closely and K_{pw} remains relatively large, a great variety of world outputs can be produced when the r's are in some one of the elementary subdivisions of K_{pw}, so that these outputs must be accompanied by factor price equality.[35]

The question naturally arises whether there is an economy free of saturation in which factor price equality is required for all possible outputs in competitive equilibrium. It turns out to be so. Suppose the number of processes, which it is ever profitable to use, is just equal to the number of factors. This allows joint production only if surplus output can be disposed of without cost. For under some demand conditions one of the joint products will not be desired and either the joint process must close down or a disposal process must be introduced.

The disposal process can be ignored if it uses no factor. Suppose, also, that the system is circular, in the sense that the production of any good requires, directly or indirectly, the use of all productive processes. In such a system two conditions must be met for competitive equilibrium. The individual r's must be in K_{pw}, so that each country may exhaust its factor supplies with activities which satisfy the profit conditions. But also the sum $\bar{r}$ of the r's must lie in $\bar{K}_{pw}$ where $\bar{K}_{pw}$ is based on integrated activities.[36] If the latter condition is not met, the supply of intermediate products is inadequate to allow the exhaustion of factor supplies by the activities in use. In this system it may happen that the r^k remain in the interior of K_{pw} for every position of $\bar{r}$ within $\bar{K}_{pw}$. Then factor prices must be equalized for all world outputs whatsoever. It is apparent that factor prices are equalized for any output that *can* be produced with equalization, since the K_y^k are identical with K_{pw} and thus do have interiors which intersect (so long as the F activities are independent and K_{pw} has an interior). No other outputs, however, are producible with these processes in competitive equilibrium, since the equilibrium outputs which are possible with factors fully mobile can still be attained, without mobility, when factor prices are equalized.[37]

This analysis exposes what is no doubt a strong tendency for the mobility of intermediate products, especially agricultural and mineral raw materials, to replace the mobility of factors. The last example, however, refers to a limiting case where the replacement of factor movement by the movement of goods is completely successful. Thus it requires the extreme assumptions, that each process, directly or indirectly, depends on every other, and that the numbers of factors and processes are equal.

13.9   The Cobb-Douglas Model

For purposes of illustration it may be useful to analyze a model in which no process becomes saturated. Consider a productive system where every production function is of the Cobb-Douglas type. For three inputs, the Cobb-Douglas production function has the form $x = a^\alpha b^\beta c^\gamma$, where x is the quantity of a good produced and a, b, and c are the quantities of the inputs used. $\alpha + \beta + \gamma = 1$ to insure homogeneity. The input proportions are given in terms of the parameters and factor prices by the relation

$$a/b = \alpha/\beta \cdot w_b/w_a.$$

The set W^k of factor price vectors consistent with factor supplies in the kth country is convex.[38] In fact, it is a polygon the vertices of which represent prices that allow the production of only one good. If we assume that the supplies of the traded intermediate products are always adequate, the set W of factor price vectors which can appear in all countries together will be the intersection of the sets W^k. We may take the production functions to be integrated with respect to intermediate products which are not traded. To allow for the limited supplies of traded intermediate products, the w^k must be intersected with the set $\overline{W}$ of factor price vectors consistent with the world resources vector $\bar{r}$ when the activities are completely integrated. This insures an adequate supply of intermediate products. The effect of trade in intermediate products will be an expansion of the set W. Consider, for instance, the case illustrated in Figure 13.5. Corresponding to the set W there is a set P of goods price vectors p which imply equalization if the productive processes are independent.[39]

If the productive processes are independent and equal in number to the productive factors, it is possible that equalization will always be implied. Then the intersection of the W^k will contain $\overline{W}$. However, this condition is not sufficient if the number of goods exceeds the number of factors.

13.10   Samuelson's Theorem

Professor Samuelson has proved a result on factor price equalization which is in the spirit of our Theorem 4, in that no direct reference is made to factor supplies and the countries are required to use at least F independent processes in common. Neither theorem, however, appears to imply the other, although the most obvious application of each is the same.

I shall present a version of Samuelson's theorem slightly different from the original and more in harmony with the approach used here. For each productive process consider the set X of ultimate factor inputs x which are consistent with a value product of \$1, where the value product is defined as $p \cdot y$ and p is some given goods price vector. We may suppose that the processes are integrated with respect to untraded intermediate products, and the prices of all other goods appearing in the processes are equalized by trade. If x^1 is in X and x^2 is in X, so also is $x = tx^1 + (1-t)x^2$ with $0 \leqslant t \leqslant 1$. For if y, y^1, and y^2 correspond to x, x^1, and x^2, then $p \cdot y = tp \cdot y^1 + (1-t)p \cdot y^2 = t \cdot \$1 + (1-t) \cdot \$1 =$

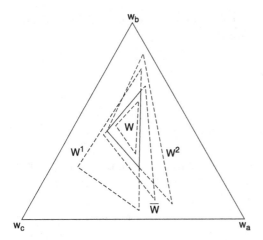

Figure 13.5
This triangle represents all possible factor price ratios. At w_a the factor price vector is $(1,0,0)$ and correspondingly at other vertices. Inside the triangle vectors are determined as in Figure 13.1. At the lower vertices of the W^k and $\overline{W}$ only x is produced. At the left vertices only y. At the top vertices only z.

The inner triangle, outlined with solid lines, represents the set W of all factor price vectors which can appear simultaneously in all countries when intermediate products are traded. The smaller triangle included inside represents the set W when intermediate products are not traded.

In deriving the sets W^k and $\overline{W}$ the following parameters were used in a Cobb-Douglas model:

	α	β	γ	ρ_x	ρ_y	ρ_z
x	.45	.05	.40		.10	
y	.10	.30	.50			.10
z	.10	.65	.05	.20		

$r^1 = (.30, .40, .30)$, $r^2 = (.25, .25, .50)$, $\bar{r} = (.27, .31, .42)$.

The ρ's refer to intermediate product inputs, which are also treated as variable. $\bar{r}$ is based on the assumption that country 2 is half again as large as country 1.

$1. Thus the set X is convex, and we shall assume that it is closed. The part of the boundary of X on which no input can be reduced without increasing some other input is analogous to the traditional isoquant,[40] and may be used in the same way. Suppose that this "isoquant" is strictly convex and differentiable.[41] There will be two distinct vectors of factor prices consistent with p and the use of the same F processes (absence of specialization in the strong sense) if there are two hyperplanes each of which is tangent to all F isoquants. In the two dimensional case, for two isoquants there are two tangent lines, perpendicular to factor price vectors w and w' respectively, where $w' \neq w$.

Samuelson has shown[42] that no such ambiguity is possible, for $w \geqslant 0$, if the activities can be numbered so that the matrix

$$
A = \begin{bmatrix} x_1^1 & \cdots & x_1^F \\ \cdot & & \cdot \\ \cdot & & \cdot \\ \cdot & & \cdot \\ x_F^1 & \cdots & x_F^F \end{bmatrix}
$$

of factor inputs always has a nonzero determinant and nonzero naturally-ordered principal minors. However, the only general condition which is known at present to lead to an A which is nonzero in this sense, and which has a ready economic interpretation, seems to be that A have a dominant diagonal, i.e., $|x_i^i| > \sum_{j \neq i} |x_j^i|$ for all i.[43] Theorem 4 also applies to this case, as we have already seen. (Both our application of Theorem 4 and this application of Samuelson's theorem can be strengthened somewhat by conditions which relax strict inequality.)

Samuelson's theorem may be given the general form of

Theorem 5 Suppose at a given price vector p the matrix A of factor inputs into a certain F processes, which are minimal for a fixed value product and which meet the profit conditions at w, is non-zero for $w \geqslant 0$. Then for any pair of countries, either factor prices are equal or one country uses less than F of these processes.

Notes

1. An earlier version of this chapter was presented to the Econometric Society in Montreal, Canada, September, 1954. I wish to acknowledge the helpful advice of Professors Samuelson, Solow, and Strotz.

2. The basic article on factor price equalization is now Paul A. Samuelson, "Prices of Factors and Goods in General Equilibrium," *The Review of Economic Studies*, Vol. XXI (1), 1953–4. References to earlier literature will be found there. Articles by A. P. Lerner, *Economica*, February, 1952, and by J. Tinbergen, *Metroeconomica*, July, 1949 were particularly suggestive to me.

3. The *locus classicus* of activity analysis is chapter 3 by Tjalling C. Koopmans in *Activity Analysis of Production and Allocation*, New York, 1951, edited by Koopmans.

4. This is similar to the "futures" model described by J. R. Hicks in *Value and Capital*, Oxford, 1939, p. 136.

5. I shall sometimes speak of them as sets of conditions.

6. The effect of the profit condition is that any equilibrium input-output vector is in the boundary of the cone of possible input-output vectors, and the price vector is normal to the cone at this point.

7. A set of vectors $x^1, \ldots, x^n$ is linearly independent if $\sum t_i x^i = 0$ implies $t_i = 0$ for all i.

8. See, for instance, W. L. Ferrar, *Algebra*, Oxford, 1941, p. 32, Theorem 11.

9. In other words, the free disposal activity has the same effect as assuming that factor supplies are fixed amounts for positive prices, anything from zero to the fixed amounts for zero prices, and zero for negative prices. Thus there need not be any actual free disposal, but the fiction is very convenient.

10. We can always, by taking sums, do with one activity, at most, from each process, and since there are only a finite number of goods and factors, there can be only a finite number of processes.

11. Whether from different processes or not. By independent activities I mean activities with linearly independent vectors of factor inputs.

12. This result generalizes a proposition of Abraham Wald, which applies to a productive system with a finite number of activities, each producing a different good, and each always in use. If A is the matrix of coefficients for ultimate factor inputs, his proposition is that $A'w = p$ determines w uniquely given p if A has rank equal to F. See Wald, "On Some Systems of Equations of Mathematical Economics," *Econometrica*, October, 1951, p. 377 (translated from *Zeitschrift für Nationalökonomie*, 1936).

13. Recall the definition of "independent." Activities are *not* independent merely because they are unrelated and produce different products. Their vectors of factor inputs must be *linearly* independent.

14. The following argument is illustrated in Figure 13.1.

15. A set of vectors Y is convex if y^1 in Y and y^2 in Y implies $y = ty^1 + (1-t)y^2$ in Y for $0 \leqslant t \leqslant 1$.

16. By definition, a point z lies in the interior of K_{pw}, if it can be surrounded by a sphere (of dimension $F - 1$) which lies in K_{pw}. It is quite obvious in 2 or 3 dimensions that the assertion in the text is equivalent to this condition.

17. We are implicitly assuming that each country possesses all factors. Otherwise, the statement of the theorem becomes a little more complicated.

18. I shall usually speak as though each country has supplies of every factor. The necessary emendations should be obvious.

19. If the strict equality $\Delta w \cdot \Delta r^k < 0$ holds, the condition of no specialization can be dropped.

20. For then $\Delta w \cdot x^i < 0$ (or > 0) for all x^i and at one of the w's no activity can meet the profit condition.

21. The condition $\Delta w \cdot \Delta r \leqslant 0$ if $\Delta p = 0$ is weaker than the condition $(\Delta p \, \Delta w) \cdot (\Delta y \, \Delta r) \leqslant 0$ which holds for the single consumer with constant real income. See Samuelson, *Foundations of Economic Analysis*, Cambridge, 1947, p. 109. The latter condition, which has been applied by Wald and Hotelling to the whole market, would result in an essentially unique equilibrium. See the author's "On Equilibrium in Graham's Model of World Trade and other Competitive Systems," *Econometrica*, April, 1954, p. 154.

22. On this matter, see the author's earlier article in *The Review of Economic Studies*, Vol. 21, No. 3, "Specialization and Efficiency in World Production," p. 177 *et. seq.*

23. By saturation for a process in a certain factor, I mean that the factor input vectors of activities efficient in the use of factors are bounded away from the corresponding vertex of S. These bounds may be more or less confining. The extreme case of processes which become saturated is the process with fixed coefficients, as used for example, by Cassel and by Leontief (when there are several ultimate factors).

24. The matrix $[x_j^i]$ is then said to have a dominant diagonal.

25. Note that if the profit conditions are met and any activity from a process earns zero profit, then there is an activity efficient in the use of factors which also earns zero profits. For any superfluous input of a factor implies that the factor has a zero price. Otherwise, a profit could be realized on the activity in which the superfluity had been discarded.

26. This is the fundamental theorem of the theory of convex sets.

27. Since one inequality holds on one side of H and the other on the other side of H. Indeed, these inequalities define the "sides" of H.

28. Else some hyperplane H would separate them. But this has been shown to be impossible. Our theorem is an extension of a theorem of Hadamard. The latter, in modern guise, may be found in O. Taussky, "A Recurring Theorem on Determinants," *American Mathematical Monthly*, Vol. 56, 1949, pp. 672–676.

29. With appropriate generalizations, however, the argument extends to any number of dimensions.

30. This condition is absurd unless we suppose, as we do, that the goods which are traded are only useful as final products, never as intermediate products. Thus the system lacks the typical Leontief feature of circularity except for the untraded intermediate goods, which disappear when the activities are integrated.

31. Unless the r's are widely dispersed, some of the divisions of S' will merge. In the resulting figure, each division is the intersection with S' of the cone of normals to a zero dimensional facet of the convex set of output vectors attainable within the resources limitations. Similarly an edge of a division contains price vectors normal to a two dimensional facet.

32. That is, a combination of activities from other processes can produce at least as much of any final good, and more of at least one, while remaining within the resource limitations.

33. As we have just seen the mere fact that continuous substitution is possible in every process does not mean that a process will always be used, even when the goods which it produces are in demand. Thus it is not necessary that K_{pw} always move continuously.

34. One can substitute for "output" in these statements "output in these proportions," since the output in given proportions which is compatible with competitive equilibrium must be maximal in the set of attainable outputs and is, therefore, unique. See Koopmans, *op. cit.*, p. 86.

35. This argument like that concerning the Leontief model will generalize to any number of dimensions. The elementary subdivisions arise from the intersection of all polygons with F different activities as vertices. Of course, there must be at least F activities present.

36. In the absence of joint production, or assuming free disposal, integrated activities will exist if anything at all can be produced.

37. This depends on the fact that the r^k and $\bar{r}$ can be expressed in only one way as linear combinations of the x^i. Thus if the number of x^i exceeds the number of factors, the conclusion does not follow.

38. The proof of this assertion is omitted in the interest of brevity. It is not difficult, however.

39. The factor input vectors will be linearly independent at every w if the coefficient vectors (α, β, γ) are linearly independent. Then we may say that the processes are independent.

40. It is also related to the efficient point set of activity analysis.

41. That is, it contains no straight line segments and no corners (points without unique tangent planes).

42. Samuelson, *op. cit.*, pp. 16–17. Differentiability is clearly not necessary. It would seem that strict convexity is also superfluous.

43. A is then non-singular by Hadamard's theorem.

14 Specialization in Production and the Production Possibility Locus

Lionel W. McKenzie

In an earlier paper[1] I have given an analysis of specialization in Graham's model of world trade[2] from the viewpoint of efficient production. It was shown there that the admission of intermediate products into world trade restricted the usefulness of the Graham model. New efficient patterns of specialization would appear. However, it was not made entirely clear how trade in intermediate products differed from allowing many ultimate factors in each country. I shall show here that the Graham model retains a certain usefulness when many factors are allowed. Indeed, Graham's approach can be regarded as a generalization of the classical discussion of specialization in terms of a smooth production possibility locus. Moreover, the international trade problem, as Prof. Hicks has pointed out,[3] is quite analogous to the problem treated by welfare economists of an efficient distribution of production between firms.

We will then enquire just how the Graham extension[4] of the traditional approach, based on the production possibility locus, becomes inadequate when either joint production or trade in intermediate products is introduced. However, the more general methods of linear activity analysis can still be applied. This represents a further generalization of the classical methods, which have depended on marginal rates of substitution. We shall see that the basic flaw in the classical treatment of specialization is neither an assumption about factor supplies nor about constant costs, but the neglect of trade in intermediate products. On the other hand, activity analysis proves to be quite as necessary for the selection of sources of output, when production functions are smooth, as for the selection of activities, when production functions are not smooth.

14.1   The Graham Analogue

Suppose there are many factors in each country and the factor supplies are given, but intermediate products are not traded and joint production is absent. Throughout the chapter we will neglect the barriers to trade. Let the entries in one of Graham's tables of comparative costs[5] represent marginal rates of substitution on the production possibility loci of the various countries, where these loci are determined from the given factor supplies. Assume, as usual in these problems, homogeneity of the production functions and the absence of external economies. Suppose that production is efficient in each country separately. Then it is necessary and sufficient for efficiency in world production[6] that the specialization of countries be efficient[7] in this corresponding Graham model.

It is essential for our result that the marginal rates of substitution should be uniquely defined, even when some goods are not produced. Of course, when a good is not produced, substitution can occur in only one direction. Thus there is not, properly speaking, any tangent plane to the production possibility locus at the corresponding output,[8] which lies on an edge of the locus. However, it may happen that there is a unique plane containing all lines along which small movements are possible. This will be true if the rate at which it is possible to replace one good in production with any good which is not produced is independent of any other simultaneous substitution. This simply means that no advantage is to be gained from joint production. In other words, if (and only if) there is no joint production, a smooth production possibility locus can be regarded as possessing a tangent plane at every point, including boundary points. Then the Graham table is defined.

Once the Graham table of comparative costs has been given a secure meaning, our conclusion may be drawn from two observations. First, homogeneity and the absence of external economies implies a nondecreasing marginal rate of substitution.[9] Therefore, the set of outputs possible in fact is contained in the set of outputs possible on the (Graham) assumption of unchanging marginal rates of substitution. Second, a movement can be made in any direction, which does not involve negative production, at these rates of substitution. This means that small changes of output which accord with efficiency in each country separately are the same for the actual system and the Graham analogue. But, by our first observation, if output can be increased[10] for the actual system, it certainly can be increased for the Graham analogue. Moreover, the converse implication is also obvious. Thus we may say that the specialization in the actual system is efficient for the output produced if and only if the Graham analogue is efficient. In the terms of the earlier paper, if the pattern of specialization is not efficient in the Graham analogue, there is a non-neutral circuit[11] which can be used to increase the production of some good while not encroaching on the production of other goods.

It should be noted that the implication from inefficiency in the Graham analogue is not that the specialization in the actual system is inefficient for all world outputs[12] that can be produced with it, but only that it is inefficient when used to produce the particular world output in question.

14.2   The Limits of the Graham Analogue

I shall now make use of a numerical example introduced in my earlier paper to indicate more precisely just where the method of the Graham analogue falls short, even when the production possibility locus is smooth. It will be seen that a more general linear activities analogue must be used. An assumption that ultimate productive factors are continuously substitutable does not remove the need for greater generality.

Three products are traded, linen, cloth, and wheat. Labor is the only ultimate factor in each country. The quantity of linen needed to make cloth is technically fixed. Linen also serves as a final good. The productive processes are integrated with respect to all intermediate products other than linen. The countries trading have the following technologies:

	A			B			C		
	l.	cl.	w.	l.	cl.	w.	l.	cl.	w.
L_A	-1	-1	-1						
L_B				-1	-1	-1			
L_C							-1	-1	-1
Linen	2	-10		5	-10		10	-10	
Cloth		10			10			10	
Wheat			7			10			10

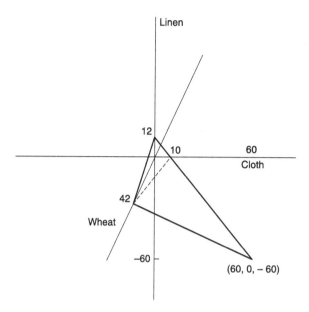

Figure 14.1
The triangle completed by dashed lines with vertices on the axes is the traditional production possibility locus for country A. Its extension to the point $(60, 0, 60)$ is based upon imports of linen.

Negative numbers represent inputs, positive numbers outputs, and L_A refers to the labor of country A. If each country provides its own supplies of linen, the table of comparative costs is:

			A	B	C
Cloth	, , ,	. . .	10	10	10
Linen	. . .	. . .	12	15	20
Wheat	. . .	. . .	42	30	20

We will extend the usual production possibility locus (an efficient point set of activity analysis) to permit negative production (in other words, input) of the traded intermediate products. Then the extended production possibility locus for country A is shown in Figure 14.1. It is assumed that country A has six units of labor so that quantities in the table represent maximum production for this country. However, if unlimited amounts of linen can be imported, the maximum production of cloth becomes 60 units.

As noted in the earlier paper, when linen is not traded, and has final as well as intermediate uses, an efficient specialization is given by A in wheat, B in cloth, and C in linen. However, it was proved there by using the basic theorem of activity analysis that this specialization is not efficient when linen is traded, for there is no set of prices which leaves the activities in use earning zero profits and the unused activities promising zero or negative profits, if put to use. An advantageous move is for B to reduce clothing production by 9 units, use the labor from $6\frac{2}{3}$ units (taken from the integrated process) to produce 10 units of linen, and use the labor from $2\frac{1}{3}$ units to produce 7 units of wheat. Then A can reduce the production of wheat by 7 units, thus releasing 1 unit of labor which can be combined with the 10 units of linen from B to produce 10 units of cloth. Thus, cloth production has been raised by 1 unit and the world production of other goods has not changed.

This improvement cannot be found by use of the Graham table alone. Suppose we remove the restriction that the production of linen in A be positive. Then let the production of cloth fall by 10 units in B and use this labor to produce 15 units of linen. "Reduce" the production of linen in A by 15 units. This allows an expansion of the production of cloth by $12\frac{1}{2}$ units. Thus the profit is $2\frac{1}{2}$ in 10 instead of 1 in 9. Thus the direct procedure, using a chain of substitutions, or a non-neutral circuit, cannot be correct. Indeed, the advantage from shift of cloth production from B to A depends partly on the relative productivities of A and B in wheat. If B is sufficiently unproductive in wheat the advantage is lost.

It is necessary to introduce explicitly the activities which produce wheat in the two countries and also the intermediate product requirements of the activity producing cloth in A (not, however, in B). Of course, this improvement is fairly easy to see through. But, more complicated cases would not be so obvious and sometimes could not be solved without much computation.

If we consult Figure 14.1, it is clear where the difficulty lies. Any movement of the output of country A does lie on the plane defined by the marginal rates of substitution in the table. However, at the vertex of the production possibility locus of country A in which it is specialized in wheat, no movement in the direction of more cloth, for linen alone, is possible. At best, it is possible to proceed along an edge of the production possibility locus in the direction of more cloth for linen *and* wheat.

If we suppose there to be many ultimate factors in each country which may be substituted continuously for each other,[13] the production possibility locus remains smooth but bulges outward from the origin. If we also assume that joint production is absent, unique "tangent" planes can be defined everywhere, even at corners. That is to say, a small movement from the wheat vertex in the direction of more cloth and linen is equal to the sum of appropriate movements in the direction of more cloth alone and more linen alone. Thus the admission of many ultimate factors has not changed the local situation. If intermediate products are not traded, the method of the Graham analogue can be applied. However, if linen is traded, traditional methods based on marginal rates of substitution fail. Several goods and activities must be considered simultaneously in both countries and the intermediate product structure of cloth production must be specified.

On the other hand, suppose joint production is present. In other words, some advantage is derived from producing linen and cloth together rather than separately. Then the production possibility locus will bend outward not only in the linen-cloth plane but also in the neighbourhood of the point of specialization in wheat. As a result, a unique tangent plane cannot be employed at the wheat vertex. The rates of substitution depend on the particular mixture of cloth and linen which is undertaken. This leads to an activities model with an infinity of activities distinguished by the proportions in which cloth and linen are produced. Obviously the Graham analogue is not helpful. However, there is a linear activities model which approximates the local situation.

One may notice further that if the inputs of intermediate products are also variable, that is, more cloth can be produced with larger linen imports even though labor is fully engaged, the point (60, 0, 60) of complete specialization in the cloth activity is replaced by an arc concave to the origin. Then once more a multiplicity of tangent planes and rates of substitution appear at the wheat vertex. In other words, joint production with variable outputs and trade in intermediate products with variable inputs have similar implications for the extended production possibility locus at its boundary points. The boundary points are, of course, the points of specialization.

The general conclusion which may be drawn from this discussion is that the method of unique marginal rates of substitution, of which the classical theory of specialization is the simplest form, and which receives its most general expression in the Graham analogue, fails inevitably in face of trade in intermediate products or of joint production, and this regardless of all varieties of continuous substitutability.

14.3   The Linear Activities Analogue

However, the full significance of the theory of specialization arises from the fact that it may be applied to any sources of output, whether regions, localities, or even firms, not merely to countries. For instance, however mobile resources may be, there is always the question of specializing their uses in the regions where they now are, so that output is a maximum,[14] and also the question of competitive equilibrium with the given distribution of resources. Furthermore, if firms are treated as sources, fixed capital, and entrepreneurial abilities, are relatively immobile. Thus an important part of the problem of efficient production, or of competitive equilibrium, is a problem of the specialization in production of firms. But if economies of scale may be neglected, the analysis corresponds to that of specialization of countries.[15] When the number of firms and products exceeds two, the method of the Graham analogue may be used to determine the efficiency of a specialization, provided joint production and trade in intermediate products are absent. Notice that one does not have joint production merely because a firm produces many products. On the other hand, if these conditions are not satisfied (and they are very strong), the efficiency of a specialization can still be tested by use of the linear activities analogue, where the activities are defined in terms of small changes. In other words, the linear activities analogue is effective in the same circumstances that lead to the efficiency of competition. However, the presence of external economies or of increasing returns to scale will require special treatment, and at the same time competition will probably be either inefficient or impossible.

The argument runs parallel to that for the Graham analogue. We will suppose for simplicity that unwanted intermediate products can be disposed of without cost. Then it cannot be advantageous to sacrifice efficiency in any country, where it is understood that traded intermediate products are treated as final goods. Therefore, we may say that a specialization is efficient for a certain world output if there is no set of changes in national outputs consistent with efficiency in each country which increases the world production of one final good (now excluding all intermediate products) unless it lowers that of another. Thus we may confine our attention to moves along the production

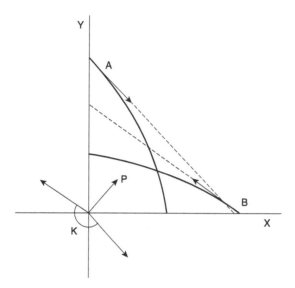

Figure 14.2
The solid curves are the actual production possibility curves. The dashed lines represent loci based on the initial tangential directions. K is the local cone when A is specialized to good Y and B to good X. The specialization is efficient since K does not overlap the positive quadrant. P is one possible price vector which eliminates profits from "arbitrage."

possibility loci. Furthermore, it is clear that so long as the production possibility locus is convex to the origin, the set of outputs in any country which are achievable in fact will lie inside the set of outputs which can be reached by extending the incipient movements which can be made. In other words, the "tangent" directions define a locus which encloses the original locus. A trivial example is given in Figure 14.2.

The possible changes in world output consistent with these tangential moves can be found by considering all combinations of movements in tangential directions. If vectors of unit length pointing in these directions are located at the origin in a space of intermediate and final goods, they may be regarded as defining linear activities. Their non-negative linear combinations form the cone of possible movements away from the existing world output. The existing world output of final goods cannot be improved upon if (and only if) every vector contained in this cone which has a positive final goods component also has a negative component. In other words, for this "local cone"[16] the origin must be an efficient point. In the case of smooth production possibility loci, it is easy to see that all countries producing a pair of final goods in common must have the same marginal rates of substitution between them. But this condition is far from sufficient. Indeed, it does not broach the real problem of specialization.

If we may suppose the number of independent tangential directions to be finite, a necessary and sufficient condition for efficiency is given by the fundamental theorem of activity analysis. Adapted to the present case, it is that there should exist a set of prices for which all tangential movements are non-profitable, where final goods prices are positive and the prices of traded intermediate products are positive or zero.[17] This means that there must be a set of prices for the goods in world trade which prevents any arbitrage operation from providing a profit, where arbitrage may involve new starts in production in a number of countries. In other words, given efficient production in each country separately, the specialization of countries is efficient if and only if there are prices for traded goods which permit the profit conditions of competitive equilibrium to be met in the sphere of international arbitrage. This means that when we analyse a trading system with the aim of identifying efficient specializations, we are at the same time determining possible competitive equilibria. Of course, for full competitive equilibrium the output produced must also be demanded.[18]

14.4 The General Theory of Specialization

In the preceding discussion it has been assumed that the supplies of ultimate resources are given in each country. If the supplies can vary, the assumption of efficiency in each country and in the activity analysis analogue may not guarantee efficiency in world production, since it gives no weight to economies in the use of factors depending on adjustments of production in more than one country. However, if the ultimate factors are continuously substitutable in processes where they are used, any release of an ultimate factor would allow an increase in the production of some final good. Thus the exception cannot occur. Also savings in the use of free factors can be ignored. Consequently, the argument needs no amendment, if factor supplies are variable, unless perhaps there are scarce factors which, for some country, are not continuously substitutable in any process used.

If the factors themselves can migrate between sources, our extension of the customary production possibility locus is inadequate. The previous argument does, indeed, apply, but it is not complete. To allow for migration, the migratory factors must appear explicitly. The production possibility locus then becomes the usual efficient point set of activity analysis.[19] Precisely the same strictures as earlier apply to the attempt to handle, in this general case, the problem of specialization with marginal rates of substitution (and transformation). Continuous variation in the rates of substitution can only remove the need for activity analysis of the local situation if specialization is not present, that is, if all the firms involved produce the same goods and use the same factors. Moreover, should more than one ultimate factor be migratory the Graham analogue will not be available, whether or not intermediate products are traded, except in that case where every firm uses every ultimate factor.

14.5   An Appendix on Specialization in Graham's Model

The characteristics which distinguish Graham's model are that each country has one ultimate factor and intermediate products are not exchanged. Let us refer to a pattern of specialization in which each country is entirely devoted to one final product as a complete specialization. In my previous article I was led to observe that efficient patterns of specialization in Graham's model could be built up from efficient complete specializations. I there referred to the set of efficient outputs consistent with an efficient specialization, a facet of the set of efficient outputs. A complete specialization results then in a zero-dimensional facet.

An *obiter dictum*, which appears on p. 175 of my earlier article, reads, "each facet of given dimension s is a polygon whose vertices are a maximal set of zero-dimensional facets, between each pair of which s countries or less specialize differently. Moreover, the points of every such maximal set form the vertices of an s-dimensional facet." It is easily seen that this statement is wrong. Indeed, the condition is neither necessary nor sufficient. However, the characterization of all specializations which are efficient by means of efficient complete specializations is, nonetheless, possible.

Let us say that a complete specialization is contained in a given specialization if it is composed of activities[20] which are used in the given specialization. Then the true theorem may be stated as follows.

(a) A specialization pattern is efficient if and only if it contains at least one complete specialization and all the complete specializations contained in it are efficient.

(b) An efficient specialization is of dimension s if and only if the number of activities in it equals $n + s + c$, where n is the number of countries and c is the number of independent neutral circuits among the activities in use.

In the terminology of facets, the facets of the set of efficient outputs are polygons whose vertices are zero-dimensional facets which can be formed from the activities present in the specialization generating the facet. If there are no circuits present, all such zero-dimensional facets will lie at a vertex. Otherwise, some will lie elsewhere within the polygon.

Part (a) of the theorem can be proved by the use of substitution circuits.[21] The only restraint on the construction of circuits is that activities not in use must only be required to provide increments of output, never decrements. It was shown in the earlier article that if a specialization is inefficient, it is possible to arrange a chain of substitutions (traverse a circuit) which increases the production of some good while reducing that of none. By continuing these substitutions, one, at least, of the activities formerly in use will be removed from use. Furthermore, such a chain of substitutions cannot be arranged if the specialization is efficient.

This shows immediately that no specialization pattern can tolerate an inefficient complete specialization pattern inside it. For the displacement of an activity from the included complete specialization will also displace an activity from the given specialization, showing it to be inefficient as well.

The more difficult question is whether when all the included complete specializations *are* efficient, the given specialization is also efficient. However, if the given specialization is not efficient, it is possible to establish a circuit which can displace an activity in use. Moreover, the circuit may be chosen so that it involves only one substitution[22] in any country. Then the activities which have their levels reduced when the circuit is traversed will occur in different countries. Since they are at positive levels, they lie in the given specialization. Thus, they may be supplemented with other activities to form a complete specialization contained in the given specialization. Since all the activities which are reduced in level in the original circuit are contained in this complete specialization, the original circuit may be used to displace an activity from it. Therefore, this complete specialization is inefficient.

That any efficient specialization in the Graham model must contain at least one complete specialization follows from the fact that the labor supply of each country must be employed.

Part (b) of the theorem has been proved on p. 175 of the earlier article.

Notes

1. "Specialization and Efficiency in World Production," *The Review of Economic Studies*, June, 1954.

2. Frank D. Graham, *The Theory of International Values*, Princeton, 1948.

3. In his Marshall Lectures, which he has kindly allowed me to see in preliminary form. I also remember reading something to the same effect a number of years ago in a set of lecture notes which Prof. Hicks lent me. I may be more indebted to the latter than I am now able to recall.

4. From a somewhat different viewpoint, Graham was quite well aware of this possibility of extension. See *The Theory of International Values*, p. 150.

5. See the example below.

6. When factor supplies are given, world production is efficient if it is not possible to increase the net production of any final good unless the net production of some other final good is reduced.

7. A specialization pattern is called efficient, in Graham's model, if it leads to efficient world production whenever the labor supplies are fully used.

8. Unless the meaning is clearly otherwise, an output means the net quantities produced of all goods, for some productive source or the whole world.

9. See, for example, K. Menger, "The Logic of the Laws of Return," *Economic Activity Analysis*, edited by Oskar Morgenstern, New York, 1954, p. 473.

10. That is, the net production of some final good increased while that of no final good is reduced.

11. A circuit is a chain of substitutions in production in which, at intermediate steps, total world production of the goods is kept constant, and which returns to the same good from which it departed. The circuit is neutral if the initial and final variations in production cancel.

12. It is no longer proper to speak of specialization patterns as efficient or inefficient in themselves.

13. It is not necessary that the production of all goods require the same factors. However, the productive system must not fall apart into sectors which employ no factors in common.

14. That is to say, production is efficient.

15. The analysis is not affected if we allow diminishing returns to scale.

16. The notion of a local cone was used by Tjalling C. Koopmans, "Analysis of Production as an Efficient Combination of Activities," chapter 3 of *Activity Analysis of Production and Allocation*, edited by Koopmans, New York, 1951. See p. 83.

17. See Koopmans, *op. cit.*, p. 82.

18. See the introduction to my earlier paper for some general considerations on the relation of efficiency to competitive equilibrium.

19. See Koopmans, *op. cit.*, for the general development of this basic notion in activity analysis.

20. The activities are integrated productive processes, converting some country's labor into a final good. It is not assumed, however, that processes are *actually* integrated.

21. See the geometrical representation of circuits in the original article. Circuits have been defined in an earlier footnote.

22. Vertical link, in the geometrical representation of the article.

15 Matrices with Dominant Diagonals and Economic Theory

Lionel W. McKenzie

A large part of the pure theory of competitive markets is deduced from a few basic propositions. First, there is Walras' Law, which asserts that the value of excess demand is zero in a trading system in which the demand and supply from each trading unit is adjusted to a given set of prices. Second, the excess demand functions for the trading system are homogeneous of zero degree in the accounting prices. Third, if production processes are linear, the processes available will promise zero or negative profits in equilibrium, and the processes actually used will show zero profits.

These propositions share the property that they lead to matrices whose elements in each column, when weighted by the corresponding prices, sum to zero. Moreover, it is sometimes reasonable to assume that the off-diagonal elements are not negative. As a result, the body of theory arising from these propositions possesses a strong mathematical unity. It is only slightly inaccurate to say that the fundamental mathematical tool is the familiar Hadamard's theorem that a matrix with a dominant diagonal is non-singular. My paper is devoted to displaying this unifying structure. In the course of the argument some new and simpler proofs will be developed.

15.1 Matrices with Dominant Diagonals

By the usual definition, an $n \times n$ matrix A is said to have a dominant diagonal if $|a_{jj}| > \sum_{i \neq j} |a_{ij}|$ for each j. However, it is convenient to generalize this definition slightly. I shall say that A has a dominant diagonal if there exist numbers $d_j > 0$ such that

$$d_j|a_{jj}| > \sum_{i \neq j} d_i|a_{ij}| \quad \text{for } j = 1, \dots, n.$$

If D is a diagonal matrix with $d_{ii} = d_i$, then DA has a dominant diagonal in the usual sense.

In some theorems it will be useful to have available an even more general type of diagonal dominance. I shall term it quasi-dominance, and the phrase "a quasi-dominant diagonal" will be abbreviated "q.d.d."

Definition   An $n \times n$ matrix A has q.d.d. if (1) there exist $d_j > 0$ such that $d_j|a_{jj}| \geqq \sum_{i \neq j} d_i|a_{ij}|$ $(j = 1, \ldots, n)$, and (2) when $a_{ij} = 0$ (given $j \in J$ and $i \notin J$ for some set of indices J), the strict inequality holds for some $j \in J$.

Matrices that may have the dominant diagonal property have been prominent in economic discussions at least since 1939. In that year J. R. Hicks [12] introduced an analysis of market stability in terms of a gross substitution matrix, whose components are derivatives of quantities demanded with respect to prices. Two years later Leontief [13] published his study of the American economy, using an input-output matrix, whose typical component is the purchase by one industry from another per dollar of output of the former. This matrix was treated as a technological datum by Leontief, but a related matrix was later interpreted by Metzler [16], Chipman [4], and Goodwin [9] to describe propensities to spend by economic sectors. The analysis of stability was further refined by Samuelson [22, pp. 257ff.] in a broader dynamic context.

The close relationship between the theories developed for these economic systems was recognized some time ago. The first systematic investigation of the underlying mathematical structure was made by Solow [24], who had the very suggestive work of Hawkins and Simon [11] and Metzler [16] to build on. Metzler had arrived at the same mathematical conditions for both the existence of a solution in the input-output system and the stability of the expenditure model. These relations were in nice accord with Samuelson's "Correspondence Principle" [22, p. 258]. Later this mathematical theory was presented in a unified fashion by Debreu and Herstein [5]. However, their connecting thread is the positive matrix with its dominant positive root rather than the matrix with a dominant diagonal. A third rather unified presentation of the mathematical theory is that of Woodbury [27, 28].[1] The treatment in this chapter will be more complete, since there have been further developments in the stability problem of Hicks and Samuelson that fall into the same pattern. These were first made by

Hahn [10], Arrow and Hurwicz [2], and Negishi [20]. Also, the dominant diagonal appears to be a good point of departure from the point of view of both mathematics and economics.

The mathematical results reached in this matter by economists were largely already present somewhere in mathematical literature. Since good references to this literature may be found in Woodbury [28], I will not attempt to trace it here. Two of the more significant papers (though not the earliest) were Frobenius [6] and Brauer [3]. It may be that one of Metzler's results—namely, that a matrix with off-diagonal elements non-negative is stable if and only if its principal minors are alternately negative and positive—was new.

15.2   Basic Mathematical Theorems

In this section we shall consider a series of mathematical theorems that relate to matrices with dominant diagonals and that are applicable to economic theory. First is a fundamental theorem.[2]

Theorem 1   If a matrix A has q.d.d., A is non-singular.

Proof   Assume the contrary. Then $q'B = 0$ for some $q \neq 0$, where $B = DA$ and D is a diagonal matrix with $d_{ii} > 0$ $(i = 1, \ldots, n)$. Let $|q_j| \geq |q_i|$ $(i = 1, \ldots, n)$ for $j \in J$, with the strict inequality if $i \notin J$. Consider $q_j b_{jj} + \sum_{i \neq j} q_i b_{ij}$ for $j \in J$. It follows that

$$|q_j|\,|b_{jj}| \leqq \sum_{\substack{i \in J \\ i \neq j}} |q_i|\,|b_{ij}| + \sum_{i \notin J} |q_i|\,|b_{ij}| \leqq \sum_{i \neq j} |q_j|\,|b_{ij}|.$$

But, since A has q.d.d., for some choice of D we have $|b_{jj}| \geqq \sum_{i \neq j} |b_{ij}|$. Then the above inequalities must be equalities, and since $|q_i| < |q_j|$ for $i \notin J$, it must be that $b_{ij} = 0$ for $i \notin J$. But, again, the fact that A has q.d.d. means that D may be chosen so that $|b_{jj}| > \sum_{i \neq j} |b_{ij}|$ for some $j \in J$. For this j, $|q_j|\,|b_{jj}| > \sum_{i \neq j} |q_i|\,|b_{ij}|$, which is a contradiction. Thus no such q exists and B, and consequently A, is non-singular.

The second theorem follows very directly from Theorem 1.

Theorem 2   If a matrix A has q.d.d. that is negative, all its characteristic roots have negative real parts.

Proof   Consider $A - sI$. If s has a non-negative real part, $|a_{ii} - s| \geqq |a_{ii}|$ for $i = 1, \ldots, n$. Thus $A - sI$ has q.d.d. and is non-singular by Theorem

1, and s cannot be a characteristic root. A more complicated proof may be found in Hahn [10].

Theorem 2 is applied in the theory of stability of a classical trading system. The following theorem is applied to the stability problem of a Keynesian multiplier model.

Theorem 3[3]   If λ is a characteristic root of a matrix A, then

$$|\lambda| \leqq m = \max \sum_{i=1}^{n} |a_{ij}| \quad \text{for } j = 1, \ldots, n.$$

If "$a_{ij} = 0, j \in J, i \notin J$" implies

$$\text{"}\sum_{i=1}^{n} |a_{ij}| < m \quad \text{for some } j \in J,\text{"}$$

then $|\lambda| < m$.

Proof   Consider $A - \lambda I$. If the theorem is false, it may happen that $|a_{jj} - \lambda| \geq |\lambda| - |a_{jj}| > \sum_{i \neq j} |a_{ij}|$ for $j = 1, \ldots, n$, where λ is a characteristic root. But this means that $A - \lambda I$ has a dominant diagonal and is non-singular. Thus λ cannot be a characteristic root. The latter part of the theorem is proved similarly by showing that if it were false, $A - \lambda I$ would have q.d.d.

The next theorem is important in the theory of Leontief input-output systems. It is also used in the static theory of the multiplier and in the static theory of market equilibrium.

Theorem 4[4]   Let B be a square matrix with $b_{ii} > 0$ for all i and $b_{ij} \leq 0$ for $i \neq j$; a necessary and sufficient condition for $Bx - y$ to have a unique solution $x \geqq 0$ for every $y \geqq 0$ is that B have q.d.d.

Proof   We first prove sufficiency. Suppose there exist $d_i > 0$ that satisfy the conditions for q.d.d. with B. Then a unique solution exists by Theorem 1. Suppose $x_j < 0$ for $j \in N$ and $x_j \geqq 0$ for $j \notin N$, where N is a set of indices. Consider $\sum_{j \notin N} b_{ij} x_j + \sum_{j \in N} b_{ij} x_j = y_i \geqq 0$ for $i \in N$. Multiplying by d_i and summing,

$$\sum_{i \in N} \sum_{j \notin N} d_i b_{ij} x_j + \sum_{i \in N} \sum_{j \in N} d_i b_{ij} x_j = \sum_{i \in N} d_i y_i \geqq 0.$$

However, the first term on the left is zero or negative. Moreover, by the assumption of q.d.d., $\sum_{i \in N} d_i b_{ij} > 0$ for some $j \in N$. Therefore, since

$x_j < 0$ for $j \in N$, the second term on the left is negative. This is a contradiction, unless N is empty.

To prove necessity consider $Bx = y > 0$. Obviously $x > 0$. This means that B' has q.d.d. Then, by the above, $B'p = \pi > 0$ can be solved for $p > 0$. Thus B also has q.d.d. Indeed, it has a dominant diagonal.

Theorem 4 shows that if a matrix A has q.d.d., it actually has a dominant diagonal. Let $b_{ii} = |a_{ii}|$ and $b_{ij} = -|a_{ij}|$. Assume q.d.d. for A, and thus for B, and consider $Bx = y > 0$. Since $x > 0$ must hold by Theorem 4, B' has a dominant diagonal. But this implies that $B'd = \delta > 0$ has a solution $d > 0$, again by Theorem 4. Thus A also has a dominant diagonal. We have

Corollary   If a square matrix A has q.d.d., A has a dominant diagonal.

This shows that the central notion is actually that of a dominant diagonal in our slightly extended sense.

The final mathematical theorem concerns an old problem, investigated by Frobenius [6], which is applicable, *inter alia*, to the theory of economic growth. A square matrix A is said to be indecomposable if there is $a_{ij} > 0$ for $i \in J$ and $j \notin J$ for any non-empty subset J of indices. Now, for any square matrix A, define the function

$$\mu_A(s) = \max_{x \in S} \min_j \sum_{i=1}^{n} x_i(s\delta_{ij} - a_{ij}),$$

where

$$S = \left\{ x \,\middle|\, \sum_{i=1}^{n} x_i = 1, x_i \geq 0 \right\},$$

$\delta_{ij} = 0$ $(i \neq j)$, $\delta_{ij} = 1$ $(i = j)$, and s is a real number. When there is no ambiguity, the subscript A will be omitted. We first prove

Lemma 1   Let $A = [a_{ij}]$ be an indecomposable square matrix and $a_{ij} \geq 0$ for $i \neq j$. If $\mu(s^*) = 0$, then s^* is a characteristic root of A, and the corresponding characteristic vectors are multiples of a positive vector x^*. Moreover, s^* is greater than or equal to the real part of λ, where λ is any characteristic root of A, and $s^* > a_{jj}$ for all j. No other characteristic root has a non-negative characteristic vector.

Proof   Let x achieve the maximum in the expression for $\mu(s^*)$. If $x_j = 0$ $(j \in J$ non-null$)$, then

$$\sum_{i=1}^{n} x_i(s^*\delta_{ij} - a_{ij}) = \sum_{i \notin J} -x_i a_{ij} < 0 \quad \text{for some } j \in J,$$

since A is indecomposable. This contradicts the definition of $\mu(s^*)$; hence $x > 0$.

Suppose $R(\lambda) > s^*$, where $R(\lambda)$ is the real part of λ. Then

$$|\lambda - a_{jj}| \geq R(\lambda - a_{jj}) = R(\lambda) - a_{jj} > s^* - a_{jj} \quad (j = 1, \dots, n).$$

However, $\mu(s^*) = 0$ and indecomposability imply $s^* - a_{jj} > 0$. Thus $\lambda I - A$ has a dominant diagonal and λ cannot be a characteristic root.

To show that s^* is a characteristic root we must prove that

$$s^* x_j^* - \sum_{i=1}^{n} x_i^* a_{ij} = y_j^* = 0 \quad \text{for all } j.$$

However, if $y_j^* > 0$ for some j, then $s^* I - A$ has q.d.d., since $x^* > 0$. Thus by Theorem 4 there is a value $x > 0$ such that $x'(s^* I - A) > 0$, and x may be chosen in S. This contradicts $\mu(s^*) = 0$. So $y^* = 0$ must hold, and s^* is a characteristic root of A with x^* as a characteristic vector.

Let $x^1 \neq 0$ be a second characteristic vector. Suppose $x^1 \neq tx^*$ for any real t. Consider $x^2 = rx^1 + (1 - r)x^*$. The value r may be chosen so that $x^2 \in S$ and $x_j^2 = 0$ for at least one index j. Then x^2 also realizes the maximum in $\mu(s^*) = 0$, contradicting the positivity of a maximizing x. Thus $x^1 = tx^*$ $(t \neq 0)$.

If there is another characteristic root λ with a non-negative characteristic vector x, then $x > 0$ must hold, for the same reasons as before. Then $\lambda > a_{ii}$ is also implied as before (λ must be real). Thus $\lambda' I - A$ has a dominant diagonal for $\lambda' > \lambda$; hence $s^* \leq \lambda$. By the same argument $\lambda \leq s^*$; hence $\lambda = s^*$.

Lemma 2   Under the conditions of Lemma 1, $|\lambda| \leq s^* + \max_j(|a_{jj}| - a_{jj})$ when $\mu(s^*) = 0$ and λ is any characteristic root of A not equal to s^*. The strict inequality holds if $a_{jj} \geq 0$ for all j, and $a_{jj} > 0$ for some j.

Proof   The matrix $\lambda I - A$ must not have a dominant diagonal. Thus $s^* - a_{jj} \geq |\lambda - a_{jj}|$ for some j. But $|\lambda - a_{jj}| \geq |\lambda| - |a_{jj}|$, with strict inequality if λ has a non-zero imaginary part or if λ and $a_{jj} \neq 0$ do not have the same signs. Thus $s^* - a_{jj} \geq |\lambda| - |a_{jj}|$, or $s^* \geq |\lambda| - (|a_{jj}| - a_{jj})$, for some j. Therefore, $s^* \geq |\lambda| - \max_j(|a_{jj}| - a_{jj})$. If $a_{jj} \geq 0$, then $s^* \geq |\lambda|$ holds, since the parentheses vanish for all j. If $a_{jj} > 0$ for some j, then λ

and a_{jj} have opposite signs, λ is complex, or λ is positive. In the first two cases we have the strict inequality as stated above, and in the third case we have the strict inequality unless $\lambda = s^*$.

Theorem 5 Let A be an indecomposable square matrix with non-negative elements. Then A has a unique characteristic root $\lambda^* > 0$ with a non-negative characteristic vector. The corresponding characteristic vectors are multiples of a unique vector $x > 0$. Moreover, $\lambda^* \geq |\lambda|$, where λ is any other characteristic root of A. If $a_{ii} > 0$ for some i, then $\lambda^* > |\lambda|$.

Proof The first part of the theorem is contained in Lemma 1. The last part is implied by Lemma 2, since $\max_j(|a_{jj}| - a_{jj}) = 0$ if $a_{jj} \geq 0$ for all j.

Corollary[5] If there is a value $n \geq 1$ such that $B = A^n$ satisfies the conditions of Theorem 5 and $b_{ii} > 0$ for some i, the conclusion of Theorem 5 holds for A with the strict inequality.

Proof If λ is a characteristic root of A with characteristic vector x, then λ^n is a characteristic root of B with the same characteristic vector. Thus $\lambda > 0$ and $x > 0$ for A implies $\lambda^n > 0$ and $x > 0$ for B; but $\lambda^n > |\lambda'|$, where λ' is any characteristic root of B not equal to λ^n. It is not possible that $\lambda^n = \lambda'''^n$, where λ'' is a characteristic root of A and $\lambda'' \neq \lambda$. For then λ'' would have a characteristic vector that was not positive by Lemma 2, and thus so would λ^n. Therefore, $\lambda^n > |\lambda''|^n$, where λ'' is any characteristic root of A not equal to λ. Thus $\lambda > |\lambda''|$.

In Lemma 1, A is indecomposable. In Section 15.8 we shall prove a result in which this condition is removed; then we can establish the converse of Theorem 2 when $a_{ij} \geq 0$ for $i \neq j$.

15.3 Existence of Positive Solutions

The mathematical theorems that we have derived from postulates of diagonal dominance will now be applied to certain basic economic problems. These are the existence, the uniqueness, and the stability of competitive equilibria. The existence question cannot be treated in its general form by these methods. However, a question of the existence type for Leontief systems can be settled by the use of Theorem 4.

A Leontief or input-output system [13] may be given by

$$Bx = y \quad \text{for } x_i \geq 0 \ (i = 1, \ldots, n),$$

$$B = [b_{ij}] \quad \text{for } b_{ij} \leq 0 \ (i \neq j), b_{jj} > 0.$$

(1)

The y_i are net outputs of goods and the x_i are activity levels in the industries. The jth column of B represents the input-output vector of the jth industry. Thus b_{ij} is the input of the ith commodity needed in producing b_{jj} units of the jth commodity; B represents the pattern of product flow between industries.

If this productive system is realized in a competitive equilibrium, a set of prices $p_i > 0$ $(i = 1, \ldots, n)$ for the n goods will be established. Furthermore, the assumption of maximum profit for producers and the linearity of the production processes (permitting $x_i = y_i = 0$) ensure that

$$\sum_{i=1}^{n} p_i b_{ij} \geq 0.$$

Since the workers in an industry must, in fact, earn a positive return in order to exist, it can be expected that the strict inequality will hold. Thus we have the following theorem:

Theorem 6[6]   If all industries appear in a competitive equilibrium with a Leontief productive system having positive activity levels, any nonnegative bill of goods can be achieved in the system.

Proof   Since $x_j > 0$ in a competitive equilibrium implies by the profit conditions that

$$\sum_{i=1}^{n} p_i b_{ij} > 0,$$

B has a dominant diagonal. Then the theorem follows directly from Theorem 4. It is clear from Theorem 1 that the existence of positive prices that permit positive returns is also a necessary condition for the conclusion of Theorem 6.

15.4   Uniqueness of Solutions

In general, competitive equilibria cannot be expected to be unique. However, uniqueness results of a limited scope can be found. One of these has been given the title "Equalization of Factor Prices." In this problem one seeks conditions implying that countries facing the same prices for goods in foreign trade will have the same factor prices. However, the basic result says that for a certain type of productive system in a competitive equilibrium the factor prices are uniquely determined when the goods prices are specified. It is applied to the original problem by assuming the appropriate productive system to be present in each country, where all countries trade goods at given prices.

Samuelson [23] has proved the following:

Lemma 3 Let $g_i(w_1, \ldots, w_n) = p_i$ $(i = 1, \ldots, n)$, where p_i and w_i are real numbers. Let P be the image under g of a region W in Euclidean n-space. If the Jacobian matrix $[g_{ij}]$ has a nested set of minors that are invariant in sign over W, then $w_i = g_i^{-1}(p_1, \ldots, p_n)$ over P.

A nested set of minors J_i, where i is the order of the minor and $i = 1, \ldots, n$, has the property that J_{i-1} is a minor of J_i, where $i = 2, \ldots, n$. Rows and columns may be permuted so that these minors all lie in the upper left-hand corner of J_n.

It is easily seen from Theorem 1 that the condition of Lemma 3 is met if there are permutations of the rows and columns of J_n such that J_n has a dominant diagonal for $w \in W$. For then J_n and its principal minors are non-singular over W. Since the values of the minors are continuous functions of w, and since W is a connected set, their signs cannot change. We may state

Lemma 4 If $[g_{ij}]$ of Lemma 3 has a dominant diagonal over W, then $w_i = g_i^{-1}(p_1, \ldots, p_n)$ over P.

These lemmas can be given several applications. However, the classical for A' use is in the problem of factor price equalization. Assume divisible goods and factors and homogeneous production functions. If n factors are used to produce n goods, in the competitive equilibrium

$$p_i = \sum_{j=1}^{n} w_j a_{ij} \quad (i = 1, \ldots, n),$$

where p_i is the price of the ith commodity, w_j the price of jth factor, and a_{ij} the input per unit of output of the jth factor in the industry producing the ith commodity. Now assume that the production functions are differentiable. The a_{ij} will be chosen so that cost is a minimum. Thus

$$\sum_{j=1}^{n} w_j \frac{\partial a_{ij}}{\partial w_k} = 0.$$

Then

$$\frac{\partial p_i}{\partial w_k} = a_{ik} + \sum_{j=1}^{n} w_j \frac{\partial a_{ij}}{\partial w_k} = a_{ik},$$

and $[a_{ij}] = A$ is the Jacobian matrix of the transformation from factor prices to goods prices. The a_{ij} are non-negative, and a dominant diagonal for A' means that each good can be identified with a factor that is uniquely important in the production of that good. This may be formulated as

Theorem 7 Suppose production functions are differentiable and homogeneous of the first degree. Let $A = [a_{ij}]$ be the matrix of inputs of n factors into the production of n goods, where A' has a dominant diagonal for all $w \geq 0$. In a competitive equilibrium, where all n goods are produced, the goods prices uniquely imply the factor prices.

Theorem 7 does not cover all the cases falling under Lemma 1, where $[g_{ij}] = [a_{ij}]$ and $a_{ij} \geq 0$. However, it does cover the two-factors, two-goods case. As we shall see in the last section, a dominant diagonal for A is equivalent to positive principal minors for the matrix B, where $b_{ii} = |a_{ii}|$ and $b_{ij} = -|a_{ij}|$. But in the 2×2 matrix A this merely involves the proper choice of the order of the columns. Then the dominant diagonal can be lost only if $|A| = 0$ for some w, with this order of columns.

15.5 Stability of a Trading System

Let $f_i(p)$ be the excess demand functions of a trading system, where $i = 1, \ldots, n$, and p_i is the price of the ith commodity. Assume $f_i(p)$ is differentiable. Suppose

$$\frac{\partial f_i(p)}{\partial p_j} = f_{ij}(p) = s_{ij} \geq 0 \quad \text{for } i \neq j.$$

We may call this the assumption of weak gross substitutability. According to Walras' Law,

$$\sum_{i=1}^{n} p_i f_i(p) = 0 \quad \text{for any } p \geq 0,$$

Differentiating, we have

$$\sum_{i=1}^{n} p_i f_{ij} = -f_j \quad (j = 1, \ldots, n).\tag{2}$$

At equilibrium, of course, $f_j = 0$ $(j = 1, \ldots, n)$.

We now assume that price changes are functions of excess demands. Suppose, for example, $dp_i/dt = k_i f_i(p_1, \ldots, p_n)$ for $i = 1, \ldots, n$, where k_i is a positive constant. Units may be chosen so that $k_i = 1$ for all i. Consider the function $V(p) = \frac{1}{2} \sum_{i \in P} f_i^2(p)$, where $P = \{i \mid f_i(p) > 0\}$. Then

$$\frac{d}{dt} V(p(t)) = \sum_{i \in P} \sum_{j=1}^{n} f_i s_{ij} f_j.$$

However, in the weak gross substitute case, $\sum_{i \in P} \sum_{j \notin P} f_i s_{ij} f_j \leqq 0$. Thus we may look at $\sum_{i \in P} \sum_{j \in P} f_i s_{ij} f_j$ alone. Using the fact that $f_i > 0$ for $i \in P$, we see that equation (2) implies that $S_p = [s_{ij}]$ $(i, j \in P)$ has a dominant diagonal. By the homogeneity of the excess demand functions we obtain

$$\sum_{j=1}^{n} p_j f_{ij} = 0.$$

Then by the assumption of weak gross substitutability, $\sum_{j \in P} p_j f_{ij} \leqq 0$. Combining these results, we find that $S_P^* = \frac{1}{2}(S_P + S_P')$ also has a dominant diagonal. This diagonal must be negative. Therefore, by Theorem 2 the characteristic roots have negative real parts. Since S_P^* is symmetric, the roots are real and S_P^* defines a negative definite quadratic form. This means that $f_P' S_P f_P$ is also negative and $dV/dt < 0$ for $f_P \neq 0$, where f_P is the vector of positive excess demands. But Walras' Law implies that f_P and f are zero together. Since $V > 0$ unless $f = 0$, we may apply Liapounoff's second method [14, pp. 255ff.] to conclude that $f \rightarrow 0$ with increasing t and that the equilibrium is stable in the large. This justifies

Theorem 8[7]   If price changes are proportionate to excess demands, in the weak gross substitute case, the equilibrium of a trading system is stable in the large.

If a numéraire is assumed, the argument may be carried through, but it involves a further step.

15.6   Stability of an Income Multiplier Model

Another application of matrices with dominant diagonals to stability problems may be found in applying the Keynesian multiplier theory to a multi-sector model of spending flows. See, for instance, Chipman [4]. Time may be divided into periods, and the spending of one period may be related to the income of the previous period. Suppose, for example, there are n countries buying one another's goods. The incremental flow of spending may be described by

$$y_i(t) = \sum_{j=1}^{n} a_{ij} y_j(t-1) \quad (i = 1, \ldots, n), \tag{3}$$

where $y_i(t)$ is the deviation from the equilibrium level of the income of the ith country in period t. Such a system of difference equations is stable if and only if the characteristic roots of $A = [a_{ij}]$ lie inside the unit circle. This suggests an application of Theorem 3.

Suppose that $a_{ij} \geq 0$ and that each country has a total marginal propensity to spend less than 1, i.e., that

$$\sum_{i=1}^{n} a_{ij} < 1.$$

Then $|\lambda| < 1$ by Theorem 3 and stability is assured. It is clear that the condition can be relaxed in the usual way. There need be but one "sink" in each set of countries for which spending circulates throughout the set.[8] We may state

Theorem 9   The multiplier model (3) is stable if the marginal propensities to spend are non-negative and the total marginal propensity of each country is less than 1.

15.7   Existence of Balanced Growth Paths

The Leontief system of (1) can also be regarded as a period model in which the output of one period supplies the inputs of the next. The formal statement is the same as (3), except that now the time lag is reversed:

$$y_i(t-1) = \sum_{j=1}^{n} a_{ij} y_j(t) \quad (i = 1, \ldots, n). \tag{4}$$

Each equation of (4) represents the distribution of the net output of the $(t-1)$th period over the lines of production of the tth period. Thus a_{ij} is the quantity of the $(t-1)$th-period output of the ith good needed to produce one unit of the jth good in the tth period. The households form an industry, with labor as its output. The existence of an equilibrium growth path is equivalent to the existence of a positive characteristic root with a positive characteristic vector for $A = [a_{ij}]$.[9] Thus we have from Theorem 5.

Theorem 10 If A is indecomposable, there is a unique path of balanced growth.

15.8 Further Mathematical Developments

In this section we shall prove the converse of Theorem 2 for matrices with non-negative elements off the diagonal. We shall also derive a modified form of Theorem 1 for matrices with non-positive elements off the diagonal. This result will be used to prove the converse of the latter part of Theorem 3 for matrices with non-negative elements. An application will be made to Leontief systems. Finally, we shall prove the equivalence of the well-known Hawkins-Simon conditions to the condition of Theorem 4.

We shall call B a component of $A = [a_{ij}]$ if $a_{ij} = 0$ for $a_{ii} \in B$, $a_{jj} \notin B$. The symbol B will also be used for the set $\{i \mid a_{ii}$ is an element of $B\}$.

Lemma 5 If B is a component of A, any characteristic root of B is a characteristic root of A.

Proof Let $\sum_{i \in B} x_i a_{ij} = \lambda x_j$ for $j \in B$, where $x_i \neq 0$ for some i. Set $x_i = 0$ for $i \notin B$. Then $x'A = \lambda x'$, and λ is a characteristic root of A.

Lemma 6 Let N be a maximal proper component of $M = [a_{ij}]$, where $a_{ij} \geq 0$ $(i \neq j)$. Let $\mu_M(s^*) = 0$. If $\mu_N(s^*) > 0$, then s^* is a characteristic root of M.

Proof Let P be the complementary minor of N. P is indecomposable since N is maximal. If $\mu_P(s^*) > 0$, a positive maximum could be achieved in $\mu_M(s^*)$, *contra* hypothesis. If $\mu_P(s^*) < 0$, a non-negative maximum in $\mu_M(s^*)$ would be excluded, again *contra* hypothesis. Then $\mu_P(s^*) > 0$, and s^* is a characteristic root of P (thus of P') by Lemma 1. But P' is a component of M' hence by Lemma 5, s^* is a characteristic root of M', and thus of M.

Theorem 2′[10] Let A be a square matrix $[a_{ij}]$ with $a_{ij} \geq 0$ for $i \neq j$; a_{ij} the characteristic roots of A have negative real parts if and only if A has a dominant negative diagonal.

Proof Sufficiency is contained in Theorem 2. Assume A does not have a dominant negative diagonal. Suppose $a_{ii} \geq 0$ for $i = i_0$. Then regardless of $x \in S$, if $y' = x'(-A)$, we have $y_{i_0} \leq 0$. Thus $\mu_A(0) \leq 0$. On the other hand, if $a_{ii} \leq 0$ for all i, then $x'(-A) > 0$ cannot hold for $x > 0$, or there would be a dominant diagonal. Hence $\mu_A(0) \leq 0$ again. Let M be a minimal component of A under the condition that $\mu_M(0) \leq 0$, and let N be a proper component of M such that $\mu_N(0) > 0$. M must exist, although it may happen that $M = A$. However, N may not exist, in which case M is indecomposable. Consider $\mu_M(s^*) = 0$. Then $s^* \geq 0$ holds, since μ is monotonic. If M is indecomposable, s^* is a characteristic root of M by Lemma 1. If M is decomposable, s^* is a characteristic root of M by Lemma 6. In either case s^* is a characteristic root of A by Lemma 5. This proves the theorem.

Corollary All the characteristic roots of a square matrix A with nonnegative elements are less than 1 in absolute value if and only if $I - A$ has a dominant positive diagonal.

Proof To show sufficiency, suppose $|\lambda| \geq 1$ and consider $|\lambda - a_{jj}| \geq |\lambda| - a_{jj} \geq 1 - a_{jj}$. Thus $\lambda I - A$ has a dominant diagonal and λ cannot be a characteristic root. On the other hand, if $I - A$ has a dominant positive diagonal, then $A - I$ has a dominant negative diagonal. Then, by Theorem 2′, the condition of the corollary can fail if and only if $A - I$ has a root with positive real part. But if λ^* is a characteristic root of $A - I$, $1 + \lambda^*$ is a root of A, and $|1 + \lambda|^*$ exceeds 1. This corollary gives a condition for the stability of the income multiplier model in Section 6 which is necessary as well as sufficient when the marginal propensities to spend are non-negative. However, the economic meaning is less transparent than the sufficient condition of Theorem 9.

Next we shall prove a result similar to Theorem 1, which is specialized to the type of matrix appearing in Theorem 4.

Theorem 1′[11] Suppose A is an $n \times n$ matrix $[a_{ij}]$ with $a_{ij} \leq 0$ for $i \neq j$, and

$$\sum_{i=1}^{n} d_i a_{ij} \geq 0 \quad (j = 1, \ldots, n)$$

for a certain set of $d_i > 0$. A is non-singular if and only if A has q.d.d. realized by these d_i.

Proof The sufficiency part is provided by Theorem 1. Suppose A does not have q.d.d. with these d_i as multipliers. By the definition of q.d.d., there is a non-empty set J of indices with $a_{ij} = 0$ for $j \in J$ and $i \notin J$, and $\sum_{i \in J} d_i a_{ij} = 0$ for all $j \in J$. Let $M = [a_{ij}]$ $(i, j \in J)$. Since M is singular, there are x_j, not all zero, such that $\sum_{j \in J} a_{ij} x_j = 0$. Put $x_j = 0$ for $j \notin J$. Then $Ax = 0$, so A is also singular.

Theorem 1' can be applied to a competitive economy with a Leontief technology. Suppose that there exist positive prices yielding non-negative returns

$$\pi_j = \sum_{i=1}^{n} p_i a_{ij} \geq 0$$

in each process. Or suppose production occurs, and net output for each commodity is

$$y_i = \sum_{j=1}^{n} x_j a_{ij} \geq 0, \quad \text{where } x' > 0.$$

In these cases, the condition of Theorem 4 can be realized for A, or A', if and only if the condition of Theorem 1' is met.

Thus the following modification of Theorem 6 may be asserted.

Theorem 6' These statements are equivalent: (1) every subset of industries that makes no purchases from the complementary subset of industries earns a return in some industry; (2) every subset of industries that furnishes no output to the complementary subset of industries has a positive net output of some good; (3) net output can be produced with goods in any proportions.

Proof The proof is immediate from Theorems 1' and 4.

Theorem 1' may also be used to prove a converse to Theorem 3 for matrices with non-negative elements.

Theorem 3' Let A be an $n \times n$ matrix $[a_{ij}]$ with $a_{ij} \geq 0$. Let

$$m = \max \sum_{i=1}^{n} a_{ij} \quad \text{for } j = 1, \ldots, n.$$

A necessary and sufficient condition for the characteristic roots of A to be less than m in absolute value is that $mI - A$ have q.d.d. realized by $d_i = 1$ $(i = 1, \ldots, n)$.

Proof Sufficiency is contained in Theorem 3. By definition of m,

$$m - \sum_{i=1}^{n} a_{ij} \geqq 0.$$

Thus, by Theorem 1', if $mI - A$ does not have q.d.d. for $d_i = 1$ (all i), then $mI - A$ is singular. It follows that m is a characteristic root.

If we consult the definition of a dominant diagonal for an arbitrary matrix, it is apparent that an arbitrary square matrix $A = [a_{ij}]$ has a dominant diagonal if and only if the matrix $B = [b_{ij}]$, where $b_{ii} = |a_{ii}|$ and $b_{ij} = -|a_{ij}|$ for $i \neq j$, has a dominant diagonal. However, it is known that a necessary and sufficient condition for B to have a dominant diagonal is that its principal minors lying in the upper left-hand corner be positive. Let us refer to B as the diagonal form of A. Then it is of some interset to prove the following theorem by use of our methods:

Theorem 4'[12] A square matrix A has a dominant diagonal if only and if its diagonal form has all principal minors positive.

Proof Let $B = [b_{ij}]$ be the diagonal form of A. We see from Theorem 1 that positive principal minors for B are necessary; the dominant diagonal is preserved as the off-diagonal elements are shrunk to zero. Then the minors preserve their signs, but in the limit these are obviously all positive.

We shall prove sufficiency by induction. It is clear that the principal minors of order 1 have dominant diagonals. Assume that the principal minor in the upper left-hand corner of order $n - 1$ is positive and has a dominant diagonal. We shall prove that the minor of order n in the upper left-hand corner also has a dominant diagonal. Denote these minors by $|B^{n-1}|$ and $|B^n|$, respectively.

Since B^{n-1} has a dominant diagonal by the induction hypothesis, Theorem 4 implies that

$$\sum_{i=1}^{n-1} x_i b_{ij} = -b_{nj} + \delta \quad (\delta > 0; j = 1, \ldots, n - 1)$$

has a solution $x_i^{\delta} > 0$ $(i = 1, \ldots, n - 1)$. Let $x_n^{\delta} = 1$. Consider

$$\sum_{i=1}^{n} x_i^{\delta} b_{ik} \quad (k = 1, \ldots, n).$$

For $k < n$,

$$\sum_{i=1}^{n} x_i^{\delta} b_{ik} = b_{nk} + \sum_{j=1}^{n-1}(-b_{nj} + \delta) \sum_{i=1}^{n-1}\left(\frac{|B_{ij}^{n-1}|}{|B^{n-1}|} b_{ik}\right).$$

But the last summation is 0 if $j \neq k$ and 1 if $j = k$. Thus, for $k < n$,

$$\sum_{i=1}^{n} x_i^{\delta} b_{ik} = b_{nk} - b_{nk} + \delta = \delta > 0.$$

For $k = n$ and $\delta = 0$,

$$\sum_{i=1}^{n} x_i^{0} b_{in} = b_{nn} - \sum_{j=1}^{n-1}\sum_{i=1}^{n-1} b_{nj}\frac{|B_{ij}^{n-1}|}{|B^{n-1}|} b_{in}.$$

By Cauchy's expansion of the determinant $|B^n|$, the right-hand side equals $|B^n|/|B^{n-1}|$, which is positive by assumption. This inequality is preserved for small positive values of δ. Thus δ may be chosen to give

$$\sum_{i=1}^{n} x_i^{\delta} b_{ik} > 0 \quad (k = 1, \ldots, n),$$

where $x_i^{\delta} > 0$. Hence B^n has a dominant diagonal.

Notes

I have benefited from casual remarks dropped between cocktails by Arrow and Samuelson. The research for this chapter was facilitated by a grant from the Ford Foundation to the Department of Economics of the University of Rochester.

1. Also see Wong [26], where many additional results are derived for input-output matrices, and Georgescu-Roegen [8].

2. For a good mathematical discussion of matrices with dominant diagonals, see G. Bailey Price [21].

3. This and other results on bounds for the norms of characteristic roots may be found in Brauer [3].

4. This result may, in retrospect, be read out of the Hawkins-Simon conditions [11]. See also McKenzie [15].

5. It is not hard to show that n always exists with $b_{ii} > 0$. Then, if the conclusion does not hold, B must be decomposable, in which case A is said to be cyclic. Acyclicity is also necessary for the conclusion. See Woodbury [27] and Solow [24].

6. Although this theorem was first stated for Leontief systems by Hawkins and Simon [11], it was also proved earlier by Mosak [19] in a different connection. Mosak was interested in a theorem of comparative statics stated by Hicks [12], namely that an increase in demand for the jth commodity at the expense of the numéraire will increase all prices when all goods are gross substitutes (see below). Both proofs involved showing the inverse of a Leontief matrix (the negative of the gross substitute matrix) to be positive if and only if its principal minors are positive. Morishima [18] has further refined Mosak's results.

7. Results of this type have been proved by Arrow and Hurwicz [2], Arrow, Block, and Hurwicz [1], and Uzawa [25], among others. Their strongest results, however, cannot be proved by the present means.

8. See the careful discussion in Solow [24]. Theorem 9 was proved by Goodwin [9] and Metzler [16].

9. Methods similar to ours were applied to this problem by Woodbury [27] and Gale [7].

10. This result can be obtained from the theorems of Metzler [17] and Hawkins and Simon [11] by combining them. Metzler showed that the roots of A have negative real parts if and only if the principal minors are alternately negative and positive.

11. See Brauer [3] and Solow [24]. These non-singularity theorems have a long history.

12. This is, in effect, the Hawkins-Simon theorem [11].

References

[1] Arrow, K. J., H. D. Block, and L. Hurwicz. "On the Stability of the Competitive Equilibrium, II," *Econometrica*, **27** (1959), 82–109.

[2] Arrow, K. J., and L. Hurwicz. "On the Stability of the Competitive Equilibrium, I," *Econometrica*, **26** (1958), 522–52.

[3] Brauer, A. T. "Limits for Characteristic Roots of a Matrix, III," *Duke Mathematical Journal*, **15** (1948), 871–77.

[4] Chipman, J. S. *The Theory of Inter-Sectoral Money Flows and Income Formation*, Baltimore, Md.: Johns Hopkins University Press, 1951.

[5] Debreu, G., and I. N. Herstein. "Nonnegative Square Matrices," *Econometrica*, **21** (1953), 597–607.

[6] Frobenius, G. "Über Matrizen aus nicht negativen Elementen," *Sitzungsberichte der Königlichen Preussischen Akademie der Wissenshaften*, **1** (1912), 456–77.

[7] Gale, D. "The Closed Linear Model of Production," in H. W. Kuhn and A. W. Tucker, eds., *Linear Inequalities and Related Systems*, Princeton, N.J.: Princeton University Press, 1956, pp. 285–304.

[8] Georgescu-Roegen, N. "Some Properties of a Generalized Leontief Model," in T. C. Koopmans, ed., *Activity Analysis of Production and Allocation*, New York: John Wiley and Sons, 1951, 165–73.

[9] Goodwin, R. M. "Does the Matrix Multiplier Oscillate?" *Economic Journal*, **60** (1950), 764–70.

[10] Hahn, F. "Gross Substitutes and the Dynamic Stability of General Equilibrium," *Econometrica*, **26** (1958), 169–70.

[11] Hawkins, D., and H. A. Simon. "Note: Some Conditions of Macroeconomic Stability," *Econometrica*, **17** (1949), 245–48.

[12] Hicks, J. R. *Value and Capital*, Oxford: Oxford University Press, 1939.

[13] Leontief, W. W. *The Structure of American Economy, 1919–1939*, New York: Oxford University Press, 1951.

[14] Liapounoff, M. A. *Problème général de la stabilité du mouvement*, reprinted as *Annals of Mathematics No. 17*, Princeton, N.J.: Princeton University Press, 1947.

[15] McKenzie, L. W. "An Elementary Analysis of the Leontief System," *Econometrica*, **25** (1957), 456–62.

[16] Metzler, L. "A Multiple Region Theory of Income and Trade," *Econometrica*, **18** (1950), 329–54.

[17] Metzler, L. "Stability of Multiple Markets: the Hicks Conditions," *Econometrica*, **13** (1945), 277–92.

[18] Morishima, M. "Gross Substitutability, Homogeneity and the Walras' Law," unpublished manuscript.

[19] Mosak, S. L. *General Equilibrium Theory in International Trade*, Bloomington, Ind.: Principia Press, 1944.

[20] Negishi, T. "A Note on the Stability of an Economy where All Goods Are Gross Substitutes," *Econometrica*, **26** (1958), 445–47.

[21] Price, G. B. "Bounds for Determinants with Dominant Principal Diagonals," *Proceedings of the American Mathematical Society*, **2** (1951), 497–502.

[22] Samuelson, P. A. *Foundations of Economic Analysis*, Cambridge, Mass.: Harvard University Press, 1947.

[23] Samuelson, P. A. "Prices of Factors and Goods in General Equilibrium," *Review of Economic Studies*, **21** (1953), 1–20.

[24] Solow, R. "On the Structure of Linear Models," *Econometrica*, **20** (1952), 29–46.

[25] Uzawa, H. "An Alternative Proof of the Stability in the Gross Substitute Case," Technical Report No. 60, Department of Economics, Stanford University.

[26] Wong, Y. K. "Inequalities for Minkowski-Leontief Matrices," in Oskar Morgenstern, ed., *Economic Activity Analysis*, New York: John Wiley and Sons, 1954, pp. 201–81.

[27] Woodbury, M. A. "Characteristic Roots of Input-Output Matrices," *ibid.*, pp. 365–82.

[28] Woodbury, M. A. "Properties of Leontief-type Input-Output Matrices," *ibid.*, pp. 341–63.

16   The Inversion of Cost Functions: A Counter-Example

Lionel W. McKenzie

16.1   The Previous History

In 1948 and 1949 Paul Samuelson began a lively modern discussion with two penetrating articles in the *Economic Journal* [9, 10] in which he showed that under certain assumptions countries that faced the same prices for goods in world trade must also have the same factor prices in competitive equilibrium.[1] The assumptions were:

(1) There are two countries equipped with the same two factors and the same production functions for each of two goods.

(2) Each country produces each good in the competitive equilibrium.

(3) There are no tariffs or transport costs, or other impediments to international trade in goods but factors are not traded.

(4) The production functions are concave and homogeneous of the first degree.

(5) Relative factor intensities for production at minimum cost are not reversed between the two lines of production as factor prices vary.

On these assumptions the equality of factor prices between the countries was proved to be a consequence of competitive equilibrium.

It might be conjectured that this theorem could be extended to n goods and n factors if assumption (5) be replaced with

(5a) The Jacobian determinant of the cost functions for the n goods is nonsingular for all admissible factor prices, not all zero.[2]

However, James and Pearce [7] pointed out that, in general, condition (5a) was effective only for a local neighborhood of a particular set of factor prices and did not guarantee that more widely separated factor prices were inconsistent with the same goods prices.

Mathematically the factor price equalization theorem (in this form) is a theorem on the existence of a unique inverse for the set of n cost functions, which have the n factor prices as arguments. This is because, in competitive equilibrium, price must equal minimum cost of production for each good, while the cost function of a good takes this minimum cost as its value at each set of admissible factor prices. Let W be an n-dimensional interval of factor prices within which all the cost functions are defined. Let P be the set of all goods prices (n-dimensional price vectors) which equal costs for some factor prices (n-dimensional price vectors) in W. Let $w^* = (w_1^*, \ldots, w_n^*)$ be a vector of factor prices at which the cost functions $f_i(w)$, $i = 1, \ldots, n$, are continuously differentiable. Write

$$p_i = f_i(w), \quad i = 1, \ldots, n. \tag{1}$$

Let $J_f(w) = |\partial f_i(w)/\partial w_j|$. Then assumption (5a) provides $J_f(w) \neq 0$. This condition is sufficient to give the existence of functions $f_j^{-1}(p)$, $j = 1, \ldots, n$, such that $w_j = f_j^{-1}(p)$, $j = 1, \ldots, n$, for p in a sufficiently small neighborhood of p^*, where $p_i^* = f_i(w^*)$, and $w_j^* = f_j^{-1}(p^*)$ [1, (267)]. However, there is no implication that such functions $f_j^{-1}(p)$ exist with all of P as their domain.

If global inversion is to be derived, additional properties of the cost functions must be used. The cost functions always have two special properties, concavity and homogeneity of the first degree, because of their dual relationship with the production functions which have these properties from assumption (4). As Samuelson showed, these properties do give the desired result for the case of two goods. However, in an attempt to establish a general theorem, in 1953 Samuelson proposed a strong additional assumption on the cost functions and thus indirectly on the production functions [11]. This assumption may be stated in the form

(5b) $J_f(w)$ has a nested set of n distinct minors none of which vanish for w in W.[3]

Subsequently Nikaido pointed out that Samuelson's proof of the adequacy of this condition was not conclusive, and he gave a counter-example. However, the counter-example is not conclusive either, since the functions used do not satisfy the conditions necessary for cost functions. Then Gale and Nikaido [3] proved that the condition

(5c) The principal minors of $J_f(w)$ are positive for all w in an n-dimensional interval W

is sufficient for a global inverse over this interval. We may rewrite (1) as

(1a) There are m countries equipped with the same n factors and the same production functions for n goods.

Then assumptions (1a), (2), (3), (4), and (5c) do imply that the global inverse functions $f_j^{-1}(p)$ exist throughout P. This result was announced by Gale and Nikaidô in 1965 [3].

Other results were established by the author in 1955, including a theorem of Samuelson's type on yet another assumption. Let $K(w)$ be the convex cone in n-dimensional Euclidean space spanned by the vectors of quantities of factor inputs into the n production processes,[4] when production takes place at minimum cost for a factor price vector w. The matrix of these input vectors is identical with the Jacobian matrix when it exists. Assume

(5d) For any w, w' in W, $K(w) \cap K(w')$ has interior points.

Then (1a), (2), (3), (4), and (5d) imply the existence of global inverse functions $f^{-1}(p)$ for p in P [5, (248)]. Also it was noted by the author that, if the Jacobian matrix has a dominant diagonal for all w in W, (5a) and (5b) are both implied [5, (249, 257)].[5] Indeed, (5c) is implied as well.

A further condition for the inversion of cost functions was noticed recently by Harold Kuhn [4]. Let $p = (p_1, \ldots, p_n)$ be the goods price system. The condition is

$$\sum_{i=1}^{n} \frac{1}{p_i} (w_i' - w_i'')(f_i(w') - f_i(w'')) > 0,$$

for all $w', w'' \neq 0$, such that $\sum_1^n w_i' = \sum_1^n w_i'' = 1$. In Kuhn's words, "this is a generalization of monotonicity and says that the effect of the unit costs that move in the direction of a change in factor costs outweighs the effect of unit costs moving in the opposite direction."

16.2 A Counter-Example to the Pearce Conjecture

A few years ago, however, Ivor Pearce argued [8] that the conjecture that a non-vanishing Jacobian (that is, assumption (5a)) is sufficient for

the global result may be correct, after all. It is the purpose of this chapter to describe a counter-example to Pearce's conjecture. The argument
may be summarized as follows: We consider identical cost functions
for $n+1$ goods which are produced by means of $n+1$ factors. We
make small perturbations in n of the cost functions, which leave them
concave and homogeneous. Thus $n+1$ different cost functions are obtained. Then we examine the Jacobian of these cost functions. An $n+1$
dimensional interval W of factor prices is determined (indeed W may
be all non-negative factor price vectors) within which the Jacobian
does not vanish. However, there may be many sets of factor prices
within W which correspond to the same goods prices.

In order that $f(w)$, where w is an $n+1$ vector, be a cost function it is
necessary and sufficient that these conditions hold

(a) $f(w)$ is defined and continuous for $w \geq 0$.
     $f(w) \geq 0$ and $f(w) > 0$ for $w > 0$.

(b) $f(\alpha w) = \alpha f(w)$ for $\alpha \geq 0$.

(c) $f(w) \geq \alpha f(w') + (1 - \alpha) f(w'')$, for $w = \alpha w' + (1 - \alpha) w''$, $0 \leq \alpha \leq 1$.

Mathematically these properties belong to the support function of a
non-empty point set which is contained in the positive orthant and
which does not include the origin.[6] This point set is the set of all combinations of factors which can be used to produce one unit of the good.
We shall wish to consider $n+1$ such functions, indexed by the integers
0 to n, representing cost functions for the $n+1$ goods and having as
arguments $w_0, w_1, \ldots, w_n$, the prices of the $n+1$ factors.
Since a cost function $f(w)$ is positive homogeneous, it is defined over
the positive orthant once its values are assigned on the unit simplex

$$S_n = \left\{ w \mid w \geq 0 \text{ and } \sum_0^n w_i = 1 \right\}.$$

We define the norm $|w|$ of a non-negative vector w by $|w| = \sum_0^n w_i$. Let
$\phi(w) = f(w)$ for $w \in S_n$. Define $f(w)$ for $w \geq 0$ by $f(w) = |w| \phi(w/|w|)$
for $|w| > 0$, $f(0) = 0$. Consider a condition, alternative to (c),

(c') $\phi(u) \geq \beta \phi(u') + (1 - \beta) \phi(u'')$ for $u = \beta u' + (1 - \beta) u''$, $0 \leq \beta \leq 1$,
      and $u', u'' \in S_n$,

it is easy to see that (c') is equivalent to (c). Indeed, using only homogeneity (c) becomes, for $w, w', w'' \neq 0$,

$$f\left(\frac{w}{|w|}\right) \geq \alpha\frac{|w'|}{|w|}f\left(\frac{w'}{|w'|}\right) + (1-\alpha)\frac{|w''|}{|w|}f\left(\frac{w''}{|w''|}\right).$$

But this relation is implied by (c′) if

$$\alpha\frac{|w'|}{|w|} + (1-\alpha)\frac{|w''|}{|w|} = 1,$$

that is, if $|w| = \alpha|w'| + (1-\alpha)|w''|$. The latter is immediate from $w = \alpha w' + (1-\alpha)w''$. Thus (c′) implies (c) when $w', w'' \neq 0$. If $w'' = 0$, we have $w = \alpha w'$, so that $f(w) = f(\alpha w') = \alpha f(w')$. Thus (c) is met, and similarly if $w' = 0$. Since (c′) is also a special case of (c), (c) and (c′) are equivalent.

We may use the fact that $u \in S_n$ implies $u_0 = 1 - \sum_1^n u_i$ to write $\phi(u)$ for $u \in S_n$ in the form $g(u^0)$ where $u^0 = (u_1, \ldots, u_n)$. Then $f(w)$ for any $w \neq 0$ satisfies $f(w) = |w|g(w^0/|w|)$. The function $f(w)$ so defined in terms of g, with $f(0) = 0$, will satisfy condition (b) regardless of the properties of g. Let $v = (v_1, \ldots, v_n)$ and define $\Delta_n = \{v \mid v \geq 0, |v| \leq 1\}$. In order to insure that (a) and (c) are satisfied, we must have that $g(v)$ satisfies

(a′) $g(v)$ is defined and continuous for $v \in \Delta_n$.
  $g(v) \geq 0$ and $g(v) > 0$ if $v \in$ interior Δ_n.

(c″) $g(v) \geq \alpha g(v') + (1-\alpha)g(v'')$, for $v = \alpha v' + (1-\alpha)v'', 0 \leq \alpha \leq 1$.

It is obvious that (a′) implies (a), and conversely. Also (c″) is clearly equivalent to (c′) which we have seen to be equivalent to (c). Therefore, we may construct our counter-example with a function $g(v)$ satisfying (a′) and (c″).

If the function $g(v)$ is twice continuously differentiable, (c″) where $v', v'' \in S$ is also equivalent to $d^2g(\alpha v' + (1-\alpha)v'')/d\alpha^2 \leq 0$ for $v', v'' \in$ interior of S and $0 \leq \alpha \leq 1$ [2, (87)]. But

$$\frac{d}{d\alpha^2}g(\alpha v' + (1-\alpha)v'') = \sum_{i=1}^n\sum_{j=1}^n\frac{\partial^2 g}{\partial v_i\partial v_j}(v_i' - v_i'')(v_j' - v_j'').$$

Let

$$H(g) = \left[\frac{\partial^2 g}{\partial v_i\partial v_j}\right].$$

Then (c″) for a twice continuously differentiable function is equivalent to

(c‴) $xH(g(v))x$, where $x = (x_1, \ldots, x_n)$, is a negative semi-definite quadratic form for $v \in$ interior Δ_n.

We must evaluate the derivative of $f_i(w)$, for $w \neq 0$, in terms of the derivatives of $g_i(v)$, where $v = w^0/|w|$, using the relation $f_i(w) \equiv |w| g_i(w^0 |w|)$. Write f_{ij} for $\partial f_i/\partial w_j$, g_{ij} for $\partial g_i/\partial v_j$. Then

$$f_{ij}(w) = g_i\left(\frac{w^0}{|w|}\right) + |w| \sum_{k=1}^{n} g_{ik}\left(\frac{w^0}{|w|}\right)\left(\frac{\delta_{jk}}{|w|} - \frac{w_k}{|w|^2}\right).$$

Since $v_k = w_k/|w|$, this becomes

$$f_{ij}(w) = g_i(v) - \sum_{k=1}^{n} v_k g_{ik}(v) + \begin{cases} g_{ij}(v), & \text{if } j \geq 1. \\ 0, & \text{if } j = 0. \end{cases}$$

Then the Jacobian $|f_{ij}|$, or $J_f(w)$, may be written

$$\begin{vmatrix} g_0 - \sum_1^n v_k g_{0k} & g_0 - \sum_1^n v_k g_{0k} + g_{01} & \cdots & g_0 - \sum_1^n v_k g_{0k} + g_{0n} \\ \vdots & \vdots & & \vdots \\ g_n - \sum_1^n v_k g_{nk} & g_n - \sum_1^n v_k g_{nk} + g_{n1} & \cdots & g_n - \sum_1^n v_k g_{nk} + g_{nn} \end{vmatrix},$$

where the functions g_i and g_{ij} are evaluated at $v = w_0/|w|$. Now subtract the first column from the other columns. Then add the resulting k-th column, multiplied by v_{k-1}, to the first column, for $k = 2, \ldots, n + 1$. The value of the determinant is not affected, so

$$J_f(w) = \begin{vmatrix} g_0 & g_{01} & \cdots & g_{0n} \\ \vdots & \vdots & & \vdots \\ g_n & g_{n1} & \cdots & g_{nn} \end{vmatrix}.$$

The method of the counter-example is to take a single cost function on Δ_n, say $g_0(v)$, and define the other cost functions by perturbing this function with factors nearly equal to 1. For sufficiently small perturbations strict concavity will be preserved. Define $g_i(v) = e^{\delta \varphi_i(v)} g_0(v)$, for $i = 1, \ldots, n$. The parameter $\delta > 0$ is introduced for convenience. The Jacobian of the cost functions $f_i(w)$ may now be written

$$J_f(w) = e^{\delta \sum_1^n \varphi_i(v)} \begin{vmatrix} g_0 & g_{01} & \cdots & g_{0n} \\ \vdots & \vdots & & \vdots \\ g_0 & \delta\varphi_{n1} + g_{01} & \cdots & \delta\varphi_{nn} + g_{0n} \end{vmatrix}.$$

Then subtracting the first row from the other rows, we derive

$$J_f(w) = e^{\delta \sum_1^n \varphi_i(v)} \begin{vmatrix} g_0 & g_{01} & \cdots & g_{0n} \\ 0 & \delta\varphi_{11} & \cdots & \delta\varphi_{1n} \\ \vdots & \vdots & & \vdots \\ 0 & \delta\varphi_{n1} & \cdots & \delta\varphi_{nn} \end{vmatrix}.$$

Therefore, $J_f(w) = \delta^n e^{\delta \sum_1^n \varphi_i(v)} g_0(v) J_\varphi(v)$. In all these formulae it is understood that $v = w^0/|w|$. The condition $g_0(v) > 0$ is always satisfied in the interior of Δ_n by condition (a').

In view of this result we may construct our example in terms of $\varphi_i(v)$ and $J_\varphi(v)$. The exponentials of the $\delta\varphi_i(v)$ are used as perturbing factors for the function $g_0(v)$ for $v \in \Delta_n$. This provides corresponding perturbations of the cost function $f_0(w) = |w| g_0(w^0/|w|)$ over the domain $w \geq 0$. In effect, the perturbation is made on the unit simplex S_n and defined on the rest of the positive orthant by postulating homogeneity of degree one in the perturbed function.

In order to construct a counter-example to the Pearce conjecture we may select $g_0(v)$ and $\varphi_i(v)$ so that

(1) The functions $g_0(v)$ and $g_i(v) = e^{\delta\varphi_i(v)} g_0(v)$ satisfy (a') and (c''').

(2) $J_\varphi(v) = 0$ for $v \in \Delta_n$.

(3) $\varphi_1(v) = \cdots = \varphi_n(v) = 0$ for at least two different values of $v \in \Delta_n$.

As we have seen (c'') is equivalent to $vH(g_i)v \leq 0$ for all v. We will choose $g_0(v) = e^{\varepsilon h(v)}$ for $\varepsilon > 0$. Then $g_0(v) = e^{\varepsilon h(v)}$ and $H(g_0) = e^{\varepsilon h}(\varepsilon H(h) + o(\varepsilon))$. Thus we may choose ε so that $xH(g_0(v))x < 0$, for $x \neq 0$, and $v \in \Delta_n$, provided that $h(v)$ is twice continuously differentiable and $xH(h(v))x < \eta < 0$, for $v \in \Delta_n$ and $|x| = 1$. Let $h_i(v) = h(v) + \delta\varphi_i(v)$, for $i = 1, \ldots, n$, and $\delta > 0$. Then for δ sufficiently small $H(h_i) = H(h) + \delta H(\varphi_i)$ is the coefficient matrix of a negative definite form if $H(h)$ is such a matrix. Thus for sufficiently small ε and δ, $g_i(v) = e^{\varepsilon h(v) + \delta\varphi_i(v_i)}$ will satisfy (c''), provided $H(h(v))$ defines a negative definite form for $v \in \Delta_n$. Then $\varphi_i(v)$ must be chosen to be twice continuously differentiable and to satisfy (2) and (3).

We now give a simple specification of functions with these properties for $n = 2$. Let $h(v) = -v_1^2 - v_2^2$. Then

$$H(g_0(v)) = \varepsilon e^{\varepsilon(-v_1^2-v_2^2)} \begin{bmatrix} -2 - \varepsilon 4 v_1^2 & \varepsilon 4 v_1 v_2 \\ \varepsilon 4 v_1 v_2 & -2 + \varepsilon 4 v_2^2 \end{bmatrix}.$$

Let

$$\varphi_1(v) = e^{v_1} \cos 4\pi v_2 - e^{1/16} \cos \frac{\pi}{4},$$

$$\varphi_2(v) = e^{v_1} \sin 4\pi v_2 - e^{1/16} \sin \frac{\pi}{4},$$

$$H(\varphi_1) = e^{v_1} \begin{bmatrix} \cos 4\pi v_2 & -\sin 4\pi v_2 \\ -\sin 4\pi v_2 & -\cos 4\pi v_2 \end{bmatrix},$$

$$H(\varphi_2) = e^{v_1} \begin{bmatrix} \sin 4\pi v_2 & \cos 4\pi v_2 \\ \cos 4\pi v_2 & -\sin 4\pi v_2 \end{bmatrix}.$$

Choose $\varepsilon = 1/8$, $\delta = 1/144$. Then $\varepsilon e^{\varepsilon(-v_1^2-v_2^2)} > 1/24$ and the column sums of $H(g_0)$ are less than $-1/24$, with non-negative off-diagonal elements. The absolute values of the elements of $\delta H(\varphi_i)$ are less than $1/48$. Then $H(g_i)$ has a dominant negative diagonal for all v, and $i = 0, 1, 2$, and thus defines a negative definite quadratic form [6, (49)]. Since the differentiability properties are obvious, this verifies (1).

$$J_\varphi(v) = \frac{1}{144} e^{2c_1} \begin{vmatrix} \cos 4\pi v_2 & -4\pi \sin 4\pi v_2 \\ \sin 4\pi v_2 & 4\pi \cos 4\pi v_2 \end{vmatrix}$$

$$= \frac{1}{144} e^{2c_1} 4\pi (\cos^2 4\pi v_2 + \sin^2 4\pi v_2) > \frac{1}{36} \pi \quad \text{for all } v.$$

Thus (2) is satisfied.

Finally, $\varphi_1(v) = \varphi_2(v) = 0$ for $v = (1/16, 1/16)$ and $v = (1/16, 9/16)$. Thus the factor price vectors $(14/16, 1/16, 1/16)$ and $(6/16, 1/16, 9/16)$ correspond to the goods price vectors $e^{1/8(-(1/16)^2-(1/16)^2)}(1,1,1)$ and $e^{1/8(-(1/16)^2-(9/16)^2)}(1,1,1)$ respectively. Or the goods price vector $(1,1,1)$ is consistent with factor price vectors

$$w = e^{1/1024} \left(\frac{14}{16}, \frac{1}{16}, \frac{1}{16} \right)$$

and with

$$w' = e^{1/1024} \left(\frac{6}{16}, \frac{1}{16}, \frac{9}{16} \right).$$

But $w \neq w'$. Since the Jacobian of the cost functions does not vanish for any $w \geq 0$, $w \neq 0$, the Pearce conjecture is thereby proved false. Note that by redefining the factor units slightly (a new unit of a factor equals $16e^{-1/1024}$ old units), we may say that the price vector for goods $(1, 1, 1)$ is consistent with the two distinct price vectors for factors $(14, 1, 1)$ and $(6, 1, 9)$. The ratio of the price of the first factor to the third factor in the first equilibrium is 21 times the ratio in the second equilibrium.

Notes

1. The economic problem of this chapter was put in an equivalent mathematical form by the author, and the mathematical problem was solved by R. G. Swan of the Mathematics Department of the University of Chicago. I would also like to thank my graduate assistant, Emmanuel Drandakis, and my colleague, Johannes Kemperman, for their help. This chapter was written while the author was supported by a grant of the National Science Foundation. Except for the reference to Gale and Nikaidô, it was completed in 1962.

2. The homogeneity of the cost functions implies that the Jacobian is not defined at zero unless it is constant.

3. That is, the minors may be ordered in a series such that the k-th minor is contained in all succeeding minors and contains all preceding minors. There is a renumbering of goods and factors which will place these minors on the main diagonal.

4. The Jacobian matrix of the cost functions is equal to the matrix of factor inputs. Thus, $K(w)$ is equal to the set of all vectors resulting from non-negative linear combinations of the columns of the Jacobian.

5. The absolute value of the diagonal element in each column exceeds the sum of the absolute values of the other elements in that column.

6. For a detailed study of the duality of cost and production functions see Shepard [12], especially sections 4 and 7.

References

[1] Dieudonné, J., *Foundations of Modern Analysis* (New York, 1960).

[2] Fenchel, W., *Convex Cones, Sets, and Functions* (Princeton, 1953).

[3] Gale, David and H. Nikaidô, "The Jacobian Matrix and Global Univalence of Mappings," *Mathematische Annalen*, Bd. 159, Heft 2 (1965), 81–93.

[4] Kuhn, Harold, "Factor Endowments and Factor Prices, Mathematical Appendix," *Economica*, XXVI (May, 1959), 142–44.

[5] McKenzie, Lionel, "Equality of Factor Prices in World Trade," *Econometrica*, XXIII (July, 1955), 239–57.

[6] ———, "Matrices with Dominant Diagonals and Economic Theory," in K. J. Arrow, S. Karlin and P. Suppes, eds., *Mathematical Methods in the Social Sciences, 1959*, (Stanford: Stanford University Press, 1960).

[7] Pearce, I. F. and S. F. James, "The Factor Price Equalization Myth," *Review of Economic Studies*, XIX, No. 2 (1952), 111–20.

[8] Pearce, I. F., "A Further Note on Factor-Commodity Price Relationships," *Economic Journal*, LXIX (December, 1959), 725–32.

[9] Samuelson, Paul, "International Trade and the Equalization of Factor Prices," *Economic Journal*, LVIII (June, 1948), 163–84.

[10] ———, "International Factor-Price Equalization Once Again," *Economic Journal*, LVIII (June, 1948), 163–84.

[11] ———, "Prices of Factors and Goods in General Equilibrium", *Review of Economic Studies*, XXI, No. 1 (1953), 1–20.

[12] Shephard, Ronald W., *Cost and Production Functions*, (Princeton, 1953).

17 Theorem and Counter-Example

Lionel W. McKenzie

17.1 Introduction

It is possible to extend the counter-example which I presented to what I took Pearce's conjecture [4] to be until it very nearly meets the theorem which he has now proved. Of course, in the nature of the case a counter-example has a narrow scope. I shall also give a proof of Pearce's basic result which does not draw upon homotopy theory, and I will extend his result somewhat. I regard the subject of our discussion to be the inversion of cost functions. This is related to the problem of factor price equalization through trade, but it is not the central issue there, as I tried to show in my *Econometrica* article [2]. Therefore, I take Pearce's various deprecating remarks on the significance of our subject to be irrelevant.

17.2 Pearce's Theorem

The cost function $f_i(w)$ is the support function of the set $X_i \subset E_n$ of combination of factor inputs which are consistent with an output of one unit of the i-th product. It is assumed that $x \in X_i$ implies $x \geq 0$ and $x \neq 0$. Then $f_i(w)$ is equal to min $w \cdot x$ for $x \in X_i$, when this minimum exists. Let D_i be the domain for w in which $f_i(w)$ is defined. Then $w \in D_i$ if and only if $w \cdot x$ is bounded below in X_i and attains its greatest lower bound. In this case there is $x' \in X_i$ such that $w \cdot x' = f_i(w)$. Also, if $\partial f_i(w)/\partial w_j$, or $f_{ij}(w)$, exists, it is equal to x'_j. Denote the vector of cost functions $f_i(w)$, $i = 1, \ldots, n$, by $f(w)$. The domain of definition of $f(w)$ is $D = \bigcap_i D_i$.

Pearce assumes that X_i is compact, which has the consequence that $D_i = E_n$. However, this is a special case. For example, if there exists a disposal process which has as inputs one unit of the i-th output and certain quantities of factors, X_i will be unbounded since all processes in these models are assumed to be homogeneous of first degree. Thus if $x \in X_i$ and $z \in E_n$ is a vector of factor inputs which can dispose of one unit of the i-th good, $x + \alpha(x + z)$ is an element of X_i for any $\alpha \geq 0$. Similarly, if factor disposal is possible, that is, there is a combination z' of factors which has no output, $x + \alpha z' \in X_i$ for any $\alpha \geq 0$. It has been customary in general equilibrium theory to assume that any single factor can be freely disposed of. This means that $x \in X_i$ implies $x' \in X_i$ for any $x' \geq x$. In this case the domain D_i of $f_i(w)$ is contained in Ω, the positive orthant of E_n.

The argument used by Pearce to establish his theorems depends on results from homotopy theory. However, his theorems may be as well derived without appealing to this theory. A very convenient point of departure is the following result from Favard [1, (295–97)].

Theorem 1   Let E and F be two simply connected bounded open sets lying in a Euclidean space E_n. Let

$$u = \gamma(v) \quad v \in E, u \in F$$

be a continuous function in closure E, mapping E on F, such that the image of every boundary point of E belongs to the boundary of F, and such finally that this function defines a local homeomorphism in every point of E, then it defines a global homeomorphism between E and F.

This theorem is proved in two pages of elementary argument. A sufficient condition for $\gamma(v)$ to be a local homeomorphism of E on F is that the Jacobian be continuous and not zero at every point of E. A necessary condition that $\gamma(v)$ be a global homeomorphism between E and F is that $\gamma(v)$ be one-to-one between E and F. Thus Theorem 1 can be restated with the condition on the Jacobian in the hypothesis and with univalence of $\gamma(v)$ as the conclusion.

I will use Favard's theorem to prove Pearce's basic result. It is assumed that X_i is convex for all i. Let F be the smallest flat (a displaced linear subspace) that contains X_i. The partial derivatives $f_{ij}(w)$ are defined and continuous in an open set E if and only if the point x' at which $w \cdot x$ achieves its minimum over X_i is unique for each $w \in E$. This is a kind of strict convexity condition which excludes the possibility that the support points for three distinct $w \in E$ be in one line. Also $|f_{ij}(w)| \neq 0$ for all $w \in \Omega$, $w \neq 0$, implies that if all goods are produced, all factors are needed. Otherwise, suppose all goods can be produced when the k-th factor is not used. Consider $w \in \Omega$, $w \neq 0$, but $w_j = 0$ for

$j \neq k$. Then there is for each i, x^i such that $w \cdot x^i = 0$. But $[f_{ij}(w)] = [x^i_j]$, so $|f_{ij}(w)| = 0$.

Pearce's basic theorem may be formulated as

Theorem 2   Let $W = \{w \mid f(w) \in \text{interior } \Omega\}$. Let D be a convex cone with vertex at the origin. Assume that $f(w)$ is defined for $w \in D$, where closure $W - \{0\} \subset \text{interior } D$, and that $|f_{ij}(w)|$ exists and is continuous and not zero for $w \in \text{interior } D$. Then $f^{-1}(p)$ exists for all $p \in \Omega$.

Proof   We suppose the units of measurement are chosen so that $\bar{x} = (1, \ldots, 1)$ lies in the interior of X, the convex hull of the X_i. Then $W = \{w \mid w \cdot x > 0 \text{ for } x \in X\}$. W is a convex cone with vertex at the origin. Since $\bar{x} \in \text{interior } X$, w and $-w$ cannot both belong to closure W, or closure W is pointed. Consider the hyperplane defined by $\bar{x}$, $H = \{w \mid w \cdot \bar{x} = 1\}$. If $w \in \text{closure } W$, $w \cdot \bar{x} > 0$, so $ww \cdot \bar{x} \in \text{closure } W \cap H$. Also closure $W \cap H$ is closed as an intersection of closed sets. Suppose closure $W \cap H$ is not bounded. Then there is a sequence $w^s \in \text{closure } W \cap H$ and $|w^s| = \sum_i |w^s_i| \rightarrow \infty$ as $s \rightarrow \infty$. The sequence $w^s/|w^s|$ is bounded and has an accumulation point $w' \in \text{closure } W$. But $w^s \cdot \bar{x} = 1$ for all s implies $w' \cdot \bar{x} = 0$. Since $\bar{x} \in \text{interior } X$, there is $x \in X$ and $w' \cdot x < 0$. Thus there is $w \in W$ and $w \cdot x < 0$, contradicting the definition of W. Therefore, closure $W \cap H$ is compact.

Let $w \in (\text{boundary } W) - \{0\}$. Suppose $f(w) \in \text{interior } \Omega$. Since closure $W \subset \text{interior } D$, there is a neighborhood U of w such that f maps U onto a neighborhood V of $f(w)$ and this map is one-to-one. Then for small $U, V \subset \text{interior } \Omega$. This implies that $U \subset W$ by the definition of W. By continuity $f(w) \in \Omega$, so $f(w) \in \text{boundary } \Omega$.

Similarly, suppose there is $p \in \text{interior } \Omega$ and $p \in f(W)$. By continuity $f(W)$ is closed relative to interior Ω. However, since $W \subset \text{interior } D$, $w \in W$ implies there is a neighborhood U of w such that $f(U) = V$ and V is a neighborhood of $f(w)$. Then $V \cap \text{interior } \Omega \subset f(W)$, so $f(W)$ is open relative to interior Ω. Since interior Ω is connected, and $f(W) \subset \text{interior } \Omega$, $f(W) = \text{interior } \Omega$.

It is clear that interior $\Omega \cap H$ is simply connected since it is convex. Also $f(w)$ and $f(w') \in \text{interior } \Omega$ implies $f(w'') \in \text{interior } \Omega$, where $w'' = \alpha w + (1 - \alpha)w'$, $0 \leq \alpha \leq 1$, from the concavity of f. This shows that W is convex. Thus $W \cap H$ is convex and simply connected.

If $f(w) = 0$, by homogeneity of first degree, $[f_{ij}]w = f(w) = 0$, so $w = 0$. This allows us to define $\bar{f}(w) = f(w)/|f(w)|$, for $w \in D \cap H$. The preceding argument implies that $\bar{f}$ maps $W \cap H$ onto interior $\Omega \cap H$. Define a mapping $\prod$ of E_{n-1} onto H by $\prod(v) = w$ where $w_i = v_i$ for

$i = 1, \ldots, n - 1$, and $w_n = 1 - \sum_{i=1}^{n-1} v_i$. Let $W^* = \prod^{-1}(W \cap H)$, $D^* = \prod^{-1}(D \cap H)$, and $P^* = \prod^{-1}$ (interior $\Omega \cap H$). Let $f^*(v) = \bar{f}(\prod(v))$ for $v \in D^*$. Then f^* maps W^* onto P^*. Also $v \in$ boundary W^* implies $f^*(v) \in$ boundary P^*. W^* and P^* are simply connected, since they are convex. f^* is continuous and locally univalent since f and $\prod$ are. That is, f^* is a local homeomorphism. Thus $f^* : W^* \to P^*$ satisfies all the conditions of Theorem 1 and f^* is a global homeomorphism of W^* on P^*. Then $\bar{f}$ is a global homeomorphism of $W \cap H$ on interior $\Omega \cap H$. By homogeneity, f is a global homeomorphism of W on interior Ω.

We must extend the homeomorphism defined by f to closure W and Ω. The properties of interior Ω used in the proof are (1) Ω is a pointed convex cone with vertex at the origin, (2) $w \in$ interior Ω implies that $w + \Omega \in$ interior Ω, and (3) closure $W - \{0\} \subset$ interior D where $W = \{w \mid f(w) \in$ interior $\Omega\}$. Let C be a pointed convex cone with vertex at the origin where $\Omega - \{0\} \subset$ interior C. Let $W(C) = \{w \mid f(w) \in$ interior $C\}$. The continuity of f implies that C may be chosen so that closure $W(C) \subset D$. C may be generated by the set resulting from a slight expansion of $\Omega \cap H$ by projection from a relatively interior point of $\Omega \cap H$. Thus by the preceding argument $f(w)$ defines a homeomorphic map of $W(C)$ on interior C. This implies that f^{-1} is defined on (boundary Ω) $- \{0\}$ and maps this set on (boundary W) $- \{0\}$. We have seen that 0 is the only point of D which maps into 0, so f maps closure W onto Ω continuously and one-to-one. Thus $f^{-1}(p)$ exists for all $p \in \Omega$.

By normalizing on $S = \{w \mid \sum_i w_i^2 = 1\}$, rather than on H, the following theorem may be proved along the same lines as Theorem 2. It includes the results of Pearce as special cases.

Theorem 3   Let D be a cone with vertex at the origin such that $f(w)$ is defined over D. Assume that $|f_{ij}(w)|$ exists, is continuous, and is not zero for $w \in$ interior D. Let P be a cone with vertex at the origin such that $P - \{0\}$ is open. Assume that $P + \Omega = P$ and that $P - \{0\}$ is simply connected. Let $W = \{w \mid f(w) \in P\}$. Assume closure $W - \{0\} \subset$ interior D. Then $f^{-1}(p)$ exists for all $p \in \bar{P}$.

$P + \Omega = P$ allows the use of concavity for f to show that W is convex and thus simply connected. These conditions together with closure $W - \{0\} \subset$ interior D are the crucial conditions for the theorem. $P - \{0\} =$ interior Ω, and $P = E_n$ are the extreme special cases for Theorem 3.

17.3   A More General Theorem

The use of concavity of f to insure that W is simply connected shows that f need not be monotone in order to derive our results. Thus X_i need not lie in Ω and $f_{ij} < 0$ is permissible. Then we not only allow goods and factors to enjoy negative prices but negative quantities of factors may be allowed, where a negative quantity indicates that the factor is an intermediate product which, in net amount, is being supplied by the process.

A very general theorem may be given. Consider a process in which $2n$ goods appear. The process is completely characterized by a closed, pointed, convex cone Y_i with vertex at the origin. y is a possible input-output combination for the i-th process if $y \in Y_i$. Positive components of y are outputs, negative components are inputs. There are no restrictions on the signs of the components of y. It is even allowed that all goods may be inputs, or all goods may be outputs. Let $p \in E_{2n}$ have n of its components, say p_j, $j \in N$, fixed in value but not all zero. Put $p_j = 0$ for $j \notin N$. Let $H = \{y \mid p \cdot y = 1\}$. Let $H_i = H \cap Y_i$, and let $k(j)$ map $\{1, \ldots, n\}$ onto the complement of N. Let $x = \rho(y) \in E_n$ where $x_j = y_{k(j)}$. Put $X_i = \rho(H \cap Y_i)$. We suppose that X_i has a non-empty interior. Then X_i may be used to define a support function $f_i(w)$. Suppose there are n such processes and we derive n sets X_i and n support functions in this way. Suppose, moreover, that the $f_i(w)$ satisfy the conditions of Theorem 3 for some P which contains $(1, \ldots, 1)$. Then the w satisfying $f_i(w) = 1$ for $i = 1, \ldots, n$, are unique. This in turn implies that the price vector p' satisfying $p' \cdot y^i \leq 0$ for $y^i \in Y_i$, all i, and $p' \cdot y^{i'} = 0$ for some $y^{i'} \in Y_i$, all i, and having $p'_j = p_j$ for $j \in N$, is unique. Thus given *these* n values for the prices with indices in N, the remaining prices that are consistent with the profit conditions are unique. This does not imply that given $\tilde{p}$ where $\tilde{p}_j = p'_j$, $j \in$ complement of N, the $\tilde{p}_j$, $j \in N$, are unique. The reverse implication requires a new argument of the same sort in the other direction. Also if the uniqueness is to hold for other p', with the same N, or another N, the assumptions must be correspondingly revised.

17.4   The Counter-Example

With the assistance of R. G. Swan I developed a counter-example to the proposition that f^{-1} exists whenever f is defined over Ω and $|f_{ij}|$ is continuous and non-zero over $\Omega - \{0\}$. I will now delimit more exactly

310   Chapter 17

the range of the counter-example. The true limit on the applicability of the general argument, which has wider scope than the particular functions used, is the condition that $f(w) > 0$ over the domain, less the origin, where f is defined. If we adapt the counter-example to E_n and let f_1 replace f_0 in the argument, $f_i(w) = |w|e^{\delta\varphi_i(w^1/|w|)}g_1(w^1/|w|)$, $i = 2, \ldots, n$, where $w^1 = (w_2, \ldots, w_n)$, and $f_1(w) = |w|g_1(w^1/|w|)$. Then $f_i(w) = 0$, if and only if $f_1(w) = 0$.

Consider the map $f: W_p \to$ interior $(p + \Omega)$ where $W_p = \{w \mid f(w) > p > 0\}$. By the argument used for Pearce's theorem, $f(W_p) =$ interior $(p + \Omega)$. Since $f(W) = \bigcup_{p>0} f(W_p)$, $f(W) =$ interior Ω. Moreover, $|f_{ij}|$ is nonsingular on $H \cap W$. Since $f(w) > 0$ on $H \cap W$, it is possible to define $\bar{f}$ on $H \cap W$. However, $f(w) = 0$ for $w \in$ boundary W, so $\bar{f}$ is not defined on boundary $H \cap W$. One might try to evade this difficulty by taking the value of $\bar{f}$ at $w \in$ boundary $H \cap W$ equal to the limit of $\bar{f}(w^s)$ as $w^s \to w$, $w^s \in H \cap W$. However, limit $f_i(w^s)/f_1(w^s) =$ limit $e^{\delta\varphi_i(w^s)} > 0$, if the limit exists. Thus the limiting value of $\bar{f}(w^s)$, as $w^s \to w$, is necessarily positive in all components, or $\bar{f}(w) \in$ interior Ω. This means that the boundary of $H \cap W$ does not map under $\bar{f}$ into the boundary of Ω and the Favard theorem cannot be applied. Therefore, there is no conflict between the counter-example and the theorem, even though the counter-example can be extended to any W defined by a closed convex cone $P \subset$ interior Ω.

As it happens, for the particular f_1 used $f_1(\prod(v)) = e^{-s(v_1^2+v_2^2)}$, and this function is no longer concave if $v_1^2 + v_2^2$ is too large. It is sufficient for concavity to have $v_1^2 + v_2^2 < 1/2\varepsilon$, as one sees from the Hessian. However, $f_1(w)$ may be defined as the support function of a sphere lying in interior Ω, say $X_1 = \{x \mid (x_1 - \xi)^2 + (x_2 - \xi)^2 + (x_3 - \xi)^2 \leq \rho^2\}$ where $0 < \xi < \rho$. The support function is $f_1(w) = \xi(\sum_{i=1}^3 w_i - (\rho/\xi)(\sum_{i=1}^3 w_i^2)^{1/2})$. This is strictly concave for all $w \neq 0$ and the set of $w \in H$ for which $f_1(w) \geq 0$ is bounded. Concavity over this bounded domain is preserved under multiplication by a perturbing function which is continuously twice differentiable and close to one. Thus concavity is not the barrier between counter-example and theorem.

17.5 Conclusions

What is the upshot of my counter-example together with Pearce's theorem? In the first place, if the classical assumption of freely disposable factors is adopted, the sets X_i are unbounded, and $f(w)$ is not defined for w if there is $w_i < 0$ for some i. Thus the conditions of the theorem cannot be met directly. The notion of an "extension" of $f(w)$ over a wider domain than the X_i allow may be useful but it is not useful in itself. One needs to know what conditions the X_i must satisfy to permit such an extension. These conditions become the object of interest. On the other hand, the counter-example does not allow $f_i(w) = 0$ for some $w \neq 0$, $w \geq 0$. This means that the counter-example depends on $x_j > \varepsilon$ for $x \in X_i$. In between is a grey area where factor disposal, which need not be free, or free goods disposal, excludes from the domain of f any w which would result, for at least one i, in $f_i(w) < 0$ (so that Pearce does not apply), but where the domain of f does include w such that $f_i(w) \leq 0$ for one or more i, so that the method of the counter-example does not apply. Note, in particular, that even so simple a case as the Cobb-Douglas cost function does not fall within the scope of either theorem or counter-example. Of course, the Cobb-Douglas cost function is written $p_j = \prod_i w_i^{\alpha_{ij}}$ or $\log p_j = \sum_i \alpha_{ij} \log w_i$, for each j, and this may be inverted if $|\alpha_{ij}| \neq 0$, but this is a special case of the cost function which arises from an X_i which is asymptotic to some coordinate hyperplane. For the general case no result is available.

Pearce's result with regard to partial equalization has limited significance. The fact that two goods price vectors belong to the same (and only) component of the inverse image of an infinite (or normalized) interval does not mean that these vectors are "close" to each other in any other sense. Of course, the idea is worth recording and may lead to further developments.

I would repeat that the present discussion is concerned with the inversion of a set of cost functions and only tangentially with factor price equalization. The latter question cannot be carried very far without considering factor supplies. Then one can discuss the range of goods prices which result in equalization of factor prices given the factor supplies and the list of traded goods. I attempted to do this at some length in my *Econometrica* article [2] under various assumptions about the production functions.

I have no serious complaint to register about Pearce's references to my work in his paper. However, there are two inaccuracies worth noting. First, the dominant diagonal case is not my basic theorem on unique inversion in the *Econometrica* paper. It is a particular example where the general theorem holds. Let K_{pw} be the cone of factor inputs which are consistent with the goods price vector p and the factor price vector w (if there is no joint production this should be written K_w since $p = f(w)$). Suppose n is the number of factors. My theorem is

Theorem 4   In a competitive equilibrium, if two countries are able to use a set of independent activities which includes one from each of n processes whose K's always intersect, factor prices must be the same in both countries. [2, (248)].

A dominant diagonal for $[f_{ij}]$ happens to imply that the K's, which are the convex cones spanned by the $[f_{ij}]$, do have interiors which intersect. But a dominant diagonal is by no means necessary for the intersection property. Second, it is not true that the dominant diagonal condition is a condition on each process separately. Pearce forgets that units of measurement for factors may be redefined. This is equivalent to post-multiplying $[f_{ij}]$ by a diagonal matrix D with a positive diagonal. Let $e_{ij} = -f_{ij}$ for $i \neq j$, $e_{ii} = f_{ii}$, all i. Then an appropriate D exists if and only if $[e_{ij}]$ has all principal minors positive [3, (60)]. This is clearly a condition which depends on all processes together.

References

[1] Favard, Jean, *Cours d'analyse de l'Ecole polytechnique*, Vol. 1 (Paris, 1960).

[2] McKenzie, Lionel W., "Equality of Factor Prices in World Trade," *Econometrica*, XXIII (July, 1955), 239–57.

[3] ———, "Matrices with Dominant Diagonals and Economic Theory," in K. J. Arrow, S. Karlin and P. Suppes, eds., *Mathematical Methods in the Social Sciences, 1959* (Stanford: Standford University Press, 1960).

[4] Pearce, Ivor, "More about Factor Price Equalization," *International Economic Review*, this issue.

Growth

18 The Dorfman-Samuelson-Solow Turnpike Theorem

Lionel W. McKenzie

In the past two years several global turnpike theorems have been established, for the Ricardian or simple Leontief model by Morishima [5] and the author [3], for a von Neumann model with strict convexity near the turnpike by Radner [6], and for a generalized Leontief model with capital goods by the author [4]. However, the original theorem of Dorfman, Samuelson, and Solow [1] dealt with a neo-classical transformation function. This transformation function allows processes to be present in which there is joint production of current output, unlike the author's local theorem for the generalized Leontief model. On the other hand, the conclusions for local behavior are stronger than those of the global theorems of Radner and the author. Also the strict convexity assumption of Radner is not needed.

The original theorem, however, was given for the case of only two goods, where the argument does not expose all the difficulties; and in the continuous model of Samuelson [7], which is stated for n goods, strict convexity is assumed. Moreover, the original proofs of the theorem do not proceed beyond the derivation of reciprocity of roots for the linear approximation to the efficiency conditions. It will be the purpose of my paper to give the original theorem (slightly weakened) a complete proof, one that does not require strict convexity and applies to any finite number of goods.

18.1 The Model

We shall start from a classical transformation function which relates the stocks of goods which may be achieved at time $t + 1$ (by efficient production) to the stocks existing at time t. Let the stock of the i-th good at time t be written S_i^t. Write ΔS_i^t for the stock increment

$S_i^{t+1} - S_i^t$ between time t and time $t + 1$. Then the transformation function, in the form

$$\Delta S_1^t = f(\Delta S_2^t, \ldots, \Delta S_n^t, S_1^t, \ldots, S_n^t), \tag{1}$$

represents the maximum increment of the first stock attainable between times t and $t + 1$ as a function of the increments of other stocks and the initial stocks. Let $S = (S_1, \ldots, S_n)$, $\Delta S = (\Delta S_1, \ldots, \Delta S_n)$, $\Delta_1 S = (\Delta S_2, \ldots, \Delta S_n)$. We make the following assumptions:

Assumption 1   The transformation function $f(\Delta_1 S, S)$ is defined and not negative over a convex set $C \subset \Omega_{2n-1}$. The interior of C is not empty.

Assumption 2 $f(\Delta_1 S, S)$ is homogeneous of the first degree and concave. It has continuous derivatives of the first two orders in the interior of C, and in this region $f_i < 0$ for $i = 2, \ldots, n$, $f_{n+i} > 0$ for $i = 1, \ldots, n$, where

$$f_i = \frac{\partial f}{\partial \Delta S_i} \quad \text{and} \quad f_{n+i} = \frac{\partial f}{\partial S_i}.$$

Ω_{2n-1} is the positive orthant of the $2n - 1$ Euclidean space.

The Hessian matrix of f is $[f_{ij}]$, $i, j = 2, \ldots, 2n$. In the case of Radner or Samuelson, where f is strictly concave except along a ray from the origin, the Hessian, when it is defined, will have rank $2n - 2$. However, in the model used for a local theorem by the author [3], there are n linearly independent and homogeneous processes, each producing a different good. These processes span an n dimensional facet of the efficient point set. The efficient point set may be identified in this model as all $(\Delta S, S)$ such that $\Delta S_1 = f(\Delta_1 S, S)$. If $(\Delta S, S)$ and $(\Delta S', S')$ both lie on the same facet the associated efficiency prices [see 2, (65 ff.)] are the same. However, these prices are proportional to the f_j. Thus the f_j are constant over the facet. Project the facet into the space of the last $2n - 1$ coordinates. Then the n dimensional linear subspace of E_{2n-1} on which the facet projects is mapped into zero by $[f_{ij}]$. Therefore, the rank of $[f_{ij}]$ is not greater than $n - 1$. On the other hand, if the number of linearly independent processes in use (which may include processes with joint production) exceeds n, the rank of $[f_{ij}]$ will be correspondingly smaller.

That the derivatives in Assumption 2 are not allowed to be zero implies that the productive system is connected in C. Similar properties play an important role in other turnpike theorems too. Connectedness, however, does not exclude the presence of self-sufficient subeconomies. Note that connectedness is a property of *efficient* production in a region where all goods appear as inputs and outputs.

Much of the interest of the Dorfman-Samuelson-Solow theorem is due to the fact that it allows the number of independent processes to be different from n, and no special assumptions are made concerning joint production. On the other hand, nonsingularity assumptions are needed in this theorem whose economic import is less clear than for the author's theorem. I should add that the author's global theorem can be extended beyond the n processes case [see 4, (22 ff.)]. This extension forms an appropriate complement to the Dorfman-Samuelson-Solow local theorem.

18.2 Maximal Balanced Growth

Define $g_i = \Delta S_i / S_i$, $b_i = S_i / S_1$. Since f is homogeneous of the first degree we may rewrite (1) in the form

$$g_1^t = f(g_2^t b_2^t, \ldots, g_n^t b_n^t, 1, b_2^t, \ldots, b_n^t). \tag{2}$$

Any path of balanced growth will satisfy an equation

$$\gamma = f(\gamma b_2, \ldots, \gamma b_n, 1, b_2, \ldots, b_n). \tag{3}$$

Let $b = (b_2, \ldots, b_n)$. Put $\Phi = \gamma - f(\gamma b, 1, b)$. Then

$$\frac{\partial \Phi}{\partial \gamma} = 1 - \sum_{i=2}^{n} f_i b_i.$$

Since, by Assumption 2, $f_i < 0$, $i = 2, \ldots, n$, in the interior of C, $\partial \Phi / \partial \gamma > 0$ in this region, and, by the implicit function theorem, (3) may be solved for γ as a function of b in a neighborhood of b' if γ' and b' satisfy (3). Moreover, $\partial \gamma(b)/\partial b_i$ exists by the implicit function theorem, and

$$\frac{\partial \gamma}{\partial b_i} = -\frac{\partial \Phi / \partial b_i}{\partial \Phi / \partial \gamma} = \frac{\gamma f_i + f_{n+i}}{1 - \sum_{j=2}^{n} f_i b_j}. \tag{4}$$

Necessary and sufficient conditions that $\gamma(b)$ enjoy a stationary value in the interior of C are that $\partial\gamma/\partial b_i = 0$, for $i = 2,\ldots,n$. However, since $f_j < 0$ by Assumption 2, these conditions are seen from (4) to be equivalent to

$$\gamma = -\frac{f_{n+i}}{f_i}, \quad i = 2,\ldots,n. \tag{5}$$

We may prove

Lemma 1   A stationary value of $\gamma(b)$ at b^* is a global maximum of γ for $(\gamma(b),b)$ satisfying (3). The set of b such that $\gamma(b) = \gamma(b^*)$ is convex.

Proof   Let (γ^*,b^*) satisfy (3). Let S_ε be a sphere of radius ε about b^* where ε is small enough that $\gamma(b)$ is defined for b in S_ε. Let $\gamma(b)$ have a stationary value at b^*. Now suppose there is any (γ',b') in C satisfying (3) where $\gamma' > \gamma^*$. Consider b'' where $|b^* - b''| = \varepsilon$ and $b^* = \alpha b' + (1-\alpha)b''$ for $\alpha = \varepsilon/|b' - b''|$. Since $\gamma(b^*)$ is a stationary value of $\gamma(b)$, the first differential of $\gamma(b)$ is 0 at b^*, and the ratio $(\gamma^* - \gamma'')/\alpha$ approaches 0 with ε, for $\gamma'' = \gamma(b'')$. On the other hand, $\gamma^* < \gamma'$ and $f_i < 0$ imply $f(\gamma^*b',1,b') > \gamma'$. Let $f(\gamma^*b'',1,b'') = \bar{\gamma}$. Then

$$\bar{\gamma} - \gamma'' = (\gamma^* - \gamma'') \sum_{i=2}^{n} b_i^* f_i(\gamma^*b^*,1,b^*),$$

plus terms of the second order in ε. By the concavity of f,

$$f(\gamma^*b^*,1,b^*) \geq \alpha\gamma' + (1-\alpha)\bar{\gamma}.$$

But for ε sufficiently small,

$$\gamma' + \frac{1-\alpha}{\alpha}\bar{\gamma} = \gamma' + \frac{1-\alpha}{\alpha}\gamma^* - (1-\alpha)\frac{\gamma^* - \bar{\gamma}}{\alpha} > \frac{\gamma^*}{\alpha},$$

since the last term is of the same order as $(\gamma^* - \gamma'')/\alpha$, which becomes small with ε, and $\gamma' > \gamma^*$. This implies $f(\gamma^*b^*,1,b^*) > \gamma*$, a contradiction. Therefore, no such (γ',b') can exist, and (b^*) is, in fact, a global maximum of $\gamma(b)$ in C.

The convexity of the set of b, where $\gamma(b) = \gamma(b^*)$, is immediate from the concavity of f. We now make

Assumption 3   There is $(\gamma^*b^*,1,b^*)$ in the interior of C such that (3) is satisfied and $\gamma(b)$ is stationary at b^*.

18.3 Efficient Growth Paths

We will say that a path $\{S^t\}$, $t = 0, \ldots, T$ is efficient, if $\Delta S_1^t = f(\Delta_1 S^t, S^t)$ for $t = 0, \ldots, T-1$, and if $\{S'^t\}$ is another path satisfying these conditions where $S'^0 \leq S^0$, then $S'^T \geq S^T$ does not hold. Suppose, however, that $(\Delta_1 S^t, S^t)$ lies in the interior of C. Then it is clear from the existence of derivatives that it is equivalent to require that $S'^0 = S^0$ and $S_i'^T = S_i^T$, $i = 2, \ldots, n$ imply $S_1'^T \leq S_1^T$. Thus we may inquire what conditions must hold if S_1^T is to be a maximum for assigned S^0 and S_i^T, $i = 2, \ldots, n$.

An equivalent problem is to maximize the Lagrangean expression

$$\sum_{t=0}^{T-1} \lambda^t [f(\Delta_1 S^t, S^t) - \Delta S_1^t] + \sum_{t=0}^{T-1} \Delta S_1^t + \sum_{i=2}^{n} \mu^i \left(\sum_{t=0}^{T-1} \Delta S_i^t - S_i^T + S_i^0 \right), \qquad (6)$$

subject to the conditions

$$S^t = S^0 + \sum_{\tau=0}^{t-1} \Delta S^\tau, \quad t = 1, \ldots, T. \tag{6'}$$

$$\Delta S_1^t = f(\Delta_1 S^t, S^t), \quad t = 0, \ldots, T-1. \tag{6''}$$

We substitute (6') in $f(\Delta_1 S^t, S^t)$, and obtain by differentiation of (6) with respect to ΔS_i^τ, $\tau = 0, \ldots, T-1$, the first order conditions

$$-\lambda^t + \sum_{\tau=t+1}^{T-1} \lambda^\tau f_{n+1}^t + 1 = 0, \tag{7}$$

$$\lambda^t f_i^t + \sum_{\tau=t+1}^{T-1} \lambda^\tau f_{n+i}^\tau + \mu^i = 0, \quad t = 0, \ldots, T-1, i = 2, \ldots, n. \tag{8}$$

Here the superscript t is transferred from the arguments to the function f for brevity. For $t = T-1$, the summations are omitted. Now subtracting the equations (7) and (8) for $t+1$ from these equations for t we obtain

$$-\lambda^t + \lambda^{t+1} + \lambda^{t+1} f_{n+1}^{t+1} = 0, \tag{9}$$

$$\lambda^t f_i^t - \lambda^{t+1} f_i^{t+1} + \lambda^{t+1} f_{n+i}^{t+1} = 0. \tag{10}$$

Next solving for λ^t in (9) and substituting in (10) we have

$$f_i^{t+1} - f_i^t = f_{n+i}^{t+1} + f_i^t f_{n+1}^{t+1}, \quad t = 0, \ldots, T-2, \, i = 2, \ldots, n. \tag{11}$$

Conditions (11) together with (6′) and (6″) are sufficient for an extremum.[2] It is a consequence of the concavity of f that these conditions are sufficient for a global maximum and, therefore, for efficiency of the path. Moreover, by the same consideration, the set of efficient paths reaching from S^0 to S_i^T, $i = 2, \ldots, n$, and realizing a maximal S_1^T is convex, while it need not be unique. We summarize these results in

Lemma 2 Conditions (11) together with (6′) and (6″) are necessary and sufficient for the path $\{S^t\}$, $t = 0, \ldots, T$ to be efficient. The set of efficient paths between S^0 and S^T is convex.

We wish to find the linear approximation to (11), (6′), and (6″) near a maximal balanced growth path. First we need

Lemma 3 In the interior of C, a maximal balanced growth path is efficient, and an efficient balanced growth path is maximal.[3]

Proof By homogeneity, in the interior of C,

$$f = f_{n+1} + \sum_{k=2}^{n} b_k(\gamma f_k + f_{n+k}). \tag{12}$$

But the parenthesis vanishes along a maximal balanced growth path lying in the interior of C by Assumption 2 and (5). Thus along such a path

$$f(\gamma b, 1, b) - \gamma = f_{n+1}(\gamma b, 1, b), \tag{13}$$

where the notation $f(\gamma b, 1, b)$ is used for the expression on the right side of (3). Using (5) and (13) we see that the right side of (11) vanishes on a maximal balanced growth path. However, the left side vanishes by the homogeneity of f_i of degree 0. This proves the first part of the lemma.

Since the left side of (11) vanishes for any balanced growth path, we may substitute (12) into the right side with $f = \gamma$ and equate to zero, obtaining

$$f_{n+i} + f_i\left(\gamma - \sum_{k=2}^{n} b_k(\gamma f_k + f_{n+k})\right) = 0. \tag{14}$$

Multiplying (14) by b_i and summing over $i = 2, \ldots, n$, we have

$$\sum_{i=2}^{n} b_i(\gamma f_i + f_{n+i}) - \sum_{i=2}^{n} b_i f_i \sum_{k=2}^{n} b_k(\gamma f_k + f_{n+k}) = 0. \tag{15}$$

Since

$$\sum_{i=2}^{n} b_i f_i < 0,$$

(15) implies that

$$\sum_{k=2}^{n} b_k(\gamma f_k + f_{n+k}) = 0.$$

Using this in (14) we immediately obtain (5). This demonstrates that any efficient balanced growth path is maximal.

18.4   The Linear System

It may be verified from routine calculations that the definitions of b_i and g_i imply

$$(1 + g_1^t)(b_i^{t+1} - b_i^t) = b_i^t(g_i^t - g_1^t), \quad i = 2, \ldots, n. \tag{16}$$

Now let $g = (g_2, \ldots, g_n)$, and write $f(g^t, b^t)$ for the right side of (2). Substituting $g_1 = f(g, b)$ and consolidating, we get

$$(1 + f^t)b_i^{t+1} - b_i^t(1 + g_i^t) = 0, \quad i = 2, \ldots, n, \ t = 0, \ldots, T - 1. \tag{17}$$

Equations (17), together with the specification of S_1^0, are equivalent to (6') and (6″).

In the neighborhood of $b_i = b_i^*$, $g_i = \gamma^*$, (16) implies, up to terms of the second order, for each i,

$$(1 + \gamma^*)(b_i^{t+1} - b_i^t) = b_i^*(g_i^t - g_1^t). \tag{18}$$

However, using $g_1 = f(g, b)$, we also have

$$g_1^t - \gamma^* = \sum_{k=2}^{n} (\gamma^* f_k^* + f_{n+k}^*)(b_k^t - b_k^*) + \sum_{k=2}^{n} (g_k^t - \gamma^*)b_k^* f_k^*, \tag{19}$$

up to terms of the second order. Here $f^* = f(g^*, b^*)$, where $g^* = (\gamma^*, \ldots, \gamma^*)$. Let (g^*, b^*) correspond to a path of maximal balanced growth in the interior of C. Such a path exists by Lemma 1 and Assumption 3. Then the first parentheses on the right side of (19) vanish by (5). Therefore, substituting (19) into (18) gives, up to terms of the second order,

$$(1 + \gamma^*)(b_i^{t+1} - b_i^t) = b_i^* \left(g_i^t - \gamma^* - \sum_{k=2}^{n} (g_k - \gamma^*) b_k^* f_k^* \right). \tag{20}$$

Hence, letting $\bar{b}_i = b_i - b_i^*$, $\bar{g}_i = g_i - \gamma^*$, we may write,

$$\bar{b}_i^{t+1} = \bar{b}_i^t + \frac{1}{1 + \gamma^*} b_i^* \left(\bar{g}_i^t - \sum_{k=2}^{n} b_k^* f_k^* \bar{g}_k^t \right), \quad i = 2, \ldots, n. \tag{21}$$

This is a set of $n - 1$ difference equations of the first order. Substituting in (17) $b_i^* + \bar{b}_i$ for b_i and $\gamma^* + \bar{g}_i$ for g_i, we obtain a set of $n - 1$ nonlinear difference equations of the first order in $\bar{b}_i$, $\bar{g}_i$. We see that (21) is the linear approximation to this system of equations near 0.

In the system (11) each term is a function of $(\Delta_1 S^t, S^t)$ or $(\Delta_1 S^{t+1}, S^{t+1})$, homogeneous of degree zero. Thus dividing the arguments of each term by S_1^t or S_1^{t+1}, as appropriate, (11) becomes a set of equations in (g^t, b^t) and (g^{t+1}, b^{t+1}), where g_1 and b_1 do not appear. Substituting $\gamma^* + \bar{g}_i = g_i$ and, $b_i^* + \bar{b}_i = b_i$, $i = 2, \ldots, n$, (11) now appears as a system of $n - 1$ difference equations in $\bar{g}_i$, $\bar{b}_i$, $i = 2, \ldots, n$. Then, by straightforward differentiation, the linear approximation to (11), in the same sense as above, is

$$\sum_{j=2}^{n} \{\gamma^*(f_{ij}^* - f_{n+i,j}^* - f_i^* f_{n+1,j}^*) + f_{i,n+j}^* - f_{n+i,n+j}^* - f_i^* f_{n+1,n+j}^*\} \bar{b}_j^{t+1}$$

$$+ \sum_{j=2}^{n} (f_{ij}^* - f_{n+i,j}^* - f_i^* f_{n+1,j}^*) b_j^* \bar{g}_j^{t+1}$$

$$= (1 + \gamma^*) \sum_{j=2}^{n} (\gamma^* f_{ij}^* + f_{i,n+j}^*) \bar{b}_j^t + (1 + \gamma^*) \sum_{j=2}^{n} f_{ij}^* b_j^* \bar{g}_j^t, \quad i = 2, \ldots, n. \tag{22}$$

Together (11) and (17) are $2n - 2$ nonlinear difference equations in the $2n - 2$ variables (g_j, b_j), $j = 2, \ldots, n$. Except for a scale factor, their solutions are uniquely associated with the efficient paths. If the solutions lie near (g^*, b^*), they will be approximately equal to (g^*, b^*) plus solutions of the $2n - 2$ linear difference equations (21) and (22) in the $2n - 2$ variables $(\bar{g}_i, \bar{b}_i)$. Our objective is to prove that when (g_i^0, b_i^0), (g_i^T, b_i^T) lie sufficiently near (g^*, b^*), and there is some corresponding efficient path, then there exists an efficient path for which the corresponding (g_i^t, b_i^t) remain near (g^*, b^*) for successive values of t comprising most of the sequence, when T is large. This will be done by proving the existence of the appropriate solution of (11) and (17).

18.5   Reciprocal Roots

We wish to prove the existence of certain solutions for

$$(1 + f(g^t, b^t))b_i^{t+1} - b_i^t(1 + g_i^t) = 0, \quad i = 1, \ldots, n - 1, \tag{17'}$$

$$f_i(g^{t+1}, b^{t+1}) - f_{n+i}(g^{t+1}, b^{t+1}) - (1 + f_{n+1}(g^{t+1}, b^{t+1}))f_i(g^t, b^t) = 0,$$

$$i = 1, \ldots, n - 1, \tag{11'}$$

where $g = (g_2, \ldots, g_n)$, $b = (b_2, \ldots, b_n)$, and $f(g^t, b^t)$ is the right side of (2). The proof that these solutions exist will depend on properties of the solutions of the linear system (21) and (22). We rewrite this system in matrix form as

$$\bar{b}^{t+1} = \bar{b}^t + K\bar{g}^t,$$

$$H_1\bar{b}^{t+1} + G_1\bar{g}^{t+1} = H_0\bar{b}^t + G_0\bar{b}^t. \tag{23}$$

In order to solve (23) for $(\bar{b}^{t+1}, \bar{g}^{t+1})$ we must add

Assumption 4 $|G_1| \neq 0$.

Solving (23) we obtain

$$\begin{pmatrix} \bar{b}^{t+1} \\ \bar{g}^{t+1} \end{pmatrix} = \begin{bmatrix} I & K \\ G_1^{-1}(H_0 - H_1) & G_1^{-1}(G_0 - H_1 K) \end{bmatrix} \begin{pmatrix} \bar{b}^t \\ \bar{g}^t \end{pmatrix}. \tag{24}$$

The solutions of the system of linear difference equations (24) depend upon the characteristic roots of the matrix on the right. If we call this matrix B, the designation of λ as a characteristic root of B means $|B - \lambda I| = 0$. However, if we multiply $B - \lambda I$ on the left by $\begin{bmatrix} I & 0 \\ 0 & G_1 \end{bmatrix}$, which is nonsingular by Assumption 4, we see that $|B - \lambda I| = 0$ is equivalent to

$$\begin{vmatrix} I - \lambda I & K \\ H_0 - H_1 & G_0 - H_1 K - \lambda G_1 \end{vmatrix} = 0.$$

Since $I - \lambda I$ and K commute, this determinant may be expanded in the form[4]

$$|G_1 \lambda^2 + (H_1 K - G_1 - G_0)\lambda + G_0 - H_0 K| = 0. \tag{25}$$

In order to simplify $H_0 K$, we will need the relation

$$\gamma^* \sum_{k=2}^{n} b_k^* f_{ik}^* + f_{i,n+1}^* + \sum_{k=2}^{n} b_k^* f_{i,n+k}^* = 0, \quad i = 2, \dots, 2n, \tag{26}$$

which is implied by the homogeneity of f_i of zero degree. From (21) the matrix K may be written

$$\frac{1}{1 + \gamma^*} [b_i^* (\delta_{ij} - b_j^* f_j^*)],$$

where $\delta_{ij} = 0$, $i \neq j$, and $\delta_{ij} = 1$, $i = j$. From (22), H_0 is $(1 + \gamma^*)[\gamma^* f_{ij}^* + f_{i,n+j}^*]$. Thus $H_0 K$ is

$$\left[\sum_k (\gamma^* f_{ik}^* + f_{i,n+k}^*) b_k^* (\delta_{kj} - b_j^* f_j^*) \right],$$

or

$$\left[\left(\gamma^* f_{ij}^* + f_{i,n+j}^* - f_j^* \sum_k (\gamma^* f_{ik}^* + f_{i,n+k}^*) b_k^* \right) b_j^* \right],$$

which, upon use of (26), becomes

$$[(\gamma^* f_{ij}^* + f_{i,n+j}^* + f_j^* f_{i,n+1}^*) b_j^*]. \tag{27}$$

Since by (22) $G_0 = (1 + \gamma^*)[f_{ij}^* b_j^*]$, we conclude that $G_0 - H_0 K = [(f_{ij}^* - f_{i,n+j}^* - f_j^* f_{i,n+1}^*) b_j^*]$. However, $G_1 = [(f_{ij}^* - f_{n+i,j}^* - f_i^* f_{n+1,j}^*) b_j^*]$. Let D be the diagonal matrix with $(b_2^*, \dots, b_n^*)$ on the diagonal and define G by $G = G_1 D^{-1}$. Then $G_0 - H_0 K = G^T D$, where G^T is the transpose of G. This is a strategic fact in the establishment of reciprocal roots.

Now consider $H_1K - G_1 - G_0$. H_1 may be written in the form

$$\{(\gamma^* f_{ij}^* + f_{i,n+j}^*) - (\gamma^* f_{n+i,j}^* + f_{n+i,n+j}^*) - f_i^*(\gamma^* f_{n+1,j}^* + f_{n+1,n+j}^*)\}. \tag{28}$$

Each of the parentheses of (28) has the form of H_0. Hence multiplication by K and use of (26) gives a term analogous to (27) except for a factor $1/(1 + \gamma^*)$. Consolidating with $-G_1 - G_0$ we get

$$H_1K - G_1 - G_0 = SD$$

$$= \left[\frac{1}{1+\gamma^*}(-(2+2\gamma^* + \gamma^{*2})f_{ij}^* + f_{i,n+j}^* + f_j^* f_{i,n+1}^*)b_j^* \right.$$

$$+ \frac{1}{1+\gamma^*}(f_{n+i,j}^* - f_{n+i,n+j}^* - f_j^* f_{n+i,n+1}^*)b_j^*$$

$$+ \left. \frac{1}{1+\gamma^*} f_i^*(f_{n+1,j}^* - f_{n+1,n+j}^* - f_j^* f_{n+1,n+1}^*)b_j^* \right].$$

Examining this expression discloses that S is symmetric. This is the second strategic fact giving reciprocal roots.

We may now write (25) in the form

$$|G\lambda^2 + S\lambda + G^T| \cdot |D| = 0. \tag{29}$$

However, D is nonsingular. It is simple to prove

Lemma 4[5] If λ is a characteristic root of B, then λ^{-1} is also a characteristic root of B.

Proof The characteristic roots of B are the roots of (29). Since $|G| \neq 0$ by Assumption 4, 0 is not a root. However, $|G\lambda^2 + S\lambda + G^T| = 0$ implies $|G + S\lambda^{-1} + G^T\lambda^{-2}| = 0$. The latter implies by the symmetry of S, $|G\lambda^{-2} + S\lambda^{-1} + G^T| = 0$. This completes the proof.

As a consequence of Lemma 4 the roots of (27) may be written λ_i, λ_i^{-1}, $i = 2, \ldots, n$, where $|\lambda_i| \leqq 1$. Of course, some roots may be repeated. We now add[6]

Assumption 5 The roots of (25) have absolute value different from unity.

Then $|\lambda_i| < 1$, $i = 2, \ldots, n$.

18.6   The Turnpike Path

As a consequence of Assumption 4 the system of equations (21), (22) may be solved for $(\bar{g}^{t+1}, \bar{b}^{t+1})$ in terms of $(\bar{g}^{t}, \bar{b}^{t})$. Let $y^{t} = (\bar{g}^{t}, \bar{b}^{t})$. Then we may write (21) and (22) in the form (24), or, using B,

$$y^{t+1} = By^{t}, \tag{30}$$

where B is a square matrix of order $2n - 2$. The characteristic roots of B appear in reciprocal pairs by Lemma 4, and have absolute values different from unity by Assumption 5. Moreover, because of the continuous derivatives assumed in Assumption 2, (30) is a linear approximation to the nonlinear system $(17')$ and $(11')$ in a neighborhood of g^{*}, b^{*}. Therefore, substituting $g^{t} = g^{*} + \bar{g}^{t}$ and $b^{t} = b^{*} + \bar{b}^{t}$, $(17')$ and $(11')$ may be written in terms of y^{t} as

$$y^{t+1} = By^{t} + e(y^{t}), \tag{31}$$

where, for any $\delta > 0$, there is $\varepsilon > 0$ such that $|y^{t}| < \varepsilon$, $|y^{t'}| < \varepsilon$, implies $|e(y^{t}) - e(y^{t'})| < \delta |y^{t} - y^{t'}|$. Also $e(0) = 0$.

Since the roots of B are in reciprocal pairs with absolute values different from unity, there is a real transformation P such that

$$P^{-1}BP = \begin{bmatrix} L_1 & 0 \\ 0 & L_2 \end{bmatrix},$$

where L_1 and L_2 are square matrices, the roots of L_1 have absolute value less than unity, and the roots of L_2 have absolute value greater than unity. Let $y = Pz$. Then we may write in place of (31)

$$\begin{pmatrix} z_1^{t+1} \\ z_2^{t+1} \end{pmatrix} = \begin{bmatrix} L_1 & 0 \\ 0 & L_2 \end{bmatrix} \begin{pmatrix} z_1^{t} \\ z_2^{t} \end{pmatrix} + h(z^{t}), \tag{32}$$

where h satisfies the condition corresponding to that satisfied by e.

We now write the matrix P of the transformation in the partitioned form $\begin{bmatrix} P_{g1} & P_{g2} \\ P_{b1} & P_{b2} \end{bmatrix}$. If the characteristic roots of B are real and distinct, the columns of P are the characteristic vectors of B, the first $n - 1$ columns being associated with roots of absolute value less than one, the last $n - 1$ with roots of absolute value greater than one. In any case, the columns of P span invariant subspaces associated with the respective λ's (or pairs of conjugate λ's when the roots are complex), and the first $n - 1$ columns span the subspaces associated with λ_i where $|\lambda_i| < 1$. If we revert to the definition of y, the matrices P_{b1} and P_{b2} may be regarded as composed of columns made up of $\bar{b}$ sub-vectors, and P_{g1} and P_{g2} may be regarded as composed of columns made up of $\bar{g}$ sub-vectors. Consider a sequence $(\bar{g}^t, \bar{b}^t)$, $t = 0, \ldots, T$, which satisfies (17′) and (11′). Then z^t satisfies (32) where, in particular,

$$\bar{b}^0 = P_{b1}z_1^0 + P_{b2}z_2^0,$$

$$\bar{b}^T = P_{b1}z_1^T + P_{b2}z_2^T.$$

(33)

In order to guarantee that (33) can be satisfied with some values of z_2^0 and z_1^T we make the following assumption:

Assumption 6 The columns of P can be so chosen that $|P_{b1}| \cdot |P_{b2}| \neq 0$.

We may now prove the basic lemma.

Lemma 5 Let k and η be arbitrary positive numbers. There are positive numbers N and ε such that $T > N$ and $|\bar{b}^0| + |\bar{b}^T| < \varepsilon$ imply the existence of a solution $y^t = (y_1^t, y_2^t)$ of (31) for $t = 0, \ldots, T$, where $y_2^0 = \bar{b}^0$ and $\bar{y}_2^T = \bar{b}^T$, and $|y_2^t| < k\varepsilon$ for $T_1 < t < T_2$ where $(T_2 - T_1)/T > 1 - \eta$.

Proof The proof will be by the method of successive approximations. Consider the functions

$$\theta_1(t) = L_1^t z_1^0 + \sum_1^t L_1^{t-s} h_1(\theta(s)),$$

(34)

$$\theta_2(t) = L_2^{t-T} z_2^T - \sum_{t+1}^T L_2^{t-s} h_2(\theta(s)).$$

$\theta(t)$ satisfies (32) for $t = 0, \ldots, T$, if the sums $\sum_1^0$ and $\sum_{t+1}^T$ are omitted. We impose the conditions that $\theta(0) = z^0$ and $\theta(T) = z^T$. These imply, by (34),

$$z_2^0 = L_2^{-T} z_2^T - \sum_1^0 L_2^{-s} h_2(\theta(s)),$$

(35)

$$z_1^T = L^T z_1^0 + \sum_1^T L^{T-s} h_1(\theta(s)).$$

Combining (33) and (35), we may write

$$\begin{pmatrix} z^0 \\ z^T \end{pmatrix} = E^{-1} \begin{pmatrix} -\sum_1^T L_2^{-s} h_2(\theta(s)) \\ \sum_1^T L_1^{T-s} h_1(\theta(s)) \\ \bar{b}^0 \\ \bar{b}^T \end{pmatrix}, \tag{36}$$

where

$$E = \begin{bmatrix} 0 & I & 0 & -L_2^{-T} \\ -L_1^T & 0 & I & 0 \\ P_{b1} & P_{b2} & 0 & 0 \\ 0 & 0 & P_{b1} & P_{b2} \end{bmatrix}.$$

Since the characteristic roots of L_2 are greater than unity and those of L_1 less than unity, $L_2^{-T}, L_1^T \to 0$ as $T \to \infty$. Then as $T \to \infty$, $|E| \to |P_{b1}| \cdot |P_{b2}|$, which is not zero by Assumption 6. Thus (36) is uniquely solvable for (z^0, z^T) when $T > N_1$ for a sufficiently large number N_1.

Define the norm $\|B\|$ of a matrix B to be the maximum of $|Bx|$ for $|x| \leq 1$. Let λ be a largest root of L_1, so that λ^{-1} is a smallest root of L_2. It may be shown[7] that there exist $\nu > 0$, $1 > \mu > |\lambda|$ such that $\|L_1^t\| < \nu \mu^t$ and $\|L_2^{-t}\| < \nu \mu^t$. Also there is $\rho > 0$ such that $\|E^{-1}\| < \rho$.

We will now develop a solution of (32). Put $\theta_{(0)}(t) \equiv 0$ and solve (36) for $(z_{(0)}^0, z_{(0)}^T)$. Use $z_{(0)}^0$, $z_{(0)}^T$, and $\theta_{(0)}(t) \equiv 0$ in the right hand side of (34) to obtain $\theta_1(t)$. Then introduce $\theta_{(1)}(t)$ in (36) to derive $z_{(1)}^0$, $z_{(1)}^T$, and so forth. Let $\Delta_{(l)}(t) = \theta_{(l+1)}(t) - \theta_{(l)}(t)$. From (34), we have, for $0 \leq t \leq T$,

$$\Delta_{1(l)}(t) = L_1^t(z_{1(l)}^0 - z_{1(l-1)}^0) + \sum_1^t L_1^{t-s}[h_1(\theta_{(l)}(s)) - h_1(\theta_{(l-1)}(s))],$$

$$\Delta_{2(l)}(t) = L_2^{t-T}(z_{2(l)}^T - z_{2(l-1)}^T) - \sum_{t+1}^T L_2^{t-s}[h_2(\theta_{(l)}(s)) - h_2(\theta_{(l-1)}(s))].$$

Write $\bar{z}_{(l)}$ for $\begin{pmatrix} z_{(l)}^0 \\ z_{(l)}^T \end{pmatrix}$. Then

$$|\Delta_{(l)}(t)| \leq v(\mu^t + \mu^{T-t})|\bar{z}_{(l)} - \bar{z}_{(l-1)}|$$

$$+ v\sum_1^t \mu^{t-s}\delta|\Delta_{(l-1)}(s)| + v\sum_{t+1}^T \mu^{s-t}\delta|\Delta_{(l-1)}(s)|, \tag{37}$$

provided $|\theta_{(l-1)}(s)| \leq \varepsilon$, $|\theta_{(l)}(s)| \leq \varepsilon$ for $0 \leq s \leq T$, and an appropriate ε. On the other hand, we have from (36) for $l \geq 1$,

$$|\bar{z}_{(l)} - \bar{z}_{(l-1)}| \leq \rho v \sum_1^T (\mu^s + \mu^{T-s})\delta|\Delta_{(l-1)}(s)|. \tag{38}$$

Assume that $|\Delta_{(l)}(t)| \leq \varepsilon_1$, $t = 0,\ldots,T$, and $|\Delta_{(l)}(t)| \leq k\varepsilon_1$ for $t_1 \leq t \leq T - t_1$. Substituting (38) into (37), we obtain

$$|\Delta_{(l+1)}(t)| \leq 2\rho v^2\delta \sum_1^T (\mu^s + \mu^{T-s})|\Delta_{(l)}(s)|$$

$$+ v\delta\sum_1^t \mu^{t-s}|\Delta_{(l)}(s)| + v\delta\sum_{t+1}^T \mu^{s-t}|\Delta_{(l)}(s)|. \tag{39}$$

From this, using only $|\Delta_{(l)}(t)| \leq \varepsilon_1$, and noting that $\sum_0^\infty \mu^s = 1/(1-\mu)$,

$$|\Delta_{(l+1)}(t)| \leq (4\rho v^2\delta + 2v\delta)\frac{1}{1-\mu}\varepsilon_1.$$

Thus if δ is chosen less than $\delta_1 = \frac{1}{2}(4v\rho + 2)^{-1}(1-\mu)/v$, it will follow that $|\Delta_{(l+1)}(t)| \leq \varepsilon_1/2$, for $t = 0,\ldots,T$.

Now consider $|\Delta_{(l+1)}(t)|$ for $t_1 \leq t \leq T - t_1$. We treat the three terms of the right side of (39) separately. Let $\Delta^i(t)$ be the i-th term. Then

$$\Delta^1(t) \leq \rho\delta v^2(4 + 2k)\frac{1}{1-\mu}\varepsilon_1.$$

$$\Delta^2(t) \leq \rho v(1 + k)\frac{1}{1-\mu}\varepsilon_1,$$

$$\Delta^3(t) \leq \delta v(1 + k)\frac{1}{1-\mu}\varepsilon_1.$$

Let $\delta_2 = (1/6)(\rho v^2(4k^{-1} + 2)/(1-\mu))^{-1}$ and $\delta_3 = (1/6)(v(k^{-1} + 1)/(1-\mu))^{-1}$. Now choose $\delta \leq \min(\delta_1, \delta_2, \delta_3)$. Then $|\Delta_{(l+1)}(t)| \leq \varepsilon_1/2$ for $t = 0,\ldots,T$, and $|\Delta_{(l+1)}(t)| \leq k\varepsilon_1/2$ for $t_1 \leq t \leq T - t_1$.

To begin the series, from (34) and (36)

$$|\Delta_{(0)}(t)| = |\theta_{(1)}(t)| \leqq v|\bar{z}_{(0)}| \leqq \rho v(|\bar{b}^0| + |\bar{b}^T|).$$

We choose $|\bar{b}^0| + |\bar{b}^T| \leqq \varepsilon_1/\rho v$. Then $|\Delta_0(t)| \leqq \varepsilon_1$. On the other hand, $|\Delta_0(t)| \leqq v(\mu^t + \mu^{T-t})|\bar{z}_0| \leqq 2v\mu^{t_1}|\bar{z}_0| \leqq 2\varepsilon_1\mu^{t_1}$ for $t_1 \leqq t \leqq T - t_1$. Therefore, if $t_1 > \log(k/2)/\log \mu$, we will also have $|\Delta_0(t)| \leqq k\varepsilon_1$ for $t_1 \leqq t \leqq T - t_1$. With these choices $|\Delta_{(l)}(t)| \leqq \varepsilon_1/2^l$ and for $t_1 \leqq t \leqq T - t_1$, $|\Delta_{(l)}(t)| \leqq k\varepsilon_1/2^l$. Therefore, $\theta_{(l)}(t)$ converges to a function $\theta(t)$ with $|\theta(t)| \leqq \varepsilon$, and $|\theta(t)| \leqq k\varepsilon$ for $t_1 \leqq t \leqq T - t_1$, where $\varepsilon = 2\varepsilon_1$. It is necessary to take ε small enough to validate the use of δ in (37). Finally, choose $N > \max\{2t_1/\eta, N_1\}$ and set $T_1 = t_1$, $T_2 = T - t_1$. To see that these choices are possible, notice that δ and t_1 depend upon k but not upon ε. Then ε may be chosen from knowledge of δ, and N may be chosen from t_1 and η. Thus the conditions of the lemma are satisfied when we set $y^t = P\theta(t)$.

It is a simple application of Lemma 5 to prove the turnpike theorem of Dorfman, Samuelson, and Solow. Suppose that $\{S^t\}$, $t = 0, \ldots, T$, is an efficient path. Let $b^0 = {}_1S^0/S_1^0$ and $b^T = {}_1S^T/S_1^T$, where ${}_1S = (S_2, \ldots, S_n)$. Suppose k, η, N, ε, T, $|\bar{b}^0|$, $|\bar{b}^T|$ satisfy the conditions of Lemma 5. Then (31) has the solution described there, to which corresponds a solution $\{g'^t, b'^t\}$ of (17') and (11'), where, $b'^0 = b^0$, $b'^T = b^T$. To this solution of (17') and (11') there corresponds a solution $\{S'^t\}$, $t = 0, \ldots, T$ of (11), (6') and (6''). Moreover, the path $\{S'^t\}$ is efficient by Lemma 2. By homogeneity we may set $S'^0 = S^0$. Then $S'^T = \alpha S^T$ for some $\alpha > 0$. But both paths are efficient paths lasting for T periods, so $\alpha > 1$ and $S'^T = S^T$. We have proved

Turnpike Theorem (Dorfman, Samuelson, and Solow) Let k and η be arbitrary positive numbers. Let $\{S^t\}$, $t = 0, \ldots, T$, be an efficient path. Then there are positive numbers N and ε such that $T > N$ and $|{}_1S^0/S_1^0 - b^*| + |{}_1S^T/S_1^T - b^*| < \varepsilon$ imply there exists an efficient path $\{S'^t\}$, $t = 0, \ldots, T$, where $S'^0 = S^0$ and $S'^T = S^T$, and $|{}_1S'^t/S_1'^t - b^*| < k\varepsilon$ for $T_1 < t < T_2$ where $(T_2 - T_1)/T > 1 - \eta$.

Notes

1. This work has been supported by a grant from the National Science Foundation.

2. These conditions are obviously the finite difference versions of Samuelson's conditions (5) [7, (79)], for zero consumptions. They reduce to his conditions in the limit as the length of the period shrinks toward 0.

3. Lemmas (2) and (3) for the case of two goods, and for a model avoiding the use of Δb, were proved, in principle, by Dorfman, Samuelson, and Solow [1, (326 ff.)].

4. If $\lambda = 1$, the upper left hand block is identically 0, and the result is obvious from substitution in (25). If $\lambda \neq 1$, then $|I - \lambda I| \neq 0$. Consider the matrix $\begin{bmatrix} A & B \\ C & D \end{bmatrix}$, where $|A| \neq 0$ and $AB = BA$. The determinant is not changed if we multiply by $\begin{bmatrix} A^{-1} & -B \\ 0 & A \end{bmatrix}$ on the right. However the product is $\begin{bmatrix} I & 0 \\ CA^{-1} & -CB + DA \end{bmatrix}$, and the determinant of this matrix is $|-CB + DA|$, which, for our case, is (25). I owe the main lines of this argument to my referee.

5. A result corresponding to this for the continuous model may be found in Samuelson's paper [7, (87–88)] (together with his *addendum*).

6. One consequence of this assumption is that b^* is unique. For the convexity of the set of maximizing b by Lemma 1 implies that if b^* is not unique, there are maximizing b in every neighborhood of b^*.

7. L_1 is similar to a matrix which may be written $M + N$, where M is diagonal with the characteristic roots of L_1 on the diagonal and N is nilpotent. Consider $(M + N)^t$. If $N^t = 0$ for $t > s$, $(M + N)^t = \sum_{\tau = t-s}^{t} \binom{\tau}{t} M^\tau N^{t-\tau}$. This formula and its analogue for L_2 can be used to derive the result. The argument depends upon $\lambda_i < 1$ for $i = 2, \ldots, n$. Thus Assumption 5 is needed at this point.

References

[1] Dorfman, Robert, Paul Samuelson, and Robert Solow. *Linear Programming and Economic Analysis*, (New York: McGraw-Hill, 1958), ch. 12.

[2] Koopmans, T. C., "Analysis of Production as an Efficient Combination of Activities," *Activity Analysis of Production and Allocation*, T. C. Koopmans, ed., (New York: John Wiley, 1951).

[3] McKenzie, Lionel, "Price-Quantity Duality and the Turnpike Theorem," paper presented to the Econometric Society, December, 1960.

[4] ———, "Three Turnpike Theorems for a Generalized Leontief Model," to be published.

[5] Morishima, Michio, "Proof of a Turnpike Theorem: The No Joint Production Case," *Review of Economic Studies*, XXVIII (February, 1961), 89–97.

[6] Radner, Roy, "Paths of Economic Growth that are Optimal with Regard Only to Final States", *Review of Economic Studies*, XXVIII (February, 1961), 98–104.

[7] Samuelson, Paul, "Efficient Paths of Capital Accumulation in Terms of the Calculus of Variations", *Mathematical Methods in the Social Sciences*, 1959, K. J. Arrow, S. Karlin, and P. Suppes, ed., (Stanford: Stanford University Press, 1960).

19 Turnpike Theorem of Morishima

Lionel W. McKenzie

Consider a closed linear model of production over time (see, for example, Gale [3]). We may term a path of maximal balanced growth in such a model a Neumann ray, since such paths were first studied by John von Neumann in one of the most original of all essays in mathematical economics [8].[1] A Turnpike Theorem is a theorem which establishes that certain classes of efficient paths in such a model remain near a Neumann ray for most of the time. These may also be termed efficient paths of capital accumulation, since in a closed model of this type only stocks of goods appear explicitly.

There are three fundamental turnpike theorems, that of Dorfman, Samuelson, and Solow announced in *Linear Programming and Economic Analysis*, chapter 12 [1], that of Morishima, proved independently by Morishima [7] and McKenzie [5], and that of Radner [9]. The credit for the initial inspiration goes, of course, to Dorfman, Samuelson, and Solow. Their theorem is local and uses a neo-classical transformation function which can allow joint production and independent processes. The Morishima theorem is global but it requires that joint production be absent from the model altogether, a very stringent requirement which leads to a generalized version of Ricardo's model of annual reproduction. The Radner theorem is global but requires something like the generation of the transformation set by a single joint production process, at least near the turnpike. If joint production were excluded from Radner's model, only one good could be produced, and the model would be trivial from the present viewpoint. Nevertheless, the Radner theorem has been extended by McKenzie [6] and seems to offer the greatest promise of a general theory of capital accumulation in closed linear models.

The interest of the Morishima theorem arises from its strength and the simplicity of its idea. The idea is to show that prices converge to the Neumann ray prices as time increases and, for the Neumann ray technology, quantities diverge from the Neumann ray as time increases (converge as time decreases). Thus after enough time has passed to allow the establishment of (essentially) the Neumann ray technology, quantities must be very near the Neumann ray if they are to remain non-negative for a long time, and this condition continues to hold as long as sufficient time remains in the whole period of accumulation. These convergence properties are easily derived from an earlier Samuelson-Solow theorem [10] on balanced growth.[2] Then the theorem follows directly.

The version of the Morishima theorem which I shall prove here differs from his in two major respects. It replaces an assumption that the number of activities is finite by an assumption that the normalized set of activities is compact. This permits a neater development of the argument. Also our theorem applies uniformly to all efficient paths, regardless of whether the terminal stocks are positive. In our argument, unlike Morishima, we appeal directly to the Samuelson-Solow theorem.[3]

The processes of our model have the goods of period $t + 1$ as outputs and the goods of period t as inputs. In addition, there is no joint production. The absence of joint production is inconsistent with the presence of durable instruments of production, since if durable goods are used, the surviving stock of goods must be included among the outputs of a process. Of course, joint production could be present even without durable, or fixed, capital, but if joint production is excluded, only circulating capital can appear. Even circulating capital can only appear in the form of semi-finished goods, not as reserve stocks of materials and components. For at the end of any period the remaining stocks of materials and components would have to be treated as joint products of the process.

We assume there are n goods whose quantities at the close of period t are given by the components of a non-negative vector $y^t \in E_n$. There is a transformation set $T \subset E_{2n}$ and $(-y^t, y^{t+1}) \in T$ implies that y^t may be transformed during one period into y^{t+1}. Let $T_i = \{(-y^t, y^{t+1}) \in T \mid y_j^{t+1} = 0, \text{ for all } j \neq i\}$. Initially we make four assumptions about T.

(I) $T = \sum_{i=1}^{n} T_i$. $T \cap (0, \Omega) = (0, 0)$.

(II) T_i is a closed convex cone with vertex at the origin. There is $(-y^t, y^{t+1}) \in T_i$ where $y_i^{t+1} > 0$.

For $(-y^t, y^{t+1}) \in T_i$ let us say that $(-y^t, y^{t+1})$ is in $\bar{T}_i$ if $(-w^t, w^{t+1}) \in T_i$ and $-w^t \geq -y^t$, $w^{t+1} \geq y^{t+1}$ imply $w^t = y^t$, $w^{t+1} = y^{t+1}$. $\bar{T}_i$ is the ith set of efficient input-output combinations, or elliptically the ith set of efficient outputs, where both inputs and outputs are treated as desired goods. $\bar{T}$ is defined in the same way for T. Define $H_i = \{(-y^t, y^{t+1}) \mid y_i^{t+1} = 1\}$. Let $\bar{I}_i = \bar{T}_i \cap H_i$. Assumptions I and II imply that $\bar{I}_i$ is not empty. Assume also

(III) $\bar{I}_i$ is compact.

(IV) $(-y^t, y^{t+1}) \in T_i$ implies $(-w^t, w^{t+1}) \in T_i$ for $-w^t \leq -y^t$, $w^{t+1} \leq y^{t+1}$, $w^t \geq 0$, $w^{t+1} \geq 0$.

We will comment on these assumptions. The effect of I is to exclude joint production or external economies, and provide that something cannot be produced from nothing. By II there are constant returns to scale, and each good is producible. By III the sets of efficient input-output combinations are compact for given outputs. IV provides for free disposal of excess supplies of goods.

We may also define a transformation set for more than one period. Let T^N be an N period transformation set. Then $(-y^0, y^N) \in T^N$ will mean there exist $(-w^t, w^{t+1}) \in T$ for $t = 0, \ldots, N-1$, and $w^0 = y^0$, $w^N = y^N$. It is now convenient to use a weaker notion of efficiency where only goods of the final period are treated as desired. Let $(-y^0, y^N)$ belong to $\bar{T}^N$ if and only if $(-w^0, w^N) \in T^N$ and $-w^0 \geq -y^0$, $w^N \geq y^N$ implies $w^N = y^N$. This definition does not require that resources be economized except to the extent that the output of final goods is increased. The elements of $\bar{T}^N$ will be called final efficient. We may prove

Lemma 1 $(-y^0, y^N) \in \bar{T}^N$ implies the existence of $p^t \geq 0$, for $t = 0, \ldots, N$, and of $(-y^t, y^{t+1}) \in T$, for $t = 0, \ldots, N-1$, such that

$$-p^t \cdot y^t + p^{t+1} \cdot y^{t+1} = 0, \quad \text{and}$$

$$-p^t \cdot w^t + p^{t+1} \cdot w^{t+1} \leq 0, \, t = 0, \ldots, N-1, \quad (1)$$

for any $(-w^t, w^{t+1}) \in T$.

The converse follows if $p^N > 0$.

Proof Let E_n^t be an n-dimensional Euclidean space whose typical vector is written z^t, x^t, etc. Let $E_N = \prod_{t=0}^N E_n^t$. E_N is the Cartesian product of the E_n^t and its typical vector is $z = \prod_{t=0}^N z^t$. Write $z^{(\tau)} = \prod_{t=0}^N z^t$, where $z^t = 0$ for $t \neq \tau$. Define the intertemporal production set $Y^t = \{-z^{(t-1)} + z^{(t)} \mid (-z^{t-1}, z^t) \in T\}$. Let $Y_N = \sum_{t=1}^N Y^t$. Y_N is a closed and pointed convex cone with vertex at the origin. Consider $y \in E_N$. In accord with our definition of final efficiency treating only final goods as desired, we may say y is final efficient relative to given initial resources $y^o > 0$ if $y^{(t)} = 0$, $t = 1, \ldots, N - 1$, and $Y_N \cap (y + \Omega^{(N)}) = y$. $\Omega^{(N)}$ is the set of all $w \in E_N$ such that $w \geq 0$ and $w^t = 0$ for $t \neq N$. The existence of such a vector is guaranteed by Assumptions II and IV.

Y_N has a non-empty interior by IV. Y_N and $(y + \Omega^{(N)})$ are closed and convex and int $Y_N \cap (y + \Omega^{(N)}) = \phi$. Thus there is $p \in E_N$, $p \neq 0$ such that $p \cdot w \leq 0$, $w \in Y_N$, $p \cdot w \geq 0$, $w \in Y + \Omega^{(N)}$ [4]. Since y is in both sets, $p \cdot y = 0$. Since $-\Omega_N \subset Y_N$, or Y_N has a disposal process for each good, $p \geq 0$. Suppose $p^o = 0$. Then the first inequality and Assumption II implies $p^1 = 0$. This may be continued until $p^N = 0$, so $p = 0$, contradicting the hypothesis that $p \neq 0$. Thus $p^o \geqslant 0$. By the definition of Y_N, $-p^t \cdot w^t + p^{t+1} \cdot w^{t+1} \leq 0$ for $(-w^t, w^{t+1}) \in T$, $t = 0, \ldots, N - 1$. Since $p \cdot y = 0$, equality holds if $w^t = y^t$, $w^{t+1} = y^{t+1}$. This gives (1).

Suppose (1) is satisfied for each t, and $p^N > 0$. Suppose there is $z \neq y$ and $z \in Y_N \cap (y + \Omega^{(N)})$. Then $z - y \in \Omega^{(N)}$ and $z - y \neq 0$. Thus $p \cdot y = 0$ implies $p \cdot z > 0$. But $z \in Y_N$, contradicting $p \cdot w \leq 0$ for $w \in Y_N$. Thus $Y_N \cap (z + \Omega^{(N)}) = y$ and y is final efficient for initial resources y^o. This ends the proof.

Since T_j is a pointed cone (pointed by virtue of the time orientation of production), it is convenient to consider a cross-section defined on a unit output. We are particularly interested in the efficient input-output combinations I_j. Write $a_{(j)} \in I_j$, where $a_{(j)} = (a_{1j}, \ldots, a_{nj})$ and $(-a_{(j)}, y) \in I_j$ where $y_j = 1$. I_j is compact by Assumption III. It corresponds to the neo-classical isoquant. Let p now be an n-dimensional vector. For given $p \geqslant 0$, let $M_j(p)$ be the set of $a_{(j)}$ such that $p \cdot a_{(j)} = \min p \cdot a$ for $a \in I_j$. Then we may write $h_j(p) = p \cdot a_{(j)}$ for any $a_{(j)} \in M_j(p)$. $h_j(p)$ is the support function of I_j defined over $p \geqslant 0$. We prove two lemmas on $M_j(p)$ and $h_j(p)$. First,

Lemma 2 $M_j(p)$ is convex and not empty for any $p \geqslant 0$, and $M_j(p)$ as a function of p is upper semi-continuous and homogeneous of degree 0.

Proof Since I_j is compact and not empty, and $h(p)$ is continuous, $h(p)$ assumes its minimum at some point $\bar{a} \in I_j$. Then $\bar{a} \in M_j(p)$. Convexity is a consequence of the convexity of T_j. Positive homogeneity is obvious. Suppose $p^k \to p'$, as $k \to \infty$, $k = 1, 2, \ldots$. Suppose $p^k \cdot a^k$ provides the minimum of $p^k \cdot a$ over I_j. Let $a^k \to a'$. Then $p' \cdot a'$ minimizes $p' \cdot a$ over I_j, so $M_j(p)$ is an upper semi-continuous function of p.

Let $h'_j(p, p')$ be the directional derivative of $h_j(p)$ with respect to p' [2, p. 79 ff]. It may be defined as

$$h'_j(p, p') = \lim_{s \to \infty} \frac{h_j\left(p + \dfrac{p'}{s}\right) - h_j(p)}{\dfrac{1}{s}}.$$

Since a support function is concave, the directional derivative exists for $p + p'$ within the region of definition, i.e., $p + p' \geqq 0$, where $p' \neq 0$ and $p \geqslant 0$. We now show that

Lemma 3 $h'_j(p, p') = p' \cdot a_{(j)}$ for some $a_{(j)} \in M_j(p)$.

Proof   For any $a_{(j)} \in M_j(p)$, $h_j(p) = p \cdot a_{(j)}$. Let $p^s = p + \dfrac{p'}{s}$ where $s = 1, 2, \ldots$. $M_j(p^s) \subset I_j$ which is bounded by Assumption III. For each s choose $a^s \in M_j(p^s)$. Thus there will be at least one accumulation point a which lies in $M_j(p)$ by upper semi-continuity. a is the limit of a sequence $a^{s'}$ where $a^{s'} \in M_j(p^{s'})$ and $s' \to \infty$. Therefore,

$$h'_j(p, p') = \lim_{s' \to \infty} \frac{\left(p + \dfrac{p'}{s'}\right) \cdot a^{s'} - p \cdot a}{\dfrac{1}{s'}} = p' \cdot a.$$

Note that when $p' \geqslant 0$, $a \geqslant 0$ implies $p' \cdot a \geqq 0$. However, $a > 0$ for all $a \in M_j(p)$, implies that $h'(p, p') > 0$ for any $p' \geqslant 0$.

According to Lemma 1, we may associate with any final efficient input-output combination (y^0, y^N) a sequence $\{p^0, \ldots, p^N\}$ of non-negative, non-zero price vectors and a sequence $(-y^t, y^{t+1})$, $t = 1, \ldots,$ $N - 1$, of elements of T such that (1) is satisfied each period. By the second condition of (1) and Assumption I, this implies $p^t_j \leqq h_j(p^{t-1})$ for each t. It may be proved further that

Lemma 4   If $y^{t+1}_j > 0$, and the conditions of Lemma 1 hold, then $p^{t+1}_j = h_j(p^t)$.

Proof By Assumption I, $(-y^t, y^{t+1}) = \sum_{j=1}^n (-y^t_{(j)}, y^{t+1}_{(j)})$, where $(-y^t_{(j)}, y^{t+1}_{(j)}) \in T_j$ for each j. By the second condition of (1), we see that $-p^t \cdot y^t_{(j)} + p^{t+1} \cdot y^{t+1}_{(j)} \leq 0$ will hold for each j. Then since the first condition of (1) holds for $(-y^t, y^{t+1})$ by assumption, it must also hold for (p^t, p^{t+1}) and $(-y^t_{(j)}, y^{t+1}_{(j)})$. Now if $y^{t+1}_j > 0$, and $p^{t+1}_j < h_j(p^t)$, $-p^t \cdot w^t + p^{t+1} \cdot w^{t+1} < 0$ for all $(-w^t, w^{t+1}) \in \bar{I}_j$. Consider the entire section $H_j \cap T_j$. For any $(-z^t, z^{t+1}) \in H_j \cap T_j$, there is $(-w^t, w^{t+1}) \in I_j$ and $-w^t \geq -z^t$, $w^{t+1} \geq z^{t+1}$. Thus $-p^t \cdot z^t + p^{t+1} \cdot z^{t+1} < 0$ for all $(-z^t, z^{t+1}) \in H_j \cap T_j$, and, therefore, for all $(-z^t, z^{t+1}) \in T_j$ unless $(-z^t, z^{t+1}) = (0, 0)$. This is in contradiction with the hypothesis that (1) holds. Thus $p^{t+1}_j = h_j(p^t)$ must follow.

We may, by use of Lemma 4, achieve a slightly stronger result than in Lemma 1. This is

Lemma 5 It is possible to choose the price sequence $p^t \geq 0, t = 0, \dots, N$, of Lemma 1, so that $p^{t+1}_j = h_j(p^t)$ for each t.

Proof It is always true that $p^t_j \leq h_j(p^{t-1})$. Then suppose $p^t_j < h_j(p^{t-1})$ and consider the implications of raising p^t_j to equality with $h_j(p^{t-1})$. By Lemma 4, $y^t_j = 0$. Thus the first condition of (1) in period t is still met. The second condition follows immediately from the definition of $h_j(p)$.

In period $t + 1$, consider any kth good. If $y^{t+1}_k > 0$, the increase of p^t_j leaves $h_k(p^t)$ unchanged. For $p^{t+1}_k = p \cdot y^t_{(k)} = h_k(p^t)$, and the jth component of $y^t_{(k)}$ must be zero by $y^t_j = 0$. On the other hand, if $y^{t+1}_k = 0$, $h_k(p^{t+1})$ may be allowed to increase from a rise in p^t_j. This will clearly not violate (1) in period $t + 1$.

There can be an effect in period $t + 2$ only in the case $y^{t+1}_k = 0$. Then a rise in $h_k(p^{t+1})$ means the revised p^{t+2}_k will be higher than otherwise, but now the considerations applying to the increase of p^t_j may be repeated. In other words, (1) will prevail in every period for the revised price sequence if it held for the original sequence.

Let $A(p)$ be the set of A, such that $A = [a_{ij}]$, $a_{(j)} \in M_j(p)$. A is an $n \times n$ matrix, and $A \geq 0$. $A(p)$ is upper semi-continuous in E_{n^2}. We make the further assumption

(V) There is an integer $s > 0$ such that $A^{(1)} \dots A^{(s)} > 0$ for any $A^{(t)} \in A(p^t)$, for any $p^1 \geq 0$ and $p^t = h(p^{t-1}), t = 2, \dots, s$.

In the light of Assumption (V) whenever N is divisible by s we may redefine the period of production so that $A > 0$ always holds for $A \in A(p)$. Let one new period comprise s old periods. The new T is the same as the old T^s, and the new $A(p)$ is the set of all $A^1 \ldots A^s$, where $A^t \in A(p^t)$ and $p^t = h(p^{t-1})$, $t = 2, \ldots, s$, and $p^1 = p$. By Assumption (V) it follows that $A \in A(p)$ in the new terminology implies $A > 0$. As it will turn out, we may with no loss of generality replace (V) by

$$A > 0 \quad \text{for } A = (a_{(1)}, \ldots, a_{(n)}) \text{ and } a_{(j)} \in I_j. \tag{V'}$$

Let us write a price sequence chosen according to Lemma 5 in the form

$$p^{t+1} = H(p^t), \quad t = 0, \ldots, N - 1. \tag{2}$$

$H(p)$ is homogeneous of degree one and continuous. As a consequence of Lemma 3, if we also make Assumption V', $H(p)$ is strictly increasing for $p \geqslant 0$. Thus $H(p)$ satisfies the conditions of the Samuelson-Solow theorem on the stability in the large of paths of balanced growth [10].[4]

Then, for given p^0, as $t \to \infty$, $\frac{p^t}{|p^t|} \to p^*$, where $p^* > 0$, and $H(p^*) = \lambda p^*$ for some $\lambda > 0$. We may prove

Theorem 1 On Assumptions I, II, III, IV, and V', with every $(-y^0, y^N) \in \bar{T}^N$ there may be associated a sequence $\{p^t\}$, $t = 0, \ldots, N$, of price vectors satisfying (2) and the conditions of Lemma 1. Let $V(p^*)$ be an arbitrary neighbourhood of p^*. There is a number N' such that $t > N'$ implies, for any such sequence with $N > N'$, that $\frac{p^t}{|p^t|} \in V(p^*)$.

Proof Define $S = \{p \mid \Sigma p_i = 1 \text{ and } p_i \geqq 0\}$. Define $H'(p^t) = \frac{H(p^t)}{\Sigma H_i(p^t)}$. I claim there is N' such that $H'^t(S) \subset V(p^*)$ for $t \geqq N'$ where H'^t is the t-fold repetition of H'. From the Samuelson-Solow theorem, for any $p \geqslant 0$ there is N_p such that $H'^t(p) \in V(p^*)$ for $t > N_p$. Since H'^t is continuous, there is a neighbourhood U_p of p in S and $H'^t(U_p) \subset V(p^*)$ for $t > N_p$. A set of neighbourhoods $\{U_p\}$ of this type for all $p \in S$ form a cover of S. Since S is compact there is a finite subcover $\{U_{p_k}\}$. Then N' may be taken equal to the maximum of N_{p_k}.

In order to proceed to Theorem 2, a final assumption is needed. Let S_i be the smallest subspace containing T_i. We assume.

(VI) If $z, z' \in \bar{T}_i$, then $z'' = \alpha z + (1 - \alpha)z'$, $0 < \alpha < 1$, lies in the interior of T_i relative to S_i, or else $z = \beta z'$ for $\beta \geqq 0$.

Assumption VI will recall Radner's assumption of "strict convexity" for T. However, whereas Radner is assuming, to be precise, that only one activity is profitable for the *whole economy* at prices associated with the Neumann ray, we are assuming that only one activity is profitable for *each industry* at prices associated with efficient paths. Thus efficient decentralized production guided by market prices is compatible with maximal balanced growth in our model, but not in Radner's model (except in a trivial sense when all firms are using the same process).

Note that Assumption VI for technology T under Assumption V will imply VI for technology T^s, which then satisfies Assumption V'.

With the aid of VI it is possible to prove

Lemma 6 For $p \geqslant 0$, $M_j(p) = \{a_j\}$, a one element set, and $a_j(p)$ is continuous.

Proof Let δ_j have $\delta_j^j = 1$, $\delta_i^j = 0$, $i \neq j$. By definition of $M_j(p)$, all points $(-y, \delta^j)$ with $y \in M_j(p)$ are efficient. Moreover, $M_j(p)$ is convex. Thus if $y \in M_j(p)$, $y' \in M_j(p)$, then $y'' = \alpha y + (1 - \alpha)y'$, $0 \leq \alpha \leq 1$, lies in $M_j(p)$, so $(-y'', \delta^j) \in \bar{Y}_j$. However, interior points of T_i relative to S_i obviously cannot be efficient. Such points are interior points in the subspace of those goods which are inputs or outputs for T_i. Thus Assumption VI is contradicted, unless $y = y'$.

Let $p^s \to p$, where $\{a^s\} = M_j(p^s)$. Since I_j is bounded there is a subsequence $a^{s'} \to a$. By upper semi-continuity $a \in M_j(p)$. Then by the above, $M_j(p) = \{a\}$ and $a^s \to a$. This completes the proof.

Now consider the sequences $\{y^t\}$ and $\{p^t\}$ which appear in Lemma 1 and satisfy (1) for $t = 0, \ldots, N$. If $\{p^t\}$ is chosen to satisfy (2), as it may be by Lemma 5, $p^t > 0$ must hold for $t > 0$ by Assumption V'. Then by Lemma 6, we may write $A(p^t) = [a_{ij}^t]$, where $\{a_{(j)}^t\} = M_j(p^t)$. We may prove

Lemma 7 With Assumptions V' and VI, for any $(-y^0, y^N) \in \bar{T}^N$ there is a unique sequence $\{y^t\}$, $t = 0, \ldots, N$, satisfying (1) for each t. For $t = 2, \ldots, N$, this sequence satisfies

$$y^{t-1} = A(p^{t-1})y^t, \tag{3}$$

where $\{p^t\}$ is chosen to satisfy (2) and the conditions of Lemma 1.

Proof From Assumption I, $(-y^t, y^{t+1}) \in T$ implies $(-y^t, y^{t+1}) = \sum_{j=1}^{n}(-y_{(j)}^t, y_{(j)}^{t+1})$ where $(-y_{(j)}^t, y_{(j)}^{t+1}) \in T_j$ for each j. Then, since $\{p^t\}$ and $(-y^t, y^{t+1})$ satisfy (1), $y_j^{t+1} > 0$ implies $p_j^{t+1} \cdot y_j^{t+1} = p^t \cdot y_{(j)}^t$. By the choice of $\{p^t\}$ to satisfy (2), $p_j^{t+1} = h_j(p^t) = p^t \cdot a_{(j)}^t$, for $t \geq 0$. Moreover, by Lemma 6, and Assumption VI, $p^t \cdot a_{(j)} > p_j^{t+1}$ for $a_{(j)} \in I_j$ and $a_{(j)} \neq a_{(j)}^t$. However, from the definition of I_j, $y_{(j)}^t = \gamma a_{(j)}$ for some $a_{(j)} \in I_j$ and $\gamma \geq 0$. Since $a_{(j)} > 0$, by V', and $p^t > 0$, it then follows from (1) and (2) that $\gamma = y_j^{t+1}$. Thus $y^t = \sum_{j=1}^n y_{(j)}^t = \sum_{j=1}^n y_j^{t+1} a_{(j)}$. This result may be written as (3) above.

The uniqueness of $\{y^t\}$ for this choice of $\{p^t\}$ is obvious if (3) is used to proceed backward from y^N. However, if a sequence $\{p^t\}$ satisfies (1) for one choice of $\{y^t\}$, it will at least satisfy the second relation of (1) for any other choice of $\{y^t\}$ compatible with $(-y^o, y^N) \in T^N$. Then $p^o \cdot y^o = p^N \cdot y^N$ implies that the first relation is satisfied as well. Thus $\{y^t\}$ is unique.

Consider (3) where $p^{t-1} = p^*$. Let $A(p^*) = A^*$. Write $G(y^t) = A^* y^t$. Then (3) becomes

$$y^{t-1} = G(y^t), \tag{3'}$$

where $G(y^t)$ satisfies the conditions of the Samuelson-Solow theorem by the fact that $A^* > 0$.[5] Thus, if $\{y^t\}$ is a solution of (3'), $\frac{y^t}{|y^t|} \to y^*$, as $t \to -\infty$, for a given $y^* > 0$.

Define $G'(y^t) = \frac{G(y^t)}{\Sigma G_i(y^t)}$. By a repetition of the argument of Theorem 1 there is N'' such that $G'^t(S) \subset W(y^*)$ for $t > N''$, where $W(y^*)$ is an arbitrary neighbourhood of y^* in S. Let $G(p^{t-1}, y^t)$ be defined by $A(p^{t-1})y^t$ where $p^{t-1} > 0$. Then $G(p^*, y^t) = G(y^t)$. By Lemma 6, $G(p, y)$ is a continuous function of p. Let $G'(p, y)$ represent the normalization of $G(p, y)$. Put $y^{t-1} = G(p^{t-1}, y^t)$, $y^{t-2} = G(p^{t-2}, y^{t-1}) = G^2(p^{t-1}, y^t)$, etc. Then there is a neighbourhood $V(p^*)$ of p^* such that $p^{\tau-t} \in V(p^*)$ for $t = 1, \ldots, N''$ implies $G'^{N''}(p^{\tau-1}, y^\tau) \subset W(y^*)$ for any $y^\tau \in S$.

Let $N > N' + N''$. Consider sequences $\{p^t\}$, $\{y^t\}$, which satisfy (1) for $t = 0, \ldots, N$. I claim $y^o, y^N \geq 0$ implies $\frac{y^t}{|y^t|} \in W(y^*)$ for the interval $N' \leq t \leq N - N''$. If necessary choose a new sequence $\{p^t\}$ to satisfy (2). Then, by Theorem 1, there is N' such that $p^t \in V(p^*)$ for all $t > N'$. Therefore, the argument of the last paragraph shows that $y^t \in W(y^*)$ for $t \leq \tau - N''$, provided that $\tau - N'' \geq N'$.

We have now the basis for

Theorem 2 We make Assumptions I, II, III, IV, V, and VI. Consider any (y^o, y^N) which is final efficient and the associated sequence $\{y^t\}$ described in Lemma 7. For any ε, $0 < \varepsilon < 1$, and any neighbourhood

$W(y^*)$, there is a positive integer N_1 such that $N > N_1$ implies that $\frac{y^t}{|y^t|} \in W(y^*)$ for an interval of length at least $(1 - \varepsilon)N$.

Proof Set $N_1 > \frac{N'+N''}{\varepsilon}$. Then the result follows immediately for Assumption V'. To establish the result on Assumption V, notice first that if (y^t, y^{t+v}) is final efficient then so is (y^{t+u}, y^{t+v}) for $u < v$. Next from Lemma 5 $p^t > 0$ holds for $t > s$, and this implies that (y^t, y^{t+v}) is final efficient by Lemma 1, when $t + v > s$. Thus by starting from y^t, $t \le s$, subsequences, containing every sth term, may be chosen from $\{y^t\}$, which are compatible with the technology T^s, satisfying V'. Each y^t, $t = 1, \ldots, N$, is contained in one such subsequence. If N_1 is chosen larger than $\frac{s(N'+N'')}{\varepsilon}$, our conclusion follows for each subsequence and therefore for the original sequence. Thus, as asserted, V' may replace V as an assumption without loss of generality.

Appendix

Let $X_i(t + 1) = H^i[X_1(t), X_2(t), \ldots, X_n(t)]$, $i = 1, \ldots, n$, where each H^i is defined for non-negative arguments, takes non-negative values, is positive homogeneous of degree 1, continuous, and strictly monotonic increasing. The Samuelson-Solow theorem says that $\lim_{t \to \infty} \frac{X_i(t)}{V_i^* \lambda^t} = x$, $i = 1, \ldots, n$, where the V_i^*, λ, and x are positive constants [10, pp. 413, 419]. Choose the V_i^* so that they sum to 1, then $\lim_{t \to \infty} \frac{X_i(t)}{\Sigma X_i(t)} = V_i^*$. Thus the applications in the text follow immediately.

Notes

1. The substance of this chapter together with a local theorem was presented to the Econometrics Society in December, 1960. My work was done independently of Morishima's, and also of the Hicks pilgrimage which eventuated in [7] and [9]. This work has been supported by a grant from the National Science Foundation.

2. This is a misnomer since the theorem primarily applies to the stability of a process of price development, not quantity development. It anticipated the arguments which led to the results on price stability by Arrow, Block, and Hurwicz, though, I believe, this was unnoticed by them.

3. I presume that in Morishima's argument he should have proved the constant c in (11), p. 93 [7], to be different from zero.

4. See the appendix for a statement of this theorem.

5. See the appendix for a statement of this theorem.

References

[1] Robert Dorfman, Paul Samuelson, and Robert Solow. *Linear Programming and Economic Analysis*, chapter 12, New York, 1958.

[2] W. Fenchel. *Convex Cones, Sets, and Functions*, Princeton, 1953.

[3] David Gale. "The Closed Linear Model of Production." *Linear Inequalities and Related Systems*, edited by Kuhn and Tucker, Princeton, 1956.

[4] Samuel Karlin. *Mathematical Methods and Theory in Games, Programming, and Economics*, vol. 1, appendix B. Reading, Massachusetts, 1959.

[5] Lionel McKenzie. "Price-Quantity Duality and the Turnpike Theorem," paper presented to the Econometric Society, December, 1960.

[6] Lionel McKenzie. "Three Turnpike Theorems for a Generalized Leontief Model," presented to the Econometric Society, August, 1961.

[7] Michio Morishima. "Proof of a Turnpike Theorem: The No Joint Production Case." *Review of Economic Studies*, February, 1961.

[8] John von Neumann. "Über ein ökonomiches Gleichungsystem und ein Verallgemeinerung des Brouwerschen Fixpunktsatzes," Ergebnisse eines Mathematischen Kolloquiums, No. 8, 1937 (translated in *Review of Economic Studies*, 1945–46).

[9] Roy Radner. "Paths of Economic Growth That Are Optimal with regard only to Final States." *Review of Economic Studies*, February, 1961.

[10] Paul Samuelson and Robert Solow. "Balanced Growth under Constant Returns to Scale." *Econometrica*, July, 1953.

20 Accumulation Programs of Maximum Utility and the von Neumann Facet

Lionel W. McKenzie

The study of optimal programs of economic growth which maximize a sum of utility was begun by Frank Ramsey (1928). He considered the case of a stationary population with no technical progress, except that which is explained by capital accumulation, no uncertainty about the future, and a single aggregate output that serves both as capital good and consumption good. His primary objective was to determine the rate of saving at any time prescribed by an optimal program of capital accumulation of unlimited duration.

Ramsey chose to consider a utility sum with no time discounting. Such a sum over an infinite future will be infinite for many programs between which it will not distinguish. To get round this difficulty Ramsey introduced a level of utility saturation and replaced the utility sum by a sum of differences between the utility enjoyed at saturation and the actual level of utility. If the saturation level can be reached by some program of accumulation, this differential sum will be finite for that program, and this program may be regarded as better than any program for which the differential sum is larger. Therefore, the criterion of maximizing the utility sum can reasonably be replaced by that of minimizing the differential sum, the shortfall from saturation, and the new problem will ordinarily have a solution.

The saturation level for utility can arise, according to Ramsey, either from an upper bound on the utility function itself or from an upper bound on the level of output that can be achieved through increasing the quantity of capital. Even if one does not wish to accept the notion of a bounded utility function, the bound on output from given population and given natural resources is entirely in accord with common sense. Indeed, if one allows for the need to replace capital as it wears out, and for the fact that this also uses labor, a bound on total capital accumulation is strongly recommended, even if output with unlimited capital supplies is not limited. However, a bound on capital accumulation would also suffice to define a saturation level of utility.

Ramsey did not bring out the point explicitly, but the appeal of his substitute criterion probably comes from the fact that a program which achieves a lower shortfall from saturation than another program will thereby also have the property that its utility sum over a finite period will exceed this sum for the same period for the other program provided the period is long enough. The criterion was explicitly phrased this way in recent work of Hiroshi Atsumi (1965) and Christian von Weizsacker (1965).

In recent years Ramsey's work has been extended in various ways. Uncertainty about the future of tastes and technology has been introduced by Mirrlees (1965). Atsumi (1965) and Koopmans (1965) have dealt with the case of an increasing population without scarce natural resources. Atsumi (1966) and Gale (1966) extended the model to consider more complicated technologies where the number of goods produced may exceed one. And simple forms of technical progress have been introduced by Weizsacker and Mirrlees. Also a straightforward extension of the Ramsey case to many goods was made by Samuelson and Solow (1956).

In this recent work two main themes have been present, the proof that infinite optimal programs converge to a saturation level and the proof that infinite optimal programs exist. Koopmans (1965) used methods very close to those of Ramsey to give these proofs for his model. The new feature of Koopman's model is a population which increases at a constant exogenous rate. Ramsey had not faced the question of summing utility over populations of different sizes, but the logic of his summation over years would seem to imply that people living in different years should be treated equally. However, Koopmans shows that the Ramsey type of argument will not work unless future utility is discounted at a rate at least equal to the rate of population growth. This is the course adopted by Koopmans and described as maximizing a sum of per capita utility over time.

Atsumi (1965) independently of Koopmans adopted the same expedient of summing per capita utilities and applying the Ramsey criterion, which he explicitly interpreted in terms of finite sums which eventually exceed the finite sums of any competing path. Atsumi did not concern himself with the existence question for infinite paths but proved the convergence of optimal paths to saturation paths in the sense of paths with maximum sustainable per capita utility. These saturation paths had already been characterized by Phelps, Joan Robinson, and others. However, Atsumi was the first to combine an expanding population with more than one produced good. Also, unlike Samuelson and Solow, he was able to avoid assuming strict convexity of the production set, apart from homogeneity, by using methods akin to those applied by Radner (1961) and myself (1963) to the von Neumann model. He proved the asymptotic convergence of optimal paths to saturation paths in a generalized Leontief model (1966). He also derived a generalization of the expression for the optimal saving ratio in a neo-classical model.

Finally, David Gale (1966) has treated both the asymptotic convergence of optimal paths defined by the Atsumi-Weizsacker criterion and the existence of such optimal paths in linear production models with a finite set of activities. However, he has avoided some of the problems incident to introducing many goods by using a strictly concave utility function, defined on activity levels rather than on goods.

My purpose in this chapter is to deal with the problems of asymptotic behavior of optimal paths using the Atsumi-Weizsacker criterion in a fully general production model. This allows an extension of Gale's result on the existence of infinite optimal paths. I follow Atsumi and Koopmans in assuming a steadily expanding population without scarce natural resources. The special limitations of the production set involved in strict convexity or in the absence of joint production are avoided. Two main results are derived. First, in a quite general model with a (weakly) convex transformation set, the finite optimal paths are shown to lie close, for all but a fixed number of periods, to a certain facet of the transformation set. This facet is characterized by the presence of the input-output combinations that provide the maximum sustainable utility. Indeed, a subset of the facet is described to which the optimal paths approach for all but a fixed number of periods. Second, it is shown that when this subset of the facet is a single point (where maximum sustainable utility will be realized) infinite paths exist which have a slightly weakened form of Atsumi-Weizsacker optimality.

20.1 The Model

We shall deal with an economy in which there are n kinds of durable and non-durable goods which can be accumulated as capital stocks. The quantities of these goods per capita at time t are the components of a vector $k(t) \geqslant 0$ in E_n, an n-dimensional Euclidean space. We assume that the development of the population over time is specified and also the rate at which natural resources are exhausted. Then it is reasonable to suppose that the per capita utility that can be achieved through consumption of goods and services during the period from t to $t + 1$ depends only on the initial and terminal capital stocks per capita $k(t)$ and $k(t + 1)$. This gives rise for each t to a transformation set $Y(t)$ in E_{2n+1} composed of points $(u(t), k(t), -k(t - 1))$ where $u(t)$ is a per capita utility level achievable in the tth period with initial capital stocks $k(t - 1)$ and terminal capital stocks $k(t)$.

In the present discussion the model will be specialized further by supposing that $Y(t)$ is a constant set Y for all t. The rationale for this specialization may be taken to be a constant rate of expansion for population, whose composition is fixed, and the absence of scarce natural resources. However, the depletion of resources, a varying rate of population growth, and technical progress could be so offsetting as to achieve the same result. The first formal assumption is

(I) Y is a closed convex subset of E_{2n+1}. Also $(u, k', -k) \in Y$ implies $(u(1), k'(1), -k(1)) \in Y$ when $u(1) \leqslant u$, $0 \leqslant k'(1) \leqslant k'$, and $k(1) \geqslant k$.

The second part of Assumption I is an assumption of free disposal. The assumption of convexity may be defended on the same grounds here as in the theory of production with linear activities. In the theory of production convexity results if the level of a productive activity may be continuously varied with all inputs and outputs changing in the same ratio, and if the productive activities are independent, so that the possibility of realizing one activity is not dependent on the levels of other activities. In the present model utility may be treated as an output resulting from combining capital goods and certain types of people.

Indeed, transformation set Y may be derived from a more basic activities cone. Suppose there are r types of people and the initial population is represented by a vector L in E_r. Let the initial capital stocks vector be K and the terminal vector K'. Let U be the utility generated over the period. Then there is a cone Y^Δ in $E_{2n+2r+1}$ whose elements have the form $z = (U, K', L', -K, -L)$. We are considering the section of this cone given by all elements of the form $z' = (U, K', \rho\bar{L}, -K, -\bar{L})$. $\bar{L}$ has the composition of the actual population and $|\bar{L}| = 1.$[1] ρ is the population expansion factor. Corresponding to z' there is a element $y = (u, k', -k) \in Y$ with $u = \rho^{-1}U$, $k' = \rho^{-1}K'$, and $k = K$.

There is no reason to expect the section of Y^Δ at $|\bar{L}|$ to be strictly convex since V is generated by independent activities involving people of differing tastes doing different jobs in various independent industries and consuming different bundles of services. On the other hand, the convexity of Y^Δ does not depend on convexity of the individual utility functions. The fact that the quantities of a finite number of types of people are made to vary continuously is an approximation of the same order of realism with the same assumption made for goods. The continuous variation of all quantities is used to provide the convexity that we need.

Let us say that k is expansible with respect to Y, or simply expansible, if there is $(u, k', -k) \in Y$ and $k' > k$. A further assumption is

(II)   There is a capital stock vector k^Δ which is expansible with respect to Y.

In other words, there is a level of capital stocks from which it is possible to accumulate larger per capita stocks of all types. Finally, we assume

(III)   (a)   For any number ξ there is a number η, depending on ξ, such that $|k| \leqslant \xi$ and $(u, k', -k) \in Y$ implies $u < \eta$ and $|k'| < \eta$.

(b)   There is a number ζ, and a number $\gamma < 1$, such that $(u, k', -k) \in Y$ and $|k| \geqslant \zeta$ implies $|k'| < \gamma|k|$.

Thus if initial stocks are bounded, terminal stocks are bounded and utility is bounded above. Also there is a limit above which accumulation per capita cannot be sustained. This is reasonable since capital goods are subject to some wear from time alone and labor services are needed to restore them.

20.2   The Turnpike Theorem

Consider the set $V = \{u, k' - k\}$ of vectors in E_{n+1}, where $(u, k', -k) \in Y$. V is convex and closed since Y is convex and closed. Consider the subset V^+ of V defined by $v \in V^+$ if $k' \geqslant k$, where $v = (u, k', -k)$. By Assumption III(b), $|k| < \zeta$ must hold for $v \in V^+$. Then, by Assumption III(a), v is bounded for $v \in V^+$. Since Y is closed, it is easily seen that V^+ is compact. Also by Assumption II, V^+ is not empty. Thus there is a point $v^* \in V^+$ where $v^* = (u^*, k^{*\prime} - k^*)$ and u^* is maximal for $v \in V^+$.

Let us say that k is not saturated, with respect to Y, if there is k' such that $(u, k', -k') \in Y$ and $k' > k$. It is useful to assume with regard to k^*

(IV) k^* is expansible, and not saturated, with respect to Y.

This says that further accumulation can occur from k^* and, moreover, there exist stocks of goods per capita, larger then those which allow maximum utility per capita to be realized, that can be sustained in a process belonging to Y. We may show

Lemma 1   There is a vector $p^* \in E_n$ such that $p^* \geqslant 0$ and, for $(u, k' - k) \in V$,

$$u + p^* \cdot (k' - k) \leqslant \mu$$

$$u^* + p^* \cdot (k^{*'} - k^*) = \mu.$$
(1)

Moreover, we may choose $\mu = u^*$ and $k^{*'} = k^*$.

Proof v^* is a boundary point of V, since $v^* \in \text{int } V$ contradicts the maximality of u^* for v in V^+. Since V is convex, there is a vector $(\pi, p) \in E_{n+1}$ such that $(\pi, p) \neq 0$ and, for $(u, k' - k) \in V$

$$\pi u + p \cdot (k' - k) \leqslant \mu$$

$$\pi u^* + p \cdot (k^{*'} - k^*) = \mu,$$
(2)

for some number μ. By free disposal, $(\pi, p) \geqslant 0$ holds and $k^{*'}$ may be assumed equal to k^*. Then it follows from (2) that $\pi u^* = \mu$. Suppose $\pi = 0$. Since k^* is expansible by Assumption IV, there is $v \in V$ where $v = (u, k' - k^*)$ and $k' > k^*$. For this v, $\pi u + p \cdot (k' - k^*) > \mu$, in violation of (2). Therefore, $\pi > 0$. We may choose $\pi = 1$. Also it is sometimes useful to choose p^* relative interior to the set of p which satisfy (2) with $\pi = 1$.

Let F be the set of $y = (u, k', -k)$ such that $y \in Y$ and

$$u + p^* \cdot k' - p^* \cdot k = u^*.$$
(3)

Since the left side of (3) is $< u^*$ for any element y of Y where $y \notin F$, we see that $(1, p^*, p^*)$ is a normal to the convex set Y in the points of F, which include $y^* = (u^*, k^*, -k^*)$. I shall refer to F as the von Neumann facet of Y and y^* as a von Neumann point. y^* may not be unique but the set N of all points $y \in F$ for which $y = (u, k', -k)$ with $k' \geqslant k$ is convex and need not exhaust F. N is the set of all von Neumann points.

I wish to consider paths of capital accumulation departing from an initial stock per capita $k(0)$. We adopt the Atsumi-Koopmans objective of maximizing the sum of per capita utility over the planning period, which in this section is finite, and reach an assigned terminal (final) stock per capita k^Δ. This may be arbitrarily chosen within limits of feasibility.

Equivalently, we will maximize $\sum_{t=1}^{T} \rho^{-t} U(t)$. That is to say, maximizing per capita utility is equivalent to discounting the sum of individual utility at the rate of population increase.

The choice of this objective can be defended in several ways. One way is to assume that each period the existing population is interested only in its own future welfare, but that each type of population grows at the rate ρ and the distribution of income over the types of people remains the same over time. Then if mortality is ignored, discounting at the rate $\rho - 1$ is justified at each moment of decision. The mortality rate would justify a higher discount rate except to the extent that it is compensated by an interest in the welfare of the unborn. That this interest should exactly offset the effects of mortality, however, regardless of the level of ρ, is clearly *ad hoc*.

There is another source of interest in a discount factor equal to the growth factor. This comes from the general theory of maximization in linear production models where the objective is to maximize terminal stocks in pre-assigned proportions. In the case where the desired goods are overproduced in the initial von Neumann equilibrium, and the surplus stocks can grow at the von Neumann growth rate also, the present theory may be applied in the derivation of asymptotic results (see McKenzie, 1967, and Winter, 1965). This is easily interpreted in the present case. The von Neumann growth factor here is ρ, the maximum rate of population growth. Population is produced in the model from population and a subsistence supply of consumption goods. Utility is produced by consumption, but it is not an input to the process of population growth. The population growth rate ρ' is a policy variable to be chosen each period. Then if utility is treated an an input to an activity whose output is ρ times the input of utility, the maximization of the terminal stock of utility,[2] when $\rho' = \rho$, is equivalent to the Atsumi-Koopmans objective, since $\sum_{t=1}^{T} \rho^{T-t+1} U(t) = \rho^{T+1} \sum_{t=1}^{T} \rho^{-t} U(t) = \rho^{T+1} \sum_{t=1}^{T} u(t)$. Moreover, it is known from earlier work that for large T, ρ' will be close to ρ most of the time in a maximal program where U is the only desired terminal stock (McKenzie, 1967). But when ρ' approaches ρ the problem of the present chapter arises, and if the assumptions are met, the asymptotic results derived here will apply.

Although this problem can arise in any closed linear model with a terminal objective, it may seem very special that the maximal growth rate ρ_1 for over-produced goods should be exactly equal to ρ in the technology which only uses over-produced goods. However, this is the unique *distinguished* case which does arise. The other possibility is $\rho_1 < \rho$, and then complications do not appear.

Let us define a path of accumulation as a sequence $\{k(t)\}$, such that there is a sequence $\{u(t)\}$, and $(u(t), k(t), -k(t-1)) \in Y$ for each t. I wish to consider paths of accumulation lasting T periods, departing from a given initial stock per capita $k(0)$ and reaching a given terminal stock per capita $k(T)$. Moreover, we will confine our attention to stocks $k(0)$ from which there exists a finite path $\{k(t)\}$, $t = 0, \ldots, \tau$, and $k(\tau)$ is expansible. The existence of a stock $k(\tau)$ is guaranteed by Assumption II. Then there is $(u, k' - k(\tau)) \in V^+$.

In order to conduct our argument we want to show that from any point in Y which allows stocks to expand we can pass by a finite path of accumulation to a von Neumann point of Y. It is convenient to prove

Lemma 2 (Gale.) Suppose $k(0)$ is expansible, and k is sustainable. Then there is an infinite accumulation path $\{k(t)\}$, $t = 0, 1, 2, \ldots$, in which $k(t) \to k$ as $t \to \infty$.

Proof Since $k(0)$ is expansible there is $y' = (u', k', -k(0)) \in Y$ and $k' > k(0)$. Since k is sustainable there is $y = (u, k, -k) \in Y$. Since Y is a convex set, $\lambda^t y' + (1 - \lambda^t) y = y(t) \in Y$ for $0 < \lambda < 1$. Write $y(t) = (u(t), k'(t), -k(t-1))$. Then $k'(t) = \lambda^t k' + (1 - \lambda^t)k$ and $k(t) = \lambda^{t+1} k(0) + (1 - \lambda^{t+1})k$. We must select λ so that $k(t') - k(t) > 0$. This is equivalent to $k' - k - \lambda(k(0) - k) > 0$, which holds for λ sufficiently near 1. Then it is implied by free disposal that $\{k(t)\}$ is an accumulation path. Since $\lambda(t) \to 0$ in the limit as $t \to \infty$, $k(t) \to k$. We shall need the

Corollary Suppose $k(0)$ is expansible and k is not saturated. Then, for τ sufficiently large, there is an accumulation path $\{k(t)\}$, $t = 0, \ldots, \tau$, such that $k(\tau) = k$.

Proof Since k is not saturated, there is $k' > k$ where k' is sustainable. By the Lemma there is a path $\{k(t)\}$, $t = 0, 1, 2, \ldots$, such that $k(t) \to k'$. Then for some τ, $t \geq \tau$ implies $k(\tau) > k$. By free disposal $k(\tau)$ may be set equal to k.

The Corollary to Lemma 2 says that any per capita stock can be reached provided that an even larger stock is sustainable and that the initial stock allows accumulation to begin. Given that these conditions are met by the initial and terminal stocks, we will first prove that when T is sufficiently large, the normalized input-output vector $(u(t), k(t), -k(t-1))$ must stay near F most of the time if the sum of per capita utility is maximized over the path. The Radner theory for closed models of growth can be applied here, as Atsumi has shown, and, indeed, the argument is simpler in the open model. Let $d(F, y) = \min|z - y|$ for $z \in F$.

Lemma 3 (Atsumi) Let $y = (u, k', -k) \in Y$. For any $\varepsilon > 0$, there is $\delta > 0$ such that $d(F, y) > \varepsilon$ implies $u + p^* \cdot (k' - k) < u^* - \delta$, given $|k| \leqslant \zeta$.

Proof If the assertion were false, there would be a sequence $y(s)$ for $s = 1, 2, \ldots$ with $d(F, y(s)) > \varepsilon$ for all s and $u(s) + p \cdot (k'(s) - k(s)) \to u^*$. However, $|k(s)| \leqslant \zeta$ and Assumption III(b) imply that $|k'(s)|$ is bounded. Then by III(a), $y(s)$ lies in a bounded region for all s. Thus there is a point of accumulation $\bar{y} = (\bar{u}, \bar{k}', -\bar{k})$, and $\bar{u} + p^* \cdot (\bar{k}' - \bar{k}) = u^*$, although $d(F, \bar{y}) > \varepsilon$. This contradicts (1) and establishes the lemma.

We may now prove an asymptotic result. Let $\{k(t)\}$ be a path of capital accumulation, lasting for T periods, with initial stocks $k(0)$ and terminal stocks (per capita) $k(T)$. We will say that $\{u(t)\}$ is a utility path associated with $\{k(t)\}$ if $(u(t), k(t), -k(t-1)) \in Y$ fro all t. We will say that $\{k(t)\}$ is an optimal path from $k(0)$ to $k(T)$ if the per capita utility sum $\sum_{t=1}^{T} u(t) \geqslant \sum_{t=1}^{T} u'(t)$, where $\{u'(t)\}$ is any utility path associated with any T-period accumulation path $\{k'(t)\}$ leading from $k(0)$ to $k(T)$. Also if $\{k(t)\}$ is an accumulation path and $\{u(t)\}$ is an associated utility path, we will call $\{y(t)\}$ a production path associated with $\{k(t)\}$ if $y(t) = (u(t), k(t), -k(t-1)) \in Y$ for all t.

We may now prove the turnpike theorem.

Theorem 1 Suppose $k(0)$ is expansible and $\bar{k}$ is not saturated. Then, for large T, there is an optimal path $\{\bar{k}(t)\}$, $t = 0, \ldots, T$, leading from $k(0)$ to $k(T) = \bar{k}$. Let $\{\bar{y}(t)\}$ be the associated production path. Then given any $\varepsilon > 0$, there is N such that $d(F, \bar{y}(t)) > \varepsilon$ holds for not more than N periods.

Proof By the corollary to Lemma 2 for T large enough a path $\{k(t)\}$ exists from $k(0)$ to $k(T) = \bar{k}$. By Assumption III(b), the set of all T-period paths from $k(0)$ to $\bar{k}$ is bounded. Then from the fact that Y is closed, a T-period path $\{\bar{k}(t)\}$ exists for which the utility sum $\sum_{t=1}^{T} \bar{u}(t)$ is a maximum for all T-period paths from $k(0)$ to $\bar{k}$.

Since, by Assumption IV, k^* is not saturated, there is also an accumulation path lasting N_0 periods, for some $N_0 \geqslant 0$, leading from $k(0)$ to k^*. Moreover, since, by Assumption IV, k^* is expansible, there is an accumulation path lasting N_1 periods, for some $N_1 \geqslant 0$, leading from

k^* to $\bar{k}$. Let $T > N_0 + N_1$. Finally, since $(u^*, k^*, -k^*) \in Y$ by the definition of a von Neumann point, from $t = N_0$ to $t = T - N_1$, there is an accumulation path $\{k(t)\}$ where $k(t) = k^*$. Let $\{k(t)\}$, $t = 0, \ldots, T$, where $k(T) = \bar{k}$, represent the combination of those three paths in sequence, and let $\{u(t)\}$ be an associated utility path with $u(t) = u^*$ for $t = N_0$ to $t = T - N_1$. Let $u' = \sum_{t=1}^{N_0} u(t)$ and $u'' = \sum_{t=T-N_1+1}^{T} u(t)$. Then the utility sum along this "comparison path" is at least $(T - N_0 - N_1)u^* + u' + u''$. This sum must not exceed $\sum_{t=1}^{T} \bar{u}(t)$ for the optimal path.

On the other hand, it follows directly from (1) that

$$\bar{u}(t) \leqslant u^* - p^* \cdot (\bar{k}(t) - \bar{k}(t-1)).$$

By Lemma 3, when $d(F, \bar{y}(t)) > \varepsilon$ and $|k(t)| < \zeta$, there is $\delta > 0$ such that $\bar{u}(t) \leqslant u^* - p^* \cdot (\bar{k}(t) - \bar{k}(t-1)) - \delta$. This provides a 'valuation ceiling' for the utility sum. However, it is a consequence of Assumption III(b) that $|\bar{k}(t)| < \zeta$ for $t > N_2$ for some $N_2 \geqslant 0$. Thus putting the utility sum between the 'floor' established by the comparison path and the 'valuation ceiling', we obtain

$$(T - N_0 - N_1)u^* + u' + u'' \leqslant \sum_{t=1}^{T} \bar{u}(t) \leqslant Tu^* - p^* \cdot (\bar{k} - k(0)) - \tau\delta, \quad (4)$$

where $N_2 + \tau$ is the number of periods when $d(F, \bar{y}(t)) > \varepsilon$. This inequality requires

$$\tau \leqslant \delta^{-1}((N_0 + N_1)u^* + p^* \cdot (k(0) - \bar{k}) - u' - u''). \tag{5}$$

Thus N may be chosen equal to $N_0 + N_1 + N_2 + N_3$ where N_3 is any number larger than the right side of (5).

Corollary   The conclusion of Theorem 1 continues to hold if $k(0)$ and k^* are not necessarily expansible, but finite paths exist leading from $k(0)$ to k^Δ where k^Δ is expansible, and from k^* to $k^{\Delta\Delta}$ where $k^{\Delta\Delta}$ is expansible.

20.3   Convergence on the von Neumann Facet

If a stronger result is to be reached than approximation to the von Neumann facet the structure of the facet must be studied.[3] The number of processes $y = (u, k', -k)$ that lie in F and are positively linearly independent can be infinite. However, the maximum number of processes that lie in F and are independent is equal to the dimension of F plus 1.

Let the dimension of F be $r - 1$, and choose r linearly independent vectors $y(j)$ which lie in F. Define

$$A = [k(1) \ldots k(r)], \quad B = \begin{bmatrix} u(1) & \cdots & u(r) \\ k'(1) & \cdots & k'(r) \end{bmatrix}.$$

Then for any $y \in F$, we may write

$$y = \begin{bmatrix} B \\ -A \end{bmatrix} x, \quad x \in E_r, \quad \sum_{j=1}^{r} x_j = 1. \tag{6}$$

The x_j are allowed to be any real numbers.

We shall say that a production path $\{y(t)\}$, $t = 1, \ldots, T$, lies on F if $y(t) \in F$ for these t. Let

$$\bar{A} = \begin{bmatrix} k(1) & \cdots & k(r) \\ 1 & \cdots & 1 \end{bmatrix}, \quad \bar{B} = \begin{bmatrix} k'(1) & \cdots & k'(r) \\ 1 & \cdots & 1 \end{bmatrix}.$$

Then the necessary condition (6) for $y \in F$, implies that the sequence $\{x(t)\}$, $t = 1, \ldots, T$, corresponding to $\{y(t)\}$ on F, satisfies

$$\bar{A}x(t+1) = \bar{B}x(t). \tag{6'}$$

From the definition of F we know there is at least one solution of (6'), $x(t) = x^* \geqslant 0$, for all t. Moreover, there is such a solution where $y^* = \begin{bmatrix} B \\ -A \end{bmatrix} x^*$ lies in the relative interior of F. Otherwise, F would not be minimal.[4] However, the fact that F is minimal follows from the choice of p^* to lie in the relative interior of the set of p such that $(1, p)$ satisfies (2). Let $X = \left\{ x \mid y = \begin{bmatrix} B \\ -A \end{bmatrix} x, \sum_{j=1}^{r} x_j = 1, \text{ and } y \in F \right\}$. Then $x^* \in \text{int } X$, the interior of X. Necessary and sufficient conditions for a production path $\{y(t)\}$, corresponding to an accumulation path $\{k(t)\}$, to lie on F are (6') and $x(t) \in X$ in each period. X is a convex set by the convexity of F.

Since $x^* \in \text{int } X$, if x is another constant solution of (6'), for small α, $x' = x^* + \alpha x$ will also lie in X and define a path $\{y(t)\}$ on F, which is constant. Indeed, if $\{x(t)\}$ is any cyclic solution of (6'), not necessarily constant, it may be combined with x^* to give another solution of (6') which lies in X and generates a path on F. These paths lie on F for arbitrarily large t, if α is chosen small enough.

In order to characterize all paths on F, it is necessary to examine the general solution of (6'). This can be done by examining the canonical form of the (possibly singular) pencil of matrices $\bar{B} - \lambda\bar{A}$. (This theory may be found in Gantmacher (1959).) The canonical form is reached by pre-multiplying and post-multiplying $\bar{A}$ and $\bar{B}$ by nonsingular real matrices P and Q of orders $n + 1$ and r respectively. This amounts to defining new composite goods and new activities in a way to simplify as far as possible the relation of $\bar{A}$ and $\bar{B}$ as linear transformations. The composite goods and activities use negative as well as positive weights. However, they often may be interpreted as variations of the quantities of goods and activities from positive levels.

We will say that a matrix L is a diagonal block of a matrix C if L is a submatrix of C and all elements of C that lie outside L and in a row or a column that contributes to L are zero. The canonical matrix for $\bar{B} - \lambda\bar{A}$ may have diagonal blocks:

$$L_1, \ldots, L_p; \quad L_1', \ldots, L_q'; \quad N_1, \ldots, N_s; \quad J - \lambda I.$$

Also, if needed, 0 columns and rows must be added, to bring the order of the block diagonal matrix up to that of $\bar{B} - \lambda\bar{A}$, which is $(n + 1, r)$. Each submatrix L_i has the form

$$L_i = \begin{bmatrix} 1 & -\lambda & & & 0 \\ & 1 & -\lambda & & \\ & & \cdot & \cdot & \\ & & & \cdot & \cdot \\ 0 & & & 1 & -\lambda \end{bmatrix}.$$

Its order is $(\varepsilon_i, \varepsilon_i + 1)$. Each submatrix L_i' has the form

$$L_i' = \begin{bmatrix} -\lambda & & & 0 \\ 1 & -\lambda & & \\ & 1 & \cdot & \\ & & \cdot & \cdot \\ & & \cdot & -\lambda \\ 0 & & & 1 \end{bmatrix}.$$

Its order is $(\eta_i + 1, \eta_i)$. Each submatrix N_i has the form

$$N_i = \begin{bmatrix} 1 & -\lambda & & & 0 \\ & 1 & -\lambda & & \\ & & \cdot & \cdot & \\ & & & \cdot & \cdot \\ & & & \cdot & -\lambda \\ 0 & & & & 1 \end{bmatrix}.$$

Its order is (u_i, u_i). Finally, $J - \lambda I$ is a rational canonical form minus λ times the identity matrix of the same order.

Write $\bar{B}_1 - \lambda \bar{A}_1 = C_1$ for the canonical form of $\bar{B} - \lambda \bar{A}$. $\bar{A}$ and $\bar{B}$ multiplying elements of E_r on the right define linear transformations from E_r to E_{n+1}. The zero columns of C_1 correspond to the common right null spaces of $\bar{A}$ and $\bar{B}$. However, since the columns of $\begin{bmatrix} B \\ -A \end{bmatrix}$ are linearly independent, the right null space of $\begin{bmatrix} \bar{B} \\ -\bar{A} \end{bmatrix}$ cannot have dimension exceeding 1, and this is the same subspace as the common right null space of $\bar{A}$ and $\bar{B}$. In this subspace of E_r the solution of (6′) is completely arbitrary, but no difference is made to the corresponding capital stock vectors k and k'. Then we see from (3) that the utility produced is not affected either.

The L_i arise from disjoint null spaces of $\bar{A}$ and $\bar{B}$ in E_r. There is a one dimensional subspace of each of these null spaces associated with a submatrix L_i. The 1 in the upper left corner of L_i represents a variation of output which needs no variation of input. Then the following columns represent the use of the preceding output variation as an input variation to produce a new output variation until finally the $-\lambda$ in the lower right hand corner represents the absorption of the last input variation without producing a further output variation. Thus ε_i is the number of transformations before the initial effect is entirely cancelled. Each submatrix L_i may give rise to a transient modification of a solution of (6′), which affects x and k and may affect u as well. By starting such transients in each period at appropriate levels a solution may be constructed that grows at an arbitrary rate, in particular at the rate 1 of the solution x^*. However, (1) implies that the utility accruing along the new constant path is again u^*.

Multiplying elements of E_{n+1} on the left, $\bar{A}$ and $\bar{B}$ also define linear transformations from E_{n+1} to E_r. The submatrices L_i' arise from disjoint left null spaces (in E_{n+1}) in the same way that the L_i arise from disjoint right null spaces (in E_r). However, the submatrices L_i' generate transient solutions of (6′) that depend on an initial input variation and cannot be continued beyond η_i periods, since the final output variation is not usable. Similarly, the submatrices N_i arise from null spaces of $\bar{A}$ to which no null spaces of $\bar{B}$ correspond. In this case, as for the L_i, an output variation occurs with no input variation. But, as for the L_i', the final output variation cannot be absorbed, so the solution cannot be continued beyond the first u_i periods.

Finally, the submatrix $J - \lambda I$ corresponds to a subspace in which $\bar{A}$ is non-singular. In this subspace the solutions of $(6')$ may be expressed in terms of the characteristic roots of J and associated characteristic vectors by classical formulas. In the case of real roots the characteristic roots are diagonal elements of J, and among the real roots is the root 1 for which $Q^{-1}x^*$ may serve as a characteristic vector.

The solutions of $(6')$ may be expressed in terms of the columns of Q and P^{-1}. First, note that $\bar{A}x(t+1) = \bar{B}x(t)$ is equivalent to

$$P^{-1}\bar{A}_1 Q^{-1}x(t+1) = P^{-1}\bar{B}_1 Q^{-1}x(t).$$

Since Q is non-singular and its order is (r, r), its columns span E_r. Thus any sequence in $x(t)$ can be expressed by means of a sequence of linear combinations of the columns $q(j)$ of Q. But $Q^{-1}q(j)$ is a vector with its jth component equal to 1 and all other components 0. Thus $\bar{A}_1 Q^{-1}q(j)$ is equal to the jth column of $\bar{A}_1$ and $\bar{B}_1 Q^{-1}q(j)$ is equal to the jth column of $\bar{B}_1$. These columns have only one non-zero component if they intersect the blocks L_i, L_i' or N_i and no more than two non-zero entries in other cases. However, a sequence $\{x(t)\}$ is already a solution if it satisfies $\bar{A}_1 Q^{-1}x(t+1) = \bar{B}_1 Q^{-1}x(t)$. The multiplication of this equation by P^{-1} will give the variation in capital stocks generated by the solution. In the simplest cases this variation is a column of P^{-1}. In the general case it is a linear combination of columns of P^{-1}, which can express any arbitrary variation of stocks, since the order of P^{-1} is $(n+1, n+1)$ and its columns span E_{n+1}.

For illustration consider a simple L block,

$$L = \begin{bmatrix} 1 & -\lambda & 0 \\ 0 & 1 & -\lambda \end{bmatrix}.$$

Let $q(1), q(2), q(3)$ be the columns of Q with the same indices as the columns of C_1 that intersect L. Then $x(t) = 0$, $t < \tau$, $x(\tau) = q(1)$, $x(\tau+1) = q(2)$, $x(\tau+2) = q(3)$, $x(t) = 0$, $t > \tau+2$, is a solution of $(6')$. In the subspace of E_r on which this L block operates

$$Q^{-1}q(1) = \begin{pmatrix} 1 \\ 0 \\ 0 \end{pmatrix}, \quad Q^{-1}q(2) = \begin{pmatrix} 0 \\ 1 \\ 0 \end{pmatrix}, \quad \text{and} \quad Q^{-1}q(3) = \begin{pmatrix} 0 \\ 0 \\ 1 \end{pmatrix}.$$

Then

$$\begin{pmatrix} 0 \\ 0 \end{pmatrix} = \bar{A}_1 Q^{-1}q(1) = \bar{B}_1 Q^{-1}\begin{pmatrix} 0 \\ 0 \end{pmatrix}$$

$$\begin{pmatrix} 1 \\ 0 \end{pmatrix} = \bar{A}_1 Q^{-1} q(2) = \bar{B}_1 Q^{-1} q(1)$$

$$\begin{pmatrix} 0 \\ 1 \end{pmatrix} = \bar{A}_1 Q^{-1} q(3) = \bar{B}_1 Q^{-1} q(2)$$

$$\begin{pmatrix} 0 \\ 0 \end{pmatrix} = \bar{A}_1 Q^{-1} \begin{pmatrix} 0 \\ 0 \end{pmatrix} = \bar{B}_1 Q^{-1} q(3).$$

The corresponding variations in capital stocks are $P^{-1}\begin{pmatrix} 1 \\ 0 \end{pmatrix} = p(1)$, $P^{-1}\begin{pmatrix} 0 \\ 1 \end{pmatrix} = p(2)$. Here $\begin{pmatrix} 1 \\ 0 \end{pmatrix}$ and $\begin{pmatrix} 0 \\ 1 \end{pmatrix}$ represent vectors in E_{n+1} whose other components are all equal to 0. The explicit components correspond to the rows of C_1 which intersect L. Suppose a solution of this type that lasts three periods is started up in every period. Then after the first three periods a constant solution $x(t) = q(1) + q(2) + q(3)$ is obtained for all subsequent time. The corresponding variation of capital stock is

$$\begin{pmatrix} k(t) \\ 0 \end{pmatrix} = p(1) + p(2).$$

Since (6') implies that $\sum_{i=1}^{r} x_i(t)$ is constant, it follows that $\sum_{i=1}^{r} q_i(j) = 0$ for $j = 0, 1, 2$, and $p_{n+1}(j) = 0$, $j = 1, 2$.
    A simple example for an L' block is

$$L' = \begin{bmatrix} -\lambda & 0 \\ 1 & -\lambda \\ 0 & 1 \end{bmatrix}.$$

Using a notation like that in the preceding example, there is a solution in the form $x(\tau) = q(1)$, $x(\tau + 1) = q(2)$, but it cannot be continued beyond $x(\tau + 1)$, and it requires an initial investment of stocks to begin. In detail,

$$Q^{-1} q(1) = \begin{pmatrix} 1 \\ 0 \end{pmatrix} \quad \text{and} \quad Q^{-1} q(2) = \begin{pmatrix} 0 \\ 1 \end{pmatrix}, \quad \text{and}$$

$$\begin{pmatrix} 1 \\ 0 \\ 0 \end{pmatrix} = \bar{A}_1 Q^{-1} q(1)$$

$$\begin{pmatrix} 0 \\ 1 \\ 0 \end{pmatrix} = \bar{A}_1 Q^{-1} q(2) = \bar{B}_1 Q^{-1} q(1)$$

$$\begin{pmatrix} 0 \\ 0 \\ 1 \end{pmatrix} = \bar{B}_1 Q^{-1} q(2).$$

The initial input is $P^{-1}\begin{pmatrix} 1 \\ 0 \\ 0 \end{pmatrix} = p(1)$. Then $P^{-1}\begin{pmatrix} 0 \\ 1 \\ 0 \end{pmatrix} = p(2)$ is produced

and used, but $P^{-1}\begin{pmatrix} 0 \\ 0 \\ 1 \end{pmatrix} = p(3)$ and $p(3)$ cannot be used on F.

An example for an N block is

$$N = \begin{bmatrix} 1 & -\lambda \\ 0 & 1 \end{bmatrix}.$$

There is a solution in the form $x(t) = 0$, $t < \tau$, $x(\tau) = q(1)$, $x(\tau + 1) = q(2)$, but it cannot be continued beyond $x(\tau + 1)$. In detail,

$$Q^{-1}q(1) = \begin{pmatrix} 1 \\ 0 \end{pmatrix}, \quad Q^{-1}q(2) = \begin{pmatrix} 0 \\ 1 \end{pmatrix}, \quad \text{and}$$

$$\begin{pmatrix} 0 \\ 0 \end{pmatrix} = \bar{A}_1 Q^{-1}q(1) = \bar{B}_1 Q^{-1}\begin{pmatrix} 0 \\ 0 \end{pmatrix}$$

$$\begin{pmatrix} 1 \\ 0 \end{pmatrix} = \bar{A}_1 Q^{-1}q(2) = \bar{B}_1 Q^{-1}q(1)$$

$$\begin{pmatrix} 0 \\ 1 \end{pmatrix} = \bar{B}_1 Q^{-1}q(2).$$

The initial output is $P^{-1}\begin{pmatrix} 1 \\ 0 \end{pmatrix} = p(1)$. This is used to produce $P^{-1}\begin{pmatrix} 0 \\ 1 \end{pmatrix} = p(2)$ which is not usable on F.

The block $J - \lambda I$ presents no special problem unless there is a zero characteristic root. This gives rise to a block that, in a simple case, takes the form

$$D = \begin{bmatrix} -\lambda & 0 \\ 1 & -\lambda \end{bmatrix}.$$

This is like an L' block with the last row missing; that is, no final output is produced. As in the case of an L' block an initial input is needed. A solution has the form $x(\tau) = q(1)$, $x(\tau + 1) = q(2)$, $x(t) = 0$, for $t > \tau + 1$. In detail

$$\begin{pmatrix} 1 \\ 0 \end{pmatrix} = \bar{A}_1 Q^{-1} q(1)$$

$$\begin{pmatrix} 0 \\ 1 \end{pmatrix} = \bar{A}_1 Q^{-1} q(2) = \bar{B}_1 Q^{-1} q(1)$$

$$\begin{pmatrix} 0 \\ 0 \end{pmatrix} = \bar{A}_1 Q^{-1} \begin{pmatrix} 0 \\ 0 \end{pmatrix} = \bar{B}_1 Q^{-1} q(2).$$

The initial input variation is $P^{-1} \begin{pmatrix} 1 \\ 0 \end{pmatrix} = p(1)$. This is used to produce a variation $P^{-1} \begin{pmatrix} 0 \\ 1 \end{pmatrix} = p(2)$ that is absorbed with no variation in output.

We find then that the only parts of the solution of (6′) which can influence the asymptotic results are those which arise from a zero column of C_1 or from the quasidiagonal blocks L_i and $J - \lambda I$. If a zero column is present, let it be the first column of C_1. Let $q(1)$ be the first column of Q, where $P(\bar{B} - \lambda \bar{A})Q = \bar{B}_1 - \lambda \bar{A}_1$. Then $x(0,t) = \alpha_t q(1)$ is a solution of (6′) for any sequence of real numbers α_t. Let $q(i,0), \ldots,$ $q(i, \varepsilon_i)$ be the columns of Q corresponding to L_i. Then $\alpha_{it} q(i,0) + \cdots + \alpha_{it-\varepsilon_i} q(i, \varepsilon_i) = x(i,t)$ is a solution where the α_{it} are arbitrary real numbers for all t. Whereas $\bar{A} q(1) = \bar{B} q(1) = 0$, $\bar{A} q(i,1) = \bar{B} q(i,0) = p(i,1)$ where $p(i,1)$ is an appropriate column of P^{-1}. Thus the solution $x(i,t)$ has an effect on the capital stock vector k. Moreover, if $\alpha_{it} = 1$ for all $t \geqslant 0$, the resulting solution $x^\Delta(i,t)$ is constant for $t > \varepsilon_i$ and $x^* + \alpha x^\Delta(i,t)$ is a constant solution of (6′) for these t and lies in X for all sufficiently small α. Since (1) implies that all constant paths of F have $u(t) = u^*$, $u^\Delta(i,t) = 0$.

The final block $J - \lambda I$ gives rise to the type of solutions recognized in the theory of systems of ordinary difference equations of the first order. J is further decomposed into blocks J_{ij}, which take two forms. If λ_j is real, the associated blocks are

$$J_{ij} = \begin{bmatrix} \lambda_j & & & 0 \\ 1 & \cdot & & \\ & \cdot & \cdot & \\ & & \cdot & \cdot \\ 0 & & 1 & \lambda_j \end{bmatrix}.$$

If λ_j is complex, its complex conjugate $\bar{\lambda}_j$ is also a root, and associated with the pair $\lambda_j, \bar{\lambda}_j$ there are blocks

$$
J_{ij} = \begin{bmatrix}
0 & 1 & 0 & & & & \\
-|\lambda_j|^2 & 2R(\lambda_j) & 1 & 0 & & & \\
& 0 & 0 & 1 & 0 & & \\
& & -|\lambda_j|^2 & 2R(\lambda_j) & & & \\
& & & & \cdot & & \cdot \\
& & & & & \cdot & \\
& 0 & & & & \cdot & \cdot \\
& & & & & -|\lambda_j|^2 & 2R(\lambda_j)
\end{bmatrix}
$$

J has zero elements outside these blocks. The order of J_{ij} is $(\delta_{ij}, \delta_{ij})$. $R(\lambda_j)$ is the real part of λ_j and $|\lambda_j|$ is the absolute value. If $\bar{A}_J$ and $\bar{B}_J$ are matrices which represent the linear transformations $\bar{A}$ and $\bar{B}$ on the subspace corresponding to $J - \lambda I$, the λ_j, and their complex conjugates, are the characteristic roots of $|\bar{A}_J^{-1}\bar{B}_J|$.

For each block J_{ij}, where $\lambda_j \neq 0$, there is a solution of $(6')$ of the form

$$
x(i, j, t) = \sum_{s=1}^{\delta_{ij}} q(i, j, s)(J_{ij}^t a)_s,
$$

where a is a vector of dimension δ_{ij} of arbitrary constants a_s and the $q(i, j, s)$ are the columns of Q corresponding to the columns of the J_{ij} block. To derive this result, note that if $x(t)$ is a solution, then $x(t) = Qz(t)$ where $\bar{A}_1 z(t) = \bar{B}_1 z(t-1)$. But, for the subspace of E_r on which J_{ij} operates, this last equation is equivalent to $z_{ij}(t) = J_{ij} z_{ij}(t-1)$, where $z_{ij}(t)$ is the part of $z(t)$ that corresponds to the columns of the J_{ij} block. Then $z_{ij}(t) = J_{ij}^t z_{ij}(0)$. Put $a = z_{ij}(0)$ to obtain the formula.

If $a \neq 0$, the expression in parentheses goes to 0 with increasing t if $|\lambda_j| < 1$, and is unbounded with increasing t if $|\lambda_j| > 1$. Since Q is nonsingular, the same behavior holds true for the corresponding solutions $x(i, j, t)$. The associated vector of capital stocks is also unbounded, since the final component of the solution vector is constant by $(6')$. However, by Assumption III(b), $|k(t)| \geq \zeta$ implies $|k(t+1)| < \gamma|k(t)|$, $\gamma < 1$. Thus ζ is eventually a bound on $|k(t)|$, and this implies that the weight of any component $x(i, j, t)$ for $|\lambda_j| > 1$ must be small in a solution of $(6')$ which describes a path of accumulation lying on F for a large number of periods.

The only remaining solutions arising from $J + \lambda I$ are those solutions $x(i, j, t)$ for which $|\lambda_j| = 1$ or $\lambda_j = 0$. In the case $\lambda_j = 0$ no output is produced after δ_{ij} periods. Thus components arising from these blocks have no effect on solutions for $t > \delta_{ij}$. The solutions for $|\lambda_j| = 1$ are cyclic, and not constant except for those associated with $\lambda_j = 1$, among which is x^*. Let $x(j,t)$ be a real solution belonging to λ_j and $\bar{\lambda}_j$ for $|\lambda_j| = 1$. Then it follows from $x^* \in \text{int } X$ that for sufficiently small α, $x^* + \alpha x(j,t)$, will also lie in X for all t with $1 \leqslant t \leqslant T$, however large T may be. Since (6') implies $\sum_i x_i(j,t) = \sum_i x_i(j,t+1)$, it follows that $\lambda_j \neq 1$ implies

$$\sum_i x_i(j,t) = 0$$

for all t. Let E^* be the subspace of the space E_r which is spanned by those columns of Q which are associated with a zero column of C_1, the quasi-diagonal blocks L_i, and the diagonal blocks J_{ij} for $|\lambda_j| = 1$. Let $X^* = X \cap E^*$. Finally, let $W = \left\{ y \,\middle|\, \begin{bmatrix} B \\ -A \end{bmatrix} x = y \text{ for } x \in X^* \right\}$. We may prove

Lemma 4 Let $\{x(t)\}$, $t = 1, \ldots, T$, be a sequence of vectors in E_r that satisfy equation (6') and the condition $\sum_{i=1}^r x_i(t) = 1$. Assume for the corresponding sequence $\{k(t)\}$ and $|k(t)| \leqslant \zeta$ and

$$y(t) = (u(t), k(t), -k(t-1)) = \begin{bmatrix} B \\ -A \end{bmatrix} x(t).$$

Then for any $\varepsilon > 0$, there is $N > 0$ such that $d(y(t), W) < \varepsilon$ for all t with $N < t < T - N$. N is independent of T.

Proof Let S_1 be the subspace of E_r which is spanned by the columns of Q that are associated with those J_{ij} whose λ_j have $|\lambda_j| > 1$. Let Q_1 be the submatrix of Q formed of these columns. Define S_2 in the analogous way for $|\lambda_j| < 1$. It is implied by the preceding analysis of (6') that after r periods $x(t)$ will be in the vector sum of S_1, S_2, and E^*. Let J_1 and I_1 be matrices representing the transformations $\bar{B}$ and $\bar{A}$ on S_1, and J_2 and I_2 similarly for S_2. Then with respect to the projection $x_1(t)$ of $x(t)$ on S_1, (6') may be written

$$x_1(t) = Q_1 z(t)$$

$$z(t+1) = J_1 z(t),$$

where all the characteristic roots of J_1 have absolute value less than 1. Then $J_1^t \to 0$ as $t \to \infty$. This implies that N_1 exists such that $|x_1(0)| < \zeta$

and $t > N_1$ implies $|x_1(t)| < \frac{1}{2}\varepsilon$. In the same way $|x_2(T)| < \zeta$ implies there is N_2 such that $|x_2(t)| < \frac{1}{2}\varepsilon$ for $t < T - N_2$. Therefore, N may be chosen to be the maximum of r, N_1, and N_2.

Since the equality in (1) is realized for any path $\{y(t)\}$ which lies on F, and $\mu = u^*$, we have, for $y(t) = (u(t), k(t), -k(t-1))$,

$$\sum_{t=1}^{s} u(t) + p \cdot k(s) - p \cdot k(0) = su^*. \tag{7}$$

Suppose $\{y(t)\}$ is generated according to (6) by a sequence of activity vectors $\{x(t)\}$ in the interior of X. Consider a modified sequence defined by $x'(t) = x(t) + \alpha q(i, t)$ for $t = 0, \ldots, \varepsilon_i$, $x'(t) = x(t)$, otherwise, where $q(i, 0), \ldots, q(i, \varepsilon_i)$ are the columns of Q corresponding to the quasi-diagonal block L_i. As we have seen, for small α, $x'(t) \in \text{int } X$ and generates a path on F, since $\bar{A}q(i, 0) = 0$, $\bar{B}q(i, 0) = \bar{A}q(i, 1), \ldots$, $\bar{B}q(i, \varepsilon_i - 1) = \bar{A}q(i, \varepsilon_i)$, and $\bar{B}q(i, \varepsilon_i) = 0$. Then $k'(0) = k(0)$ and $k'(\varepsilon_t + 1') = k(\varepsilon_t + 1)$. Moreover, by (7) $\sum_{t=1}^{\varepsilon_i} u(t') + p \cdot k(\varepsilon_i + 1) - p \cdot k(0) = \varepsilon_i u^*$, so

$$\sum_{t=1}^{\varepsilon_i} u(t') = \sum_{t=1}^{\varepsilon_i} u(t).$$

The introduction of solutions associated with the L_i makes no difference to the utility sum after the transient fluctuation in capital stocks has passed. Thus maximizing utility in choosing a path on F will not eliminate the arbitrary element due to an L_i block. By the same type of argument it has already been shown that modification of $\{x(t)\}$ by $q(1)$ has no effect on utility, where $q(1)$ spans a common null space of $\bar{A}$ and $\bar{B}$ on E_r. The same considerations indicate that the effects of cyclic modifications of $x(t)$ will cancel out over a full cycle. Thus in the absence of specific initial conditions the result of Lemma 4 is as definite an asymptotic result as we can reach for paths on F.

In order to prove an asymptotic result for arbitrary optimal paths by means of Theorem 1 and Lemma 4, we must show that a path $\{y(t)\}$ which lies near the von Neumann facet F must also lie near a path $\{y'(t)\}$ satisfying the conditions of Lemma 4. We prove

Lemma 5 Let $\{y(t)\}$, $t = 1, \ldots, T$, be a production path in Y. Let $\{y'(t)\}$ be defined by $y'(t) = \begin{bmatrix} B \\ -A \end{bmatrix} x'(t)$, where $\{x'(t)\}$ satisfies (6') for

$t = 1, \ldots, T$. For any $T \geqslant 1$, $\delta > 0$, there is an $\varepsilon > 0$ such that if $d(y(t), F) < \varepsilon$ for all t, then there is a sequence $\{y(t')\}$ where $|y(t) - y(t')| < \delta$ for $t = 1, \ldots, T$.

In the general case, a difficulty arises in proving this lemma that does not occur when $\bar{A}$ and $\bar{B}$ both possess inverses. Thus it would not be possible simply to appeal to the analogous lemma proved for the generalized Leontief model in my former chapter (1963). The difficulty is that $\bar{B}x = \bar{A}w$ may have no solution in w for some choices of x. The corresponding formula for the normalized matrices is $\bar{B}_1 Q^{-1} x = \bar{A}_1 Q^{-1} w$. The obstacle to a solution arises when there is a row of $\bar{B}_1$ which contains a non-zero element while the same row of $\bar{A}_1$ is zero throughout. This may happen in two cases. First, it holds for the last row of any L_i' block. Thus if a solution is to exist for w, it is necessary that $(Q^{-1}x)_s = 0$ if the sth column is a last column of an L_i' block. The second case arises for the last row of an N_i block. It is also necessary that $(Q^{-1}x)_s = 0$ if the sth column is the last column of an N_i block.

Proof of Lemma 5   By the fact that $d(y(t), F) < \varepsilon$, $y'(1)$ which satisfies $|y(1) - y'(1)| < \delta$ can be found by putting $\varepsilon = \delta$. Suppose a sequence $\{y'_{\tau-1}(t)\}$ can be found for any δ_1 for $t = 1, \ldots, \tau - 1$, where $\tau - 1 < T$, and $|y(t) - y'_{\tau-1}(t)| < \delta_1$ for each t. To prove the lemma we must show that this implies that a sequence $\{y'_\tau(t)\}$ also exists with $|y(t) - y'_\tau(t)| < \delta$ for $t = 1, \ldots, \tau$. Let $\{y'(t)\}$ be defined for $t = 1, \ldots, \tau - 1$, and choose ε so that $|y(t) - y'(t)| < \delta_1$ for $t < \tau$. Let $y'(\tau - 1) = (u'(\tau + 1), k'(\tau - 1), -k'(\tau - 2))$. Then

$$\begin{pmatrix} k'(\tau - 1) \\ 1 \end{pmatrix} = \bar{B}x'(\tau - 1).$$

Assume $(Q^{-1}x'(\tau - 1))_s = 0$ for all s such that the sth column of $\bar{A}_1 + \lambda\bar{B}_1$ intersects the last $T - \tau + 1$ columns of submatrices L_i' or N_i when these columns are present. We will say that such an $x'(\tau - 1)$ is feasible. Then $P\begin{pmatrix} k'(\tau-1) \\ 1 \end{pmatrix}$ lies in the subspace spanned by the columns of $\bar{A}_1$. Therefore, there exists $x'(\tau)$ such that $\begin{pmatrix} k'(\tau-1) \\ 1 \end{pmatrix} = P^{-1}\bar{A}_1 Q^{-1}x'(\tau) = \bar{A}x'(\tau)$. We define $y'(\tau) = \begin{bmatrix} B \\ -A \end{bmatrix}x'(\tau)$.

Assume $d(y(\tau), F) < \varepsilon$. Then there is $y \in F$ for which $|y - y(\tau)| < \varepsilon$ and $y = \begin{bmatrix} B \\ -A \end{bmatrix}x$. Let $y = (u, k', -k)$ and $y(\tau) = (u(\tau), k(\tau), -k(\tau - 1))$. Then $|k(\tau - 1) - k| < \varepsilon$, so $|k'(\tau - 1) - k| < \varepsilon + \delta_1$. By the continuity of the linear transformation defined by A, for $k'(\tau - 1)$ near k, we may choose $x'(\tau)$ near x. In turn this implies $y'(\tau)$ near y, using the definition of $y'(\tau)$. This shows that ε and δ_1 may be chosen, which is to say, ε may be chosen, so that $|y'(\tau) - y(\tau)| < \delta$. Notice also that the definition of $x'(\tau)$ implies that $(Q^{-1}x'(\tau))_s = 0$ for all s such that sth column intersects the last $T - \tau$ columns of submatrices L'_i or N_i, when these columns are present. Thus if a sequence $\{y'_{\tau-1}(t)\}$ can be found for any $\delta_1 > 0$ and if $x'(\tau - 1)$ is feasible, a sequence $\{y'_\tau(t)\}$ can be found and $x'(\tau)$ can be chosen to be feasible. It only remains to show that $x'(1)$ can be chosen to be feasible for any $T > 0$.

Let $y(t) = (u(t), k(t), -k(t-1))$, $t = 1, \ldots, T$. In the way described earlier, the proximity of $y(1)$ to F allows the choice of $y = (u, k^\Delta, -k) \in F$ such that k is near $k(0)$ and k^Δ is near $k(1)$, where $\begin{pmatrix} k \\ 1 \end{pmatrix} = \bar{A}x$, $\begin{pmatrix} k^\Delta \\ 1 \end{pmatrix} = \bar{B}x$. Then the proximity of $y(2)$ to F allows the choice of $y' = (u', k'^\Delta, -k')$ so that k' is near $k(1)$, and k'^Δ is near $k(2)$, where $\begin{pmatrix} k' \\ 1 \end{pmatrix} = \bar{A}x'$, and $\begin{pmatrix} k'^\Delta \\ 1 \end{pmatrix} = \bar{B}x'$, and so forth. Although $\begin{pmatrix} k^\Delta \\ 1 \end{pmatrix}$ may not be expressible by $\bar{A}z$ for any z, $\begin{pmatrix} k' \\ 1 \end{pmatrix}$ is so expressed with $z = x'$. Moreover, k^Δ is near k', since both are near $k(1)$. Let us refer to an L'_i block or an N_i block as an infeasible block. The components of $w^\Delta = P\begin{pmatrix} k^\Delta \\ 1 \end{pmatrix}$ which correspond to the last rows of infeasible blocks can be made as small as we like through making $(k^\Delta - k(1))$ small. Suppose a component w_i^Δ is large relative to the approximation of w^Δ to $w(1) = P\begin{pmatrix} k(1) \\ 1 \end{pmatrix}$, where $(\bar{A}_1 z)_i = \delta$ implies $(\bar{B}_1 z)_j = \delta$ and the jth row of $\bar{A}_1$ is zero. That is, the ith component of w^Δ corresponds to the next to last row of an infeasible block. Since k^Δ is near k', w^Δ is near w' and $w_j'^\Delta$ is large relative to the approximation of w'^Δ to $w(2) = P\begin{pmatrix} k(2) \\ 1 \end{pmatrix}$. But this contradicts $k(2)$ near k'' where $\begin{pmatrix} k'' \\ 1 \end{pmatrix}$ is expressible as $\bar{A}x''$, for some x''. Continuing this argument until $t = T$, if necessary, it must be that by the choice of ε the absolute value of a component of $w = P\begin{pmatrix} k^\Delta \\ 1 \end{pmatrix}$ which corresponds to any of the last $T + 1$ rows of an infeasible block can be made as small as desired. These are the only components of w that can lead to a capital stock $k'(T)$ that is not expressible as $Ax'(T)$. We may term them the infeasible components. Not all components of w can be infeasible since w near $w(0)$, w^Δ and w' near $w(1)$, and so forth, would then imply $\left| \binom{k(T)}{1} \right|$ could be reduced below 1 by choosing ε small enough. We now choose $\binom{k'(0)}{1} = P^{-1}w'(0)$, where $w_i'(0) = w_i$ when the ith component is feasible and $w_i'(0) = 0$, otherwise. Then $x'(1)$ is chosen so that $(Q^{-1}x'(1))_j = 0$ if the jth column intersects one of the last T columns of an infeasible block, and $(Q^{-1}x'(1))_j = (Q^{-1}x)_j$, otherwise. Thus $\binom{k'(0)}{1} = P^{-1}A_1Q^{-1}x'(1)$ will hold. Since $x'(1)$ is feasible and $|x(1) - x'(1)|$, and therefore $|y(1) - y'(1)|$, can be made arbitrarily small, the induction is successfully begun. This completes the proof of Lemma 5.

We now have it that optimal paths of accumulation where the technology is given by Y will lie near the von Neumann facet F for all save a certain number N_1 of the total number of periods, given the initial and terminal capital stock vectors, regardless of the length of the path $T \geqslant N_1$. Also a path $\{y(t)\}$ which remains near enough to F for a number of periods T_1 will stay near a sequence $\{y'(t)\}$ of vectors whose associated $x'(t)$ satisfy $(6')$ during these periods. Finally, $\{y'(t)\}$ will stay near the subset W of F for all periods save initial and terminal sequences of length N_2 independent of T_1. This suggests that the production vector associated with an optimal path with assigned initial and terminal stocks can stay outside a given neighbourhood of W for no more than a fixed number of periods, however long the accumulation path may be. This is the substance of the second theorem.

Theorem 2 Let $\bar{y}(t) = (\bar{u}(t), \bar{k}(t), \bar{k}(t - 1))$. Suppose that $k(0)$ is expansible and $k(T)$ is not saturated. Then for any $\varepsilon > 0$, there is N such that if $\{\bar{y}(t)\}$, $t = 1, \ldots, T$, is associated with an optimal path $\{\bar{k}(t)\}$ with initial and terminal stocks equal to $k(0)$ and $k(T)$, then $d(W, \bar{y}(t)) > \varepsilon$ for not more than N periods. N depends upon ε.

Proof The proof requires assembling the results of Theorem 1, Lemma 4, and Lemma 5. We may fix N_1 according to Theorem 1 so that $d(F, \bar{y}(t)) \geqslant \delta$ for no more than N_1 periods, where δ is a positive number which may be chosen arbitrarily small and N_1 depends on δ. From the proof of Theorem 1 we see that N_1 may be chosen so that during the remaining $T - N_1$ periods, $|\bar{k}(t)| \leqslant \zeta$ also holds.

By Lemma 5 for any $N_2 \geqslant 0$ and $\varepsilon > 0$ there is a $\delta > 0$ such that $d(F, \bar{y}(t)) < \delta$ for N_2 (or fewer) consecutive periods ensures that there is a sequence $\{y'(t)\}$ for these periods where $y'(t) = \begin{bmatrix} B \\ -A \end{bmatrix} x'(t)$ and

$(x'(t), x'(t+1))$ satisfies $(6')$ for all pairs of immediate successors, and $|\bar{y}(t) - y'(t)| < \frac{1}{2}\varepsilon$ for each t.

By Lemma 4 for any $\varepsilon > 0$ there is N_3 such that during any consecutive sequence of periods $d(W, y'(t)) < \frac{1}{2}\varepsilon$ for all t except N_3 periods at the beginning and end of the sequence. Select $N_2 > 2N_3$. Suppose $d(F, y(t)) < \delta$ holds from period t_1 to period t_2. Then $d(W, y'(t)) < \frac{1}{2}\varepsilon$ provided that there is $\tau_1 \geqslant t_1$ and $\tau_2 \leqslant t_2$ and $\tau_1 + N_3 < t < \tau_2 - N_3$. Thus for such t, $d(W, y(t)) < \varepsilon$. But appropriate τ_1, τ_2 exist for all t which satisfy $t_1 + N_3 < t < t_2 - N_3$. Consequently $d(W, y(t)) < \varepsilon$ must hold for all periods in a sequence of periods between times when $d(F, y(t)) \geqslant \delta$ except for $2N_3$ periods in the sequence. But the number of such sequences cannot exceed $N_1 + 1$. Thus an upper bound on the number of periods when $d(W, y(t)) > \varepsilon$ can hold is $2N_3(N_1 + 1)$. We may take N to be this number. Note that for any ε an N_3 may be chosen, and for any N_3 an N_2 may be chosen. Then for N_2 and ε, there is an appropriate δ from which N_1 may be determined. Thus there is N for any arbitrary $\varepsilon > 0$, and the theorem is proved.

20.4   Efficiency Prices

In order to prove the existence of infinite optimal paths we must derive the efficiency prices which are associated with an optimal program according to the theory of activity analysis. The goal of the program is the maximization of $\sum_{t=1}^{T} u(t)$ given $k(0)$ and $k(T)$, where $y(t) = (u(t), k(t), -k(t-1)) \in Y$.

Let $E(t)$ be an $n+1$ dimensional Euclidean space with a basis whose first component represents a quantity of utility and whose remaining n components represent stocks of goods. For example, $(u, k') \in E(t)$, and $(0, -k) \in E(t)$. Let $E = \prod_{t=0}^{T} E(t)$. E is the Cartesian product of the $E(t)$. Thus $z = \prod_{t=0}^{T} z(t) \in E$ where $z(t) \in E(t)$ for $t = 0, \ldots, T$. Write

$$z((\tau)) = \prod_{t=0}^{T} z(t)$$

where $z(t) = 0$ for $t \neq \tau$. We may write $z(t) = (z_u(t), z_k(t))$. We will say $y = (u, k', -k) \in Y$ corresponds to $(z(t), z(t-1))$ when $z(t) = (u, k')$ and $z(t-1) = (0, -k)$. Define the intertemporal production set $Y((t)) = \{z((t)) + z((t-1)) \mid y \in Y \text{ and } y \text{ corresponds to } (z(t), z(t-1))\}$.   Let $Y_T = \sum_{t=0}^{T} Y((t))$. Define the feasible set $Z = \{z \in Y_T \mid z(0) = (0, z_k(0)), z_k(0) \geqslant -k(0), z_k(t) \geqslant 0, t = 1, \ldots, T-1, z_k(T) \geqslant k(T)\}$. Suppose $Z \neq \emptyset$.

We wish to consider a point $\bar{z} \in Z$ such that $\sum_{t=1}^{T} \bar{z}_u(t)$ is maximal over Z. The existence of such a point is guaranteed if Z is bounded above in $z_u(t)$. However, this is easily seen by use of Assumption III. We also define a preferred set

$$B = \left\{ z \in E \middle| \sum_{t=1}^{T} z_u(t) > \sum_{t=1}^{T} \bar{z}_u(t), z_k(0) \geqslant -k(0), z_k(t) \geqslant 0 \text{ for} \right.$$
$$\left. t = 1, \ldots, T - 1, z_k(T) \geqslant k(T) \right\}.$$

Suppose $z' \in Y_T \cap B$. Then by the definitions of B and Z, $z' \in Z$. Moreover $\sum_{t=1}^{T} z'_u(t) > \sum_{t=1}^{T} z_u(t)$, which contradicts the maximality of $\bar{z}$ in Z. Therefore, no such point z' can exist.

Both Y_T and B are convex sets. By the Minkowski separation theorem there is a vector $\bar{q} \in E$ and a real number μ such that $\bar{q} \cdot z > \mu$ for $z \in B$ and $\bar{q} \cdot z \leqslant \mu$ for $z \in Y_T$. Write $\bar{q}(t) = (\bar{q}_u(t), \bar{q}_k(t))$. Since $z_k(t)$ is unbounded above for $z \in B$, it must be that $\bar{q}(t) \geqslant 0$. Let $\bar{B}$ be the closure of B. Since $\bar{z} \in \bar{B} \cap Y_T$, $\bar{q} \cdot \bar{z} = \mu$. Also $\bar{q}_u(t) = \alpha$, a given number, for all t. Otherwise, there would be points $z \in B$ near $\bar{z}$ with $\bar{q} \cdot z < \mu$. We choose $\bar{q}$ and μ so that $\alpha = 1$.

Any $z \in Y_T$ may be expressed $\sum_{t=1}^{T}(z((t)) + z((t-1)))$, where $z((t)) + z((t-1)) \in Y((t))$. Let $\mu(t) = \bar{q}((t)) \cdot \bar{z}((t)) + \bar{q}((t-1)) \cdot \bar{z}((t-1))$. Then $\mu = \sum_{t=1}^{T} \mu(t)$. Also $\bar{q}((t)) \cdot z((t)) + \bar{q}((t-1)) \cdot z((t-1)) \leqslant \mu(t)$ for all $z((t)) + z((t-1)) \in Y((t))$. But $z((t)) + z((t-1)) \in Y((t))$ is equivalent to $y \in Y$ where $y = (u, k', -k)$ and $z(t) = (u, k')$, $z(t-1) = (0, -k)$. Therefore, replacing $\bar{q}_k$ by $\bar{p}$, we have

$$u + \bar{p}(t) \cdot k' - \bar{p}(t-1) \cdot k \leqslant \mu(t)$$
$$\bar{u}(t) + \bar{p}(t) \cdot \bar{k}(t) - \bar{p}(t-1) \cdot \bar{k}(t-1) = \mu(t), \quad t = 1, \ldots, T, \tag{8}$$

for any $(u, k', -k) \in Y$. In (8) we have taken $\bar{z}(t)_k = 0$, $t = 1, \ldots, T-1$. This is permissible by the assumption of free disposal. Thus we have proved

Lemma 6 Let $\{\bar{y}(t)\}$ be an optimal path of T periods where $\bar{y}(t) = (\bar{u}(t), \bar{k}(t), -\bar{k}(t-1))$, $\bar{k}(0) \leqslant k(0)$, and $\bar{k}(T) \geqslant k(T)$. Then there exists a sequence of prices of goods $\bar{p}(t)$ and real numbers $\mu(t)$ such that (8) is satisfied for all $y = (u, k', -k) \in Y$.

We will refer to $\{\bar{p}(t)\}$ as a sequence of efficiency prices for the optimal sequence $\{\bar{y}(t)\}$.

It is convenient (though not essential) for the subsequent argument to have infinite price sequences for infinite production paths. Consider an infinite production path $\{y(t)\}$, $y(t) = (u(t), k(t), -k(t-1))$, $t = 1$, $2, \ldots$, every initial segment of which is an optimal finite path given the terminal stock vector of the segment. By Lemma 6 there is for each initial segment a sequence of efficiency prices which satisfy (8). An infinite path with optimal initial segments will be said to have finite optimality. We may prove

Lemma 7 (Malinvaud, 1953; 1962) Suppose $\{y(t)\}$, $t = 1, 2, \ldots$, is a production path that has finite optimality. If the associated efficiency prices are bounded over all initial segments, there is a price sequence $\{p(t)\}$, $t = 0, 1, \ldots$, whose initial segments are efficiency prices for the initial segments of $\{y(t)\}$.

Proof Let $\{y_T(t)\}$ and $\{p_T(t)\}$ be an initial segment of $\{y(t)\}$ terminating at $y(T)$ and an associated sequence of efficiency prices. There is a sequence $\{\mu_T(t)\}$ associated with $\{p_T(t)\}$ satisfying (8). Moreover, $\mu_T(t)$ is bounded over t and T, since $p_T(t)$ is bounded, and also $y(t)$ is bounded by Assumption III. Consider the sequence $\{p_T(0)\}$, $T = 1, 2, \ldots$. Since $p_T(0)$ is bounded, there is a convergent subsequence $p(0)_{T_i} \to p(0)$, where $i = 1, 2, \ldots$, and $T_{i_1} > T_{i_2}$ for $i_1 > i_2$. Then there is a further subsequence of $\{p_{T_i}(0)\}$ that we may write $\{p_{T_j}(0)\}$, $j = i_1$, $i_2, \ldots$, with $p_{T_j}(0) \to p(0)$, $p_{T_j}(1) \to p(1)$, and $\mu_{T_j} \to \mu(1)$. Continuing this procedure we derive infinite sequences $\{p(t)\}$, $t = 0, 1, \ldots$, and $\{\mu(t)\}$, $t = 1, 2, \ldots$. By continuity these sequences satisfy (8) with $y(t) = (u(t), k(t), -k(t-1))$. Thus the initial segments of $\{p(t)\}$ give efficiency prices for the initial segments of $\{y(t)\}$.

20.5 Existence of Optimal Paths

In a model with a transformation set Y that is not strictly convex it is necessary to weaken the Atsumi-Weizsacker definition of optimality. Let $\{y(t)\}$, $t = 1, 2, \ldots$, $y(t) = (u(t), k(t), -k(t-1))$, be an infinite production sequence. We will say that $\{y(t)\}$ is optimal if the following in true: Let $\{y'(t)\}$, $t = 1, 2, \ldots$, $y'(t) = (u'(t), k'(t), -k'(t-1))$, be any other production path where $k'(0) = k(0)$. Then for any $\varepsilon > 0$ there is T such that $t > T$ implies $\sum_{t=1}^{T}(u'(t) - u(t)) < \varepsilon$. This weakening does not seem to be significant unless the utility function is merely ordinal. However, the fact that we sum utilities over time implies that the utility function is defined except for an affine transformation, and thus it is not merely ordinal.

Even with the weaker criterion of optimality infinite optimal paths will not always exist in our model. A deep reason for this failure seems to be the fact that some points of W may have "larger" terminal stocks than others, so that it is worthwhile to go from the point with 'larger' stocks to another. But this may not be possible on F. Then the closer the transition hugs F the better it may be, and the longer it will take. Thus there will be an infinite sequence of paths each better than the last, while the limit path never leaves the initial point and is the worst path of all. Gale has given examples that fit this description. To avoid the difficulty we will assume

(V)   The set $W = \{y^*\}$.

In other words, the set W is a unique von Neumann point on F. This means that in the block diagonal canonical form of $\bar{B} - \lambda\bar{A}$ there are no L blocks and no blocks $J_{ij} + \lambda I$ where $|\lambda_j| = 1$ and $\lambda_j \neq 1$. Moreover, 1 is a simple root of $\bar{A}_J^{-1}\bar{B}_J$. Then $\bar{A}_J^{-1}\bar{B}_J$ is a Frobenius matrix by the definition of Uzawa (1961).

In order to use Lemma 7, it will be necessary to bound the efficiency prices associated with any infinite production sequence whose initial segments are optimal. This will require a slightly stronger version of Assumption IV. Let us say that k is a subsistence stock if there is $(u, k', -k) \in Y$ and there is no $(u', k'', -\alpha k) \in Y$ for $\alpha < 1$. The revised assumption is

(IV')   With respect to the transformation set Y, k^* is expansible, not saturated, and not a subsistence stock.

In addition to IV' we will need a direct corollary of Theorem 2,

Lemma 8   Any infinite path which is finitely optimal converges to W.

Proof   Suppose $\{y(t)\}$, $t = 1, 2, \ldots$, is finitely optimal and does not converge to W. Then there is $\varepsilon > 0$ and $d(y(t), W) > \varepsilon$ for $t = t_1, t_2, \ldots$, where the t_i are all distinct. But by Theorem 2, there is N such that $d(y(t), W) > \varepsilon$ for no more than N periods for a finite optimal path $\{y(t)\}$, $t = 1, 2, \ldots, T$. If $T > t_N$, there is a contradiction, so $d(y(t), W) \to 0$ as the lemma asserts.

As a consequence of Lemma 8, it is sufficient to bound the efficiency prices in some neighborhood of W, that is, in view of Assumption V, in some neighborhood of y^*. This is proved in

Lemma 9   There are $\eta > 0$ and $\bar{p} \geqslant 0$ such that $d(y^*, \bar{y}) < \eta$,

$\bar{y} \in Y$, $\bar{y} = (\bar{u}, \bar{k}', -\bar{k})$, and

$$u' + p' \cdot k' - p \cdot k \leqslant \mu \tag{8'}$$

$\bar{u} + p' \cdot \bar{k}' - p \cdot \bar{k} = \mu$, for all $(u', k', -k) \in Y$,

imply $p' < \bar{p}$.

Proof Suppose the lemma is false. Then there is a sequence

$$(p'(s), p(s), \mu(s)), \quad s = 1, 2, \ldots,$$

that satisfies (8') with $\bar{y}$ replaced by $y(s) = (u(s), k'(s), -k(s))$ where $y(s) \to y^*$ and $|p'(s)| \to \infty$. But by Assumption IV' there is a point $y^\Delta \in Y$ where $y^\Delta = (u^\Delta, k^\Delta, -k^*)$ and $k^\Delta > k^*$. Then $u^\Delta + p'(s) \cdot k^\Delta - p(s) \cdot k^* \leqslant \mu(s)$ must hold. Let $q(s) = (1, p'(s), p(s), \mu(s))$ and

$$q^\Delta(s) = q(s)/|q(s)|.$$

There is a subsequence $\{q^\Delta(r)\}$, $r = s_1, s_2, \ldots$, of $\{q^\Delta(s)\}$, such that $q^\Delta(r) \to q^\Delta = (q_u^\Delta, q_k'^\Delta, q_k^\Delta, \mu^\Delta)$. But q^Δ satisfies (8') when $\bar{y}$ is replaced by the limit y^* of the sequence $\{y(s)\}$, or

$$q_u^\Delta u^\Delta + q_k'^\Delta \cdot k^\Delta - q_k^\Delta \cdot k^* \leqslant \mu^\Delta$$

$$q_u^\Delta u^* + q_k'^\Delta \cdot k^* - q_k^\Delta \cdot k^* = \mu^\Delta.$$

Subtracting the second of these relations from the first, we obtain $q_u^\Delta(u^\Delta - u^*) + q_k'^\Delta \cdot (k^\Delta - k^*) \leqslant 0$. If $|q^\Delta(s)|$ is unbounded, $q_u^\Delta = 0$, $q_k'^\Delta \cdot (k^\Delta - k^*) \leqslant 0$. Since $q_k'^\Delta \geqslant 0$ and $(k^\Delta - k^*) > 0$, this implies that $q_k'^\Delta = 0$, and $q_k^\Delta \cdot k^* + \mu^\Delta = 0$. Then $q_k^\Delta \cdot k \geqslant q_k^\Delta \cdot k^* > 0$ must hold for all $k \geqslant 0$, where $(u, k', k) \in Y$. However, by Assumption IV' there is $(u, k', \alpha k^*) \in Y$ where $\alpha < 1$. This is a contradiction, since $q_k^\Delta \cdot \alpha k^* < q_k^\Delta \cdot k^*$. Thus $q(s)$ is bounded, which implies that $p'(s)$ is bounded and the lemma follows.

The final preparation needed for the proof that an infinite optimal path exists is to show that an infinite path exists that is finitely optimal.

Lemma 10   Assume that $k(0)$ is expansible. There is a path $\{y(t)\}$, $t = 1, 2, \ldots$, where $y(t) = (u(t), k(t), -k(t-1))$ and every initial segment of $\{y(t)\}$ is optimal.

Proof   Let $\{k(T)\}$, $T = 0, 1, \ldots$, be a sequence of stock vectors where $k(T) \to k^*$. According to Lemma 2, $\{k(T)\}$ may be chosen so that there exists a production path $\{y_T(t)\}$, $t = 1, \ldots, T$, for every $T \geqslant 1$ and $y_T(1) = (u(1), k(1), -k(0))$, $y_T(T) = (u(T), k(T), -k(T-1))$. Then by closure of Y, there is an optimal path of T periods between $k(0)$ and $k(T)$ for every $T \geqslant 1$. Since $\{y_T(0)\}$, $T = 1, 2, \ldots$, is bounded by Assumption III, there is a convergent subsequence $\{y_{T_s}(1)\}$, $s = 1, 2, \ldots$, say $y_{T_s}(1) \to \bar{y}(1)$. Then a subsequence of this sequence $\{y_{T_r}(0)\}$ may be chosen such that $y_{T_r}(2) \to \bar{y}(2)$. Continuing this selection, we may derive a sequence $\{\bar{y}(t)\}$, $t = 1, 2, \ldots$, where $\bar{y}(t) = (\bar{u}(t), \bar{k}(t), -\bar{k}(t-1))$ and $\bar{y}(t) \in Y$ for all t by closure of Y. Moreover, $\{\bar{y}(t)\}$, $t = 1, \ldots, T$ is the limit of a sequence of optimal T periods paths. Thus by closure of Y it is an optimal T period path, given the terminal stock $\bar{k}(T)$. The sequence $\{\bar{y}(t)\}$, $t = 1, 2, \ldots$, satisfies the conditions of the lemma.

We are now ready to prove the existence of an optimal path by the method of Gale.

Theorem 3 Under Assumptions I, II, III, IV', and V, if $k(0)$ is expansible, there is an infinite optimal path $\{\bar{y}(t)\}$,

$$\bar{y}(t) = (\bar{u}(t), \bar{k}(t), -\bar{k}(t-1)) \in Y, \quad \bar{k}(0) \leqslant k(0).$$

Proof We will show that a path $\{\bar{y}(t)\}$ that satisfies Lemma 10 is optimal. Let $\{y(t)\}$, $t = 1, 2, \ldots$, where $y(t) = (u(t), k(t), -k(t-1))$, be any other path in Y. By the proof of Theorem 2, if $d(y(t), y^*) > \varepsilon > 0$ for an infinite number of periods, $\sum_{t=1}^{T}(u(t) - u^*) \to -\infty$, as $T \to \infty$. On the other hand, Theorem 2 implies $\bar{y}(t) \to y^*$. Also, (4) implies that

$$\sum_{t=1}^{T}(\bar{u}(t) - u^*) \geqslant u' + u'' - (N_0 + N_1)u^*.$$

In this formula u' and N_0 are fixed independently of T. Let u be derived from $y' = (u, k', -k^*) \in Y$ where $k' > k^* \cdot y'$ exists by Assumption IV. Then for sufficiently large T, the convergence of $\bar{y}(t)$ to y^* will give $k' > \bar{k}(T)$. Thus N_1 may be chosen equal to 1, and $u'' = u$. This justifies $\sum_{t=1}^{T}(\bar{u}(t) - u^*) \geqslant u' + u - (N_0 + 1)u^*$ for all $T > T_1$, where T_1 is a fixed number. Thus infinite paths for which $\sum_{t=1}^{T}(u(t) - u^*) \to -\infty$ as $T \to \infty$ need not be considered, that is, it is sufficient to consider paths $\{y(t)\}$ where $y(t) \to y^*$.

By Lemma 9, we may apply Lemma 7 to obtain a sequence of goods prices $\{\bar{p}(t)\}$, $t = 0, 1, \ldots$, whose initial segments are efficiency prices for the initial segments of $\bar{y}(t)$. Then $\bar{p}(t)$ and $\bar{y}(t)$ satisfy relations (8) with some sequence of real numbers $\{\bar{u}(t)\}$. Summing the second relation, we obtain $\sum_{t=1}^{T} \bar{u}(t) = \bar{p}(0) \cdot \bar{k}(0) - \bar{p}(T) \cdot k(T) + \sum_{t=1}^{T} \bar{u}(t)$. Summing the first relation, we obtain $\sum_{t=1}^{T} u(t) \leqslant \bar{p}(0) \cdot k(0) - \bar{p}(T) \cdot k(T) + \sum_{t=1}^{T} \bar{u}(t)$. Therefore, subtracting the first sum from the second, we obtain $\sum_{t=1}^{T}(u(t) - \bar{u}(t)) \leqslant \bar{p}(T) \cdot (k(T) - \bar{k}(T))$. This inequality holds for every $T = 1, 2, \ldots$, and $|k(T) - \bar{k}(T)| \to 0$, as $T \to \infty$ by the fact that both sequences of stock vectors converge to k^*. Then for any $\varepsilon > 0$ there is N such that $\sum_{t=1}^{T}(u(t) - \bar{u}(t)) < \varepsilon$ for $T > N$, and $\{\bar{y}(t)\}$ is an optimal path by the definition we have adopted. Note from the proof of Theorem 3 that the set of infinite optimal paths is precisely the set of infinite paths that are finitely optimal.

Acknowledgments

The research on this chapter was begun at the Rochester Conference on Mathematical Models of Economic Growth, sponsored by the Social Science Research Council in the summer of 1964. It was continued at the Stanford Conference on Optimal Growth, sponsored by the Mathematical Social Science Board of the Center for Advanced Research in the Behavioral Sciences in the summer of 1965. In the course of my research I have benefited greatly from the advice of David Gale and Johannes Kemperman. During both the Conferences and in other periods my work was supported by the National Science Foundation.

Notes

1. If x is a vector in n dimensional Euclidean space, $|x| = \sum_{i=1}^{n} |x_i|$, where $|x_i|$ is the absolute value of x_i.

2. The idea of accumulating utility as a stock was suggested to me by a remark made by Roy Radner at the Cambridge Conference on Activity Analysis in the Theory of Growth and Planning sponsored by the International Economic Association in the summer of 1963.

3. The analysis of paths on the von Neumann facet found in this section was stimulated by a paper (1964) delivered to the Faculty Seminar of the Department of Economics of the University of Rochester by Michio Morishima. He in turn gives much credit for the stimulation of his ideas to Sir John Hicks.

4. F is minimal in the sense that it is the smallest facet of Y that contains all the von Neumann points of Y.

References

Atsumi, H. (1965) Neoclassical growth and the efficient program of capital accumulation. *Review of Economic Studies* 32, 127–36.

——— (1966) Efficient capital accumulation in open models. (Doctoral dissertation, University of Rochester.)

Gale, D. (1966) *On optimal development in a multi-sector economy.* (Mimeographed.)

Gantmakher, F. R. (1959) *Applications of the theory of matrices.* New York.

Koopmans, T. C. (1965) On the concept of optimal growth. In *Semaine d'Etude sur le Rôle de l'Analyse Econométrique dans la Formulation de Plans de Développement* 1ᵉ partie. (Pontificiae Academiae Scientiarum Scripta Varia, 28, i.)

Mirrlees, J. A. (1965) Optimum accumulation under uncertainty. (Mimeographed).

McKenzie, L. W. (1963) Turnpike theorems for a generalized Leontief model. *Econometrica* 31, 165–80.

——— (1967) Maximal paths in the von Neumann model. In E. Malinvaud and M. O. L. Bacharach (eds.) *Activity analysis in the theory of growth and planning,* chapter 2, London.

Malinvaud, E. (1953) Capital accumulation and efficient allocation of resources. *Econometrica* 21, 233–68.

——— (1962) Efficient capital accumulation: a corrigendum. *Econometrica* 30, 570–3.

Morishima, M. (1964) *Theory of growth: the von Neumann revolution.* (Institute for Mathematical Studies in the Social Sciences, Technical Report No. 130) Stanford.

Radner, R. (1961) Paths of economic growth that are optimal with regard only to final states: a turnpike theorem. *Review of Economic Studies* 28, 98–104.

Ramsey, F. P. (1928) A mathematical theory of savings. *Economic Journal* 38, 543–59.

Samuelson, P. A. & Solow, R. M. (1956) A complete capital model involving heterogeneous capital goods. *Quarterly Journal of Economics* 70, 537–62.

Uzawa, H. (1961) Causal indeterminacy of the Leontief input-output system *Kikan Riron Keizaigaku* 12, 49–59.

Weizsacker, C. C. von (1965) Existence of optimal programs of accumulation for an infinite time horizon. *Review of Economic Studies.*

Winter, S. G. Jr. (1965) Some properties of the closed linear model of production. *International Economic Review* 6, 199–210.

21 Capital Accumulation Optimal in the Final State

Lionel W. McKenzie

This chapter is concerned with capital accumulation in a closed linear model of production where the accumulation program is optimal with respect to the final stocks. This is the context of the so-called turnpike theory of Dorfman, Samuelson, and Solow [1], and the production model is that associated with the name of John von Neumann [11], as generalized by Gale [2] and Kemeny, Morgenstern, and Thompson [5]. A turnpike theorem for the von Neumann model was first proved by Radner [12]. It was shown by the author [6] that the general turnpike problem falls naturally into two parts, a convergence to a subset of the production set, which was called the von Neumann facet, and convergence on the facet, perhaps to a unique ray. A rather comprehensive treatment of convergence of optimal paths to the facet in polyhedral models was given by the author [7]. A theory for the general convex model, which is similar to the first part of this chapter, was developed, independently, by Movshovich [10].

The further convergence on the facet was discussed in the context of a generalized Leontief model by the author in the paper that introduced the idea [6]. The analogous theorem for a Ramsey problem where current consumption is in the utility function was later proved by the author for a general convex model [8]. A related result was obtained by Inada [4] for the von Neumann model with a terminal objective. In the present paper the previous results are extended and at the same time the method of proof is simplified. The mathematical theorem on the simultaneous reduction of two rectangular matrices to normal form which underlies the analysis of convergence on the facet may be found in Gantmacher [3].

21.1   The Production Model

The production model is given by a set Y of $2n$-tuples of real numbers which we will write $(-x, y)$. Here x and y are n-tuples of non-negative real numbers, and x_i is the quantity of the ith capital good in the initial stock of a period and y_i is the quantity of the ith capital good in the terminal stock. If Ω_n is the positive orthant of the Euclidean space E_n, $(-x, y) \in -\Omega_n x \Omega_n \subset E_n^2$ or $E_n x E_n$. When $(-x, y) \in Y$ holds, the transformation of the initial stock represented by x into the terminal stock represented by y is compatible with the technology available over a period of given duration. We assume

Y1 Y is a closed convex cone with vertex at the origin. $Y \subset (-\Omega_n x \Omega_n)$.

Y2   There is $(-x, y) \in Y$ such that $y > 0$.

Y3 $(-x, y) \in Y$ and $x = 0$ implies $y = 0$.

Y4 $(-x, y) \in Y$ implies $(-w, z) \in Y$ for $w \geqq x, 0 \leqq z \leqq y$.

21.2   The Comparison Paths

An accumulation path is a sequence of input-output combinations $(-x^t, y^t)$, $t = 1, 2, \ldots, T$, where $x^t \leqq y^{t-1}$. We are concerned with T-period paths that start from a certain initial stock y^0 and reach a final stock y^T. In view of Y4, the accumulation path may also be characterized by the output sequence $\{y^t\}$, $t = 1, 2, \ldots, T$, and the initial stock y^0.

For the valuation of terminal stocks we postulate a homothetic preference relation R on Ω_n. Let $S_n = \{z \mid z_i \geqq 0 \text{ and } \sum_{i=1}^n z_i = 1\}$. We assume

R1 R is transitive and complete, i. e. xRy and yRz imply xRz, and for any $x, y \in \Omega_n$ either xRy or yRx, or both.

R2 R is homothetic, i. e. xRy implies $\alpha x R \alpha y$ for any $x, y \in \Omega_n$ and $\alpha > 0$.

R3   There is $x \in \Omega_n$ such that $0Rx$ does not hold.

R4   If $0Rx$ does not hold, for any $y \in S_n$ there is $\beta > 0$ such that $\beta x R y$.

These assumptions allow us to define a utility function $u(z)$ on Ω_n such that xRy if and only if $u(x) \geqq u(y)$. Choose $\tilde{x}$ such that $0R\tilde{x}$ does not hold. Define $u(z)$ by $u(z) = \inf \beta$ such that $\beta \tilde{x} R z$ holds.

We define a maximal rate of balanced growth α_i for the ith stock by $\alpha_i = \sup \beta$ such that there is $(-x, y) \in Y$ and $y \geq \beta x$, $y_i > 0$. Let I be a subset of indices $I \subset \{1, \ldots, n\}$. It is immediate to prove

Lemma 1 Let $\alpha(I) = \min \alpha_i$ for $i \in I \neq \Phi$. Then for any $\beta < \alpha(I)$, there is $(-x, y) \in Y$ such that $y \geq \beta x$ and $y_i > 0$ for $i \in I$.

Proof By definition of α_i, for any $\varepsilon > 0$, there is $(-x^i, y^i) \in Y$ such that $y^i \geq (\alpha - \varepsilon)x^i$ and $y_i^i > 0$. Let $(-x, y) = \sum_{i \in I}(-x^i, y^i)$. Then $y = \sum_{i \in I} y^i \geq \sum_{i \in I}(\alpha_i - \varepsilon)x^i \geq [\alpha(I) - \varepsilon]\sum_{i \in I} x^i = [\alpha(I) - \varepsilon]x$.

Now define $\alpha = \max \alpha(I)$ over all $I \subset \{1, \ldots, n\}$ such that there is y with $y_i = 0$ for $i \notin I$ and $u(y) > 0$. There is no loss of generality in assuming

Y5 $y^0 > 0$.

A comparison path is defined for some $\beta \leq \alpha$. By definition of α, for any β, $0 < \beta < \alpha$, there is $x^1 \neq 0$ such that $(-x^1, y^1) \in Y$ and $y^1 = \beta x^1$. Moreover, $u(x^1) > 0$. We may choose $x^1 \leq y^0$. Then in the tth period the input-output combination along the comparison path is $\beta^{t-1}(-x^1, y^1) = (-x^t, y^t)$. There may, or may not, exist a comparison path for $\beta = \alpha$.

21.3 The Valuation Ceilings

An optimal T-period path starting from initial stocks y^0 is a path from y^0 reaching stocks y^t in T periods such that $u(y^T) \geq u(z^T)$ for any path $z^0, \ldots, z^T$, of T periods with $z^0 = y^0$. It is clear that $u(y^T) \geq u(z^T)$ must hold, in particular, when $z^0, \ldots, z^T$ is a comparison path.

Let $I_\alpha = \{i \mid \alpha_i \leq \alpha\}$. A critical result for establishing the valuation ceilings is

Lemma 2 For any $\beta > \alpha$, there is $p \in S_n$ such that $\beta p \cdot x \geq p \cdot y + \varepsilon$, for some $\varepsilon > 0$, for all $(-x, y) \in Y$ for which $\sum_{i \in I_\alpha} x_i = 1$. Also $p_i > \varepsilon$ for $i \in I_\alpha$, and $\beta p \cdot x \geq p \cdot y$ for all $(-x, y) \in Y$.

Proof Define a reduced transformation set $Y_\alpha = \{(-x, y) \mid x_i = y_i = 0$ for $i \notin I_\alpha$, and there is $(-w, z) \in Y$ such that $x_i = w_i$, $y_i = z_i$ for $i \in I_\alpha\}$. Y_α is derived from Y by putting equal to 0 the inputs and outputs with indices outside I_α for processes in Y. The assumptions Y1–Y4 may be seen to hold for Y_α.

Let $\alpha_i' = \sup \beta$ such that there is a process $(-x, y) \in Y_\alpha$, and $y \geq \beta x$ where $y_i > 0$. It is clear that $\alpha_i' \geq \alpha_i$ for $i \in I_\alpha$, since a process $(-w, z)$ in

Y with $w_i \geqq \beta z_i$, for $i = 1, \ldots, n$, is represented by a process $(-x, y)$ in Y_α with $x_i = w_i \geqq \beta z_i = \beta y_i$, for all $i \in I_\alpha$. We will show that equality holds. Suppose, on the contrary, that $\alpha'_j > \alpha_j$ held for some $j \in I_\alpha$. Let $(-x', y') \in Y_\alpha$ where $y' \geqq \beta' x'$, $\beta' > \alpha_j$, $y'_j > 0$. Choose β' so that $\beta' < \alpha_i$ for all $i \notin I_\alpha$. We may suppose $I_\alpha \neq \{1, \ldots, n\}$, or else $Y = Y_\alpha$ and the result follows. Then by Lemma 1 there is $(-w, z) \in Y$ and $z \geqq \beta' w$ where $z_i > 0$ for all $i \notin I_\alpha$, $z_i = 0$ for $i \in I_\alpha$. Let $(-\tilde{x}, \tilde{y}) \in Y$ be a predecessor of $(-x', y') \in Y_\alpha$. Then $\tilde{y}_i \geqq \beta' \tilde{x}_i$, for $i \in I_\alpha$. Consider $(-w', z') \in Y$, where $w' = w + \gamma \tilde{x}$ and $z' = z + \gamma \tilde{y}$, $\gamma > 0$. For small γ, $z'_i > \alpha_j w'_i$, which contradicts the definition of α_j. Thus $\alpha'_i = \alpha_i$ for all $i \in I_\alpha$.

Let $\beta > \alpha$. Otherwise, β may be arbitrary. Define $C_\beta = \{z \mid z = y - \beta x$ for $(-x, y) \in Y_\alpha\}$. Let $E_\alpha = \{z \mid z \in E_n$ and $z_i = 0$ for $i \notin I_\alpha\}$. Y_α is the projection of Y on $E_\alpha \times E_\alpha$. Define $S_\alpha = S_n \cap E_\alpha$, and $\Omega_\alpha = \Omega_n \cap E_\alpha$. The definition of α implies that $C_\beta \cap \Omega_\alpha = \{0\}$, and $z = 0$ for $z \in C_\beta$ implies $z = y - \beta x$ where $x = y = 0$.

We will show that C_β is closed. Suppose not. Then there is $z^s \in C_\beta$ and $z^s \to z \notin C_\beta$, $s = 1, 2, \ldots$ Consider $\bar{z}^s = \frac{y^s}{|x^s|} - \beta \frac{x^s}{|x^s|} = y^s - \beta \bar{x}^s$. It is not possible that $\bar{y}^s$ is unbounded for that would provide an accumulation point of the sequence $\tilde{z}^s = \frac{\bar{y}^s}{|\bar{y}^s|} - \beta \frac{\bar{x}^s}{|\bar{y}^s|}$, say $\tilde{z} = \tilde{y} - \beta \tilde{x}$, where $\tilde{x} = 0$ in contradiction to Y3. Thus $\{\bar{z}^s\}$ lies in a compact set and there is an accumulation point $\bar{z} \in C_\beta$ by closure of Y. If $\bar{z} \neq 0$, $\frac{\bar{z}}{|\bar{z}|} = \frac{z}{|z|} \in C_\beta$, contradicting the hypothesis. Thus $\bar{z} = 0$. But $\bar{z} = \bar{y} - \beta \tilde{x}$, where $|\tilde{x}| = 1$ and $(-\tilde{x}, \bar{y}) \in Y_\alpha$. This contradicts the definition of Y_α. Thus C_β is closed.

Let $\bar{C}_\beta = \{z \mid z \in C_\beta$ and $z = y - \beta x$ for $x \in S_\alpha\}$. Then $\bar{C}_\beta \cap \Omega_\alpha = \Phi$. $\bar{C}_\beta$ is closed since S_α and C_β are closed, and $\bar{C}_\beta$ is bounded from Y3. By a separation theorem for closed convex cones there is $p \subset E_\alpha$ such that $p \cdot z \geqq 0$ for $z \in \Omega_\alpha$ and $p \cdot z < -\varepsilon < 0$ for $z \in \bar{C}_\beta$. By assumption Y4, $-S_\alpha \subset \bar{C}_\beta$. Thus $p_i > \varepsilon > 0$ for $i \in I_\alpha$. The condition $p \cdot z < -\varepsilon$ for $z \in \bar{C}_\alpha$ is equivalent to $p \cdot y - \beta p \cdot x \leqq 0$, for all $(x, y) \in Y_\alpha$ and $x \in S_\alpha$. Since $p_i = 0$ for $i \notin I_\alpha$, this implies that $p \cdot y - \beta p \cdot x \leqq 0$, for all $(-x, y) \in Y$ and $\leqq -\varepsilon$, when $\sum_{i \in I_\alpha} x_i = 1$.

When $\beta = \alpha$, it is simple to show

Lemma 3 There is $p \in S_n$ such that $\alpha p \cdot x \geqq p \cdot y$ for all $(-x, y) \in Y$.

Proof Let $C = \{z \mid z = y - \alpha x$ for $(-x, y) \in Y_\alpha\}$. The definition of α implies that $C \cap$ interior $\Omega_\alpha = \Phi$. Then by a separation theorem for convex sets there is $p \in E_\alpha$, $p \neq 0$, such that $p \cdot z \leqq \gamma$ for $z \in C$ and $p \cdot z \geqq \gamma$

for $z \in \Omega_\alpha$. Since $0 \in C \cap \Omega_\alpha$, $\gamma = 0$. Also $p_i = 0$ for $i \notin I_\alpha$ implies $p \cdot y - \alpha p \cdot x \leq 0$ for all $x, y \in Y$. However, it may not be possible to find p satisfying $p \cdot y - \alpha p \cdot x \leq 0$ where $p_i > 0$ for all $i \in I_\alpha$.

21.4   Convergence to a Facet

The asymptotic theorems on optimal T-period paths are proved by combining the comparison paths and the valuation ceilings. Three inequalities must be used. Let $\{\bar{y}^t\}$, $t = 1, \ldots, T$, be the optimal path. The first inequality is

$$\beta^T u(x^1) \leq u(\bar{y}^T), \text{ where } T \geq 1, x^1 \leq y^0, \beta \leq \alpha, \text{ and } u(x^1) > 0. \tag{1}$$

Lemma 1 provides for the existence of the comparison path for any $\beta < \alpha$. However, it may be that no such path exists for $\beta = \alpha$.

The second inequality relates utility to valuation. However, another assumption will be needed to strengthen $R4$. This is

R5   There is $\delta > 0$ such that $y \in S_n$ implies $u(y) < \delta \sum_{i \in I_\alpha} y_i$.

$R5$ is equivalent to the condition that $u(y)$ be bounded over all values of y_i, $i \notin I_\alpha$, given the values of y_i, $i \in I_\alpha$. With the aid of $R5$ we may prove

Lemma 4   Let $p \geq 0$ have $p_i > 0$ for all $i \in I_\alpha$. Then there is $\gamma > 0$ such that $u(y) - \gamma p \cdot y \leq 0$ for all $y \in \Omega_n$.

Proof   We choose γ such that $\gamma p_i > \delta$ for all $i \in I_\alpha$. Then $\gamma p \cdot y > \delta \sum_{i \in I_\alpha} y_i > u(y)$ for $y \in S_n$. This guarantees (2) for an appropriate choice of p.

Since we will be free to choose the length of p the second inequality may be written

$$u(y) - p \cdot y \leq 0, \text{ for all } y \in \Omega_n. \tag{2}$$

The third inequality establishes the valuation ceiling. It is

$$p \cdot y - \beta p \cdot x \leq 0, \text{ for any } (-x, y) \in Y, \text{ where } p_i > 0 \text{ for } i \in I_\alpha, \beta \geq \alpha \tag{3}$$

Lemma 2 provides (3) for any $\beta > \alpha$. In particular, we may apply (3) to the optimal path to obtain $p \cdot \bar{y}^T < \beta^T p \cdot y^0$.

Now take $\beta = \beta_1 < \alpha$ in (1) and $\beta = \beta_2 > \alpha$ in (3). Then p satisfying (3) with $\beta = \beta_2$ may be used in (2). With these substitutions the three inequalities may be applied to a comparison path $\{\beta^t x^1\}$, $t = 0, \ldots, T$, to give

$$\beta_1^T u(x^1) \leqq u(\bar{y}^T) \leqq p \cdot \bar{y}^T \leqq \beta_2^T p \cdot y^0. \tag{4}$$

These inequalities may be established for any $\beta_1 < \alpha < \beta_2$ with p such that $p_i > 0$ for $i \in I_\alpha$.

We will define a set of neighborhoods of comparison paths in Y within which the optimal path must lie most of the time for sufficiently long times of accumulation. Choose $0 < \delta < 1$, $0 < \Theta < 1$, both arbitrarily small. Then take ε so that $\frac{\alpha-\varepsilon}{\alpha+\varepsilon} > (1-\delta)^\Theta$. Choose p to satisfy (2) and (3) with $\beta = \alpha + \varepsilon$. The neighborhood is defined by $N(\Theta, \delta, \varepsilon, p)$ $= \{(-x, y) \mid (-x, y) \in Y$ and $p \cdot y \geqq (1-\delta)(\alpha+\varepsilon)p \cdot x\}$. With N so defined it follows that

Lemma 5 The neighborhood $N(\Theta, \delta, \varepsilon, p)$ contains any comparison path associated with $\beta \geqq \alpha - \varepsilon$.

Proof Let $(-x, y)$ satisfy $y \geqq \beta x$. Then $p \cdot y - (1-\delta)(\alpha + \varepsilon)p \cdot x \geqq p \cdot (\alpha - \varepsilon)x - (1-\delta)(\alpha+\varepsilon)p \cdot x \geqq p \cdot (\alpha - \varepsilon)x - (\alpha - \varepsilon)p \cdot x = 0$, using the inequality satisfied by ε.

The first asymptotic result is

Theorem 1 There is τ such that $T > \tau$ implies that an optimal path $\{y^T\}$, $t = 1, \ldots, T$, satisfies $(-y^t, y^{t+1}) \in N(\Theta, \delta, \varepsilon, p)$ for at least $(1 - \Theta)T$ periods. τ depends on Θ, δ, ε, and p.

The proof of Theorem 1 merely involves an application of inequalities (4) with a slight modification. When the path is outside the neighborhood $N(\Theta, \delta, \varepsilon, p)$, inequality (3) with $\beta = \alpha + \varepsilon$ is replaced by the inequality

$$p \cdot y - (1-\delta)(\alpha + \varepsilon)p \cdot x \leqq 0. \tag{5}$$

Then we obtain from the definition of Θ,

$$(\alpha - \varepsilon)^T u(x) \leqq u(\bar{y}^T) \leqq p \cdot \bar{y}^T \leqq (1-\delta)^{\Theta T}(\alpha + \varepsilon)^T p \cdot y^0. \tag{6}$$

It follows that $(1-\delta)^{\Theta T}\left(\frac{\alpha+\varepsilon}{\alpha-\varepsilon}\right)^T p \cdot x' \geqq u(x') > 0$ must hold for all $T > 0$. However, by choice of ε, $(1-\delta)^\Theta \frac{\alpha+\varepsilon}{\alpha-\varepsilon} < 1$. Thus for large T, the inequality (6) must be violated. This implies the existence of τ.

We define a cone P dual to Y. Let $P = \{(p,q) \mid p \cdot x \geqq q \cdot y$ for all $(-x, y) \in Y\}$. For any $(p,q) \in P$ a subset $F(p,q)$ of Y is defined by $F(p,q) = \{(-x, y) \mid (-x, y) \in Y$ and $p \cdot x = q \cdot y\}$. Consider a sequence of neighborhoods $\{N(s) = N[\Theta, \delta, \varepsilon(s), p(s)]\}$, where $\varepsilon(s) \to 0$, $s = 1$, $2, \ldots$ Let $[-x(s), y(s)]$ be the initial input-output combination of a comparison path for $N(s)$. In other words, $x(s) \leqq y^0$, $y(s) = (\alpha - \varepsilon^s)x(s)$, and $[-x(s), y(s)] \in Y$. Choose $x(s)$ so that $x_i(s) = y_i^0$ for some i. Then

Lemma 6 There are points of accumulation $\tilde{p}$ and $\tilde{x}$ of $\frac{p(s)}{|p(s)|}$ and $x(s)$, such that $(-\tilde{x}, \alpha\tilde{x}) \in F(\alpha\tilde{p}, \tilde{p})$.

Proof The existence of the accumulation points follows immediately since the sequences are bounded. Then $(-\tilde{x}, \alpha\tilde{x}) \in Y$, since Y is closed. Also $(\alpha + \varepsilon^s)p(s) \cdot x \geqq p(s) \cdot y$, from (3), implies $\alpha\tilde{p} \cdot x \geqq \tilde{p} \cdot y$ for any $(-x, y) \in Y$. Then $\alpha\tilde{p} \cdot \tilde{x} = \tilde{p} \cdot \alpha\tilde{x}$ implies $(-\tilde{x}, \alpha\tilde{x}) \in F(\alpha\tilde{p}, \tilde{p})$. We will write $F_\alpha(\tilde{p})$ for $F(\alpha\tilde{p}, \tilde{p})$.

Define $N(\delta, p) = \{(-x, y) \mid (-x, y) \in Y$ and $p \cdot y \geqq (1 - \delta)\alpha p \cdot x\}$. In the relative topology of Y, $N(\delta, \tilde{p})$ is a neighborhood of $F_\alpha(\tilde{p})$. We see that

Lemma 7 For any $\delta' > \delta$, there is a number $\sigma > 0$ such that $N[\Theta, \delta, \varepsilon(s), p(s)] \subset N(\delta', p)$ for $s > \sigma$.

Proof Consider normalized neighborhoods $\tilde{N}(s)$ where $(-x, y) \in \tilde{N}(s)$ implies $|x| = 1$. For small $\varepsilon(s)$, $(1 - \delta')\alpha < (1 - \delta)[\alpha + \varepsilon(s)] \leqq \frac{p(s) \cdot y}{p(s) \cdot x}$ when $(-x, y) \in \tilde{N}(s)$ and $p(s) \cdot x \neq 0$. But $\frac{p(s)}{|p(s)|} \to \tilde{p}$ implies that for large s, $(1 - \delta')\alpha\tilde{p} \cdot x < \tilde{p} \cdot y$ will hold for $(-x, y) \in \tilde{N}(s)$ and $\tilde{p} \cdot x \neq 0$. If $\tilde{p} \cdot x = 0$, then $\tilde{p} \cdot y = 0$ since $(\alpha\tilde{p}, \tilde{p}) \in P$, and again $(-x, y) \in N(\delta', \tilde{p})$. This completes the proof for $x \neq 0$. However, $x = 0$ implies $y = 0$ by Y3, and $(0, 0)$ lies in all the neighborhoods.

Define $P_\alpha = \{p \mid \alpha p \cdot x \geqq p \cdot y$ for all $(-x, y) \in Y\}$. If $p \in P_\alpha$, $(-x, \alpha x) \in Y$ implies $(-x, \alpha x) \in F_\alpha(p)$. Moreover, by Lemma 6 there is $(-x, \alpha x) \in Y$ where $x \neq 0$. Thus $\bigcap_{p \in P_\alpha} F_\alpha(p) = F_\alpha \neq \Phi$. Also,

Lemma 8 Let $p\varepsilon$ relative interior P_α. Then $F_\alpha = F_\alpha(p)$. We omit the proof, which is elementary.

In order to combine the ideas of Lemmas 7 and 8, we also need

Lemma 9 Let $p \in P_\alpha \cap S_n$. Then for any Θ, $0 < \Theta < 1$, and δ, $0 < \delta < 1$, there are sequences $\varepsilon(s) \to 0$ and $\frac{p(s)}{|p(s)|} \to p$ such that $N[\Theta, \delta, \varepsilon(s), p(s)]$ are well defined.

Proof Take $\varepsilon(1) > 0$ and let $\tilde{p}(1)$ be a price vector given by Lemma 2 such that (3) is satisfied with $\beta = \alpha + \varepsilon(1)$. Let $\tilde{p}(s) = \gamma_s \tilde{p}(1) + (1 - \gamma_s)p$, where $0 < \gamma_s \leqq 1$, and $\gamma_s \to 0$, $s = 1, 2, \ldots$ Define $\varepsilon(s) = \gamma_s \varepsilon(1)$. Then condition (3) is met since it is met by $p(1)$, $\varepsilon(1)$ and by $p, \varepsilon = 0$. Choose ζ_s large enough so that $p(s) = \zeta_s \tilde{p}(s)$ satisfies (2). This is possible since $p_i(s) > 0$ for $i \in I_\alpha$. Then $N(s) = N[\Theta, \delta, \varepsilon(s), p(s)]$ are the required neighborhoods.

We want to show that an optimal path that is long enough spends most of the time in an arbitrary neighborhood of F_α. We will refer to a neighborhood U of F_α in the relative Euclidean topology of Y as a homogeneous neighborhood if $(-x, y) \in U$ implies $\zeta(-x, y) \in U$ for any $\zeta \geqq 0$. Our result is

Theorem 2 For any Θ, $0 < \Theta < 1$, and any homogeneous neighborhood U of F_α, there is τ such that $T > \tau$ implies that an optimal path $\{\bar{y}^t\}$, $t = 1, \ldots, T$, satisfies $(-y^t, y^{t+1}) \in U$ for at least $(1 - \Theta)T$ periods. τ depends on Θ and U.

Proof It is sufficient to consider normalized vectors in F_α. Let $\tilde{F}_\alpha = \{(-x, y) \mid (-x, y) \in F_\alpha \text{ and } |x| = 1\}$. $\tilde{F}_\alpha$ is compact from Y1 and Y3. We may define normalized subsets $\tilde{Y}$ and $\tilde{U}$ of Y and U respectively in the same way. $\tilde{Y} \supset \tilde{U} \supset \tilde{F}_\alpha$, and $\tilde{U}$ is a neighborhood of $\tilde{F}_\alpha$ in the relative Euclidean topology of $\tilde{Y}$. Choose $p\varepsilon$ rel int P_α and $|p| = 1$. Then $\tilde{F}_\alpha = \tilde{F}_\alpha(p)$, by Lemma 8, where $\tilde{F}_\alpha(p)$ is a normalized cross-section of $F_\alpha(p)$. I claim that δ may be chosen so small that $\tilde{N}(\delta, p) \subset \tilde{U}$, where $\tilde{N}(\delta, p)$ is a normalized cross section of $N(\delta, p)$ for $|x| = 1$. Suppose not. Then there is a sequence $(-x^s, y^s) \in \tilde{N}(\delta^s, p)$ and $\notin \tilde{U}$ such that $\delta^s \to 0$ and $(-x^s, y^s) \to (-x, y)$. The latter follows from the fact that $N(\delta_s, p) \subset \tilde{N}(\delta, p)$ for $\delta^s < \delta$ and $\tilde{N}(\delta, p)$ is compact by Y1 and Y3. But then by definition of $\tilde{N}(\delta^s, p)$ and continuity of the inner product, $p \cdot y = \alpha p \cdot x$, so $(-x, y) \in \tilde{F}_\alpha$. Since $(-x, y) \notin \tilde{U}$, this is a contradiction of the hypothesis that $\tilde{U}$ is a neighborhood of $\tilde{F}_\alpha$.

By Lemma 9, there is a sequence of neighborhoods $\{\tilde{N}[\Theta, \delta', \varepsilon(s), p(s)]\}$ for any admissible Θ and δ' with $\varepsilon(s) \to 0$ and $\frac{p(s)}{|p(s)|} \to p$. By Lemma 7, for $\delta' < \delta$, there is σ such that $\tilde{N}[\Theta, \delta', \varepsilon(\sigma), p(\sigma)] \subset \tilde{N}(\delta, p)$. By Theorem 1, there is then τ such that $T > \tau$ implies that $(-\bar{y}^t, \bar{y}^{t+1}) \in N[\Theta, \delta', \varepsilon(\sigma), p(\sigma)]$ for at least $(1 - \Theta)T$ periods. But by homogeneity of these neighborhoods, this implies that $(-\bar{y}^t, \bar{y}^{t+1}) \in U$ for these periods.

It may happen that there are accumulation points $\tilde{p}$ and $\tilde{x}$ of sequences like those in Lemma 6 where $\tilde{p}_i > 0$ for $i \in I_\alpha$ and $u(\tilde{x}) > 0$. In this case ε may be set equal to 0. But $\varepsilon = 0$ allows the replacement of ΘT by a fixed number say $\tau > 0$. The new form of (6) is

$$\alpha^T u(\tilde{x}) \leqq u(\bar{y}^T) \leqq \gamma \tilde{p} \cdot \bar{y}^T \leqq (1 - \delta)^\tau \alpha^T \gamma \tilde{p} \cdot y^0. \tag{7}$$

Then we may prove

Theorem 3 If there is x such that $u(x) > 0$ and $(-x, \alpha x) \in Y$, and p such that $p_i > 0$ for $i \in I_\alpha$ and $p \in P_\alpha$, then for any homogeneous neighborhood U of F_α, there is $\tau > 0$ such that an optimal path $\{\bar{y}^t\}$, $t = 1$, $2, \ldots, T$, can remain outside U for no more than τ periods.

Proof It is clear that for large τ the inequalities (7) will be violated. Thus τ_1 exists such that $\bar{y}^t$ lies in $N(\delta, p)$ for all but τ_1 periods. Then the argument in the proof of Theorem 2 implies that $N(\delta, p) \subset U$ for δ sufficiently small.

21.5 Convergence on the Facet

Further convergence properties of optimal paths may be derived from convergence properties of arbitrary paths which lie on F_α. Let W be a set of rays from the origin that lie in F_α. We will say a path $\{y^t\}$, $t = 0$, $1, 2, \ldots, T$, is in F_α if $(-y^t, y^{t+1}) \in F_\alpha$ for all t. Assume

F1 For any homogeneous neighborhood V of W (in the relative topology of Y) there is a number $v > 0$ such that if $\{y^t\}$, $t = 0, 1, \ldots, T$, is a path in $F_\alpha(-y^t, y^{t+1}) \in V$ for all t such that $v < t < T - v$.

An assumption of this type will later be derived from our previous assumptions. We may prove, using F1,

Lemma 10 For any homogeneous neighborhood V of W, there is a neighborhood U of F_α and a number v such that if $\{y^t\}$, $t = 0, 1, \ldots, T$, is a path in U, $(-y^t, y^{t+1}) \in V$ for all t such that $v < t < T - v$.

Proof Let v be determined in accordance with F1. By homogeneity it is sufficient to consider paths $\{y^t\}$, $t = 0, 1, 2, \ldots, T$, where $|y^0| = 1$. Suppose that the lemma is false. Then we may select a sequence of paths $\{y^t(s)\}$, $s = 1, 2, \ldots$, of length T and neighborhoods U_s of F_α, such that $[-y^t(s), y^{t+1}(s)] \in U_s$, for each t, $U_s \subset U_{s-1}$, and $\bigcap U_s = F_\alpha$, but, for each s, $[-y^t(s), y^{t+1}(s)] \notin V$ for some t where $v < t < T - v$. Y3 implies that all these paths lie in a bounded set. Thus for some t, $v < t < T - v$, say t_1, there is a sub-sequence $\{y^t(r)\}$, $r = 1, 2, \ldots$, such that $y^t(r) \to y^t$ for $t = 0, \ldots, T$, and $[-y^{t_1}(r), y^{t_1+1}(r)] \notin V$ for all r. But, $(-y^t, y^{t+1}) \in U_r$ for all r, and thus $(-y^t, y^{t+1}) \in F_\alpha$. This implies $\{y^t\}$, $t = 0, 1, 2, \ldots, T$, is a path in F_α, although $(-y^{t_1}, y^{t_1+1}) \notin V$. This contradicts F_1, so the lemma follows.

Lemma 10 allows stronger versions of Theorems 2 and 3 to be proved. These are

Theorem 2′ For any Θ, $0 < \Theta < 1$, and any homogeneous neighborhood V of W, there is τ such that $T > \tau$ implies that an optimal path $\{\bar{y}^t\}$, $t = 0, 1, \ldots, T$, satisfies $(-\bar{y}^t, \bar{y}^{t+1}) \in V$ for at least $(1 - \Theta)T$ periods. τ depends on Θ and V.

Proof Using Theorem 2 we obtain τ such that $(-y^t, y^{t+1}) \in U$ for all but $\Theta'T$ periods for $T > \tau$. For given Θ' choose U and thus T so that Lemma 10 may be applied using the V of Theorem 2′. Then there is a number v such that $(-\bar{y}^t, \bar{y}^{t+1}) \in U$ for v periods before t_1, and v periods after t_1, implies that $(-\bar{y}^{t_1}, \bar{y}^{t_1}) \in V$. However, from Theorem 2 this condition cannot fail in more than $\Theta'T$ times $2v$ periods. Thus it suffices to choose Θ' so that $2v\Theta' < \Theta$ to establish the conclusion.

In the same way we may prove a stronger version of Theorem 3.

Theorem 3′ If there is x such that $u(x) > 0$ and $(-x, \alpha x) \in Y$, and p such that $p_i > 0$ for $i \in I_\alpha$ and $p \in P_\alpha$, then for any homogeneous neighborhood V of W, there is $\tau > 0$ such that an optimal path can remain outside V for no more than τ periods.

Proof Using Theorem 3, we obtain $(-\bar{y}^t, \bar{y}^{t+1}) \in U$ for all but τ' periods. Then applying Lemma 10 as before we find that $(-\bar{y}^t, \bar{y}^{t+1})$ can lie outside V for no more than $2v\tau'$ periods. Choose $\tau = 2v\tau'$.

We now turn to the justification of F1. First, normalize Y by replacing every $(-x, y) \in Y$ by $(-\alpha x, y)$. Then $\alpha = 1$ and we will write F for F_α. Define $A = [x(1) \ldots x(r)]$, $B = [y(1) \ldots y(r)]$, where $\{-x(j), y(j)\}$, $j = 1, \ldots, r$, is a set of linearly independent vectors in F which span F. Let $Z = \{z \mid (-x, y) = (-Az, Bz), \text{ and } (-x, y) \in F\}$. Then $(-x, y) \in F$ is equivalent to

$$(-x, y) = (-Az, Bz) \text{ for } z \in Z \tag{8}$$

There exist non-singular real matrices P and Q of orders $k{\times}k$ and $r{\times}r$ respectively which reduce A and B to simple canonical forms $A_1 = PAQ$ and $B_1 = PBQ$. The matrices B_1 and A_1 are block diagonal with corresponding blocks of the following types:

Type L, in B_1, $\begin{bmatrix} 1 & 0 & 0 \\ 0 & 1 & 0 \end{bmatrix}$, or $[I_{h-1} \quad 0]$, where h is the number of columns in the block,

in A_1, $\begin{bmatrix} 0 & 1 & 0 \\ 0 & 0 & 1 \end{bmatrix}$, or $[0 \quad I_{h-1}]$.

Type M, in B_1, $\begin{bmatrix} 0 & 0 \\ 1 & 0 \\ 0 & 1 \end{bmatrix}$, or $\begin{bmatrix} 0 \\ I_{h-1} \end{bmatrix}$, where h is the number of rows in the block,

in A_1, $\begin{bmatrix} 1 & 0 \\ 0 & 1 \\ 0 & 0 \end{bmatrix}$, or $\begin{bmatrix} I_{h-1} \\ 0 \end{bmatrix}$

Type N, in B_1, $\begin{bmatrix} 1 & 0 \\ 0 & 1 \end{bmatrix}$, or I_h, where the block is square of order h,

in A_1, $\begin{bmatrix} 0 & 1 \\ 0 & 0 \end{bmatrix}$, or $\begin{bmatrix} 0 & I_{h-1} \\ 0 & 0 \end{bmatrix}$.

Type J_R, in B_1, $\begin{bmatrix} \varrho & 0 \\ 1 & \varrho \end{bmatrix}$, or $\varrho I_h + \begin{bmatrix} 0 & 0 \\ I_{h-1} & 0 \end{bmatrix}$,

in A_1, $\begin{bmatrix} 1 & 0 \\ 0 & 1 \end{bmatrix}$, or I_h.

Type J_C, in B_1, $\begin{bmatrix} 0 & 1 & 0 & 0 \\ -\varrho\varrho^* & \varrho+\varrho^* & 0 & 0 \\ 0 & 1 & 0 & 1 \\ 0 & 0 & -\varrho\varrho^* & \varrho+\varrho^* \end{bmatrix}$,

in A_1, $\begin{bmatrix} 1 & & & \\ & 1 & & 0 \\ & & 1 & \\ 0 & & & 1 \end{bmatrix}$.

In J_R, ϱ is a real number, while in J_C, ϱ is complex. If A is nonsingular, only these blocks appear and B_1 is a real canonical form for $A^{-1}B$. We are then concerned with the ordinary system of difference equations $z^{t+1} = A^{-1}Bz^t$.

The goods space is transformed by P and the activities space by Q. Each column of B_1 is an output vector and the corresponding column of A_1 is an input vector for an activity in the transformed spaces. The columns of P^{-1} represent "composite commodities" corresponding to the rows of A_1 and B_1. The columns of P^{-1} associated with a particular pair of blocks of A_1 and B_1 span an invariant subspace of E_n^2 which is transformed by the activities in these blocks. We may write $E_n^2 = S_1 + S_2 + S_3 + S_L + S_M + S_N$ where S_1 is transformed by J_R blocks with $|\varrho| = 1$, S_2 by J blocks with $|\varrho| < 1$, S_3 by J blocks with $|\varrho| > 1$, S_L by L blocks, S_M by M blocks, S_N by N blocks.

Let p be the price vector obtained in Lemma 8. It is an immediate consequence of the condition $p \cdot x = p \cdot y$ for $(-x, y) \in F$ that the columns of P^{-1} that span S_L, S_N, S_2, and S_3 lie in the orthogonal subspace S^* of p in E_n^2. For example, let u be the column of P^{-1} corresponding to the last row of a J_R block. Then $p \cdot u = \varrho p \cdot u$, which implies that $\varrho = 1$ or $p \cdot u = 0$. Now the same argument applies to each earlier row. On the other hand if u is the column of P^{-1} corresponding to the first row of an L or an N block, $p \cdot u = 0$ from the first activity, and using this fact the same argument extends to the other rows. Finally, if u and v are the columns of P^{-1} corresponding to the first and second rows of a J_C block, the first two activities give $(1 - \varrho)\varrho^* = (1 - \varrho)$, or $\varrho = 1$, if $p \cdot u$ and consequently $p \cdot v \neq 0$. However, $\varrho = 1$ contradicts the definition of J_C. When $p_i = 0$, there is a simple L block transforming the ith coordinate subspace. Thus one column of P^{-1} is a vector on the ith coordinate axis. Since the columns of P^{-1} are linearly independent, the columns that span the other invariant subspaces of S^* always contain ith components which are non-zero and for which $p_i > 0$. Thus $p \cdot v = 0$ where v is such a column implies that v contains negative as well as positive components. Indeed, v will be selected so that $v_i = 0$ for $p_i = 0$. Finally S_M cannot contribute to a path on $\bar{F}$ after the first k periods. These facts and the non-negativity of the capital stock vectors along an accumulation path are used to prove an asymptotic theorem for paths $\{y^t\}$ on F. Define $W = F \cap [(S_1 + S_L) x (S_1 + S_L)]$. We prove

Theorem 4   If V is any homogeneous neighborhood of W, relative to F, and $\{y^t\}$, $t = 0, 1, \ldots, T$, is a path on F, there is a number of v such that $(-y^t, y^{t+1}) \in V$ for all periods, except possibly for v initial periods and v terminal periods. v depends on V but not on T.

Proof   We may assume that y^0 lies in the unit simplex S_n of E_n. Write $y^t = z_1^t + z_2^t + z_3^t + z_L^t + z_M^t + z_N^t$, where $z_1^t \in S_1$, $z_2^t \in S_2$, and so on. Since the blocks M and N have outputs which cannot be inputs on F, $z_M^t = z_N^t = 0$, for all t. S_2 is transformed by J blocks with $|\varrho| < 1$. Denote this transformation by Φ_2. Then $\Phi_2^t z_2^0 \to 0$ as $t \to \infty$. Moreover, by linear independence of the subspaces $|z_2^0| < \zeta_2$ for some number ζ_2, for any

y^0 with $y^0 \in S_n$. Thus for any $\varepsilon_2 > 0$ and $y^0 \in S_n$, there is N_2 such that $|z_2^t| < \varepsilon_2$ for $t > N_2$.

S_1 may be decomposed further into S_1' and S_1^* where $S_1^* \subset S^*$. S_1' is spanned by the columns of P^{-1} corresponding to the first rows of J blocks with $\varrho = 1$. It is easily seen by the method of argument used before that $p \cdot v = 0$ when v is a column of P^{-1} corresponding to any row of a J_1 block other than the first. Then, for $t > n$, we may write $y^t = z_1'^t + z^{*t}$ where $z_1'^t \in S_1'^t$, $z^{*t} \in S^*$, and $z_1'^t = z_1'^0$ for all t. However, $y^0 \in S_n$ implies $0 \leq p \cdot y^0 \leq \max p_i$, for $i = 1, \dots, n$. Since $p \cdot z^{*0} = 0$ and $z'^t = z'^0$, for all t, $p \cdot y^t = p \cdot z'^t = p \cdot y^0$, for all t, and $0 \leq p \cdot z'^t \leq \max p_i$, for $i = 1, \dots, n$, independently of the choice of $y^0 \in S_n$. On the other hand, $y^t \geq 0$ holds for all t, so that z_i^{*t} is bounded below. By $p \cdot z^{*t} = 0$, this implies that z_i^t is also bounded above when $p_i > 0$. Suppose z_3^t is unbounded with t. Since $z_3^t \in S^*$, by linear independence of the subspaces z^{*t} is also unbounded. When $p_i = 0$, there is a simple L block provided by the disposal activities for output and input of the ith good. Thus $z_{3i}^t = 0$ for $p_i = 0$. Thus z^{*t} is unbounded in some component i where $p_i > 0$. This contradicts the condition $y^t \geq 0$ given that y^0 is chosen in S_n. Thus there is $\zeta_3 > 0$ such that $|z_3^t| < \zeta_3$ for all t. Denote the transformation of S_3 by the J blocks with $|\varrho| > 1$ by Φ_3. Then $z_3^{T-} = \Phi_3^{-\tau} z_3^T \to 0$, as $\tau \to \infty$. Thus for any $\varepsilon_3 > 0$, there is N_3 such that $|z_3^t| < \varepsilon_3$ for all $t < T - N_3$, for $T > N_3$.

We now choose $\varepsilon_2 < \frac{\varepsilon_1}{2}$, $\varepsilon_3 < \frac{\varepsilon_1}{2}$, and $v > \max(n, N_2, N_3)$. Then $|z_2^t + z_3^t + z_M^t + z_N^t| < \varepsilon_1$ for all t such that $v < t < T - v$. If $p \cdot y^0 = 0$, $y_t^0 > 0$ implies $p_i = 0$, and similarly for y^t. Then $y^t \in S_L$ for all t and there is nothing to prove. On the other hand, $p \cdot y^t = p \cdot y^0 > \varepsilon$ implies that there is $\delta > 0$ such that $|y^t| > \delta$ for all t. Then by choice of ε_1, $\frac{\varepsilon_1}{\delta}$ may be made arbitrarily small. We define a homogeneous neighborhood V_ε of W, relative to F, by $V_\varepsilon = \{(-x, y) \mid |z_2 + z_3 + z_N + z_M|/|x| < \varepsilon, |w_2 + w_3 + w_M + w_N|/|y| < \varepsilon\}$, where z_2 is the S_2 component of x, w_2 is the S_2 component of y, and so on. For any neighborhood V of W relative to F, there is ε such that $V_\varepsilon \subset V$. But for any V_ε the number v exists. This proves the theorem.

Let $\tilde{S}_1$ be subspace transformed by the columns of P^{-1} corresponding to the last rows of J_R blocks with $|\varrho| = 1$ and the last two rows of J_C blocks with $|\varrho| = 1$. This subspace is invariant. Define $\tilde{W} = [(\tilde{S}_1 + L) x (\tilde{S}_1 + L)]$. We may also prove a stronger version of Theorem 4 in which W is replaced by $\tilde{W}$.

Theorem 5   Theorem 4 is valid with $\tilde{W}$ in place of W.

Proof   Let $S_1 = \tilde{\tilde{S}}_1 + \tilde{S}_1$, and let z_1^t, $\tilde{\tilde{z}}_1^t$, and $\tilde{z}_1^t$ be the corresponding summands in an expression for y^t. In order to extend Theorem 4 to the set $\tilde{W}$, we must show that for any $\varepsilon_4 > 0$, a number N_4 exists such that $|\tilde{\tilde{z}}_1^t| < \varepsilon_4$ must hold for all $t < T - N_4$ for $T > N_4$. We assume $y^0 \in S_n$ so that $z_1^{t\prime} = z_1^{0\prime}$ is bounded as before. However, by examining the powers of J blocks with $|\varrho| = 1$, we may discover that the transformation Φ_1^τ that they define on S_1 is unbounded with τ for inputs that lie in $\tilde{S}_1$. Write $S_1 = S_1' + S_1''$, where S_1' has the earlier definition and S_1'' is spanned by the remaining columns of P^{-1} which correspond to J blocks with $|\varrho| = 1$. Then $\tilde{\tilde{z}}_1^t \neq 0$ implies that $\Phi_1^\tau z_1^t = z_1^{t+\tau}$ is unbounded in its projection $z_1^{\prime\prime t+\tau}$ on S_1''. But $S_1'' \subset S^*$ and the argument used for z_3^t applies here to give $\zeta_4 > 0$ such that $|z_1^{\prime\prime t}| < \zeta_4$ for $0 \leqq t \leqq T$. This implies that N_4 exists for any $\varepsilon_4 > 0$. The fact that Φ_1^τ is unbounded for the domain $\tilde{S}_1$ in the range S_1'' is easily seen for J blocks with $\varrho = \pm 1$ by observing that the subdiagonal terms have absolute values at least as large as $t - n$. Closely analogous facts govern the other J blocks with $|\varrho| = 1$ as well.

Our results are given more intuitive meaning by the

Remark   If all paths of balanced growth on F lie on a unique ray (y), and no cyclic paths (except balanced paths) have constant amplitude, $\tilde{W} = y$.

The proof is immediate from the definition of $\tilde{W}$ and the conditions cited. This is essentially the case described by Morishima for the polyhedral model [9, ch. 10]. It means that the convergence properties given in Theorem 3′ imply convergence of optimal paths to the von Neumann ray.

Note

This research was supported by the National Science Foundation of the United States of America.

References

[1] Robert Dorfman, Paul A. Samuelson, and Robert M. Solow: *Linear Programming and Economic Analysis*, New York 1958.

[2] David Gale: The Closed Linear Model of Production, in H. W. Kuhn and A. W. Tucker (eds.), *Linear Inequalities and Related Systems*, Princeton 1956.

[3] F. R. Gantmacher: *Applications of the Theory of Matrices*, Inter-science Publishers, New York 1959.

[4] Ken-ichi Inada: Some Structural Characteristics of Turnpike Theorems, *The Review of Economic Studies 31* (January 1964).

[5] J. G. Kemeny, O. Morgenstern, and G. L. Thompson: A Generalization of the Von Neumann Model of an Expanding Economy, *Econometrica 24* (April 1956).

[6] Lionel W. McKenzie: Turnpike Theorems for a Generalized Leontief Model, *Econometrica 31* (January–April 1963).

[7] Lionel W. McKenzie: Maximal Paths in the Von Neumann Model, in E. Malinvaud and M. O. L. Barach (eds.), *Activity Analysis in the Theory of Growth and Planning*, London 1967.

[8] Lionel W. McKenzie: Accumulation Programs of Maximum Utility and the Von Neumann Facet, in J. N. Wolfe (ed.), *Value, Capital, and Growth*, Edinburgh 1968.

[9] Michio Morishima: *Theory of Economic Growth*, Oxford 1969.

[10] S. M. Movshovich: Turnpike Theorems in Von Neumann-Gale Models (Weak Form), *Ekonomika i Matematicheskie Metody (Economics and Mathematical Methods)*, 1969 (in Russian).

[11] John von Neumann: Über ein ökonomisches Gleichungs-System und eine Verallgemeinerung des Brouwerschen Fixpunktsatzes, in K. Menger (ed.), *Ergebnisse eines Mathematischen Kolloquiums, 8*, 1937. Translated as A Model of General Equilibrium, *The Review of Economic Studies 13* (1945/46).

[12] Roy Radner: Prices and the Turnpike, III. Paths of Economic Growth that are Optimal with Regard Only to Final States, *Review of Economic Studies 28* (February 1961).

22 Turnpike Theorems with Technology and Welfare Function Variable

Lionel W. McKenzie

The model is given by a sequence of production sets Y_t, $t = 1, 2, \ldots,$ where an element of Y_t is written (x, y), and a sequence of utility functions $u_t(x, y)$ defined on Y_t. The element (x, y) of Y_t is an input-output vector of capital stocks, where $x \in E_{t-1}$, a Euclidean space of dimension n_{t-1}, and $y \in E_t$. Also $x \geq 0$, $y \geq 0$. The function $u_t(x, y)$ is real valued. The vector x represents the initial stocks of period t and y the terminal stocks. Capital stocks may be interpreted to include any state variables, such as quantities of pollutants in the environment or levels of skill in the population. $Y_t \subset \Omega_{t-1} \times \Omega_t$ the positive orthant of a Euclidean space of dimension $n_{t-1} + n_t$.

We assume with respect to Y_t

(I) Y_t is convex and closed for all $t \geq 1$.

(II) Given t, for any $\zeta_1 \geq 0$, there is ζ_2 such that $(x, y) \in Y_t$ and $|x| < \zeta_1$ implies $|y| < \zeta_2$.

(I) provides a convex technology. (II) bounds the productivity of the technology for each t. We assume with respect to $u_t(x, y)$

(III) u_t is concave and continuous on Y_t.

Loosely speaking (III) provides that marginal utilities are non-increasing and utility is bounded over bounded subsets of Y_t.

Define a path of accumulation as a sequence (k_t), $t = 0, \ldots, T$, where $T \geq 1$, and there is $(k_{t-1}, k_t) \in Y_t$ for $t = 1, \ldots, T$. We may refer to (u_t), $u_t = u_t(k_{t-1}, k_t)$, as an associated utility sequence. We choose an initial stock $\underline{k}$ and say that a path of accumulation is feasible if $k_0 = \underline{k}$. We may also say that the associated utility sequence is feasible. Assume

(IV) There is a feasible path of accumulation (k_t), $t = 0, \ldots, T$, for every $T \geq 1$, such that $(k_{t-1}, k_t) \in$ interior Y_t, $t = 1, \ldots, T$.

(IV) requires that $\underline{k}$ be positive and that production can be carried forward and the capital stock vector produced be such that one is never forced to the boundary of the production set in the subsequent period.

An infinite path of accumulation is a sequence (k_t), $t = 0, 1, \ldots$, where there is $(k_{t-1}, k_t) \in Y_t$ for $t = 1, 2, \ldots$ An infinite path is said to be feasible if $k_0 = \underline{k}$.

Lemma 1   There is an infinite accumulation path that is feasible.

Proof   Let (k_t^T) be a T period path of accumulation. By (IV) there is a feasible path (k_t^T) for $T = 1, 2, \ldots$ By (II) k_t^T is bounded for $T \geqq t$ if k_{t-1}^T is bounded for these T. But $k_0^T = \underline{k}$ for all feasible paths. Therefore, (k_t^T) is bounded for $T \geqq t$ for all $t \geqq 1$. By the Cantor diagonal process we may choose a subsequence $T_1, T_2, \ldots$, such that $k_t^{T_i} \to k_t$ for all t. By (I) Y_t is closed, and $(k_{t-1}, k_t) \in Y_t$ for all t. Also $k_0 = \underline{k}$, so (k_t) is an infinite path of accumulation that is feasible.

22.1   The Existence of Optimal Paths

A finite accumulation path (k_t), $t = 0, \ldots, T$, is *optimal* if it is feasible and its associated utility sequence (u_t) satisfies $\sum_{t=1}^T u_t \geqq \sum_{t=1}^T u_t'$ where (u_t') is any feasible utility sequence. An infinite accumulation path is optimal if it is feasible and its associated utility sequence satisfies $\limsup \sum_{t=1}^T (u_t' - u_t) \leqq 0$ as $T \to \infty$, where (u_t') is any feasible infinite utility sequence. This is the overtaking criterion which is implicit in Ramsey [1928] and Koopmans [1965], and explicitly formulated by Weizsäcker [1965] and Atsumi [1965].

It is clear from the fact that Y_t is closed for all t, that if there is a feasible path of T periods, there is an optimal path of T periods. Thus from assumption (IV) there exists an optimal path of T periods for every $T > 0$. However, the existence of infinite optimal paths is not obvious, nor indeed true, without further assumptions. Perhaps the simplest example occurs when there is a natural resource in given initial supply which cannot be replenished but keeps without deterioration. Suppose that the utility obtained from the consumption of the resource is larger the later the consumption occurs. Then there is no optimal plan for using this resource since any plan proposed can be exceeded by postponing consumption. We note that the difficulty is not avoided if utility from the consumption of the resource is bounded above unless the bound is attained in some period. However, a bound would imply that paths exist which are nearly optimal, that is, for any $\varepsilon > 0$, there is a path which cannot be surpassed by more than ε. Such paths were called ε-optimal by McFadden [1967].

With any accumulation path of T periods, $T > 0$, which is optimal we can associate a sequence of prices (p_t) where $p_t \in E_t$, $t = 0, \ldots, T$, which support the path over the Y_t in a sense made specific in the following

Lemma 2   Let (k_t), $t = 0, \ldots, T$, be an optimal accumulation path. Then there exists a sequence of price vectors (p_t), $p_t \in E_t$, such that

$$u_t(k_{t-1}, k_t) + p_t k_t - p_{t-1} k_{t-1} \geqq u_t(x, y) + p_t y - p_{t-1} x,$$

for all $(x, y) \in Y_t$ and all $t \geqq 1$.

Note that it is not assumed that $p_t \geqq 0$ holds. Thus it is possible that some goods are harmful to utility, that is, bads or sources of pollution. Also it is possible to include population among the goods, differentiated by natural abilities and acquired skills. Lemma 2 is a well known result. We later prove a similar proposition here.

From the example already mentioned, we know that it will not necessarily be the case that an infinite optimal path can be found by taking limits of optimal T period paths as $T \to \infty$. In each T period optimal path the resource will be consumed in the T-th period, but for any limit of such paths as $T \to \infty$ the resource is never consumed. This is the worst possible infinite path. Moreover, it is not clear that the price systems associated with the T period optimal paths will themselves have a limiting price sequence, though if they do, any limiting price sequence will support some limiting accumulation path.

The existence of price sequences supporting infinite production paths was considered by Malinvaud [1953]. Let (p_t^T), $t = 0, \ldots, T$, support the T period initial segment of the infinite path. It was found necessary to introduce assumptions to prevent any price vector p_t^T from being unbounded as $T \to \infty$. Our problem is similar if u_t is treated as an output of the t-th period. However, we have the difficulty that a price of unity is assigned to u_t in every period. Thus Malinvaud prices may exist when ours do not if the Malinvaud prices assign a price of zero to utility in some period.

The method of Weizsäcker [1971] for proving that an infinite path is optimal is to suppose that prices exist that support the infinite path in the sense of Lemma 2, and to show that under some further conditions on the values of capital stocks at these prices, the path is optimal. We will first develop a theory of this type. Three assumptions are needed.

(W1)   There is an infinite feasible accumulation path (k_t) supported by a price sequence (p_t) in the sense of Lemma 2.

(W2)   Lim sup $p_t k_t = M < \infty$, and if (k_t') is an infinite feasible path lim inf $p_t k_t' > M' > -\infty$.

Let $\delta_t(x, y) = u_t(k_{t-1}, k_t) + p_t k_t - p_{t-1} k_{t-1} - (u_t(x, y) + p_t y - p_{t-1} x)$, for any $(x, y) \in Y_t$.

(W3)   For any $\varepsilon > 0$, there is a $\delta > 0$, such that $|p_t(x - k_t)| > \varepsilon$ implies $\delta_{t+1}(x, y) > \delta$ for any $(x, y) \in Y_{t+1}$.

(W2) places bounds on the limiting values of the capital stocks as $t \to \infty$, along feasible paths and along the path given by (W1). (W3) provides for a value loss for the input-output combination in period t when the value of input differs from the value of input on the given path. This assumption is weaker than a uniform strict concavity of the utility function, but it plays the same role.

With these assumptions it is easy to prove that (k_t), $t = 0, 1, \ldots$, is indeed an optimal infinite path of accumulation. Consider any feasible path (k_t'). Let $\delta_t = \delta_t(k_{t-1}', k_t')$. Then $u_t' - u_t = p_t(k_t - k_t') - p_{t-1}(k_{t-1} - k_{t-1}') - \delta_t$. Summing, we obtain

$$\sum_1^T (u_t' - u_t) = p_0(k_0 - k_0') + p_T(k_T - k_T') - \sum_1^T \delta_t. \tag{1}$$

However, $k_0 = k_0' = \underline{k}$ by feasibility. Then by (W2)

$$\limsup \sum_1^T (u_t' - u_t) \leq M - M' - \lim \sum_1^T \delta_t.$$

Suppose for some number γ lim sup $\sum_1^T (u_t' - u_t) > \gamma$, then $\delta_t \to 0$. But $\delta_t \to 0$, together with (W3) implies that for any $\varepsilon > 0$ sufficiently large t implies that $|p_t(k_t' - k_t)| < \varepsilon$. Thus lim sup $\sum_1^T (u_t' - u_t) \leq 0$, and (k_t) is an optimal path of accumulation by the definition. We have proved

Theorem 1   Under assumption (W1), (W2), (W3), the path (k_t) is optimal.

22.2   Other Initial Stocks

Once an optimal path (k_t) has been proved to exist from the initial stock $\underline{k}$, optimal paths may be derived for a set of alternative initial stocks. This set may be very large. In particular there will then exist an optimal path from any initial stock k such that a path of accumulation exists of some length T from k to k_T. Indeed, even when no such finite path is available, the existence of an optimal path from k will still be implied if there is an infinite path from k with a finite value loss relative to the optimal path (k_t) from $\underline{k}$ and its supporting price sequence. A finite value loss means that $\lim \sum_1^T \delta_t < \infty$ as $T \to \infty$ in (1). The condition is obviously met if a T period path is available from k to k_T. This part of our theory is an application of the methods of Brock [1970].

Let us define the set K of all capital stocks from which there are infinite paths with finite value loss. K is convex as a consequence of Assumption (I). However, K may not be closed. Let $L(k) = \inf(\lim \sum_1^T \delta_t, T \to \infty)$ over infinite paths from k. Then $L(k^s)$, $s = 1, 2, \ldots$, may be unbounded as $k^s \to k$, even though it is finite for each k^s. An obvious example occurs when some good is needed in the initial stocks if the value loss is to be finite but this good is lacking at k.

We wish to prove

Theorem 2   If there is a path from $\underline{k}$ that satisfies Assumptions (W1), (W2), (W3), there is an infinite optimal path from any $k \in K$.

Proof   Let $s = 1, 2, \ldots$ index a sequence of paths and let $L^s(k)$ be the value loss on the s-th path. We may assume that the sequence is chosen so that $L^s(k) \to L(k)$. Let (k_t^s), $t = 1, 2, \ldots$, be the s-th path. By Assumption (II), k_t^s, $s = 1, 2, \ldots$, is bounded for each t. Thus we may choose a subsequence such that (retain notation) $k_t^s \to \bar{k}_t$ for each t. By Assumption (I) $(\bar{k}_t)$, $t = 1, 2, \ldots$, is also an accumulation path from k. I claim that $(\bar{k}_t)$ is an optimal path from k.

Let $\bar{L}$ be the value loss associated with $(\bar{k}_t)$, it is clear that $\bar{L} \geq L(k)$. Also $\bar{L} < \infty$ since the $L^s(k)$ are bounded. Suppose $\bar{L} > L(k)$. Then for all large s, $\bar{L} - L^s > \varepsilon$ for some $\varepsilon > 0$. Choose T so large that

$$\bar{L} - \sum_1^T \delta(\bar{k}_{t-1}, \bar{k}_t) < \varepsilon/4.$$

Choose S so large that

$$\sum_1^T \delta_t(\bar{k}_{t-1}, \bar{k}_t) - \sum_1^T \delta_t(k_{t-1}^s, k_t^s) < \varepsilon/4 \quad \text{for } s > S.$$

Then

$$\bar{L} - \sum_1^T \delta_t(k_{t-1}^s, k_t^s) < \varepsilon/2 \quad \text{for } s > S.$$

But $L^s \geq \sum_1^T \delta(k_{t-1}^s, k_t^s)$, so $\bar{L} - L^s < \varepsilon/2$ for $s > S$ in contradiction to $\bar{L} - L^s > \varepsilon$ for all large s. Therefore, $\bar{L} = L(k)$, or the limit path realizes minimal value loss for all infinite paths from k.

Let us say that path (k_t') from k is good if there is a number γ such that $U_T = \sum_1^T (u_t' - u_t) > \gamma$ for all $T > 0$, where (u_t) is the utility sequence associated with an optimal path (k_t) from $\underline{k}$, and (u_t') is the utility sequence associated with (k_t'). Let us say the path (k_t') is bad if $U_T \to -\infty$, as $T \to \infty$. In order to complete the proof of Theorem 2 we need

Lemma 3 Every path from k is either good or bad. If (k_t'), $t = 0, 1, \ldots$, is a good path from k, $p_t(k_t - k_t') \to 0$ as $t \to \infty$.

Proof Since $\delta_t \geq 0$, $\sum_1^T \delta_t$ is either bounded as $T \to \infty$ or else converges to ∞. But from (1) and (W2) and (W3) (k_t') is good in the former case and bad in the latter case. If $p_t(k_t - k_t')$ does not converge to 0, it must be the case that $|p_t(k_t - k_t')| > \varepsilon$ an infinite number of times where ε is some positive number. By (W3) this implies $\delta_t > \delta > 0$ for an infinite number of times. Thus $\sum_1^T \delta_t \to \infty$ and (k_t') is bad. Thus $p_t(k_t - k_t')$ must converge to 0.

To complete the proof of Theorem 2, suppose (k_t') is any accumulation path from k. By Lemma 3, we may assume that (k_t') is good, since $(\bar{k}_t)$, having finite value loss, is good. Then in the right-hand side of (1) the second term goes to 0 as $T \to \infty$, and this is also true when $\bar{k}_t$ replaces k_t'. Also $\bar{k}_0 = k_0' = k$. Thus

$$\sum_1^T (u_t' - \bar{u}_t) = \sum_1^T (u_t' - u_t) - \sum_1^T (\bar{u}_t - u_t) \to \sum_1^T \bar{\delta}_t - \sum_1^T \delta_t' \quad \text{as } t \to \infty.$$

But $\lim \sum_1^T \bar{\delta}_t \leq \lim \sum_1^T \delta_t'$, so $\lim \sup \sum_1^T (u_t' - \bar{u}_t) \leq 0$. This proves the optimality of the limit path $(\bar{k}_t)$ from k.

22.3   A Stationary Case

A particular case to which Theorems 1 and 2 are easily applied is a model described by Gale [1967] and McKenzie [1968]. In this model the technology and the utility function are stationary, that is, $Y_t = Y$ and $u_t = u$ for all t, and free disposal of surplus stocks is assumed. Then it is easy to show that the constant path that provides maximum sustainable utility can be supported by constant prices and thus satisfies (W1) and the first part of (W2). The latter part of (W2) and (W3) must be added, but their force is especially clear in this case.

We may present the model formally by adding to Assumptions (I), (II), and (III) three additional assumptions.

(G1) $Y_t = Y$, $u_t = u$, for all t.

(G2)   There is $\eta > 0$ such that $|k| > \eta$ implies $|k'| < |k|$ for all $(k, k') \in Y$. Let $B_\varepsilon(x, y)$ be the open ball of radius $\varepsilon > 0$ about (x, y).

(G3)   There is an infinite feasible path (k_t), $t = 0, 1, 2, \ldots$, such that $B_\varepsilon(k_t, k_{t+1}) \subset Y$ for some $\varepsilon > 0$ for all t.

(G1) asserts that the model is stationary. (G2) places a limit on the size of capital stocks that can be sustained. A model including (G2) as an assumption is sometimes said to be labor constrained since a limited population might be thought to limit the size of maintainable capital stocks. (G3) prevents the infinite path that is assumed to exist from approaching the boundary of Y, and implicitly requires $\underline{k} > 0$.

In order to apply Theorems 1 and 2 we must find an infinite path that is supported by prices. We first prove the existence of a balanced path.

Lemma 4   On Assumption (G1), (G2), and (G3) there is a point $(k, k) \in$ interior Y.

Proof   Consider

$$k^s = \frac{1}{s} \sum_0^{s-1} k_t, \quad k^{s'} = \frac{1}{s} \sum_1^{s} k_t,$$

where (k_t) is given by (G3).

By convexity of Y, $(k^s, k^{s'}) \in Y$. Since k_t is bounded as a consequence of (G2), there is a point of accumulation (k, k'). Then boundedness also implies $k' = k$. By (G3), $(k, k) \in$ interior Y.

Define the set $V = \{v \mid v = y - x, \text{ where } (x, y) \in Y\}$. V is contained in E^n. By Lemma 4, 0 is an interior point of V, and by (G2), the set of $(k, k') \in Y$ with $k = k'$ is bounded. Define $f(v) = \max u(x, y)$ for $v = y - x$, $v \in V$. Let $W = \{(u, v) \mid u \leq f(v) \text{ and } v \in V\}$. W is convex and closed, also $(\bar{u}, 0)$ is a boundary point of W, where $\bar{u} = f(0)$. Thus there is $(\pi, p) \in E_{n+1}$ and $(\pi, p) \neq 0$, such that $\pi u + pv \leq \pi\bar{u}$ for all $(u, v) \in W$. Suppose $\pi = 0$. Then $pv \leq 0$ for all $v \in V$, or since 0 is interior to V in $E^n \cdot p = 0$. Thus $\pi \neq 0$, and we may choose (π, p) so that $\pi = 1$. Then $u + pv \leq \bar{u}$ for all $(u, v) \in W$. This implies immediately

Lemma 5 There is $p \in E^n$, $p \neq 0$, such that $u + py - px \leq \bar{u}$ for all $(x, y) \in Y$, where $u = u(x, y)$ and $\bar{u} = \max u(x, x)$ for $(x, x) \in Y$.

Let $u(\bar{k}, \bar{k}) = \bar{u}$. Then the path (k_t), $t = 0, 1, 2, \ldots$, where $k_t = \bar{k}$ for all t is an infinite path that is supported by the price sequences (p_t), $t = 0, 1, 2, \ldots$, where $p_t = p$ for all t. This path may be described as the optimal stationary program.

Lemma 5 implies Assumption (W1) and the first part of (W2). However, there is no avoiding the latter part of (W2), as well as (W3), which is a weak kind of strict concavity for $u(x, y)$. That is, the surface in $2n + 1$ dimensional Euclidean space defined by $u(x, y)$ is not flat at $(\bar{k}, \bar{k})$ in directions for which px changes. Of course, this assumption is protected by an assumption of strict concavity for $u(x, y)$, but strict concavity is not needed unless the value of the inputs at the prices p changes. Indeed, it is possible in the stationary case to give up strict concavity altogether and show that concavity plus uniqueness of the balanced path, and the absence of cyclic paths along which δ_t is equal to 0, suffices to give the results of Theorems 1 and 2 (McKenzie [1968]). (W3) may be restated as

(G4) For any $\varepsilon > 0$, there is $\delta > 0$, such that $|p(x - \bar{k})| > \varepsilon$ implies $\delta(x, y) > \delta$ for any $(x, y) \in Y$.

In (G4), $\delta(x, y) = u(\bar{k}, \bar{k}) - u(x, y) - p(y - x)$.

Now Theorems 1 and 2 may be applied to this case. By Theorem 1, (k_t), $k_t = \bar{k}$, all t, is an optimal path for initial stocks equal to $\bar{k}$. By Theorem 2, for any initial stock k from which there is a path (k_t) satisfying $\sum_{t=1}^{T} \delta_t < \gamma$, for all $T \geq 1$, for some number γ, where value loss $\delta_t = \bar{u} - u_t - p(k_t - k_{t-1})$, there exists an optimal path $(\bar{k}_t)$, $t = 0, 1, 2, \ldots$, where $\bar{k}_0 = k$. The hypothesis is equivalent to $k \in K$ by the earlier definition. K contains, *inter alia*, all k from which there are paths that reach $\bar{k}$.

If we add an assumption of free disposal, which eliminates the problem of pollution from the model, we may dispense with the latter part of (W2) since $p \geq 0$ will hold and capital stocks are non-negative by definition. In any case, it is reasonable to suppose there is an upper bound to the accumulation of nuisances along feasible paths. However, with an assumption of free disposal it is also possible to characterize further the set K. Assume

(G5) If $(x, y) \in Y$, then $(z, w) \in Y$ for all $z \geq x$, $0 \leq w \leq y$, and $u(z, w) \geq u(x, y)$.

Let us say that x is expansible if there is $(x, y) \in Y$ where $y > x$. Then we may prove (Gale [1967])

Lemma 6 If k is expansible, then $k \in K$.

Proof Consider $\alpha^t(k, k') + (1 - \alpha^t)(\bar{k}, \bar{k}) = (k_t, k'_{t+1})$, where $k' > k$, $0 < \alpha < 1$, $t = 0, 1, 2, \ldots$. For $t = 0$, $(k_t, k'_{t+1}) = (k, k')$, as $t \to \infty$, $(k_t, k'_{t+1}) \to (\bar{k}, \bar{k})$. But $k'_{t+1} = \bar{k} - \alpha^t(\bar{k} - k')$ and $k_{t+1} = \bar{k} - \alpha^{t+1}(\bar{k} - k)$. Then $k'_{t+1} > k_{t+1}$ if $k' - \alpha k > \bar{k} - \alpha \bar{k}$, which holds for α near 1 since $k' > k$. Thus by free disposal (k_t) is an infinite feasible path approaching $\bar{k}$. The value loss $\delta_{t+1} = \delta(k_t, k_{t+1})$, where δ is a convex function since u is concave. Also

$$(k_t, k_{t+1}) = (\bar{k}, \bar{k}) - \alpha^t((\bar{k}, \bar{k}) - (k_0, k_1)).$$

Thus

$$\delta_t \leq (1 - \alpha^t)\delta(\bar{k}, \bar{k}) + \alpha^t \delta(k_0, k_1) = \alpha^t \delta_1 \quad \text{and} \quad \sum_1^\infty \delta_t \leq \frac{1}{1 - \alpha} \delta_1,$$

proving that $k \in K$.

One can go even further, with Gale, to assume there exists an expansible stock $\tilde{k}$ and the point $(0, 0)$ is in Y. Then the points between $\tilde{k}$ and 0 are expansible by convexity, and one of them may be reached from any positive, initial stocks by free disposal. Thus $k > 0$ implies $k \in K$. Also (G3) becomes superfluous if we assume

(G3′) The origin $(0, 0) \in Y$, and there is a point $(\tilde{k}, k') \in Y$ where $k' > \tilde{k}$.

(G5) and (G3′) imply the conclusion of Lemma 4, since $(y, y) \in$ interior Y for any y where $\tilde{k} < y < k'$. We may now state

Theorem 3   With Assumptions (G1), (G2), (G3′), (G4), and (G5), there is an optimal path from any positive initial stocks.

However, the assumption that $(0,0) \in Y$ seems a bit extreme. Also it would be enough to be able to reach positive stocks from the initial stocks.

22.4   Turnpike Theorems

We know from Lemma 3 that Assumptions (W1), (W2), and (W3) imply that the values of the capital stocks along optimal paths from initial stocks in K approach one another as $t \to \infty$. That is, $p_t k_t' \to p_t k_t''$ for infinite optimal paths, with $k_0' \in K$ and $k_0'' \in K$, $t = 0, 1, 2, \ldots$ However, the convergence need not be uniform over K. Also there may be many such sets K defined for different optimal paths in the same model of capital accumulation. This is a rather weak form of turnpike theorem. It results directly from the statement of (W3). Indeed, our asymptotic results will all depend on the condition that implies $\delta_t > \delta$, for it is this condition that is eliminated along a good path. In the proof of existence we only needed to make $|p_t k_t - p_t k_t'|$ small, and this explains the condition that was used in (W3).

The turnpike theorem that will be our chief concern, however, is of a different type. We will introduce a terminal objective in the form of a capital stock vector $\bar{k}$ to be achieved at time T, sufficiently far in the future, and we will consider finite paths of accumulation starting from a given initial stock $\underline{k}$. Our purpose is to show that under certain assumptions the early stages of such paths may stay on the infinite optimal path from $\underline{k}$ with only a small loss of utility compared with an optimal program of T periods reaching the assigned capital stock vector $\bar{k}$.

The critical issue in "straight-down-the-turnpike" theorems (Winter [1965]) is the ability to switch between the T period optimal path with terminal objective $\bar{k}$ and the infinite optimal path, with little loss of utility. Suppose (p, q) are support price vectors for $(x, y) \in Y_t$. That is,

$$u(x, y) + qy - px \geq u(z, w) + qw - pz \quad \text{for all } (z, w) \in Y_t.$$

Define $\delta(z, w)$ by reference to (x, y) and (p, q). We assume

(T1)   For any $\varepsilon > 0$, there is $\delta > 0$, such that $\delta(w, z) < \delta$ implies (x, z) and $(w, y) \in Y$ and

$$|u(w, z) - u(x, z)| + |u(x, y) - u(w, y)| < \varepsilon.$$

Let $\underline{k}$ be a vector of initial stocks for an infinite optimal path (k_t), $t = 0, 1, \ldots$, that is supported by a price sequence (p_t), $t = 0, 1, \ldots$ We assume that (k_t) satisfies Assumptions (W1), (W2), and (W3) with respect to (p_t). Consider a T period optimal path (k_t'), $t = 0, \ldots, T$, where $k_T' = \bar{k}$. In order to prove the turnpike theorem we also need to assume that $\bar{k}$ can be reached from k_τ for any $\tau \geq 0$ by means of a path of bounded length and bounded utility loss compared with the utility accumulated along the infinite optimal path over the same sequence of periods from τ. Assume

(T2)   There are numbers N and U such that for $\tau \geq 0$ there is an accumulation path (h_t), $t = 0, \ldots$, where $h_t = k_t$, $t \leq \tau$, $h_{\tau+n} = \bar{k}$, $n < N$ and

$$\sum_{1}^{\tau+n} (u_t(k_{t-1}, k_t) - u_t(h_{t-1}, h_t)) < U.$$

Using (W1), (W2), (W3), and (T2) we may prove

Lemma 7   For any $\delta > 0$, there is N such that $T > N$ implies there is $t > T - N$ and $\delta_t(k_{t-1}', k_t') < \delta$.

Proof   Choose $\varepsilon > 0$. By optimality of the T-period path, using (h_t) as defined in (T2),

$$\sum_{t=1}^{T} u_t(h_{t-1}, h_t) \leq \sum_{t=1}^{T} u_t(k_{t-1}', k_t'). \tag{2}$$

Combining (1) and (2) gives

$$\sum_{t=1}^{T} u_t(h_{t-1}, h_t) \leq \sum_{t=1}^{T} u_t(k_{t-1}', k_t') = \sum_{t=1}^{T} u_t(k_{t-1}, k_t) + p_T(k_T - \bar{k}) - \sum_{t=1}^{T} \delta_t. \tag{3}$$

Suppose $\delta_t > \delta$ for all $t > T - N$. Then we may write, in place of (3),

$$\sum_{1}^{T} u_t(h_{t-1}, h_t) \leq \sum_{1}^{T} u_t' \leq \sum_{1}^{T} u_t + M - M' - N\delta, \tag{4}$$

where (W2) has been used. However, by (T2), $\sum_{1}^{T}(u_t - u_t(h_{t-1}, h_t)) < U$. Thus (4) implies $N\delta < U + M - M'$. Since this is a contradiction for large N, the t of the lemma must exist.

Combining (T1) with Lemma 7 allows the proof of a straight-down-the-turnpike theorem. Let $h_t^{t_0} = k_t$ for $t < t_0$ and $h_t^{t_0} = k_t'$ for $t \geq t_0$. We may prove

Theorem 4 For any $\varepsilon > 0$ there is N such that $T > N$ implies there is t_0, $T - N < t_0 \leq T$, and $(h_t^{t_0})$, $t = 0, \ldots, T$, is a feasible path of accumulation and

$$\sum_{t=1}^{T} u_t(k_{t-1}', k_t') - \sum_{t=1}^{T} u_t(h_{t-1}^{t_0}, h_t^{t_0}) < \varepsilon.$$

Proof By Lemma 7 for an arbitrary $\delta > 0$, we may choose an N, such that if $T > N$, there is $t_0 > T - N$, for which $\delta_{t_0}(k_{t_0-1}', k_{t_0}') < \delta$. But for any $\varepsilon > 0$, (T1) allows the choice of δ so that

$$(k_{t_0-1}', k_{t_0}) \in Y_{t_0} \quad \text{and} \quad |u_{t_0}(k_{t_0-1}, k_{t_0}) - u_{t_0}(k_{t_0-1}', k_{t_0})| < \varepsilon/2.$$

Since (k_t), $t = 0, \ldots, t_0$, is a finite optimal path for the objective k_{t_0} at time t_0,

$$\sum_{t=1}^{t_0-1} u_t(k_{t-1}, k_t) \geq \sum_{t=1}^{t_0-1} u_t(k_{t-1}', k_t') + u_{t_0}(k_{t_0-1}', k_{t_0}) - u_{t_0}(k_{t_0-1}, k_{t_0})$$

$$> \sum_{t=1}^{t_0-1} u_t(k_{t-1}', k_t') - \varepsilon/2.$$

But by (T1), the choice of δ can be made so that it also holds that

$$(k_{t_0-1}, k_{t_0}') \in Y_{t_0} \quad \text{and} \quad |u_{t_0}(k_{t_0-1}, k_{t_0}') - u_{t_0}(k_{t_0-1}, k_{t_0}')| < \varepsilon/2.$$

Then

$$\sum_{t=1}^{t_0-1} u_t(k_{t-1}, k_t) + u_{t_0}(k_{t_0-1}, k_{t_0}') > \sum_{t=1}^{t_0} u_t(k_{t-1}', k_t') - \varepsilon.$$

Thus

$$\sum_{t=1}^{T} u_t(h_{t-1}^{t_0}, h_t^{t_0}) > \sum_{t=1}^{T} u_t(k_{t-1}', k_t') - \varepsilon,$$

since these paths coincide after $t = t_0$. This completes the proof.

22.5   Support Prices

Since optimal paths from $k \in K$ converge to (k_t), the optimal path from $\underline{k}$, and also finite optimal paths whose objective $\bar{k}$ can be reached from (k_t) converge to (k_t), it would be possible to use (T1) and (T2) to derive straight-down-the-turnpike theorems for paths starting from $k \in K$ when only (k_t) is price supported. The possibility of switches between (k_t) and (k_t'), optimal from k, and between (k_t) and (k_t^T), T period optimal from k, implies the possibility of switches between (k_t') and (k_t^T) when both are near (k_t). Thus a complete theory of existence and convergence can be built up when only (k_t) is supported by prices. However, the turnpike results may be derived somewhat more effectively if support prices are available for the optimal paths from initial stocks $k \in K$. The purpose of this section is to prove that, with some additional assumptions, such prices do exist and the capital values are bounded over time. The method of proof is due to Weitzman [1971].

Define K_t as the set of all capital stock vectors x from which there are infinite paths starting from time t with finite value loss. Let V_t be the set of capital stock vectors y such that there is $(x, y) \in Y_t$ for some x. Let $T_t(x)$ be the set of all terminal stocks y such that $(x, y) \in Y_t$. We assume

(S1) $T_1(k) \cap K_1$ has an interior. Also $V_t \cap K_t$ has an interior for $t > 1$.

It is clear that (S1) is satisfied if there is an infinite path $(\tilde{k}_t)$, $t = 0$, $1, \ldots$, from initial stocks in K with $(\tilde{k}_t, \tilde{k}_{t+1}) \in$ interior Y_{t+1} for $t \geq 1$, and if interior $T_1(k) \cap K_1$ is not empty. However, the existence of the path $(\tilde{k}_t)$ is not necessary. A somewhat stronger assumption than (S1) is

(S1') $k \in$ interior K and, for $t \geq 1$, $V_t \cap K_t$ has an interior.

With (S1) support prices may be derived from $t = 1$, while (S1') gives support prices beginning with $t = 0$.

We consider an optimal path (k_t'), $t = 0, 1, \ldots$, from $k_0' = k \in K$. We may write $-L_t(x) = \sup(-\sum_{t+1}^{\infty} \delta_\tau)$, over the collection of all infinite accumulation paths (h_τ), $\tau = t, t+1, \ldots$, where $h_t = x \in K_t$. Then

$$-L_t(k) = -\sum_{t+1}^{\infty} \delta_\tau(k_{\tau-1}', k_\tau'),$$

as we have already seen. By the definition, we have, for $x \in K_t$,

$$-L_t(x) = \sup(-\delta_{t+1}(x, y) - L_{t+1}(y))$$

over all y such that $(x, y) \in Y_{t+1}$ and $y \in K_{t+1}$. Make the induction assumption there exists $q_t \in E_t$ such that

$$-L_t(k'_t) - q_t k'_t \geq -L_t(x) - q_t x \quad \text{over all } x \in K_t.$$

Substituting for L_t we obtain

$$-\delta_{t+1}(k'_t, k'_{t+1}) - L_{t+1}(k'_{t+1}) - q_t k'_t \geq -\delta_{t+1}(x, y) - L_{t+1}(y) - q_t x, \tag{5}$$

for all $(x, y) \in Y_{t+1}$ with $y \in K_{t+1}$. Denote the left-hand side of (5) by v_{t+1}. Then

$$v_{t+1} + \delta_{t+1}(x, y) + q_t x \geq -L_{t+1}(y).$$

We define two sets,

$$A = \{(w, y) \mid (x, y) \in Y_{t+1}, \text{ for some } x, \text{ and } w > v_{t+1} + \delta_{t+1}(x, y) + q_t x\},$$

and

$$B = \{(w, y) \mid y \in K_{t+1} \text{ and } w \leq -L_{t+1}(y)\}.$$

A and B are disjoint by the inequality (5). They are also convex. A is convex since δ_{t+1} is convex over Y_{t+1} as a consequence of the concavity of u_{t+1} and the convexity of Y_{t+1}. B is convex since $-L_{t+1}$ is concave over the convex set K_{t+1}. This A and B may be separated by a hyperplane in E^{n+1} defined by a vector $(\pi, -q_{t+1})$. Then $\pi w - q_{t+1} y \geq \pi w' - q_{t+1} y'$ for all $(w, y) \in A$ and $(w', y') \in B$. From (5) and the definitions of w and w' this implies

$$\pi\{-\delta_{t+1}(k'_t, k'_{t+1}) - L_{t+1}(k'_{t+1}) - q_t k'_t + \delta_{t+1}(x, y) + q_t x\} - q_{t+1} y$$

$$\geq -\pi L_{t+1}(y') - q_{t+1} y', \tag{6}$$

for any $(x, y) \in Y_{t+1}$, and $y' \in K_{t+1}$. Put $x = k'_t$, $y = k'_{t+1}$ and (6) becomes

$$-\pi L_{t+1}(k'_{t+1}) - q_{t+1} k'_{t+1} \geq -\pi L_{t+1}(y') - q_{t+1} y', \tag{7}$$

for all $y' \in K_{t+1}$. Put $y' = k'_{t+1}$ in (6) and we obtain

$$\pi\{-\delta_{t+1}(k'_t, k'_{t+1}) - q_t k'_t\} + q_{t+1} k'_{t+1} \geq \pi\{-\delta_{t+1}(x, y) - q_t x\} + q_{t+1} y, \tag{8}$$

for all $(x, y) \in Y_{t+1}$. If $\pi = 0$, (7) and (8) together would imply $q_{t+1}k'_{t+1}$ $= q_{t+1}y$ over a set W equal to all $y \in K_{t+1}$ such that there is x and $(x, y) \in Y_{t+1}$. This equality is impossible if W contains an open set. However, W equals $V_{t+1} \cap K_{t+1}$ which has an interior by (S1) or (S1'). Thus we may choose $(\pi, -q_{t+1})$ so that $\pi = 1$. Then (8) becomes

$$-\delta_{t+1}(k'_t, k'_{t+1}) + q_{t+1}k'_{t+1} - q_t k'_t \geqq -\delta_{t+1}(x, y) + q_{t+1}y - q_t x, \qquad (9)$$

for all $(x, y) \in Y_{t+1}$. Using (S1), the induction may be started with a parallel argument for the determination of q_1 where the terms $q_0 k'_0$ and $q_0 x$ are omitted. The relation (5) is replaced by

$$-\delta_1(k, k'_1) - L_1(k'_1) \geqq -\delta_1(k, y) - L_1(y), \qquad (5')$$

for all y such that $(k, y) \in Y_1$ and $y \in K_1$. Then the relation (7), with $\pi = 1$, is established beginning with $t = 1$ together with an initial relation

$$-\delta_1(k, k'_1) + q_1 k'_1 \geqq -\delta_1(k, y) + q_1 y, \qquad (10)$$

for all $(k, y) \in Y_1$. As it turns out, q_0 is not needed. However, use of (S1') allows the induction to begin with q_0.

In order to derive the price sequence that supports (k'_t), $t = 0, 1, \dots$, it is merely necessary to replace δ_{t+1} in (9), by its definition, that is,

$$\delta_{t+1}(x, y) = (u_{t+1}(k_t, k_{t+1}) + p_{t+1}k_{t+1} - p_t k_t) - (u_{t+1}(x, y) + p_{t+1}y - p_t x). \qquad (11)$$

Substituting in (9), we obtain

$$u_{t+1}(k'_t, k'_{t+1}) + (p_{t+1} + q_{t+1})k'_{t+1} - (p_t + q_t)k'_t$$

$$\geqq u_{t+1}(x, y) + (p_{t+1} + q_{t+1})y - (p_t + q_t)x, \qquad (12)$$

for all $(x, y) \in Y_{t+1}$. Setting $p'_t = (p_t + q_t)$ in (12) gives the desired relations for a price sequence (p'_t), $t = 1, 2, \dots$, that supports the infinite optimal path (k'_t), $t = 0, 1, \dots$, with $k'_0 = k \in K$. It is understood that K is defined relative to (k_t), $t = 0, 1, \dots$, when (k_t) is supported by the price sequence (p_t), $t = 1, 2, \dots$ The prices p_0 are not needed since k_1 is sufficiently characterized by the relation $u_1(k_0, k_1) + p_1 k_1 \geqq u_1(k_0, y) + p_1 y$ for all $(k_0, y) \in Y_1$, and similarly for k'_1 and p'_1.

It remains to prove that $p'_t k'_t$ is bounded above. Since (k'_t) is an optimal path departing from $k \in K$, we obtain from (7), $L_t(k'_t) + q_t k'_t \leqq$

$L_t(x) + q_t x$ for any $x \in K_t$. Put $x = \alpha k'_t$ for $\alpha < 1$, and suppose $\alpha k'_t \in K_t$. Then

$$(1 - \alpha) q_t k'_t \leqq L_t(\alpha k'_t) - L_t(k'_t). \tag{13}$$

However, $L_t(k'_t) \to 0$ as $t \to \infty$. Thus if $L_t(\alpha k'_t)$ is bounded for $t \to \infty$, $q_t k'_t$ will also be bounded. This can be arranged if an appropriate property holds for the Y_t. For example, assume

(S2)   There are $\delta > 0$, $\zeta > 0$, $0 < \alpha < 1$, such that $L_t(y) < \delta$ implies $L_t(\alpha y) < \zeta$, uniformly for all sufficiently large t.

We know that $L_t(k'_t) \to 0$ as $t \to \infty$, since $L_0(k)$ is finite. Thus $L_t(k'_t) < \delta$ can be satisfied for any $\delta > 0$, for large t. Then by Assumption (S2), there is $0 < \alpha < 1$ such that $L_t(\alpha k'_t) < \zeta$ for all large t. This implies that the right-hand side of (13) is bounded as $t \to \infty$, or $\limsup q_t k'_t < \infty$. We have proved

Theorem 5   Assumptions (W1), (W2), (W3) and (S1) imply that a supporting price sequence (p'_t) exists for every infinite optimal path (k'_t) from $k \in K$. If Assumption (S2) also holds, then $p'_t k'_t$ is bounded for $t \geqq 1$.

We found it necessary to introduce additional assumptions to obtain price supports for paths from $k \in K$ and to bound the capital values. However, the assumptions we used in proving existence for the stationary case are strong enough to imply (S1') for all positive initial stocks. We may show

Lemma 8   Under Assumptions (G1), (G2), (G3'), and (G5), (S1') is satisfied if k is positive.

Proof   As a consequence of (G3') and (G5), we may use free disposal to reach an expansible stock $\tilde{k}$. Then Lemma 6 implies $\tilde{k} \in K$, so $k \in K$ also. Since this argument holds for any positive stock, $k \in$ interior K. Also in the proof of Lemma 6, k' may be chosen interior to the set $T(k)$. Then, using the notation of that proof, $k'_{t+1} \in$ interior $T(k_t) \cap K_{t+1}$ for all $t \geqq 0$. Thus (S1') is satisfied and support prices are derivable beginning with q_0.

In order to bound the capital values over time it is necessary to strengthen the assumptions that were used for existence in the stationary case, since they do not imply (S2). One approach is to amend Assumption (G4) to obtain convergence to $\bar{k}$ for good paths and then provide for the application of (13) near $\bar{k}$. Assume

(G4′) For any $\varepsilon > 0$ there is $\delta > 0$ such that $|x - \bar{k}| > \varepsilon$ implies $\delta(x, y) > \delta$ for any $(x, y) \in Y$.

This is only slightly weaker than assuming strict concavity of the utility function in input coordinates. Also assume

(G6) There is $\delta > 0$, $\zeta > 0$, $0 < \alpha < 1$, such that $|(x, y) - (\bar{k}, \bar{k})| < \delta$ implies $(\alpha y, \bar{k}) \in Y$ and $\delta(\alpha y, \bar{k}) < \zeta$.

Then we may prove

Lemma 9   Under Assumptions (G1), (G2), (G4′), (G5), and (G6), (S2) is satisfied.

Proof   In the stationary case L_t is independent of t and we may write L for L_t. Then $L(k_t') \to 0$ implies $|k_t' - \bar{k}| \to 0$ by (G4′), which implies $\delta(\alpha k_t', \bar{k}) < \delta$ for large t by (G6). But then $L(\alpha k_t') \leqq \delta(\alpha k_t', \bar{k}) < \zeta$ for large t and (S2) holds.

Finally, we may state

Theorem 6   Assumptions (G1), (G2), (G3′), and (G5) imply in the stationary model that a supporting price sequence (p_t') exists for every infinite optimal path (k_t') from $k > 0$. If Assumptions (G4′) and (G6) also hold, $p_t' k_t'$ is bounded for $t \geqq 0$.

References

H. Atsumi, 1965, Neoclassical growth and the efficient program of capital accumulation, *Rev. Econ. Studies* **32**, 127–136.

W. Brock, 1970, On existence of weakly maximal programmes in growth models, *Rev. Econ. Studies* **37**, 275–280.

D. Gale, 1967, On optimal development in a multi-sector economy, *Rev. Econ. Studies* **34**, 1–18.

T. C. Koopmans, 1965, On the concept of optimal economic growth, Pontificae Academia *Scientiarum Scripta Varia*, pp. 225–300.

E. Malinvaud, 1953, 1962, Capital accumulation and efficient allocation of resources, Econometrica **21**, 233–238; and Efficient capital accumulation: a corrigendum, *Econometrica* **30**, 570–573.

D. McFadden, 1967, On the evaluation of development programs, *Rev. Econ. Studies* **34**, 25–50.

L. W. McKenzie, 1968, Accumulation programs of maximum utility and the von Neumann facet, in: *Value, capital, and growth*, ed. J. N. Wolfe (Edinburgh), pp. 353–383.

F. Ramsey, 1928, A mathematical theory of savings, *Economic Journ.* **38**, 534–559.

M. L. Weitzman, 1971, Duality theory of convex programming for infinite horizon economic models, Cowles Foundation Discussion Paper, November 1971.

C. C. von Weizsäcker, 1965, Accumulation for an infinite time horizon, *Rev. Econ. Studies* **32**, 85–104.

S. Winter, 1965, Some properties of the closed linear model of production, *Internat. Econom. Rev.* **6**, 199–210.

23 A New Route to the Turnpike

Lionel W. McKenzie

There has recently appeared a genuine alternative to the method of Liapounov functions in proving turnpike theorems for optimal growth programs. The new approach achieves global results without appealing to the method of value loss. Instead the problem is imbedded in a Banach space and the results come from an application of an implicit function theorem. This method is due to Araujo and Scheinkman [1977]. Our purpose here is to indicate how the approach can be extended to models of growth with time dependent utility functions and, at the same time, strengthened to give exponential convergence.[1]

We use a reduced model in which the utility achieved in the tth period is represented as a function $u^t(x, y)$ of the initial stocks x at time $t - 1$ and the terminal stocks y at time t. The utility function u^t is real valued, strictly concave, and defined on a convex subset Y_t of $R_+^n \times R_+^n$. Here R_+^n is the Cartesian product of n copies of the nonnegative real line, endowed with the Euclidean topology. To prepare for the use of the implicit function theorem we assume that Y_t has a non-empty interior and u^t is twice continuously differentiable on the interior of Y_t.

We call a sequence $\{k^t\}$, $t = 0, 1, \ldots$, a path of capital accumulation if $(k_t, k_{t+1}) \in Y_{t+1}$ for each t. We say that the path $\{\bar{k}_t\}$ catches up to $\{k_t\}$ if for any $\varepsilon > 0$ there is some T such that $\sum_1^t u^t(\bar{k}_{t-1}, \bar{k}_t) > \sum_1^t u^t(k_{t-1}, k_t) - \varepsilon$ for all $t > T$. A path $\{\bar{k}_t\}$ is optimal if it catches up to every alternative path $\{k_t\}$ with $k_o = \bar{k}_o$. If $\{\bar{k}_t\}$ is a path of positive stocks, consider alternative paths $\{k_t\}$ where $k_t = \bar{k}_t$ for $t \neq \tau$ and $k_\tau = x > 0$. Then $\{\bar{k}_t\}$ catches up to $\{k_t\}$ if and only if $u^\tau(\bar{k}_{\tau-1}, x) + u^{\tau+1}(x, \bar{k}_{\tau+1}) \leq u^\tau(\bar{k}_{\tau-1}, \bar{k}_\tau) + u^{\tau+1}(\bar{k}_\tau, \bar{k}_{\tau+1})$. But the differentiability assumption implies that this condition will be violated for some choice of x unless the equation

$$u_2^t(\bar{k}_{t-1}, \bar{k}_t) + u_1^{t+1}(\bar{k}_t, \bar{k}_{t+1}) = 0 \tag{1}$$

is true for $t = 1, 2, \ldots$, where u_1^t denotes the vector of derivatives of u^t with respect to initial stocks and u_2^t the vector of derivatives with respect to terminal stocks. Thus (1) is a necessary condition for optimal paths, and corresponds to the Euler-Lagrange condition of the calculus of variations.

The Araujo-Scheinkman trick is to treat (1) as defining a transformation between Banach spaces depending on initial stocks $\bar{k}_0$ as parameters and then use the implicit function theorem to obtain the path as a continuous function of k_0. Depending on the particular Banach space chosen, the continuity of this function will imply a local turnpike theorem. In their paper the space of bounded sequences of n vectors ℓ_∞^n is used, and the local theorem gives Liapounov stability of the optimal path for k_o near $\bar{k}_o$.

However, in a stationary model the optimal stationary state has a special status. Using another argument with an additional assumption they obtain local asymptotic stability of the optimal stationary state. Then combining these results they prove global asymptotic stability for a certain set of optimal paths. We will be able to dispense with stationarity. Nevertheless with assumptions analogous to those of Araujo and Scheinkman we will derive global stability with an exponential rate of convergence.

Let $\{\bar{k}_t\}$ be a path satisfying (1) where the distance of $\bar{k}_t$ from the boundary of Y_t is at least $\varepsilon > 0$ in all periods. Represent an arbitrary path $\{k_t\}$ by $\{z_t\}$ where $z_t = k_t - \bar{k}_t$. Also rewrite (1) as

$$v_2^t(z_{t-1}, z_t) + v_1^{t+1}(z_t, z_{t+1}) = 0, \quad t = 1, 2, \ldots, \tag{2}$$

setting $v^t(z_{t-1}, z_t) = u^t(k_{t-1}, k_t)$. Then v^t is real valued and twice continuously differentiable. We will also refer to $\{\tau_t\}$ as a path when it corresponds to a path $\{k_t\}$. We will consider paths $\{z_t\}$ such that the corresponding k_t remain in the interior of Y_t.

For a given $\beta < 1$, let $x_t = \beta^{-t} z_t$. Let F_z be the set of sequences $|z_t| < \frac{\varepsilon}{2}$ and $\beta^{-t}|z_t| < \infty$, for all t. Let F_x be the corresponding set of sequences $\{x_t\}$. Then F_x is contained in the Banach space ℓ_∞^n of bounded sequences of vectors in E_n. The norm $|x|_\infty$ of $x \in \ell_\infty^n = \sup_t |z_t|$, where $|z_t|$ is the Euclidean norm in R_+^n. The set F_x is not empty since it contains the zero path. By the assumption that $(\bar{k}_{t-1}, \bar{k}_t)$ is bounded interior to Y_t over t, F_x has a non-empty interior in ℓ_∞^n.

By analogy to Araujo and Scheinkman, we define a function ξ by

$$\xi(x_0, x)_t = \alpha_t \beta^{-t} v_2^t(\beta^{t-1} x_{t-1}, \beta^t x_t) + \alpha_t \beta^{-t} v_1^{t+1}(\beta^t x_t, \beta^{t+1} x_{t+1}),$$

for $t = 1, 2, \ldots$, where $x = \{x_t\}$, $t = 1, 2, \ldots$, and $\alpha_t > 0$ will be chosen later. Since $\xi(0,0)_t = 0$ for all t, if ε is chosen small, ξ maps F_x into ℓ_∞^n provided the functions $\xi(x_0, x)_t$ have derivatives that are bounded and uniformly continuous over t. (The symbols x, y, etc. are used to denote by context elements of R^n or ℓ_∞^n.)

We will say that a path $\{k_t\}$ is *regular* if it satisfies the Euler-Lagrange equations, and also

(a) There exists $\varepsilon > 0$ such that $|(k_{t-1}, k_t) - (x, y)| > \varepsilon$ for all $(x, y) \in$ boundary Y_t for all t.

(b) There exist numbers $\alpha_t > 0$ such that the second partial derivatives $\alpha_t u_{ij}^{t+2-i}(x, y)$, $i, j = 1$ or 2, are bounded from 0 and ∞, and are uniformly continuous near the path $\{k_t\}$.

In a quasi-stationary model where $u^t = \rho^t u$ for $0 < \rho < 1$, the choice $\alpha_t = \rho^{-t}$ is always effective for an interior path.

We now assert

Lemma 1 If $\{\bar{k}_t\}$ is a regular path, and ξ is defined as above, the derivative $D_x \xi(x_0, x)$ at $(0,0)$ is given by

$$[D_x \xi(x_0, x)h]_1 = \alpha_1 [v_{22}^1 + v_{11}^2]h_1 + \alpha_1 \beta v_{12}^2 h_2,$$

$$(3)$$

$$[D_x \xi(x_0, x)h]_t = \alpha_t \beta^{-1} v_{21}^t h_{t-1} + \alpha_t [v_{22}^t + v_{11}^{t+1}]h_t + \alpha_t \beta v_{12}^{t+1} h_{t+1},$$

for $t = 2, 3, \ldots$, where $h \in \ell_\infty^n$ and v_{ij}^t is evaluated at $(0,0)$. Moreover, $D_x \xi$ is continuous at $(0,0)$.

Proof I will summarize the proof of Araujo and Scheinkman. Let $L(h)$ be the linear map given by the right hand side of (3). Let $r(h) = \xi(0,h) - \xi(0,0) - L(h)$. If $\lim |r(h)|_\infty / |h|_\infty = 0$, as $|h|_\infty \to 0$, then $L(h)$ is the derivative of ξ at $(0,0)$.

Write $[\xi(x_0, x)]_t = \phi^t(x_{t-1}, x_t, x_{t+1})$. Then $\phi^t(x, y, w) = \alpha_t \beta^{-t} v_2^t (\beta^{t-1} x, \beta^t y) + \alpha_t \beta^{-t} v_1^{t+1} (\beta^t y, \beta^{t+1} w)$. Since ϕ^t is differentiable at $(0,0,0)$ uniformly over t, given $\gamma > 0$, there exists $\eta > 0$ such that $|(p, q, u)|$ implies $|\phi^t(x + p, y + q, w + v) - \phi^t(x, y, w) - \alpha_t \beta^{-1} v_{21}^t (\beta^{t+1} x, \beta^t y) p - \alpha_t v_{22}^t (\beta^{t+1} x, \beta^t y) q - \alpha_t v_{11}^{t+1} (\beta^t y, \beta^{t+1} w) q - \alpha_t \beta v_{12}^{t+1} (\beta^t y, \beta^{t+1} w) u| < |(p, q, u)| \frac{\gamma}{2}$. Hence given $\gamma > 0$ there exists $\eta > 0$ such that $|r(h_0, h)|_\infty = \sup_t |[\xi(0,h)]_t - [\xi(0,0)]_t - [L(0,0)h]_t| \leq \frac{\gamma}{2} \sup_t |[(0,h)]_t| = \frac{\gamma}{2} |(0,h)|_\infty$, provided $|(0,h)|_\infty < \eta$. The continuity of the derivative $D_x \xi$ follows from the continuity at $(0,0)$, uniform over t, of $\alpha_t v_{ij}^{t+2-i}$, $i, j = 1$ or 2.

Our objective is to use the implicit function theorem for the equation $\xi(x_o, x) = 0$ to express x as a function $\psi(x_o)$ in the neighborhood of $x_o = 0$, where ψ is continuous and differentiable in ℓ^n_∞. This will imply that there exists a function $k(k_o)$ for k_o near $\bar{k}_o$ such that (k_o, k) corresponding to $\{k_t\}$ satisfies (1) and k_t converges to $\bar{k}_t$ at an exponential rate. In other words, there is a path starting from any initial stocks near $\bar{k}_o$ that satisfies the necessary conditions for an optimum and converges exponentially to $\{\bar{k}_t\}$.

However, in order to invoke the implicit function theorem, we must show that the Jacobian of the map ξ, that is, the derivative $D_x\xi(x_o, x)$ evaluated at $(0,0)$, defines a linear homeomorphism of ℓ^n_∞ onto ℓ^n_∞ [Dieudonnée, 1960, p. 265]. Then $D_x\xi$ will be said to be invertible. Our objective can only be reached with additional restrictions on ξ. In particular, we may assume that $D_x\xi(x_o, x)$ has dominant diagonal blocks at $(0,0)$ when β is chosen sufficiently near 1.

An infinite matrix M formed of $n \times n$ blocks M_{ij}, with M_{ii} invertible, has row dominant diagonal blocks if $\sup_i |M_{ii}^{-1}| < \infty$ and $\sup_i \sum_{j \neq i} |M_{ii}^{-1}M_{ij}| = \delta < 1$. Here $|M_{ij}|$ is $\sup|M_{ij}y|$ for $y \in R^n$, $|y| = 1$. M defines a transformation of ℓ^n_∞ into ℓ^n_∞ when $\sum_j |M_{ij}|$ is bounded over i, since $|Mx|_\infty = \sup_i \sum_j |M_{ij}x_j| \leq \sup_j \sum_j |M_{ij}| |x_j| \leq |x|_\infty \cdot \sup_i \sum_j |M_{ij}|$. However, the boundedness over t of $\alpha_t v_{ij}^{t+2-i}$ implies this condition for $D_x\xi$. The invertibility of $D_x\xi$ will follow when the diagonal blocks are dominant.

Lemma 2 If M, mapping ℓ^n_∞ into ℓ^n_∞, has dominant diagonal blocks, M is invertible.

Proof Again I will summarize the proof of Araujo and Scheinkman. Since M is bounded on the unit ball in ℓ^n_∞, it is a continuous linear map. Thus it is only necessary to show that M^{-1} exists and is continuous over ℓ^n_∞. This follows if M is one to one and onto [Taylor, 1958, p. 179]. Let M_1 be the matrix of diagonal blocks M_{ii}^t with 0's elsewhere. The assumption that $|(M_{ii}^t)^{-1}|$ is bounded over t implies that M_1^{-1} exists and is continuous. Let $M_2 = M_1^{-1}M$. Then the assumption of dominant diagonal blocks implies $|M_2 - I| = \sum_{i \neq j} |(M_{ii})^{-1}|M_{ij}| = \delta < 1$. It follows from this that M_2 has a continuous inverse over ℓ^n_∞ [Taylor, 1958, p. 164]. Thus $M = M_1M_2$ has a continuous inverse over ℓ^n_∞.

We will now prove a preliminary turnpike result.

Lemma 3 If $(\bar{k}_o, \bar{k})$ is a path of accumulation that is regular and the Jacobian of the map ξ, derived from the Euler-Lagrange equation, has dominant diagonal blocks, then there is a neighborhood of $\bar{k}_o$ from each point of which there starts a path of accumulation that is regular and converges to $(\bar{k}_o, \bar{k})$ exponentially as $t \to \infty$.

Proof We will make use of the implicit function theorem. By the assumption of regularity $\xi(x_o, x)$ maps a neighborhood of $(0,0)$ in $R^n \times \ell_\infty^n$ into ℓ_∞^n with $\xi(0,0) = 0$. Moreover $D_x \xi(0,0)$ is a linear homeomorphism of ℓ_∞^n onto ℓ_∞^n from Lemmas 1 and 2. This implies that a continuous function $\psi(x_o)$ exists in a neighborhood of $x_o = 0$ such that $\xi(x_o, \psi(x_o)) = 0$ where $\psi(x_o)$ is continuous and differentiable.

The continuity of ψ implies that $|x_o|$ may be chosen small enough to place x near 0, that is, $\sup_t |x_t| < \varepsilon$ for a small positive ε. Then $z_t = \beta^t x_t$ for $\beta < 1$ implies that z_t converges exponentially to 0, that is, k_t converges exponentially to $\bar{k}_t$. This proves the lemma.

In Araujo and Scheinkman ξ is defined directly from (2) without introducing β^t ($\alpha_t = \rho^t$ for their quasi-stationary model). They then assume dominant diagonal blocks for $D_x \xi$ with this definition of ξ, that is, $|[v_{22}^t + v_{11}^{t+1}]^{-1} v_{21}^t| + |[v_{22}^t + v_{11}^{t+1}]^{-1} v_{12}^{t+1}| < \delta < 1$, for all t. However, it is easily seen that this condition is satisfied for a certain δ if and only if our condition is satisfied for a choice of β with $\delta < \beta < 1$.

It should be noted that we do not know that $\psi(x_o)$ is the only regular path from x_o, nor do we know that $\psi(x_o)$ is optimal. Optimality considerations require that $k + \psi(x_o)$ be compared with *all* other paths from $\bar{k}_o + x_o$, not just those that are regular or remain close to k. In order to make this comparison effectively we need some further definitions. First we normalize the utility functions u^t by adding an appropriate constant in each period so that $u^t(\bar{k}_{t-1}, \bar{k}_t) = 0$ for each t. Then we say that $\{\bar{k}_t\}$ is *reachable* from a path $\{k_t\}$, $t = 0, 1, 2, \ldots$, if from any k_t there is a path $\{k'_\tau\}$, $\tau = t, t+1, \ldots$, and a number μ, such that $k'_t = k_t$ and, for some $T > t$, $k'_T = \bar{k}_T$, where $\sum_{\tau=t+1}^{T} u^\tau(k_{\tau-1}, k_\tau) < \mu$. The normalization is inessential, but convenient. We will say that a path $\{k_t\}$ is *bad* if for any number v there is T such that $\sum_{\tau=1}^{t} u(k_{\tau-1}, k_\tau) < v$ for all $t > T$. We now make the assumption

I. The path $\{\bar{k}_t\}$ is reachable from every path $\{k_t\}$, $t = 0, 1, 2, \ldots$, that is not bad.

Next define the value loss of the stocks (x, y) relative to (z, w) by $\delta_t(x, y; z, w) = u^t \cdot (z, w) - u_2^t w - u_1^t z - (u^t \cdot (x, y) - u_2^t y - u_1^t x)$, where derivatives are evaluated at (z, w). Since u^t is strictly concave $\delta_t > 0$ will hold for any choices $(x, y) \neq (z, w)$ in Y_t. We will say that the concavity of u^t is *weakly uniform* if for any ε, there is $\delta > 0$, such that $|u_1^t \cdot (x - z)| > \varepsilon$ implies $\delta_t(x, y; z, w)$ for all t and δ for any choices of (x, y) and (z, w) in Y_t, where $u_1^t = u_1^t(z, w)$, and $t = 1, 2, \ldots$. Weak uniformity of concavity is similar to an assumption of uniform absolute risk aversion for the utility functions u^t, although risk does not enter our argument. Note that weak uniformity is not sufficient to imply a turnpike theorem in itself by the value loss approach. In particular, weak uniformity is consistent with $u^t = \rho^t u$ for $0 < \rho < 1$, which allows the condition $|u_1^t \cdot (x - z)| > \varepsilon$ to fail for large t even though $|x - z|$ is large. We add the assumption

II.   The concavity of u^t is weakly uniform, over t and Y_t.

We will say that an optimal path $\{k_t\}$ that is regular satisfies the dominant diagonal condition if the Jacobian $D_x \xi$ of the function $\xi(x_0, x)$, defined relative to $\{k_t\}$, has dominant diagonal blocks. Now with the aid of Assumptions I and II we can prove a turnpike theorem for optimal paths whose initial stocks lie close together.

Theorem 1   Suppose $\{\bar{k}_t\}$, $t = 0, 1, \ldots$, is an optimal path that is regular and satisfies the dominant diagonal condition. And Assumptions I and II are met. Then every capital stock k_o near $\bar{k}_o$ initiates a unique optimal path, and this path converges exponentially to $\{\bar{k}_t\}$.

Proof   We will show that the paths proved to exist in Lemma 3 are optimal paths. Define the value function $V^t(x) = \sup \sum_{\tau=t+1}^{\infty} u^\tau(k_{\tau-1}, k_\tau)$ over all paths $\{k_\tau\}$, $\tau = t, t+1, \ldots$, with $k_t = x$, for which the sum exists. For an optimal path $\{\bar{k}_t\}$ it is shown that a sequence of prices $\{\bar{p}_t\}$ exists that satisfy the relations

$$V^t(\bar{k}_t) - \bar{p}_t \bar{k}_t \geq V^t(x) - \bar{p}_t x, \text{ and} \tag{1}$$

$$u^{t+1}(\bar{k}_t, \bar{k}_{t+1}) + \bar{p}_{t+1}\bar{k}_{t+1} - \bar{p}_t\bar{k}_t \geq u^{t+1}(x, y) + \bar{p}_{t+1}y - \bar{p}_t x,$$

for $(x, y) \in Y_t$, $\tag{5}$

when $\{\bar{k}_t\}$ is regular and $V^t(x)$ is well defined [McKenzie, 1976]. However, in our case the differentiability of u^t implies that $\bar{p}_t = -u_2^t(\bar{k}_{t-1}, \bar{k}_t) = u_1^{t+1}(\bar{k}_t, \bar{k}_{t+1})$. (Benveniste and Scheinkman [1976] have also proved that $u_1^{t+1} = dV^t/dx$ at $x = \bar{k}_t$.)

Now consider the path $\{k^t\}$ from k_o near $\bar{k}_o$ proved to exist in Lemma 3 and any alternative path $\{k_t'\}$ from $k_o' = k_o$ that is not bad. From (5) we obtain

$$u^{t+1'} - \bar{u}^{t+1} = \bar{p}_t(k'_t - \bar{k}_t) - \bar{p}_{t+1}(k'_{t+1} - \bar{k}_{t+1}) - \delta_t \tag{6}$$

where $u^{t+1'} = u^{t+1}(k'_t, k'_{t+1})$, $\bar{u}^{t+1} = u^{t+1}(\bar{k}_t, \bar{k}_{t+1})$ and $\delta_t \geqq 0$. Summing (6) gives

$$\sum_1^T (u^{t'} - \bar{u}^t) = \bar{p}_o(k'_o - \bar{k}_o) + \bar{p}_T(\bar{k}_T - k'_T) - \sum_1^T \delta_t. \tag{7}$$

From (5) and the normalization of u^t, we have $-V^T(k'_T) \geqq \bar{p}_T(\bar{k}_T - k'_T)$. But $V^T(k'_T) > v$ for some number v holds by Assumption I since $\{k'_t\}$ is not bad. Thus the right hand side of (7) is bounded except for δ_t. However, if $\sum_1^T \delta_t$ is unbounded $\{k'_t\}$ is bad, a contradiction. Thus $\delta_t \to 0$, and by Assumption II it must be true that $\bar{p}_T(\bar{k}_T - k'_T)$ converges to 0 as $T \to \infty$.

Since (k_t, k_{t+1}) is interior to Y_t and u^t is strictly concave, the analog of (6) holds for $\{k_t\}$ and $\{k'_t\}$, that is, (7) holds in the form

$$\sum_1^T (u'_t - u_t) = p_o(k'_o - k_o) + p_T(k_T - k'_T) - \sum_1^T \delta'_t, \tag{8}$$

where $u_t = u_t(k_{t-1}, k_t)$, $p_t = -u_2^t(k_{t-1}, k_t)$, and $\delta'_t \geqq 0$. However, $k'_o = k_o$. Also $k_T \to \bar{k}_T$, and $p_t \to \bar{p}_t$, from Lemma 3 and the continuity of u_2^t, which is uniform over t along $\{\bar{k}_t\}$ by regularity. Thus $p_T(k_T - k'_T) \to \bar{p}_T(\bar{k}_T - k'_T) \to 0$, and the right hand side of (8) converges to $-\sum_1^T \delta'_t \leqq 0$, and < 0, if k'_t differs from k_t for any t. This shows that $\{k_t\}$ is an optimal path, since $\{k'_t\}$ is an arbitrary path that is not bad. The optimal path is unique by strict concavity of u^t. This finishes the proof of the turnpike theorem where initial stocks are close.

Our task now is to extend this result to a global analog. Define the loss function $L_t(x) = \inf \sum_{\tau=t+1}^{\infty} \delta_\tau(k_{\tau-1}, k_\tau; \bar{k}_{\tau-1}, \bar{k}_\tau)$ over all accumulation paths with $k_t = x$. $L_t(x)$ is defined on R_+^n but $L_t(x) = \infty$ if there is no path from x. Let $K = \{x \,|\, x \in R_+^n$ and $L_o(x) < \infty\}$. K contains an open set since it contains all x such that $(x, \bar{k}_1) \in Y_1$.

Lemma 4 Suppose $\{\bar{k}_t\}$ is an optimal path that is regular and Assumptions I and II hold. Then there is a unique optimal path from any $k_o \in K$.

Proof The proof of this lemma is made by showing that there is a path from $x \in K$ realizing the loss function $L_o(x)$ and that this path is optimal. The method of proof was discovered by Brock [1970] and applied to the present case by McKenzie [1974]. The proof that a path exists that realizes the minimum value loss is just as in these references. It involves taking the limit of a sequence of paths whose value losses approach $L_o(x)$ and showing that the limit path has a value loss equal to $L_o(x)$. Then we may consider once more the expression (7) where $\{k'_t\}$ is the limit path. Since $\sum_1^\infty \delta_t$ is finite, Assumption II implies that $\bar{p}_t(\bar{k}_T - k'_T) \to 0$. Now consider (7) with an alternative path $\{k''_t\}$ substituted for $\{k'_t\}$ where $k''_t = k'_t = x$, where $\{k''_t\}$ is not bad. By Assumption I we may deduce as in the proof of Theorem 1 that $\bar{p}(\bar{k}_T - k''_T) \to 0$. Subtracting (7) for $\{k'_t\}$ from (7) for $\{k''_t\}$ gives

$$\sum_1^T (u''_t - u'_t) \to \sum_1^T \delta'_t - \sum_1^T \delta''_t \leqq 0, \tag{9}$$

since $\{k'_t\}$ minimizes value loss. Here δ'_t is the value loss for (k'_t, k'_{t+1}) and δ''_t for (k''_t, k''_{t+1}). This demonstrates the optimality of $\{k'_t\}$. Uniqueness follows from the strict concavity of u^t.

Let K' be the subset of K whose optimal paths are regular and satisfy the dominant diagonal condition. We will find, using the method of Araujo and Scheinkman, that Theorem 1 can be extended to the connected component C of K' that contains $\bar{k}_o$. Let S be the subset of C such that the optimal path from $x \in S$ converges exponentially to $\{\bar{k}_t\}$. By Theorem 1, and the hypothesis on $\{\bar{k}_t\}$, C contains an open set that is not empty. We will show that S is open and closed in C, and, therefore, $S = C$. Suppose $k_o \in C$. By Lemma 4 there is a unique optimal path $\{k_t\}$ from k^o, and this path is regular and satisfies the dominant diagonal condition by definition of K'. Thus the hypothesis of Theorem 1 is met for $\{k_t\}$, and from every point in a small neighborhood of k_o the unique optimal path converges exponentially to $\{k_t\}$. Since $k_o \in C$, k_t in turn converges to $\bar{k}_t$ exponentially. Thus $|k'_t - \bar{k}_t| \leqq |k'_t \quad k_l| + |k_t - \bar{k}_t| \leq \beta^t |k'_o - k_o| + \beta^t |k_o - \bar{k}_o|$, and k'_t also converges exponentially at rate β^t to $\bar{k}_t$, as $t \to \infty$. Thus S is open.

Now suppose that $k_o \in \text{bdry } S$ and $k_o \in C$. Then once more Theorem 1 applies so that the unique optimal path $\{k'_t\}$ departing from k'_o near k_o converges to $\{k_t\}$ departing from k_o. But some of these k'_o belong to S and the optimal paths they start converge exponentially to $\{\bar{k}_t\}$. Therefore, k^t must converge exponentially to $\bar{k}_t$ and S is closed in C. But C is a connected set, so $S = C$. We have proved

Theorem 2 Suppose $\{\bar{k}_t\}$ is an optimal path of capital accumulation that is regular, and Assumptions I and II are met. Let K be the set of capital stocks from which there are paths with finite value loss relative to $\{\bar{k}_t\}$. Then there are unique optimal paths from each $k_t \in K$. K is a convex set with non-empty interior. Assume the optimal paths $\{k_t\}$ from $k_o \in K'$ satisfy the dominant diagonal condition and C is the connected component of K' containing $\bar{k}_o$. Then $k_t \to \bar{k}_t$ as $t \to \infty$ at an exponential rate for any path $\{k_t\}$ with $k_o \in C$. C has a non-empty interior.

The crucial feature of the argument leading to the turnpike result is the invertibility of the Jacobian of (2) after multiplying by the α_t. We treated (2) as defining a transformation of ℓ_∞^n into itself. However, other Banach spaces may also be used and, given other assumptions, may be more effective. For example, if uniform strict concavity is assumed in the strong sense that is appropriate for value loss arguments, the appropriate space is Hilbert space ℓ_∞^n. The invertibility lemma follows if the Jacobian is negative definite. But consideration of the block diagonal form shows that the Jacobian is negative definite if $\begin{bmatrix} \alpha_{t-1} u_{11}^t & \alpha_{t-1} u_{12}^t \\ \alpha_t u_{21}^t & \alpha_t u_{22}^t \end{bmatrix}$ is negative definite uniformly over t and Y_t. In the quasi-stationary case $u^t = \rho^t u$, $\alpha_t = \rho^{-t+1}$ and the critical form is given by $\begin{bmatrix} \rho u_{11} & \rho u_{12} \\ u_{21} & u_{22} \end{bmatrix}$. But as Brock and Scheinkman [1975] have shown this is the condition for applying the value loss method to the case of discounted utility in the manner of Cass and Shell [1976]. Thus for differentiable utility and interior paths, the method of Araujo and Scheinkman includes the value loss approach as a special case.

Note

1. This chapter was presented in an earlier version to the American Summer Meeting of the Econometric Society in Madison, Wisconsin, June, 1976. The revision has benefited from suggestions of José Scheinkman.

References

[1] Araujo, A., and J. A. Scheinkman. Smoothness, Comparative Dynamics, and the Turnpike Property, forthcoming in *Econometrica*, 1977.

[2] Benveniste, L., and J. A. Scheinkman. Differentiable Value Functions in Concave Dynamic Optimization Problems, University of Chicago Working Paper, October, 1975.

[3] Brock, W. A. On Existence of Weakly Maximal Programmes in a Multi-Sector Economy, *Review of Economic Studies*, 37, 2, April, 1970, pp. 263–288.

[4] Brock, W. A., and J. A. Scheinkman. On the Long-Run Behavior of a Competitive Firm, *Equilibrium and Disequilibrium in Economic Theory*, ed. G. Schwödauer, Springer-Verlag, Vienna, 1975.

[5] Cass, D., and K. Shell. The Structure and Stability of Competitive Dynamical Systems, *Journal of Economic Theory*, 12, 1, February, 1976, pp. 31–70.

[6] Dieudonnée, J. *Foundations of Modern Analysis*, Academic Press, New York, 1960.

[7] McKenzie, L. W. Turnpike Theorems with Technology and Welfare Function Variable, *Mathematical Models in Economics*, ed. J. Łoś, and M. W. Łoś, American Elsevier, New York, 1974, pp. 271–287.

[8] McKenzie, L. W. Turnpike Theory, *Econometrica*, 44, 5, September, 1976, pp. 841–865.

[9] Taylor, A. E. *Introduction to Functional Analysis*, John Wiley, New York, 1958.

A Bibliography of the Work of Oskar Morgenstern

Books

Wirtschaftsprognose, eine Untersuchung ihrer Voraussetzungen und Möglichkeiten, Vienna: Julius Springer Verlag, 1928, iv + 129 pp.

Edit. and Preface to: *A. de Viti de Marco, Grundlehren der Finanzwirtschaft*, Tübingen, 1932.

Ed.: *Beiträge zur Konjunkturforschung*, Vol. 4 and subsequent, Vienna: Julius Springer Verlag, 1934.

Die Grenzen der Wirtschaftspolitik, Vienna: Julius Springer Verlag, 1934, 136 pp.

The Limits of Economics, Translation by Vera Smith, London: W. Hodge and Co., Ltd., 1937, v + 151 pp. (Revised edition of No. 4).

Theory of Games and Economic Behavior, (with John von Neumann) Princeton: Princeton University Press, 1944, xviii + 625 pp.

Theory of Games and Economic Behavior, (with John von Neumann), 2nd edition, revised and enlarged, Princeton: Princeton University Press, 1947, xviii + 641 pp.

On the Accuracy of Economic Observations, Princeton: Princeton University Press, 1950, ix + 101 pp.

Theory of Games and Economic Behavior, (with John von Neumann), 3rd edition, revised, Princeton: Princeton University Press, 1953, xx + 641 pp.

Ed. and contributor, *Economic Activity Analysis*, New York: John Wiley and Sons, Inc., 1954, xviii + 554 pp.

Studi di Metodologia Economica, ed. F. di Fenizio, trans. M. Talamona, Milano, 1955, pp. 152.

International Financial Transactions and Business Cycles, National Bureau of Economic Research, Princeton: Princeton University Press, 1959, xxvi + 591 pp.

The Question of National Defense, Random House, New York, November, 1959, xii + 306 pp.

The Question of National Defense, 2nd revised edition, Vintage-Books, V-192, New York, 1961, xiv + 328 pp.

Spieltheorie und Wirtschaftliches Verhalten, Würzburg, 1961, xxiv + 668 pp. (Translation of No. 7), with new preface.

Strategie-Heute, (enlarged and new preface), Frankfurt, 1962, 323 pp. (Translation of No. 14.).

Beikoku Kobubo no Shomondai Kigima Institute of Research, Tokyo, December, 1962, 383 pp. (Translation of No. 13).

On the Accuracy of Economic Observations, 2nd completely revised edition, Princeton: Princeton University Press, September, 1963, v–viii, ix–xiv, and 322 pp.

"Über die Genauigkeit Wirtschaftlicher Beobachtungen," trans. by V. Trapp, with Preface by K. Wagner, *Einzelschriften der Deutschen Statistischen Gesellschaft,* No. 4, Munich, 1952, 129 pp. (Revised translation of No. 18).

Spieltheorie und Wirtschaftswissenschaft, Vienna: R. Oldenbourg Verlag, 1963, 200 pp.

24 A Primal Route to the Turnpike and Liapounov Stability

Lionel W. McKenzie

In virtually all proofs of turnpike results, that is, proofs of theorems on the asymptotic convergence of optimal paths of capital accumulation, duality considerations play a critical role. This is natural in an economic context, where the problem in continuous time is to maximize $\int_0^\infty u(k, \dot{k})\, dt$, since the basic Euler relation from calculus of variations,

$$\frac{d}{dt} \frac{\partial u(k, \dot{k})}{\partial \dot{k}} - \frac{\partial u(k, \dot{k})}{\partial k} = 0,$$

can be interpreted to say that the rate of change of the price of capital goods (in utility units) equals the rental on capital goods; see Samuelson (1965). In the global analysis of continuous time models the Hamiltonian function $H(p, k)$ is often used where p is a price vector for capital goods. See Cass and Shell (1976), or Brock and Scheinkman (1976). In discrete time models, various Liapounov functions appear such as the sum of value losses $\sum_1^T \delta(k_{t-1}, k_t)$, which is defined using the prices that support a concave utility function. See Gale (1967), McKenzie (1968), Scheinkman (1976) and Bewley (1980). Another Liapounov function also based on value loss is the product $(p'_t - p_t)(k'_t - k_t)$ of the price differences and the capital stock differences between two optimal paths. See Cass and Shell (1976) or McKenzie (1976).

So far as I am aware the only exception to this rule in the literature is a brief passage in Jeanjean (1974), which is adopted in McKenzie (1979) for the case of undiscounted utility. His method uses the property of concave functions that a chord of the graph of the function lies below the graph. I will show in this paper how Jeanjean's method may be applied using a Liapounov function similar in other ways to that of Bewley to prove turnpike theorems for the discounted case as well. We will concentrate on quasi-stationary models where $u_t(x, y) = \rho^t u(x, y)$.

The basic theorem proves Liapounov stability for an optimal path relative to an optimal stationary path. That is, for a discount factor near enough to 1, an optimal path eventually remains in a small neighborhood of the stationary optimal path. However, this theorem can be strengthened. Assuming differentiability of certain functions, asymptotic stability can be proved.

24.1 The Reduced Model

The argument will be phrased in terms of the reduced model, in which the utility achieved over a period of time by the optimizing agent (society, firm, or household, for example) is expressed as a function of the initial and terminal state variables. The control variables (investment, consumption, activity levels, for example) have been chosen to maximize the utility achieved in the period given the assignment of initial and terminal values of the state variables. Then to achieve an optimal plan for a series of periods it is only necessary to choose the sequence of state variables corresponding to the ends of periods at appropriate levels within the range of feasible variation. These are the levels of the state variables at the beginnings of the subsequent periods, so all utility levels are determined.

This reduction avoids the need to specify the time pattern of control variables within periods, which will normally be very complex and no doubt in some cases irreducible to the choice of levels at a finite number of times. Indeed, it is almost never the case that initial stocks and the amount of goods consumed over a time period will identify both the utility achieved and the terminal value of the capital stocks. To have a well defined optimization problem for the single period it would be necessary to specify the terminal stocks, as well as the total consumption over the period. But it is also sufficient to specify the initial stocks together with the terminal stocks.

The most serious defect of the reduced model is the implicit assumption that the utility experienced in one period is independent of events in other periods, where similar myopic optimizations of period-wise utility have taken place. However, this assumption is customary in the turnpike literature, whatever model is used. Also it is slightly less serious in discrete time since the influence of one period on the following period presumably comes more heavily from the end than from the beginning of the earlier period. Thus as the period is lengthened the influence of earlier periods should tend to vanish.

For the sake of concreteness we will describe our model as a model of accumulation of capital by an economy which acts to maximize a social utility function over an infinite horizon. However, it should be remembered that other kinds of state variables are admissible, such as the levels of pollutants, the size and skills of the population, or the stores of technical knowledge, although one should be wary that the assumptions placed on the utility function do not become too implausible, even as approximations, when some of these interpretations are made. See Starrett (1972).

The basis of our model is a utility function $u_t(x, y)$, which takes real values, where x is a vector of initial capital stocks, at time $t - 1$, y is a vector of terminal capital stocks, at time t, and t is an integer. More precisely, $x \in R^{n_{t-1}}$ and $y \in R^{n_t}$, where n_τ is the number of possible kinds of capital goods in period τ and R^{n_τ} is the Cartesian product of n_τ copies of the real line with the Euclidean topology. Let $D_t \subset R^{n_{t-1}}_+ \times R^{n_t}_+$ be a convex set where $R^{n_\tau}_+$ is the non-negative orthant of R^{n_τ}. We assume

I.   The utility functions u_t map D_t into the real line. They are concave and closed for all t.

II.   If $(x, y) \in D_t$ and $|x| < \xi < \infty$, then there is $\zeta < \infty$ such that $|y| < \zeta$.

I say that a concave function $f(x)$ is closed if $x^s \to x$, where $x \in$ boundary D and D is the domain of definition, implies $f(x^s) \to f(x)$ for $x \in D$, or $f(x^s) \to -\infty$ otherwise. A concave utility function defined on capital stocks is implied by the neoclassical model, where utility is defined on consumption and consumption is given as the difference between the output and terminal stocks, if the utility function is concave in consumption goods, and the production function, which represents the maximum output of one good, given the outputs of other goods and the initial stocks, is concave. This model is described in Burmeister and Dobell (1970). The subscript t on the utility function indicates that both the neoclassical utility function and the production function may be changing over time. Also endogenous technical change may in some cases be treated as a form of capital accumulation.

A path of capital accumulation is a sequence of capital stock vectors $\{k_t\}$, $t = t_0, t_0 + 1, \ldots$, where $(k_{t-1}, k_t) \in D_t$ for all t. If $\{k'_t\}$ is another path of accumulation, with $k'_{t_0} = k_{t_0}$, we say that $\{k_t\}$ catches up to $\{k'_t\}$ if for any $\varepsilon > 0$, there is a time $T(\varepsilon)$ such that $\sum_{t_0+1}^{T} u_t(k'_{t-1}, k'_t) -$

$\sum_{t_0+1}^{T} u_t(k_{t-1}, k_t) < \varepsilon$ for all $T > T(\varepsilon)$. We say that $\{k_t\}$ is *optimal* if it catches up to every alternative path starting from the same initial stocks k_{t_0}. This criterion may be found in Gale (1967). There are several variants of it which need not concern us.

24.2   Uniform Strict Concavity

It is convenient to define a *value* V_t for capital stocks. If $x \in R_+^{n_t}$ and there is a path of accumulation beginning from x, define $V_t(x) = \sup(\lim \inf \sum_{t+1}^{T} u_\tau(h_{\tau-1}, h_\tau), T \to \infty)$ over all paths $\{h_\tau\}$ with $h_t = x$. If no path of accumulation beginning at x exists, put $V_t(x) = -\infty$. This value function was used by Peleg and Zilcha (1977) in a stationary model. The concavity of V_t follows directly from Assumption I. Also define $K_t = \{x \mid V_t(x) > -\infty\}$, that is, K_t is the set of $x \in R_+^{n_t}$ which have values that are finite or $+\infty$.

The notion of uniform strict concavity is applied to the utility functions along a path of accumulation. We say that the u_t are *uniformly strictly concave* along the path $\{k_t\}$ if $|(x, y) - (k_{t-1}, k_t)| > \varepsilon > 0$ implies there exists $\delta > 0$ such that $u_t\left(\frac{1}{2}(x + k_{t-1}, y + k_t)\right) > \frac{1}{2}(u_t(x, y) + u_t(k_{t-1}, k_t)) + \delta$, independently of t. Using this notion we may prove a turnpike theorem.

Theorem 1   Let $\{k_t\}$ and $\{k_t'\}$, $t = 0, 1, \ldots$, be optimal paths where the u_t are uniformly strictly concave along $\{k_t\}$. Assume $k_0 \in$ relative interior K_0, and $k_0' \in K_0$. Then for any $\varepsilon > 0$, there is a number $N(\varepsilon)$ such that $|k_t' - k_t| > \varepsilon$ can hold for at most $N(\varepsilon)$ periods.

Proof   We define a utility gain achieved in each period by the average of the two paths compared with the average of the utilities along the two paths. Let the capital stocks along the average path $\{k_t''\}$ satisfy $k_t'' = 1/2(k_t + k_t')$. By the convexity of D_t, $\{k_t''\}$ is well defined. The *utility gain* $\gamma_t = u_t(k_{t-1}'', k_t'') - \frac{1}{2}(u_t(k_{t-1}, k_t) + u_t(k_{t-1}', k_t'))$. We also define the total prospective gain from the time t by $G(t) = \sum_{t+1}^{\infty} \gamma_\tau$, where $G(t) = \infty$ is allowed.

By $k_0 \in$ relative interior K_0 we mean that $k_0 \in$ interior K_0 in the relative topology of the smallest affine subspace containing K_0. It is a consequence of this assumption that $\bar{k}$ exists where $\bar{k} \in K_0$ and $k_0 = \alpha \bar{k} + (1 - \alpha)k_0''$, for some α with $0 < \alpha < 1$. We may choose the origin of utility independently in each period so that $u_t(k_{t-1}, k_t) = 0$ for all t, and $V_0(k_0) = 0$. Thus $k_0 \in K_0$ in any case. Also the concavity of V_0 over K_0 implies that $V_0(k_0) \geqslant \alpha V_0(\bar{k}) + (1 - \alpha)V_0(k'')$. Since $V_0(k_0) = 0$, this inequality is equivalent to

$$V_0(k_0'') \leqslant \frac{\alpha}{\alpha - 1} V_0(\bar{k}). \tag{1}$$

But the definition of V_0 and $G(0)$ implies, since $\{k_t''\}$ is a feasible path, that $V_0(k_0'') \geqslant \frac{1}{2}(V_0(k_0) + V_0(k_0')) + G(0)$, or

$$V_0(k_0'') \geqslant \frac{1}{2} V_0(k_0') + G(0). \tag{2}$$

It is immediate from (1) and (2) that

$$G(0) \leqslant \frac{\alpha}{\alpha - 1} V_0(\bar{k}) - \frac{1}{2} V_0(k_0'). \tag{3}$$

It may be verified that the right side of (3) is non-negative. On the other hand, given $\varepsilon > 0$, there is $\delta > 0$ such that $G(0) \geqslant N(\varepsilon)\delta$ where $N(\varepsilon)$ is the number of periods when the distance of the two paths exceeds ε. Thus $N(\varepsilon) \leqslant G(0)/\delta$, which is a finite number. This is the desired result. Its method of proof illustrates the primal approach to turnpike theorems. The first use of this approach, so far as I know, was due to Patrick Jeanjean.

If the dual method were used to prove a theorem of the same type as Theorem 1, it would be necessary to prove that support prices exist for at least one of the optimal programs, preferably Weitzman prices (1973) that support the value function as well as the utility function in each period. The assumption that would serve in place of uniform strict concavity is uniform value loss of the other path relative to the price supported path. This is an assumption that could be met even though the utility were generated by a finite set of activities in each period if the price supported path lay on a vertex. It would be an optimal stationary path in a stationary model that sits on a given vertex of the graph of the utility function. On the other hand, uniform strict concavity along the path would not be met. However, a way around this difficulty exists in the present case through smoothing the graph of u_t while preserving the vertex on which the stationary path is located as a facet of the graph.

24.3 The Quasi-Stationary Model

Theorem 1 will not apply to a model in which the utility of given stocks tends to vanish in the far future. In particular, it cannot be used to establish the stability of a stationary optimal path in the model with discounted utility. However, the utility gain approach can still be ap-

plied to prove stability for values of the discount factor close enough to
1. Our first task is to prove that non-trivial stationary optimal paths exist in the quasi-stationary model under appropriate assumptions.

The *quasi-stationary* model is a model satisfying Assumptions I and II
that also satisfies

1. $D_t = D$ and $u_t = \rho^t u(x, y)$ for $0 < \bar{\rho} < \rho < 1$, for all t. $D \subset R^{2n}_+$,
where n is the number of capital goods.

In addition, we will make the following assumptions.

2.   There is $\zeta > 0$ such that $|x| \geqslant \zeta$ implies for any $(x, y) \in D$, $|y| < \gamma|x|$,
where $\gamma < 1$.

3.   If $(x, y) \in D$, then $(z, w) \in D$ for all $z \geqslant x$ and $0 \leqslant w \leqslant y$. Moreover,
$u(z, w) \geqslant u(x, y)$.

4.   There is $(\bar{x}, \bar{y}) \in D$ such that $\bar{\rho}\bar{y} > \bar{x}$.

Assumption 2 implies that all paths are bounded. Assumption 3
provides for free disposal of surplus stocks. This assumption excludes
the consideration of harmful goods such as pollutants in the quasi-
stationary model. Assumption 4 says that a stock exists which can be
expanded in one period beyond the levels given by multiplying the
stock by the reciprocal of the discount factor. Thus there are no ex-
haustible and nonproducible resources in the quasi-stationary model.
However, a steady growth of population is not excluded if the utility
function and its arguments are interpreted as per capita.

Under these Assumptions we may prove

Theorem 2   The quasi-stationary model has a stationary optimal path.

Proof   First, we define a subset Δ of the diagonal of $R^n \times R^n = R^{2n}$,
which contains all stationary paths. Let Δ be all $(x, x) \in R^n \times R^n$ such
that $x \geqslant 0$ and $|x| \leqslant \zeta$. Let f be a correspondence from Δ into D, where
$f(x, x) = \{(z, w) \mid \rho w - z \geqslant (\rho - 1)x \text{ for } (z, w) \in D\}$. Assumption 4 implies that $(\bar{x}, \bar{y}) \in f(x, x)$ for any $(x, x) \in \Delta$. Thus $f(x, x)$ is not empty for
$(x, x) \in \Delta$.

We will need

Lemma 1   If $(z, w) \in f(x, x)$, for $(x, x) \in \Delta$, then $|z| < \zeta$.

Proof   If $(z, w) \in f(x, x)$, the definition of f implies that

$$|z| \leqslant \rho|w| + (1 - \rho)|x|, \tag{1}$$

where $\rho < 1$. Suppose $|z| = \zeta$. Then by Assumption 2 $|w| < \zeta$. But by (1), $\zeta \leqslant \rho|w| + (1 - \rho)\zeta$, or $|w| \geqslant \zeta$, which is a contradiction. If $|z| > \zeta$, consider $(\bar{x}, \bar{y}) \in f(x, x)$ by Assumption 4 with $|\bar{x}| < \zeta$ by Assumption 2. Let $(z', w') = \alpha(\bar{x}, \bar{y}) + (1 - \alpha)(z, w)$, $0 < \alpha < 1$. Then $(z', w') \in f(x, x)$ by the convexity of $f(x, x)$. For an appropriate choice of α, $|z'| = \zeta$, which leads once again to a contradiction. This proves the lemma.

Lemma 2 The correspondence f is lower semicontinuous.

Proof Suppose $(z, w) \in f(x, x)$ and $(x^s, x^s) \to (x, x)$, where $(x^s, x^s) \in \Delta$, $s = 1, 2, \ldots$. Let (z^s, w^s) be the point on the line segment from (z, w) to the point $(\bar{x}, \bar{y})$ assumed to exist in Assumption 4, which is closest to (z, w) and also contained in $f(x^s, x^s)$. The existence of (z^s, w^s) follows from the fact that $(\bar{x}, \bar{y}) \in f(x^s, x^s)$. Suppose $(z^s, w^s) \nrightarrow (z, w)$. Then there is a point of accumulation $(\bar{z}, \bar{w})$ at a distance of at least ε from (z, w) such that a subsequence (z^s, w^s) (retain notation) converges to $(\bar{z}, \bar{w})$ with $\rho w^s - z^s = (\rho - 1)x^s$. Since $\rho\bar{y} - \bar{x} > (\rho - 1)x$ and $\rho w - z \geqslant (\rho - 1)x$ it follows that $\rho\bar{w} - \bar{z} > (\rho - 1)x$. This implies $\rho w^s - z^s > (\rho - 1)x^s$ for large s, contradicting the choice of (z^s, w^s). Thus $(z^s, w^s) \to (z, w)$ and f is lower semicontinuous.

Let g be a correspondence from the collection of subsets of D to D defined by $g(U) = \{(z, w) \in U \mid u(z, w) \geqslant u(z', w') \text{ for all } (z', w') \in U\}$ for $U \subset D$. Consider $(g \circ f)(x, x)$ for $(x, x) \in \Delta$. Assumptions 2 and 3 imply that $|w| < \zeta$ if $|z| \leqslant \zeta$ and $(z, w) \in D$. Then Lemma 1 implies that $f(x, x)$ is bounded. Moreover, the set $B = \{(x, y) \in f(x, x) \mid u(x, y) \geqslant u(\bar{x}, \bar{y})\}$ is compact and contains $(\bar{x}, \bar{y})$. Since $u(x, y)$ is closed in B by Assumption I, it follows that $(g \circ f)(x, x)$ is convex, compact, and not empty.

Let h be a correspondence from the collection of subsets of D to Δ defined by $h(U) = \{(z, z) \mid (z, w) \in U\}$. Thus h is a projection on Δ along the first factor of the Cartesian product $E^n \times E^n$. The correspondence h is continuous. Finally, define the correspondence $F = h \circ g \circ f$. F maps Δ into the set of non-empty, convex, compact subsets of Δ. The closedness of u and the lower semicontinuity of f imply that $g \circ f$ is upper semicontinuous (Berge, 1963, p. 116). Since h and $g \circ f$ have compact range, F is also upper semicontinuous. Since Δ is compact and convex and F maps Δ into convex subsets, the Kakutani fixed point theorem (Berge, 1963, p. 174) implies there is (k, k) such that $(k, k) \in F(k, k)$. It is clear that (k, k) maximizes utility over $f(k, k)$. These results may be summarized as

Lemma 3   There is $(k, k) \in D$ such that $u(k, k) \geq u(x, y)$ for all $(x, y) \in D$ that satisfy $\rho y - x \geq (\rho - 1)k$.

In order to show that the (k, k) of Lemma 3 defines a stationary optimal path we require

Lemma 4   If (k, k) satisfies the conditions of Lemma 3, there is $q \in R_+^n$ such that $u(k, k) + (1 - \rho^{-1})qk \geq u(x, y) + qy - \rho^{-1}qx$ for all $(x, y) \in D$.

Proof   Let $V = \{v \mid v = \rho w - z, \text{ for some } (z, w) \in D\}$. It follows from Assumptions 3 and 4 that $(\rho - 1)k \in \text{interior } V$. Indeed, $(\rho - 1)k < 0$, while $\rho \bar{x} - \bar{y} > 0$ for the $(\bar{x}, \bar{y})$ mentioned in Assumption 4. Let $D_v = \{(z, w) \in D \mid \rho w - z \geq v\}$. I claim D_v is bounded for $v \in V$. Suppose not. Let $\bar{v} = \rho \bar{y} - \bar{x} > 0$. Choose α, $0 < \alpha < 1$, such that $v' = \alpha \bar{v} + (1 - \alpha)v \geq 0$. Let $(x, y) = \alpha(\bar{x}, \bar{y}) + (1 - \alpha)(z, w)$ for $(z, w) \in D_v$. Then (x, y) is unbounded as well. But $v' \geq 0$ implies $|y| > |x|$, which implies that $|x| \leq \zeta$ by Assumption 2, which in turn bounds $|y|$ by Assumption II. This contradiction establishes the claim.

Define $\phi(v) = \sup u(x, y)$ for $(x, y) \in D_v$. Since u is concave and closed by Assumption I and D_v is bounded, the sup is attained for any $v \in V$. Let $W = \{(u, v) \mid u \leq \phi(v) \text{ and } v \in V\}$. W is convex since ϕ is concave. Let $v^* = (\rho - 1)k$, where k satisfies Lemma 3, and let $u^* = u(k, k) = \phi(v^*)$. Then (u^*, v^*) is a boundary point of W. Thus by a separation theorem for convex sets (Berge, 1963, p. 163) there is $(\pi, p) \in R^{n+1}$ and $(\pi, p) \neq 0$, such that $\pi u + pv \leq \pi u^* + (\rho - 1)pk$ for all $(u, v) \in W$. Since v is unbounded below by Assumption 3, $p \geq 0$ must hold. Suppose $\pi = 0$. Then $pv \leq (\rho - 1)pk$ for all $v \in V$. However, $(\rho - 1)k$ is interior to V, which implies $p = 0$. This contradicts $(\pi, p) \neq 0$, so $\pi \neq 0$. We may choose (π, p) so that $\pi = 1$. Then $u + pv \leq u^* + (\rho - 1)pk$ for all $(u, v) \in W$. This is equivalent to the assertion of the lemma since we may set $q = \rho p$.

We are now in position to complete the proof of the theorem. Let (k, k) satisfy Lemma 3. Consider the stationary path $k_t = k$, $t = 1, 2, \ldots$, and any competing path $\{k_t'\}$ where $k_0' = k$. From Lemma 4 we have

$$\rho^t u(k, k) + \rho^t qk - \rho^{t-1}qk \geq \rho^t u(k_{t-1}, k_t) + \rho^t qk_t - \rho^{t-1}qk_{t-1}, \tag{2}$$

for all t. Summing (2) from $t = 1$ to T gives

$$\sum_1^T \rho^t u(k, k) + \rho^T qk - qk \geq \sum_1^T \rho^t u(k_{t-1}, k_t) + \rho^T qk_T - qk. \tag{3}$$

Assumption 2 implies that k_t is bounded as $t \to \infty$. Thus (3) implies in the limit, which exists since $\rho < 1$, $\sum_1^\infty \rho^t u(k, k) \geqslant \sum_1^\infty \rho^t u(k_{t-1}, k_t)$, or $k_t = k$ is an optimal path.

Let K^ρ be the set of capital stocks x with $V_0(x) > -\infty$. It follows from the compactness of the set of paths from x, in the product topology, and the continuity of the discounted utility sum that an optimal path exists from any $x \in K^\rho$. Moreover, it is easily seen that all sustainable stocks belong to K^ρ. If $(x, x) \in D$, one feasible path from x is $k_t = x$, all t. Thus $V_0(x) \geqslant \sum_1^\infty \rho^t u(x, x) = (1/(1 - \rho))u(x, x) > -\infty$. The use of duality in establishing the existence of an optimal stationary path seems harder to avoid than in proving asymptotic theorems. The proof used here that an optimal stationary path exists was developed by McKenzie (1979). A very similar proof was independently developed by Flynn (1980).

24.4 A Neighborhood Turnpike Theorem

We will prove turnpike theorems for the quasi-stationary model. First, we will prove global stability in the sense of Liapounov for a stationary optimal path. Liapounov stability means that an optimal path is eventually confined to a neighborhood of the stationary optimal path, which can be made small by choosing ρ near to 1. It will turn out that asymptotic stability holds, if certain functions are differentiable, for a ρ sufficiently close to 1. Asymptotic stability means that an optimal path converges to a stationary optimal path as $t \to \infty$.

The only optimal stationary paths that will concern us are those that were proved to exist in Theorem 2. We will refer to these paths as non-trivial. A *non-trivial* optimal stationary path is a path $k_t = k$, all k, such that $u(k, k) \geqslant u(x, y)$ for all (x, y) such that $\rho y - x \geqslant (\rho - 1)k$. Let $\{k_\tau(\rho)\}$, $\tau = 0, 1, \ldots$, be an optimal path with $k_0(\rho) = \bar{x}$. We may represent $\{k_\tau(\rho)\}$ as an element $\mathbf{k}(\rho)$ of the Banach space l_∞^n. Let $k_\tau = k^\rho$, $\tau = 0, 1, \ldots$, be a stationary optimal path. Define the utility gain in period τ by $\gamma_\tau(\mathbf{k}(\rho), k^\rho) = u(k'_{\tau-1}(\rho), k'_\tau(\rho)) - \frac{1}{2}u(k_{\tau-1}(\rho), k_\tau(\rho)) - \frac{1}{2}u(k^\rho, k^\rho)$, where $k'_\tau(\rho) = \frac{1}{2}(k_\tau(\rho) + k^\rho)$. Define the Liapounov function $G_t(\mathbf{k}(\rho), k^\rho) = \sum_1^\infty \rho^\tau \gamma_{t+\tau}(\mathbf{k}(\rho), k^\rho)$. Then $G_{t+1}(\mathbf{k}(\rho), k^\rho) - G_t(\mathbf{k}(\rho), k^\rho) = \sum_1^\infty \rho^\tau \gamma_{t+\tau+1} - \sum_1^\infty \rho^\tau \gamma_{t+\tau}$, omitting the arguments of the γ functions. Thus, omitting arguments for the G functions,

$$G_{t+1} - G_t = (\rho^{-1} - 1)G_t - \gamma_{t+1}. \tag{1}$$

From the definition we note that the utility gain γ_t depends only on the components (k_{t-1}, k_t) of $\mathbf{k}(\rho)$.

Let $\bar{u} = u(\bar{x}, \bar{y})$, where $(\bar{x}, \bar{y})$ satisfies Assumption 4. Let $\bar{\Delta}$ be the set of $(x, x) \in \Delta \cap D$ such that $u(x, x) \geqslant \bar{u}$. We will say that u is *uniformly strictly concave in* $\bar{\Delta}$ if for any $(x, x) \in \bar{\Delta}$ and any $(w, z) \in D$, the following holds. For any $\varepsilon > 0$ there is $\delta > 0$ such that $|(x, x) - (w, z)| > \varepsilon$ implies $u(w', z') - \frac{1}{2}u(x, x) - \frac{1}{2}u(w, z) > \delta$, where $(w', z') = \frac{1}{2}((x, x) + (w, z))$. We now assume

5. The utility function u is uniformly strictly concave in $\bar{\Delta}$.

Let (k, k) satisfy $u(k, k) \geqslant u(z, w)$ for $(z, w) \in D$ and $w \geqslant z$. We will refer to the stock k as an optimal stationary stock. It is easily seen from the proof that Lemma 3 holds for $\rho = 1$. Thus there is such a stock. We are now able to show that the set of non-trivial optimal stationary paths for ρ, non-empty for $\bar{\rho} < \rho < 1$ by Theorem 2, converges to the unique optimal stationary stock k, as $\rho \to 1$.

Theorem 3   There is an optimal stationary stock k such that if $\rho \to 1$, for $\rho < 1$, then $\sup|k^\rho - k| \to 0$, where the sup is taken over all k^ρ that correspond to non-trivial optimal stationary paths.

Proof   We have seen that there is such a (k, k). From Assumption 5 it is unique. Also if we define, for $\bar{\rho} < \rho \leqslant 1$, $f'(x, \rho) = \{(z, w) \mid \rho w - z \geqslant (\rho - 1)x$ for $(z, w) \in D\}$, a slight extension of the argument for Lemma 2 shows that f' is lower semicontinuous in x and ρ'. Then the theorem of Berge applies and $g \circ f'$ is upper semicontinuous. Note that (k^ρ, k^ρ) satisfies $(k^\rho, k^\rho) \in (g \circ f')(k^\rho, \rho)$, where k^ρ defines an optimal stationary path.

Suppose there were $\rho_s \to 1$ and k^{ρ_s} such that $|k^{\rho_s} - k| > \varepsilon > 0$ for all $s = 1, 2, \ldots$. Then there would be a point of accumulation $\bar{k}$ such that $(\bar{k}, \bar{k}) \in (g \circ f')(\bar{k}, 1)$. But $u(\bar{k}, \bar{k}) \geqslant u(k, k)$ and $\bar{k} \neq k$, contradicting the uniqueness of the element of Δ maximizing utility over $f'(\bar{k}, 1)$. This proves the theorem.

Let $k_t = k^\rho$, all t, be a non-trivial optimal stationary path for the discount factor ρ and let q^ρ support k^ρ in the sense of Lemma 4. Let $v(\rho) = \sup|q^\rho|$ over supports of k^ρ belonging to ρ. We have

Lemma 5   The function $v(\rho)$ is bounded as $\rho \to 1$.

Proof   Suppose not. Then by Theorem 3 there is a sequence $k^{\rho_s} - k$, $\rho_s \to 1$, where $v(\rho_s) \to \infty$, $s = 1, 2, \ldots$. From Lemma 4 we obtain

$$u(k^{\rho_s}, k^{\rho_s}) + (1 - \rho_s^{-1})q^{\rho_s}k^{\rho_s} \geq u(x, y) + q^{\rho_s}y - \rho_s^{-1}q^{\rho_s}x,$$

for all $(x, y) \in D$. (2)

The sequence ρ_s may be chosen so that $|q^{\rho_s}| \to \infty$ by the assumption. Divide (2) through by $|q^{\rho_s}|$ and consider a subsequence, retaining notation, for which $q^{\rho_s}/|q^{\rho_s}|$ converges to q, where $|q| = 1$. From (2) we obtain $0 \geq qy - qx$ for all $(x, y) \in D$. This contradicts Assumption 4 and proves the lemma.

From Lemma 5, $v(\rho^s)$ is bounded as $s \to \infty$. Thus if we consider the limit of (2) for a converging subsequence, as described above, the result is

$$u(k, k) \geq u(x, y) + qy - qx, \qquad \text{for all } (x, y) \in D. \quad (3)$$

In other words, the support formula of Lemma 4 also applies to the point (k, k), where k is an optimal stationary stock. It will not be surprising to learn that $k_t = k$ can be proved to be a stationary optimal path for $\rho = 1$. However, we do not need this fact. Indeed, without Assumption 5 it is not true, although a weakened form of Theorem 3, where k is not unique, still holds.

We are free to choose the origin of utility so that $u(k, k) = 0$. Let $V^\rho(x) = \sup(\lim \sum_1^T \rho^t u(k_{t-1}, k_t))$ as $T \to \infty$ over paths $\{k_t\}$ with $k_0 = x$. The limit exists since paths are bounded by Assumption 2. Thus $u(k_{t-1}, k_t)$ is bounded above and the sum of positive terms in the series $\{u(k_{t-1}, k_t)\}$ exists from $0 < \rho < 1$. Thus the limit of the full sum exists and is finite or $-\infty$. V^ρ is the value function for the discount factor ρ.

We will say that a capital stock x is *expansible* if there is $(x, y) \in D$ where $y > x$. We will say that a capital stock x is *sufficient* if there is a finite path $\{k_t\}$, $t = 0, \ldots, T$, such that $k_0 = x$ and k_T is *expansible*. Given any expansible stock x, Gale (1967) showed how to construct a path $\{h_t\}$, $t = 0, 1, \ldots$, where $h_0 = x$ and $h_t \to k$, as $t \to \infty$ such that $\sum_1^\infty u(h_{t-1}, h_t) > -\infty$. Let $K^\rho = K$ for $\rho = 1$. We have

Lemma 6 If x is expansible, $x \in K$.

Proof Consider $\alpha^t(x, y) + (1 - \alpha^t)(k, k) = (h_t, h'_{t+1})$, where $y > x$, $0 < \alpha < 1$, $t = 0, 1, \ldots$. Then $(h_0, h'_1) = (x, y)$, and as $t \to \infty$, $(h_t, h'_{t+1}) \to (k, k)$. Note that h_{t+1} and h'_{t+1} are not the same. Indeed, $h'_{t+1} = k - \alpha^t(k - y)$, while $h_{t+1} = k - \alpha^{t+1}(k - x)$. Then $h'_{t+1} > h_{t+1}$ if $(y - \alpha x) > (k - \alpha k)$. This holds for α near 1 since $y > x$. Thus by free disposal $\{h_t\}$ is a path approaching k. Also $(h_t, h_{t+1}) = (k, k) - \alpha^t((k, k) - (h_0, h_1))$.

Therefore, $u(h_t, h_{t+1}) \geq (1 - \alpha^t)u(k,k) + \alpha^t u(h_0, h_1)$ by the concavity of u, and $u(h_t, h_{t+1}) \geq \alpha^t u(h_0, h_1)$ by the choice of origin. Thus $\sum_1^\infty u(h_{t-1}, h_t) \geq (1/(1-\alpha))u(h_0, h_1) > -\infty$, so $h_0 = x \in K$.

We now prove

Lemma 7   Assume that x is sufficient. Then $V^\rho(x)$ is bounded for $\bar{\rho} < \rho \leq 1$.

Proof   If k_t is any path with $k_0 = x$ and $t = 0, 1, \ldots$, we have from (3) that

$$u(k_{t-1}, k_t) \leq q(k_{t-1} - k_t). \tag{4}$$

Multiplying (4) by ρ^t and summing we have

$$\sum_1^T \rho^t u(k_{t-1}, k_t) \leq \sum_1^T \rho^t q(k_{t-1} - k_t)$$

$$= \rho q k^0 + \sum_1^{T-1} \rho^t(\rho - 1)qk^t - \rho^T qk^T \leq \rho q k_0. \tag{5}$$

The left-hand side of (5) is bounded above for $0 < \rho \leq 1$ by qk_0 independently of ρ and T. Thus $V^\rho(x)$ is bounded above as $\rho \to 1$.

On the other hand, to show that $V^\rho(x)$ is bounded below, we may as well assume that x is expansible. From the proof of Lemma 6 there is an infinite path (h_t, h_{t+1}) from $h_0 = x$ where $u(h_t, h_{t+1}) \geq \alpha^t u(h_0, h_1)$ and $0 < \alpha < 1$. Then $\sum_1^\infty \rho^t u(h_{t-1}, h_t) \geq (\rho/(1 - \rho\alpha))u(h_0, h_1) > -\infty$. Since $V^\rho(x) \geq \sum_1^\infty \rho^t u(h_{t-1}, h_t)$, it follows that $V^\rho(x)$ is bounded below and, in particular, bounded below as $\rho \to 1$. Thus the lemma is proved.

For the proof of the neighborhood turnpike result we require the assumption

6.   Let $k_t = k^\rho$, $t = 0, 1, \ldots$, be a non-trivial optimal stationary path for $\bar{\rho} < \rho < 1$. Let $(z, w) \in D$. Then there is $\eta > 0$ and $\varepsilon > 0$ such that $|z - k^\rho| < \eta$ implies there is w' such that $(z, w') \in D$ and $(w'_i - z_i) > \varepsilon$ for $i = 1, \ldots, n$.

We may say that stocks near the stocks of optimal stationary paths are uniformly expansible for $\bar{\rho} < \rho < 1$. The neighborhood turnpike is given by

Theorem 4   Let $k_t = k^\rho$, $t = 0, 1, \ldots$, be a non-trivial optimal stationary path for $\bar{\rho} < \rho < 1$. Assume that x is sufficient. If $\{k_t(\rho)\}$, $t = 0$,

1, ..., is an optimal path with $k_0(\rho) = x$, given an ε-ball $S_\varepsilon(k^\rho)$ about k^ρ, there is ρ' and T such that $k_t(\rho) \in S_\varepsilon(k^\rho)$ for all $t > T$ and all $\rho' < \rho < 1$.

Proof By uniform strict concavity over $\bar{\Delta}$, for any $\varepsilon > 0$ and all k^ρ, $\bar{\rho} < \rho < 1$, we may choose $\delta > 0$ such that $u(z', w') - \frac{1}{2}(u(z, w) + u(k^\rho, k^\rho)) > 2\delta$ when $|(z, w) - (k^\rho, k^\rho)| > \varepsilon$, where $(z', w') = \frac{1}{2}((z, w) + (k^\rho, k^\rho))$ and (z, w) is an element of D. Consider the right side of (1) for $t = 0$. We may choose ρ near enough to 1 to give $(\rho^{-1} - 1)G_0(\mathbf{k}(\rho), k^\rho) < \delta$, provided $G_0(\mathbf{k}(\rho), k^\rho)$ is bounded as $\rho \to 1$. However, $G_0 \leqslant V^\rho(\frac{1}{2}(x + k^\rho)) - \frac{1}{2}(V^\rho(x) + V^\rho(k^\rho))$, since $\{\frac{1}{2}(k_t + k^\rho)\}$ is a feasible path with $k_0 = x$.

As $\rho \to 1$, $V^\rho(x)$ is bounded by Lemma 7, and $V^\rho(\frac{1}{2}(x + k^\rho))$ is bounded above by the first part of the proof of Lemma 7. In the light of Theorem 3, it is sufficient to bound $V^\rho(k^\rho)$ in a compact neighborhood B of k. For $k^\rho \in B$, by Assumption 6 there is $\varepsilon > 0$ such that $(k^\rho, k^\rho + \varepsilon e) \in D$, where $e = (1, \ldots, 1)$, and ε is independent of k^ρ. Then α in Lemma 7 may be chosen independently of k^ρ and the proof of the lemma implies that $V^\rho(k^\rho) \geqslant (\rho/(1 - \rho\alpha))u(k^\rho, k^\rho + \varepsilon e)$. However, $u(k^\rho, k^\rho + \varepsilon e)$ is bounded for $k^\rho \in B$ by Assumption I. This implies that $V^\rho(k^\rho)$ is bounded below as $\rho \to 1$. Thus G_0 is bounded above. On the other hand, $G_0 \geqslant 0$ from the concavity of u. Thus G_0 is bounded. Then if $|(k_0(\rho), k_1(\rho)) - (k^\rho, k^\rho)| > \varepsilon$, so that $\gamma_1(\mathbf{k}(\rho), k^\rho) > 2\delta$, it follows from this choice of ρ that the left side of (1) for $t = 0$, $G_1(\mathbf{k}(\rho), k^\rho) - G_0(\mathbf{k}(\rho), k^\rho)$, is less than $-\delta$.

Suppose $|(k_{t-1}(\rho), k_t(\rho)) - (k^\rho, k^\rho)| > \varepsilon$. Then $(\rho^{-1} - 1)G_t < \delta$ implies $(\rho^{-1} - 1)G_{t+1} < \delta$. In fact, we have

$$(\rho^{-1} - 1)G_t - \gamma_{t+1} < -\delta, \tag{6}$$

omitting arguments of functions. Then (1) implies $G_{t+1} - G_t < -\delta$, or $(\rho^{-1} - 1)G_{t+1} < (\rho^{-1} - 1)G_t < \delta$. On the other hand, if $|(k_{t+1}(\rho), k_{t+2}(\rho)) - (k^\rho, k^\rho)| > \varepsilon$ holds, $\gamma_{t+2} > 2\delta$ by uniform strict concavity and the choice of δ. Thus (6) implies $(\rho^{-1} - 1)G_{t+1} - \gamma_{t+2} < -\delta$. In other words, (6) continues to hold so long as $(k_t(\rho), k_{t+1}(\rho))$ remains outside an ε-neighborhood of (k^ρ, k^ρ). Consequently (1) implies

$$G_T(\mathbf{k}(\rho), k^\rho) \leqslant G_0 - T\delta, \tag{7}$$

if $(k_t(\rho), k_{t+1}(\rho))$ is outside the ε-neighborhood from $t = 0$ to $t = T$. Since G_T is non-negative by definition, (7) compels $(k_t(\rho), k_{t+1}(\rho))$ to enter this neighborhood eventually to avoid a contradiction. Note that the argument implies the result uniformly for all ρ' with $\rho < \rho' < 1$. Also all non-trivial stationary optimal paths for these ρ' must lie in an ε-neighborhood of any one of them.

To complete the proof we require

Lemma 8 If $\mathbf{k}(\rho)$ is an optimal path from k_0, then for any $\delta > 0$ there is $\varepsilon > 0$ such that $|(k_0, k_1(\rho)) - (k^\rho, k^\rho)| < \varepsilon$ implies $G_0(\mathbf{k}(\rho), k^\rho) < \delta$, uniformly for $\bar{\rho} < \rho < 1$ and all non-trivial optimal stationary paths for ρ.

Proof By the definition of G_0 and the feasibility of the intermediate path,

$$G_0(\mathbf{k}(\rho), k^\rho) = u\left(\tfrac{1}{2}(k_0 + k^\rho), \tfrac{1}{2}(k_1(\rho) + k^\rho)\right)$$

$$- \tfrac{1}{2}\left(u(k_0, k_1(\rho)) + u(k^\rho, k^\rho)\right)$$

$$+ \rho V^\rho\left(\tfrac{1}{2}(k_1(\rho) + k^\rho) - \tfrac{1}{2}\rho(V^\rho(k_1(\rho)) + V^\rho(k^\rho)). \tag{8}$$

It is implied by Assumption 4 that $u(k^\rho, k^\rho) \geqslant u(\bar{x}, \bar{y})$ for all k^ρ, $\bar{\rho} < \rho < 1$, or $(k^\rho, k^\rho) \in \bar{\Delta}$. I claim u is uniformly continuous over $\bar{\Delta}$. Suppose not. Then there are sequences (z^s, w^s) and (x^s, x^s) where $|(z^s, w^s) - (x^s, x^s)| \to 0$ and $|u(z^s, w^s) - u(x^s, x^s)| > \varepsilon > 0$. However, we may assume that $(x^s, x^s) \to (y, y) \in \bar{\Delta}$. Then $(z^s, w^s) \to (y, y)$ as well and $|u(z^s, w^s) - u(y, y)| > \varepsilon > 0$. Thus u is not continuous at (y, y) in contradiction to Assumption I.

Thus, from (8), we see that G_0 is small for $(k_0, k_1(\rho))$ near (k^ρ, k^ρ), provided $\mathbf{k}'(\rho)$ an optimal path from k_0' and $(k_0', k_1'(\rho)) \to (k^\rho, k^\rho)$ implies $V^\rho(k_1'(\rho)) \to V^\rho(k^\rho)$. However, Assumption 6 implies that k^ρ is uniformly expansible for $\bar{\rho} < \rho < 1$. Expansibility of k^ρ and free disposal imply that $(k^\rho, k_1'(\rho)) \in D$ for $k_1'(\rho)$ near k^ρ. Thus $u(k^\rho, k^\rho) + \rho V^\rho(k^\rho) \geqslant u(k^\rho, k_1'(\rho)) + \rho V^\rho(k_1'(\rho))$, and $V^\rho(k_1'(\rho)) \leqslant V^\rho(k^\rho) + \varepsilon$ may be assured for any assigned ε for any ρ, $\bar{\rho} < \rho < 1$, and any k^ρ, by bringing $(k_0'(\rho), k_1'(\rho))$ near to (k^ρ, k^ρ).

A repetition of this argument may be made from the viewpoint of a switch from k_0' to k^ρ, since Assumption 6 applies to any k_0' near k^ρ. Then k_0' is expansible, uniformly over k^ρ and $\bar{\rho} < \rho < 1$, and k^ρ may be reached. This gives $V^\rho(k^\rho) \leqslant V^\rho(k_1'(\rho)) + \varepsilon$ for any assigned ε when $(k_0', k_1'(\rho))$ is sufficiently near (k^ρ, k^ρ). Thus $V^\rho(k_1'(\rho)) \to V^\rho(k^\rho)$ as needed and the lemma follows.

We may now complete the proof of Theorem 3. By (1), $G_{t+1} \leqslant \rho^{-1}G_t$. For any $\zeta > 0$, there is by Lemma 8 an $\varepsilon > 0$ such that $|(k_t, k_{t+1}) -$

$(k^p, k^p)| < \varepsilon$ implies $G_t < \zeta$. Choose $\zeta < \rho G_0$. By Assumption 5, for ζ sufficiently small there is ε' such that $|(k_{t+1}, k_{t+2}) - (k^p, k^p)| > \varepsilon'$ implies $G_{t+1} \geqslant \gamma_{t+2} > \rho^{-1}\zeta$, uniformly for $\bar{p} < \rho < 1$. Therefore, $(k_{t+1}, k_{t+2}) \in S_{\varepsilon'}(k^p, k^p)$, the ε'-ball about (k^p, k^p). It is clear that $S_\varepsilon \subset S_{\varepsilon'}$. If $(k_{t+1}, k_{t+2}) \notin S_\varepsilon$, the first part of the proof implies that G_τ decreases for $\tau > t + 1$, until $(k_\tau, k_{\tau+1})$ re-enters S_ε. Thus $(k_\tau, k_{\tau+1})$ cannot leave $S_{\varepsilon'}(k^p, k^p)$, and k_τ cannot leave $S_{\varepsilon'}(k^p)$.

The theorem is proved if we can show that ε' may be chosen arbitrarily small by choosing ζ and ε sufficiently small. Suppose not. Then there are sequences ρ_s and t_s, and a sequence $\zeta^s \to 0$, such that $G_{t_s+1} \leqslant \rho_s^{-1}\zeta^s$ while $|(k_{t_s+1}, k_{t_s+2}) - (k^s, k^s)| > \varepsilon' > 0$, where k^s corresponds to a non-trivial optimal stationary path for ρ_s. But $G_{t_s+1} > \gamma_{t_s+2} > \gamma > 0$ for $|(k_{t_s+1}, k_{t_s+2}) - (k^s, k^s)| > \varepsilon'$ by Assumption 5. Thus no such sequence can exist and the theorem is proved.

The order in which the choices of small quantities are made is first ε'. Then ζ, ε, and δ are chosen uniformly over k^p and $\bar{p} < \rho \leqslant 1$. Choose $\zeta < \rho G_0$ so that $G_{t+1} \leqslant \rho^{-1}\zeta$ implies $(k_{t+1}, k_{t+2}) \in S_{\varepsilon'}(k^p, k^p)$. Then ε so that $(k_t, k_{t+1}) \in S_\varepsilon(k^p, k^p)$ implies $G_t < \zeta$ by Lemma 8. Then δ so that $\gamma_t > 2\delta$ when $(k_{t-1}, k_t) \notin S_\varepsilon(k^p, k^p)$. Finally ρ so that $(\rho^{-1} - 1)G_0 < \delta$. This last choice is possible since the earlier choices are valid uniformly over k^p and $\bar{p} < \rho < 1$, and G_0 is bounded as $\rho \to 1$.

Some results related to Theorem 4 in the context of a differentiable model in continuous time may be found in Nishimura (1979). My first use of Liapounov stability was in the Handbook chapter (1979).

24.5   An Asymptotic Turnpike Theorem

I regard the neighborhood turnpike theorem as the basic result of the subject. However, a stronger result is available, at least when certain functions are twice differentiable. A first derivative for the value function when the utility function has a first derivative has been proved by Benveniste and Scheinkman (1979).

7.   The utility function u is strictly concave over $\Delta^0 \supset \bar{\Delta}$, where Δ^0 is open in the relative topology of D.

Assumption 7 and Theorem 4 imply that the optimal path from a stock x where there is y and $(x, y) \in \Delta^0$ is unique. Therefore, $G_0(\mathbf{k}(\rho), k^p)$ for $k_0(\rho) = x$ may be written $G^p(x, k^p)$. Then $G^p(x, k^p) \leqslant V^p\left(\frac{1}{2}(x + k^0)\right) - \frac{1}{2}(V^p(x) + V^p(k^p))$. Also $\gamma_1(\mathbf{k}(\rho), k^p) = u\left(\frac{1}{2}(x, k_1) + (k^p, k^p)\right) - \frac{1}{2}(u(x, k_1) + u(k^p, k^p)) = \gamma(x, k^p)$ since k_1 depends on x.

Unfortunately it has not been proved that the existence of a second differential for u implies the existence of a second differential for V^p, much less for $G^p(x, k^p)$ or $\gamma^p(x, k^p)$. Let D^0 be an open set containing D. We assume

8. The utility function u may be extended to a function u' on D^0, so that the utility gain $\gamma^p(x, k^p)$ and the prospective utility gain $G^p(x, k^p)$ have non-singular second differentials at all x such that $(x, x) \in \bar{\Delta}$.

Write the matrices of coefficients of the differentials given by Assumption 8 as $[G^p_{ij}]_{i, j=1,\dots,n}$, and $[\gamma^p_{ij}]_{i, j=1,\dots,n}$. Note that Assumption 5 implies $G^p(x, k^p) > 0$ for $x \neq k^p$, while $G^p(k^p, k^p) = 0$. Similarly $\gamma^p(x, k^p) > 0$ for $x \neq k^p$, and $= 0$ if $x = k^p$. Therefore, the non-singularity of the differentials of G^p and γ^p_1 at k^p implies that the differentials are positive definite.

We may now prove

Theorem 5 Under the conditions of Theorem 4 there is ρ' such that the optimal path $\{k_t(\rho)\}$, $t = 1, 2, \dots$, converges asymptotically to k^p for all $\rho' < \rho < 1$, where $k_t = k^p$ is the unique optimal stationary path for ρ.

Proof By Theorem 4, $k_t(\rho)$ can be confined to an arbitrarily small neighborhood U of k^p for all $t > T$ by a choice of ρ sufficiently near 1. The line of proof is to make the neighborhood U small enough that the development of $G^p_t(\mathbf{k}(\rho), k^p)$ is governed by the second differentials at (k^p, k^p). Once it established that G^p_t is decreasing at a rate bounded below zero outside any small neighborhood of (k^p, k^p) contained in U it follows, since G^p_t is non-negative, that $k_t(\rho)$ must converge to k^p to avoid contradiction.

From (4.1) we have

$$G_{t+1}(\mathbf{k}(\rho), k^p) - G_t(\mathbf{k}(\rho), k)$$

$$= (\rho^{-1} - 1)G_t(\mathbf{k}(\rho), k^p) - \gamma_{t+1}(\mathbf{k}(\rho), k^p)$$

$$= (\rho^{-1} - 1)(k_t - k^p([G^p_{ij}](k_t - k^p))$$

$$- (k_t - k^p([\gamma^p_{ij}](k_t - k^p) + o(|(k_t - k^p)|^2), \tag{1}$$

where G^p_{ij} and γ^p_{ij} are evaluated at k^p and the final term is of order smaller than the second in the difference of k_t and k^p. We choose ρ, first, near enough to 1 to render the matrix $[(\rho^{-1} - 1)G^{\rho}_{ij} - \gamma^{\rho}_{ij}]$ negative definite, then smaller if need be, so that the neighborhood U, to which $k_t(\rho)$ is eventually confined by Theorem 4, is small enough that the right side of (1) is negative in U and of absolute value at least twice the remainder term. Then the continuity of the differentials in k_t implies, if k_t is outside a small ball $S_{\epsilon}(k^0)$, there is a negative upper bound on $G_{t+1} - G_t$. Thus to avoid contradicting $G_t \geqslant 0$, k_t must eventually lie in $S_{\epsilon}(k^{\rho})$. Since this argument applies to any $\epsilon > 0$, k_t must, in fact, converge to k^{ρ}, and the theorem is proved. It is easily shown by an argument due to Bewley (1980) that the asymptotic approach is in fact exponential.

Note

I would like to thank Makoto Yano and the referee for a number of improvements in the argument. This chapter was written while the author was Taussig Professor of Economics at Harvard University.

References

Benveniste, L., and Scheinkman, J. (1979), On the differentiability of the value function in dynamic models of economics, *Econometrica* **47**, 727–732.

Berge, C. (1963), "Topological Spaces," Oliver and Boyd, London.

Bewley, T. (1980), "An Integration of Equilibrium Theory and Turnpike Theory," Discussion Paper No. 405, Northwestern University.

Brock, W. and Scheinkman, J. (1976), Global asymptotic stability of optimal control systems with applications to the theory of economic growth, *J. Econ. Theory* **12**, 164–190.

Burmeister, E., and Dobell R. (1970), "Mathematical Theories of Economic Growth," Macillan & Co., London.

Cass, D., and Shell K. (1976), The structure and stability of competitive dynamical systems, *J. Econ. Theory* **12**, 31–70.

Flynn, J. (1980), The existence of optimal invariant stocks in a multi-sector economy, *Rev. Econ. Studies* **47**, 809–811.

Gale, D. (1967), On optimal development in a multi-sector economy, *Rev. Econ. Studies* **34**, 1–18.

Jeanjean, P. (1974), Optimal development programs under uncertainty: The undiscounted case, *J. Econ. Theory* **7**, 66–92.

McKenzie, L. (1968), Accumulation programs of maximum utility and the von Neumann facet, *in* "Value, Capital and Growth" (J. N. Wolfe, Ed.), Edinburgh Univ. Press, Edinburgh.

McKenzie, L. (1976), Turnpike theory, *Econometrica* **44**, 841–865.

McKenzie, L. (1979), "Optimal Economic Growth and Turnpike Theorems," Discussion Paper No. 79-1 University of Rochester; also *in* "Handbook of Mathematical Economics" (Arrow and Intriligator, Eds.), North-Holland, New York, in press.

Nishimura, K. G. (1979), "A new Concept of Stability and Dynamical Economic Systems," unpublished, Yale University.

Peleg, B., and Zilcha, I. (1977), On competitive prices for optimal consumption plans, *SIAM J. Appl. Math.* **32**, 627–630.

Samuelson, P. (1965), A catenary turnpike theorem, *Amer. Econ. Rev.* **55**, 486–495.

Scheinkman, J. (1976), On optimal steady states of n-sector growth models when utility is discounted, *J. Econ. Theory* **12**, 11–20.

Starrett, D. (1972), Fundamental nonconvexities in the theory of externalities, *J. Econ. Theory* **2**, 180–199.

Weitzman, M. (1973), Duality theory for infinite horizon convex models, *Manag. Sci.* **19**, 783–789.

25 Turnpike Theory, Discounted Utility, and the von Neumann Facet

Lionel W. McKenzie

Asymptotic theory for optimal paths of capital accumulation is more difficult when the utility function for the single period is concave, but not strictly concave. However, in the case of stationary models where future utility is not discounted, the theory is rather fully developed [5, 7]. There is convergence to a subset of processes which span a flat on the epigraph of the utility function. This flat is often referred to as the von Neumann facet. Then if the optimal paths that lie on the von Neumann facet converge to a stationary optimal path, the same property is shown to hold for other optimal paths. The first result is proved using the concavity of the utility functions. Either prices that support the optimal paths are used to determine value losses for other paths, or the utility gains of a path intermediate between optimal paths are defined and shown to lead to a contradiction if convergence does not occur. If prices are used, a Liapounov function is defined that is the sum of the value losses suffered by the paths at each other's support prices. The Liapounov function is nonpositive but increasing off the von Neumann facet. Again, convergence must occur to avoid contradiction. The second result, convergence to the stationary optimal path, is based on the fact that asymptotic convergence to the facet of optimal paths implies that these paths inherit the stability properties of the optimal paths that lie on the facet.

In the case of discounted utility and quasi-stationary models this order of proof does not succeed, because convergence of optimal paths to the facets on which optimal stationary paths lie cannot be proved to be asymptotic on the basis of arguments from value losses, or utility gains. The stability that is available from these arguments is Liapounov, or neighborhood, stability [8]. The proof of Liapounov stability of the von Neumann facet for a discount factor less than 1 depends on the assumptions that support prices for points on the facets are unique, and that the utility function is uniformly strictly concave in directions leaving the facets. In order to carry the argument further, we must use the convergence of the von Neumann facets associated with discount factors to the von Neumann facet of the undiscounted model as the discount factor approaches 1. Then, as before, it is possible to appeal to the stability properties of the optimal paths for the undiscounted case that lie on the von Neumann facet. We may prove that optimal paths are confined to smaller neighborhoods of an optimal stationary path as the discount factor approaches 1 if the von Neumann facet for undiscounted utility is stable, that is, contains no infinite cyclic paths. Finally, in a differentiable case, the optimal paths are proved to converge asymptotically to an optimal stationary path for discount factors close enough to 1. The argument is illustrated with an example which is an elaboration of an example due to Weitzman [9].

25.1   The Model

We will be concerned with the quasistationary model in reduced form. That is, the technology and the social utility function, except for discounting, are unchanging over time, and they are summarized in utility functions $\rho^t u(x, y)$ defined on initial stocks x at time $t - 1$ and terminal stocks y at time t. The discount factor ρ satisfies $0 < \rho < 1$. It is assumed that utility within the period is maximized subject to the constraints of initial and terminal stocks. This approach is entirely consistent with the neoclassical growth model where social utility and technology are introduced separately although it is more general than that model.

The assumptions concern $u(x, y)$ and its domain of definition D. They are:

Assumption 1   The function u maps $D \subset R_+^n \times R_+^n$ into the real line. D is convex and u is concave and closed.

Assumption 2   For any $\xi < \infty$, if $(x, y) \in D$ and $|x| < \xi$, there is $\eta < \infty$ such that $|y| < \eta$.

Assumption 3   There is $\zeta > 0$ such that $|x| \geqslant \zeta$ implies for any $(x, y) \in D$, $|y| < \gamma |x|$, where $\gamma < 1$.

Assumption 4   If $(x, y) \in D$, then $(z, w) \in D$ for all $z \geqslant x$ and $0 \leqslant w \leqslant y$. Moreover, $u(z, w) \geqslant u(x, y)$.

Assumption 5   There is $(\bar{x}, \bar{y}) \in D$ such that $\bar{p}\bar{y} > \bar{x}$, where $0 < \bar{p} < 1$.

A concave function $f(z)$ defined in a convex set D is called closed if $\limsup f(z) = -\infty$, as $z \to w$, for $w \notin D$, and $\limsup f(z) = f(w)$, as $z \to w$, for $w \in D$. Assumptions 1 and 2 imply that u is bounded for given x. We will say that $\{k_t\}$, $t = \tau, \tau + 1, \ldots$, is a path of capital accumulation if $(k_t, k_{t+1}) \in D$ for all t. Assumptions 2 and 3 imply that a path of accumulation from k_τ is bounded. Assumption 4 is free disposal of surplus stocks. Assumption 5 provides an initial stock that can grow in one period by a factor larger than $\bar{p}^{-1}$. The number $\bar{p}$ will serve as a lower bound on the discount factors that are considered.

Let us refer to a capital stock x as *expansible* if there is y such that $y > x$ and $(x, y) \in D$. Let us refer to a capital stock x as *sufficient* if there is a finite sequence $k_0, \ldots, k_T$, where $k_0 = x$, $(k_{t-1}, k_t) \in D$ for $t = 1, \ldots, T$, and k_T is expansible. We will be concerned with paths from stocks that are sufficient. This permits our using somewhat simpler definitions than customary in optimal growth literature. First, we note that if $\{k_t\}$, $t = 0, 1, \ldots$, is a path, $\sum_1^\infty p^t u(k_{t-1}, k_t) = \lim \sum_1^T p^t u(k_{t-1}, k_t)$ as $T \to \infty$ always exists if the value $-\infty$ is allowed. For we may separate the series, $u(k_{t-1}, k_t)$, $t = 1, 2, \ldots$, into a series, $u(k_{t_i-1}, k_{t_i})$, $i = 1, 2, \ldots$, all of whose terms are positive or zero, and a series, $u(k_{t_j-1}, k_{t_j})$, $j = 1, 2, \ldots$, all of whose terms are negative. Since k_{t-1} is bounded by Assumptions 1 and 3, $u(k_{t-1}, k_t)$ is bounded above by Assumption 1. Thus $\lim \sum_{i=1}^N p^t u(k_{t_i-1}, k_{t_i})$ exists, as $N \to \infty$, and $\lim \sum_{j=1}^N p^t u(k_{t_j-1}, k_{t_j})$ exists as a finite number or $-\infty$, as $N \to \infty$, since both these sequences are monotone. But the original limit is the sum of these limits and exists as well, as a finite number or $-\infty$.

Using the existence of the sum of discounted utilities along any path we may define a *value* for a capital stock x by $V(x) = \sup \sum_1^\infty p^t u(k_{t-1}, k_t)$ over all paths $\{k_t\}$, $t = 0, 1, \ldots$, with $k_0 = x$. Put $V(x) = -\infty$ if no such path exists. Let us say that $\{k_t\}$ is an *optimal* path from x if $V(x) > -\infty$ and $\sum_1^\infty p^t u(k_{t-1}, k_t) = V(x)$. We will prove

Theorem 1   There is an optimal path from any capital stock which is sufficient.

Proof   Let x be a sufficient capital stock. Then there is a path from x whose utility stream is bounded below, since there is a path that goes to an expansible stock and stays there. Thus $V(x) > -\infty$. We need to prove that there is a path whose utility sum equals $V(x)$. By definition of supremum, there is a sequence of paths $\{k_t^s\}$ with $k_0^s = x$, $s = 1$,

2,..., such that $\sum_1^\infty \rho^t u(k_{t-1}^s, k_t^s) \to V(x)$. By Assumptions 2 and 3, k_t^s is bounded over s for all t. Thus there is a subsequence $\{k_1^s\}$ (retain notation) such that $k_1^s \to k_1'$. Also choosing further subsequences there is for any $T > 0$ a subsequence $\{k_t^s\}$ (retain notation) such that $k_t^s \to k_t'$ for $t = 1,\ldots,T$. By the Cantor process, we may choose a subsequence $\{k_t^s\}$ (retain notation) which converges to $\{k_t'\}$ for all t. Then (k_{t-1}', k_t') is the limit of a sequence $\{k_{t-1}^s, k_t^s\}$, where $(k_{t-1}^s, k_t^s) \in D$ for every s. Thus $(k_{t-1}', k_t') \in D$ provided that $u(k_{t-1}', k_t') > -\infty$. Since k_t^s is bounded over s and t by Assumptions 2 and 3, Assumption 1 implies $u(k_{t-1}^s, k_t^s) \leq \beta$ holds for some $\beta > 0$. This gives $\sum_{\tau=1, \tau \neq t}^\infty \rho^\tau u(k_{\tau-1}^s, k_\tau^s) \leq (1/1 - \rho)\beta$ for all s and all t. Since $\sum_{\tau=1}^\infty \rho^\tau u(k_{\tau-1}^s, k_\tau^s) \to V(x) > -\infty$, as $s \to \infty$, it follows for each t that $u(k_{t-1}^s, k_t^s) > -\beta'$ holds for some $\beta' > 0$ for all s. Therefore, by Assumption 1, we have that $(k_{t-1}', k_t') \in D$. Since this is true for all t, $\{k_t'\}$ is a path.

We will show that

$$V(x) = \sum_1^\infty \rho^t u(k_{t-1}', k_t'). \tag{1}$$

Since the maximization problem is unaffected by adding a constant to the utility function, and $u(k_{t-1}^s, k_t^s) \leq \beta$ holds for all s and t, we may suppose that the utility function has been chosen so that $u(k_{t-1}^s, k_t^s) \leq 0$ for all s and t.

Then the partial sums $\sum_1^T \rho^t u(k_{t-1}', k_t')$ form a monotone sequence which converges to $V' = \sum_1^\infty \rho^t u(k_{t-1}', k_t')$. For any $\varepsilon > 0$ we may find T such that

$$\sum_1^T \rho^t u(k_{t-1}', k_t') < V' + \frac{\varepsilon}{4}. \tag{2}$$

Now choose S so large that for $s > S$

$$\sum_{t=1}^T \rho^t u(k_{t-1}^s, k_t^s) - \sum_1^T \rho^t u(k_{t-1}', k_t') < \frac{\varepsilon}{4}. \tag{3}$$

Substituting (2) in (3), we obtain

$$\sum_{t=1}^T \rho^t u(k_{t-1}^s, k_t^s) - V' < \frac{\varepsilon}{2}, \tag{4}$$

for all $s > S$. But (4) implies immediately

$$\sum_{t=1}^{\infty} \rho^t u(k_{t-1}^s, k_t^s) - V' < \frac{\varepsilon}{2}. \tag{5}$$

Since the first term of (5) converges to $V(x)$ as $s \to \infty$, we may conclude, using the definition of V', that

$$V(x) - \sum_{1}^{\infty} \rho^t u(k_{t-1}', k_t') < \frac{\varepsilon}{2}. \tag{6}$$

Since the argument is valid for any $\varepsilon > 0$, and $\sum_{1}^{\infty} u(k_{t-1}', k_t') \leqslant V(x)$ by definition of $V(x)$, it must be that (1) holds, or $\{k_t'\}$ is an optimal path from x.

25.2   Preliminary Results

I will cite some results for the quasi-stationary model from previous papers. Let us say that a path $\{k_t\}$, $t = 0, 1, \ldots$, is stationary if $k_t = k$ for all t. The following result has been proved (McKenzie [8]).

Proposition 1   The quasi-stationary model, for $\bar{\rho} \leqslant \rho < 1$, has a stationary optimal path, $k_t = k$, which satisfies the condition $u(k, k) \geqslant u(x, y)$ for all $(x, y) \in D$ such that $\rho y - x \geqslant (\rho - 1)k$.

The condition of Proposition 1 is not empty because of Assumption 5. We will refer to optimal stationary paths that satisfy the condition of Proposition 1 as *nontrivial*. It is not implied that a nontrivial stationary optimal path is unique, or even isolated.

A further result establishes the existence of proportional price supports for nontrivial stationary optimal paths (McKenzie [8]).

Proposition 2   If $k_t = k$ is a nontrivial stationary optimal path, for $\bar{\rho} \leqslant \rho < 1$, there is $q \in R_+^n$ such that

$$u(k, k) + (1 - \rho^{-1})qk \geqslant u(x, y) + qy - \rho^{-1}qx, \tag{7}$$

for all $(x, y) \in D$.

We may note that both Proposition 1 and Proposition 2 hold for stationary models where $\rho = 1$, provided Assumption 1 is strengthened so that u is strictly concave at a point (k, k) that satisfies the condition of Proposition 1 for $\rho = 1$. However, even without this strengthening we may define a set of optimal stationary stocks for the stationary model. We will say that k is an *optimal stationary stock* if $(k, k) \in D$ and

$u(k, k) \geqslant u(x, y)$ for all $(x, y) \in D$ satisfying $y \geqslant x$. The optimal stationary points (k, k) are also price supported in the sense of Proposition 2, but they need not correspond to optimal paths. We have

Proposition 3 There is an optimal stationary stock. There is $q \in R_+^n$ such that, if k is an optimal stationary stock,

$$u(k, k) \geqslant u(x, y) + q(y - x), \tag{8}$$

for all $(x, y) \in D$.

It is not only stationary optimal paths that may be given price supports. Indeed, in this model we may show that any optimal path from a sufficient stock may eventually be supported by prices. Since our interest lies in asymptotic theorems, it does not matter whether the initial segments of optimal paths have price supports. To be exact, we may show

Proposition 4 If $\{k_t\}$, $t = 0, 1, \ldots$, is an optimal path, for $\bar{p} \leqslant \rho < 1$, and k_0 is sufficient, there is $\tau > 0$ such that there exists a sequence of price vectors $q_t \in R_+^n$, $t \geqslant \tau$, which satisfy

$$V(k_{t+1}) - q_{t+1}k_{t+1} \geqslant V(y) - q_{t+1}y, \tag{9}$$

for all y such that $V(y) > -\infty$, and

$$u(k_t, k_{t+1}) + q_{t+1}k_{t+1} - \rho^{-1}q_t k_t \geqslant u(x, y) + q_{t+1}y - \rho^{-1}q_t x, \tag{10}$$

for all $(x, y) \in D$, for all $t \geqslant \tau$. Also τ is independent of ρ.

Proof This Proposition is implied by the argument for Lemma 1 in McKenzie [7], with small modifications. Let the set K be the set of capital stocks y such that $V(y) > -\infty$. Let P be the set of capital stocks y for which there is $(x, y) \in D$. It is immediate from Assumptions 4 and 5 that interior $(P \cap K) \neq \varnothing$. This is the condition used in the argument for the induction step of Lemma 1 of [7]. To start the induction at time τ, we may use a condition like the condition $(S1)$ in McKenzie [6]. Let $T_\tau(k_0)$ be the set of capital stocks y such that there is a path $\{h_t\}$, $t = 0, \ldots, \tau$, where $h_0 = k_0$ and $h_\tau = y$. $T_\tau(k_0)$ is convex by the convexity of D. Since k_0 is sufficient, $T_\tau(k_0)$ is not empty, and we may choose τ so that there is $y \in T_{\tau-1}(k_0)$, where y is expansible. Then by Assumptions 4 and 5 we have that interior $(T_\tau(k_0) \cap K) \neq \varnothing$.

Let $u_\tau(x, y) = \sup \sum_1^\tau \rho^t u(h_{t-1}, h_t)$ over all paths $\{h_t\}$, $t = 0, \ldots, \tau$, such that $h_0 = x$ and $h_\tau = y$. Then from the definitions we have

$$u_\tau(k_0, k_\tau) + \rho^\tau V(k_\tau) \geqslant u_\tau(k_0, y) + \rho^\tau V(y), \tag{11}$$

for all $y \in T_\tau(k_0)$. Let v_τ equal the left side of (11). Then

$$v_\tau - u_\tau(k_0, y) \geqslant \rho^\tau V(y). \tag{12}$$

Define two sets,

$$A = \{(w, y) \mid y \in T_\tau(k_0) \text{ and } w > v_\tau - u_\tau(k_0, y)\},$$

and

$$B = \{(w, y) \mid y \in K \text{ and } w \leqslant \rho^\tau V(y)\}.$$

A and B are not empty, but by (12) they are disjoint. They are also convex. Thus by a separation theorem for convex sets [1, p. 163] A and B may be separated by a hyperplane contained in R^{n+1}, defined by a vector $(\pi, -p_\tau) \neq 0$. Then $\pi w - p_\tau y \geqslant \pi w' - p_\tau y'$ for all $(w, y) \in A$ and $(w', y') \in B$.

Using the definitions of w, w', and v_τ and relation (12), the separation of A and B implies

$$\pi\{u_\tau(k_0, k_\tau) + \rho^\tau V(k_\tau) - u_\tau(k_0, y)\} - p_\tau y \geqslant \pi\rho^\tau V(y') - p_\tau y', \tag{13}$$

for any $y \in T_\tau(k_0)$ and $y' \in K$. If $\pi = 0$, (13) implies $p_\tau \cdot (y' - y) \geqslant 0$ for all $y' \in K$, $y \in T_\tau(k_0)$. Since interior $(T_\tau(k_0) \cap K) \neq \varnothing$, this implies $p_\tau = 0$ as well, contradicting $(\pi, -p_\tau) \neq 0$. Thus $\pi \neq 0$ and we may put $\pi = 1$. Put $y = k_\tau$ and (13) may be written

$$V(k_\tau) - \rho^{-\tau}p_\tau k_\tau \geqslant V(y') - \rho^{-\tau}p_\tau y', \tag{14}$$

for all $y \in K$. Put $y' = k_\tau$, and we obtain

$$u_\tau(k_0, k_\tau) + p_\tau k_\tau \geqslant u_\tau(k_0, y) + p_\tau y, \tag{15}$$

for all $y \in T_\tau(k_0)$. This p_τ can be used to start the induction argument.

The induction step is entirely parallel to the argument for p_τ, except that $\rho^\tau V_\tau(k_\tau)$ is replaced by $\rho^{\tau+1}V_{\tau+1}(k_{\tau+1}) - p_\tau k_\tau$, and τ is replaced by $\tau + 1$ in each use. Also P replaces $T_\tau(k_0)$ in the argument, and $u_\tau(k_0, k_\tau)$ and $u_\tau(k_0, y)$ become $u(k_\tau, k_{\tau+1})$ and $u(x, y)$. Then when y is put equal to $k_{\tau+1}$ in the argument, x is put equal to k_τ. The conclusion which is drawn will appear as (9) and (10), with q_t replaced by $\rho^{-t}p_t$. Thus Proposition 4 is established. The details of the induction step, which uses interior $P \cap K \neq 0$, may be found in McKenzie [7].

Proposition 5 In case of a nontrivial stationary optimal path $k_t = k$, all k, relations (9) and (10) are satisfied by $k_t = k_{t+1} = k$ and $q_t = q_{t+1} = q$.

Proof There is nothing to prove in the case of (10), which is the same as (7) after the substitutions are made. To derive (9), let $\{h_\tau\}$, $\tau = t$, $t+1, \ldots$, be an optimal path from initial stocks $h_t \in K$. Multiply (7) through by ρ^τ and substitute $h_{\tau-1}$ for x and h_τ for y. Then add the resulting inequalities from $\tau = t+1$ to $\tau = \infty$.

25.3 Liapounov Stability of the Facet

The epigraph G of the utility function $u(x, y)$ is defined as all $(\zeta, x, y) \in R^1 \times R_+^n \times R_+^n$ such that $(x, y) \in D$ and $\zeta \leqslant u(x, y)$. Since u is concave, G is convex. Since u is closed, G is closed (see Fenchel [2, p. 78]). A nontrivial stationary optimal path $k_t = k(\rho)$, $t = 0, 1, \ldots$, corresponds to a point $(\zeta^*, k(\rho), k(\rho))$ of the boundary of G, where $\zeta^* = u(k(\rho), k(\rho))$. According to Proposition 2, any such point has a supporting price vector of the form $(1, -\rho^{-1}q, q)$. Let $S \subset R^n$ be the set of vectors q that appear in supporting price vectors of this form, and let $q(\rho)$ be chosen in the interior of S relative to the smallest flat of R^n that contains S. We will also refer to $q(\rho)$ as a supporting price vector. Define the *von Neumann facet* $F(k(\rho))$ for the optimal stationary path, $k_t = k(\rho)$, to be the set of $(\zeta, x, y) \in G$, such that

$$\zeta + q(\rho)y - \rho^{-1}q(\rho)x = u(k(\rho), k(\rho)) + (1 - \rho^{-1})q(\rho)k(\rho). \tag{16}$$

It is easily seen that $F(k(\rho))$ is well defined. Indeed, write k for $k(\rho)$, and let $\phi(q, q) = \{(\zeta, x, y) \in G \mid \zeta + qy - \rho^{-1}qx = u(k, k) + (1 - \rho^{-1})qk\}$ for $q \in S$. Then $F(k(\rho)) = \bigcap_{q \in S} \phi(q, q)$ is an alternative characterization of the von Neumann facet.

In order to prove that an optimal path from a sufficient initial stock eventually converges, in an appropriate sense, to a von Neumann facet, we will use a Liapounov function which is symmetric with respect to a nontrivial stationary optimal path and another optimal path from a sufficient stock. Let $k(\rho)$ define a nontrivial stationary optimal path for the discount factor ρ satisfying $\bar{p} \leqslant \rho < 1$. Let $q(\rho)$ define a supporting price vector, where $q(\rho)$ is chosen in the way described above. Let $\{k_t(\rho)\}$ be another optimal path from a sufficient stock $x = k_0(\rho)$, for the discount factor ρ and a given x. Let $\{q_t(\rho)\}$ be a sequence of price vectors from $t = \tau$ which satisfy relations (9) and (10) of Proposition 4 with respect to $\{k_t(\rho)\}$, $t = 0, 1, \ldots$, and an appropriate $\tau > 0$. We will refer to the $q_t(\rho)$ as support prices for the path. Recall that τ depends on x, but not on ρ. Define the Liapounov function, $L_t(\rho)$, relative to a particular $k(\rho)$, by

$$L_t(\rho) = (q_t(\rho) - q(\rho))(k_t(\rho) - k(\rho)). \tag{17}$$

In order to use the function $L_t(\rho)$, some additional results will be needed. Let $p, q \in R_+^n$. If $u(z, w) + qw - pz$ achieves a maximum $\sigma(p, q)$ on the epigraph G of u, define the facet $\phi(p, q)$ of G by $\phi(p, q) = \{(\zeta, x, y) \in G \mid \zeta = u(x, y) \text{ and } u(x, y) + qy - px = \sigma(p, q)\}$. In this terminology, the von Neumann facet $F(k(\rho)) = \phi(\rho^{-1}q(\rho), q(\rho))$ for an appropriate choice of $q(\rho)$. If B is a set and z is a vector, let $d(z, B) = \inf |(z, w)|$ for $w \in B$, that is, the distance of z from B. Also let ϕ' or F' be the projection of ϕ or F, respectively, on the space of initial and terminal stocks. We will also refer to $\phi'(p, q)$ or $F'(k(\rho))$ as a facet of G. The value loss lemma is

Lemma 1 Let $\phi'(p, q)$ be a facet of G. For any $\xi > 0$, $\varepsilon > 0$, there is $\delta > 0$, such that $(x, y) \in D$, $|x| < \xi$, and $d((x, y), \phi'(p, q)) \geq \varepsilon$ implies $u(x, y) + qy - px \leq \sigma(p, q) - \delta$.

Proof If the conclusion were false, there would be a sequence (x^s, y^s), $s = 1, 2, \ldots$, such that the distance of each member of the sequence from F' exceeds ε, but the corresponding value losses $\delta^s \to 0$. Since the sequence lies in a bounded region by Assumption 2, we may assume that $(x^s, y^s) \to (\bar{x}, \bar{y})$. Since $\delta^s \to 0$, $u(\bar{x}, \bar{y}) \geq \lim \sup u(x^s, y^s) = \sigma(p, q) - q\bar{y} + p\bar{x}$, as $s \to \infty$, and $(\bar{x}, \bar{y}) \in D$. Therefore, $u(\bar{x}, \bar{y}) = \lim \sup u(x^s, y^s)$ and $u(\bar{x}, \bar{y}) + q\bar{y} - p\bar{x} = \sigma(p, q)$. Thus $(\bar{x}, \bar{y}) \in \phi'(p, q)$, contradicting the assumption that (x^s, y^s) is bounded away from ϕ'. This establishes the lemma.

Recall that an optimal stationary stock k satisfies $u(k, k) \geq u(x, y)$ for all $(x, y) \in D$ with $y \geq x$. Let k be an optimal stationary stock. Choose the origin of the utility function so that $u(k, k) = 0$. For $\bar{\rho} \leq \rho < 1$, write the value function as $V(\rho, x)$ with this normalization. It has been shown earlier [8] that

Lemma 2 For given x that is sufficient, the value function $V(\rho, x)$ is bounded over ρ such that $\bar{\rho} \leq \rho < 1$.

Using Lemma 2 it is possible to bound the prices, and therefore the Liapounov function, as $\rho \to 1$. Indeed,

Lemma 3 If x is sufficient and $\{k_t(\rho)\}$, $t = 0, 1, \ldots$, is an optimal path with $k_0(\rho) = x$, there is τ such that the prices $q_t(\rho)$ given by Proposition 4 are bounded for each t, over $\bar{\rho} \leqslant \rho < 1$, for $t \geqslant \tau$.

Proof We choose τ as in Proposition 4. Then interior $T_\tau(x) \cap K \neq \varnothing$. Suppose $q_\tau(\rho)$ is unbounded for $\bar{\rho} \leqslant \rho < 1$. Then there is a sequence $q_\tau(\rho^s)$, $s = 1, 2, \ldots$, such that $|q_\tau(\rho^s)| \to \infty$. Recalling that $q_\tau = \rho^{-\tau} p_\tau \neq 0$, divide (14) through by $|q_\tau(\rho^s)|$. Let $q^s = q_\tau(\rho^s)/|q_\tau(\rho^s)|$, and $k^s = k_\tau(\rho^s)$. The sequence (q^s, k^s), $s = 1, 2, \ldots$, will have a point of accumulation $(\bar{q}, \bar{k})$, since k^s is bounded from Assumption 3. Since $V(\rho^s, x)$ is bounded over s by Lemma 2, we obtain from (14)

$$\bar{q}(y - \bar{k}) \geqslant 0, \text{ for all } y \in K. \tag{18}$$

Similarly, we may divide (15) through by $|q_\tau(\rho^s)|$. Since $V(\rho^s, x)$ is bounded over s, $u_\tau(x, k_\tau(\rho^s))$ is bounded over s by the argument used in the proof of Theorem 1. Also, there is an open set $B \subset T_\tau(x) \cap K$ such that $u_\tau(x, y)$ is bounded for $y \in B$. Choosing the same accumulation point of (q^s, k^s) as before, we obtain

$$\bar{q}(y - \bar{k}) \leqslant 0, \text{ for all } y \in B. \tag{19}$$

Together (18) and (19) imply $\bar{q}(y - \bar{k}) = 0$ for $y \in B$. Since B is open and $\bar{q} \neq 0$, this is a contradiction. Thus $q_\tau(\rho)$ is bounded over $\bar{\rho} \leqslant \rho < 1$.

To complete the proof, we establish the induction step, assuming that $q_t(\rho)$ is bounded. We arrive at the same contradiction again using (9) and (10) in place of (14) and (15), and using an open set $B \subset P \cap K$, to which there corresponds a bounded open set $B' \subset D$ such that $y \in B$ implies there is x with $(x, y) \in B'$. B and B' may be chosen so $u(x, y)$ is bounded for $(x, y) \in B'$. Also $u(k_t, k_{t+1})$ is bounded independently of ρ from the fact that $V(\rho, x)$ is bounded. Then the analogue of (18) arises from (9), and the analogue of (19) arises from (10). Thus $q_{t+1}(\rho)$ is also bounded over $\bar{\rho} \leqslant \rho < 1$, and the lemma is proved.

We may now derive some properties of the function $L_t(\rho)$ that will be useful for proving convergence to the facet. First, $L_t(\rho)$ is bounded along an optimal path at each $t \geqslant \tau$, uniformly over the choice of $k(\rho)$ and $\bar{\rho} \leqslant \rho < 1$. By Lemma 3, the $q_t(\rho)$ are bounded for $t \geqslant \tau$ and $\bar{\rho} \leqslant \rho < 1$ for an assigned initial stock x that is sufficient. We will also need a bound on $q(\rho)$ for $\bar{\rho} \leqslant \rho < 1$, which is independent of the choice of $k(\rho)$. To this end, we prove

Lemma 4 The prices $q(\rho)$ that support a nontrivial optimal stationary path $k_t = k(\rho)$, $t = 0, 1, \ldots$, are bounded over $k(\rho)$ and $\bar{\rho} \leqslant \rho < 1$.

Proof If $q(\rho)$ is not bounded, there is a sequence ρ^s, $k(\rho^s)$, $q(\rho^s)$, $s = 1, 2, \ldots$, such that $|q(\rho^s)| \to \infty$. Since ρ^s and $k(\rho^s)$ lie in bounded sets, the sequence may be chosen so that $\rho^s \to \rho$ and $k(\rho^s) \to k$. If $\rho < 1$, $V(k(\rho^s))$ is bounded, and the argument of the proof of Lemma 3 may be repeated to show that $q(\rho^s)$ is bounded, using Proposition 5 in place of Proposition 4 and an open set $B \subset D$. If $\rho = 1$, relation (10) implies

$$u(k(\rho^s), k(\rho^s)) + q(\rho^s)(1 - (\rho^s)^{-1})k(\rho^s) \geqslant u(x, y) + q(\rho^s)(y - (\rho^s)^{-1}x) \tag{20}$$

for all $(x, y) \in D$. Dividing (20) by $|q(\rho^s)|$ and passing to the limit for an appropriate subsequence gives

$$q(y - x) \leqslant 0 \tag{21}$$

for all $(x, y) \in D$, where q is the limit of $(q(\rho^s))/(|q(\rho^s)|)$ (retain notation) as $s \to \infty$. Since $q \neq 0$, relation (21) contradicts Assumption 5. Thus once again $q(\rho^s)$ is bounded. This implies that $q(\rho)$ is bounded over all choices of $k(\rho)$, and $\bar{\rho} \leqslant \rho < 1$.

We may now establish

Lemma 5 $L_t(\rho)$ is bounded along an optimal path from any sufficient stock at each $t \geqslant \tau$ uniformly with regard to the choice of $k(\rho)$ and $\bar{\rho} \leqslant \rho < 1$.

Proof By the definition $L_t(\rho) = (q_t(\rho) - q(\rho))(k_t(\rho) - k(\rho))$, where $k_t(\rho)$, $t = 0, 1, \ldots$, is an optimal path supported by the $q_t(\rho)$ and $k(\rho)$ defines a nontrivial stationary optimal path supported by $q(\rho)$. The stock vectors are bounded from Assumption 3, and the price vectors are bounded from Lemmas 3 and 4, with the necessary uniformities. Thus $L_t(\rho)$ is bounded and the lemma follows.

A second property that is needed is that $L_t(\rho)$ is not positive, that is,

Lemma 6 $L_t(\rho) \leqslant 0$, for $\bar{\rho} \leqslant \rho < 1$, when $L_t(\rho)$ is well defined.

Proof Consider relation (9) for the optimal path $\{k_t(\rho)\}$, $t = 0, 1, \ldots$, with $k_0(\rho) = x$ with x sufficient, and for the nontrivial stationary optimal path $k(\rho)$. Then for $t \geqslant \tau$, from Propositions 4 and 5,

$$V(k_{t+1}(\rho)) - q_{t+1}(\rho)k_{t+1}(\rho) \geqslant V(k(\rho)) - q_{t+1}(\rho)k(\rho), \tag{22}$$

$$V(k_{t+1}(\rho)) - q(\rho)k_{t+1}(\rho) \leqslant V(k(\rho)) - q(\rho)k(\rho). \tag{23}$$

Subtracting (22) from (23) gives

$$(q_{t+1}(\rho) - q(\rho))k_{t+1}(\rho) \leqslant (q_{t+1}(\rho) - q(\rho))k(\rho). \tag{24}$$

But (24) implies immediately $L_{t+1}(\rho) \leqslant 0$.

From Proposition 2, we have for a nontrivial stationary optimal path $k_t = k(\rho)$ that $q(\rho)$ supports $k(\rho)$ in the sense of (7), or (10). Similarly from Proposition 3, if k is an optimal stationary stock, k is supported by q in the sense of (8) or (10). The von Neumann facet $F(k(1))$ is the set of $(\zeta, x, y) \in G$ such that

$$\zeta + q(y - x) = u(k,k), \tag{25}$$

where k is an optimal stationary stock and q satisfies Proposition 3 with k. $F(k(1))$ is the analogue of $F(k(\rho))$ when $\rho = 1$, where $k(1)$ is understood to be any optimal stationary stock. When the supporting price vector is chosen to be relative interior in the manner described above for $q(\rho)$ it will be denoted by $q(1)$.

We recall that $(\eta, -\rho^{-1}p, q)$ are support prices for the point $(u(x, y), x, y)$ of the epigraph G of u if $\eta u(x, y) + qy - \rho^{-1}px \geqslant \eta u(z, w) + qw - \rho^{-1}pz$, for all $(z, w) \in D$. If $\eta = 1$, we may also say in this case that (p, q) with the discount factor ρ supports (x, y).

The third property of $L_t(\rho)$ that is needed is that $L_t(\rho)$ equals 0 on $F'(k(\rho))$ and becomes small in a neighborhood of $F'(k(\rho))$. To establish this property we make the further assumption,

Assumption 6 If (p, q) are support prices for some point of the von Neumann facet $F'(k(\rho))$, where $\bar{\rho} \leqslant \rho \leqslant 1$, then $(p, q) = (q(\rho), q(\rho))$.

Assumption 6 is equivalent to the requirement that $u(x, y)$ be ~~smooth at all $(x, y) \in F'(k(\rho))$. That $L_t(\rho) = 0$~~ in $F'(k(\rho))$ is immediate from the definitions and Assumption 6. A further consequence of Assumption 6 is

Lemma 7 Let $(x, y) \in D$, $|x| \leqslant \xi$, and let (p, q) be support prices for (x, y) when the discount factor is ρ. If $k(\rho)$ defines a nontrivial optimal stationary path for $\bar{\rho} \leqslant \rho < 1$, or an optimal stationary stock for $\rho = 1$, for any $\lambda > 0$ there is $\varepsilon > 0$ such that $d((x, y), F'(k(\rho))) < \varepsilon$ implies $(p - q(\rho))(x - k(\rho)) > -\lambda$, uniformly over $k(\rho)$ and $\bar{\rho} \leqslant \rho \leqslant 1$.

Proof Suppose not. Then there is $\lambda > 0$, and sequences $(x^s, y^s) \in D$, (p^s, q^s), $k(\rho^s)$, $q(\rho^s)$, $s = 1, 2, \ldots$, such that $d((x^s, y^s), F'(k(\rho^s))) \to 0$ and $(p^s - q(\rho^s))(x^s - k(\rho^s)) \leqslant -\lambda$, where (p^s, q^s) supports (x^s, y^s) with the discount factor ρ^s, and $q(\rho^s)$ supports $k(\rho^s)$. By Assumption 2, (x^s, y^s) is bounded, and by Assumption 3, $k(\rho^s)$ is bounded. Also by Lemma 4, $q(\rho^s)$ is bounded. Let $(\eta^s, -\rho^{s-1}\bar{p}^s, \bar{q}^s) = (1, -\rho^{s-1}p^s, q^s)/$

$|(1, -\rho^{s-1}p^s, q^s)|$. Then $(\eta^s, -\rho^{s-1}\bar{p}^s, \bar{q}^s)$ supports $(u(x^s, y^s), x^s, y^s)$, and has unit norm. Thus there is a subsequence for which $(x^s, y^s) \rightarrow (x, y)$, $\rho^s \rightarrow \rho, k(\rho^s) \rightarrow k(\rho), q(\rho^s) \rightarrow q(\rho)$, and $(\eta^s, -\rho^{s-1}\bar{p}^s, \bar{q}^s) \rightarrow (\eta, -\rho^{-1}\bar{p}, \bar{q})$. If $\eta > 0$, $p = \eta^{-1}\bar{p}$, and $q = \eta^{-1}\bar{q}$ are well defined, and $(1, -\rho^{-1}p, q)$ are support prices for $(u(x, y), x, y)$ if $(x, y) \in D$. In this case, (p, q) with the discount factor ρ supports (x, y). We will shortly establish both $\eta > 0$ and $(x, y) \in D$.

Note that $(k(\rho^s), k(\rho^s))$ all lie in the compact set $\bar{\Delta} = \{(x, x) \in D \mid u(x, x) \geqslant u(\bar{x}, \bar{y})\}$, where $(\bar{x}, \bar{y})$ is the point mentioned in Assumption 5. Then $(k(\rho), k(\rho))$ is also in $\bar{\Delta}$ and thus in D. The continuity of the relation (7) implies that $q(\rho)$ supports $k(\rho)$ and, by Assumption 6, it is the unique support of $k(\rho)$. If $\rho < 1$, the support property implies (see [6]) that $k(\rho)$ defines a stationary optimal path for the discount factor ρ. Also the conditions of Proposition 1 will be satisfied in the limit so that the optimal path is nontrivial. If $\rho = 1$, it is clear from Proposition 1 that $k(\rho)$ is an optimal stationary stock. Let (z^s, w^s) be the closest point of $F'(k(\rho^s))$ to (x^s, y^s). Then $d((z^s, w^s), (x^s, y^s)) \rightarrow 0$ and $(z^s, w^s) \rightarrow (x, y)$. Since $(q(\rho^s), q(\rho^s))$ supports (z^s, w^s), $(q(\rho), q(\rho))$ supports (x, y) if $(x, y) \in D$. However, if $(x, y) \notin D$, $u(z^s, w^s) \rightarrow -\infty$, while (z^s, w^s), $k(\rho^s)$, and $q(\rho^s)$ are bounded. Thus $(q(\rho^s), q(\rho^s))$ and (z^s, w^s) do not satisfy (16) for large s, which contradicts the assumption that $(z^s, w^s) \in F'(k(\rho^s))$. Since $F'(k(\rho))$ is closed in D, it follows that $(x, y) \in F'(k(\rho))$. Then by Assumption 6, $(q(\rho), q(\rho))$ is the unique price support for (x, y). On the other hand, if $\eta = 0$, $\alpha(\bar{p}, \bar{q}) + (1 - \alpha)(q(\rho), q(\rho))$ would also support (x, y). Thus $\eta > 0$ must hold, and it must be that $p = q = q(\rho)$. Then $(p - q(\rho))(x - k(\rho)) = 0$, which contradicts $(p^s - q(\rho^s))(x^s - k(\rho^s)) \leqslant -\lambda < 0$ for large s. Thus no such sequence can exist, and the lemma is proved.

The application of Lemma 7 to $L_t(\rho)$ is contained in the

Corollary If $\{k_t(\rho)\}$, $t = 0, 1, \ldots$, is an optimal path and $k_0(\rho) = x$ is sufficient, then for all $\lambda > 0$ there are $\varepsilon > 0$ and τ, such that $t \geqslant \tau$ and $d((k_t(\rho), k_{t+1}(\rho)), F'(k(\rho))) < \varepsilon$ imply $L_t(\rho) > -\lambda$, uniformly with respect to t, $k(\rho)$, and $\bar{p} \leqslant \rho < 1$.

Proof By Assumption 3, all $k_t(\rho)$ lie in a bounded set. By Proposition 4, there is τ such that price supports $(q_t(\rho), q_{t+1}(\rho))$ exist for $(k_t(\rho), k_{t+1}(\rho))$ when $t \geqslant \tau$. Thus the conditions of Lemma 7 are met, and the conclusion follows from the definition of $L_t(\rho)$. Note that $L_t(\rho)$ is defined relative to a particular $k(\rho)$, so the notation is not complete.

We have now shown that $L_t(\rho)$ is bounded, not positive, and small near $F'(k(\rho))$. In order to prove that the optimal path approaches every $F'(k(\rho))$, we will need to apply Lemma 1 to the facets $F'(k(\rho))$ uniformly for ρ satisfying $\bar{\rho} \leqslant \rho < 1$. Define the value loss $\delta(\rho^{-1}p, q; x, y)$ by

$$\delta(\rho^{-1}p, q; x, y) = \sigma(\rho^{-1}p, q) - (u(x, y) + qy - \rho^{-1}px),$$

where $\sigma(p, q)$ was defined above. Let $k_t = k(\rho)$, $t = 0, 1, \ldots$, be a nontrivial stationary optimal path, which, by Assumption 6, is supported in the sense of Proposition 2 by the unique price vector $q(\rho)$. We assume

Assumption 7   For any $\xi > 0$, $\varepsilon > 0$, there is $\delta > 0$, such that $|x| < \xi$ and $d((x, y), F'(k(\rho))) > \varepsilon$ implies $\delta(\rho^{-1}q(\rho), q(\rho); x, y) > \delta$ for any ρ with $\bar{\rho} \leqslant \rho < 1$, and any choice of $k(\rho)$.

Assumption 7 together with Assumption 6 implies that u is strictly concave near $F'(k(\rho))$ uniformly with respect to ρ and $k(\rho)$. We may now prove a crucial result.

Lemma 8   Given an optimal path $\{k_t(\rho)\}$, $t = 0, 1, \ldots$, where k_0 is sufficient, for any $\varepsilon > 0$, there is τ such that $t \geqslant \tau$ and $d((k_t(\rho), k_{t+1}(\rho)), F'(k(\rho))) \geqslant \varepsilon$ implies there is $\delta > 0$ such that $L_{t+1}(\rho) - \rho^{-1}L_t(\rho) \geqslant \delta$, uniformly for $\bar{\rho} \leqslant \rho < 1$ and all $k(\rho)$.

Proof   Let $t \geqslant \tau$ in Proposition 4, so the prices $q_t(\rho)$ exist. For any nontrivial optimal stationary path $k(\rho)$, Lemma 1 and the definition of $F'(k(\rho))$ imply there is $\delta > 0$ such that

$$u(k_t(\rho), k_{t+1}(\rho)) + q(\rho)k_{t+1}(\rho) - \rho^{-1}q(\rho)k_t(\rho)$$

$$\leqslant u(k(\rho), k(\rho)) + q(\rho)k(\rho) - \rho^{-1}q(\rho)k(\rho) - \delta, \qquad (26)$$

$$u(k_t(\rho), k_{t+1}(\rho)) + q_{t+1}(\rho)k_{t+1}(\rho) - \rho^{-1}q_t(\rho)k_t(\rho)$$

$$\geqslant u(k(\rho), k(\rho)) + q_{t+1}(\rho)k(\rho) - \rho^{-1}q_t(\rho)k(\rho). \qquad (27)$$

Subtracting (26) from (27) gives

$$L_{t+1}(\rho) - \rho^{-1}L_t(\rho) \geqslant \delta, \qquad (28)$$

as desired. Then uniformity follows immediately from Assumption 7.

Lemma 8 will be used to bring the optimal path into a neighborhood of each $F(k(\rho))$. Let τ be chosen to satisfy Proposition 4. Suppose $d((k_\tau(\rho), k_{\tau+1}(\rho)), F'(k(\rho))) > \varepsilon$, for $\bar{\rho} \leqslant \rho < 1$. Then we have from Lemma 8 that

$$L_{\tau+1}(\rho) - L_\tau(\rho) > (\rho^{-1} - 1)L_\tau(\rho) + \delta, \tag{29}$$

for some $\delta > 0$, uniformly over $k(\rho)$ and $\bar{\rho} \leqslant \rho < 1$. As $\rho \to 1$, the term $(\rho^{-1} - 1) \to 0$. Thus the right-hand side of (29) converges to δ, and ρ_1 may be chosen so that $(\rho_1^{-1} - 1)L \geqslant -\delta/2$, where L is a lower bound on $L_\tau(\rho)$ for $\bar{\rho} \leqslant \rho < 1$. This bound exists by Lemma 5. Then $(\rho^{-1} - 1)L_\tau(\rho) + \delta > \delta/2$ holds for $\rho \geqslant \rho_1$. By (29), for $\rho \geqslant \rho_1$, $L_{\tau+1}(\rho) - L_\tau(\rho) > \delta/2$, and the lower bound L is still effective. Consequently, $(\rho^{-1} - 1)L_{\tau+1}(\rho) > -\delta/2$.

Again by (29), for $\rho > \rho_1$, $L_{\tau+2}(\rho) - L_{\tau+1}(\rho) > \delta/2$ if $d((k_{\tau+1}(\rho), k_{\tau+2}(\rho), F'(k(\rho))) > \varepsilon$. Indeed, L remains a valid lower bound on $L_t(\rho)$ for all $t > \tau$, so long as $d((k_t(\rho), k_{t+1}(\rho)), F'(k(\rho))) > \varepsilon$. Thus for such t we have

$$L_t(\rho) - L > \tfrac{1}{2}(t - \tau)\delta. \tag{30}$$

But by Lemma 6, $L_t(\rho) \leqslant 0$ holds for all $t \geqslant \tau$. To avoid contradiction, $(k_t(\rho), k_{t+1}(\rho))$ must enter the ε-neighborhood of $F'(k(\rho))$ before $t_1 = \tau - 2L/\delta$. This justifies

Lemma 9 Let x be a sufficient capital stock, and $\{k_t(\rho)\}$ an optimal path from x, and $k(\rho)$ a nontrivial optimal stationary path. Then for any $\varepsilon > 0$, there is ρ_1, $\bar{\rho} \leqslant \rho_1 < 1$, and $t_1 > 0$, such that $d((k_t(\rho), k_{t+1}(\rho)), F'(k(\rho))) \leqslant \varepsilon$ for some $t < t_1$ when $\rho_1 \leqslant \rho < 1$. Here t_1 is independent of ρ and $k(\rho)$.

By Lemma 9, given k_0, we may choose an ε_1 as small as we like and still find a $\rho_1 < 1$ such that $\rho \geqslant \rho_1$ but less than 1 implies that the optimal path $k_t(\rho)$ from k_0 eventually enters the ε_1-neighborhood of $F'(k(\rho))$. Then, by the Corollary to Lemma 7, for any $\lambda > 0$ we may find an ε_1 such that $L_t(\rho) > -\lambda$ holds for $k_t(\rho)$ in the ε_1-neighborhood of $F'(k(\rho))$. A final lemma is needed to provide that $L_{t+1}(\rho)$ near 0 implies that (k_{t+1}, k_{t+2}) remains near $F'(k(\rho))$. Let τ be chosen as in Proposition 4.

Lemma 10 For any $\varepsilon > 0$ there is $\lambda > 0$ such that $L_t(\rho) > -\lambda$ implies $d((k_t(\rho), k_{t+1}(\rho)), F'(k(\rho))) < \varepsilon$, uniformly over $k(\rho)$, $\bar{\rho} \leqslant \rho < 1$, for $t \geqslant \tau$.

Proof By Assumption 7, for any $\varepsilon > 0$ there is $\lambda > 0$ such that, if the value loss $\delta_{t+1} = \delta(\rho^{-1}q(\rho), q(\rho); k_t(\rho), k_{t+1}(\rho))$ is less than $\bar{\rho}^{-1}\lambda$, then

$d((k_t(\rho), k_{t+1}(\rho)), F'(k(\rho)))$ is less than ε, uniformly over $k(\rho)$ and $\bar{\rho} \leqslant \rho < 1$. However, by the proof of Lemma 8, we have $t \geqslant \tau$ implies $L_{t+1}(\rho) \geqslant \bar{\rho}^{-1} L_t(\rho) + \delta_{t+1}$. Moreover, by Lemma 6, we have $L_{t+1}(\rho) \leqslant 0$. Thus $\delta_{t+1} \leqslant -\bar{\rho}^{-1} L_t(\rho)$. If $L_t(\rho) > -\lambda$, it follows that $\delta_{t+1} \leqslant \bar{\rho}^{-1}\lambda$. Then it must be that $d((k_t(\rho), k_{t+1}(\rho)), F'(\rho))) < \varepsilon$, which completes the proof of the lemma.

We may now prove the first main result.

Theorem 2 For any $\varepsilon > 0$ there is ρ' such that $\bar{\rho} \leqslant \rho' \leqslant \rho < 1$ and x sufficient implies that any optimal path $\{k_t(\rho)\}$ for $k_o(\rho) = x$ eventually lies in the ε-neighborhood of $F'(k(\rho))$. The convergence is uniform with respect to ρ and $k(\rho)$.

Proof We choose $\varepsilon > 0$ arbitrarily small. Then by Lemma 10, for $t + 1 > \tau$ and $\bar{\rho} \leqslant \rho < 1$ there is λ such that $L_{t+1}(\rho) > -\lambda$ implies $d((k_{t+1}(\rho), k_{t+2}(\rho)), F'(k(\rho))) < \varepsilon$. By the proof of Lemma 8, we have $L_{t+1}(\rho) \geqslant \bar{\rho}^{-1} L_t(\rho)$. Thus $L_{t+1}(\rho) > -\lambda$ if $L_t(\rho) > -\bar{\rho}\lambda$. By the Corollary to Lemma 7, we may choose ε' so that $L_t(\rho) > -\bar{\rho}\lambda$, uniformly for $\bar{\rho} \leqslant \rho < 1$, when $(k_t(\rho), k_{t+1}(\rho))$ lies in the ε'-neighborhood of $F'(k(\rho))$. Finally, by Lemma 9, ρ' may be chosen with $\bar{\rho} \leqslant \rho' \leqslant 1$ so that $(k_t(\rho), k_{t+1}(\rho))$ enters the ε'-neighborhood of $F'(k(\rho))$ before a fixed time t_1 for any ρ with $\rho' \leqslant \rho < 1$.

The argument implies that once $(k_t(\rho), k_{t+1}(\rho))$ lies in the ε'-neighborhood of $F'(k(\rho))$, $(k_{t+1}(\rho), k_{t+2}(\rho))$ lies in the ε-neighborhood. If $(k_{t+1}(\rho), k_{t+2}(\rho))$ is not in the ε'-neighborhood and $L_{t+1}(\rho) \geqslant L$, where L is the lower bound on $L_\tau(\rho)$ used in the proof of Lemma 8, it follows from the proof of Lemma 8 that $L_{t+2}(\rho) > L_{t+1}(\rho)$, so that $(k_{t+2}(\rho), k_{t+3}(\rho))$ lies in the ε-neighborhood of $F'(k(\rho))$ as well, and subsequent input-output vectors lie in this neighborhood by the same argument until they enter the ε'-neighborhood once again. Then they are confined to the ε-neighborhood by a repetition of the argument. Thus, the only requirement needed to guarantee convergence to the ε'-neighborhood and subsequent confinement to the ε-neighborhood is that ε be chosen small enough so that we have $-\lambda > L$. By the Corollary to Lemma 7, this is possible, so the proof is complete.

25.4 Liapounov Stability of the Optimal Stationary Point

We have now established that an optimal path from a sufficient stock can be confined eventually to a neighborhood of a facet $F'(k(\rho))$ of the graph G, for an arbitrary choice of a stock $k(\rho)$ that defines a nontrivial optimal stationary path, and ρ larger than some ρ', $\bar{\rho} \leqslant \rho' \leqslant \rho < 1$. Moreover, the neighborhood may be made as small as desired by choosing ρ sufficiently near 1. We will now show that stability on the von Neumann facet $F^* = F'(k(1))$ implies that the optimal path may be confined to an arbitrarily small neighborhood of $k(\rho)$ by choice of ρ sufficiently near 1.

The idea of the proof is to combine three stability results: the convergence of optimal paths for $\rho < 1$ to a neighborhood of the facets $F'(k(\rho))$; the convergence of the facets $F'(k(\rho))$ to F^* as $\rho \rightarrow 1$; and the convergence of optimal paths on F^* to $k^* = k(1)$. It is shown that the optimal path for $\rho < 1$ must then converge to a neighborhood of $k(\rho)$, which may be made arbitrarily small by choosing ρ near enough to 1.

We will first prove the convergence of $F'(k(\rho))$ to F^* as $\rho \rightarrow 1$. The set of optimal stationary stocks is convex and compact as a consequence of Assumptions 1 and 3. We assume

Assumption 8   There is a unique optimal stationary stock k^*.

It is immediate from the results of an earlier paper [8] that the following lemma holds. In its original form it was proved by Scheinkman [10].

Lemma 11   Let k^* be the unique optimal stationary stock. Then $\sup |k(\rho) - k^*| \rightarrow 0$ as $\rho \rightarrow 1$, where the sup is taken over all $k(\rho)$ that define nontrivial optimal stationary paths for given ρ.

Let $F''(k(\rho))$ be all $(x, y) \in F'(k(\rho))$, such that $|x| \leqslant \zeta$, where ζ is from Assumption 3. $F''(k(\rho))$ is not empty since it contains $(k(\rho), k(\rho))$. We will say that a set A converges to a set B if $\sup d(z, B) \rightarrow 0$ for $z \in A$. This relation is not symmetric. With use of Lemma 11 and Assumption 8 we may easily prove

Lemma 12   Let $k(\rho)$ be the stock of an optimal stationary path for ρ with $\bar{\rho} \leqslant \rho < 1$. If $\rho \rightarrow 1$, then $F''(k(\rho)) \rightarrow F^*$.

Proof   By Lemma 11, $\rho \rightarrow 1$ implies $k(\rho) \rightarrow k^*$. By Lemma 3, $q(\rho)$ is bounded as $\rho \rightarrow 1$, where $q(\rho)$ supports the path defined by $k(\rho)$. Thus there is a convergent sequence $q(\rho^s) \rightarrow q$, $s = 1, 2, \ldots$. From continuity of the inner product, q supports the path defined by k^*. Then Assumption 6 implies $F(q, q) = F^*$.

Suppose the lemma is false. Then there is a sequence $(x^s, y^s) \in F''(k(\rho^s))$ where $\rho^s \rightarrow 1$, with $\bar{\rho} \leqslant \rho^s < 1$, such that $d((x^s, y^s), F^*) > \varepsilon >$

0 for all s. By Assumption 2 and $|x^s| \leqslant \zeta$, (x^s, y^s) lies in a bounded region. Thus there is a convergent subsequence (retain notation) (x^s, y^s) $\rightarrow (x, y)$. Since (x^s, y^s) and $q(\rho^s)$ are bounded, the support property implies that $u(x^s, y^s)$ is bounded below. Therefore, $(x, y) \in D$ by Assumption 1. By closedness of u, (q, q) supports (x, y) so that $(x, y) \in F^*$. This contradicts the assumption that $d((x^s, y^s), F^*) > \varepsilon > 0$. Thus no such sequence can exist, and the lemma follows.

Let us say that the von Neumann facet F^* is stable if for any $\varepsilon > 0$ there is T such that a path $\{k_t\}$, $t = 0, 1, \ldots$, with $|k_0| \leqslant \zeta$ and (k_t, k_{t+1}) $\in F^*$ for all t must satisfy $|k_t - k^*| < \varepsilon$ for all $t > T$. It may be shown that this will be so in the absence of cyclic paths that lie on F^* [4]. We may prove

Theorem 3   Assume that the von Neumann facet F^* is stable. Then for any $\varepsilon > 0$ there is ρ' such that $\bar{\rho} \leqslant \rho' \leqslant \rho < 1$ and x sufficient implies that any optimal path $\{k_t(\rho)\}$ for $k_0(\rho) = x$ eventually lies in the ε-neighborhood of $k(\rho)$.

Proof   By Theorem 2, $(k_t(\rho), k_{t+1}(\rho))$ converges to an ε-neighborhood of $F'(k(\rho))$, when ρ is chosen near enough to 1. Since $|k_t(\rho)| < \zeta$ must hold eventually by Assumption 3, the convergence is actually to $F''(k(\rho))$. Also by Lemma 12 we have that ρ may be chosen near enough to 1 to case $F''(k(\rho))$ to lie eventually in the ε-neighborhood of F^*.

Suppose, in contradiction to the statement of the theorem, $k_t(\rho)$ does not eventually remain in an ε-neighborhood of $k(\rho)$ for some $\varepsilon > 0$. Let T be an arbitrary positive integer. Then there are sequences $\rho^s \rightarrow 1$, $\varepsilon^s \rightarrow 0$, and τ^s, $s = 1, 2, \ldots$, so that $(k_t(\rho^s), k_{t+1}(\rho^s))$ lies in the ε^s-neighborhood of F^* for $t \geqslant \tau^s$, but for which there is $t^s = \tau^s + T$ and $|k_{t^s}(\rho^s) - k(\rho^s)| > \varepsilon$. Let $h_t^s = k_{\tau^s + t}$ for $t = 0, 1, \ldots$. Since the paths $\{h_t^s\}$ lie in a bounded set, we may choose, by the Cantor process, a subsequence (retain notation) such that $\{h_t^s\}$ converges to a sequence $\{h_t\}_{t \geqslant 0}$ in the sense that $h_t^s \rightarrow h_t$ as $s \rightarrow \infty$, for all $t \geqslant 0$. Then $d((h_t, h_{t+1}), F^*)$ $= 0$, for $t \geqslant 0$. Since F^* is closed, and the boundary points of F^* lie in D as a consequence of Assumption 1, $\{h_t\}$ is an infinite path on F^*, but $|h_T - k^*| \geqslant \varepsilon$. Since this construction is possible for T arbitrarily large, the stability of $F'(k(1))$ is violated. Thus no such sequences can exist, or $k_t(\rho)$ does eventually remain in the ε-neighborhood of $k(\rho)$, where ε may be chosen arbitrarily small if ρ is then chosen near enough to 1. The theorem is proved.

25.5   Asymptotic Stability of the Optimal Stationary Point

We have been able to show on the basis of a stable von Neumann facet F^* that the optimal paths from sufficient stocks converge to a neighborhood of the unique optimal stationary stock. Moreover, this neighborhood may be made arbitrarily small by choosing ρ near enough to 1. Also the following result is known from previous work [5].

Lemma 13   On the basis of Assumptions 1, 2, 3, 4, 5, and 8, if the von Neumann facet F^* is stable, then $k_t = k^*$, $t = 0, 1, \ldots$, is a stationary optimal path for $\rho = 1$, and all optimal paths for $\rho = 1$, whose initial stock is sufficient, converge asymptotically to k^*.

In order to strengthen the stability of $k(\rho)$ to be asymptotic for the case $\rho < 1$, we will introduce a differentiability assumption. Let k^* be the unique optimal stationary stock.

Assumption 9   The optimal stationary point $(k^*, k^*) \in$ interior D. The utility function u has continuous partial derivatives in a neighborhood of (k^*, k^*). The second differential of u at (k^*, k^*) is negative for the argument (z, w) if $(k^*, k^*) + \alpha(z, w) \notin F^*$ for all $\alpha > 0$. Also $\det([(\partial u(x, y))/\partial x \partial y]_{(k^\rho, k^\rho)}) \neq 0$.

The second part of Assumption 9 says that $(D^2 u)\,(z, w)$ evaluated at (k^*, k^*) is negative when the direction (z, w) from (k^*, k^*) leads out of F^*, in every neighborhood of (k^*, k^*). The last part of Assumption 9 says that the determinant of the block of cross derivatives in the Hessian is different from 0.

Assumption 9, together with Lemma 11, implies that u has continuous partial derivatives at any nontrivial stationary optimal path for ρ near to 1. The partial derivatives of u may be used to define necessary conditions for an optimal path that correspond to the Euler conditions of the calculus of variations. Let $u_1(x, y) = (\partial u(z, w))/\partial z$ evaluated at (x, y), and similarly for $u_2(x, y)$. Then a necessary condition for the optimality of a path $\{k_t(\rho)\}$, $t = 0, 1, \ldots$, which is interior to D, is

$$u_2(k_{t-1}, k_t) + \rho u_1(k_t, k_{t+1}) = 0, \tag{31}$$

for all $t \geqslant 1$. The Eqs. (31) must be satisfied, in particular, by a stationary optimal path, $k_t(\rho) = k(\rho)$, $t = 0, 1, \ldots$. Since a unique optimal stationary stock also defines an optimal path for $\rho = 1$, these equations are also satisfied by $k_{t-1} = k_t = k_{t+1} = k^*$ and $\rho = 1$.

The linearization of (31) at $k_{t-1} = k_t = k_{t+1} = k(\rho)$ may be written

$$\rho u_{12}^p z_{t+1} + (\rho u_{11}^p + u_{22}^p)z_t + u_{21}^p z_{t-1} = 0, \tag{32}$$

where $z_t = (k_t - k(\rho))$ and $u_{11}^p = (\partial^2 u(x, y))/\partial x \partial x$, evaluated at $x = y = k(\rho)$, and similarly for the other expressions u_{ij}^p. If $\det(u_{12}^p) \neq 0$, (32) may be transformed to

$$z_{t+1} = -(u_{12}^p)^{-1}(u_{11}^p + \rho^{-1}u_{22}^p)z_t - \rho^{-1}(u_{12}^p)^{-1}u_{21}^p z_{t-1}. \tag{33}$$

Then putting $y_t = z_{t-1}$, the second order system of n linear difference Eqs. (33) may be expressed as the system of $2n$ linear difference equations

$$z_{t+1} = -(B^\rho)^{-1}(A^\rho + \rho^{-1}C^\rho)z_t - \rho^{-1}(B^\rho)^{-1}(B^\rho)^T y_t,$$
$$\tag{34}$$
$$y_{t+1} = z_t,$$

where $B^\rho = u_{12}^p$, $A^\rho = u_{11}^p$, $C^\rho = u_{22}^p$, T indicates transpose, and use is made of the fact that $u_{21}^p = (u_{12}^p)^T$.

The solutions of (34) are determined by the characteristic roots and characteristic vectors of the matrix

$$M^\rho = \begin{bmatrix} 0 & I \\ -\rho^{-1}(B^\rho)^{-1}(B^\rho)^T & -(B^\rho)^{-1}(A^\rho + \rho^{-1}C^\rho) \end{bmatrix}.$$

The product of the characteristic roots equals $\det(M^\rho) = \rho^{-n}$, so 0 is not a characteristic root. This depends on the fact that B^ρ has been assumed nonsingular. However, by Assumption 9 and Lemma 11, B^ρ will be nonsingular for ρ near 1. The characteristic equation of M^ρ is

$$|\lambda^2 I + M_{22}^\rho \lambda + M_{21}^\rho| = 0, \tag{35}$$

where $M_{22} = (B^\rho)^{-1}(A^\rho + \rho^{-1}C^\rho)$ and $M_{21} = \rho^{-1}(B^\rho)^{-1}(B^\rho)^T$. If the matrix that appears in (35) is multiplied by B^ρ on the left and $((B^\rho)^T)^{-1}$ on the right and the transpose is taken of the product matrix, the result is the same matrix as (35) with $(\rho\lambda)^{-1}$ substituted for λ. Also the determinant of this matrix is 0. Thus if λ is a characteristic root, so is $(\rho\lambda)^{-1}$. The argument is due in the present case to Levhari and Liviatan [3].

It has been shown in detail by Scheinkman [10] that these properties of the linearization of (31) at $\rho = 1$ together with two further properties to be described imply that (31) is locally stable at a stationary optimal point (k^ρ, k^ρ) when ρ is sufficiently near 1. The first property that is needed is that (35) have no roots λ with $|\lambda| = 1$, so the linear system has a saddle point at the origin, which corresponds to (k^p, k^p), with half its roots of norm less than 1. The subspace corresponding to these roots is the stable subspace for the linear system.

A second property that is needed is that the projection of the stable subspace of the linear system on the space of initial stocks have the origin as an interior point. Scheinkman shows that this property will hold if no point (o, v) with $v \neq 0$ lies in the stable subspace. He shows that this will be true when u is strictly convex near (k^p, k^p) with a negative definite second differential. However, in our case, a nontrivial von Neumann facet implies a singular second differential. Moreover, there seems no good reason why a point (o, v) with $v \neq 0$ should not lie on the von Neumann facet. Such a point corresponds to a variation in terminal stocks without a variation in initial stocks. And it would seem possible that such a (o, v) be in the stable subspace.

Scheinkman's argument for the local properties of the multisector Ramsey model is analogous to my argument for the von Neumann model [4]. In my case, I did not make the assumption of strict concavity that would exclude a nontrivial von Neumann facet. However, I did simply assume that no root λ had $|\lambda| = 1$, and that the appropriate property, corresponding to the property described above for the stable manifold, held. In view of Assumption 9, it suffices here to assume

Assumption 10a   For $\rho = 1$, there are no cyclic paths on the von Neumann facet F^* except $k_t = k^*$, all t.

Assumption 10b   For $\rho = 1$, there is no path $\{k_t\}$ on the von Neumann facet with $k_0 = k^*$, $k_1 = k^* + v$, where $v \neq 0$, such that $k_t \to k^*$ as $t \to \infty$.

The assumptions suffice to establish the conditions used by Scheinkman. The argument of Levhari and Liviatan excludes a characteristic root λ of (35) with $|\lambda| = 1$, unless the corresponding invariant subspace is spanned by vectors (z_1, z_2) such that $(k^*, k^*) + (z_1, z_2) \in F^*$, and this possibility is excluded by 10a. Indeed, value loss considerations confine cyclic paths for $\rho = 1$ to F^*, and the negative definite second differential of u at (k^*, k^*) for directions leading off F^* ensures that the linearization preserves this property.

Scheinkman's argument excluding (o, v) with $v \neq 0$ from the stable manifold of (35) is also valid here for any (o, v) such that $(k^*, k^*) + \alpha(o, v) \notin F^*$ for all $\alpha > 0$. Thus 10b is precisely the addition needed to exclude other (o, v), given the properties of the second differential in

Assumption 9. Scheinkman's argument is also based on value loss considerations. Thus we may use the strong strict concavity remaining in the model to reduce the *ad hoc* character of Assumptions 5 and 6 in my earlier paper [4] somewhat, but an *ad hoc* element remains.

Using the Hirsch–Pugh stable manifold theorem for equilibria whose linearizations are hyperbolic, that is, display generalized saddlepoints, Scheinkman shows that (k^ρ, k^ρ) is locally stable for the nonlinear difference equation system (31) when ρ is near 1. I had proved the analogous result for a von Neumann model by use of a process of successive approximations [4]. Moreover, he proves by means of the Hirsh–Pugh theorem that the radius of the stable neighborhood may be chosen uniformly for $\rho' < \rho < 1$ for some ρ' near 1. However, Theorem 3 implies that any optimal path from a sufficient stock eventually remains within a neighborhood of k^ρ, which may be made arbitrarily small by choosing ρ near enough to 1. Combining these results, we may conclude that every path from a sufficient stock converges *asymptotically* to k^ρ under Assumptions 1 to 10 when ρ is near enough to 1. This implies, of course, that the stationary optimal path is unique in this case. We may assert

Theorem 4 On the basis of Assumptions 1 through 10, there is $\rho' \geqslant \bar{\rho}$ such that $\rho' \leqslant \rho < 1$ and x sufficient implies that any optimal path $\{k_t(\rho)\}$ for $k_o = x$ converges asymptotically to k^ρ, where k^ρ defines the unique stationary optimal path for ρ.

25.6 An Example

This investigation of the turnpike properties of optimal paths in the presence of a nontrivial von Neumann facet and a discount factor less than 1, has been guided by an example due to Martin Weitzman and reported by Paul Samuelson [9]. Put in our terms, their model with one capital good is based on utility functions $\rho^t u(x, y) = \rho^t x^{1/2}(1 - y)^{1/2}$, where x is the initial stock and y is the terminal stock. The stocks x and y are constrained to lie between 0 and 1. The graph of u is a truncated cone with vertex at $(0, 0, 1)$ in the (u, x, y) space. They find cyclic paths to exist for all values of ρ between 0 and 1, so that stability does not hold, despite the presence of a unique stationary optimal path for each value of ρ. Samuelson points out that local stability of the stationary optimal path is restored if both exponents $\frac{1}{2}$ are slightly reduced so that u is strictly concave.

Let us generalize the model somewhat in another direction by setting $u(x, y) = x^\beta(1 - y)^{1-\beta}$, for $0 < \beta < 1$. Then the utility function remains a cone with vertex at $(u, x, y) = (0, 0, 1)$, so the von Neumann facet is still nontrivial for all ρ with $0 < \rho \leqslant 1$, and β with $0 < \beta < 1$. The matrix of the linear system of first order difference equations that determines the local stability properties near the stationary optimal path is

$$M^\rho = \begin{bmatrix} 0 & 1 \\ -\rho^{-1} & -\dfrac{\beta}{1-\beta} - \dfrac{1-\beta}{\rho\beta} \end{bmatrix} \tag{36}$$

The stationary optimal path is $k^t = k^\rho = \rho\beta/(1 - (1 - \rho)\beta)$ for all t.

The characteristic roots of M^ρ are $\lambda_1 = -(1 - \beta)/\rho\beta$ and $\lambda_2 = -\beta/(1 - \beta)$. The characteristic vectors are $(1, \lambda_1)$ and $(1, \lambda_2)$. The root λ_1 corresponds to the characteristic vector $(1, \lambda_1)$, where $(k^\rho, k^\rho) + \alpha(1, \lambda_1)$ lies on the von Neumann facet for α small. Then the path described by this root and its accompanying vector provides a solution of the Euler equation (31). If $\beta > \frac{1}{2}$, the root λ_2 has $|\lambda_2| > 1$, and the root λ_1 has $|\lambda_1| < 1$, for ρ near enough to 1. In this case, the von Neumann facet provides a stable solution of the Euler equation from any initial stock, and from the general theory [6] we know that this is an optimal path. If $\beta < \frac{1}{2}$, $|\lambda_2| < 1$ and $|\lambda_1| > 1$ for all values of ρ. Then the path on the von Neumann facet is explosive, but in our terminology F^* is still referred to as stable since it gives stability to the model when $\rho = 1$. Finally, in the case where $\beta = \frac{1}{2}$, $\lambda_2 = -1$ regardless of ρ, and this corresponds in the linear system to the cyclic path that Weitzman found for the original model. Also in this case, when $\rho = 1$, $\lambda_1 = -1$ as well, so F^* has cyclic paths and Theorem 4 cannot be applied. As we have seen, for any other value of β there is local stability for ρ near 1. Then, loosely speaking the neighborhood theorem, our Theorem 3, allows local stability to be exploited for global stability when ρ is near enough to 1.

The example is illustrated in Figure 25.1 for the case in which $\beta = \frac{1}{3}$ and $\rho = 1$ or $\frac{1}{2}$.

Note

I am indebted to Truman Bewley for raising some questions to which this chapter is addressed, and to Paul Samuelson [8] and Martin Weitzman for an example which greatly illuminated the issues involved. I also wish to thank Swapan DasGupta, Keisuke Osumi, José Scheinkman, and Makoto Yano for their assistance.

This research was done, in large part, while the author was Taussig Research Professor in Economics at Harvard University.

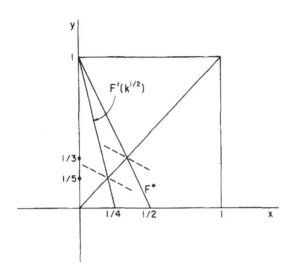

Figure 25.1

$\beta = \frac{1}{3}$, $\rho = \frac{1}{2}$, implies $\lambda_1 = -4$, $\lambda_2 = -\frac{1}{2}$, $k^{1/2} = \frac{1}{5}$, $\beta = \frac{1}{3}$, $\rho = 1$, implies $\lambda_1 = -2$, $\lambda_2 = -\frac{1}{2}$
$k^* = \frac{1}{3}$. Dashed lines indicate directions corresponding to characteristic vectors for λ_2.

References

1. C. Berge, "Topological Spaces," Oliver & Boyd, London, 1963.

2. W. Fenchel, Convex cones, sets, and functions, mimeo, Department of Mathematics, Princeton University, 1953.

3. D. Levhari and N. Liviatan, On stability in the saddle-point sense, *J. Econ. Theory* **4** (1972), 88–93.

4. L. W. McKenzie, The Dorfman–Samuelson–Solow turnpike theorem, *Int. Econ. Rev.* **4** (1963), 29–43.

5. L. W. McKenzie, Accumulation programs of maximum utility and the von Neumann facet, *in* "Value, Capital and Growth" (J. N. Wolfe, Ed.), Edinburgh Univ. Press, Edinburgh, 1968.

6. L. W. McKenzie, Turnpike theorems with technology and welfare function variable, *in* "Mathematical Models in Economics" (J. Łós and M. W. Łós, Eds.), American Elsevier, New York, 1974.

7. L. W. McKenzie, Turnpike theory, *Econometrica* **44** (1976), 841–865.

8. L. W. McKenzie, A primal route to the turnpike and Liapounov stability, *J. Econ. Theory* **26** (1982), 194–209.

9. P. A. Samuelson, Optimality of profit-including prices under ideal planing, *Proc. Nat. Acad. Sci. U.S.A.* **70** (1973), 2109–2111.

10. J. A. Scheinkman, On optimal steady states of n-sector growth models when utility is discounted, *J. Econ. Theory* **12** (1976), 11–30.

Sources

Equilibrium

3. On equilibrium in Graham's model of world trade and other competitive systems, *Econometrica*, April 1954, pp. 147–161.

4. Competitive equilibrium with dependent consumer preferences, *Second Symposium in Linear Programming*, vol. I, edited by H. A. Antosiewicz, National Bureau of Standards, Washington DC, 1956, pp. 277–294.

5. Demand theory without a utility index, *Review of Economic Studies*, June 1957, vol. XXIV (3), pp. 185–189.

6. On the existence of general equilibrium for a competitive market, *Econometrica*, January 1959, pp. 54–71.

7. Stability of equilibrium and the value of excess demand, *Econometrica*, July 1960, pp. 606–617.

8. On the existence of general equilibrium: Some corrections, *Econometrica*, April 1961, pp. 247–248.

9. Why compute economic equilibria? In *Computing Equilibria: How and Why*, edited by J. Los and M. Los. North Holland, Amsterdam, 1976, pp. 3–19.

10. The classical theorem on existence of competitive equilibrium, presidential address to the Econometric Society, *Econometrica*, July 1981, pp. 819–841.

11. The existence of competitive equilibrium over an infinite horizon with production and general consumption sets, with J. H. Boyd III, *International Economic Review*, February 1993, vol. 34, pp. 1–20.

Trade

12. Specialization and efficiency of world production, *Review of Economic Studies*, June 1954, pp. 165–180.

13. Equality of factor prices in world trade, *Econometrica*, July 1955, pp. 239–257.

14. Specialization in production and the production possibility locus, *Review of Economic Studies*, October 1955, vol. XXIII (1), pp. 56–64.

15. Matrices with dominant diagonals and economic theory, in *Mathematical Methods in the Social Sciences*, edited by K. J. Arrow, S. Karlin and P. Suppes, Stanford University Press, 1959, pp. 47–62.

16. The inversion of cost functions: A counter-example, *International Economic Review*, October 1967, pp. 271–278.

17. Theorem and counter example, *International Economic Review*, October 1967, pp. 279–285.

Growth

18. The Dorfman-Samuelson-Solow turnpike theorem, *International Economic Review*, January 1963, pp. 29–43.

19. Turnpike theorem of Morishima, *Review of Economic Studies*, June 1963, pp. 169–176.

20. Accumulation programs of maximum utility and the von Neumann facet, in *Value, Capital, and Growth*, edited by J. N. Wolfe, Edinburgh University Press, 1968, pp. 353–383.

21. Capital accumulation optimal in the final state, in *Contributions to the von Neumann Growth Model*, edited by G. Bruckmann and W. Weber, Springer-Verlag, New York, 1971, pp. 107–120.

22. Turnpike theorems with technology and welfare function variable, in *Mathematical Models in Economics*, edited by J. Los and M. Los. North Holland, Amsterdam, 1974, pp. 271–288.

23. A new route to the turnpike, in *Mathematical Economics and Game Theory*, edited by R. Henn and O. Moeschlin, Springer-Verlag, New York, 1977, pp. 683–694.

24. A primal route to the turnpike and Liapounov stability, *Journal of Economic Theory*, June 1982, vol. 27, pp. 194–209.

25. Turnpike theory, discounted utility, and the von Neumann facet, *Journal of Economic Theory*, August 1983, vol. 30, pp. 330–352.

Index